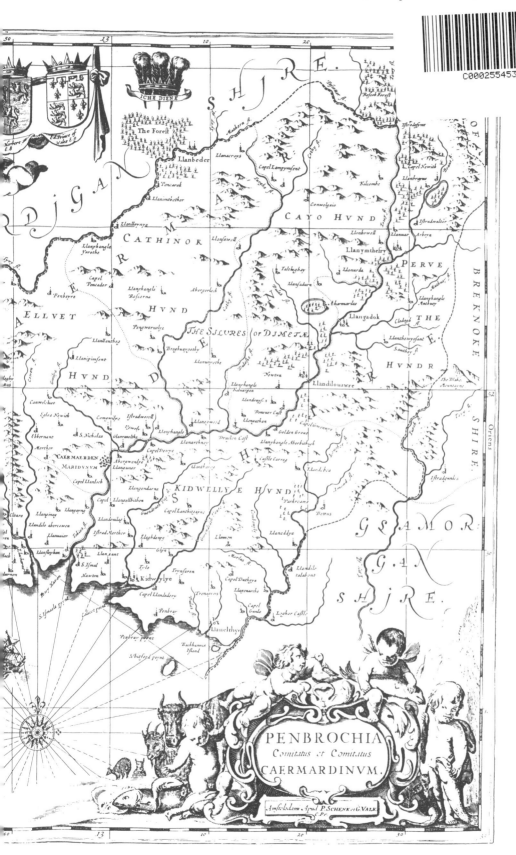

THE FRANCIS JONES TREASURY
OF
HISTORIC PEMBROKESHIRE

Major Francis Jones, late Wales Herald at Arms and his wife, Ethel.
Preparations for the Knights of the Garter ceremony at Windsor Castle.

Dedicated to the memory of Francis and Ethel Jones,
for the gloriously happy childhood they gave their children.
For their example, humour and love,
of which this book is a result.

TREASURY
OF
HISTORIC
PEMBROKESHIRE

By MAJOR FRANCIS JONES,
C.V.O., T.D., D.L., F.S.A., M.A., K.St.J.
Late Wales Herald Extraordinary
1908 - 1993

Editor
CAROLINE CHARLES-JONES

Format and additional Editorial
HUGH CHARLES-JONES

Published by
BRAWDY BOOKS, PEMBROKESHIRE
1998

Published by
Brawdy Books, Plas yr Wregin, Dinas, Newport
Pembrokeshire, SA42 0YH
Telephone: 01348 811450

ISBN 0 9528344 21

Illustrations
Leon Olin, Sylvia Gainsford
Sue James, Stan Rosenthal

Front Cover Design
Leon Olin, Sylvia Gainsford

Design and Make-up
ARTdesigns
Meiros Hill, Felingwm Uchaf
Carmarthen SA32 7BB
Telephone 01267 290670

Printed and Bound by
Redwood Books
Kennet House, Kennet Way
Trowbridge
Wiltshire BA14 8RN

CONTENTS

CHAPTER I

TRIBUTES TO THE MAN BEHIND THE PEN

CHAPTER II

IN THE BEGINNING

First memories . . . Childhood inspiration . . . St. Mary's Church, Haverfordwest . . . Heraldry, His first holy well . . . Schooldays . . . Early researches . . . Herbert Vaughan . . . Schoolmaster days . . . Saving Haverfordwest records . . . Work at National Library of Wales . . . War Service, Africa, Italy and the Middle East . . . Historical section of the War Office . . . Association with the College of Arms . . . County Archivist . . . Retirement

CHAPTER III

EARLY DAYS

Anglo-Norman occupation . . . Towns and boroughs established . . . Linguistic divide . . . Pembroke Castle rises . . . Days of stability . . . Pembrokeshire becomes 'premier' Welsh county . . . The princes in the Tower . . . St. Dogmael's Abbey built . . . Lordships north and south . . . Henry VII born on Welsh soil . . . Haverfordwest's first charter . . . The Flemings . . . Pembrokeshire surnames . . . Wars of the Roses . . . Giraldus Cambrensis, Henry VIII . . . The Dissolution . . . Act of Union 1536 . . . A form of 'Home Rule'. . . Merchant trade . . . The wool trade . . . Coal mining . . . Importance of George Owen, The Civil War . . . A royal mistress . . . A flourishing economy . . . Education . . . The French landing . . . Industrial Revolution . . . the Rebecca Riots . . . The railways . . . The end of the Squirearchy . . . Fast economic changes . . . Galaxy of Pembrokeshire Historians

Folk-lore and medieval religious observances . . . Names . . . Destruction of holy wells . . . The bulldozer's progress . . . The importance of local research . . . The early well cult . . . Wells, Ffynnon Carreg . . . Canna's . . . Ffynnon Ddewi . . . St. Owen's . . . Llandrichian . . . Nine wells . . . Penarthur . . . Ffynnon Fair . . . Healing, wishing and rag wells . . . Origins of well names . . . Council of Arles in 452 AD . . . Well worship outlawed . . . Old gods expelled and the True God replaced . . . Wells down the medieval ages . . . Bathing in a chapel well . . . God given well to St. David . . . The plumber and a holy well . . . A well-head quarrel . . . Discovering a holy well . . . A holy well ritual . . . Fairs at wells . . . Hermit's wells . . . Healing wells . . . Well cults and their traditions . . . Drinking from a human skull . . . Blessed Virgin wells . . . A well cure for madness . . . The leper's well . . . Good luck well . . . Rituals . . . Cursing wells . . . Ghost wells

Chapter IV

A MEDLEY OF PEMBROKESHIRE HOUSES
AND THEIR FAMILIES

Chapter V

IN THE COUNTRYSIDE

CHAPTER VI
A REVIEW OF PEMBROKESHIRE MILITARY MEN

CHAPTER VII
SOME ANCESTRAL HALLS AND THEIR FAMILIES

CHAPTER VIII

OF GHOSTS AND GHOULS, OF HAUNTINGS AND HORRORS

CHAPTER IX

MATTERS ECCLESIASTICAL, PRIESTS, PARSONS AND PARISHIONERS

CHAPTER X

LITIGATION, VEXATIOUS MATTERS AND VARIOUS WRONGDOERS

CHAPTER XI

SOME VANISHED PEMBROKESHIRE SPLENDOURS

CHAPTER XII

SOME PEMBROKESHIRE SPORTS AND SPORTSMEN

CHAPTER XIII

HERBERT VAUGHAN – THE MAN I KNEW

CHAPTER XIV

JOTTINGS FROM THE FRANCIS JONES ARCHIVES

CHAPTER XV

THE PATAGONIAN PAPERS

CHAPTER XVI

MY UNFORGETTABLE PEMBROKESHIRE COMPANION

ACKNOWLEDGEMENTS

Books like ships, only travel with many willing hands. We have been blessed with a many-talented crew who helped launch the good ship *Treasury*. Our thanks and gratitude to the following:

Typing and sensible suggestions
Mrs. Pam Davies of Argoed, Mrs. Kathy Rollinson for typing and Mrs. Laurie Widgery for proof reading.

Design and illustrations
Leon Olin and Sylvia Gainsford for the brilliant dust jacket and the many hours they devoted to drawings – quite beyond the call of duty and copy dates.

Stan Rosenthal for his unique vignettes.

Sue James for her delightful wildlife drawings.

Thomas Lloyd of Stone Hall, a staunch friend, for his collection of Pembrokeshire Coats of Arms, as well as his unfailingly kind encouragement.

Our gratitude also to the National Library of Wales for permission to use all the prints, maps and posters in this book. The unstinting help of Mr. Francis and his staff in selecting them, photocopying them and sending them to us.

Editorial layout and advice
Robert Innes-Smith, yet again for his expertise and good humour when the going got tough. Gwylon Phillips for his great knowledge of Pembrokeshire place names and generous advice.

Our Special Decoration for Valour
To Andy Taylor whose patience, dedication and skill in producing our camera-ready manuscript and illustrations for the printers is beyond praise.

Marketing
Mrs. Mary Burdett-Jones for her support and efficiency which was most appreciated. Our family friend, Leonard Rees of Cerbid gave valuable advice. Thanks also to all West Wales bookshops, as well as W.H. Smith, Waterstones, Ottakar's, and especially Victoria Books of Haverfordwest. They all did us proud.

Patron Subscribers All
Without whose confidence and practical support not one page, let alone three books would have been published. They came from Tenby to Tokyo, Crymych to China, Amroth to Australia and Angle to America and many other parts of the globe.

To all those unnamed people who have helped us along the way, and who have let us use material, articles and illustrations for this book, many thanks.

Finally thanks to our children, Guy and Tileri, for sticking it out during long days and evenings when their parents talked of nothing except "The Book".

EDITOR'S INTRODUCTION

TWO writers at their desks. Nearly two thousand years separate them, from Ancient Greece to the remote north Pembrokeshire of the early 1920's. On discovering Plutarch's words, a slim blue eyed school-boy finds a life long philosophy. His name is Francis Jones. Carefully and neatly he copies out these words.

"I record not history, but human destiny. The evidences of vice or virtue are not confined to famous accomplishments, but often some trivial event, a word, a joke will serve better than great campaigns and battles as a revelation of character". Plutarch.

After Francis Jones's death in 1993 we viewed the awesome legacy of his huge archives. His words seem to whisper, 'the responsibility of an historian is to make his findings known to all'. So from our remote hillside home we became learner publishers. Our two volumes – The Historic Houses of Pembrokeshire and their Families and Historic Carmarthenshire Homes and their Families, now at the end of their print runs, triggered a demand for yet more books. This book is the result of popular demand from west Wales and all over the world. The vital creative vision for it came from Francis Jones's daughter-in-law, Caroline.

We hope the *Treasury* coming from the pen of a master historian will inform and entertain you and that it might also inspire young students to take up a rewarding study of antiquity.

At best Welsh place-name spellings are contentious, a veritable quagmire of differing opinion. So we have used Francis Jones's spellings, this doubtless will provoke happy hours of debate in our wake. Meanwhile we press on with the reality of book publishing.

Often people speak to us of Francis Jones. "I met him when he was researching" or "I heard him give a talk". No longer can we hear his voice but we can give you his words.

Hugh and Caroline Charles-Jones
Brawdy Books, 1998

Notice to all researchers of Welsh history

The National Library of Wales is a vast treasure house of Welsh records. We highly recommend their efficient and supremely helpful staff and up-to-date facilities for any imaginable facet of past Welsh historical records.

The National Library of Wales, Aberystwyth, Ceredigion, Wales SY23 3BU

Tel.: 01970 632800. Fax: 01970 615709. E-mail: holi @ llgc.org.UK

LIST OF PATRON SUBSCRIBERS

Mr. & Mrs. P. Addison, Lagos, Portugal.

Mrs. G. E. Aitchison, The Crown Inn,
Axbridge, Somerset.

Mrs. M. M. L. Akehurst, Little Melbreck,
Stock, Ingatestone, Essex.

Capt. D. G. Anderson, Caeffynnon Road,
Llandybie, Carms.

Mr. D. Ayers, Milton Cres., Pill, Pembs.

Mr. & Mrs. Grahame Barratt, Carew, Pembs.

Grenville Barrett, Cannon Hill Farm,
New Moat, Pembs.

Mrs. E. M. Barry, Shilton House, Shilton, Oxon.

Mr. S. R. Beesley, Hill Lane,
Haverfordwest, Pembs.

Mr. & Mrs. A. R. Bentham, Fron House,
Whitland, Pembs.

Mr. & Mrs. S. B. Beresford-Davies,
Glasdir Bach, Nevern, Pembs.

Mrs. M. C. Berry, Friends Cottage,
Barham, Kent.

Mrs. S. A. Berry, Roch Castle,
Haverfordwest, Pembs.

Mr. F. Bevan, Glanmorfa, Ferryside, Carms.

Mrs. D. Bevan, Ty Picton, Llansteffan, Carms.

Mr. & Mrs. M. Beynon-Isaac,
King Edward Road, Swansea.

Dr. J. H. L. Birchall, High Barn,
Gressingham, Lancs.

Mr. R. Blacklaw-Jones, Rock House,
Haverfordwest, Pembs.

Mrs. V. C. N. Boardman, Hillside Close,
Goodwick, Pembs.

Mr. H. M. Boggis-Rolfe, Plâas Pontfaen, Pembs.

Mr. R. Bowen, Holywell Cres.,
Abergavenny, Gwent.

Mrs. P. M. Bowen, Mount Pleasant,
Penffordd, Pembs.

Miss M. Bowen-Evans, Rock Villa, Trelech, Carms.

Mr. A. ap I. Bowen-Jenkins, Ravens Park Lodge,
Haverfordwest, Pembs.

Mr. M. Brown, Rhosgranog, Llandeloy, Pembs.

Mr. W. C. Brown, St. Michael's Road,
Llandaff, Cardiff.

Mrs. G. G. Brown, Hazel Hill,
Llanstadwell, Pembs.

Revd. R. L. Brown, The Vicarage, Welshpool,
Powys.

Mr. P. C. & Mrs. S. C. Budden, Penygroes,
Llanelli, Carms.

Mr. J. H. Burgess, Portman Rd., Kings Heath,
Birmingham.

Mrs. D. C. Burland, Norman Hill, Dursley, Glos.

Mr. O. Bushell, New Moat, Pembs.

Mr. M. P. Butler, Whitsome East Newton, Duns,
Berwick.

Mr. P. G. V. Campbell, Brynderi, Llangoedmor,
Ceredigion.

Mrs. G. D. Chamberlain, Reibey Pl., Curtin, Aust.

Mr. A. W. H. Charles, Henllys, Llanrhian, Pembs.

Alexander Charles-Jones, Fulbrook, Oxon.

Gareth Charles-Jones, The Coach House Stables,
Wantage.

Guy Charles-Jones, Wycliffe College,
Stonehouse, Glos.

Jeremy Charles-Jones, Charlham,
Ampney St. Peter, Glos.

Mr. & Mrs. R. W. Charles-Jones, Keepers,
Oddington, Glos.

Tileri Charles-Jones, Brynhyfryd, Dinas, Pembs.

Dr. R. E. Chilcott, Hill House, Keston, Kent.

Mr. M. J. Childs, Windermere Ave., Roath Park,
Cardiff.

Dr. W. E. Church, Mannering House,
Bethersden, Kent.

Mr. S. J. Coker, Mountain, Clarbeston Road,
Pembs.

Sir Colin Cole, Burstow, Surrey.

Mr. & Mrs. J. Collier, The Pink House, Sutton,
Pembs.

Mr. P. Cook, John Street, Neyland, Pembs.

Mr. G. Coulter, Altadena, U.S.A.

Canon A. Craven, The Rectory, Nolton, Pembs.

Mr. M. A. J. B. Craven, Carlton Road, Derby.

Mr. D. Iwan Dafis, Llain Pren Afalau,
Llandudoch, Aberteifi.

Col. D. L. Davies, Withybrook, Haverfordwest,
Pembs.

Dr. Glan R. Davies, Glyneiddan, Nantgaredig,
Carms.

Dr. J. D. Davies, Llwyn y Celyn, Llanwrda, Carms.

Dr. M. Glan Davies, Summerleas, Yelverton,
Devon.

Dr. Paul G. Davies, Rose Barn, Little Dunmow,
Essex.

Major & Mrs. R. Davies, Hillcrest Gardens,
Hinchley Wood, Surrey.

Mr. H. E. Davies, Brunt Farm, Dale, Pembs.

Mr. J. B. Davies, Cerrig Llwyd, Lisvane,
Cardiff.

Mr. J. E. Davies, Church Road, Whitchurch,
Cardiff.

Mr. R. Davies, North Gate, Little Newcastle,
Pembs.

Mrs. P. Davies, Argoed, Newport, Pembs.

R. Glan Davies, Quay de la Seine, Paris.

Mr. & Mrs. H. G. G. Devonald, St. Lawrence,
Fishguard, Pembs.

Mr. T. Picton Devonald, Delffordd, Pontardawe,
Swansea.

Mr. G. D. Dobbins, Brynbanc, Brynberian,
Pembs.

Mr. J. Downs, Fairoakland, Wineham, W. Sussex.

Mr. & Mrs. J. Dowson, Brockington Drive,
Tupsley, Hereford.

Lord Dynevor, Cilsane, Llandeilo, Carms.

Mrs. J. E. Eagles, Bryn Eryri, Llanilar,
Aberystwyth.

Mr. & Mrs. R. M. Eastham, Dolau, Dwrbach,
Pembs.

Mr. D. Ellis, Poyston Hall, Rudbaxton, Pembs.

Mr. P. L. Evans, Bryncoed, Llangunnor, Carms.

Mrs. R. Evans, Hafod-y-dail, Llanychaer, Pembs.

P. G. Evans, Victoria, Australia.

Mr. J. W. A. Fackrell, Bruges, Belgium.

Mrs. M. Fletcher, Norbury, London.

Mr. D. T. R. Francis, Briar Walk, London.

Mrs. S. Francis, Alclud, Penbanc, Fishguard,
Pembs.

Mr. B. G. Fuller, Hunters Mead, Sarratt, Herts.

Miss V. E. Gabriel, Harries Street, Tenby, Pembs.

P. Galland, Lausanne, Switzerland.

Mr. R. & Mrs. P. Garnon Peters, Victoria, B.C.,
Canada.

Mrs. C. George, Milton Meadows, Milton,
Pembs.

Mr. F. M. Gibbs, Brynmor Road, Gowerton.

Mr. W. D. S. Gibby, Boltons Lane, Pyrford,
Surrey.

Col. R. H. Gilbertson, Coed-y-ffynnon,
Lampeter Velfrey, Pembs.

Mr. R. W. Giles, Glendower, Gt. Mongeham,
Deal, Kent.

Mrs. G. A. Gill, Milton Farm, Burton, Pembs.

Mr. A. C. Gladitz, Brettingham Court,
Hinton St. George, Som.

Mr. D. R. Gorman, Lulworth Pl.,
Walton-le-Dale, Lancs.

Mrs. P. R. Gould, Tredefaid, Llantood, Cardigan.

Miss E. O. Griffiths, Heol Bethel, Pontyberem,
Carms.

Mr. & Mrs. R. J. Griffiths, New Road,
Haverfordwest, Pembs.

Mr. J. R. Griffiths, School Rd., Evesham, Worcs.

Mrs. M. A. Griffiths, Blaencorse, St. Clears,
Carms.

Mr. T. Gwyn-Jones, Hamstead Pk., Newbury,
Berks.

Mr. S. L. Hancock, Queen Elizabeth Ave.,
Neyland, Pembs.

Dr. & Mrs. D. Harris, Sprucedale Ave., London,
Ontario, Canada.

J. & D. Harries, Brisbane, Queensland, Australia.

Mr. E. D. & Mrs. J. M. Harries, McCartheys Rd.,
Maleny, Australia.

Linzi Harrison, Rose Cottage, Tenby, Pembs.

Mr. H. W. Harrison, Ashridge Drive,
Bricket Wood, St. Albans, Herts.

Mr. D. M. F. & Mrs. L. M. Harvey, The Slough,
Jameston, Pembs.

Mrs. S. Henry, Ger-y-dre, Johnston, Pembs.

Mr. A. R. Henniker-Gotley, Guildford, Surrey.

Mr. D. Herring, Ballynoe, Eire.

Mr. C. R. Hitchings, Hitchin, Herts.

Mrs. I. V. Hewitt, Elmhurst Road, Thatcham,
Berks.

Mrs. S. Hewitt, Spring Wells, Spittal, Pembs.

Miss J. A. Hoare, Spielplatz, Bricket Wood,
St. Albans, Herts.

Mr. & Mrs. J. Hogg, Meadow Cottage,
Lords Meadows Farm, Pembroke, Pembs.

Mrs. S. E. M. Hollands, Berkeley Court,
Eastbourne, E. Sussex.

Mr. H. B. Holt, Newport Castle, Pembs.

Mrs. E. A. Horne, La Vielle Fontaine, St. Ouen,
Jersey.

Dr. D. C. & Mrs. S. M. Horsman,
Gower Rd., Swansea.

Hugh Owen Library, The University of Wales,
Aberystwyth.

Mr. E. E. Hughes, Xalet del Far, Juberri, Andorra.

Mr. J. V. Hughes, Rice Street, Port Talbot,
W. Glam.

Mr. D. J. Hughes-Davies, Hfinchiu. Taiwan.

Mr. R. Innes-Smith, The Old Vicarage, Derby.

Mrs. S. J. Jackson, Temeraire, Weymouth,
Dorset.

Mr. A. James, The Weir, Cross Park,
Pembroke Dock, Pembs.

Mrs. D. James, The Weir, Cross Park,
Pembroke Dock, Pembs.

Mr. P. F. James, Homewood, Swallowcliffe,
Salisbury, Wilts.

Brig. R. James, Upper Court, Colwall, Malvern.

Mr. R. J. James, Henry's Moat, Pembs.

Mr. P. K. Jenkins, Cefn Goleu, Llandeilo, Carms.

Mrs. M. B. Jenkins, Trearched Farm, Croesgoch, Pembs.

Mr. D. M. John, Carreg Onnen, Fishguard, Pembs.

Lt. Col. Sir J. Johnston, Windsor Great Park, Berks.

D. Skeel Jones, Bedford.

Miss A. L. Jones, Hendre, Carmarthen.

Miss E. C. Jones, Bryn Dissil, Llandissilio, Pembs.

Mr. D. M. Jones, Tal-y-Werydd, Aberarth, Ceredigion.

Mr. J. Alun G. Jones, The Havens, Orton Brimbles, Peterborough.

Mrs. C. Jones, Gurrey Manor, Nantyrhibo, Sir Gaerfyrddin.

Mrs. M. Jones, 10 Stradey Hill, Llanelli.

The Rev. Dr. & Mrs. Jones, New Street, St. Davids, Pembs.

Mr. P. E. C. Jones, Loveston Cross, Loveston, Pembs.

Mr. A. F. Jones-Lloyd, Lancych, Boncath, Pembs.

Mr. N. King, Honeygrove, Laugharne, Carms.

Mr. P. I. King, Bachau, Carreg Wen Village, Boncath, Pembs.

Mr. R. G. King, Stackpole, Nairn, Scotland.

Mrs. B. J. Kirkwood, Sheather Ave., St. Ives, N.S.W., Australia.

Mr. & Mrs. J. Lane Fox, Arlington Farm House, Bibury, Glos.

Mrs. E. M. Leat, Woodstock Close, Kingswood, Bristol.

Mr. B. C. Lewis, Old Post Office, Stackpole, Pembs.

Mr. & Mrs. Skyrme Lewis, North Nash, Pembs.

Mrs. F. L. Lewis, Clover Park, Haverfordwest, Pembs.

Mr. G. T. Lewis, Fairfield, Cholsey, Wallingford, Oxon.

Mr. R. W. A. P. Lewis, Caermaenau Fawr, Clynderwen, Pembs.

Mr. S. R. Lewis, Amroth Castle, Pembs.

The Hon. T. O. Lewis, Hean Castle, Saundersfoot, Pembs.

Mrs. R. V. Lilwall, Main Street, Pembroke.

Mr. M. R. Lippiatt, Clos Croft, Croesgoch, Pembs.

Mrs. D. Llewellyn, Cefn Colstyn, Cardiff.

Mr. J. E. Lloyd, Ashwood, Camrose, Pembs.

Sir Ian Lloyd, Bakers House, Priors Dean, Hants.

Mr. M. & The Hon. J. Lloyd-Faulkner, Llanwnda, Pembs.

Prof. & Mrs. D. A. Long, Brawdy, Pembs.

The Hon. J. Long, Highworth, Wilts.

H. Longhorne, Philadelphia, U.S.A.

Sir David Mansel-Lewis, Stradey Castle, Llanelli.

Mr. A. G. Marriner, Avenue Road, Dorridge, W. Midlands.

Christopher Marshall, Pemberton, Pont St., London.

Mr. J. Martin, Joliment, W. Australia.

Mrs. J. M. Martin, Subiaco, W. Australia.

Lt. Col. H. P. S. Massy, Long Acre, Owermoigne, Dorset.

Mr. P. Matthews, St. David's House, Swansea.

Mr. C. Mathias, Hazelbrook Farm, Carew, Pembs.

Viscountess Melville, Frith Wood, Chalford, Glos.

Mr. J. F. Meyler Williams, St. Katharine's Parmoor, Oxon.

Mr. D. Miles, St. Anthony's Way, Haverfordwest, Pembs.

Mr. M. & Mrs. J. Millington, Ryles Cres., Macclesfield, Cheshire.

Mr. R. E. Mogg, Dryslwyn, Llandeloy, Pembs.

Mr. A. J. R. Moon, Trewern Mansion, Whitland, Pembs.

Mr. H. P. G. Morgan, Siena Lodge, Ynystawe, Clydach.

Mr. D. Morris, Ramsden Road, London.

Mr. H. Morse, Church Row, Tontêg, Pontypridd.

Mrs. J. Mount, Hawtree Cottage, Tenby, Pembs.

Miss Mount, The Green, Tenby, Pembs.

Mr. I. Nagai, Sengawa-machi, Tokyo, Japan.

Mr. & Mrs. G. R. Nicolle, Rising Sun Cottage, Nolton Haven, Pembs.

Mr. M. Noott, Grafton Cottage, Chaddesley Corbett, Worcs.

The Duke of Norfolk, Arundel Castle, Sussex.

Mr. T. Oldham, Rhychydwr, Crymych, Pembs.

Mr. & Mrs. R. Outwin-Flinders, Wycliffe College Junior School, Stonehouse, Glos.

Mr. J. Owen, The Pembrokeshire Record Office, The Castle, Haverfordwest.

Mrs. S. Paravicini, Glyn Celyn House, Brecon, Powys.

Ms. V. Parcell, Paskeston, Pembroke Dock, Pembs.

Mrs. B. Parker, Castle Reach, Newport, Pembs.

Mr. J. R. Parnell Davies, Cheriton, Chesham, Bucks.

The Misses E. A. Y. & L. A. Parry, Tir-y-Nant, Ammanford, Carms.

Mr. A. D. Payne, Boldmere Road, Sutton Coldfield, W. Midlands.

Mrs. Z. J. Pearce, Myrtle Cottage, Carrow Hill, Magor, Mons.

Mr. Juan Peel, Uruguay, South America.

Mr. P. G. V. Pegge, Llwynbedw, Boncath, Pembs.

Mr. E. H. Perkins, Llysgwyn, Bethesda, Narberth, Pembs.

Mr. & Mrs. G. Phillips, Briscwm, Cardigan.

Mr. W. & Mrs. S. Phillips, Highfield,
New Hedges, Pembs.

Mr. & Mrs. P. Pocock, Entraygues, France.

Mr. J. S. Powell, Lilac Cottage, Penmaen,
Gower.

Mr. R. W. Price, Irlwyn, Wolfscastle, Pembs.

Mr. R. Pugh, Cwm Overnant House, Carmarthen.

Major D. Rankin-Hunt, The Royal Collection,
St. James Palace, London.

Miss E. Rees, Brynhedydd, Llansteffan, Carms.

Mr. A. J. H. Rees, Felinfoel, Llanelli, Carms.

Mr. L. Rees, Cerbid, Solva, Pembs.

Mrs. N. Rees, Treasury Cottage, St. Davids, Pembs.

Mr. A. T. Rees Jones, Cemaes y Graig, Burry Port.

Mrs. D. L. Rhind, Four Winds, Court, Hartlepool.

Miss M. A. Richards, Marlborough House,
Llandrindod Wells, Powys.

Mr. J. Roach, Addison Road, Haverfordwest,
Pembs.

Mrs. E. G. Roberts, Tudor Close, Penarth,
Vale of Glam.

Mr. G. V. Robinson, Green Castle, Llangain,
Carmarthen.

Mrs. B. E. Rosenfeld, Clwyd, Penarth, S. Glam.

Mr. W. D. A. Rowlands, Trefelin,
St. Brides Major, Bridgend.

Mr. & Mrs. M. H. B. Ryder, Broadlands Farm,
Tiers Cross, Pembs.

Mrs. O. R. S. Scott-Goddard, Solveig, Cuffley,
Herts.

Mr. M. R. Sheppard, Mole Bridge Cottage,
Rusthall Common, Kent.

Mrs. K. Silcox-Butt, Hendy, Pontarddulais,
Swansea.

Mr. I. F. Skyrm, Lodge Farm, Broadheath, Worcs.

St. Davids Cathedral Library, St. Davids, Pembs.

The Viscount St. David.

Mr. & Mrs. P. Stanley, Cheltenham, Glos.

Mr. B. Picton Swann, Durlston Cl., Camberley,
Surrey.

Mr. A. R. & Mrs. A. Taylor, Meiros Hill, Carms.

Miss P. Thomas, Presely View, Pembroke Dock,
Pembs.

Mr. E. H. Thomas, Finchampstead Road,
Wokingham, Berks.

Mr. E. R. Thomas, Yardley, Leominster,
Hereford.

Mr. R. Thomas, Lampit Mawr, Fishguard, Pembs.

Mr. M. & Mrs. S. J. Thompson, Ramsey House,
St. Davids, Pembs.

Mr. R. Thorne, Little Green, London.

Mrs. M. N. E. Tiffany, Old High St., Headington,
Oxford.

Mr. J. S. Towers, Foster Court, Witham, Essex.

J. Towyn-Jones, Brynsiriol, Carmarthen,
President of the Carmarthenshire Antiquarian
Society.

Mr. A. A. Tremellen, Tremoilet Farm, Pendine,
Carms.

Mr. P. J. Ungoed, Neath Road, Maesteg, M. Glam.

Mr. S. C. Van Dulken, Green Road, London.

Canon G. J. Vaughan-Jones, Bryn-y-Mor Terr.,
Aberystwyth.

Mr. B. Voyle, Queen Victoria Rd., Llanelli,
Carms.

Mr. & Mrs. R. J. Walmsley, Ysgarwen, Cilgwyn,
Pembs.

Mr. J. Walford, Rhoslyn, Talley, Carms.

Mr. T. M. Ll. Walters, Sandalwood Rd.,
Loughborough, Leics.

Dr. H. Walters, Llyfrgell Genedlaethol Cymru,
Aberystwyth.

Mr. I. Walters, Church Terr., Goodwick, Pembs.

Mrs. E. F. E. Warlow, Castle Way, Dale, Pembs.

Mr. S. Watkins, Trewern, Nevern, Pembs.

Mr. R. I. Webb-Bowen, The Orchard,
Sixpenny Handley, Wilts.

Mrs. L. Widgery, Jordanston, Fishguard, Pembs.

Mr. R. de Wilde, Strand, London.

Mr. P. Williams, Cavendish Meads, Sunninghill,
Berks.

Mrs. E. M. Williams, Thornton Hse., Thornton,
Pembs.

Mrs. F. G. Williams, Llanbadarn Fawr,
Aberystwyth.

Mrs. S. A. Williams, Radley, Grosvenor Rd., Glos.

Mrs. N. L. Willis (nee Reynish), Pyle, Bridgend,
Glam.

Mr. T. Woodcock, Norroy & Ulster King of Arms,
College of Arms, Queen Victoria St., London.

GLOSSARY OF USEFUL TERMS

BOVATE: Area an ox can plough in a season.

CARUCATE: 64 acres. See PLOUGHLAND.

COCKROAD: Clear cut road through a wood across which a net is hung from opposite trees to catch woodcock. Cockshoot-time is dusk when birds are most likely to fly into the nets.

CULM: The slack of anthracite coal mixed with beaten clay and water and made into 'balls' and used on the fire; it burned very slowly and the fire could be kept in all night.

DEMESNE: Land retained by the lord of the manor for his own use and upon which tenants give free labour as part of their obligations in return for their holdings.

FEIDR/ BEIDIR: Found mainly in Pembrokeshire, meaning literally cow crossing. Dyfed was colonised by the Déisi from Co. Waterford in the third century who continued to rule until the tenth century. A former King of Munster, Cormac Mac Cuilleanáin (901-7) had declared that every road should be the width of a cow, plus the length of a cow. The Irish equivalent is 'bothar'.

FOREST: Originally used to describe an open area with trees and pasture, moorland and mountain reserved for hunters.

GAVELKIND: Equal succession to land of all heirs.

HUSBANDMAN: Tenant farmer.

INTER ALIA: Among others.

KNIGHT'S FEE: Land held by a knight in return for military service being roughly
640 acres (10 ploughlands).
20 knight's fees held of the King make a Barony.
5 knight's fees held of Earldom of Pembroke make a Barony.

MESNE: Subordinate lord holding estate from superior feudal lord.

MESSUAGE: Dwelling house with outbuildings and land assigned to its use.

OXLAND: 8 acres but variable from place to place.

PLOUGHLAND: The amount of land that could be ploughed in a year. It varied from 60-180 acres from place to place.

PROTONOTARY: Chief clerk or registrar in a law court.

STANG: Measure of land, a quarter of a Welsh acre.

SUIT OF COURT: Obligation to attend the lord's court.

TOWNRED: Township or cluster of homesteads.

IURE UXORIS: In right of his wife.

VIDE: See.

YEAR: Given as 1748/9 for example. The year is written in this way to denote dates between 1 January and 24 March in the years from 1582 to 1752. In 1582 the Gregorian Calendar was introduced in Catholic Europe by Pope Gregory XIII to replace the old Julian Calendar. Britain did not change until 1752 when the start of the official year was moved from 25 March to 1 January. For example 9 February 1715 in Europe is written as 9 February 1714/5 in Britain.

Ref: G. Owen, *Elizabethan Pembrokeshire*. Ed. Brian Howells, 1973. Pembs. Record Office.

CHAPTER I

TRIBUTES TO THE MAN BEHIND THE PEN

F.J.'s son Hugh Charles-Jones writes:

MY FATHER said "The duty of an historian is to make his findings known to all". He was true to this code all his life. Inheriting his archives I felt a strong duty to both my parents that his work should continue to be published.

One of the very first to encourage us was His Grace the Duke of Norfolk, KG, Premier Duke and Earl of England, Earl Marshal and head of the College of Arms.

The Duke of Norfolk

The Duke of Norfolk writes:

"Francis Jones, Wales Herald at Arms Extraordinary was under my cousin's command, and mine during State Occasions for thirty years. In both ceremonial and executive duties it was obvious we had a man of talent and quality. I always enjoyed his company, his knowledge, wit and good humour. Francis was commissioned into the army in 1931, and held appointments to the Crown until his death in 1993. A total of sixty-two years service.

"In his twenties he rescued Haverfordwest's county records, and the present Record Office there is but one of his pioneering legacies. His learned achievements continued. For example he single-handedly catalogued every Welsh manuscript in the College of Arms. This is shortly to be published.

"I am pleased to see Francis's books produced by his family. He richly deserves such recognition, for he was a credit to his country which he served with lasting distinction, and to his native county of Pembrokeshire."

Norfolk

Sir Colin Cole, former Garter King of Arms, writes:

IF THERE had not been a herald six hundred years ago who took his name from Wales this name would not have been revived as that of a Herald Extraordinary in 1963 when, to the immense pleasure of the people of Wales, Major Francis Jones was created Wales Herald of Arms.

This was in large measure a tribute to his exceptional achievements as an antiquarian, an archivist, an historian, and a genealogist.

To these skills he added those of heraldic scholarship which he shared with and taught to his friends and colleagues among the heralds of England so that they came to have a greater understanding of the heraldry of Wales than ever they had before. I learnt about Francis Jones as we became friends that he prefered to explain and instruct by bardic discourse rather than by what he wrote, although the sound groundwork of his own specialist knowledge was obvious by his co-authorship of *Royal and Princely Heraldry in Wales* published in 1969, the year of the Investiture of the Prince of Wales at Caernarvon Castle. This great event was for Francis the high point of his career as Wales Herald. On 1 July 1969 he was, with dignity and delight, on parade participating in a ceremony which was the epitome of ancient ritual of which Francis had himself with historical insight made a telling contribution.

Another earlier notable event was also of deep meaning to F.J., especially as a Herald bearing the name of his native land. This was the devising and grant of his badge of office as "Wales", royally approved in 1967, in the designing of which Francis played a big part. Its components were an open Royal Crown of the thirteenth century and the Welsh *Croes Naid*. The whole history of Wales entwined with that of England, I am sure, was symbolised for Francis by this special cross believed to contain a small piece of the True Cross and particularly treasured by the Welsh. It came to be the chief relic at St. George's Chapel, Windsor and the representation of it there, carved on a roof-boss, inspired Wales Herald, imbued with affection towards both countries, to seek it as part of his badge of office, a badge by which assuredly he will be remembered as a dedicated herald, of real ability, courteous, mellow, amiable, always companionable and a faithful friend to his fellow heralds and other professional colleagues.

Francis Jones, his wife Ethel, and Sir Colin Cole at a picnic at Runnymede

Sir David Mansel Lewis writes:

WITH my fellow citizens of Pembrokeshire I welcome and take heart from another volume from the posthumous pen of Francis Jones, our champion and compatriot. He was born and bred in Mathry, an ancient and traditional farming locality to which he held strong allegiances throughout his life. I first met him while we were both researching and was struck by his thoroughness as he pored through manuscripts his pencil poised, like the rod of an angler waiting to strike when some significant fact swam up into his keen gaze from the faded pages before him. As is often the case with countrymen, he had about him an atmosphere of timelessness, something which no doubt enabled him to live happily in the past among his papers and cardboard boxes full of records, and to view them through the eyes almost of their contemporaries, attaching the same kind of urgency and emphasis as would have been imparted to them by their original writers. Indeed one sometimes felt that he had actually walked out of the document himself in order to illuminate and enlarge upon the points which were made in it.

Perhaps it was his sheer talent that first attracted him to the attention of Herbert Vaughan, the late Edwardian scholar and dilettante, who wrote that immortal work, *The South Wales Squires*. It was through Vaughan's good influence that Francis Jones joined the National Library of Wales, where, released from school-mastering, he woke and wandered more or less uninterrupted through that remarkable storehouse of Welsh antiquity. More or less, because in fact like many Welshmen, Francis never really did quite what he said he was going to do. Or, to use a double negative, didn't do it in the way that other people would have expected. Diligent, painstaking, accurate and dutiful he certainly was in carrying out the wishes of his various mentors and employers, but alongside this was always the compulsive search for idiosyncrasy, for character, for the mannerisms and curiosities which he knew to be the hallmarks of the heroes and heroines which he conjured up from these dusty papers.

There is something enormously satisfactory about great scholarship, particularly when it is described in simple understandable terms. "You see I am something of a squirrel" he told me. "I keep nearly everything, a trait which I think I must have inherited from my mother. When she died we found among her effects several boxes containing string, all labelled roughly as to their contents. Very long, long, medium and short. There was one remarkable box", he said, "and this was labelled 'pieces of string too short to be of any use'."

His experience of human nature had led him to believe almost passionately in heredity and in the genetics of breeding, and for eminent men he would invariably trace a distinguished forebear pointing triumphantly to the logic of the succession.

Neither egalitarian nor snob he moved as easily among the crowds of the Eisteddfodwyr, with whom he conversed in fluent Welsh, as among the Garter Knights at Windsor Castle, wearing his tabard with great dignity and regaling them with scholarly, occasionally unscholarly, anecdotes of which he had an enviable supply. In short he was ubiquitous, and from his wide experience of life was able to achieve a unique social balance within the corridors of power at Whitehall, through the Officers' Mess at Larkhill, in the Common Rooms of the University of Wales, the canteens of the South Wales Steel Works, the cattle mart at Haverfordwest, or the leather armchairs of the Athenaeum. And so his discourse and his contribution was known everywhere and is well remembered by those who attended his many lectures and talks or who were lucky enough to enjoy his enormously stimulating company.

"I always use a pencil" he would say "because, you see, you can rub it out." You never quite knew which direction his conversation was going to take; and as he talked on, jotting the while, I would think about this meticulous man with his remarkable ability to discover and assemble the evidence that brings to life our own social history. I think now also about that frugal collection of boxes which he inherited. It may have been a pointer to his work among the archives. His great collections of documents and papers which he amassed throughout his life were always stored in neat cardboard boxes too, and duly numbered and labelled.

And that last box; why did he keep it? Was it, perhaps, because he thought that one day someone would go carefully through it and join up all those loose ends?

Roscoe Howells writes:

ROSCOE HOWELLS, journalist, novelist and local historian is the much loved and admired doyen of Pembrokeshire writers. With his distinctive charm and wit he writes of Francis Jones:

It could sound odd perhaps that one of my happiest memories of Francis Jones should also be one of the last I have of him is before his death, in 1993. The memory of which I speak now was at the end of March 1987.

Frank always maintained that he did not drive and what did it matter anyway as long as his beloved Ethel was there to indulge him? By 1987, however, she was no longer there to chauffeur him so he came by bus to Kilgetty. My wife had prepared a lovely lunch and we cracked a bottle of wine. We drove to Pembroke after lunch to call at the Riverside Nursing Home to see Miss Winnie Vaughan. I was deeply in love with her when I was ten years old but, since she was thirty-seven at the time, I hardly stood much of a chance. She was from my native Saundersfoot and taught at the old Tenby Council School. That was back in 1930 or thereabouts and the student teacher at that time was one Francis Jones. I remember him as very dapper with a neat moustache and, wearing the fashionable plus-fours of that era. That day in 1987 when we called at the Riverside Nursing Home Frank and my beloved Miss Vaughan had not seen each other for nearly sixty years. She was then in her ninety-fourth year and as bright as a button. There was so much talk of that happy time in all our lives as the two of them reminisced. There was much hilarity too and I remember Miss Vaughan saying, "So you see, Francis" (it was always Francis), "I remained a spinster to the end". And with all that marvellous charm of his, Frank said, "Not spinster, Winifred, my dear, perish the thought. Say rather, Unclaimed Jewel." No wonder I remember the day with such gratitude.

My friendship with Frank grew from those long ago days in school at Tenby. In later years, when I was doing some writing I could always turn to him. There would, invariably, also be a laugh. I laughed all the way home one night after I had called on Francis and Ethel when they lived at the little house inside Carmarthen's old castle walls. It was a moonlight night and as we stood outside, so calm and quiet was it in the midst of the town beyond, I remarked what a peaceful, convenient spot it was to live, he said "Indeed Roscoe. It is very satisfying for a man to be able to come out in the moonlight and pee against his own wall if he wants to. Like Ahab in the Old Testament you know. I'm sure you remember Ahab? All schoolboys love reading about Ahab."

Puckish, I suppose, would be the term for his sense of humour. I was in his study once when he was on the telephone. I browsed through his marvellous library. A book on Greek mythology appealed to me immensely. When he finished on the telephone I said "This is a lovely little book, Frank. Could I borrow it with you?" As a Pembrokeshire man I would, of course, have said 'with' and not 'from'.

"Certainly not," he said.

"Yes, you're quite right," I said. "That's the trouble with lending books. Half the time you forget who borrowed them and you never have them back."

"My dear fellow," said he, "where d' you think half these books came from?"

Nor did his humour stop short at a little bit of facetious philosophy. Once I was bemoaning some error of omission in some piece of research. He said, "Roscoe, it's God's fault of course. He brings us into the world knowing nothing, we acquire all this knowledge, and at the end, when we could make use of it, it's too late. I'm sure He's a frightfully decent type and means well but He's got it all wrong. If He asked me I would have say, "Now listen to me Old Sport. You should bring us into the world knowing everything and let it run down at the end, then we could really put up a distinctly good show."

I remember him as a friend, helpful and encouraging towards one whose scholarship was as nothing compared with his, and that he somehow made you feel special. I miss him because he is irreplaceable.

Major David Rankin-Hunt, Norfolk Herald, writes:

ALTHOUGH my interest in history has been with me for as long as I can remember, it was Francis Jones who broadened my interest and knowledge. Our first meeting came about as a result of a schoolboy letter. During the many years that followed, we exchanged countless letters and had many happy meetings, at which I experienced that special brand of Welsh hospitality. In turn, I would entertain him in London. We often spoke in our native Welsh which puzzled many an Anglo-Saxon. His inspirational stories and his wise counsel encouraged me to explore new areas of history, including heraldry, which was to provide the seed that led to my being appointed Norfolk Herald in later life. More than anyone else, he encouraged me to join the T.A. which I did in 1974. This lead to my joining the Regular Army which was to have a profound influence on the course of the rest of my life.

Major Francis Jones was the quintessential Welsh gentleman who moved with ease through every stratum of society. He was a combination of many things, an intellectual, a soldier, a countryman, a family man, and above all a friend who helped me in every way he could. Indeed, some of the successes I have enjoyed are as a direct result of his influence and help.

CHAPTER II

IN THE BEGINNING

IN THE FOOTSTEPS OF AN ANTIQUARY

Presidential Address delivered by Francis Jones at the one hundred and thirty-second annual summer meeting at Carmarthen, 1985

I CONSIDER the invitation to become President of The Cambrian Archaeological Association to be the crowning glory of a lifetime devoted to antiquarian pursuits. To have been elected to follow in the footsteps of the illustrious holders of this office is one of the greatest honours that can be bestowed, and I can only hope that acceptance will be justified by my future conduct. I offer you my sincere thanks for the confidence you have placed in me. Having witnessed the passing of more decades than I care to count, nevertheless I do not plead guilty to old age despite an occasional suspicion of a feeling that perhaps might be described as a mild senescence which, however, will in no way deter me from pursuing historical and archaeological studies with the dedication that governed my more sprightly days. Presidency of the Association provides a spur to continuing effort. Mingled with the pleasure of the occasion is the perplexity attending choice of a subject appropriate for this address. After much thought, and guided by experienced friends, I propose to offer you some reflections on an antiquary's pilgrimage through the storied land which is the heritage of every Briton.

I was born in north Pembrokeshire, at seaside Trefin in the Hundred of Dewsland, Cantref Dewi, a purely agricultural territory, so that the environment of the dwellers was dominated by the farming scene. After two-and-a-half years we moved to the inland village of Llandeloy, situated midway between my grandparents' homes, the farms of Grinston and Clawddcam, and it was on the hearths of those homesteads that I spent most of the first ten years of my life, and it is to those years that I owe the lasting interests that decided my future conduct. Both my grandmothers possessed an unending store of local lore, old songs, poems, tales, legends, traditions, which became the staple diet of a voracious youth. My mother had inherited similar interests, and not only did she add to my knowledge but directed my footsteps towards antiquarian pastures. Thus, it was among feminine cossettings that I embarked on my pilgrimage. Certain youthful happenings, seemingly minor, can have a lasting effect on one's career, often leading to an unexpected denouement. These fragmentary events remain in the mind like vignettes that decorate chapter-headings in old leather-bound folios, or the engraved scenes that formed so popular a feature of Victorian publications. However insignificant, seemingly forgotten, they lie coiled in one's memory, which later a chance word, a sound, a fragrance, a shaft of sunlight, or the sigh of the wind, will evoke. Among them is one that I never forgot, which profoundly influenced

Tales of Chivalry

my subsequent conduct, forming the start-line of a pursuit that I have never abandoned, and of which I have never wearied.

I was six years of age at the time. One day brought boundless excitement. My mother dressed me with care, informing me that we were off to her old home, Clawddcam. In due course one of my uncles arrived in a pony-trap, and away we bowled along dusty lanes, with occasional cries of merriment as the vehicle swayed when wheels ran over a pot-hole or missed a rut, for those lanes still lay outside Macadam's tarry authority. It appeared that my grandfather intended on the morrow taking a load of wool to the annual fair, *ffair ŵlan*, at Haverfordwest some ten miles away, and my mother and I were to accompany him. In later years my mother described how we had made ourselves comfortable among the bales in the big cart, as snug as any feather-bed, while my grandfather sat behind the horses. What with the early hour and the movement of the vehicle, I soon fell asleep, and have no remembrance of any sights or sounds as we rumbled past the sentinel oaks of Caswilia, splashed through the fords of Trewilym and Dwr Mŵntan, and toiled up the hill that winds over heather-clad Plumstone, separating the Welshry from the Englishry, and so on till we reached Haverfordwest.

Here I awoke. I recall the bustling crowds. I gazed with awe at what seemed to be gigantic beings, lanky men with oaken staffs, kinsmen from a hill-farm in the Preseli foothills I was told. There was much shaking of hands, cheerful conversation, and from time to time a tall figure would pat my head, the menfolk pressed pennies into my hands, the womenfolk gave me sweets. The recollection is fragmentary, but what comes next is etched as sharply as an engraving by Dürer, as firmly as a design by Burne-Jones. We were back among the bales, farmers, dealers, kinsfolk. It was then that the engraver took the impressionable wax of my memory into his complete possession. And this is what he engraved:-

I wandered away from my mother's side and found myself walking down a short, steep street flanked with towering houses. Though I had never been in the town before and all was strange, yet I was unafraid. I crossed the road and came to some railings. These I followed, running my hand along them in the manner of small boys till I came to an iron gate. Unlatched, it yielded to my touch. A paved way led to a lofty cyclopean building. I descended a short flight of steps and entered a porch. A nail-studded door stood ajar, I passed into an enormous hall, the biggest I had ever seen. And I was alone.

It must have been high noon, for the vast silent building was full of a gentle diffused light. What impressed me even more than the massive columns, the serried seats, and carved ceilings, were the windows – windows aflame with glorious colours – gold, silver, blue, green, red, which seemed to chant a welcome and to dance like the waters of the rill near my country home. On the wall I beheld a lozenge-shaped panel, its main feature a black lion, red in tooth and claw, around its neck a golden crown fastened to a long trailing chain; there were also heads of boars and bulls, new moons, silver lilies, crosses, and a blood-red hand severed at the wrist. Bewildered, yet delighted, I walked slowly along the aisle. I saw the black animal again, this time in a long pointed window alive with the sparkling hues. Shields of various shapes and sizes decorated the walls, and high above hung a panoply of streaming banners with strange devices, and a gilded helmet.

What were these enchanting pictures? What were they called? Why were they here? Enthralled, I gazed at the windows and from the windows to the walls. Then the sunlight melted away as a cloud rolled blanket-wise over the town without. The friendliness of the windows waned like the fading smile on the face of one who wishes to intimate that the audience is at an end. I hastened to the door, bounded up the steps and scurried towards the market-place, my mind dominated by desire to tell my mother about these beautiful objects. How I found my way I know not, but find it I did. Happily the distance was short and I soon reached an anxious mother, for some kinsfolk were even then searching for the one who had strayed like a lost sheep. In tremulous excitement I tried to describe what I had seen, my treble tale interspersed with breathless questions, and all in the Welsh tongue, for I knew no English then.

And there the engraver laid down his tool. I do not recall the homeward journey. Worn out by the excitements of the day, I slept soundly on a pile of sacks, for the billowy wool had been exchanged for golden sovereigns which my grandfather carried in a small leathern scrip.

Some years later when my mother presented me with an illustrated book on heraldry explaining the mysteries of blazonry, crests, lions rampant, griffons segreant, chevrons and bends, fleurs-de-lys, argent, gules and azure, I began to appreciate the meaning of what I had seen within St. Mary's Church, Haverfordwest. That book remains a treasured memento.

Thenceforth I lived in the glow of heraldry. During schooldays a cultured master taught me to draw and paint shields and ensigns. I haunted solicitors' offices where I pored over armorial seals; transcribed manuscripts in national and private archives; tramped to remote churches to consult tablets and tombstones; explored the dim recesses of cathedrals, and hailed medieval effigies as my present friends. The eagles of Owain Gwynedd became as well-known

High Street, Haverfordwest

to me as the barnyard fowls at home, the golden lion of the Lord Rhys as familiar as Moss our faithful sheep dog. No man, however far he may travel, however long he may live, whatever successes he may enjoy, whatever reverses he may suffer, ever cuts himself wholly adrift from childhood influences and experiences. The memory of the brief encounter has remained with me as my ark of heraldic covenant. And so it was that the journey of an uncomprehending child in a farmer's cart jolting through a grey dawn to the wool fair at Haverfordwest, well over 70 years ago, early in the reign of King George V, marked the beginning of the road that was to lead to a herald's tabard in the reign of Queen Elizabeth the Second.

Some 80 yards across a green sward before my rural home, I could see ruins of ancient Llandeloy church (since restored), and just below it a holy well whose waters were said to cure many ailments when accompanied by a recital of the Lord's Prayer. But the well had another use. The holy well that provided water for our homes where it was used unaccompanied by prayer or invocation. In my eleventh year, we moved to Goodwick in Llanwnda parish, to enable me to go to Fishguard County School. My new home stood on the northern outskirts of the township, bordered by a farm, in one of whose fields a little well bubbled unobtrusively. As the field was called Parc Ffynnon Wnda, here then was the holy well of the saint after whom the parish had been named. It seemed that I was not to escape the watery piety of my early environment. Such were the origins of a pilgrimage that ended in 1954 with the publication of a minor work called *The Holy Wells of Wales*.

About this time, 1919-20, I came to know a delightful old lady. Marged Hughes was the daughter of the third generation of millers on the nearby estate of Trellewelyn. One of her narrations concerned the last of the ancient gentry there; namely three sisters known as "Tair Ladi Trellewelyn", admirable horsewomen famed for exploits in the hunting field, owning their own pack of hounds. Eventually, the estate passed to the surviving sister who married someone "from away" whose name my informant could not recall, but who lived at a place called "Bush or something similar". Over twenty years later I became friendly with J. W. Phillips, solicitor, and member of this Association. One day he invited me to dine at his pleasant home at Haverfordwest. We entered the dining room whose walls were adorned with numerous family portraits. I took my seat, and soon noticed on the opposite wall the portrait of a winsome lady in early eighteenth century attire. I asked who she was. My host replied, "She married an ancestor of mine, her name was Mary Phillips, heiress of Trellewelyn, who lived with her husband near this town at the mansion of Withybush". Here, at last, was my elusive Diana of the Chase. I raised my glass and drank a silent toast, not to the alluring heiress, but to Marged Hughes, long gone, whose tales had lingered in my mind. My kindly host afterwards loaned me deeds and documents enabling me to compile a history of the Trellewelyn estate and its former owners.

During my time at the Fishguard County School in the early 1920s, our masters often took us for country walks to study shrubs, trees, flowers; also to see archaeological remains, cromlechs, stone circles, old churches, mansions, and farmhouses, for the area was laden with relics of long, long ago. On our return we had to compose an essay describing what we had noted on our perambulations. Equally exciting were the "tasks", as they were known, to be carried out during summer holidays. One of mine was a dissertation, illustrated by sketches, on historical features in Llanwnda parish, which, for some reason, brought a cautious commendation.

These antiquarian rambles inspired me to compose short articles for local newspapers, a ploy that led to introductions to elderly, experienced persons with similar tastes and a tolerant attitude to tumbling youth. In 1926 my review of *The South Wales Squires* led to an agreeable correspondence with the author, Herbert Vaughan, then of Tenby, and when some years afterwards I settled at that seaside town, he gave me the freedom of his library where I made my first acquaintance with the volumes of Dwnn's *Heraldic Visitations,* to become constant companions of my adult life. Another early patron, Sir Evan Davies Jones, Lord Lieutenant, lived in a house overlooking Fishguard Bay, and he too gave me the run of his select library and extensive collection of heraldic bookplates. During one visit he presented me with the fourteen volumes of *West Wales Historical Records* edited by that enduring antiquary, Francis Green of St. Davids, whose friendship and guidance I was later to enjoy.

Such, then, are some memories of my youngling days. Eventually I became a schoolmaster, and made fresh acquaintances, many of them esteemed Cambrians like E. H. Leach, Dr. David Salmon, Sir Henry Stuart-Jones, Lord Merthyr, Professor W. F. Grimes and several solicitors who gave me access to ancient documents, all enriching my slowly accumulating historical experience.

In 1934 I was appointed to a boys' school in Haverfordwest, and further, instructed by the Pembrokeshire County Council to compile a schedule of their vast, hitherto neglected muniments housed within the castle, with a view to establishing a Record Office. In the adjoining building were the headquarters of the Pembrokeshire police, presided over by Capt. A. T. N. Evans, Chief Constable. I organised my office among the muniments, and had been there barely a week when a young friend, a local curate, called and, appalled at the amount of dust my suit was absorbing, departed, but returned within a few days and presented me with a raiment to protect my clothes, namely a white surplice, and it was in that garb, screening me from neck to foot, like a monk from a medieval monastery, that I greeted startled researchers who ventured to invade my dusty domain.

But an even stranger experience was to come my way. Now, in a room next to my archives were stored contemporary police records, some of a confidential nature. The question arose – should I, not being a member of the force, be allowed access to a building wherein such delicate material was kept? I became somewhat apprehensive. Nothing happened until one day a solemn policeman looked in, informing me that "the Chief" wished to see me immediately. I was ushered into the imperious presence, at a table stood a towering stern-faced Captain Evans. I trembled. Was the axe about to fall? He handed me a book, saying "Repeat after me: I swear by Almighty God" and so on till the end. Then, his face wreathed in a smile he said "Welcome, Mr. Jones. You are now a Special Constable, and can delve in your office without more ado". I believe I am the only archivist in Britain to have held the post of a Special Constable to enable archival duties to be accomplished. It is perhaps unnecessary to remind you that Captain Evans was an honoured member of this Association, and for many years its very efficient local secretary.

In due course I was advised to apply for a post in the Department of Manuscripts and Records in the National Library of Wales, then being advertised. This I did. Soon afterwards I received a visit from a stranger, a very pleasant gentleman indeed. He saw some of the work on which I was engaged, looked at the archives, and asked quite a number of questions, seemingly of an innocent nature. We got on splendidly, and following the usual civilities, he took his leave. At the time, all I knew of him was that he came from Cardiganshire, and his name, eternally Jones. A week or so later I received instructions to present myself at the National Library at a certain date, for interview. The event proved propitious, and I was among two applicants selected to fill the post, the other being my old school friend, Dr. B. G. Charles, born in the same parish as myself and a kinsman of my wife. Imagine my surprise when I discovered that my new governor, Keeper of the Department, was none other than the genial gentleman who had called at my Haverfordwest office. He is with us this evening, a distinguished former President of this Association namely Dr. E. D. Jones, who finally became Librarian of our National Institution. Holy Writ informs us that Moses dispatched twelve men to spy out the land of Canaan, an enterprise that took them forty days and forty nights. The National Library of Wales dispatched one man only who took but a few hours to amass the necessary information.

Hitherto, the Hundred of Dewsland had been my history tutor, its rural parishes my diligent instructors; Haverfordwest Castle had presided over my apprenticeship and now the National Library was to undertake my graduation. My time in that institution proved to be the most significant and rewarding of my antiquarian career, and I acknowledge my indebtedness to proficient colleagues whose indulgence and co-operation enabled me to deal more professionally with those interests which by now had become my way of life. I would like to mention one particular colleague whose co-operative responses added materially to my progression. He was then Keeper of the Department of Maps, Prints, and Drawings, his name, Mr Noel Jerman, whose contribution to contemporary studies, and especially to the Association, of which he became President, will be known to you all. Another felicitous association was the fact that one of the secretaries of the Library was Mrs. Blodwen Jerman who has also benefited the Cambrians in ample measure.

Then came the war, to take me away from the halcyon pastures of learning and research. The military experience taught me that however hostile the terrain, however engaged our energies, however difficult the circumstances, the antiquary need never be lonely or bereft, for through dark clouds shafts of sunlight break through to stimulate the imagination and bring contentment to the eye. Whatever the language of the land, historic remains are never dumb, but address the onlooker with an eloquence that requires no words. Campaigns in North Africa, the Middle East and Italy, provided opportunities, however brief, to extend, albeit cursorily, one's knowledge of relics of various civilisations as well as the more modern exhibit provided by those distant lands.

Towards the end of hostilities I was posted to the Historical Section of the War Office (later placed under the Cabinet Office), to commence writing the official history of the

Second World War. I duly reported to Whitehall, met my new chief, Brigadier Latham, an experienced military historian, and to my astonishment and delight, discovered that one of his secretaries was none other than Mrs. Blodwen Jerman, friend of Aberystwyth days. There was further joy in store, for her husband, Squadron-Leader H. N. Jerman was also stationed in London in the Ministry of Defence. Further, my department included Dr. Nash-Williams, whose early demise was later mourned by us all.

Fifteen years in London enabled me, during spare time, to consult the endless resources of the Public Record Office, British Museum, Society of Antiquaries, College of Arms and (equally important) to meet people whose scholarship augmented my increasing harvest. Alas, many have departed, like W. J. Hemp, J. D. K. Lloyd, J. Conway Davies, Sir Goronwy Edwards, Major Lloyd-Johnes, Sir John Cecil-Williams, Wynne Griffith, Sir Idris Foster, while others, happily still with us contributing to our journals, like Dr. A. J. Taylor, Dr. Ralegh Radford, Sir Anthony Wagner, Professor Glanmor Williams, Professor W. F. Grimes and many more.

My association with the College of Arms extends back to 1947 when I made the acquaintance of a distinguished herald, later to become Garter Principal King of Arms, Sir Anthony Wagner, a scholar and author with a comprehensive view of heraldry and all the various aspects associated with that art. Here too I met the other heralds, and owe much to their unfailing kindness and support over the years. I was invited by chapter to compile a report on the Welsh MSS in the College, which I duly made and presented in 1957. Among the large collection I discovered a chest full of such documents, some in the Welsh tongue, which had been sold by their indefatigable collector, Edward Protheroe, to the College in 1826, among them manuscripts by George Owen, the Pembrokeshire antiquary (d. 1613), others by the painstaking north Wales scholar, the Revd. Richard Thomas (d. 1780). This was the first time they had been unveiled since their purchase, and were of prime importance to antiquaries. With the College's permission, I invited my old friend, Dr. B. G. Charles, to examine the Owen items, some of which he used in his definitive biography, *George Owen of Henllys, a Welsh Elizabethan*, published in 1973. What a delight it was to study these yellowing papers that had slumbered undisturbed for some 130 years. Aladdin's cave is not wholly a thing of the past.

Fortunately, at an early stage I had appreciated the importance of friendship in the antiquarian world. No student of our historical heritage stands on his own, and neither does a specialised subject. Take for example numismatology: the subject concerns a number of factors that contribute to the whole. We ask, of what metals were the coins made? How and when did mints come into being?

Visiting ancient monuments between battles

How were the artisans trained in necessary skills? What is the significance of the designs? Why were certain emblems chosen as decorations? What do we know of the monarchs whose heads adorn them? What were the circumstances that led to the selection of such designs? Why do emblems vary so much? How were they controlled? Indeed many more aspects also call for elucidation. And so when one looks at a coin, ancient or modern, a whole concourse of circumstances is involved, and it becomes necessary to have, at least, an acquaintance with them. This is true of all the subjects that command our interest. No historian, no researcher stands on his own. We are all "fellows" whether elected or not. Conversation, correspondence, discussion, participation, these are the essential ingredients of our questing lives. I find that antiquaries are prepared always to help and to share. This, my masters, is the world of the true antiquary – and what a wonderful world!

In 1959 I returned to Wales to be archivist of Carmarthenshire, which afforded further opportunities for specialised research, and expanded my acquaintance with people of similar tastes, like Sir Frederick Rees, Sir Grismond Philipps of Cwmgwili, Canon Jones-Davies of Llywel, editors of learned journals like Dr. Prys Morgan of the Cymmrodorion and Mr. Gwyn Thomas of our Cambrians, successive editors of the journal of the National Library, Canon E. T. Davies and Canon Walker of the Church in Wales Historical Journal, Mr. George Boon and Geraint Jenkins of our National Museum, Messrs. Peter Smith and Tony Parkinson of RCAM, Mr. Donald Moore, and many members of our county antiquarian societies and of local record offices. I would particularly like to mention our former President, Sir Cennydd Traherne who helped substantially when I was compiling a list of Glamorgan historic houses, and including Lady Traherne who made visits to Coedarhydyglyn so pleasurable to my wife and myself, and Mr. Mansel Lewis, Lord Lieutenant of Dyfed and Lady Mary, who have given me unstinting support. To a man engaged in these studies, it is essential continually to widen one's sphere of friends. The field of historical and antiquarian research has no limit. We are for ever finding something new.

> *For there is good news yet to hear and fine things to be seen*
> *Before we go to Paradise by way of Kensal Green.*

And so the hurrying years swept on. In 1974 I retired from my official post, having devoted nearly all my life to research in the hope that one day I might find that elusive crock of gold at the end of an equally elusive rainbow. But there is no crock of gold, no *crochan aur*; if we desire it we must manufacture it ourselves.

Believing as I do that those engaged in research have a duty to make the results available to the public, through lectures, books, and essays, I have continued to offer my "widow's mite", trusting such productions may be regarded as contributions to subjects that interest us. This I hope to continue during the years that remain to me.

My own efforts have been directed largely to Welsh families and homes, many of the latter having been, within my lifetime, either demolished or reduced to a pale reflection of their former semblance. I have listed over 7,000 in our thirteen counties, which I visited from time to time. House and family should be studied together, for it was the dwellers who gave character and style to the dwelling, and, accordingly, I perused available genealogical works which exist in various repositories. As well as main residences we must include the lesser-known, many having survived as farmsteads, the history of their owners obscured, sometimes forgotten, but may often be retrieved from genealogical data. Much useful information can be provided by medieval poetry, odes of praise and dolorous elegies, while legal records, particularly lawsuits, taxation lists, are equally productive, and of course family deeds and documents. In more modern times, estate maps, terriers, and rent-rolls can be invaluable. Maps of cartographers from the days of Humphrey Lhuyd onwards, especially those of the eighteenth century, Emanuel Bowen and Kitchin's series for example, are often revealing. Early nineteenth century Ordnance Survey maps produced by Lieut.-Colonel Thomas Colby, are noteworthy, inasmuch as he sometimes marks the original site of a mansion that had been later re-erected some distance away.

A dreary feature of our century is the destruction of historical remains even where they have been officially listed. A few months ago a farmer in this county was fined for destroying an ancient fortification on his land. Such features can never be restored. Another example is provided by field-names, a most rewarding adjunct of historical studies, names like Parc y Castell, Parc y Gaer, Parc y Twmp, Parc y Meirw, Parc y Gromlech, Parc Ffynnon Fair, and the like, often the only clues to long-lost memorials. But many of these useful witnesses are disappearing due to changes in agricultural practices which require larger fields, even small farms being absorbed into the bigger units. A few years ago I visited a farm that had been sold to a landowner in England who had appointed a Scots bailiff to administer day-to-day concerns and found that the former field-names had been discontinued and replaced by numbers. Not long afterwards I visited what had been the residence of a landowning family, now sold to a distant farmer who settled there. I was standing on the lawn in front of the dwelling with the farmer's wife, a most co-operative lady. I had invited her to tell me the names of the fields. She was sorry, they no longer knew the original names, their pronunciation was too complicated, and now the fields had no names at all. I then pointed to a field before us and said "If a bull broke into that field how would you describe it to your husband or workers?" She promptly answered: "I'd say the bull has broken into the field in front of the house." "But what if he broke in there?" said I, pointing to the adjacent meadow. She replied, "I'd say that the bull had broken into the field next to the field in front of the house." For this indomitable lady there was no U-turn.

It is true that such names can be rescued by chats with old workmen and neighbours, but they, too, are becoming fewer. The Tithe Schedules and Maps of 1836-47, can be helpful, but unfortunately a number do not include all the field-names, some none at all, so that chances of recovery may well be nullified. In this county, some Women's Institutes have amassed a most comprehensive collection of field names, and they deserve warmest congratulations for safeguarding our heritage by their admirable exertions.

Whenever compiling a narrative of a family and its residence, I try to include the local setting, for human affairs - our way of life - are determined by history, environment, climate, occupation, language, religion, education, traditions and legends, all of which should be taken into account. Nothing stands on its own – castles, mansions, homesteads, cottages, *cromlechau*, architecture – all form part of the tapestry that destiny weaves around us.

Such are some of the delights and difficulties confronting antiquaries and historians. But we can offer a lifetime, and if we concentrate on rescue and protection, much vital information may yet be safeguarded and our store of knowledge increased. In these days of rapid change, the antiquary has no time to stand and stare.

Finally, Mr. Chairman, Ladies and Gentlemen, I would like to pay a tribute to one who for some fifty-three long and pleasant years was the mainstay of my endeavours, namely my wife who departed from amongst us earlier this year. She was thrilled to learn that I had been selected to become your President, and had looked forward to this occasion. So, it is appropriate that I am allowed to render homage to her this evening. My tribute will be short, it will not be mournful, but I hope will illustrate the joyousness that characterised her journey through life.

Ethel also had enjoyed a country upbringing. She came from a farming background and was interested in her forebears, the families of Charles, Lawrence, Skeel and Dedwydd, particularly the last-named, who bore this unusual, indeed unique, surname, meaning "happy". This Dewsland patronymic is first found in 1326. The last of the male line was William Dedwydd whose daughter, Margaret Dedwydd, was my wife's grandmother. She liked to recall the family tradition relating to the origin of the name. Early one morning, a Dewsland farmer, on opening the outer door, was amazed to find on the threshold, a bundle containing a child attired in silks and ribbons. He lifted the bundle, whereupon the little one looked up and gave him a cheerful smile. The farmer exclaimed, "Dedwydd wyt, a Dedwydd fydd dy enw" (Happy thou art, and Happy will be thy name), and carried him into the homestead where he was nurtured, in due course married, the name Dedwydd being borne by his yeomen successors, and, although now extinct in the male line, the name and its qualities continue to distinguish descendants. My wife certainly inherited a happy sunlit nature. Her modesty and unassuming ways were basic ingredients of her personality as many here this evening will know. Although not trained in historical and antiquarian studies, an intelligent interest enabled her to become proficient in such matters. She drew and painted heraldic shields, accompanied me to ancient churches, copied entries from parish registers, helped to measure buildings, and being adept with camera, took pictures of scores of country houses, farmsteads, earthworks and the like, often directing my attention to details that had escaped my observation. She read my essays, made useful corrections and improvements. She drove me, a non-driver, to sites throughout Wales, often places I would never have seen otherwise. She was my Good Companion.

All these travels were pleasureable, except one which proved less attractive perhaps. I vividly recollect this most unusual experience that befell us several years ago. And a strange event it was. She had driven me to a remote mansion on a wooded hillside which had been sold to a local farmer who inhabited the domestic wing of the residence. We entered by a drive, one side bounded by a large meadow, and owing to the very bumpy surface of the route, my charioteer suggested pulling on to the meadow, and then proceed on foot. We did so, and walked towards a gate secured with a piece of cord. The mansion stood just below, an impressive eighteenth century building, from which a wing extended to the rear, and whose door was half ajar. As I drew near, the door seemed to move towards me, then closed with a click, and I heard the rattling of chains being secured by an unseen hand. Mystified, I knocked. No answer, and my hesitant call "Anyone at home?" met with a serene silence. Gloomily I returned to my wife who comforted me by saying we might call again some time. We retraced our steps to the meadow, almost reached the car when suddenly the air was rent by a tumultuous bellowing from an enraged

The manic moo

cow careering across the grass. We hurriedly entered and secured the doors. Luckily the animal swerved past, darted towards the gate which it shattered and continued towards the mansion proclaiming its advent with a most horrendous fanfare. Unperturbed, my wife turned the car and sped like a rally driver towards the outer entrance. As we passed safely through, I noticed a roadside well just below the ancient parish church. My antiquarianism immediately took over, and I asked her to stop so that I could examine it as I had heard of its healing properties. A man was filling a pail at the well, who, I thought might tell me something of interest. I got out and walked towards him, and when I spoke he turned sharply, and I soon realised that the poor man was clearly defective and almost inarticulate. I hastily entered the car. All I could say was "Down the road". It proved to be the steepest hill in the county, with bends like fiddlers' elbows, steep falls on one hedgeless side of the alarming route, but my driver's skilful manoeuvring enabled us to reach the low ground safely. We then passed over a small stone bridge, beyond which lay a sleepy hamlet with an old-fashioned tavern where I decided to call to enjoy some refreshment to restore my spirits. Alas, the tavern was shut. It was the last note in a litany of catastrophe. Clearly it was not my day.

Such was my acquaintance with the unexpected. My wife then drove up a long hill on the further side and gained the airy uplands, but after a few miles her cheerful comments brought me out of my depression and soon we were both laughing merrily about the buffets that had come my way. Whenever she was around there was always balm in Gilead. With her at my side I never walked alone. My years with her had been a Dance to the Music of Time.

A companion of kindly, gentle ways, Ethel now lies in the lap of legends, among the tranquil acres of her ancestral Dewsland which had always been her abiding scene.

For many years this Association too has walked by my side. I profited from opportunities of attending lectures delivered by well-informed and experienced members, of participating in discussions and exchange of information, while it enabled some of my literary efforts to be published in our valued journal. My connection with the Cambrian Archaeological Association has been long and fruitful, so that it is a privilege indeed to become your President, and, in your company, savour again endless enjoyments from the antique world. *Da bo'ch a Dedwydd.*

CHAPTER III

EARLY DAYS

PEMBROKESHIRE FROM NORMAN TIMES ONWARDS

ON THE eve of the Norman invasion, the territory known to us today as Pembrokeshire, formed part of the Kingdom of Deheubarth, ruled by Rhys ap Tewdwr, descendant of the law-giver Hywel Dda. Although the earlier Kingdom of Dyfed has been incorporated into Deheubarth it continued to retain its older land divisions as units of administration. In the north and north-west lay the *cantrefi* of Emlyn, Cemais, and Pebidiog; in the centre lay those of Rhos and Daugleddyf; below the haven of Milford lay Penfro, a long curved promontory that stretched from the shores of Castlemartin to the woodlands of Narberth; and on the east lay the cantref of Gwarthaf extending eastwards to the gates of the town of Carmarthen.

It is worth noting that these divisions were disturbed very little by the Normans who based their feudal units on the earlier Welsh ones, and that several centuries later, when Pembrokeshire was formed into a shire on the English pattern, the earlier divisions survived as administrative hundreds and indeed continue so to this day. Thus despite superimposition by the conquerors, the older territorial divisions survived, a circumstance that gave stability to the basic population, and, as we shall see, resulted in the remarkable survival of the native aristocracy and the farming families.

A rapid Norman thrust in the latter half of the eleventh century altered the whole political structure of West Wales, and the land known to us as Pembrokeshire became severed from Deheubarth, so that by the twelfth century it consisted of a conglomeration of feudal lordships forming part of those occupied lands known as the marches of Wales. This arrangement lasted until 1536, so that throughout the Middle Ages, Pembrokeshire never achieved any unity, and its history is that of fragments, each under its own feudal lord who held the land of the King, often retaining many of the older Welsh customs like *cymortha* for example, local officials such as the *maer* and *rhaglaw* and elements of Welsh administration that the Norman lords incorporated into the feudal structure. And so the way of life of the people – particularly in the rural areas – was not unduly disturbed. It was a change of masters rather than a change of population. Even in south Pembrokeshire where Anglo-Norman occupation was more pronounced, the native population was not so much displaced as absorbed, as shown by the names of Welshmen in early deeds and documents and by Welsh place-names, like Tenby, Pembroke, Pwllcrochan, Llangwm and others which would not have survived had the occupation been as ruthless and thorough as it is sometimes alleged to have been. The most significant of the changes wrought by the conquerors was the establishment of towns and boroughs, almost exclusively Anglo-

Norman, and as these were more numerous in south Pembrokeshire, their influence there was more marked than in the agricultural north. Furthermore, intermarriage between the invaders and the native population, such as Martin, Mortimer, Cantington, de Windsor, Stackpole, and Perrott, to name but a few, led to an early intermingling of the races, and so to a lessening of tension, and a general stabilis-

Manorbier Castle

ation. The difference between "Little England beyond Wales" and the rest of the county is not racial but linguistic.

The Norman arrival was heralded by the advance of Roger de Montgomery (created Earl of Shrewsbury in 1071), who from Cardiganshire thrust boldly into Pembrokeshire with forces that proved sufficiently powerful to retain those areas that the rapidity of their onset had gained. These lands were conferred upon Earl Roger's younger son, Arnulph de Montgomery, who established his *caput* at Pembroke, where a fortalice, hurriedly built, was later extended into a formidable stone castle and entrusted to the care of his chief follower, Gerald de Windsor.

Encouraged by this success, other Norman thrusts followed, and the land parcelled out among the adventurous invaders. In the south the native population was partly displaced, although not on so large a scale as commonly supposed, while those who remained were absorbed by the Anglo-Norman followers who engaged in the arts of peace; farming, trading and fishing as well as those of war.

These settlements were not established without opposition and even after castles were erected and the settler population reinforced, they had to struggle to maintain their foothold against the Welsh under the princes of Deheubarth, and both the King and his barons often found themselves engaged in wars of re-conquest. However, the superior military equipment and discipline of the Anglo-Normans, their reinforcement from England both by sea and by land, coupled with the internecine rivalries between the native princes, rendered the final outcome inevitable.

Consequently there is no unified history of Pembrokeshire during the Middle Ages, although at some points it sometimes touched national history. It was from Pembrokeshire that the initial conquest of Ireland was carried out; it was the lordships of the county that formed a firm base for campaigns against the Welsh princes and it was from Milford Haven that Henry Tudor set forth for the field of Bosworth, an adventure that changed the course of our national history. To appreciate the significance of this development it becomes necessary to review the lordships in a little more detail. These lordships did not come into being at one particular date; their boundaries often changed, and there were occasional creations of new lordships and sub-infeudation. Nevertheless the pattern of the political mosaic remained constant, namely the superimposition of the feudal structure on the older territorial divisions.

By far the most important of the lordships was that of Pembroke. As already indicated it owed its early existence to Earl Roger and his son, Arnulph. Originally, the territory under its direct rule included the land south of the Haven, that is the old cantref of Penfro, a name retained by the conquerors and which took the form of Pembroke. In the early part of the twelfth century, the lordship came to include the cantrefi of Rhos and Daugleddyf to the north of the Haven, but further changes confined it to the earlier cantref of Penfro. In later times the Earls of Pembroke extended their domination, even to include the more northerly lordship of Cemais, but this was always opposed and the overlordship was but shadowy. Its chief stronghold, the fortress of Pembroke, was first built about 1190, and others were raised later within its boundaries – Carew, Manorbier, Tenby and the smaller outpost of Upton. Pembroke was organised as a shire, much along the pattern already established in England, with its own jurisdiction, administered by a sheriff, coroner, and other administrative officers. It was certainly organised as a county palatine in 1138, and possibly earlier. This was the first area of the conquered lands to be so organised to the west of Severn and forms the root of Pembrokeshire's claim to be the premier county in Wales. Nevertheless, it must be remembered that this county included only a part of the territory that comprises modern Pembrokeshire. The holders of this fief were earls, considerably more important than the barons or lords of the neighbouring lands. The Earls of Pembroke were national figures and their names, Montgomery, Clare, Marshal, Valence, Hastings, and Herbert form part of British history. It must be appreciated that none of these was ever resident in Pembroke, and few of them ever visited the county whence they derived their title and revenues. The first Earl of Pembroke was Gilbert de Clare who received the dignity in March 1138. On the death of the third earl without issue soon after 1185, his sister, Isabel de Clare, carried the earldom to her husband, William Marshal. Six of the name of Marshal bore the title, until eventually it passed to the de Valence family who held it for two generations. From de Valence it passed to Hastings, the last of whom, John de Hastings, died as Earl of Pembroke in 1389, when the earldom reverted to the Crown. In 1414 Henry IV conferred the dignity on his younger son, Humphrey of Lancaster, who held it until 1447, and in that year it was granted to William de la Pole, Earl of Suffolk. The next Earl, Jasper Tudor, was invested in 1452, but was attainted some nine years later. In 1468 it was conferred on William Herbert whose tenure was brief as he was beheaded in the following year. His only son, William Herbert, succeeded to the earldom, but in 1479 resigned it at the request of King Edward IV who created him Earl of Huntingdon. The reason for the resignation was that the King wished to bestow the title on his son and heir apparent. Accordingly on 8 July 1479, the King conferred the Earldom of Pembroke on Edward, Prince of Wales, who held it until he succeeded to the Throne as King Edward V on 9 April 1483. This Earl of Pembroke is better known in history as one of the "Princes of the Tower," where he was murdered about five months after his accession. Another association of the Prince with Pembrokeshire is that he was also Lord of Haverfordwest, the lordship having been conferred on him by his father.

After this the earldom slumbered awhile. In 1532 Henry VIII erected it into a marquessate which he conferred on his wife, Queen Anne Boleyn. On the execution of the marchioness four years later the dignity reverted to the Crown. However, the title Earl of Pembroke was revived and on 11 October 1551, was conferred on William Herbert in whose descendants it has remained to this day. The present incumbent is the sixteenth Earl of the last creation and the thirty-fifth who has held the ancient title of Earl of Pembroke.   The history of the other lordships follow a similar pattern. The lords marcher bowed the knee only to the King and in their marcherdoms they were kings themselves.

In the last decade of the eleventh century or the beginning of the twelfth – the date is uncertain, Robert FitzMartin, a fiefholder in Devon, established himself in the Nevern district where he appropriated the lands and fortified dwelling of a Welsh regulus who had been unable to withstand the onset.

Rapacity and piety were twin characteristics of the Normans and one of FitzMartin's first acts after acquiring power over an extensive part of the cantref of Cemais was to found the Abbey of St. Dogmael, probably in 1118. Although his troops were superior both in armament and discipline to the pastoral Welshmen, he had to take the field constantly and in 1135 was fighting desperately to resist the sons of Cyhylyn and the princes of Deheubarth. Nevertheless he weathered the difficulties, a temporary peace was arranged, and with true Norman perspicacity he sought firmer assurance for the future by marrying his son, William, to Angharad, daughter of Rhys ap Gruffydd, one of Deheubarth's most illustrious princes. For some time the alliance resulted in more settled conditions, but he was to find that family relationship was not a certain basis for lasting harmony. Owing to some disagreement Rhys ap Gruffydd marched against his son-in-law and in 1191 expelled him from his stronghold at Nevern. Whereupon William settled at nearby Newport and on a knoll overlooking the sea built a strong stone castle which thenceforth became the caput of his barony of Cemais.

The lords of Cemais suffered from their Norman friends as much as from their Welsh relations, for the earls of Pembroke sought, and often succeeded in establishing overlordship over their neighbours' affairs. Accordingly Cemais occasionally came under the suzerainty of the earls, as for instance in 1273 when Nicholas Martin acknowledged that he owed suit to the Earl for his lordship of Cemais.

The Martins seem to have resided on their lands far more than most of the other lords and after 1282 we find William Martin being ordered by the King, "to dwell continuously," in the Welsh marches. On the death of the last male of the family in 1326, the barony passed to James, Lord Audley, a descendant through the female line from the builder of Newport castle. The lordship remained in the Audleys until the death of Nicholas, Lord Audley. In 1391, it fell into abeyance and remained in that uncertain state until 1405-8 when it passed to his great-nephew, John Tuchet, who held the title of Lord Audley. The baronial rights and franchises of Cemais were alienated in 1543 when John, Lord Audley sold them to William Owen of Henllys, a local landowner enriched by practice of the law, father of Pembrokeshire's celebrated antiquary, George Owen. By that time however, the prerogatives and realities of the medieval lordships together with all others in the marches of Wales, had been vested in the Crown so that what William Owen in fact acquired were the rights and status of an ordinary lord of the manor.

The neighbouring lordship of Cilgerran on the banks of the Teifi in north-east Pembrokeshire had been carved out of parts of the old cantref of Emlyn, probably founded by the Montgomerys or the Clares, and was under the domination of the Earls of Pembroke. During the first half of the thirteenth century the Cantilupes were the lords, from whom Cilgerran passed to the Hastings family which held it in 1277. In the fifteenth century it became part of the possessions of the Crown. The caput of the lordship of Cilgerran, stood on a steep bluff overlooking a narrow gorge through which runs the river Teifi.

The lordship of Haverford owed its origin to the Norman invaders and the powerful castle that dominated the tidal Cleddau at this spot, is believed to have been built in the twelfth century by Gilbert de Clare, father of the first Earl of Pembroke. Like other Pembrokeshire lordships it was from time to time held as part of the Earldom and occasionally by the Crown. In 1317 Edward II specifically granted Haverford to Aylmer de Valence, Earl of Pembroke. It often changed hands and was held at different times by de Braose, de Bohun, Hastings and Mortimer. It was held by the Prince of Wales (son of Edward IV), and it was as Edward Prince of Wales and Lord of Haverford, that he granted a charter conferring important liberties on the burgesses and enacting that the town should be incorporated.

The smaller lordship of Narberth was never so important as the others, although its castle occupied a strategic position in eastern Pembrokeshire. It was held at various times by the families of Mortimer and Devereux, and in 1477 was held by the Prince of Wales.

The lordships of Dewsland (Pebidiog) and Llawhaden differed from the others inasmuch as they were episcopal fiefs whose overlord for the time being, was the Bishop of St. Davids. The ancient cantref of Pebidiog had been granted by the Welsh princes to the See of St. Davids, a circumstance that had an important effect on those who lived there. It is the only part of Wales that has never been conquered either by the English or the Normans. Its inhabitants are the oldest free folk in Britain. The Normans, pious if nothing else,

respected the property of the Church so that Dewsland was spared the battles and sieges that accompanied the annexation of other parts of Pembrokeshire. No stone fortress was built on its soil; no alien garrison stood ward and watch over its inhabitants. The fact that it was the land of Dewi, the patron saint, proved sufficient to preserve it from the grasping hands of ambitious invaders. To its caput, the cathedral church of St. Davids, came thousands of pilgrims throughout the Middle Ages when two such pilgrimages were held to be equal to one to the Eternal City. From the bay of Goodwick to the strand of Newgale, from the grey crags of Pencaer to the bold cliffs of Penmaendewi, agricultural folk passed tranquil days. While all the Norman castles are in ruins, the Cathedral of St. Davids remains an enduring monument to the

Celtic Cross at Nevern

arts of peace. It is true that the once magnificent Episcopal palace on the banks of Alun is now nothing more than a picturesque relic, but that change was encompassed by the vicissitudes of administration rather than the battering ram and siege gun.

The smaller lordship of Llawhaden also belonged to the see and its castle was built as a fortified residence for the Bishops in the

St. Dogmaels

penultimate decade of the thirteenth century. The Bishops had two other residences, neither being fortified, namely Trefin in Dewsland, and Lamphey, "below the water," in Castlemartin.

Such was the political complexion of Pembrokeshire throughout the Middle Ages – a mosaic of lordships each under its own lord with its own laws and customs. Thus the medieval history of the county is a history of fragments, there was no cohesion, no central control. It was a western Balkans. Accordingly no history of Pembrokeshire as such can be attempted for this period, we can only glance at certain facets of life, the main ingredient of which was a sturdy individualism.

Another Norman feature, the relics of which are still with us, was the building of religious houses. Among these were St. Dogmaels Abbey and Pill Priory (Reformed Benedictines), Haverfordwest Priory (Augustinian Canons), Haverfordwest Friary (Black Friars), Monkton Priory (Benedictine), Caldey Priory, Llawhaden Hospital and Whitwell Hospital at St. Davids. All of these owed their origin to the Normans such as William Martin, who founded Caldey and St. Dogmaels, Robert FitzTankard, founder of Haverfordwest Priory, Arnulph of Montgomery, founder of Monkton Priory and Adam de Rupe (Roch), founder of Pill Priory. In addition there were numerous subordinate chapels and chantries, dating from the age of Celtic saints, built in characteristic Welsh form and often endowed and enriched by the Norman settlers. Among these we find the chapel at the holy well of Cwmwdig, St. Justinian's chapel, St. Mary's College at St. Davids, St. Non's chapel and many more. Prominent among them and enjoying considerable wealth and power, was the Commandery of the Knights of St. John at Slebech, above the waters of Cleddau. Together with the parish priests, the good monks were the main, indeed the only, civilising agents of that barbarous age, giving succour to the needy, aid to the sickly and infirm, welcoming to their cloisters the wandering bards, the illuminators of manuscripts, as well as training and encouraging the voices of young and old to give praise to the Heavenly Master, to serve whom was their mission in life.

However, there were two features which taken together help to form the larger picture, although they developed independently and largely in isolation. The first was the establishment and development of towns, the second was the basic industry of the county, agriculture. Trade and industry in addition to sustaining the wants of society, also provide a sense of unity and common purpose, often helping to allay racial animosities. A "Welsh black" among the pastures of Daugleddy and a pony on the slopes of Preseli, have no nationality. Growing and raising, buying and selling, farming, fishing, trading – this was the common denominator that governed men's daily lives.

The Welsh had never been dwellers in towns. Prior to the Norman arrival there had been no towns in Pembrokeshire, only a few villages of no consequence. The formation of towns was an alien activity introduced into the county by the Normans. Apart from siting castles in places that gave them natural protection, the Normans were also careful to site them so that their garrisons had access to the sea and could be supported by sea-borne reinforcements. This meant that they were often sited at places equally suitable for sea-borne trade with the result that during the Middle Ages many developed into flourishing trading town, such as Pembroke, Tenby, Haverfordwest and Newport. The Norman retainers built their habitations around the walls of the castles to which they could retire in troublous times and the Norman lords protected their followers by granting privileges and liberties to them. Charters were granted, sometimes by the local lord, sometimes by the King and invariably confirmed, sometimes extended, by successive monarchs. The towns themselves were protected by strong walls and gateways, excellent examples of which can still be seen at Tenby.

Pembroke can justly claim to be the first county town in Wales, being *caput* of the first county organised to the west of Severn. It received its first charter in the reign of Henry I (1100-35) and the first Earl incorporated the inhabitants of the town which he surrounded with an embattled wall defended by several bastions and entered by well-guarded gateways. The town flourished and although it often suffered from warlike incursions, its castle never fell into the hands of an attacker. Within the castle walls Henry VII was born – the last of the three Kings of England who had been born on Welsh soil.

Haverfordwest, on the banks of the tidal Cleddau, received its first charter from Henry II (1154-89) who confirmed the liberties of the townsfolk as they had been in the time of Henry I, so it is certain that the town was built early in the twelfth century and that it possibly had received an earlier charter. Subsequent charters were granted to Haverfordwest by two Earls of Pembroke and by fifteen monarchs, the last being from the hands of William and Mary. Governed by a mayor who also bore the title of Admiral of the Port, and a Corporation, it became the most important trading centre in Pembrokeshire. The right to have a sheriff and two bailiffs was granted in 1479 by the

Pembroke Castle

Prince of Wales, who then held the dignity of Lord of Haverford. In 1545 Henry VIII granted a statute erecting it into a town and county of itself which later enjoyed its own assizes, courts of Great Sessions, with a Lord Lieutenant and *Custos Rotulorum*. Its prosperity and geographical position made Haverfordwest an ideal county town after the Act of Union which organised Pembrokeshire as a shire.

Other towns such as Newport, whose earlier charter was confirmed by Nicholas Martin about the year 1240, and Tenby whose inhabitants were incorporated by William de Valence with the consent of his wife in whose right he had succeeded to the palatinate, developed along similar lines, while lesser castle-towns like Narberth and Cilgerran became thriving centres for local trade.

The racial composition of Pembrokeshire was greatly affected by medieval events. In the train of the Norman lords came Englishmen, later to be reinforced, particularly in the southern half of the county by families from Somerset, Devon and Cornwall, counties which always enjoyed a brisk coastal trade with south Wales. In the eleventh century a number of Flemings settled there, mainly in the Roose and Haverfordwest area, described by Giraldus as "a people brave and robust, ever most hostile to the Welsh . . . well versed in commerce and woollen manufactories". They were too few in numbers to maintain a separate identity for long and became absorbed into the general population. It is ironic that the only family which has a proven descent in the male line from a Fleming, lives in the Welsh part of Pembrokeshire, whose ancestors forsook their Germanic tongue for that of the native population. In time these elements, to which was added later an Irish infusion, became welded into Pembrokeshire men described by the poet Drayton as, "those men of Pembroke of the mixed breed".

It is interesting to note that the northern part of the county retained its Welsh speech throughout the centuries, whereas the southern part is entirely English-speaking. The line dividing these linguistic communities stretches roughly from Roch on the west to Narberth on the east. George Owen, the Pembrokeshire historian, has discussed this division in some detail and sometimes used the old legal term land-scar (that is, boundary) to express himself. Unfortunately some modern writers have interpreted this as a proper name and have tried to impose the name "landsker" or "landscar" on this dividing line. However, no Pembrokeshire man has ever used the term in that sense and it is time that this "cuckoo's egg" should be expelled from the writings of enthusiastic but ill-informed writers of the mid twentieth century.

In fact the difference between north and south Pembrokeshire is not racial, but linguistic. In the north we still find Welsh speaking families bearing the Norman names of Martell, Mortimer, Devereux and Reynish and English names of Picton, Sayce, Selby, Miles, Mabe and Batin, while in the south, monoglot English families answer to the names Griffith, Howell, Craddock, Bowen and Rees. Thus does genealogy confound racial and nationalistic unrealities and in Pembrokeshire the language of a man is no indication of his ancestral origin. The man whose ancestors were harried by Normans now keeps a shop in the shadow of Pembroke castle, while another whose ancestors lorded it over medieval Haverfordwest herds his sheep on the uplands of Freni Fawr.

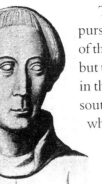

Gerald of Wales

Throughout the Middle Ages the people of Pembrokeshire pursued a reasonably settled life. It is true that until the final eclipse of the Welsh princes in 1282, the land was often harried by warbands, but there was no re-conquest and the castles and lordships remained in the hands of the advenae. Its geographical position at the extreme south-west meant that it was far removed from those parts of Wales where the political decisions were decided in field and court. Even during the rising of Owain Glyndŵr whose armies thrust into the very heart of the west, Pembrokeshire was never as completely in his grasp as the rest of Wales. Glyndŵr had good Norman blood in his veins, for he descended from the family of de Vale who held lands in the lordship of Haverfordwest and he himself inherited the manor of Trefgarn in the right of that descent. The county also suffered from the ravages of the Wars of the Roses, but the people were content to leave the issues of state to their lords whose main concern was the retention of the castles. Some of them, like Harry Dwnn of Picton Castle, took the field on the Yorkist side which led to his death at the battle of Banbury in 1469. Another Pembrokeshire Yorkist was more fortunate. This was Jenkyn Lloyd of Blaiddbwll in Llanfyrnach, a descendant of early chieftains and who bore as his coat of arms a golden lion rampant between eight golden roses on a blue shield. To demonstrate his loyalty to the House of York, he changed the colour of the roses to white. So long as the Yorkists were in the ascendant he did well and was rewarded with some local appointments. However, after the Lancastrian triumph in 1485 we hear no more of Jenkyn and his white roses – an example of the hazards of displaying one's politics in heraldic form.

During the Middle Ages, Pembrokeshire produced two of Wales's greatest literary men. The first, in point of time was Gerald de Barri, better known as Giraldus Cambrensis or Gerald the Welshman. Born at Manorbier about 1146, he was the youngest son of William de Barri and Angharad, daughter of Gerald de Windsor by Nest, daughter of the prince, Rhys ap Tewdwr. He became an eminent cleric and wrote numerous books, still regarded as valuable sources of historical information, perhaps the best known being *Intinerarium Kambriae*. He died in 1223. The other literateur was Wales's greatest medieval poet, Dafydd ap Gwilym, who flourished in the period 1340-70. Dafydd was very much a Pembrokeshire man, being descended from its ancient princes who had come to terms with the Normans and whose descendants became King's men, and held important royal appointments in west Wales. His great-great-grandfather had been Constable of Cemais in 1241 and a decade later held the appointment of King's Bailiff. It is necessary to emphasise his ancestry, for Dafydd's connection with Pembrokeshire is conveniently overlooked by writers who wish to associate him more intimately with a neighbouring county. His poems have survived and, as Dr Thomas Parry has written, "his conception

Henry Tudor

of the unity of the poem as the ordered production of a single mood is not matched in the works of any other Welsh poet until the present century".

The accession of Pembrokeshire-born Henry Tudor, Earl of Richmond, as King Henry VII in 1485 was the beginning of a long period of peace for a country that had been cruelly racked by internal dissension for nearly a century. The political structure of Wales – principality, crown lands, marcherdoms – and the fragmentary character of its local government, remained unchanged, seemingly unchanging. But winds of change were blowing over the land and during the reign of the next monarch rose to a veritable hurricane.

There were several reasons for the impending changes. The economic position of Britain had become stronger and her overseas trading interests added daily to her growing wealth. The Renaissance had inspired new ideas, but more important still was the attitude of the Crown towards its responsibilities. The Tudors quickly realised that the only way to eliminate civil disorders was to centralise government and control directly under the Crown, and to deprive the feudal nobility of the ability to muster troops and to wage war under their own banners. Served by able administrators and an efficient bureaucracy, the trend was towards centralisation of authority thus increasing the power of the Crown. The Statute of Livery and Maintenance was passed to prohibit the great lords assembling and maintaining armed retainers so that private wars and a possible threat to central government was effectively reduced. A new spirit was becoming evident, the spirit of English nationalism, typified in the person of the able, ambitious, energetic Henry VIII. He was the herald of the modern age – a John Bull in Tudor bonnet.

But it was not until the fourth decade of the sixteenth century that Britain was pulled, squealing and struggling, from its outworn medieval background and brought into a world that demanded new men and new measures. Between 1530 and 1540 a revolution took place in Britain which was to determine its future position in the European structure. Its main architect was Henry VIII, the greatest crowned revolutionary in British history and certainly its most successful.

The first step was the complete severance of the native Church from the dominance of Rome. The substitution of the monarch as head of the Church was an act of supreme significance and the ruthlessness with which the policy was carried out bore ample witness to the determination of the reforming King and his ministers. The dissolution of the monasteries followed. Although most religious houses were in need of reform there can be no doubt that their suppression was a violent measure and, some might consider, went beyond the demands of reasonable correction. In Pembrokeshire, the abbeys of St. Dogmaels, Haverfordwest, Monkton, the College of St. Mary at St. Davids and the chantries, were emptied of their venerable tenants, of their treasures, lands, and revenues, while the outward expression of religious exercises, pilgrimages to holy wells and altars of saints, adoration of relics and veneration of images, were declared idolatrous practices, not to be tolerated by a monarch who, ironically, had once been declared "Defender of the Faith" by a former occupant of the throne of St. Peter. The people were stunned, but generally acquiesced in the new order which afforded them little opportunity for defying the dictates of their masterful ruler. When, over a decade later, Queen Mary attempted a counter-reformation, it found strong opposition from those who had accepted the new Protestantism, and William Nichol of Haverfordwest, preferred to suffer at the stake rather than renounce his convictions.

But the measure that affected Pembrokeshire most was the so-called Act of Union of 1536, and the supplemental act passed four years later. This was the moment in history when Pembrokeshire as we know it was born. Here again, the ruthless axe fell with devastating effect. The distinction between Crown lands, the lord Marcherdoms and their separate jurisdictions, was swept away and the whole county came under the rule of English law. While it is true that many of the feudal incidences remained in that some of the older divisions survived as manors – Cemais and Dewsland, for example – this had only a minor significance, for their incumbents could no longer raise troops, levy taxes, or execute felons. They had been cut down to size. The King was supreme over all.

Inevitably, boundaries were rearranged. The eastern half of the lordship of Emlyn and nearly all of the fertile cantref of Gwarthaf, were torn from medieval Dyfed and incorporated into the new shire of Carmarthen. Then, indeed as now, angry growls were heard on the slopes of Preseli and on the banks of Cleddau, in the council chambers of Haverfordwest and Tenby and the court leet at Newport but these in no way lessened the determination of the monarch and his ministers to implement the new policy. Pembrokeshire came into being – its traditional cantrefi and lordships transformed into seven administrative hundreds; in the north Cilgerran, Cemais and Dewsland; in mid-county, Roose, Dungleddy and Narberth; and, "below the water", the long curving horn of Pembroke, which gave its name to the new political structure. By further arrangements made in 1542, Haverfordwest was formed into a county of its own (as well as remaining the "county town" of the whole shire), while Laugharne and Llanstephan (initially included in the new Pembrokeshire), were transferred to Carmarthenshire. This settlement, which re-arranged the rump of the old Dyfed, has remained substantially unchanged to the present day.

As we have seen, by an accident of history, Pembrokeshire became divided into Welsh and English-speaking areas. Under the new dispensation the division remained as clear as ever and, indeed, has never been eliminated. However, there is not, and has never been, any line of demarcation.

A south Pembrokeshire man has as much loyalty and affection for the Prince of Wales as his northern neighbour, and the burghers of Haverfordwest will cheer the Welsh rugby XV as ecstatically as the ploughmen of Llandeloy.

King Henry VIII who affected these changes had close family associations with the county. Among his ancestors were the Welsh princes of Dyfed, the later lords of Trefgarn and the Norman family of de Vale. His grandfather had been buried near the high altar in St. David's Cathedral. His father had been born in Pembroke Castle in 1456 and had found refuge among Pembrokeshire folk when Yorkist rulers were baying at his heels and it was to Milford Haven that he returned in 1485, and from there, with an army swelled by Pembrokeshire supporters, marched to decisive victory at Bosworth. Henry VIII was the first to fortify the Haven whose waters had borne his father to the sceptre and the orb.

The new organisation allowed Pembrokeshire people to participate more intimately in the governing of their local affairs. For the first time the people were able to elect Members of Parliament, provide High Sheriffs and Justices of the Peace from among their own kith and kin. They had access to the King's courts at Westminster and to the King's Assizes and Great Sessions held on their doorstep. Numerous lesser officials, coroners, clerks of the courts, customs officers, commissioners, captains of array, and many more were selected from the men on the spot. The people of Pembrokeshire were now participating in self-government. It was a form of home rule.

Mention must also be made, in passing, of an important event in the reign of Queen Elizabeth, since it had a profound effect on the northern half of the county. This was the translation of the Bible into Welsh, and this more than any other single factor contributed to the preservation of this ancient language.

As a maritime county Pembrokeshire had a two-fold interest – seaborne trade and agricultural production. Through Tudor (and later) times, agriculture continued to be the basic industry, and with its ancillaries constituted the backbone of local economy. Production, particularly of grain, was greater than has been supposed and the surplus, in addition to supplying the local markets, was exported by sea to other parts of Britain. The charter towns with access to the sea had enjoyed a flourishing existence throughout the Middle Ages, and now, with the general rise in national prosperity became important ports in their own right. The title, Admiral of the Port, still borne by the Mayor of Haverfordwest, bears testimony to the maritime activities of that town in earlier times. Ships came to the ports of Pembroke and Tenby, and to Haverfordwest, on the tidal Cleddau laden with merchandise, homely commodities and necessities and more exotic items like spices and wines, and bore away cattle, grain, wool, pelts and manufactured goods produced by the industry of Pembrokeshire folk.

Ships built in Pembrokeshire yards, owned and manned by local men, traded as far afield as the Baltic and Mediterranean. Such voyaging could sometimes be hazardous as William Scourfield of Moat discovered during Elizabeth's reign.

The woollen trade flourished in the Middle Ages and several families, such as the Laugharnes and Voyles, profited so well that they bought large estates and so entered the ranks of the landed gentry. However, by late Tudor times the woollen trade had passed its peak and coal-mining, tanning and other ancillaries were providing opportunities for energetic and ambitious men. Thomas Cannon of Haverfordwest was another who participated successfully in trade, which led to a seat in Parliament and the joys of a knighthood and an extensive landed estate. Coal-mining was carried on, mostly as the result of capital invested by the gentry, in the areas of Brawdy, Roch and particularly in the south of the county, but it was not for another century that developments in mechanical techniques enabled the industry to become a significant factor in the life of west Wales.

The Tudor period witnessed an influx of newcomers to the county. Some profited by the dissolution of the religious houses whose lands were sold or leased to laymen. Among them were the Barlows of Slebech. Others arrived as officials, such as the Stepneys of Prendergast who intermarried with heiresses of Welsh families, so that their descendants became leading magnates in west Wales. Two other distinguished arrivals were Dr. Thomas Phaer of Forest, Cilgerran, physician to Queen Mary Tudor, and who translated Virgil's *Aeneid* into English, and Robert Recorde of Tenby, the mathematician and inventor of some mathematical signs still in use.

The old traditional families with roots deep in medieval times, continued to hold vast estates, and indeed to increase them and it was they who effectively dominated all aspects of local government – the influential and able houses of Wogan of Wiston, Owen of Orielton, Philipps of Picton Castle, Bowen of Llwyngwair and Trefloyne, Warren of Trewern, Lloyd of Cilciffeth, Perrott of Haroldston, the Laugharnes, Adams of Paterchurch, Butler of Coedcanlas, Catharne of Prendergast, and many more.

No account of Elizabethan Pembrokeshire can be complete without mention of George Owen of Henllys (1552-1613), and recourse to his unique and invaluable *Description* of the county. George Owen was a conceited, learned, litigious, biased and wholly delightful individual. His father, a successful lawyer descended from a minor north Pembrokeshire family, had bought the manorial jurisdictions of the lordship of Cemais and set himself up as a magnate in the Newport-Nevern area. The gifted son, George, who walked with a limp, inherited the fruits of his father's speculation and, dominated by a *folie de grandeur*, spent most of his time advancing the claims of his lordship to primacy in Pembrokeshire. An outstanding antiquary he was interested in all aspects of history, present and past, and amassed a huge corpus of manuscript material which he arranged as a *Description of Pembrokeshire*. This veritable treasure-house full of curious lore, contains vivid pen-pictures of life in bygone Pembrokeshire. His exciting commentary on the game of *cnapan* – a barbaric form of rugby-football played between parishes – is something which the most expert modern commentators can hardly rival. Little of consequence escaped his inquisitive attention, his buccaneering pen probed into the most unlikely corners, his industry and energy were prodigious, and his work remains, not only a landmark, but a basis for any historical enquiry into the bygones of Pembrokeshire.

The seventeenth century witnessed the consolidation of the efforts of the previous century. The growing prosperity that marked the Tudor period did not end with Elizabeth's death in 1603. The county continued to flourish under the Stuarts and, despite the dislocations caused by the Civil Wars, emerged without appreciable damage to its economy. It is interesting to note that the Welsh parts of Pembrokeshire were, with few exceptions, strongly Royalist, whereas the anglicised parts produced enthusiastic Roundheads. It was south Pembrokeshire that kept the flame of opposition alive when all other parts of the county lay in the King's hands. Pembroke castle was the only fortress that did not capitulate to the Royal forces, and the waters of the Haven enabled Parliamentary vessels to relieve the beleaguered garrison and to support land operations on behalf of Cromwell. Foremost among the Roundhead leaders stood Major-General Rowland Laugharne of St. Brides, one of the ablest tacticians thrown up during the unhappy conflict.

However, constancy was not a lasting quality in those tumultuous days, and men changed their political allegiances as nonchalantly as changing their shirts. When the second Civil War broke out in 1648, Rowland Laugharne, Colonel Powell and Mayor Poyer (a respectable tradesman of Pembroke) abandoned their earlier partisanship, declared for the King and garrisoned Pembroke castle, the key to military success in the west. The importance of such a move may be gauged by the fact that Cromwell deemed it necessary to lead an expedition into Pembrokeshire. The castle's defenders soon felt the presence of his military genius and Laugharne capitulated after a short siege. The conqueror decreed that one of the three leaders must forfeit his life, the decision to be made by lot. Laugharne, Powell and Poyer nervously drew the papers from a Parliamentarian casque. The hapless Poyer drew the blank and he fell before a firing squad in Covent Garden. Thereafter, his descendants bore the motto "Destiny is against me" in memory of the melancholy fate of their ancestor.

Another association with this cyclonic period proved less lethal. Lucy Walter, one of Pembrokeshire's most permissive daughters, attracted the notice of the Prince of Wales (later King Charles II), and consequently became the mother of the Duke of Monmouth. Her father, William Walter of Haverfordwest and Roch, who had married a cousin of the Royalist Earl of Carbery, came from a line of wealthy burgesses in the county town.

As a result of the rising of 1648, Cromwell ordered the destruction of certain castles in Pembrokeshire, so that they could never again become a challenge to the new regime. The castles of Tenby, Roch, Benton, Haverfordwest and Pembroke suffered in various degree as a result of this rigorous mandate, but their formidable ramparts defied total demolition, a tribute to the work of the medieval masons who had erected them.

Although several local magnates suffered through fines and confiscations, the Civil War did not disturb the balance of the ruling families unduly and at the Restoration in 1660 they were still firmly in the saddle. The agricultural interest, that abiding basis of Welsh life, had not been dislocated, and the towns of Haverfordwest, Pembroke, Tenby and to a lesser degree, Narberth and Newport, continued to flourish as centres of trade and commerce.

One of the most notable features of this century was the rise of religious dissent. This occurred in the latter half of the century and although the nonconformists as they became known, were not particularly numerous and extended their influence but slowly, they were destined to become a vital religious and political force in the nineteenth century.

The eighteenth century was tranquil so far as Pembrokeshire was concerned, a period of steady economic progress. Landowners consolidated and improved their properties, farmers benefited from the general prosperity and improved marketing facilities. The towns, particularly Haverfordwest, continued to flourish, and the ports were playing an even more leading role in the economy. Landing stages, quays, kilns and storehouses were built at remote creeks like Abercastell, Solva, Porthgain, Fishguard and Stackpole Quay. The sea was one of Pembrokeshire's great highways and at the ports and creeks, vessels discharged cargoes of coal, limestone and other goods and took away grain and other produce to markets further afield. Many landowners and farmers held shares in the small craft which plied their trade along the coast of Wales and beyond. Pembrokeshire accents were heard on the quaysides of Liverpool, Dublin, Bristol and London. It was during this period that the two lighthouses were built to guide mariners, namely St. Anne's, constructed mainly through the exertions of the Allen family, and the Smalls, created in 1773.

This seagoing trade continued to grow during the succeeding centuries and was displaced only after road and rail communications became so developed that the competition proved ruinous to the small ship owners. The writer's family has been intimately connected with the coastal trade. One of his ancestors was engaged in carrying cargoes of grain in the eighteenth century (to which he added the illicit but eminently profitable, smuggling of salt); another found a watery grave at Cefn Sidan sands during a great storm; a kinsman owned and captained one of the very last vessels to trade in Pembrokeshire ports, the *Ben Rein*, which only ceased her peaceful operations shortly before the outbreak of the Second World War.   (In which the author sailed as a small boy. – *Ed.*)

The same century produced valiant sea-dogs whose names continue to adorn our naval annals – Admiral Thomas Tucker of Sealyham (who slew the notorious pirate "Bluebeard"), Admiral Vaughan of Trecwn, Admiral Sir Erasmus Gower of Glandyfan, and Admiral Sir Thomas Foley of Ridgeway (a friend of Nelson). Neither must we overlook that other, though less respectable, sea-dog namely Bartholomew Roberts of Casnewydd Bach, *Barti Ddu*, swashbuckling buccaneer, terror of the Spanish Main.

But man does not live by bread alone. The eighteenth century saw the first concerted move to improve the educational lot of the people. Not that the county had been without schools; there had been a school at St. David's cathedral in the Middle Ages and another was established there before 1563 which continued to flourish into the nineteenth century. A grammar school had been founded in Haverfordwest by Thomas Lloyd of Cilciffeth in 1613 and another had been established there by Mary Tasker in 1684. Sir Hugh Owen of Orielton, had founded a similar school at Pembroke in 1690. The wealthier families sent their sons to grammar schools at Cardigan, Carmarthen, Swansea and Bristol and later to the public schools in England.

Few facilities had existed for the poorer people but more attention was paid to them in the eighteenth century. Philanthropic public-spirited people like Sir John Philipps of Picton Castle, the devout Griffith Jones, Vicar of Llanddowror, Madam Bevan of Laugharne and the Bowens of Llwyngwair took a prominent part in establishing circulating charity schools with the object of imparting elementary education to the lowly, both children and adults. These schools were held in various places – in farmhouses, cottages, barns, churches and other buildings, mainly in the villages and country districts. Between 1699 and 1736, no fewer than twenty-eight schools of all kinds existed in the county. Neither must we forget the laudable efforts of the Revd. John Griffith of Fagywr-goch in north Pembrokeshire (1732-1825), a poor curate passing rich on £42 a year, who established, in 1761, a lending library of over one thousand volumes purchased from his own slender resources, and in addition gave private tuition to the children of cottagers and farmers in his locality.

Porthmawr chimney

Both the Church and the Nonconformists (now a strongly organised body) made strenuous efforts to spread education and succeeded in achieving much despite the limitations of their resources. The evangelical tours of Howell Harris, John Wesley and Whitfield, all of whom laboured in Pembrokeshire for a time, were an important influence on the people, refining their mode of life and directing their steps towards truer Christian witness.

The improvement in agriculture was due mainly to the interest of the landowners whose prosperity was indissolubly linked with the land. Enlightened landowners like Thomas Lloyd of Cwmgloyn, and Mirehouse of Brownslade, active land-agents like Thomas and Charles Hassall, were introducing new systems of farming, establishing better breeds of cattle, helping to form farmers' clubs and writing essays and pamphlets on various aspects of the industry.

The acceleration of the Industrial Revolution led to greater productivity in Pembrokeshire coal mining which was becoming a major industry particularly in the Kilgetty-Saundersfoot area (where the Philipps's of Picton Castle provided capital for further expansion), Hook, Freystrop, Landshipping and Cresswell. Slate and stone quarrying was developed at Cilgerran, Llangolman, Rosebush, Porthgain, and later at Trefgarn. The quarries of Porthgain were near to the little cove which soon became a lively port with quay, storehouses and cottages built specially for the quarrymen.

The founding of the Royal dockyard, first at Milford, then at Pembroke Dock, and the founding of Milford as a fishing port by Charles Greville and Sir William Hamilton towards the end of the century, led to the development of the Haven which in due course gave employment to thousands of people. Tenby, which had sunk into torpid gentility suddenly came to life again, and through the exertions of Dr. Jones and Sir William Paxton became a fashionable resort for holiday makers and for the ailing who sought relief from their ills in the sea bathing it afforded.

The annals of the eighteenth century are not complete without reference to the event known as "the landing of the French". In 1797 a force of some 1,400 men, which included a high percentage of jailbirds and other unsavoury characters under command of General Tate, landed at Carreg Wasted near Aberfelin, a small cove below the hamlet of Llanwnda. Before they could achieve any objective, a force of volunteers consisting of the Castlemartin Yeomanry, Fishguard Fencibles and militia units, commanded by the energetic Lord Cawdor, marched against them, with the result that the enemy capitulated unconditionally. They were allowed to march to Goodwick sands where they

Fishguard

Milford Haven

piled their arms. The landing caused great alarm and spurred the central government to expedite measures for the more effective protection of our shores. In the struggles with Napoleon, numerous Pembrokeshire men played a worthy part, chief among them General Sir Thomas Picton of Poyston, who fell at Waterloo, leading his troops in repelling a desperate French attack.

Perhaps of all the periods in Pembrokeshire's history none was more important than the nineteenth century. It was an age of tremendous advance on the home front, politically and economically. Changes came fast and furious, generally to the good. The development of the coal industry and agricultural prosperity is again clearly reflected in the activity at the ports and the increasing sea-borne trade. Haverfordwest and Tenby continued to be the main ports, but were closely rivalled by Milford Haven, Fishguard, and even Solva. For instance, in 1837 there were 28 shipowners and 42 Master Mariners belonging to the port of Fishguard alone, and at one time some 200 vessels had landed cargoes at Solva. Among the shipowners of Fishguard in 1837 were merchants like Levi Vaughan, farmers like John Morgan Mortimer of Penysgwarne and Hugh Harries of Cefnydre and landowners like William Gwynne of Court. The market-house and the quay was improved and Fishguard became a flourishing town.

Among the most important innovations was one which was to influence Pembrokeshire life to a remarkable degree, namely the reorganisation of land communications. In 1850 the railroad came to the county and Neyland was selected as the terminus of the Great Western railway. Accordingly the packet station and the Irish trade were transferred from Milford to the new terminus, and as a result a new town arose at Neyland. Ironically, the same causes that led to the little town's foundation and prosperity led to its decline. In 1904-6 a harbour was constructed at Goodwick (on which the inappropriate name of Fishguard Harbour was bestowed), and soon superseded Neyland as the port for Ireland. It was now Goodwick's turn to prosper and in a short time it grew from a sleepy hamlet into a bright little town, the only unimaginative intrusion being the newly erected, "company houses," called Harbour Village.

At the same time, a great improvement took place in road communications, proving particularly helpful to the farming community. A slump occurred in agriculture in the late 1830's and in the 1840's, and this, together with other difficulties, led to outbreaks of violence known an the "Rebecca Riots". Farmers and workers assembled at nightfall, some being disguised as women, and attacked and destroyed toll-gates and toll-houses, one of the main grievances being the excessive tax levied on road-users. These outrages were only suppressed by bringing troops and extra police into the area. Fortunately agriculture improved and more settled conditions resulted. A feature of this century is the formation of large numbers of farmers' societies and clubs, the holding of cattle shows, ploughing matches, and other co-operative and competitive events, which gave encouragement to all branches of the agricultural industry.

Population statistics are usually a good guide to the state of a nation's prosperity and become more obvious when studied at county level. It is only since the beginning of the nineteenth century that we have reliable population figures, which permit us to discern the trends. In 1801 the population of the county was 56,280, which gradually increased until in 1861, it stood at 96,278, the highest figure it ever reached. By 1901 it had fallen to 87,894, due partly to emigration of workers from the countryside to the industrial areas of Glamorgan where higher wages were the lure. Thereafter an appreciable increase occurred, and in 1921 there were 91,480 people in the county. During the depression between the two World Wars the population sank again and by 1941 had fallen to 85,400.

From the Act of Union of 1536 down to 1889 the county had been governed and administered by its ancient land-owning families – Philipps of Picton Castle, Owen of Orielton, Edwardes and Tucker of Sealyham and Trefgarn, Lort of Stackpole, Barlow of Slebech, Bowen of Llwyngwair, Elliot of Narberth, Harries of Tregwynt, and a host more. Their services were voluntary and they held all the important appointments, the levers of power, appointments like Lords Lieutenant, Deputy Lieutenants, High Sheriffs, Justices of the Peace, Members of Parliament, Clerks of the Peace, County Treasurers and other similar posts. Patronage lay entirely in their hands. Most important of all were the Justices of the Peace who, through the Quarter Sessions, were responsible for the whole administration of the county. For over three-and-a-half centuries the system had worked remarkably well, and it must be emphasised that the Justices were unpaid, their services entirely voluntary. The political and economic developments of the eighteenth and nineteenth centuries, the increase in population and the growing complexities of administration made a change desirable, even necessary. What had given one good service in 1580, was no longer effective to deal with the situation in 1880. Changed circumstances demanded new techniques. The three great reform bills – 1832, 1867 and 1884 – were the harbingers of the new era. Most significant of all was the Bill passed in 1888, which reorganised local government and set up the machinery of County Councils. It was a bell that tolled for the squires and marked the end of an age. Power now passed from the Justices of the Peace into the hands of the County Council whose members, drawn from all walks of life, were the elected representatives of the people. The Council with paid staff trained in administration, took over the responsibilities that had hitherto been the concern of comparatively few men. Henceforth the Quarter Sessions confined its work to legal matters. Thus from 1889 onwards the history of Pembrokeshire to a considerable degree is the history of its County Council, the Rural and Urban District Councils and to a lesser degree the parish Councils, set up in 1894.

During the early part of the twentieth century Pembrokeshire life jogged on without any important changes. The Second World War and its aftermath brought radical alterations, such as the advent of larger military and other government installations, and the massive oil terminals on the shores at Milford Haven. The acceptance of the tourist trade as a source of income. The change from subsistence farming into a profit-making industry, for example, the production of turkeys and other fowl on an immense scale, all helped to balance the losses caused by the dwindling fishing industry at Milford, the closure of numerous railway installations and the loss of the dockyard at Pembroke Dock. New attitudes and skills are transforming Pembrokeshire life. It is an age of large concerns. The fashionable word is "viable". A farm is now a "unit". Many mourn reductions in small farms and holdings and one can only hope that the new world will not lack the humanity that characterised the old.

I conclude this brief review by reminding readers of the long literary tradition of the, "premier county," of Wales. We start with Asser, bishop and scholar, a Pembrokeshire man, who may have come from Trefasser in Pencaer, and a friend of Alfred the Great. From Cemais came Dafydd ap Gwilym, one of the greatest poets of medieval Wales. Manorbier was the birthplace of Giraldus Cambrensis, "patron saint" of Pembrokeshire historians, whose *Itinerary* and *Works* are standard requirements for those who would unravel the mysteries of the twelfth century. Taking a long leap forward we come to George Owen, witty, gifted, provocative, who laid the basis of a study of our Antiquities; and his son, also named George, who became York Herald of Arms, and his disciples, the Revd. George Owen Harry of Dinas and George William Griffith of Penybenglog, skilled in the unravelling of genealogies and heraldic intricacies. In the eighteenth century Dr. Erasmus Saunders threw a vivid light on the condition of the See of Davids, while the elegant prose of Richard Fenton of Glynymel has preserved much curious lore for our delectation; the poet Anna Williams of Rosemarket, friend of Dr. Johnson, the hymn-writer William Lewis of Abermawr, the Shakespearean commentator, Maurice Morgann of Blaenbylan, were honoured by their contemporaries. Nearer our times we find Dr. Thomas Nicholas of Brawdy parish, secretary of the committee whose labours led to the establishment of the first University College of Wales and author of *The County Families* and *Pedigree of the English People;* Edward Laws of Tenby whose *Little England Beyond Wales* is essential reading for everyone interested in Pembrokeshire.

In the early part of the present century, a talented series of writers added their quota of publications, among them the Revd. Meredith Morris of Cwmgwaun, James Phillips of Haverfordwest, J. Rowland Phillips of Cilgerran, Dr. Henry Hicks and Francis Green, both of St. Davids, Arthur Leach of Tenby, Principal David Salmon of Narberth, Sir Frederick Rees, Edgar Phillips (the Archdruid, "Trefin"), Commander E. H. Stuart Jones and the three gifted sons of Fishguard, the brothers T. H. Evans ("Igloo Habs"), the Revd. J. T. Evans and the late Revd. A. W. Wade Evans. Among those happily still with us adding to their own reputation while providing literary delights for others, we can number Professor W. F. Grimes, Dr. B. G. Charles, Mr. B. G. Owens, Dr. Brian Howells, Dr. David Howell, Mr. Waldo Williams, Mr. Stanley Richards, Mr. E. T. Lewis, Mr. Douglas James and Mr. Roscoe Howells. All these writers have been inspired by the land that gave them birth and have given back to Pembrokeshire, in generous measure, sparkling gems polished by intellectual qualities which many envy and which all acclaim.

THE HOLY WELLS OF PEMBROKESHIRE

Lecture delivered before the Pembrokeshire Local History Society at Haverfordwest, 28 November 1969

THE SUBJECT on which I am going to speak this evening is one that hitherto has not received the attention I feel it deserves. This is less true of England where it has engaged the attention of antiquaries and scholars, but in Wales it has excited the attention only of a few local historians. In fact, until my book *The Holy Wells of Wales* appeared in 1954, no effort had been made to study its significance outside isolated areas, restricted both in terms of time and locality, that is more or less in isolated and often unrelated terms.

In the past the subject of wells has been considered (1) as a facet of folk-lore or (2) a side-light on medieval religious observances, or (3) as an aspect of popular superstition. To one of Roman Catholic sympathies the cult of holy wells was a permissive religious exercise sanctioned by the Church. To the Puritan, and particularly the Non-conformist, it was a Popish practice designed to perpetuate the ignorance of an illiterate people dominated by a priestly caste. To the folk-lorist it formed an ingredient in the picturesque hot-pot that formed the diet of a rural population, providing an innocent entertainment at certain seasons of the year.

In fact the history of holy wells includes all these, and more. However, if we are to understand its full significance, the subject must be discussed as a whole, for no one facet can provide a balanced and reasonably accurate conspectus.

The proposition I place before you is this – that at one time all wells were considered holy and it was only changes in religious, social and economic life, at various periods in history, that deprived them of their status and respect so it is important that an effort be made to collect information about as many of them as we possibly can. Experience has shown that the very names of wells may contain clues to their former condition and, indeed, sometimes may contain the only record of an historical occurrence otherwise nearly forgotten.

The question of names is extremely important and often the sole memorials of holy wells. Numerous fields in Pembrokeshire comprise well-names which they have often retained centuries after the well itself has dried up or become hidden by undergrowth.

Owing to rapid changes this century, and in particular to advanced mechanical techniques, our well-names and field-names are in peril of being completely obliterated. Let us briefly review the enemies who are not merely at our gates but actually within them. The most formidable of these are government installations – formidable because of the vast resources behind them and because of the large acreage they require. The main ones being the airfield at Brawdy, the depot at Trecwn, the artillery school at Manorbier, and the tank training area at Castlemartin. As a result whole farms and large agricultural tracts have been transformed into a different kind of landscape. Farmhouses, cottages, even historic mansions, have been razed; fields have disappeared and over them new houses and other necessary installations have risen. Former war-time installations such as at Withybush and between Solva and St. Davids took further toll of large tracts of land.

Then we have industrial projects that have revolutionised life along the shores of Milford Haven. These petrol and oil leviathans have also taken toll of our agricultural land. Schemes considered necessary by waterboards have added to the erosion. The Forestry Commission provides a further blanket for landscape and names, as does the constant urban sprawl that has taken place, and is taking place. Every day we are losing bits of our countryside in England and Wales. When I lived in Haverfordwest, I was in the country at the top of City Road: in those days the Haven Road was a country lane flanked by a few houses wherein dwelt the more genteel burgesses of this ancient town. Look at it today. Look at the environs of Tenby, Milford, Fishguard and Goodwick – everywhere the spearheads are thrusting into the farmlands.

Modern conveniences have rendered most wells obsolete. When I was young all farms, cottages, and villages, drew water from nearby wells. A well stood a few yards from the house in which I was born in Trefin, and I remember helping to carry water from the churchyard-well when I lived at Llandeloy, and from a well in a corner of a field near my paternal grandfather's farm at Grinston in Brawdy parish. But the introduction of modern amenities such as piped water from reservoirs which brings the commodity into the house at the mere turn of a tap, has resulted in a large number of wells becoming totally neglected.

Another factor, which has become increasingly significant since the last war, is the tendency for more people to live in the country and to work in the towns. As one in every two of the population now own motor cars – the question of wider and better roads becomes paramount. The local railway system, immolated on the altar of Lord Beeching's alleged efficiency, the Tourist Board's policy of attracting yet more visitors, the heavy traffic to and from our industrial and government installations, all add to the difficulties of travel, so that new and better roads and bridges become an imperative.

More subtle, even more devastating, is erosion from within due to the changing pattern of agriculture. The post-war tendency is to form large farms – or units – a hideous word with a hideous connotation, now much in fashion. I know of numerous small farms in my home district, in Dewsland, which have been thus incorporated. And not only incorporated, but have completely disappeared – hedges of the fields taken down, for another tendency is to have larger fields and the homesteads swept away. With bulldozers, and so on, this physical transformation can be effected in a remarkably short space of time. It is not only faith that can move mountains.

Another enemy of field-names is a tendency to use numbers rather than names. In some areas, Poles and Englishmen have taken over farms, and there are cases where they have re-named fields in their own language. It is only fair to say that only a minority do this, for a good many Englishmen who have settled in wholly-Welsh areas have retained the earlier names.

It is important to make a record of such names in time. It may be too late in some instances, but in others valuable work may still be accomplished. For instance, have the names in the area of the Llysyfran reservoir been recorded? In another generation it will be too late.

I would like to quote an example of what can be done in this matter, partly because it falls within my own experience, and partly because it may encourage my friends in Pembrokeshire to act along similar lines. Last year the Carmarthenshire Women's Institutes decided to embark on some project to celebrate Investiture Year. They did me the honour of asking my opinion. I said that I felt that it would be a sound idea if they considered some project which would have a permanent value and might benefit future generations. I suggested that a collection of the field-names of the county might be suitable. They agreed to this.

The ladies of over sixty Institutes set to work with the efficiency and enthusiasm that distinguishes all their undertakings. The result was a veritable triumph. Thousands of field-names were recorded – many illustrated by sketches and maps – including areas awaiting the attention of the Coal Board and the Water Engineers. Future historians will have reason to bless the Women's Institutes for celebrating Investiture Year in this manner. I went through the final collection and was rewarded by numerous names of wells whose existence were unknown to me.

The collection of all the well-names within a county is far too Herculean a task for one person, but if the load is shared it becomes a practical arrangement capable of achievement. Co-operation is an ingredient of success. Once done, it is done for ever.

In view of the changes we see around us, it is imperative that Pembrokeshire should embark on a similar scheme. There is no time to be lost. Perhaps the Pembrokeshire Community Council, the Local History Society, the Women's Institutes, the County Education Authority (through the schools), or Young Farmers' Clubs, could take the matter in hand. I respectfully suggest that this proposal is worthy of your consideration.

The study of wells in this county is particularly interesting. In the north we have Welsh-speaking Pembrokeshire, in the south English-speaking Little England, each with its own particular and diverse traditions. However, the difference is linguistic rather than racial as anyone with a knowledge of the genealogical structure of the county knows. The line of demarcation is not, and never has been as clearly defined as some would have us believe. There has never been a *landsker* and there has never been such a place-name in Pembrokeshire, although efforts have been made by some outsiders to impose it upon us. The blood of the ancient Welsh, the Normans, Flemings, English, with a dash of Irish is found in all parts of the county. We are a mixed breed, a successful amalgam of different peoples, a racial cocktail of some potency. Our only difference is the language, together with a few idiosyncrasies mainly imposed by geographical considerations. I am prepared to eat porridge prepared by a cook from either north or south Pembrokeshire, and so am safe from the attentions of the hawk-eyed vigilantes who administer the Race Relations Act.

Accordingly, there is no difference in the attitude of Pembrokeshire people towards holy wells, and their history is much the same in all areas. This is probably because the origin was exclusively religious, a feeling akin to all nationalities, and because after the religious significance had paled, the subsequent development was uniform.

Before I enter into details it may be useful if I define the terms used. A well was usually a small circular pool fed by springs in its bed. It could also be a mere spring, sometimes, spout, sometimes fountain. These are the names we find – well, spring, spout, and fountain. The Welsh forms are *ffynnon* (the overflow being called *gofer*) and *pistyll*, while *tarddiad*, *llygad*, *blaen* and *codiad* were used for spring.

The well cult is part of the veneration of water which characterised most early religious observances. Wells were regarded as the abodes of gods and associated with purification ceremonies, sacrifice, divination, fertility, healing and weather charms. Striking examples occur in the Old Testament, such as the holy wells of *En Gihon, Beersheba, En haq qoreh*, to name but a few. Similar veneration of the well is found in Egypt, Babylon, Greece, Rome and by Celts and Teutons, indeed throughout the whole ancient world. Sometimes wells themselves were regarded as gods, also rivers that flowed from them, and an example of the latter exists in the river Alun that flows below St. David's Cathedral, whose name is derived from the Celtic goddess Alauna.

Great megaliths, groves, sometimes single trees and burials, are found near or alongside holy wells. A mound called Bedd Samson stands near Ffynnon Garreg in the parish of Nevern. Sick visitors to Canna's Well in Llangan West parish, offered a pin at the well, then drank or bathed, and afterwards tried to sleep on Canna's Chair, a great megalith a few yards away. These megaliths later bore the name of Christian saints and a record dated 1483, mentions a megalith called Maen Dewi that stood near Ffynnon Ddewi in Fishguard parish. Lluyd, the antiquary, writing in 1698, mentions an inscribed stone near St. Owen's Well in Narberth parish. During the last century a *cromlech* near the holy well at Llandridian in Pencaer, and another at Nine Wells near Solva, were destroyed. In 1846 a stone called Mesur-y-Dorth served as a gatepost to Penarthur Farm near St. Davids, which previously had stood with two other ornamented stones around the holy well of Penarthur. Mesur-y-Dorth is now in the Cathedral – where it is known as the "Gurmarc stone" after the name incised on it. Near Ffynnon Fair in Maenclochog parish, are great boulders believed to have formed part of a *cromlech* and tradition states that one of them, when struck, gave forth a loud ringing sound which did not cease until water from Ffynnon Fair had been carried into the parish church. In Pembrokeshire I have found 17 wells associated with megaliths, but there are probably others that have escaped my attention.

These few examples from among many establish that veneration for wells existed in early times. Thus wells were sacred sites, and when Christian missionaries came to Britain they adapted those sites to Christian usages and often built churches or chapels alongside and sometimes over them. Numerous examples occur in Pembrokeshire as I shall show later on. The missionaries and priests introduced Christian rites and ceremonies at the wells, which continued to be observed until the Reformation, although in many places they survived in a debased form as "healing", "wishing" and "rag" wells.

Thus it will be seen that originally all wells were sacred, so an effort must be made by historians to list as many as possible, whether their names are indicative or not, and there are several wells with humdrum names like Ffynnon Las, Red Well, or even just the Well, concerning which legends have survived or which once had a reputation for possessing healing properties. Accordingly, a brief look at the names we are likely to encounter will assist us in our enquiry.

These fall into eight main classes:

1. Wells with holy names: These are named after saints, priests, or have some other religious associations. This class is by far the most numerous, and such wells are found in all parts of the county – Ffynnon Ddewi on the border of Brawdy parish, Pistyll Meugan in Llanfair Nantgwyn, St. Caradoc's well in St. Thomas, Haverfordwest, St. Govan's well on the coast of Bosherston parish, St. Mary's well at Tenby, to name but a few named after Celtic saints. An example of a holy well with a chapel built over it is to be found in Cwmwdig farmyard. Others are called Ffynnon Capel, Ffynnon Eglwys, indicating a similar origin. I have found 82 wells bearing saints' names in Pembrokeshire. I have also a list of 34 healing wells, undoubtedly holy wells in origin. The fact that many wells contain healing properties, rendered them a subject of veneration to an unlettered people. The healing qualities were ascribed to a god or a saint, a perfectly natural consequence.

2. Wells named after lay people: Although these bear the names of lay people, it is possible that some of them commemorate holy men who have left no other record. In Meline parish we have Ffynnon Adda, in Clydey Ffynnon Arthur, in Mathry parish Ffynnon Llywelyn, and in Dinas parish Ffynnon Ofi. These should be carefully noted, for further evidence may be found in due course to establish their true origin.

3. Occupational names: These are named after people who lived near, or who habitually used, certain wells. Thus we have Ffynnon Ceisied in Llanglydwen, retaining an old Welsh word now obsolete, *cais ceisied*, meaning steward or local officer. Many others are found such as Ffynnon-y-gof, Ffynnon-y-saer, Ffynnon-y-meddyg, and so on.

4. Adjectival names: These are very common, such as Ffynnon las, wen, -goch, -felen, -deg, -oer, and many more.

5. Tree names: These too are fairly common, and usually owe their names to a certain type of tree or trees that grew alongside. It is likely that many are religious in origin, for in some known cases, rags and other symbolic offerings were hung by devotees on trees or bushes that grew alongside a holy or healing well. Among these we find Ffynnon cyll, -gollen, -ddrain, -helyg, -ysgawen and -ywen.

6. Animal and bird names: Wells bearing such names derive from the fact that they were a favourite haunt of certain animals or birds, and, doubtless, this explains most of them. But it must also be borne in mind, that certain animals were sacred to the Celts, and it is possible that an echo of that early association may have lingered in some of the names. For instance, Ffynnon y blaidd, -ceiliog, -gath, -gog, -barcud, -march and -milgi.

7. Topographical names: These are self-explanatory, being names after their geographical location, such as Ffynnon y ddol, -y mynydd, -y wern, -y grib, and so on.

8. Miscellaneous names: Some names have defied classification. Probably because they have reached us in corrupt and mutilated forms. To attempt to interpret them without earlier examples of the spelling would be dangerous, indeed fruitless, and so the only course is to note them in the hope that further research may provide explanatory material. The most outstanding example I have found in Pembrokeshire is a well in Llanddewi

Felffre called Ffynnon-well-na-buwch near an old Baptist chapel formerly known by that name and now simply as Ffynnon. Translated literally, Ffynnon-well-na-buwch means "the well that is better than a cow", which defies interpretation, and I am convinced that in its original form it was something quite different.

In all I have been able to list 236 wells in Pembrokeshire, but as this represents my own researches, it is clear that there must be very many more. I have come across many of their names in ancient manuscripts, in deeds and other documents and on old maps and plans, particularly in Tithe maps and Schedules made for each Pembrokeshire parish between the years 1836 and 1845. Special mention must be made of the Tithe maps. They are extremely valuable as the majority of them contain the name of each field, a number of which are no longer in use. As the list of fields are accompanied by a large scale parish map it is possible to locate them with precision, and this has enabled me to discover several wells, particularly those of saints. I have been through the Tithe maps and Schedules of every parish in Pembrokeshire, and they contain, in addition to names, other useful historical information.

I now propose to discuss wells with religious associations, by far the most numerous of those included in our enquiry. Veneration for wells had been a prominent feature of the pagan world and the difficulty which Christian missionaries found in leading the people away from them, is reflected in early ecclesiastical councils. The Council of Arles in 452 A.D., of Rouen and of Toledo, denounced those who offer vows to trees or well or stones, as they would at altars. The Council of Tours in 567, explicitly forbade the worship of fountains and Gildas, in the same century, denounced the beliefs in wells to which people paid divine honour in earlier times.

Appreciating how deeply attached the people were to ancient forms, the Church decided to adopt a new policy, both subtle and realistic. This was reflected in Pope Gregory's letter to Mellitus in 601, which instructed missionaries in future procedure. It stated that the idols in Britain were to be destroyed, but the temples that housed them were to be purified with "holy water"; altars were to be erected and then, "converted from the worship of devils to the worship of the true god". It is important to note that this ensured the continuity of the earlier site – the old gods were expelled, the true God installed – the site remained.

Accordingly many churches and chapels came to be built near holy wells and numerous examples occur throughout England and Wales. Thirty-three are to be found in Pembrokeshire and doubtless there are others.

Under the medieval church, wells were no longer worshipped, but dedicated to saints, and those who made pilgrimages to them and partook of the waters either by drinking or bathing, now returned their thanks to God and the saints for the benefits they expected. They offered money and gave other gifts at the well, which in later times, after the religious element had been suppressed, became symbolic gifts such as pins or some forms of metal. Certain wells acquired a reputation for working miracles. As some wells, by their nature, contain curative elements which relieved rheumatism, poor eyesight, internal and other complaints, it was a natural step for the sufferer to ascribe the cure to the patron of the well.

Today there are wells whose waters contain valuable medicinal properties – Lourdes, Llandrindod, Builth and many others nearer home.

An example of belief and ritual is provided by Ffynnon Degfel. This well stood on the boundary of Brawdy and St. Elvis parishes, and tradition states that Degfel on a pilgrimage to St. Davids drank from this well and bathed his eyes there. It has been visited within living memory for the cure of warts: these were bathed in the well before dawn on Sunday and the treatment was continued on the following seven mornings before the dew had gone. It was also believed that a single strand of hair thrown into it would result in a certain cure.

The most popular dedications in Pembrokeshire were to the Blessed Virgin Mary (Ffynnon Fair), St. David, St. Non, St. Peter, St. Meugan, and St. Michael (Mihangel).

In Gumfreston churchyard, just below the church, is a worn flight of steps leading to three wells, two of which are chalybeate in nature. These were visited by many people in bygone days and bent pins thrown into them on Easter day, known as "throwing Lent away". In Burton churchyard is a well which had been used occasionally as a baptistry. Once a small chapel stood at Carswell in Jeffreston parish, mentioned in a record of 1564. A writer stated in 1851 that there was "a holy well in Warren churchyard on the west of the tower, on the steps of which once stood a cross".

A small chapel was built over a well in what is today the farmyard of Cwmwdig between Llanrhian and St. Davids. In 1715 Browne Willis recorded what he had been told about the Cwmwdig well. He wrote "there is a gentleman now living of the age of ninety who saw the west end doorway of this chapel up, and that he remembered a gentlewoman of the name of Butler lodging at his father's house, who would be at her devotion often in the chapel, and came every Thursday night to bathe in the chapel well which was firmly arched over; and on Wednesday night she went to Non's chapel and bathed in the well adjoining it".

There were numerous such wells in St. Davids and adjoining parishes. The cult of St. David – Dewi Sant – was particularly strong in Pembrokeshire, as shown by the churches and wells dedicated to him.

According to Giraldus, St. David prayed to God for a new well; it immediately arose and, so we are told, sometimes ran with wine and milk. Called Pistyll Dewi, it lay near the east end of St. David's Cathedral until Sir Gilbert Scott destroyed it during restoration work in 1866. There was another Pistyll Dewi at the ruins of Capel y Pistyll at Porthclais, and according to tradition, it was there that St. David was baptised. On the borders of Brawdy and Whitchurch parishes is a Ffynnon Dewi and, according to Giraldus, St. David caused this well to come into existence by turning the sod with his bachal during a time of prolonged drought.

In a field still called Parc Ffynnon Ddewi near Llanreithan is another neglected well of the saint. On Mabws farm in Mathry parish there is also a

Typical Holy Well

field called Park Ffynnon Dewi. A cottage in Hayscastle parish with a well beside it was known as Ffynnon Ddewi, but by today the cottage has completely vanished and the name forgotten by all but the oldest inhabitants. Another lost well, formerly Ffynnon Ddewi was in Fishguard parish; it was so called as late as 1894, but by today no one remembers it. Other wells of St. David are found in the parishes of Dinas, Llanychllwydog, Manordeifi, Llanddewi Felffre and Cosheston. The one in Llanddewi Felffre has long dried up but is still commemorated by the field name Parc Ffynnon Ddewi, about half a mile west of the parish church. In the field behind Llys Dewi on the Dinas-Newport road is a Pistyll Dewi, near which stood the medieval Capel Dewi, mentioned by George Owen in his *Description of Pembrokeshire.* According to Haverfordwest Corporation Deeds dated 1315, 1333 and 1461-83, the *Fontem Sancti Davidi*, the well of St. David, stood between Fountain Row and Dewi Street, today known as Dew Street. In 1697 the Corporation leased it to a plumber named William Yearnold and thereafter it supplied water for domestic purposes for the town. It may be argued that the pious expressions that characterise the burgesses of this ancient town, which the more discerning among you will have observed, is largely due to consumption by their ancestors of water supplied by the obliging font of our patron saint.

St. David's mother is also commemorated. Non's well continues to flow near the ruins of the little medieval chapel and was famous for curing all kinds of complaints. It was reputed to ebb and flow with the tide, although it stood some hundreds of feet above the sea. Fenton mentions coins being thrown into it as offerings. The Roman Catholics have restored this ancient well and in July 1951 it was solemnly re-dedicated and a pilgrimage made to it.

Mention of the waters of holy wells used for domestic purposes reminds me of my youth. Between the ages of two and ten I lived at Llandeloy and all the water was carried in pails and cans from the churchyard well. This holy well had once been covered by a cupola of dressed stone. The stones were still to be seen when I was a boy and my friend, the Rev. Haydn Parry, once vicar there, also remembers seeing them strewn on the ground. It is merely known as ffynnon, but if its original name could be discovered it might throw light on the dedication of Llandeloy church that stands beside it.

Another well whose name and very existence had long been lost was that of St. Wnda, and it may be of interest to hear about its re-discovery. A Pembrokeshire tradition states that the saints Aedan and Gwynda, on their way to St. Davids, stopped to drink at Ffynnon Tregroes near Solva. Each wished to bestow his name on the well, tempers became uncontrollable, with the unsaintly sequel that poor Gwynda received a good hiding. Aedan then smugly dedicated the well to himself, and pleased with the turn of affairs wended his way to the Cathedral city. But Gwynda took a different direction, travelled quickly northwards till he came to Pencaer. Having put this distance between himself and his muscular conqueror he felt safer and proceeded to establish a church at Llanwnda and to sanctify a well within the parish bounds. For a long time it was believed that his well was in the hamlet of Llanwnda itself. True there is a well there, but it had no name, legends or traditions associated with it. Some years ago when searching through some old wills, I came across one dated 1777. One of the bequests concerned a field called Parc Ffynnon

Wnda. The address of the testator was not given, only the parish, but from the properties mentioned it seemed clear that it was somewhere between Tresisillt Fach and Stop-and-Call, just above Goodwick. Later, I consulted the Tithe Commutation Schedule for Llanwnda parish compiled in 1843. Going through the hundreds of field names it contained, I found Parc Ffynnon Wnda among them – a field on the little farm of Penfeidr just above Stop-and-Call. The field was also numbered, and on consulting the Tithe Map, I was able to locate it precisely. When I visited the field I found the well completely hidden among brambles and bushes, with some traces of stones around it, which may have been the remains of a cupola or even a small chapel. Here then, was the holy well of St. Wnda, and it may be that this was his first settlement and that he later moved to where the parish church now stands. It illustrates the importance of preserving field-names which I emphasised at the beginning of my talk. Numbers of Council houses have been built nearby which in due course may extend over the field and so obliterate this interesting record of religious life in early Pembrokeshire. The path of the antiquary is long and arduous and it does not always lead to such a desirable journey's end.

A well that has defied my efforts to locate is St. Caradog's well in the parish of St. Thomas, Haverfordwest. Corporation deeds of 1315 refer to "the well of St. Caradog near the well of St. David". We have an idea where the latter was, but the former remains a mystery. Fenton calls it "the noted St. Cradock's well", whose sanctity and supposed virtue were derived from its having been a favourite haunt of that hermit saint whose cell was at Haroldstone, and adds that it was visited by lovers on the morning of the fair held there on Easter Monday.

Divination in connection with matrimonial future was another feature of St. Caradog's well. On the morning of Easter Monday, a young woman who pined for a husband, came to the well, offered three pins and then gazed intently into the water. If the ritual had been properly observed, it was believed that the face of her future husband would be mirrored in the water. One tale relates how the hopeful young lady was scared out of her wits by the appearance of the evil face of a great hairy monster.

 Carlisle writes in 1811 that Caradog's well "till within these few years, there was a sort of vanity fair, where cakes were sold, and country games celebrated". Some of you will recall Giraldus's interesting account of the conveying of Caradog's body over Newgale sands.

Several examples exist of well-chapels disappearing without trace. One of them was Capel Meugan. No traces of the chapel remain, but Pistyll Meugan on the borders of Bridell and Llanfair Nant-gwyn parishes still flows strongly in the yard of Pistyll Meugan farm. Many references to it exist, and George Owen of Henllys has included it in his writings. We know exactly when, why, and how this little well-chapel was destroyed. George Owen has recorded that on 14 July 1592, men were ordered "to repair to the place called St. Meigans where somtyme offringes & superstitious pilgrimages have been used, and there to cause to be pulled downe and utterlie defaced all reliques and monuments of that chappell, not leaving one stone thereof upon an other & from tyme to tyme to cause to be apprehended all such persons of what sexe kinde or sorte whatsoever that shall presume hereafter contrarie to the tenor and purporte of the said honorable commission, to repair either by night or daie to the said chappell or well in superstitious manner & to bringe or send before us or enie of us . . .". So thoroughly was the work carried out that no trace of the chapel remains, but the waters of Pistyll Meugan and its name continue to bear testimony to the saint. However, ruthless destruction did not wholly eradicate the respect that the well had inspired in the people. In Llyfr Plygain in 1618 it is called *Sainct Meugan yng-Hemys*, where fairs were said to have been held on Ascension Day, Thursday after Trinity Sunday and the Monday after St. Martin's Day. The Rural Dean of Cemais who assisted my enquiries wrote to me some years ago, "The reason commonly attributed for the building of the church at Meigan is that there are several streams of water to the south of the church's traditional site, which are said to contain three distinct types of water which will never mix. One is said to be good for the eyes and the cure of warts, another for rheumatics and crippled joints, and the third for *clefyd y galon*" (heart ailment).

Sometimes the cult of a saint was confined to a particular district. For instance St. Brynach who was popular in the north of the county. There was a Brynach's well or Ffynnon Frynach (today called Bernard's well) in Henrys Moat parish: it stood near the old chapel of St. Brynach about three-quarters of a mile north-east of the parish church. It is protected by a hood of masonry, and adjoining it are traces of a well-chamber. Another was in Llanfair Nant-gwyn parish, and is known only from a deed about 1665 which mentions a field called Park y ffynnon Vernach near Trefach. Another Ffynnon Brynach was in Llanfyrnach parish. In 1603 a Pistyll Brynach is mentioned in Nevern parish, which may have been near a stone enclosure called Buarth Brynach near Cernydd Meibion Owen.

A number of these holy wells and chapels are found in lonely places. Many of the early Celtic saints desired peace and seclusion to meditate, while some were of hermit disposition. One of the best known of these is St. Govan's chapel and well, in a narrow cleft

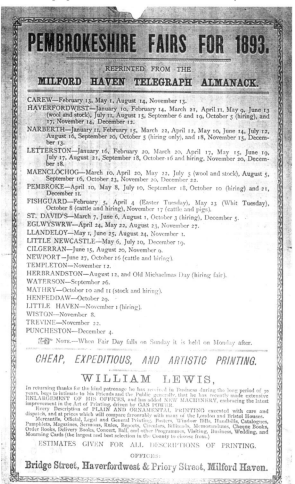

Notice of Fair

in the rocky coast below Bosherston. In 1662 John Ray the naturalist saw "St. Gobins well by the sea side, where under the cliff stands a little chapel sacred to that saint, and a little below it a well famous for the cure of all diseases". In the late 1690s one of Edward Lluyd's correspondents wrote "Within the Chappell there's a spring & another below the Chappell towards the sea. The watter of these springs is found to be good for many distempers". In 1775 Sir Thomas Gery Cullum saw a man from Carmarthen who had pains in his hip bathing the afflicted part and drinking the water from a limpet shell, after which he left money on a stone altar in the chapel. Fenton and Carlisle mention it as a popular resort of those suffering with ill-health. Near the well is a deposit of red clay formed by rock decomposition to which great virtue was attached; a poultice of this was applied to limbs and eyes, and the patients then lay by the well for several hours.

In 1860 we learn from Murray's Handbook that St. Govan's well still attracted "patients even of the upper classes, some of them from far afield". In that century, John Cain Jones wrote from North Wales to the Rev. Mr. Rowlands of Carmarthen – "I profess that I am one of the outcasts, far from my native part, having had illness, and in straightened circumstances, but possessing the will to go to the well of St. Govans, Pembrokeshire, to seek a cure".

St. Govans was spared the fate of St. Meugan's and the little chapel is in fair repair, and its well still bears testimony to ancient belief. Perhaps remoteness proved its salvation.

Another remote coastal well and chapel were less fortunate. This was Ffynnon Degan above Porth Sychan, a little cove near Strumble Head. The holy well is about half a mile inland near Tai Bach. The site of the chapel is still called Capel Degan and there is a Cnwc Degan in a field called Parc y Capel nearby. In 1720 Gough wrote "the ruined chapel, above the well is a tumulus called St. Degan's Knwc or Knoll, where people resort to seat themselves on holidays and Sundays. There is a remarkable habit of this said St. Degan, preserved for several ages; the person that has it now having had it in his custody for forty years to whom it was handed down by an elderly matron of upwards of ninety years of age. This habit, a piece whereof, I have sent you enclosed, I had the curiosity to see; it is much in the form of a clergyman's cassock but without sleeves. There were two of them of the same make near a yard in length, but having the like slit or hole at every corner on each end, and on the brim of each side were loops of blue silk". According to Fenton faint traces of the chapel could be seen in his day, and he says "I recollect an old man who said he remembered the chapel up, and in part of it, then roofed, the same sacred vest was preserved and shown, which was purchased many years after by a stranger; with the removal of his robe the fame of his sanctity died away". He also says that local people still tell a "thousand miraculous stories" of Degan, and point out on the rocks the print of the hoof of his horse when he escaped from the ocean. Here it is possible we have an echo of the inundation of Cantre 'r Gwaelod and Degan's escape to the higher land.

Remote wells are not confined to the coast by anymeans. A famous inland example is provided by Ffynnon Deilo in the hill parish of Llandeilo Llwydiarth. This sequestered district has always been sparsely populated and provided peace and tranquillity for scholars and holy men to pass an undisturbed existence. It is said that St. Teilo lived there for a time and the holy well near the church is named after him, but it is possible that this reflects an extension of his cult rather than residence. Two megaliths in the churchyard bear Ogam and Latin inscriptions. Concerning the well, Sir John Rhys has written "I would now only point out that we have here an instance of a well which was probably sacred before the time of St. Teilo: in fact, one would possibly be right in supposing that the sanctity of the well and its immediate surrounding was one of the causes why its site was chosen by a Christian Missionary".

The waters of Ffynnon Deilo (also called Ffynnon yr Ychen) were drunk from a skull called Penglog Teilo, of which the family of Melchior who lived in the adjacent farm were hereditary keepers. This was a brain-pan which, filled to the brim with water, was handed to the devotee by one of the Melchiors. Legend says that Teilo, on his death-bed, instructed a servant to take his skull from the Carmarthenshire Llandeilo where he then lay, to Llandeilo Llwydiarth, adding that thereby God and man would be glorified.

About 1840 a consumptive youth from Glamorgan came to the well, drank directly from it, and departed without benefit. His father brought him there a second time when the boy drank the water from the skull and was in due course completely cured. The earliest reference to this relic is in Carlisle's book in 1811. *Mor iached a dwr ffynnon Deilo* is still a Pembrokeshire saying. (As healthy as the water of Teilo's well.)

The well, about one hundred yards northeast of the church, was protected by a stone enclosure, while the overflow passed into a pond. It enjoyed a high reputation for curing tuberculosis (decline), whooping cough and certain respiratory diseases. The family of Melchior who farmed Llandeilo from 1591 until well on into this century were the traditional custodians of the well, and the virtue of drinking the draught of water from the skull was supposed to consist of its being administered by the eldest son of the house of Melchior.   Thornhill Timmins wrote in 1895 that the skull, which he describes as "this curious relic formerly held in high esteem as a cure for all manner of sickness", was kept clean and shining on the shelf of the home farm.   The old skull disappeared early in this century and, is said, with what truth I know not, to have been sold to an acquisitive and persuasive caller for £50 in 1927.

Hereditary custodians of relics are frequently found in the history of the Celtic church. The Melchiors were descended from a yeoman called Melchior ap Ieuan ap Howell of Newport who died in 1591. His son, who took his father's Christian name as his permanent patronymic, came to Llandeilo Llwydiarth by marriage and his descendants remained there for many generations. There is another Ffynnon Deilo, once known for its healing properties, on the boundaries of the parishes of Crinow and Lampeter Velfrey. Sometimes a special cup was used, and at some wells, like Ffynnon Aaron in Llanreithan parish, the water had to be drunk out of the palm of the hand.

Several wells were dedicated to female saints. St. Non we have already mentioned. Then, there were Ellen's well in the parishes of Angle and Llawhaden, and Margaret's well near Templeton. St. Bride was also a patron of wells. Near Henllys in Nevern parish was Pistyll San Ffraed, mentioned in a document of 1418, near which stood a small chapel known as Capel St. Ffraed, and according to George Owen, pilgrimages were made to it.

Wells were also associated with inundation tales. One legend says that the tarn called Llyn Llambed y Moch near Mathry was formed by a well overflowing as its guardian had been affronted by the owner of the field in which it stood. Doubtless such tales had been produced in the first instance to impress upon the mind the necessity of treating wells and the well-cult with due respect.

But the most popular of all were the wells of the Blessed Virgin Mary, and 15 of them have been located in the county. Some I have been able to identify from field names in the old Tithe Maps, such as Parc Ffynnon Fair on Sychpant farm in Llanychllwydog parish; Parc Ffynnon Fair on Pencnwc farm near Castle Morris and St. Mary's Wellback a field in Camrose parish. Several of her wells were known as Lady's well – Our Lady being a popular way of referring to her. There is a Lady well on Cresswell hill and there are others in the parishes of Spittal, Roch, Hamlet of St. Thomas, Haverfordwest and in St. Mary-out-Liberty, Tenby. In many cases the well was near the church, also dedicated to the Virgin Mary. Some of these wells are said to be haunted by a white lady (*Ladi Wen*) which is a folk-lorish corruption which came into being after the Reformation and intensified in Puritan and Non-conformist times, when everything connected with the Catholic church was held to be superstitious and unworthy of credence.

Pembrokeshire possessed a well reputed to cure mental disorders in the churchyard of St. Edrins and said to cure madness. Tradition relates that the well dried up because a woman washed clothes in it on a Sunday and a variant says it was because a farmer had brought a mad dog to drink from it – the dog recovered, but the master died. However, the virtue of the water was miraculously transferred to the grass growing around the base of the church walls. The grass was eaten between bread in the form of a sandwich and a money offering was placed in a stone trough in the churchyard wall, the prerequisite of the parish clerk. My grandmother, Mrs Elizabeth Francis of Clawddcam, remembered a boy who had been bitten by a dog, being given such a sandwich to eat. The grass around the walls of St. Edrins church is still called *porfa'r cynddeirog* (rabid grass).

Many wells which do not bear holy names were famous for curative waters, but there can be no doubt that in pre-Reformation times they too formed part of the well-cult based on religious considerations. Many were known for relieving afflicted eyesight, which seems to have been a common complaint in olden times. Among them we find Ffynnon Lygad in St. Davids parish, and another Ffynnon Lygad in St. Dogmaels parish, and in a field called Holy Well Field on Rhyndaston farm near Hayscastle was a well once visited by people from great distances looking for a cure for eye infections. There is a Ffynnon Claf in Lampeter Velfrey – *claf* being the old Welsh word for leprosy, Hotwells in Little Newcastle, Ffynnon Ofy in Dinas parish, all of which were believed to relieve various illnesses.

Rituals and ceremonials carried out at the wells, even those in quite modern times, are in essence based on religious observances, relics of the old Catholic days too deeply rooted in the minds of the people to be totally extinguished.

Wells were visited at all times of the year, but there were some very special occasions the most important being *Calan Mai* (1 May) and *Calan Gaeaf* (1 November). St. Caradog's

Well at Haverfordwest was visited on Easter Monday. On May Day, people dressed Priest's Well, near Narberth, with sprigs of mountain ash (rowan, *cerddinen*).

In South Pembrokeshire the use of what was called "New Year's Water," was a practice clearly derived from medieval days, and survived to this century. Children drew the water in cups which they carried to various houses, sprinkled the water over people with sprigs of evergreen or box. These lustrations were said to bring good luck during the ensuing year. During the lustrations the children chanted the following lines:

> *We bring new water from the well so clear,*
> *For to worship God with, this happy new year;*
> *Sing levy dew, sing levy dew, the water and the wine,*
> *With seven bright gold wires, the bugles that do shine;*
> *Sing reign of fair maid, with gold upon her toe,*
> *Open you the west door, and turn the old year go;*
> *Sing reign of fair maid, with gold upon her chin,*
> *Open you the east door and let the new year in.*

These lines have a Christian and medieval ring. The "fair maid" would seem to represent the Virgin. Some people have interpreted the words "*levy dew*" as the Welsh, "*llef i Dduw*" (cry to God), but without earlier forms it would be unwise to accept it. When I lived in Tenby during the years 1930-4, I was personally stopped in the street by bands of little children who sprinkled me with the water as described above. Thus, what had once been a solemn observance, had degenerated into a childish pastime.

As the rituals and ceremonies became debased and secularised, tales of fairies and ghosts replaced those of the saints and priests. Fairies were believed to live beneath some wells, and this was said of a well in Llanreithan parish – probably reflecting an ancient belief in the well as an entrance to a subterranean land. Occasionally folk-lore associated some wells with the Devil. He was said to haunt the well at Gerddi Bach Trewilym in the parish of St. Lawrence so that few wayfarers would pass that way alone on dark nights. Sometimes ghosts were said to appear such as at Ffynnon Ysbryd in the parish of Little Newcastle.

Another legend concerning this well, said that when the well was approached at night, the hoof beats of a galloping horse could be heard, becoming clearer the nearer one came to the well; and as one moved away, the sounds became fainter until they finally died away. Sometimes the fiendish cries of its rider also added to the din. An equally sinister denizen, in the form of a winged

The holy well of St. Nons

serpent of dragon type, covered with red and gold scales was believed to lurk in the bottom of the well at Grinston in Brawdy parish.

A few wells possessed a malevolent quality.

For instance, people who wished to lay a curse on their enemies threw bent pins into a well just outside Llanllawer church, after uttering an incantation. The interesting point about this well is that it was also a beneficial well. A watery version of Dr Jekyll and Mr Hyde.

Everything that has had an influence on the human mind and behaviour is worthy of study. It is easy for us who reap the benefits conferred by experience and a liberal education, to denigrate the limitations of our ancestors, and to dismiss their beliefs and customs. However, we must remember that they lived in an age of faith, when Holy Writ and the teachings of the Church, the existence of angels and devils and supernatural agencies, were accepted without question and when events and experiences which could not be explained by logic were assigned to the will of God or a benevolent saint. What was but imperfectly understood, was readily explained by invoking the supernatural. We must remember that such explanations were acceptable not only to the illiterate and inarticulate multitude, but to the greatest minds of the ancient and medieval world. Many of these beliefs which we term "pious frauds", often brought comfort and repose to troubled minds and we should pause before condemning any custom, however strange and illogical it may now appear, which in its day helped the stumbling steps of our forebears along their journey through life. That we do not believe or accept them now is no reason for condemnation.

THE WELLS OF ST. DAVID

INQUIRIES reveal 30 Welsh wells dedicated to our patron saint. A few others have been discovered in England, especially along the border in Cheshire, Shropshire and Herefordshire. It is singular that not one example has been found in north Wales.

A distribution map of these wells shows that they lie within the boundaries of the medieval See of St. Davids. This is what we expect, for this was the main area of his cult and confirms what we already know about St. David's movements. Taken in conjunction with church dedications these wells are valuable indications of the areas where the saint was most popular.

There is no doubt that the Dewi wells are all very old. Some, indeed, may have been dedicated to the saint during his lifetime, and it is possible that he had personal associations with them. Others were posthumous dedications, but made before the twelfth and thirteenth centuries when the *Lives of the Saints* as we have them, were written.

Earlier manuscripts, such as the *Book of Llandaff,* show that some of the wells were known in pre-Norman days. In any case, they must all be older than the time of the Reformation.

Of the 30 Welsh wells of St. David, 17 are in Pembrokeshire, the greater number of which is concentrated in the Dewsland hundred, Pistyll Dewi at Porthclais (St. Davids parish) is said to have miraculously appeared for David's baptism, and afterwards it enjoyed a great reputation for cures. It still flows amidst the ruined masonry of its chapel.

Answer to prayer

At Glyn Hodnant, in the same parish, the saint prayed for a well which immediately gushed forth. This, we are told by the medieval writers, periodically flowed with wine, a fact which did not fail to ensure its popularity in an age untroubled by licensing laws.

A well arose in Brawdy parish where his tears fell. This well, which still flows, was always visited by pilgrims to St. Davids. The "well of the holy Dewi", mentioned in early Haverfordwest deeds, was put to utilitarian uses in 1697 when pipes were laid to convey its water for domestic purposes in the town of Haverfordwest. The well has disappeared, but its name is still commemorated in Dew-street, where it was located.

Wells bearing St. David's name were also found in Whitchurch, Llanreithan, St. Dogwells, Hayscastle, Fishguard, Newport, Llanychllwydog, Maenclochog, Llanddewi Felffre, Cosheston and Manordeifi.

In Cardiganshire six of David's wells have been identified. One, near Tregaron, was inside a cottage. It is said to have flowed after the Saint had restored to life the only child of a peasant woman. His wells are also to be seen at Llanddewibrefi, Llandysul, Llandygwydd, south of Llanarth, Bangor and in Henfynyw.

The Henfynyw well is near the church, and in its depths is said to be imprisoned the spirit of an ancient "Cardi" whose life had not been particularly exemplary.

Annual fair

Near Ffynnon Ddewi, in Llandysul parish, an annual fair was formerly held in March – obviously a relic of a *Gŵylmabsant* (wake). It was discontinued after complaints had been made that the water of Ffynnon Ddewi was being used for brewing an extremely potent beverage.

Two of his wells flow in Carmarthenshire – one near Llanarthney and the other in the Vale of Towy. In Glamorgan are three of his wells – north of Newton Nottage, St. Bride's Major, and near Maen Cetti, in Gower.

One legend relates that Maen Cetti was a pagan monument which St. David split in two in order to prove that it was not sacred, and sealed his action by commanding a holy well to appear. In Breconshire there is a St. David's well in Llangamarch, and in Radnorshire there is one in Llanbadarn Fynydd.

Among the wells of our patron saint in England was one near Glastonbury where he established a church. There was a well "full of poison" near this church, which, after David had blessed it, became noted for its medicinal properties.

The wells of St. David and of St. Non, his mother, are sometimes found close together in the same locality, such as those near St. Davids, Pembrokeshire, in the adjoining parishes of Altarnon and Davidstowe, in Cornwall, and near Dirinon in Brittany.

I hope that my talk has indicated the importance of holy wells in the life of bygone Pembrokeshire, and I trust that some future historian will consider the subject worthy of deeper and wider treatment. To me, every aspect of Pembrokeshire history is important. Not least the silent, neglected, wells in distant fields, for in their depths too, lies knowledge.

Chapter IV

A MEDLEY OF PEMBROKESHIRE HOUSES
AND THEIR FAMILIES

Picton Castle and the Philippses

1938

IN THE hundred of Dungleddy in Pembrokeshire, between the ancient town of Haverfordwest and the manor house of Slebech, stands Picton, one of the many castles of the premier county. Situated on a headland it overlooks the confluence of the eastern and western Cleddau, a river that has played an important part in the military annals of West Wales, and which has been an equally important factor in the commercial development of those parts. It is a historic district in the very centre of Pembrokeshire and abounds in historic houses of feudal splendour. To the north is Wiston, formerly the stronghold of Wizo the Fleming and the mighty Wogans; to the east lies Canaston Wood and Canaston House, the home of the Poyers, and Ridgeway, the charming seat of the Foley family; Llawhaden, a castle belonging to the See of St. Davids; and Narberth, the old home of the Mortimer and Elliott families. Nearby is Slebech, the former establishment of the Knights of St. John, afterwards of the great Royalist family of Barlow, and later of the Barons de Rutzen. To the south is ruined Boulston, another nest of the Wogans, and over the water snug in a bend of the Cleddau, lies the unique village of Llangwm. To the west is Haverfordwest – "Honey Harfat" – the very heart of Pembrokeshire – a town that has more than once decided the history of the county. To those of us who are Pembrokeshire men born and bred, the Picton Castle district and its family means a great deal.

Here, then, in the fairest and richest part of the county is Picton, one of the earliest castles in the country which can claim the unique and proud distinction of being the only castle in Britain which has never been dismantled or forfeited or untenanted, and which has never passed out of the possession of the descendants of its original founder. It was built in the early part of the twelfth century by William de Picton, a Norman Knight in the following of Arnulph de Montgomery. Along the centuries many alterations and additions have been made, but these changes have not been entirely injudicious and the building still presents an aspect of venerable antiquity and lordly grandeur. The old entrance retains the deeply-recessed portal, the rounded arches, corbel heads and narrow windows that mark the handiwork of the Norman builders. Above the massive entrance porch rise the deep-set windows of the chapel with its handsome painted glass. The interior contains numerous apartments disposed around a spacious hall on whose lofty walls historic family portraits of various periods remain the silent sentinels of an ancient clan. The moat has long since been filled up and its place is now occupied by pleasant walks and *parterres*.

Picton Castle – Buck's view

By marriage with an heiress of the Pictons, the Castle became the property of the influential family of Wogan which has played a prominent part in the history of our nation. Sir John Wogan of Picton was Justiciary of Ireland and died in 1311. A great benefactor of the Church, he founded the Wogan chapel in St. David's Cathedral where his effigy may still be seen. His son, also a John Wogan, was Justiciary of Ireland until 1313. The next son, Sir Thomas Wogan, also held high offices in that island. The Wogans of Picton ended in heiresses and to Katherine, who married Owen Dunn of Muddlescombe, near Kidwelly, fell the inheritance of Picton Castle. The Dunns were an old landowning stock ever to the fore when there was fighting and hard knocks. Henry Dunn, grandfather of this Owen, was an ally of Owain Glyndŵr, and Glyndŵr's letters to him are still preserved in Paris.

Owen Dunn's son was Henry Dunn of Picton, who, true to his warlike traditions, met death in a skirmish at Banbury on Monday, in the vigil of St. James the Apostle, 1469, two days before the main battle, leaving a son and heir, William Dunn (born 1465) and two daughters. The son died young and the elder daughter and co-heiress, Jane, married Thomas Philipps of Cilsant who became in right of his wife the lord of Picton Castle, and since that time – over 400 years – West Wales has known the family of Philipps of Picton – the name being always spelt with one *l* and two *p*'s.

Pembrokeshire has produced more landed families than any other shire in the Principality, but the great majority of them, like the Owens of Orielton, the Scourfields, the Barlows, the Lorts, the Perrots, the Wogans, and many others have become extinct or sunk from their high estate. The family of Philipps however still retains its prestige, acres, and influence in West Wales.

The family was numerous in all its early generations and the younger sons established over thirty flourishing cadet branches in Pembroke, Carmarthen, and Cardigan. They gave 52 High Sheriffs to those counties, 25 Members of Parliament, besides Lords Lieutenant, Magistrates and other officials. The Philippses married into practically every well-known county family and many of the younger sons also married into non-land-owning families with the result that a great number of Pembrokeshire people today can justly claim kinship with the noble house of Picton, and the vigorous blood of the clan can be found throughout the county. The main cadet branches settled at Pentypark, Haythog, Castle Bythe, Southfield, Woodstock, Nash, Tregibby, Cwmgwili, Rushmoor, Coedgain and Llangunnor.

Thomas Philipps, the first of Picton Castle, was descended from Cadifor Fawr, Lord of Blaencych. One of Cadifor's descendants was Sir Aaron ap Rhys ap Bledri, who exchanged the homespun robes of the Welsh squire for the armour of the Crusader, and followed Richard I to the Holy Land. For his services he was made a Knight of the Holy Sepulchre, and it is said that he added the golden collar and chain to his black lion rampant, which is still the coat-armour of the family. Lewys Glyn Cothi addresses several odes to members of this family and in a laudatory poem to Thomas Philipps, gives Thomas's parentage and describes his wife as the "Rose of Pembroke" and compares her to the beauty of the Northern Lights. He ends with a spirited description of the cellars of Picton which he says were full of the wine of Mound (sic), the wine of Normandy, the wines of Bordeaux and Rochells, and sparkling Muscatel, the wines of Speyer-on-the-Rhine and the grape of Spain, and also the home-made wines of Britain. Lewys stayed often at the castle and no doubt the mellow contents of the cellar were no inconsiderable aid to his versatile muse.

Thomas Philipps carried the lion banner of his family successfully over the battlefields of France. Documents in the British Museum contain numerous references to him. In June 1513, an order for Protection was made by Charles, Earl of Worcester, for "Sir Thomas ap Philipps about to serve in the war with France, having done like service in the last voyage with 100 men". He was knighted about 1512. He was one of the coroners for Pembrokeshire, Steward of Llanstephan and Oysterlowe, and Squire of the Body of Henry VIII.

His son, Richard Philipps, was a lover of the Welsh language and a manuscript book belonging to him is now in the National Library of Wales.

Sir Thomas's grandson, Morgan Philipps, had an interesting matrimonial experience. Anne Morris, heiress of Henry Morris of Castle Villa in Brawdy parish, Pembrokeshire, married William Scourfield of Moat, a prominent land magnate of his day. William was also a great traveller and ventured to what was then the little known territory of Barbary. Years passed by and no news was received of him. Anne, at last, not unnaturally believed herself to be bereaved and decked herself in the coy weeds of a widow. Morgan Philipps of Picton successfully laid siege to her heart, married her, and she came to Picton Castle. However, a terrible day arrived, for William Scourfield

Philipps of Picton Castle

returned in the flesh, having been a long time a prisoner of the Moors. Not being the complete Enoch Arden he immediately demanded the restitution of his wife and instituted proceedings in the Court of Great Sessions in 1576, with the result that Anne had to leave the stately Castle of Picton and return to Mr. Scourfield. There is no record of the reactions of Morgan Philipps, but he lost no time in seeking a new wife and this time made no mistake, for he married Elizabeth Fletcher, whose spinsterhood was above reproach, the undoubted unmarried daughter of the Registrar of Bangor, and they had eleven children. His eldest son, Sir John Philipps, was created a Baronet by James I. The Civil War saw great activity at Picton. Like most of the Pembrokeshire gentry, Sir Richard the Second Baronet, was in turn a Royalist and a Roundhead. He garrisoned his castle for the King but shortly afterwards turned his coat. In 1643, Gerrard the Royalist commander, stormed the castle and captured Sir Richard's son and two daughters, besides three barrels of powder, 150 arms, 12 trunks of plate and a large sum of money. There is a tale that one of the children, a small child in its nurse's arms was watching the hostile troops from a window near the ground. While a parley was on, a Royalist trooper got into conversation with the nurse and suddenly snatched the child from her arms, thereby giving the besiegers additional bargaining power.

During this period many a local bride and bridegroom were united in holy matrimony at the castle. Llawhaden, Wiston and Bletherston were consolidated parishes, and although banns were still published in church, the ceremony of marriage was celebrated at Narberth Castle and Picton Castle and performed by a civil magistrate.

Sir Richard's first wife was Elizabeth Dryden, daughter of Sir Erasmus Dryden and cousin of John Dryden, the poet, and had a son, Sir Erasmus Philipps, who entertained the Duke of Beaufort to dinner at Picton while on his progress through Wales in 1684. His son, Sir John Philipps, became known as a man of good works and especial enlightenment. He took a deep and practical interest in all philanthropic and educational movements which earned him the title of "the good Sir John", and his good deeds deserve a volume to themselves. He was closely associated with the Charity Schools and was mainly responsible for 29 schools established in Pembrokeshire between 1705 and 1727. He helped Griffith Jones of Llanddowror by advice and money, and in 1721 that popular cleric married Margaret Philipps, Sir John's sister. A member of many societies for improving the morals and welfare of the people, Sir John gave considerable financial assistance to those societies. The late Mr. Shankland wrote justly these words: "Few men can be found in the United Kingdom during this period whose personal labour and charitable designs were at once so varied and lofty in character and so benevolent and far-reaching in their results." He was a friend of John Gambold and John Wesley, and it was through his financial aid that George Whitfield completed his University career. The good Sir John died in 1736.

The "good Sir John" had three sons – Sir Erasmus, the eldest, who was drowned in the Avon near Bath in 1743 by a fall from his horse while hunting; Sir John, who succeeded his brother, and Bulkeley Philipps of Abercyfor in Carmarthenshire.

Sir Erasmus Philipps, while an undergraduate at Oxford, kept a diary which throws much light on the educational and social life of the early eighteenth century. He was a keen sportsman and was frequently seen on the Turf. On 22 September 1720, he writes: "Walked to Portmead where Mr. Freeman's horse run against Mr. Jerningham's and Mr. Garret's mare, and won the £20 plate. After this was a Foot race between several Taylors for Geese. At night went to the Ball at the Angel. A Guinea Touch."

On 5 January 1721, he writes, "my sister Katherine died at Picton Castle in the 23rd year of her age and was in a few days after interred in Prendergast Church (Haverfordwest). This funeral was extremely handsome (the expense of it amounting to about £600) and was attended by the Chief Gentry of the Countrey . . . I was informed from a good hand, that upon this occasion there was a struggle between Orielton and Colby Coaches about precedency".

Sir Erasmus, as I have said, was drowned in the Avon in 1743, and was succeeded by his next brother, Sir John Philipps, who was a well-known Jacobite. He was a stern Tory, a member of the country party and also a member of the West Wales Jacobite Union called the Society of the Sea Sergeants, whose activities however were more social than political in character. He was cousin of the famous Horace Walpole who once described him as, "a notorious Jacobite". Despite his sympathy for the Stuart cause he was greatly respected in and out of the House and held high offices in Parliament. He was made a Privy Councillor. Like his father he showed an interest in education and in 1749 founded a scholarship at Pembroke College, Oxford. He died in 1764, aged 63.

Dr. Samuel Johnson made an interesting reference to Picton Castle. The learned doctor said: "A Chief and his Lady should make their home like a court. They should have a

Picton Castle – A Victorian view

certain number of gentlemen's daughters to receive their education in the family, to learn pastry and such things from the housekeeper, and manners from my Lady. That was the way in the great families in Wales . . . at Lady Philipps's . . . There were always six young ladies at Sir John Philipps's when one was married, her place was filled up. There was a large schoolroom where they learnt needlework and other things."

The only son of the Jacobite was Sir Richard Philipps, the seventh baronet, who was created Lord Milford in the Peerage of Ireland in 1776. He followed in the family tradition and took an active part in public life, being Lord Lieutenant of the county and Member of Parliament. He married his kinswoman, Mary Philipps of Pentypark.

A Mrs. Morgan who, with her husband, toured Pembrokeshire in 1795 gives an interesting picture of Lord Milford and his lady. His lordship then gave a ball at Haverfordwest.

The writer says "Lord and Lady Milford stood near the door and received the company as they entered. We were introduced and Lady Milford was very polite to me. There is in her manner and countenance all that ease and sweetness which belong to a person of fashion, and she is besides very handsome. His Lordship is handsome too, but he is not as easy as she is. He walked about during tea to see that everything was properly regulated".

Mrs. Morgan attended another ball in a few days time when she had an experience, which she says, made her "very uncomfortable for some time, though the incident in itself was very trifling". While dressing for the ball she left her purse in her room. And she writes "on having lost a rubber to Lord Milford I had no money to discharge the debt. Mr. Morgan not being near, I was obliged to go and seek for him at the bottom of the room, and it was some time after the table was broken up before I could pay his Lordship".

Lord Milford died without issue in 1823 and the baronetcy went to a distant relation, and Picton Castle and the estates to a descendant of Bulkeley Philipps, youngest son of "the good Sir John". The present owner (1938) of Picton, Sir Henry Philipps, Bt., is a descendant by maternal descent, whose members adopted the name Philipps on succeeding to the property. At one time the family owned nearly a third of the county of Pembroke, besides lands in Cardiganshire and Carmarthenshire. In the last century they owned over twenty-two parishes.

Thus the name and blood of the Philippses of Picton Castle remain to us, and their pedigree imparts a sense of historical continuity, stability and pride of race. The family inherited great traditions and great responsibilities, and they well fulfilled the obligations which birth and breeding impose. The motto of the Philippses is DUCIT AMOR PATRIAE – THE LOVE OF COUNTRY LEADS ME ON – and it is because they have lived up to that motto that they have nobly justified the existence of the independent country gentleman.

And so we leave the home of the medieval knights, the crusaders, the Sheriffs and Magistrates, the home of ancient chivalry and steadfast patriotism – Picton Castle – the Pride of Pembroke.

GRIFFITH OF PENYBENGLOG

O N THE brow of a hill in Meline parish, Pembrokeshire, stands the house of Penybenglog. Once the home of a family that played a prominent part in the life of the county, it shared the fate of many of our manorial halls, and today there is little to indicate its former glory. The family has passed into oblivion as though it had never existed. Yet its members were distinguished men, descendants of powerful Marcher chieftains, successful soldiers, and kinsmen to Dafydd ap Gwilym, Owain Glyndŵr, the Royal Tudors, and James I of England. One was a well-known antiquary and a patron of bards. But the family history is widely scattered, and after many years of patient searching the present writer is able to publish a coherent memorial to Griffith of Penybenglog.

There are five very interesting seventeenth century manuscripts[1] in the Llanstephan Collection in the National Library of Wales, and a careful study of them convinced me that there was a close connection between the volumes. The connecting link is Penybenglog. It is clear that they were composed by a man capable of writing five distinct types of penmanship, namely, the cursive, italic script, large print, ornate capitals, and the legal hand. In many instances the writer used four of the types in one sentence. The first word would be in large print or ornate capitals; then would follow the cursive hand until a place, or personal name was encountered which would be entered in the legal hand or italic script. Examination proved that the writer was a first-rate genealogist with a fondness for writing, that he had a sound knowledge of English, Welsh and Latin, and that he was either a lawyer or had received a legal education. The manuscripts are genealogical and mostly concern Griffith family of Penybenglog. We find numerous pedigrees of the Griffith clan, the Reeds, the Warrens, Bowens of Pentre Ifan and Llwyngwair, Hearle, Reynolds of Blaiddbwll, Jenkin Lloyd of Kemes (Cemais), all of whom were related to the Penybenglog family. Further, the Griffith trees contain more details and are far more accurate than the others, which suggests that the writer was at least a near friend if not a member of the Griffith household. It will later be shown how the authorship was determined.

Llanstephan MS. 38 contains poems by various Welsh bards to north Pembrokeshire squires – Owen of Henllys, Bowen of Llwyngwair, Warren of Trewern, and Griffith of Penybenglog. Fourteen poems are addressed to the Penybenglog family, some of which contain dates and interesting architectural details. The last folio, once the outside cover, bears the legend *William Griffith* with some words which defied all efforts to read. However, the fluorescence cabinet clearly revealed the following written in the legal hand *William Griffiths est verus possessor hujus libri donatem per patrem . . .* The volume also contains several entries in the hand of Iago ap Dewi, who is known to have been at Penybenglog in 1715.[2]

Llanstephan MS. 58 contains writing in the five hands we have noted, and also has an entry on folio one in the autograph of Iago ap Dewi. *Llanstephan MS.* 62 contains a folio pasted on the inside cover giving a pedigree of the descendants of Owain Gŵynedd with a brief account of his life and times, and is in the same cursive hand. *Llanstephan MS.* 101 contains pedigrees of north

Pembrokeshire and Carmarthenshire families. Nearly all of these trees relate to Penybenglog, and are written in the five styles of handwriting. Most of them are undated save where they are Griffith pedigrees[3] which are brought down to 1626. The use of the legal hand wherever the name George William Griffith occurs is noteworthy.

The most interesting is *Llanstephan MS. 138.* Some 35 folios contain copies of very early trees of north Wales families, coats of arms, poems, astronomy, and Bonedd Saint Cymru, in the hand of David Parry. Folios 23-35 are in a different hand having no connection with the other part of the volume. Three kinds of writing are used: the cursive, italic script, and capitals, being identical with the handwriting in the foregoing manuscripts. Folios 23-30 contain the descendants of Noah the first monarch of the world to Rhys ap Tewdwr, Prince of South Wales – a copy of an older manuscript. Folio 31 contains coroners' challenge pedigrees and a letter asking George William Griffith to help to make out this descent. Folio 32 contains a chart of the descendants of Bleddyn ap Kynvyn and Rhodri Mawr. Folio 33 contains the descent of the Penybenglog. At this stage it is sufficient to say that a short account is given of every male member of the family in agnatic line, and in the account of George William Griffith the personal pronoun *I* is used.[4] Folio 34 contains the descents of Jenkin Lloyd of Kemes, and folio 35 is a private draft letter by Frances Griffith of Penybenglog. Obviously some of these were personal family papers, the blank parts of which were used for genealogical purposes.

But who is the writer of these manuscripts? How genealogy can be of use in determining the authorship of manuscripts will be shown as we unfold the history of the Griffith family, and the way in which the present writer was able to prove that they were written by George William Griffith, will be given when we reach the seventeenth century part of the pedigree. George William Griffith of Penybenglog lived between 1580 and 1655, and was a well-known antiquary of his day. As there is a modern tendency to decry ancient trees as useless fabrications, a critical examination of the tree on folio 33 of *Llanstephan MS. 138* is interesting. The subsequent pages will show that there was an honest effort to record the truth, and when the genealogy was put to the test of historical records it was found that the seventeenth century scribe was, in the main, accurate.

George William Griffith, described in the *Golden Grove MS.* as "the famous antiquary", is the author of the pedigrees in *Llanstephan MS.* 138 and the other manuscripts we have examined. Added to this he also wrote the first 16 folios in the *Vairdre Book,* giving a genealogical history of the Lords of Kemes. In the course of that history many deeds are cited, and several of them have an important bearing on the Penybenglog family of which a detailed knowledge is shown. A large number of pedigrees in the *Golden Grove, Dale Castle,* and *Peniarth MSS.* quote his name as authority for descents, which proves that he was a compiler of genealogies. It is known that there were old deeds at Penybenglog, that he had searched the records of the Barony, and possessed a sound knowledge of Latin. Of all the early genealogists he is the only one who has given authorities for his statements, and may thus be truly described as a pioneer of modern scientific research. In an age when genealogists were more or less mere copyists, he stands apart, following his own methods, and disdaining to adopt the more easy-going methods of his contemporaries.

The Bronwydd Documents throw important light on his career. In *Estreat Rolls (Kemes, 1614-17)* we find entries in his own hand, in which he describes himself as George William,[5] attorney to the said court. These entries are in two kinds of writing – italic script and legal, the latter being used for his own name and his description, a characteristic we have already noted in the other manuscripts. The fact that he was an attorney accounts for his knowledge of Latin and skill in penmanship, particularly the legal hand. He was witness to a deed of partition,[6] dated 2 September 1630, relating to lands in Manordivy and Kenarth, and it is noteworthy that the signature "Geori' Wm' Gr' " is in the legal hand. *Brogyntyn MS.* 12 (in N.L.W.) is a copy of the laws of Hywel Dda, and the fly-leaf bears the inscription in the same hand, *liber' ex dono Geor' Wm Gri de Pen y Benglog in com' Pembr' xvii Augusti* 1640. We now understand his able handling of ancient deeds in relation to genealogy and his skill in compiling pedigrees that will stand the test of examination.

An inquisition held at Newport on 29th August, 15 Charles I, describes George William Griffith, gent., as an escheator for the county of Pembroke *(Vairdre Book,* fo. 224a).

Penybenglog had a welcome for the bards who never wearied of singing the praises of the family, as the following brief extracts from *Llanstephan MS.* 38 show. Robert Dyfi addressed a poem to Meistr Siors Wm Gruffyth o Ben y benglog yng Hemais

> *Dyn doeth wyd dawn Duw i'r hudh*
> *Difalch o Rees ap Dafydh.* (fo. 169.)

Richard Gruffith *alias* Clerke Eynon sings on folio 181

> *Siors ddwysglod hynod or hen; Iachay*
> *Pur ychel waed bryden,*
> *Ath gywely ddoeth gy olwen*
> *Pur Iawn had y penrhyn hen.*

On folio 182, Robert Dyfi describes the coat-armour of the family as

> *llew gwar yn kario lliw gwyn*
> *llew ku hael llew Kyhelyn.*

However, Griffith takes him to task, and in a marginal note says that Robert has wrongly described the arms *(kam ddoskrio'r bais arfau),* but the bard – on his next visit perhaps – corrected his error, and in an additional englyn sings

> *Llew brytan fyan bob awr, gwyl feirddion*
> *Glew fawr ddysg perffeidd fawr,*
> *Llew llawfaeth a llu lliwfawr*
> *Llew Kyhelyn melyn mawr.*

"Melyn" *(or)* not "lliw gwyn" *(argent)* was the metal of the Penybenglog lion. Siams Emlyn is obviously a gallant and pays a compliment to Mistress Maud, the lady of the house. He sings

> *Dyrvy iechyd yr byd ar benn y bennglog*
> *Byw arogl byr wenn*
> *A llewych foyd llawenn*
> *Gida mawd y gadw a menn.* (fo. 183.)

Dafydd Llwyd Mathe brackets George William Griffith with George Owen and George Owen Harry, and refers to our man as a genealogist and translator

Dau Siors oedd ar goedd dau ga – un drad
Heb dryddudd oi dvall
Yn awr mae un arall
O iachwr Cyfieythwr call.
A hwnnw ar henw rhudd, a elwyr
Siors Wiliam Gryffydd
Ar ol y ddau arwul ddudd [7]
Hwn a droidiwd yn drydudd. (fo. 184.)

Among the bards who paid their tribute were Dafydd Emlyn, Siams David William, Harry Howel the genealogist, Y Prydydd Coch, and Morgan Gwyn.

He also wrote part of *Llanstephan MS.* 130. On folio 29 there are trees by him of the families of Perrott, Philipps of Picton, Stepney, Pryse of Gogerddan, Jones of Harmeston, and Vaughan of Golden Grove. On folios 27b-28 there is a chart of the Hall family of Trewent. Our antiquary has added material to this in the legal hand. Where the entry of William Gr. of Penybenglog = Elizabeth Thomas, occurs, he has added *"pater G. Wm.Gr. de Penybenglog 1649"*. His signature also occurs on folio 114 of *Llanstephan MS.* 101 and several other manuscripts.

Owning a large estate, George William Griffith had a distinct taste for arts and antiquities, and knew George Owen of Henllys, who lived nearby. The Civil War brought trouble and George William Griffith left his antiquities and bardic friends for the council chamber of the Roundheads. In June, 1644, a committee nominated by an ordinance of Parliament, for the mutual defence and safety of the counties of Pembroke, Carmarthen, and Cardigan, and amongst its members was George William Griffith, Esquire.[8] Penybenglog suffered as a result of his partisanship and was plundered by the Cavaliers. We can do no better than to quote Griffith's own description in the manuscript containing his family history: *George Wm Gruffyth, son & heyre to Wm. Gr., after the death of his father lived at Penybenglog, repayred the Ruines of the decayed buyldeinges, erected & bestowed charge upon ffences, hedges, & moundes upon the dem'[9] thereof, & for enlargeinge the same dern' purchased certeyne tenants & Lands in Meliney & Nevarne, amounteinge to the value of £300 & upwards. He for his affection to the Parlt was plundered by the kinges party to his damage £250. He was one of the Comtee for the associated com' of Pembr Carm'then & Cardigan. Commissiond for the monethly assessmts in the com' of Pembr' & now in the moneth of March by comon[10] from Oliver, Lo: P'tector of the Comon wealth of England, Scotland & Ireland, unto John Haggad[11] chiefe justice of the corn' of Pembr Carm'then & Cardigan, directed sommoned to appeere before him to take the oath of Justice of the peace wthin the com' of Pembr' wch I tooke before him at Cardigan 22 Martii 1653.*

It is strange that a man of repute and culture like George William Griffith threw in his lot with a party who had scant respect for the ancient things so dear to the heart of the antiquary. But his will suggests an answer and also corroborates the foregoing quotation. In giving directions relating to trust money, he says: "I do heerby wholly referre my selfe to be considered and proportioned to the judgement and Rule of those most worthy and noble gentlemen . . . that is to saie Sr. Hugh Owen and Arthur Owen, Esq., whome since my ffirst acquaintance with them I ever found to be towards me friendly and lovinge." Now these "ffriendly and lovinge" men were active Roundheads and greatly attached to the Parliamentary party, so it is very likely that they influenced Griffith in no small degree. In a bequest to his daughter, he says " . . . she well knoweinge (how that by the Kinges party under commaund of Gerard[12] then prevalent in theis partes) I was totally plundered and since could not recover anie considerable estate in gooddes".

He was married and had four children in 1613. He was born 21 April 1584, married on 22 November 1605. His account states that his wife was *Mathildam f. Jacobi Bowen de Llwyngwair,* and Dwnn and the bards give Mawd (i.e. Maud) – Mathildam being Griffith's Latin rendering of the name. Her mother was Elen, daughter of John Gruffydd ap Sir William Gruffydd of Penrhyn, North Wales. James Bowen of Llwyngwair was born in the last year of Henry VIII, and died on 20 October 1629. His wife Elen Griffith died in March 1624. When the parish church of Meline was restored in 1865, the ancient pews were demolished, and an old pew-back, bearing the inscription SED : MATHILD : Ux GEO: PER: PENEBENGLOG : GE : 1626, was taken away to Penybenglog.[13] She died in the Feast of Pentecost 1647.

The last entries in the pedigree were made in 1654 and give the names of the children of the writer:

1. William, born 29 August 1610, son and heir, "duxit Franciscam f. Hugonis Bowen de Upton, Ar., married Dec. 6. 1649";
2. James, second sonne. Born 18 September 1611;
3. George, third sonne, b. 17 November 1612, married Mary only daughter to Richard Vaughan of Penbryn, Sept. 15. 1649;
4. Robert, 4 sonne, b. 30 September 1615, of Grayes Inne, Esq., Admitted Barrister X Februarii 1650;
5. Morgan, fifth sonne, b. 5 October 1618, a bachelor, Mar. 26. 1654;
6. Thomas, 6 sonne b. 15 July 1620, infirmus, and youngest, mar. Elin Jones da: and sol: heir to Geo: Jones, Jan. 3 1649, hath yssue, Charity Gruffyth, liveinge Ao. 1654;
7. Elin, only daughter, b. 27 July 1609, married on 4 Aug. 1648, Jo. Bowen, youngest son of George Bowen of Llwyngwair, and had a son George Bowen alive in 1654. On 13 Dec. 1629, Dafydd Llwyd Mathe sings her praises:

> *Elen Gruffydh sydd nawswych – anwyl*
> *Einioes hir y geffych*
> *A da mawr gwir dymer gwych*
> *Ar gwr mwya'r y gerych'.*
> *(Llanst. MS. 38, fo. 185.)*

Here endeth George William Griffith's account. The last entry is apparently on 26 March 1654, four days after he had taken the oath of magistrate, and he must have died in that year or early in 1655. The last reference to him in the *Kemes Court Rolls* is an entry on 20 April 1654, in the list of suitors and free tenants of the High Court. His will, dated 12 May 1651, was proved at London on 29 August 1655, by his eldest son and executor. A [photostat] copy of the will[14] "written with myne owne hand upon severall tymes when I found my bodie prepared and in perfect memory," shows that the same hand had written the manuscripts discussed in the opening of this essay. It is a cursive hand with the trick of ornamental capitals, using the italic script when he comes to a place, or personal name. Another characteristic of both will and manuscripts is the writer's fondness for marginalia, while the spelling of personal names is identical, the name Gruffyth always having two dots over the letter *u*. The commencement of the will is in the nature of a sermon in which testator expresses his willingness to leave "with a free Harte . . . this vile and wretched world", and directs that he is to be buried in Meline "with the bones of my Decessed consorte, and many others my decessed Auncestors". However, in the disposal of his worldly goods he shows himself to be a sound attorney and the puritanism of the sermon gives place to the legal formula of the indenture. To his eldest son, William, he leaves all his real estate; to James, £2 5s. and live stock; to George, now of Penbryn, Cardigan, £10; to Robert of Grays Inn £10; to Morgan "who unto me was never more charge than his homely breedeinge and country educon," £10 and live stock; to Thomas, £7 10s.; to Helin[15] Bowen alias Gruffyth "my sole and onely daughter . . . yet eldest of all my children, £10." Then follows lengthy and detailed instructions as to his share of £1,500 for renouncing the executorship of Sir Thomas Canon's last will and testament.[16]

Little is known of William Griffith the eldest son. An interesting document amongst the *Papers of Great Sessions* for Cardiganshire for 28 Charles II, shows that he had inherited the antiquarian aptitude of his father. It is the humble petition of William Griffiths, of the parish of Melyney (sic) in the county of Pembroke, one of the antiquaries belonging to the counties of Pembroke, Cardigan, and Carmarthen, which shews that "your petitioner is an aged man and sole antiquary bellonginge to the Counties as afforesaid, and doth humbly beseech your lordshippes to discharge him . . . from appearinge att any Leete or Leetes or any other Courtes within the Countyes afforesd by reason of his beinge an antiquary and age as afforesaid & to bee dischardged of & from any Fine or Fines that may or might bee Imposed in any Courte or Courtes as afforesd by reason of his non appearance". The petition was granted on 26 May 1676.

This document has more than ordinary interest, for apart from showing that William Griffith was an antiquary, it suggests that the antiquaries of that time had a standing in a court of law. He could not have been more than 67 years of age when the petition was presented and was apparently in good health, and so the plea of being "aged" alone would not have been a sufficient reason for excusal. There is evidence, however, that the genealogists prepared pedigrees for challenging sheriffs and coroners in the Great Sessions, and I have seen several lawyers' bills of costs where these pedigrees are entered and charged as separate items, the charges varying from two shillings to six shillings. Added to this legal work the genealogists and antiquaries were continually working at transcriptions and family trees. That William Griffith was "sole" antiquary in the three counties at that time is open to question. It would be interesting to know whether any specimens of his work remain.

William Griffith lived in comfortable circumstances and was assessed at six hearths in

1670.[17] He had no issue and died before 13 September 1677, when probate of his will (dated 25 July 1677) was granted at Carmarthen to his widow and executrix, Frances. The widow was financially distressed some time after her husband's decease, and on folio 35 of *Llanstephan MS.* 138 is a draft letter to a "worthy Sir" (whose son was "my cuz. Col. Ja: Lewes") asking him to help her in her present trouble. She writes that "want makes the poor woman trott" and adds that owing to debts and legacies she has not been able to put "plough nor harrowe going this year". Whether "your most humble servant and neece Ffrances Gruffyth" received assistance from her uncle is not stated. As he was succeeded by his youngest brother, Thomas, it follows that James, George, Robert, and Morgan were probably dead and without surviving issue in 1677.

Thomas Griffith (heir of his brother William) was twice married. As we have seen from his father's chronicle, his first wife was Elin, daughter of George Jones, by whom he had a daughter, Charity, living in 1654. His second wife was Elizabeth, daughter and heiress of John Thomas of Treclyn, by Margaret, daughter of Philip Bowen of Llanycefn, whose wife was a daughter of Sir James Bowen, of Llwyngwair.[18] Thomas Griffith was buried on 24 May 1684, and his will, dated 20 April 1684, was proved at Carmarthen on 3 July in the same year.[19] His widow survived him until 1706, when her will (dated 1 August 1705) was proved.[20] He left the following issue: 1. Ajax Griffith; 2. Charity; 3. Judith, living in 1735; 4. Maud.

Ajax Griffith, of Penybenglog, married Frances, daughter of John Lloyd, of Trerees in Kemes (Golden Grove says, of Cwmgloyne). Ajax and Frances Griffith, widow (his aunt) were assessed at £9 2s. 0d. per quarter for Land Tax in Meliney parish in 1704. He is mentioned in a suit in the Great Sessions for Pembrokeshire for 8 Anne as party to a bond made on 15 July 1690; and he participated in the Parliamentary election for co. Pembroke in 1715, when he exercised his vote in favour of Owen, of Orielton. He died before 20 March, 1734-35, when his will (dated 15 February 1734-35) was proved at Carmarthen[21]. He had four children, all living in 1735:

1. Elizabeth, baptised at Nevern 10 February 1683, married in 1719 Griffith Twyning, and had issue;
2. Robert Griffith;
3. Anne married Thomas Merchant of Manorbier Newton. She died on 26 November 1761, aged 74, M.I. in Lamphrey church;
4. Lettice married John Williams, of Cardigan. The marriage bond of John Williams and Latitia Griffith of Meline, Pems., is dated 2 January 1720-21.[22]

Robert Griffith, of Penybenglog, to whom his father bequeathed a pair of wheels and a sledge, was the last male representative of his race. He married in 1713, Elizabeth, daughter of George Lloyd of Cwmgloyne,[23] by whom he had no issue. He survived his father some two years, and died before January, 1737-38, when administration of his goods was granted at Carmarthen to his widow. "And his estate came between his sisters and co-heirs, namely, Elizabeth, Anne, Lettice." [24] Penybenglog became the seat of the Revd. Watkin Lewes (father of Sir Watkin, Lord Mayor of London), who was related to the Griffith family through its union with the Lloyds.

A footnote in Owen's *Pembrokeshire*[25] reads: "In 1715, it [*i.e.* Penybenglog] was the seat of Piers William Griffith, who owned a MS. *History of Wales,* founded on Powel, which was copied in that year by Iago ap Dewi of Llanllawddog." The owner of Penybenglog in 1715, as we have seen was Ajax, not Piers William Griffith, no such person ever having existed. As noted earlier, Iago ap Dewi was responsible for marginalia in some of the Penybenglog manuscripts. On folio 66, of *Cardiff MS. 36,* the ancestry of Llawddog is given in the hand of Iago, who writes: *"Cymeint a hyn am Lawddog o lyfr Siors William Gryffydd o Ben y Benglog. Awst 9ed 1714."* [26]

In *Cardiff MS. 58* occurs the following note: *Terfyn pryd Tywysogion y Bryttanieid ynghymry wedi ei scrifennu allan o hen Lyfr-scrifen o Law un Siors William Gr. gynt o Benybenglog gan Jaco ab Dewi Ebrill 24. 1717. Ar waith hon drachefn o scrifen law Jaco ab Dewi gan Wiliam Bona o Llanpumpsaint Mai 22. 1766.*[27]

Fenton has a reference to heraldic windows, and he writes in 1811 ". . . another mansion, Penybenglog, ranked with the first in its day, which, though it has long ceased to be inhabited by any of the descendants of its ancient possessors, and has often changed masters, yet by having had the good fortune to find a succession of respectable tenants, it has been kept in a state of decent repair, and till within these few years, one of its windows exhibited the pride of ancestry in painted glass."[28]   Now there is a poem in *Llanstephan MS.* 38, folio 180, composed by Harri Howel, on 23 April 1642, containing a description of this "painted glass". It reads:

Penn benglog rowiog reiol i harfau	*Arfau'r prif lwythau helaethwych ydynt*
Wiw lunian olynol	*Breintiedig gampus wych*
Ar y ffenest orchestol	*Llawn wiwdrym pob lliw'n edrych*
Pedwar glain arhigain rhol.	*Yn loew lawn draw lana drych.*
Perffaith du odiaith nodedig iawn teg	*Arwyddfardd waithhardd i'th ddydd siwr seilad*
Aur-breintiad urddedig	*Wyd Siors Wiliam Gryffydd,*
Pob lliw draw pob' llew a drig	*Cain gu er sy fu ag fydd*
Pen ty o wydr paintiedig.	*Glau dro gwiw glod dragywydd.*

These stanzas show that the heraldic windows were in existence – prior to 1642 – which according to Fenton, had survived until the opening of the last century. But they too have been sacrificed to that strange spirit of change which periodically afflicts the less stable elements of the population of Wales. The name, Griffith of Penybenglog, has also passed away, and its only memorials are a few manuscripts, scattered references in genealogical tables, and the glowing effusions of unpublished bards.

After the Griffith family, Penybenglog became the home of Revd. Watkin Lewes, father of Sir Watkin Lewes, Lord Mayor of London. The freehold passed from the Leweses to the Hughes family who were gentlemen farmers.

In June 1946, I again visited Penybenglog. The house was then unoccupied, and had been bought by a Major Wilson who was going to renovate the house. It was in a good state of preservation, but the drawing-room floor had collapsed in part: below it was a good cellar. Above the kitchen door was a tablet which read: "J. Hughes, Esq., Rebuilt 1828. William Lewis, Tenant."

I desire to acknowledge my indebtedness to Evan D. Jones, Esq., Keeper of the MSS. and Records in the National Library of Wales, for help with the Welsh poetry and for placing his expert knowledge of palaeography at my disposal; to Dr. B. G. Charles, for most useful suggestions; and to Francis Green, Esq., of St. Davids, for his valuable assistance with the early portions of the pedigree, and for genealogical transcripts of the Penybenglog wills.

NOTES AND REFERENCES

[1] Nos. 38, 58, 62, 101, and 138.

[2] Owen's *Pembrokeshire,* ii, 468, footnote. *Vide* also *Historical MSS. Commission,* p. 265.

[3] Folios 6, 29, 34, 63, 66 – 8, and 71.

[4] Where "Griffith" is given as the authority in this essay, the reference is to folio 33 of this MS., unless otherwise stated.

[5] Prior to his father's death he is generally described as George William, and as such signed for Dwnn A: but after 1618 he is described consistently as George William Griffith.

[6] *Misc. Pem. Deeds,* No. 16, N.L.W.

[7] The three George's referred to were: 1. George Owen Harry, Clerk in Holy Orders, of Dinas, Pems., author of *The Well-Spring of True Nobilitie,* and a good antiquary, vivens 1597; 2. George Owen, of Henllys, Lord of Kemes; and 3. George William Griffith.

[8] Laws' *Little England beyond Wales,* p. 327.

[9] Demesne.

[10] Commission.

[11] Sir John Haggett, C.J. See Williams, *The Welsh Judges.*

[12] Col. Charles Gerard, the Loyalist commander, was in Pembrokeshire in 1644.

[13] See *Commission of Ancient Monuments in Wales,* Pembroke, p. 226, where this is translated as "the pew of Matilda, wife of George Perrot of Penybenglog, gentleman, 1626". The word PER has obviously been misread. It was probably GRI or some like abbreviation of Griffith. Unfortunately the pew-back has disappeared, although at the moment I have reason to believe it is in an English county.

[14] N.L.W. MS. 10, 933D.

[15] Called *primogenita* in Llanst. 101, fo. 66.

[16] Sir Thomas Canon was a noted antiquary, four times mayor of Haverfordwest, and Member of Parliament in 1625 and 1626; he was knighted in 1623. His will, dated 20 October 1638, was proved P.C.C. 23 February 1654-55 – *penes* Capel St. Leonard. See Owen's *Pem.* iii, 356.

[17] *West Wales Historical Records,* IX, 227.

[18] *Golden Grove MS.*

[19] *penes* Francis Green, Esq.

[20] *West Wales Historical Records,* i, 254.

[21] *penes* Francis Green, Esq.

[22] *West Wales Historical Records,* iii, 166.

[23] *Golden Grove MS.* A note in MS. of Sir Thomas Phillipps of Middle Hill calls her his "cos. German".

[24] Addition to a MS. of Sir Thomas Phillipps (Dr. Henry Owen's Collection, N.L.W.). Nicholas, *County Families,* ii, 629, gives *Janet* as one of the co-heiresses and traces the descent of a certain family from her. This, however, is a flight of the imagination.

[25] ii 468.

[26] *penes* G. H. Hughes, Esq., of the University College of Wales, Aberystwyth.

[27] *Historical MSS. Commission,* Vol. 11, p. 265.

[28] *Tour,* 565.

COATS OF ARMS OF PEMBROKESHIRE GENTRY

Allen of Cresselly

Barlow of Llawrenny

Bowen of Llwyngwair

Bowen of Upton Castle

Campbell of Stackpole

Callen of Merrixton

Colby of Ffynone

Morgan Davies of Grove

Saunders Davies of Pentre

Fenton of Glyn Y Mel

Fowler of Robeston Hall

*Gower of Castle Malgwyn
(Castell Maelgwn)*

Holcombe of Brownsslade

le Hunte of St. Botolphs

Davies-Lloyd of Cilrhiwe

Lloyd of Pentypark

Jones of Pentower

Jones of Brawdy

Mathias of Fern Hill

Meare of Eastington

Mirehouse of Angle Hall

Owen of Orielton

Stevenson-Owen of Poyston

Perrott of Haroldston

Phillips of Slebech

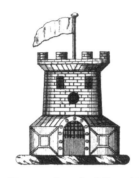

Harcourt Powell of Greenhill

James of Pantsaison

George Roch of Butterhill

Nicholas Roch of Paskeston

Rutzen of Slebech

*The Editor
gratefully acknowledges
Thomas Lloyd's
permission to reproduce
Coats of Arms
from his collection*

Scourfield of New Moat

Stepney of Prendergast

THE CANDLE-MAKERS OF HAVERFORD

Lead kindly light

NO-ONE has yet written the history or the ballad of Haverfordwest Goal, an unfortunate but necessary part of social life both past and present. At one time the gaol of the town and county of Haverfordwest was in a large old house that stood at the bottom of Tower Hill, near the Mariners' Inn. At a later date the town and county used the county gaol which was the castle. It was in the year 1728. The main *dramatis personae* were Mr. Joseph Prust, the Mayor, and his wife, Mr. Thomas Hoare, the sheriff, and his wife, and Richard Clince, Supervisor of the Excise, Henry Roberts, William Bowen, and William Jones, officers of the Excise in the town and county of Haverfordwest.

Mr. Clince was an efficient person, and after a time he noticed that though everyone in the town used candles, there were very few to be seen exposed for sale in the shops. There was a tax on candles and Mr. Clince had a feeling that King George II was not receiving his due from the burgesses of "honey Harfat". He decided to make enquiries but the answers he received were so vague and unsatisfactory, and in some cases downright rude, that he soon realised that there was a conspiracy. He was up against a brick wall. The houses were well-lit with candles but despite his night rambles he failed to find any households manufacturing them. However, one of the officers got a hint and immediately reported it to Mr. Clince. Mr. Clince was shocked to hear that the candles were manufactured under his very nose in the town gaol. They were made by the prisoners and sold in the town, and he also remembered that at no time had he heard of a prisoner escaping from Haverfordwest gaol. They were extremely happy there. Indeed the prisoners, living at the expense of the King, had become manufacturers and capitalists. What Mr. Clince's political views were I don't know, but he decided at once that this was a form of private enterprise he would not tolerate. He reported to his superiors that "a clandestine trade for the making of Candles for which no Duty or Excise was paid was carried on in the gaol of the town and county of H'west". He was ordered to suppress it.

Mr. Clince and his officers set to work, but they soon realised that they were not only up against the prisoners and the gaolers, but also against the Mayor and the Sheriff and other respectable members of the community. They then decided to keep watch.

On 23 January 1728, Mr. Clince and Henry Roberts crept up to the gaol door. It was locked. There was a hole in the door and Roberts peered in, and saw a candle mould with drops of fresh tallow on it. Mr. Clince then peered in, but one of the prisoners spotted him and spat into his eyes. However, he had another peep and saw three or four very rough bearded fellows coming towards the door. Mr. Clince and Mr. Roberts decided that they had had enough of this bo-peep business and ran away as fast as they could, "fearing that harm should befall them". However, later on, fortified by some brandy on which excise had been paid, they stealthily returned. There at the gaol door they saw Margaret Morgan, a well-known housewife, receiving something into her apron. Margaret spotted Mr. Clince and Roberts and immediately took to her heels. The excisemen pursued and as she ran she dropped a pound of candles. But they managed to catch her and, in her apron which she still clutched, they found six pounds of candles.

This was a "fair cop", but to complete the case it was necessary to enter the gaol with witnesses to get evidence of manufacture of the candles which was the vital and important matter. They immediately called on Thomas Hoare, the Sheriff, and demanded entry to the gaol. Mr. Hoare said he could not dream of allowing such a thing until he had consulted Mr. Prust, the Mayor. So Mr. Clince, Mr. Roberts and the sheriff called on the Mayor. The Mayor was quite friendly, and said he would hand over the keys so long as Mr. Clince put down a very considerable sum of money to indemnify the Mayor and the Sheriff should any prisoner escape while Mr. Clince was searching the gaol. Mr. Clince did not have the money and in any case regarded the request as unreasonable. So the excisemen had to retire in a very unsatisfactory state of mind without having searched the gaol.

Next morning the Sheriff called on Mr. Clince, and invited him to come with him to search the gaol. But Mr. Clince gave him "rude and uncivil speeches", telling him in an especially rude way what he could do with the keys. Mr. Clince realised that all traces of the evidence would have disappeared overnight.

But Mr. Clince and his excisemen, though baffled, did not throw in the sponge, and they continued their peeping-Tom act around the gaol. One night in May 1728, they saw John Jenkins leaving the gaol door with a box under is arm. As soon as he saw Mr. Clince he was galvanised into action and fled through the streets and darted into a house. After battering at the door for a while they were admitted, and saw John Jenkins seated on a chair puffing his pipe. They asked him about the box, but he denied all knowledge of it. They then searched the house and found the box with six pounds of candles in it hidden in the vault.

They then went to the Sheriff's house. The door was opened by the Sheriff's wife who told them that the Sheriff was away and had taken the keys with him. They then called on the Mayor. The door was opened by the Mayor's wife who told them that the Mayor had gone away and sweetly invited them to call again tomorrow. The excisemen had experienced this sort of thing before and had to retire defeated.

In the morning the Sheriff called on Mr. Clince and told him that he could search the gaol if he liked. Mr. Clince gave him a sour sort of reply and the Sheriff went away laughing heartily.

However, they did succeed at long last. Hiding near the gaol, they waited till the door was opening to admit someone, and they rushed in. However, they were immediately tackled by the prisoners, and bustled into a cell, where Mrs. Catherine Hoare, the Sheriff's wife locked them in. Despite their howls and yells they were kept there while the evidence of the candle making was removed. Mrs. Hoare, when releasing them, apologised, and told the angry excisemen that she had mistaken them for prisoners, and had locked them in for fear they would escape.

I am sorry to say that I do not know how this affair eventually ended. But this we can say, I think, that Mr. Joseph Prust, the Mayor, and Mr. Thomas Hoare, the Sheriff, and their wives, were the first Free Traders whose names are known to us in Pembrokeshire.

THE MAYORS OF WISTON – THE VANISHED BURGESSES

Written in the late 1940s

TODAY the ancient borough of Wiston is but a memory, and one cannot say that, "every schoolboy knows", that it was once a seat of local government with its own civic heads. Whilst the histories of Haverfordwest, Tenby and Pembroke have been written, little notice has been taken of the smaller centres such as Newport, Fishguard, St. Davids and Wiston; yet they too have their own story to unfold; Newport and Wiston had their mayors, while Fishguard and St. Davids had their Prepositi. There is reason to believe that the chief officer of St. Davids was a Mayor and not a Prepositus and it is by the former name that he is generally described in old documents. However, in this essay we will confine ourselves to a brief survey of the Borough of Wiston.

The main source of the following information is derived from the little known *Papers of Great Sessions of Pembrokeshire* deposited in the Public Record Office in Chancery Lane [now in N.L.W.]. These papers consist of Plea Rolls as the main records, with the Gaol Files, Prothonotaries Papers, etc., as subsidiary documents. They are written in Latin and in the palaeography known as the "court hand". They are extremely well preserved and are of very great importance to Pembrokeshire historians. It is sad to relate that, despite decades of free education and its worship in Wales, no-one (with the exception of the late Mr. Francis Green, J.P.), has even consulted them and made known their interesting contents to a public which is nowadays alleged to be enlightened and emancipated. It is correct to say that no history of Pembrokeshire can be rendered complete without reference to these important documents. They cover the period 1542-1830.

Prior to 1542 Wales was ruled by a large number of Lords Marcher, being some 143 altogether. Laws and their application varied considerably, with the result that conditions had become chaotic. *Brevis domini regis non currit in Wallia* was true of all the land except the County Palatine of Pembroke, which included, roughly, the area known to us as Castlemartin. However, the Tudor monarchs changed all this. They abolished the Lord Marcherships, abolished the ridiculous Welsh land tenure of gavelkind, the dangerous customs of *arddel* and *cymhortha*, and divided Wales into shire-ground. Two courts were established – The Council of Wales and the Marches, and the King's Court of Great Sessions in Wales. All this took place in the year 1542 – a date of which every Welshman should be proud. Prior to this date Wales was not a nation, and not even a geographical expression.

The Court of Great Sessions was held twice every year in the Spring and in the Autumn. It was directed to hold all manner of pleas of the Crown "in as large and ample a manner", as the Court of King's Bench in England, and also to hold Pleas of Assizes, and all other Pleas and Actions, real, personal and mixed. It was also given complete criminal jurisdiction. The Court of Great Sessions also had an equitable jurisdiction, but when and how it was acquired is not clear. It was not specifically conferred by the Act of 1542, but evidence exists in the documents in the Public Record Office to show that equity work was transacted in these courts in Elizabeth's time. The suggestion by the late Dr. Henry Owen of Poyston, that there was doubt whether the Court of Great Sessions had any equitable jurisdiction before 19 Charles II, is not justified.

The Great Sessions were general purposes courts and it is from their records that we find the names of the administrators of bygone Pembrokeshire. In the Spring and Autumn Sessions the names of all the officers of the county were returned. This list was normally a long parchment and contained the names – the Sheriff, Magistrates, Escheators, Coroners, Mayors, Prepositi, Stewards of Lordships, High Constables and Bailiffs of Hundreds, Portreves and others. Thus we can discover the names of the men who assisted in governing the county from 1542 to 1830 when the Great Sessions were abolished. Although there are very few rolls and files missing, sometimes the names of "all" the officials were not entered, with the result that there are certain gaps. However, lists of the Mayors of Haverfordwest, Tenby, Pembroke and Newport are nearly perfect, but the lists for Wiston, St. Davids and Fishguard are far from complete. In this essay the Mayors of Wiston are listed, and it is to be hoped that further research will succeed in producing a fuller list. It is possible that records of the Borough of Wiston may still be found within the county, and that they have not been totally destroyed.

Nothing is known of the origin of the Borough of Wiston and little is known of its history. Some say that it was co-extensive with the parish of Wiston, and others that it was co-extensive with the Manor of Wiston. The Manor extended two-and-a-half miles to the north, and about half-a-mile to the south of the parish boundaries. No record has been found which establishes the extent of the borough. The centre of the manor was Wiston House (home of Wizo the Fleming, and later of the mighty Wogans), and it is extremely probable that it was also the seat of government of the borough. The style of the courts was "The Manor and Borough of Wiston", and this tends to favour the belief that the Manor and the Borough were co-extensive. On the other hand, the constables of the borough acted throughout the parish of Wiston only, and had no jurisdiction on any lands beyond the parish confines. Until fresh evidence comes to hand the extent of the borough will have to remain an open question.

At no time has there been any trace, tradition, or suggestion that Wiston ever had a charter. It was called a borough by prescription. Its only records extant in 1833, were the rolls of the Court Leet, and the books containing the stamped admissions of the burgesses. It had a yearly court, by the style of "The Court Leet of the Manor and Borough of Wiston in the County of Pembroke". As the bailiff was commanded by his warrant to summon the Court Leet and view of frankpledge and also the court baron, it would appear that the court baron was held at the same time. Such being the case, the Leet jury would be the homagers. The jury composed of twelve burgesses named by the town clerk and returned by the bailiff. The jury elected a mayor and two constables, and also elected further burgesses, and made the normal presentments. The steward of the manor of Wiston, was appointed by the lord, and he took the title of Town Clerk of the Borough of Wiston without further appointment. He attended the court as an officer, kept the court books, swore in the mayor, and appointed a bailiff for the borough. He was entitled to a fee of two shillings on the admission of every new burgess.

The mayor of Wiston was presented by the jury at the suggestion of the steward. After serving for one year, he bore the title of alderman for the ensuing year. His duties do not appear to have been onerous. He presided at the Court Leet and signed the proper forms and records. Among the mayors of Wiston we find the names of great landowners like Lloyd of Cilciffeth, Wogan of Wiston, Bateman, Grant, Skyrme and Jones. But towards the end of the existence of the borough, it was reported by Mr. C. Austin that the mayors were seldom able to read or write, and that they were normally poor burgesses who were made mayors to enable them to receive by way of relief, the tolls of the small annual fair of Wiston (8 November), for the sale of cattle, sheep and horses. The fair was held in the village and the tolls amounted to some £8 -£10 per annum. This may have been true of some mayors, but the majority certainly were men of substance and ability.

Two constables were presented in the same way as the mayor. The bailiff called and attended the courts and summoned the jury, and was entitled to a fee of sixpence on admission of a new burgess. The burgesses were presented by the jury and sworn before the mayor. Originally they were people who lived within the boundaries of the borough, but later there was no qualification as to residence or the number of burgesses.

Before 1832 they voted for members of parliament in conjunction with the freemen of Tenby and Pembroke, and there is little doubt that the vote was considerably influenced by the lord of Wiston manor. The last large batch of burgesses to be made was on the eve of an expected contest in 1812. In 1832 there were between 500 and 600 burgesses of Wiston.

It would be interesting to know who the last surviving burgess was. There may be people living in Pembrokeshire today who knew some of the old burgesses of Wiston.

The parish of Wiston is agricultural and itself consisted of some 6,000 acres. In 1801 the population was 569 with 98 houses; in 1821, it was 753 with 134 houses; and in 1831 it was 745 with 129 houses.

It will be seen that this list is far from complete, but I hope that these names will become a permanent record, and may perhaps inspire some Pembroke antiquary to search local records which may fill some of the gaps.

The Mayors of Wiston

1628	David Lloyd of Cilciffeth [1]	1669	David Grant
1630	John Saunders	1670	Rowland Wogan
1631	Richard Barnard	1671	Rowland Wogan
1632	Nicholas Devereux	1672	Nicholas Smyth
1633	James Phillips	1673	Griffith Morgan
1634	James Phillips	1674	William Skyrme
1636	Rowland Griffith	1675	Rowland Wogan
1638	John Smith	1677	Nicholas Smith
1641	Mervin Callan	1679	James Wogan
1641	(Spring) Henry Jones	1680	Nicholas Smith
1642	Nicholas Smith	1681	Arthur Jones
1650	John Vougler	1682	Thomas Skyrme
1653	John Smith	1683	Compton Gwyther
1654	John Smith	1684	John Barnard
1655	John Smith	1686	John Skyrme
1656	Richard Barnard	1688	James Lloyd
1657	Richard Barnard	1689	John Skyrme
1658	Richard Barnard	1731	John Phelps, Esq.
1659	Thomas James	1732	Joseph Blundell, Esq.
1661	(Spring) John Protheroe	1733	Roger Prichard
1661	Richard Barnard	1740	Edward Hitchings, Esq.
1663	Compton Wogan	1741	Thomas Phillipps, Esq.
1664	Humphrey Bateman	1742	Morris Gibby
1665	Mervin Callan	1816	William Gibby Yeoman
1666	Nicholas Smyth	1821	John Bartlett
1667	Owen Adams	1828	Thomas Lloyd
1668	Owen Adams		

FOOTNOTE

[1] David Lloyd of Cilciffeth was second son of Thomas Lloyd of Penygegin in Llanychllwydog by Anne, daughter of Owen Jones of Trecwn. He was 18 years 10 months and 4 days of age on 10 March 1624-5, and was thus Mayor at the early age of 22. He married Mary daughter of John Wogan of Wiston, by whom he had three daughters:

a. Sibyl, married Sir Herbert Perrott; she died on 9 January 1640-1.

b. Mary, born 1629, married Richard le Hunte of Arstramont, near Wexford.

c. Joan, born in 1631, married firstly George Barlow of Slebech; secondly Walter Vaughan of Derwydd, Carms: thirdly, Walter Middleton of Carms.

David Lloyd died on 4 October 1631, and was buried at Wiston, his I.P.M. was held on 5 November 1631, (P.R.O.). It is interesting to note that his grandfather, Thomas Lloyd, liberally endowed the Grammar School, Haverfordwest in 1613. The Lloyd arms were, *argent,* a lion rampant, regardant *sable,* armed and langued *gules,* which exists today as the badge of the Grammar School. Richard Fenton, the Pembrokeshire historian, and an old Grammar School boy, was a descendant of a younger branch of Lloyd of Cilciffeth.

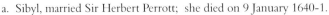

THE PETTICOAT

A Mention of the Unmentionable

This pattern was discovered in the family library, and is dated from 1890, in my great grandmother's hand.

Full sized warm petticoat

Materials required: 1 lb. petticoat yarn or Fleece; A coarse wooden crochet needle.

Allow 17 stitches for each scallop. Make a chain of 272 stitches; for convenience of counting put a white thread at each 50. Join this long chain in one round and (+) 7 double chain, 3 double chains into 8th chain; 7 double chains, miss 3, repeat from + to the end of this round, join to top of 1st double chain and turn the work.

   Crochet back in the same way, taking the back loop, so as to make ribbed crochet; continue this till it is sufficiently long, 40 rows or 20 ribs is a good length, fasten off. The last row is the bottom of the petticoat, put an edge. Begin again at the original chain and work round one way and then back again in the same way, ribbed crochet, but without any increase or decrease so as to get rid of the scallops. When this is done and the crochet quite straight, the petticoat must be decreased for the waist, and an opening for placket hole made, the latter is simple, instead of joining the rounds turn back without joining, and decrease where necessary by taking two together. Crochet along the two edges of placket hole and put the petticoat into a band or run in a string. Finish off petticoat with fancy rows.

GWISG SIR BENFRO
(o ddarlun gan Lady Llanover, tua 1830)

GWISG SIR ABERTEIFI
(o ddarlun gan Lady Llanover, tua 1830)

GWISGOEDD CYMREIG
(Trwy garedigrwydd y LLYFRGELL GENEDLAETHOL)

GWISG ARALL O SIR BENFRO
(o ddarlun gan Lady Llanover, tua 1830)

A TORPEDOED PEDIGREE

Letter from Francis Jones to College of Arms 1973

Please convey my compliments to Garter.

The pedigree you sent me is a familiar one. In the early 1930s I was plagued by the descendants of Griffith J . . . of A . . . , by the late . . . , and others who wished to prove descent from the aristocratic family of L . . . e of St. B . . . , P . . . n, Fenton, etc. And now they return to haunt me again.

I can tell you categorically that the descent as given in the enclosed pedigree is bogus. I have made a particular study of the L . . . s and their family papers have passed through my hands, and I can assure you that the descent as asserted cannot be sustained.

The whole crux of your client's pedigree revolves around Thomas L . . . e of Fishguard (1729-1808). If he is descended in the manner it is claimed, then he is an important gatekeeper ancestor. Although I have researched intensively nothing whatsoever has been found concerning his paternity. He appears out of nowhere as an innkeeper in the town of Fishguard and a pretty unsatisfactory one at that, if we are to believe the severe strictures made by a late eighteenth century tourist concerning the squalid state of the pub over which Thomas presided. Nothing whatsoever is known of his parentage, and even the maiden name of his wife is in doubt.

The history of the landowning L . . . es is well known, as is the history of the devolution of the estate. However, there were, and are plebeian families surnamed L . . . e in this county having no connection with the landed families, and I have no doubt that the inn-keeper of Fishguard must be numbered among them.

A Pembrokeshire Peregrine of impeccable pedigree

CHAPTER V

IN THE COUNTRYSIDE

THE BOX TREE

I WAS about five years of age when I first became acquainted with Prifin Enoch, or perhaps it would be more correct to say conscious of his unseen might and potential capacity for meting-out swift punishment to erring humanity. For I never saw him in the flesh despite long vigils waiting for him to emerge from his lair in the box-tree growing in the garden of my mother's old home, a farm in northern Pembrokeshire.

The garden lay behind the house. One side was bounded by the dwelling-house and the dairy, the other three sides by high tree-topped hedges, necessary bulwarks against savage gales that swept inland from the channel beyond the headland of St. Davids. During summer the garden was a veritable suntrap and from its rich warm soil sprang a variety of vegetables, fruits, herbs and flowers, all contributing to the attractions of the dining table of the farmhouse. Although small, measuring roughly 80 paces by 40, it was so admirably planned and cultivated that its output exceeded that of many a garden twice its size. Every inch supported some form of growth.

Flowers grew in profusion, a colourful pageant for human eyes and a feast without end for the bees that poured from the conical hives beneath the shelter of the walls. Along the borders and in carefully tended parterres grew lavender, violets, daffodils and primroses, while roses twined around a few rickety arches raised by the hands of some unskilled enthusiast. Herbs grew in orderly abundance – mint, marjoram, parsley, thyme and sage – used to flavour the steaming cawl, speciality of the Welsh farmhouse, and wormwood which provided bitter tea to cure many a childish ailment.

In the hedge grew agrimony "good for them that have naughty livers" as I once read in an Elizabethan manuscript; vervain said to have been used by the Druids to combat plague; camomile whose flowers could be made into a poultice to rout toothache; elecampane that cured kidney troubles in man and coughs in horses and the joyous little celandine whose sole purpose seemed to be to bring pleasure into our remote rural world. An impetus to herb cultivation in the district had been provided by a well-loved vicar, a devotee of Culpepper, who shortly after his arrival in 1907 electrified the parishioners by his addiction to sandwiches made from dandelion leaves and an appetite for plants and grasses traditionally reserved for animals. Apple trees, gooseberry, raspberry and currant bushes produced generous harvests. Beds of leeks and cabbages provided more homely fare and there were a few rows of early potatoes in the western end of the garden. Neat paths, their surface hardened by reddish ashes from generations of culm fires, ran between the plots.

An embowered cloister, a Garden of Eden, you might say. Not quite. For in this haven of flower and fruit and fragrance crouched a hidden terror whose malevolence was directed particularly at small boys of just my age.

Most of the fruit grew in the eastern end, its main feature a glorious strawberry bed. At the edge of this attractive territory grew the box-tree, some ten feet or more in height, whose dark, glossy, evergreen leaves retained their glistening brightness throughout the year, summer and winter. The box is uncommon in these parts. It is the heaviest of European timber and if placed in water will sink like a stone. An early writer speaks of the tree as one of "great beautie" whose wood was "fitt for dagger haftes". I could never learn who had planted it, but it was very old when I was a boy.

Predatory instincts awaken quickly in the young, especially at the prospect of a succulent dish. As a toddler I used to walk around the garden, somewhat timid and well-behaved, clasping my mother's hand. As I grew I became more unruly and adventurous, and when about five I suddenly awakened to the charms of the strawberry-bed; however, I lacked the hypocrisy that, alas, maturity and sophistication bring in their wake and my intentions, if not stated in as many words, were certainly telegraphed by my behaviour. The family became uneasily aware of the presence of a rogue elephant, albeit a diminutive one, which, could he get into that garden unperceived, would soon wreak devastation among the good things earmarked for the table. I had been observed gazing wistfully over the wicker gate leading to the garden and caught trying to clamber over one of the high hedges. However, I was soon stopped dead in my predatory tracks, not by sermon or spanking, but by a far more effective deterrent.

I learnt that the garden contained a monster, by the side of which the awful guardian of the Hesprides was no more than a frolicsome pup. The name of this fearsome being, so they told me, was Prifin Enoch.

He seemed to have been capable of changing his form, at least so I concluded after hearing detailed descriptions from various members of the family. To one, he appeared as a small, tawny, bristly, four-legged creature, possessing a singularly long lasso-like tongue with which he dragged his prey within range of powerful jaws. Another said he had three eyes and six legs – one informant gave him ten legs and fifty claws, claiming that he could kick and leap like a kangaroo. My dear empirical grandmother agreed with all versions. An old serving man, whose grey hair and solemn visage vouched for his veracity to my way of thinking, went so far as to tell me he had actually seen a severed hand lying near the box-tree, sole remains of some juvenile gadabout who had tried to raid the strawberry-bed.

Prifin Enoch's abode was the heart of the box-tree, his life a dedication to the protection of fruit. All agreed he was completely harmless so long as one did not take the fruit, especially the strawberries, without my grandmother's permission. One could walk and play along the paths, around the bushes, indeed around the box-tree itself, without incurring the custodian's wrath.

Later, it dawned on me that this strange creature seemed to be totally unknown outside the family. I mentioned Prifin Enoch to my fellows at Sunday School and to grown-ups on neighbouring farms, but they had never heard of him, while a few were frankly sceptical of his existence. But I knew the doubting Thomases were quite wrong, quite ill-informed. To me he was as real as the box-tree in which he lurked, as real as the luscious fruit his ceaseless vigilance protected.

I spent long hours among the ferns on top of the hedge. I crouched behind the privet near the wicket gate. I gazed from a window overlooking the garden, hoping I might espy the fell sentinel emerge from his leafy den, but he never moved, my vigils were in vain. I usually entered the garden as bold as a grenadier, but as I approached the box-tree my courage wavered and waned. I peered cautiously into its dark heart, and on one occasion fled headlong believing I had glimpsed a pair of baleful eyes glaring at me from among the leaves. It was only in summer and harvest-time that his name was invoked. In the winter and unproductive seasons he apparently hibernated for there was no fruit to guard.

As I grew older, faint doubts arose in my mind, not of the animal's existence, but of his efficiency. On one occasion, when the bushes heavily laden, I momentarily forgot all about the sinister sentinel and plucked at the forbidden fruit. Realisation of the mortal peril in which I stood came immediately, and I tore frantically from the scene of my temerity until I reached the safety of the farmyard, for I had been told he would never leave the confines of the garden. I was amazed to realise I was alive at all. Perhaps he had been asleep? Or had moved away? When I related the affair to my kinsfolk, they congratulated me on my providential escape and assured me he was certainly still in residence and would hardly be so tolerant in future. I never tested his efficiency again.

Following my tenth birthday, my parents moved to a town many miles away and thereafter our visits to the farm became more desultory. I formed new friendships, new interests, and the memory of the guardian of the garden became a topic of laughter rather than consternation. I do not remember exactly when I ceased to believe in Prifin Enoch's existence, probably about the same time as my belief in Father Christmas evaporated, but while I gave up the latter with reluctance, I gave up the former with relief.

I reached manhood and left the shire of my birth. Now and then I recalled the garden, the fruit, the box-tree, smiled to myself and related the tale of the unseen abomination to my wife and children, which caused much hilarity.

After returning from the War, having encountered among Tunisian djebels and Italian valleys enemies far more malevolent than Prifin Enoch, I made a pilgrimage to those memory-hallowed acres so long held by my ancestors, pathways I had trod as a child, hedgerows where I had found nests of wren and robin and finch, streams where sticklebacks had succumbed to my youthful cunning, meadows where I had gambolled among the hay-makers, and of course to the old farmhouse, home of my early jollities, now owned by my cousin.

The house itself remained much the same. After some hours around the hospitable hearth, I took a stroll by myself to try to recall the early raptures and enchantments. Much was changed. The cowshed with its wooden stalls and posts had been "converted" to meet the requirements of an authoritative government board, concrete covered the pebbled causeway in the yard, taps had exiled the pump, the coachhouse sheltered a tractor, the chaff-cutter had disappeared and so had the antiquated scales on which I had seen so much wool, grain, potatoes and other produce weighed in the distant days of "mixed" farming. The stable stood silent, the horses I had known and the descendants of those horses, far far away as fairyland.

I entered the garden. I will not dwell on the scene. My paradise was lost. The strawberry bed had vanished; so had the box-tree. I returned to the wicket gate and standing there, watching me, was the ten-year-old son of my cousin, a bright lad, wise in the ways of television and smart up-to-date school learning. Smilingly, I asked him, "Have you seen Prifin Enoch?" He stared, then asked "Is he a footballer or a film-star?"

I then knew that Prifin Enoch was dead – very dead.

※   ※   ※

F.J. adopted many pen names as his work was published so often in West Wales newspapers; De Loy, Llandeloy, Brawdy, Someone Else, Audax, Essex Harries and Dewisland.

He spent much time deciphering dusty parchments and faded records. However, he always found time to sit and admire the beauty of nature. He often wrote poetry to mark the memory of those moments. Here is an example.

Dŵr yr Hendre
In a cloudless course where stars shone bright,
The moon rode gaily in her deep-dark sky,
The shades of bushes were sentries last night
When by Hendre's flow I wandered by.

Far, far from the warring cries of life
I sat, and harkened to the river's word
And found content; so let me linger yet awhile
By Hendre's flow where fairies' chants are heard.

Francis Jones, November 22 1930

Disaffection and Dissent in Pembrokeshire

HISTORICAL research has proved that political disaffection and religious dissent were closely allied in bygone days. The former led to the Civil War and the formation of the two great political parties of Whig and Tory, while the latter culminated in the Nonconformist upsurge of the seventeenth and eighteenth centuries. The history of both movements has been carefully written, but they are not always so clear-cut as we imagine them to have been. Motives were obscure or mixed, and there was much crossing of the floor. Thus the Civil War in Pembrokeshire is an example of intricate political apostasy and, apart from a few steadfast families, most of the leaders turned their coats, some twice, and some even thrice. These twisted threads have been deftly disentangled in a recent work by Mr. Arthur L. Leach, while the story of dissent has been fully given in the vast number of books that have been, and continue to be, published on that subject. This renders unnecessary a detailed discussion of the origins and development of both movements in these pages. It has been my main concern to give further examples, hitherto unpublished, which illustrate and support the previous findings on these subjects. Unless otherwise stated, all these examples are drawn from the Papers of Great Sessions for Pembrokeshire, deposited in the Public Record Office (now in N.L.W.). These documents, largely untouched by West Wales historians, contain a wealth of information on a variety of subjects, and throw considerable light on the daily lives of our forebears. I would like, at the outset, to acknowledge my indebtedness to the officials of that important institution in Chancery Lane, whose ready kindness at all times made my researches there a real pleasure.

Among these papers occur quite a number of cases of "utterances tending to treason". Measured by present-day standards, they often amount to little more than a candid criticism of the government of the day, but it will be seen that some were closely linked with religion which made their enormity loom all the more in the eyes of the prevailing powers. Unfortunately, the verdicts are not recorded in the majority of lawsuits, but independent evidence shews that the defendants certainly escaped with their lives. Fines and imprisonment were the general consequences, and several of the accused survived to take a prominent part in the public life of the county. In some instances only indictments are preserved, which were returned as true bills or were thrown out by the Grand Juries, but in several cases depositions of witnesses are attached. In this essay all the examples relate to Pembrokeshire.

The earliest of these cases concerns one Thomas David Morris, a yeoman of St. Edrins in the Hundred of Dewsland who lived when James I was King. The first Stuart monarch was far from popular, and his attitude towards sports, smoking and native pastimes, was not calculated to endear him to his subjects south of the border. In 1612, Prince Henry, the Heir Apparent, and in many ways a remarkable youth, died, just short of his eighteenth year. An interesting account of the Prince's death is given on folio 10 of Harl. MS. 1977 in the British Museum. The news of his death soon reached distant Pembrokeshire, and on 10 December 1612, Thomas David Morris left his plough and strolled into an alehouse in his native parish, kept by one David Lewis. The yeoman entertained somewhat strong views about the reigning monarch, and it was not long before he was discussing the Prince's death with the innkeeper and Annis John ap Ieuan. As a result of his remarks the yeoman found himself indicted at the Great Sessions at Haverfordwest in Spring 1613. The document has an additional interest as the disloyal words are reproduced in the Welsh language.[1] The indictment states that "Thomas David Morris, not having the fear of God before his eyes, but at the instigation of the devil, spoke the following malicious, seditious, and traitorous words "Y newydd kynta ar glowon ni a fo y wenwyno ynte hefyd. ni cheyson ni ddim byd da gwedy y ddowad ef yn frenin, a mellteth ddyw yr awr y dayth ef yn frenin"; i.e., "I wishe the next newes wee heare may be that he (meaning our Lord the King) may be poysoned also. Wee have had no good worlds since he came to be Kinge, and gods curse be upon the houre that he came to be kinge". From these words it would appear that there was a rumour that Prince Henry had died of poisoning. What happened to the outspoken yeoman of St. Edrins is not disclosed.

There can be little doubt that the government as well as the King, was unpopular. The laws against Roman Catholics, whose position had not been improved by the Gunpowder Plot (1605), were strictly enforced. In the Autumn Sessions of 1613 the following recusants were cited as excommunicated and denounced. Alice, the wife of Thomas Bowen[2] of Trefloyne, Esq., Bridgett the wife of Thomas Tullye[3] [*recte* Tooley] gent., and Gwenllian Lewis, and Janet, her maidservants. In the Spring Sessions of 1620, Mary Tooley (she married Charles Bowen of Trefloyne) and Katherine Tooley of Slebech parish (Arnolds Hill), papists, were presented as recusants. John Gwyther of Manorbier, gent., was presented for harbouring "a seminarye preeste" in his house in 1625, while a large number of other Pembrokeshire folk were in trouble for failing to attend the parish church. The laws against the Catholics did not affect the Protestants, but King James's attitude towards smoking certainly affected people of every religious belief, and in particular, William Downe of St. Davids, who found himself in trouble in 1620, "for using and taking of tobacco in his house" – contraband perhaps.

The Word of the Lord

The King's unpopularity is again reflected in 1625 when John Loughor and Gwyn Hawkins of Tenby were committed to gaol for "speakinge of disloyall words against his majestie and his crowne".

The next rumble of disaffection in Pembrokeshire was again connected with religion, but this time it was the Quakers and Dissenters that troubled established authority. In Autumn 1642, Richard Walter and another Haverfordwest magistrate, committed a number of people taken "at an unlawful meeting, pretence of Religious worship and evil principles in great disobedience to His Majesties government". All these people were from Haverfordwest and its district, and were committed until sureties could be found for their attendance at the next Sessions. This is one of the earliest known lists of Pembrokeshire Dissenters, some of whom later became leading Quakers and nonconformists. Their names deserve being placed on record as the earliest fighters for religious toleration in West Wales. They were as follows: Edward Lord and Mary his wife; Henry Relly and Elizabeth, his wife; Elinor, wife of Jacob Woolford;[4] Hester wife of Richard Stafford; John Burdge; Thomas Jenkins; Francis Lloyd; Peregrine Musgrave;[5] Evan Bowen;[6] Humphrey Williams;[7] John Howell; William Davids; Jenkin Evan; Phillip Price; Henry Evan; William Harry; Francis Symmins;[8] Edmund Williams; Young Morgan; Samuel Hill; Ellinor Dawkins; Dorothy Grinfield; Gwenllian Evan; Magdalen Barnes; Margaret Relly; and Jane Gwyn. Some of these were rich burgesses of Haverfordwest and connected with county families. The most prominent were the Musgraves and the Symmins who came in for constant attention by the authorities in the years following. Peregrine Musgrave married in 1674 Alice, daughter of Lewis David, a landowner of Llanddewi Felffre, an active and astute Quaker. Lewis David and other Welsh Quakers bought considerable property in Pennsylvania, which they sold to emigrants from Pembrokeshire and Cardiganshire in 1682. It will be shown later how this emigration precipitated an economic crisis in Pembrokeshire.

On 22 August 1642, King Charles I raised his banner at Nottingham, and before long we find political prosecutions appearing in West Wales. Thus in 1647 John Eddowe, 'shearman' of Haverfordwest was indicted for slandering His Majesty and "speaking unfitting speeches of him". The changing fortunes of the warring parties in Pembrokeshire led to considerable disorder, and there was the inevitable tale of paying-off old scores. Griffith Twyning[9] of Llanycefn, gent., had a sorry tale to tell in 1648. He stated that in July 1643, Thomas ap Owen and Owen ap Owen sold to him the two farms of Nantygof and Cilfach Gwenith for £130. During the "unhappie tymes of distractions", Griffith Twyning declared for Parliament and the Word, and served as a soldier under command of Major Hugh Philipps[10] in the army of Major General Rowland Laugharne,[11] while Owen ap Owen served the King in the regiment of Colonel Thomas Butler.[12] Owen ap Owen and others, taking advantage of the temporary Royalist ascendancy in Pembrokeshire, forcibly entered Twyning's house which they plundered, took away the title deeds of the said two farms, reoccupied them, and now refused to acknowledge Twyning's right. They also plundered his lands and gardens which were sown with corn, turnips, pasturnips, carrots and cabbages. (Chanc. Proc. Ser II, C. 3. 464/83.) References to these root crops at this early date is interesting, but the turnips (later to revolutionise husbandry) were probably confined to Mr. Twyning's gardens.

However, by 1649 the Parliamentary party was paramount, and it was the turn of the Royalists to appear in the dock. The appearance of one Captain Richard Burton in Pembrokeshire in 1653 caused some suspicion, and the following charges were made against him: (1) That he had been an active officer in the King's army, and had been wounded either at Pontefract, Colchester, or Worcester. (2) That he had come to

Pembrokeshire as a spy, "to act some design for the enemys of the Commonwealth". He was described as a former captain under the command of General Gerrard. The depositions were taken at Newport before Thomas Jones of Brithdir and Wenallt, J.P., on 18 August 1653. Burton said that about 1647 he was serving as an officer in the Spanish army at Catalonia against the French King, where he was wounded, and as a result he was now infirm and lame. He denied being wounded during the Civil War, and was not present at the three places mentioned, being then at his house in Worcestershire. About May 1653 he met Walter Lloyd[13], gent., of Cardiganshire, in London, and lent over £20 to him. Lloyd arranged that the money should be repaid by Elizabeth Lloyd of Trefach in north Pembrokeshire. He came to the county in July 1653 to collect the money, and stayed at the house of Mr. Alban Owen,[14] who was the father of the said Elizabeth. He denied being a spy. This story was supported by David Owen[15] of Henllys, gent., who gave his evidence before Mr. Jones on the same day. The jury found there was no case to answer, and Captain Burton limped back to Henllys, where, no doubt, he described his experiences in Catalonia to the Lord of Cemais, and received, we trust, the money he had so kindly loaned to Walter Lloyd.

The next instance on record involved a burgess of Haverfordwest, who had a very poor opinion of the Vicar of St. Mary's, and also, apparently, of the Commonwealth. On 3 June 1653, David Watts of Haverfordwest, chapman, was examined before William Bowen and Thomas Davies, Justices of the Peace. It was stated that about three or four weeks previously, Watts was having a chat with his brother-in-law, John Thomas, mercer, and said that he did not come to church to listen to the Reverend Stephen Love, as he did "not edifie" anything that parson said. He was further charged with telling John Thomas "that he would have another world shortly", and that Mr. Arthur Owen,[16] Major General Laugharne, Colonel Powell,[17] Major Hugh Laugharne,[18] and Captain William Powell[19] "did meete att a private Alehouse comonly once a weeke, and that they had received Letters from France, and that upon the first disturbance they would raise the Country for the King". In addition he was also charged with abusing John Thomas's wife in language which I omit from this essay in order to conform with the proprieties of the twentieth century. Watts denied all this, saying that the charges were invented and brought against him by the malice of John Thomas. Evan Thomas, a Haverfordwest baker, supported David Watts. His objection to Mr. Love was that he had an impediment of speech which prevented him speaking with the clarity that Watts expected to find in a parish priest. No doubt this prosecution had its origin in a family quarrel.

Stephen Love was Vicar of St. Mary's in 1651-62 and Rector of St. Thomas, Haverfordwest, from which he had been ejected by the Mayor and Corporation. However, early in 1656, the Corporation was ordered to restore him and pay the arrears of his stipend, which they did with an ill grace. But the business had ceased to exercise the minds of the Mayor and Burgesses by July 1656, for Mr. Love then died.

In 1654 one of the country gentlemen at a Tenby alehouse chose to spread despondency by making some curious statements and an alarming prophesy. The central figure was John Jones[20] of Llawhaden, gent., a kinsman of the great families of Philipps and Skyrme.

He was drinking on 16 June 1654 in the company of Rees Edwards, yeoman, John Lewis, gent., both of Tenby, at the alehouse of Roger Peters. Mr. Jones, being drunk, said that he had heard from Thomas Feild of Llawhaden that Mr. James Philipps[21] of Tregibby had been killed by apprentices at their rising in London, for which he was sorry, as he was his kinsman; he hoped that Charles Stuart, King of England and Scotland, would be in England before Christmas Day; that he had seen a letter from the King to Colonel Massee, and that the Earl of Carbery[22] had the letter now; and, turning to John Lewis, who was a soldier of the Tenby garrison, said the King would "shortlie scoure your coate before it be longe", and, "after nodding at the Table, says, that the Lord Protector was a Rogue". John Jones denied most of this, but admitted saying that Thomas Feild had told him of the rising of the apprentices and of James Philipps' death. Feild, however, denied ever telling him such a thing. A true bill was returned against John Jones, but his punishment could not have been heavy as his name appears later as a respectable juror at the Sessions where he had previously been a defendant.

Disaffection was not confined to the gentry, for at the same Sessions a poor labourer from Trefgarn Owen in Brawdy, was indicted for his attachment to the Royal cause. Examination was made at Penybenglog on 24 June 1654, before a strong Parliamentarian magistrate, George William Griffith,[23] who wrote the depositions down in his own neat hand. It was on account of "certain speeches, languages and words, spoken, uttered and delivered by Rees ap Jenkin of Trefgarn Owen, labourer, touching Treason and the death of His Highness the Lord Protector of England, Scotland, Ireland &c. In the previous month Rees had said many uncivil and scandalous things to William Dean of Trefgarn, to wit "Thou art a Roundhead Rogue. I doe hope to see thy throate cutt or it be Longe"; and also that the Lord Protector had gone to Scotland and he hoped that his throat would be cut also, so that he should not return. Rees denied using these words, but a true bill was brought in at the Sessions, and he was committed for trial. At the same Sessions, William Price, alehouse-keeper, of Slebech was indicted for calling Roundheads "all Rogues and Tinkers" on 12 July 1654.

In the Autumn Sessions of 1655, Thomas Grey of Pwllcrochan, gent., found himself in trouble for making rather incautious remarks.

In December 1654 Grey had declared himself an enemy to the Protector and the Commonwealth, and had said to Thomas Powell[24] of Greenhill "There is as stately a Court kept at Whitehall as ever, and what is it to take off the Head of one King and set up another. And as well have sett him upp so wee could set him downe". But

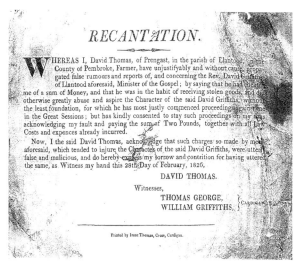

"I take it all back . . ."

Thomas Grey was a gentleman-servant to the influential Colonel le Hunte,[25] and the jurors threw out the bill, and Mr. Grey was allowed to go in peace.

The house of Thomas Elliott in Narberth was the scene of treasonable talk in December 1657. At the Spring Sessions of 1658, Thomas Walker of Crunwere, yeoman, and Thomas Davids of Lanteague, gent., commonly called Captain Davids, were indicted for vilifying and debasing the honour and authority of the Lord Protector. From the bill of indictment, and the evidence of witnesses taken before Sampson Lort and Richard Castle, Justices of the Peace, it appeared that on 2 December 1657, Walker challenged a certain Joseph Sheene to a duel, which was refused. Walker then said that he had served better men than the Lord Protector, namely, Prince Rupert, Prince Maurice and Charles Stuart, and would serve them as long as he lived, and, given the opportunity, he would cut the Lord Protector's throat. Captain Davids said that he would support his friend. Later Walker said he wished he had with him a thousand of Prince Rupert's men so that he could make them "shine Charcole", and also wished that he had a thousand men to fight for the King of Spain.

Both denied using such words or offering a challenge, and Walker added that he had served the Lord Protector since the time of "Ustere fight". They were committed to gaol without alternative of bail, and at the Sessions a true bill was returned against them.

In 1659 a descendant of Sir Rice ap Thomas found himself at variance with the government, when Perrot ap Rice[26] of Scotsborough and Rickeston was charged with speaking and publishing words tending to treason. His prosecutor was William Walter, gent., one of whose relations was later to become a very close friend of Charles II. John ap Rice of Scotsborough and John Sherburne of Tenby became sureties for Perrot, but unfortunately there is no further information on the matter.

In 1660 the boot was on the other foot for the King had come into his own again, and it was now the turn of the Royalists to wield the whip. Nor were they slow about the business. On 23 April 1660, John Evans of Roch, husbandman, made a remark which brought him before the Justices of the Great Sessions. On that day he was at Sodbury, talking to Elizabeth the wife of John Wilkin of Walwyns Castle, who mentioned to him that she had just been to Walwyns Castle church. This evidently infuriated John Evans, who blurted out "If I had been there I would have prayed that the Divell should goe with him (that is, our Lord the King)". David Brown of Walton also deposed that he had heard this remark. A true bill was the result, and Anthony Stokes and Nicholas Thomas went bail for the forthright husbandman.

One of the strongest Roundhead families in the county was that of Lort of Stackpool Court and Eastmoor. The most prominent was Sampson Lort,[27] who had held several offices under Parliament which he had served with much vigour in West Wales. He had been High Sheriff in 1649, and was Member of Parliament for Pembroke Borough in 1658-59 when Richard Cromwell was Lord Protector. In 1660 he decided to change his seat, and cast his eye on the town and of Haverfordwest, whose castle he had helped to destroy in 1648. The Mayor and burgesses were immediately in arms, and said that should Sampson Lort offer himself as a candidate, he should not be heard, as he had mulcted the town upwards of £200, and that he had issued, after the unhappy business in Worcester, a warrant to seize the person of King Charles, and had joined with Hugh Peters ("that firebrand of the nation") to "root out the orthodox clergy and to supply them with lay ignoramuses and scismatickes".[29] Haverfordwest then proceeded to elect William Philipps who was related to the Picton Castle family.

Rice Meyler, a corvisor of Haverfordwest, possessed strong views on Church and State. He was indicted in the Spring Sessions of 1661 for abusing the Court of Great Sessions and saying to William Browne of Haverfordwest "The Court is A base court and they doe give oaths to Churchwardens that they can not, nor are able to performe. Let ye Court be What itt will bee, itt can nott be baser then whatt Imployment you had under Olliver, as an Informer, for when you Informed against A poore minister he was presently putt out of his livinge, not knowing his Accuser, and tubb preachers putt in their Roomes. There was better Order and Government then in Olliver's tyme then there is now, for they sett up a Company of Drunken priests". These remarks horrified the jurors and they returned a true bill against Meyler for using words tending to treason.

The oath of Allegiance and Supremacy was not palatable to many. In 1661, William Sparkes[30] of Prendergast, corvisor, became surety for Thomas Jenkins and Owen Thomas, two saddlers of Haverfordwest who refused to take the oath.

Lawrence Edward, David Symmins, Thomas Symmins and Hugh Symmins, of Puncheston, gentlemen, the Woolfords, James Picton, gent., and many others also refused and were presented in the same year. Most of these persons were Quakers who met regularly at the house of William Bateman,[31] mercer, at Haverfordwest. Richard Davies, the Welshpool Quaker, stayed at William Bateman's house when he visited Haverfordwest in 1663-64, where he had "several brave meetings".

Under Charles II several acts were passed against those who were not members of the Established Church. The Corporation Act (1662) forbad Dissenters from holding office in corporate towns, by enacting that no person should be elected to any office in a Corporation unless he received Holy Communion in the Church of England. The term Nonconformist includes all who absent themselves from the Established Church, and in this sense is synonymous with the term Dissenter. In the stricter sense it is applied to all those ministers who were deprived of their livings on their refusal to submit to the Act of Uniformity of 1662. Their burdens were increased by the Conventicle Act of 1664, by which they were prohibited from meeting in any number greater than five. This was followed in 1665 by the Five Mile Act, and in 1673 by the Test Act, which acts were intended to deprive them of any political and religious influence. The Test Act required all officers, civil and military, to take the oaths and make their declarations against transubstantiation within six months after their appointment.

In the Spring Sessions of 1663, Thomas Tydd and John Fisher, mariners, both of Pwllcrochan parish, were presented for saying on 2 January 1662-3 "This government is worse than the Government of the Protector", and a loyal jury returned a true bill in the case. In the following Autumn Sessions we find that Philip Thomas of St. Davids had placed himself on the wrong side of the law by remarking "By God, the King shalbe broken once again", in the hearing of those fervent Royalists, Lewis Lloyd of Treferfin and William Parry. In 1663 there are numerous references to the man who became a pioneer of Pembrokeshire dissent, namely, the Reverend Peregrine Phillips[32] of Dredgeman Hill. Peregrine Phillips, together with John Luntley of Haverfordwest, feltmaker, Griffith Howell, John Hawkins, Samuel Roberts and William Jones, all yeomen of Narberth parish, refused to attend church, and on 4 June 1663, held unlawful assemblies, conventicles and meetings under colour and pretence of exercising religion at Narberth. The Quakers also came in for attention, and a large number of them were indicted for meeting at the house of William Bateman and Sarah his wife, at Haverfordwest. Elinor, the wife of Jacob Woolford, was one of the most enthusiastic members at these meetings. Nevertheless the Quakers gained adherents and continued to flourish under the persecution.

The main wrath of the Royalists was turned against Colonel Thomas Wogan, the Regicide. He was the third son of John Wogan of Wiston by Jane Colclough his wife. An active Roundhead, he was Member for Cardigan Borough in the Long Parliament in 1646. In 1647-68 he served in Pembrokeshire under Colonel Horton, and sat in the Rump Parliament of 1659. The high spot of his career was the year 1649, when he sat as one of King Charles's Judges, and affixed his signature to the death warrant. He was summoned to trial at the Restoration, being excepted from the Act of Oblivion, on 6 June 1660. He gave himself up on 27 June following, and on 13 August 1662 a warrant was issued for the sequestration of his property. He was a prisoner in the Tower of London in 1664, but on 27 July of that year he managed to escape with George Romford of Durham, Robert Davers alias Danvers, and John Mason. The circumstances of his escape are unknown, but it certainly had repercussions in his native county. To be a Wogan meant a great deal in Pembrokeshire in those days, as it was the most powerful and influential family in the country, and allied by marriage to practically all the leading families in West Wales. It is not unreasonable to assume that Pembrokeshire people had a hand in assisting him in some manner to effect his escape. At any rate, in the Great Sessions files for 1664 and 1665 are recorded the recognisances of a number of people, who were bound over to appear to give evidence touching "the escape of Collonell Thomas Woogan one of the Judges of our late sacred Majestie King Charles the first". They were as follows: Henry Howell of Templeton, Robert Holland[33] of Monkton, Owen Philipps[34] of Slebech, Rice Barrowe of Tenby, Richard Thomas of Fletherhill, John Elliott[35] of Narberth, John Protheroe of Tenby, Thomas Davids of Haverfordwest, Lewis Beynon of Kilgetty, Thomas Jones[36] of Brithdir, John Bell[37] of Arnolds Hill, Richard Lewis of St. Issels and Joana, his wife.

Unfortunately no further record of the proceedings is to be found and we do not know in what particular way these people were involved in Colonel Wogan's escape. He succeeded in reaching Holland, and a letter written on 25 September 1666 refers to "Wogan" having gone to Utrecht. According to the late Mr. Francis Green (West Wales Historical Transactions, Vol. VI), this is the last authentic mention of the Colonel. However, the Papers of Great Sessions contain one further note which shews that he was alive in 1669. In that year, one Sybil Protherough,[38] was committed to gaol by Sir Erasmus Philipps, Bart., of Picton Castle, and Richard Walter, Esq., for applying to several persons for contributions for a relief towards "Thomas Woogan one of his late Majesties murderers".

What eventually happened to Wogan is not known, but he probably died on the Continent. There was a tradition in Pembrokeshire, that some time after the Restoration, an unknown man came to the Walwyns Castle district, who, always melancholy and dejected, shunned all society. He lived in the church porch where he was relieved by the local people who said that he had the appearance of a gentleman. When asked his name, he said it was Drinkwater. He was ultimately found dead in the porch, and it was suggested that he was none other than Colonel Thomas Wogan himself. It is impossible to accept this story. Wogan was well-known in the county and would soon have been recognised had he been foolish enough to have adopted the church porch, then the most public place in the parish, as his refuge. His history shows that he was far too astute a man to risk his life in this ridiculous way, and there can be no doubt that once he was out of England, he remained out.

Perhaps one of the "star" performers on the side of Dissent and Parliament was Henry Hake, who appears to have given as much trouble to his own friends and co-religionists as to the civil authorities and the Established Church. He was a humble corvisor in Goat Street, Haverfordwest, and at one time followed his trade as a good burgess and did not concern himself with religious tenets or affairs of state. However, in 1641, he declared for Cromwell and Dissent, and from that time on, this stormy petrel's name appears in the Great Sessions Papers with a monotonous regularity. In 1641 he was in gaol for making seditious remarks. In 1655 his conscience was troubled, and he was brought before the Justices for saying "That God would not nor could not forgive a sinner". On that occasion the Reverend Peregrine Phillips, and others, came to his support and handed a written statement to the court, testifying to Henry's good character, and saying that he was "an ignorant man, but enthusiastic". The loyal burgesses however kept a close eye on him, and in 1656 presented him for keeping "a Dunge Miskin" outside his house in Goat Street. Two years later he was presented for being "a common gamester" and for playing a game called "tennis" on several occasions. Despite his sporting activities he remained a Nonconformist and stoutly refused to attend his parish church. One can well imagine his reactions to the Restoration, but although he was constantly in trouble over other matters, it was not until 1665 that the authorities clapped him in gaol for speaking dangerous words tending to treason. He also possessed strong views on such matters as tolls, and in 1682 the turbulent corvisor was charged for obstructing the collection of the "toll-corn" of the town and county of Haverfordwest. This is but a tithe of his peccadilloes, and I feel that his punishments could not have been heavy, and perhaps the Justices were lenient to one whose enthusiasm was so considerably in excess of his learning, and, most certainly of his self-control.

Several members of the Established Church were in trouble. At the Spring Sessions of 1668, the Reverend Anthony Jones, M.A.,[39] clerk, was committed by Richard Walter, Esq., Mayor of Haverfordwest, for speaking "wordes of High Treason justifying that our Sovereign Lord Kinge Charles the second is nott supream head of the Church of England". The Dissenters were also carefully watched. In 1669, the Reverend Peregrine Phillips, Moses Longman of Langum, gent., John Luntley of Haverfordwest, hatter, Marcus

Boulton[40] of Steynton parish, gent; Henry Seare of Llanstadwell, yeoman; Anthony Stokes[41], of Roch, gent.; Hugh Harries[42] of Brawdy, yeoman and Jenkin Ferrior[43] of Pembroke, yeoman; were indicted for meeting under colour of religion, etc., at Dredgeman Hill on 11 July 1669. In 1671 the Reverend Phineas Whitefote, clerk, of Haverfordwest, was bound over to appear for speaking blasphemous words and several other misdemeanours.

In 1676 Whitefote was again in trouble, for having assembled riotously with the Reverend David Rees, clerk, David Adams and Thomas Higgin, gentleman, all of Haverfordwest, and assaulting one Owen Lysence in St. Thomas ward. Dissent flourished, and the Quakers and Nonconformists were becoming stronger despite all repressive measures. The Roman Catholics, on the other hand, had lost all hopes of recapturing West Wales for the ancient faith, but continued to appear in the county where they were constantly harried by the Protestant powers. In 1679, James Higgon of Amroth, Thomas Eustance, John Dowdale, Laughlin Keogh and Thomas Conray, were committed for refusing to take the oath of allegiance and supremacy, confessing themselves to be "Popish Priests – and Fryers and of the popish Religion". By 1681 Nonconformity had become a real force in Pembrokeshire and had numbers of the county-families in its ranks. In that year a very large number of Dissenters were presented at the Sessions for refusing to attend the services of the Established Church, and among them were William Barlow of Martletwy, gent.; Richard Castle[44] of Narberth, gent.; Griffith Howell of Narberth, yeoman; John Poyer[45] of Robeston, yeoman; Hugh Harries, gent., Margaret Harries, and Catherine Harries, widow, all of Eweston, Abel Phillips,[46] of Brawdy, yeoman; Abraham Hendy of Lamphey, yeoman; Peregrine Phillips,[47] yeoman; Hugh Symmins of Puncheston, the Quaker; Moses Longman of Langum, yeoman; Henry Miles[48] of Eglwyswrw, yeoman, and many others. The government associated the Dissenters with Roundhead politics and undoubtedly this view was justified, which is clearly shewn by some of the lawsuits. In the Spring Sessions of 1685, a true bill was returned against Howell Phillip, a prominent Nonconformist yeoman from Brawdy, for saying the following words tending to treason "That they that killed the old King (meaning Charles I) did the people of the Presbyterian faith a good service". These words were uttered before three loyal parishioners, Llewellin David, George Synnet and Bartholomew Wade, who gave evidence against him. His sureties were Abel Phillips, gent., and Griffith David of Camrose. John Freeman of Bosheston, husbandman was equally outspoken. His wrath was directed against the reigning King and he was indicted at the Autumn Sessions of 1685, for saying to Henry Poyer "For whome doest thou carry armes? I would not pay thee nor noe one else a farthing for carrying armes for such a papish fellow as hee is (meaning King James II) that for aught I knowe hee (meaning King James II) will have our Throates cut shortly, or doe us a worse shroud Turne".

The Rebellion of 1688 removed "the Papist menace," and William III and his advisers were strongly Protestant and held more liberal views on the question of dissent. The Toleration Act (1689) exempted all Protestants dissenting from the Church of England from the penalties of the Act of Uniformity, the Conventicle, and the Five Mile Acts. Nonconformists, on taking the oaths to the government were allowed free exercise of their religious opinions, and those already imprisoned under the Acts were freed. Papists were to derive no benefit from the Act, nor were those sects denying the doctrine of the Trinity. No meetings were to be held behind closed doors, and places of worship were to be registered at the Bishop's or Archdeacon's court, and then certificates were to be granted. However, the oath of allegiance to William and Mary was unpalatable even to many in the Established Church, with the result that an enormous number of parish priests became non-jurors and were consequently deprived of their livings. The Roman Catholic interest had supported King James (1685/8), and under the new regime we find the Catholics appearing in treason or near-treason cases. Alexander FitzGerrard of Haverfordwest was very probably of Irish extraction, and most certainly of the Roman faith. On 1 August 1689, he used somewhat incautious words, which were not only an affront to the new monarch, but also to the good magistrates of the town and county of Haverfordwest. He said, "that he had a Commission from King James, and that he was a profest Roman Catholic: and that he had but a life to loose which he valued not; and that the Magistrates of this town were all Rebells, traytors and Murtherers, and that if the devill came to reign over them they would obey him". Mr. Morgan Walter and Thomas Wrighton heard these words, with the result that Alexander was indicted in the Autumn Sessions of 1689 and a true bill returned against him.

Several Irishmen were in difficulties after the defeat of James II. Large numbers tried to escape to France, while others, stranded in England, tried to return to their native land. However, the vigilance of the English men-o-war foiled many attempts, and a number of prisoners were landed in Pembrokeshire ports and handed over to the civil authorities. In autumn 1689, Robert Nelson, John Wilson and Constant Docherty, were committed to gaol by Robert Prust, Mayor of Haverfordwest, for "being soldiers in the service of the late King James and intending for Ireland, having no pass, and owning themselves to be popish recusants". John Smith, Daniel Morgan, John Fox and John Jones, "being vagrant Irish soldiers" were committed by George Lort, J.P. In the same year, William Mordaunt, J.P. of Scovaston, committed to gaol one Richard Brown, an Irish papist, late in arms under the command of Colonel Markeebymddy (sic), and attempting to travel to Ireland. On 22 April 1689, Arthur Laugharne,[49] J.P., of Llanreithan, committed "Helver Brace and Lewy Norma, being French men lately arrived in Ireland to fight against the Protestants in that Kingdom".

The Navy intercepted some ships. On 24 March 1689/90, Jasper Stafford, John Codd, Arthur Morphey, Robert Cavell, and Anne Macerley, were brought before George Lort and John Courcy, deputy-mayor of Pembroke, by Sir Cloudesley Shevell, Commander of their Majesties' Frigate Ye Muncke, who took the said prisoners at sea, as a prize in a barque, and who confessed themselves to be Irish men and of the popish religion. In the same month, Griffith Dawes[50] and George Lort committed ten men brought before them by Captain John Jennings, Commander of their Majesties ship, The Experiment, and lately captured aboard a catch off Kingsale in Ireland, by their own confession flying to France, and having been present in "the late battle near the River Boyne in the late King James army".

Many of the clergy refusing to take the oath of allegiance and fidelity were prosecuted. The Reverend Nicholas Roberts, M.A.,[51] of Llanddewi Felffre, a noted antiquary and naturalist, refused to take the oath and aggravated his offence by stating publicly, "That the present parliament was not a loyall parliament, and doubted the Government went on in an ill Course, and offered several arguments that the present king was not a loyal king, and said it was not lawful to take the Oath by any that had taken the oath of Allegiance to the late King James". The jury returned a true bill against him in the Autumn Sessions of 1689. The Reverend Humphrey Collins of Narberth, clerk, also felt very strongly on these matters and found it impossible to keep the still tongue which makes a wise head. The eloquent expression of his views brought him to the notice of the authorities in the autumn of 1691. He said at Narberth to one Phillip Morgan "King William is utterly Routed and all the Confederat Princes have left him, and also the Dutch, and he is come home with a Shitten Britches. And King James is landed in Scotland with several thousand men marching with speed for England. And Rebellion is worse than the Sinne of Witchcraft, and the Judgement of God will fall upon all disobedient Children. Were I to dye this moment for it, could I come at my disobedient Children (meaning the present King and Queen), that were soe develish as to disinherit their parents (meaning King James and Queen Mary), I would Cutt their Throates with my own hands. Nay more, I would pick the flesh from the Bones of them". Mr. Collins was still boiling with indignation when he met Johanna the wife of Thomas Kymer, a local landowner, at Robeston Wathen. He aired his views by remarking to her "Your King is tumbling down and you shall see alteracons suddenly. The Dutch have left him and alsoe the Confederat princes. Bee not troubled for you shall see Glorious Times very soone". He then met Mr. Thomas Kymer, and continued to spread alarm and despondency by telling him, "Your King is coming down. The Confederat Princes have left him and the States of Holland. And the Duke of Savoy has made peace with France".[52] Mr. Collins, deeply moved by the events of the times, concluded his tirade by saying "Had I a disobedient Child I would put his neck under my foot". His eloquence resulted in a true bill being brought against him.

Another clergyman who entertained strong views on the new monarch was the Reverend Evan Evans,[53] Vicar of Clydey. He had subscribed to the King's supremacy on 21 June 1688, but by 1693 his oath had worn a bit thin. Towards the end of June 1693, he was drinking with John Thomas James, a yeoman of Clydey, and James Morgan of Whitchurch, at the tavern of Andrew Havard of Clydey. Mr. Evans presently, "dranke ye health of King James and would have others drinke it. He said Evan Evans sang then a song, in these wordes, 'King James shall have his owne againe.' He said Evan Evans among other discourses there then sayd King William is no king at all". And being asked why he did not pray for King William, replied "he did not nor never would pray for King William - ye word William not being in ye comon prayer book, but Charles". Having expressed his loyalty to the Stuarts in speech and song, Parson Evans rounded off his visit to the tavern by administering (helped by John Lewis of Clydey, gent.) a thorough hiding to John Thomas James. These misdemeanours were the reason of his appearance at the Autumn Sessions at Haverfordwest.

Many of the landed gentry, as well as the parsons, were not well disposed towards Dutch William, and in 1693 Lewis Mathias[54] of Llangwarran, and John Owen the younger[55] of St. Kennox, gentlemen, appeared at the Great Sessions for "the Drinkeinge of the Health of the Late King James and of his son the Prince of Wales". The evidence shews that about 12 May 1693, John Philipps of Cilrath and Isaac Philpin,[56] gentlemen, were partaking of ale in the tavern of Griffith Morgan in Narberth parish. They were sitting quietly like respectable citizens chatting over their ale, when in swaggered Lewis Mathias and John Owen. As soon as he had a drink before him, Mr. Mathias, "began the health of the Late King James and drank to the said Isaac Philpin". Isaac, however, immediately countered this by drinking to King William's health. John Philipps then cautioned Mr. Mathias telling him to have a care not to speak treason. The jolly squire answered that there was no harm in it, and then proceeded to drink twice to King James again! Mr. Owen supported his kinsman by drinking to the Prince of Wales. Phillipps said that King James, "had no such son," but the said Mr. Owen answered and said he had, and that "he had kissed his hand, and then laying his hatt upon the Table, stood up and Dranke the Prince of Wales his health". Their punishment at the Sessions, if any, could not have been severe and both squires were pleased to repeat their offence in a few months' time.

Some of the gentry adopted an obstructionist and non-cooperative attitude to William's government. On 29 June 1693, Captain William Barlow of Slebech, Lewis Mathias of Llangwarran, Richard Owen[57] of Robeston Wathen, John Owen the elder and John Owen the younger, John Foley[58] of Llawhaden, gentlemen, Mallet Bateman[59] of Narberth, mercer, George Owen of Narberth, the Reverend Thomas David of Minwere, clerk, William Barlow[60] of Martletwy, and Will Rochford of Wiston, gentlemen, assembled at Narberth with many others, armed with swords and pistols, tending to disturb the peace, "the said Captain William Barlow being a known enemy to their Majesties and their government". At the same Sessions the following gentlemen were presented for refusing to take the Oath of Supremacy and allegiance: Sir John Barlow, Bart.[61] Rowland Laugharne of St. Brides, Lewis Wogan[62] of Boulston, William Mordaunt[63] and his son Cole Mordaunt, of Scovaston, John Bowen of Benton,[64] Thomas Bowen of Cosheston, the Reverend Thomas Davids of Minwere, clerk, Morris Davids of Crunwere, the Reverend John Howell and Robert Howell, of Trenewydd,[65] James Laugharne of Pontfaen,[66] Mallet Bateman, mercer; George Roch of Robeston Wathen, George Owen of Narberth, mercer, Phillip Harrys,[67] William Morgan and Morris Morgan[68] all of Clydey parish. In August 1693, the jury presented Sir John Barlow,[69] Lewis Wogan of Boulston, Essex Meyrick[70] of Bush, Rowland Laugharne of St. Brides, William Scourfield[71] of New Moat, Lewis Wogan of Wiston, James Lloyd of Cilrhue,[72] George Bowen[73] of Llwyngwair, and William Mordaunt of Scovaston who, having been appointed magistrates by their Majesties on 11 June 1689, had refused to take the oath and accept the appointment. Practically all these landowners were united by the bonds of kinship as well as of political sentiment.

In order to embarrass the disgruntled squires and the non-jurors still further, additional presentments were made against them in the Great Sessions. Sir John Barlow was charged with damming the river at Canaston so that it overflowed on to the highway, and also of destroying a causeway there, much to the discomfort and annoyance of their Majesties liege subjects. Mallet Bateman was also indicted for worrying his neighbours. The Reverend Thomas Davids of Minwere was further charged for holding divine service in Minwere church, he having deprived as a non-juror; and also for keeping a private school at Minwere for instructing the youth, he not being qualified so to do. Lewis Mathias of Llangwarran came in for special attention, and the indictments were framed to represent him as a veritable ogre. He was additionally presented as "a litigous and Contentious person, and one that doth generally oppress his neighbors by troublesom and vexacious law suits for trifling matters, and one that lends money to severall persons uppon Corrupt Bargains and uxurious Contracts, to ye ruine of some of their Majesties poor subjects, and also for drinking at his own house at Llangwarran, at Slebech, and at Narberth, saying 'The King shall have his owne again' ". Mr. Mathias, however, was quite unconcerned about it all, and in the following year he was again presented for singing his favourite refrain.

In 1696 some of these landowners were still being presented for failing to take the oath after being repeatedly summoned to do so. Among them we find Lewis Wogan of Boulston, James Laugharne of Pontfaen, Morris Bowen[74] of Upton, the Reverends Thomas Davids and John Howell, Robert Howell of Trenewydd, John Bowen and Thomas Bowen of Burton, William Mordaunt and Cole Mordaunt, Charles Dolson of Llanstadwell, the Reverend William Pritchard[75] of Llanfihangel Penbedw, the Reverend John Lewis of Boulston, George Owen and Mallet Bateman of Narberth, mercers. The diehard of Llangwarran seems to have capitulated by 1696 and abandoned singing his political ditty in the inns and country houses, for he does not appear again in the calendar.

After the final defeat of King James' forces in Ireland, the navy was not employed in any great strength to protect the western approaches to the British Isles, and it became quite possible again for agents from the Continent to come and go as they wished in West Wales. This led the Grand Jury to petition as follows on 6 April 1696, " We present it to be agreed grievance to the inhabitants of this country, being his Majesties Loyal Subjects, That there is noe Crusar or Convey appointed from Millford Haven northwards to Holly Head, being about 30 leagues, and several vessels [have been] taken by Privateers, laden with salt and other merchandise from Liverpool, Chester, and other Northern Ports, to ye great damage of our King and his subjects of this and the neighbouring counties, it being the common haunts of Privateers who very well know, as wee find by woofull Experience, that there is noe Crusar appointed for the said Coast, and that there is severall cricks between Millford Haven and Holly head where the French Privateers doe commonly Anchor Inn, viz, Studwell Road and under Barsey Iland Ramsey Sound, and the Ilands of Millford". Although this refers to piracy, it is well-known that the privateers would also, and in fact did, carry human cargo provided that a satisfactory sum of money had been paid. It will later be seen how the neglect of the west coast by naval patrols led to several wild rumours and alarms, culminating in a successful landing of French troops in Pembrokeshire.

The remainder of William's reign, and that of Queen Anne, did not witness any political or religious stirs in Pembrokeshire. The Roman Catholic faith had very few adherents left and the records do not contain further examples of prosecutions. The Nonconformist and Quaker movements continued to flourish, but were no longer so closely associated with politics. The authorities were content to prosecute only for assemblies and conventicles in unlicenced houses, but very rarely refused a licence for religious meetings.

The rising of 1715 did not disturb the West Wales squirearchy, and Mr. Mathias of Llangwarran, the Barlows, and the Laugharnes had become reconciled to the government of the day. There remained a few who were still prepared to further the Jacobite cause and had confidence in its ultimate success. One such person lived in Haverfordwest, namely Owen Keefe, who still hankered after the old dynasty. He was presented at the Great Sessions for saying on 10 June 1714 "That our Sovereign Lady Queen Ann was no Lawfull Queen of this Realm, and that he was sent as a Messenger from his Master James the third, King of England, and of Scotland the Eighth, and that he did not doubt but that in a fortnights tyme Some Thousands of people would Come to assist him, the said Owen Keefe, for that purpose, and that he would Stand by his Master whilst he had one drop of blood in his body". Two Haverfordwest burgesses, William Ayleway and John Hussey, gave evidence against him. The jury however, threw out the bill, and Keefe quietly departed to await the arrival of James "the third of England, and of Scotland the Eighth".

The events of 1715 gave rise to comment only in Pembrokeshire, and there can be no doubt that this Protestant county never seriously contemplated assisting the Old Pretender. A few people passed remarks which brought them before their betters, but they were of a very minor nature.

Thomas Griffith of St. Davids, gent., said on 24 September 1715, "the Pretender hath entered into Scotland and now our king pretends himselfe to be Lawfull to the Crown. But he is not. There are Seaven heires Lawfull to the Crown before he be. Therefore I hope he shall not remaine long". Thomas Harry testified to having heard Griffith say this, but the jury ignored the bill, and the student of royal genealogy returned to St. Davids, no doubt to ponder anew over the intricacies of monarchical remaindership.

In the early eighteenth century a social club was formed in West Wales called "The Society of Sea Sergeants," and there was a suspicion that it had Jacobite sympathies. Its members were mostly squires, with their wives and daughters, and a list of them is given in Fenton's "Historical Tour through Pembrokeshire" (1811).[76] It is true that among the members were two acknowledged Jacobites, namely the able politician Sir John Philipps[77] of Picton, and his kinsman the hard-drinking fox-hunter of Pentypark, James Philipps.[78] But no evidence has been forthcoming to support the charge, and the Society seems to have confined its activities to assemblies, dinners, cards and snuff-taking. There is nothing to show that Sir John or his kinsman disputed the Hanoverian succession, but the fact that they were High Tories, like the majority of Sea Sergeants, would cause their Whig opponents to suspect them of the worst. There is a tradition in the Hundred of Dewsland that the Young Pretender once visited Pembrokeshire, and he is said to have stayed secretly at the home of the ancient family of Propert of Trevigan.[79] The story goes that a hunting horn was always blown when any anti-Jacobites were in the vicinity, and Charles would then immediately retire into hiding. One day pretty little Miss Propert, who was of a mischievous nature, got hold of the horn, and played some lively calls on it, which sent the royal visitor precipitately into his hiding hole! My late friend, Mr. Francis Green, a descendant of the Properts, investigated the story, and was told that it was not impossible for Charles to have been in Pembrokeshire on several occasions.

As previously mentioned, the growth of Nonconformity did not alarm the authorities or lead to that persecution which is sometimes averred by Nonconformist historians. No doubt several examples of sufferings can be adduced, but the eighteenth century records shew that these were exceptions. What really caused alarm was not Nonconformity itself but the emigration that sometimes accompanied it. A large number of West Wales people, especially Quakers, had sailed for America, a land which promised full freedom of conscience and the unfettered practice of religion. These colonists (for economic as well as religious reasons), were anxious that some of their countrymen should join them, and several agents were employed to recruit emigrants. This caused acute labour problems in Pembrokeshire, which led the Grand Jury to petition the Justices of Great Sessions on 11 April 1729 in the following terms: " We present a very pernicious practice that for several years been carried on by wicked and designing persons in this county in deluding great numbers of Ignorant Inhabitants and Labouring people, to transport them and their families without licence for so doing, to the province of Pensilvania in America, under false persuasions of great advantages, and in violation of a statute made in 5 Richard II [1381-82] caput 2nd. This practice has had very ill consequences and has put the farmers of Pembrokeshire under great difficulties in harvest time, and sufficient labour cannot be got to save their corn, and they are obliged to hire labourers at great and excessive rates, whereby the price of corn is greatly increased." The Jury prayed that the said statute be read in open court, and put into effect. It was signed by John Symmins of Llanstinan. John Vaughan of Trecwn, John Skyrme of Llawhaden, Nicholas Roch of Robeston Wathen, John Laugharne of Llanreithan, William Bowen of Burton, Samuel Harries of St. Davids, David Hughes of Harmeston, William Jones of Llether, James Willy of Lampeter Velfrey, John Foley of Ridgeway, Thomas Jones of Brawdy, William Hawker of Dale, and James Phillips of Rudbaxton – all of whom were landed proprietors. The effect of this shortage of man power forms an interesting comparison with present-day labour conditions.

There seems to have been no difficulty in obtaining a licence to hold religious meetings for dissenters. Licences were granted by the Quarter Sessions. On 10 July 1739, a licence was given to the dissenters to meet at the house of George Morris of Trefin[80] on 15 January 1739-40, the house of Evan David at Treglemais[81] was similarly licenced. On 4 October 1743, it was ordered that house called West Trefgarn Meeting House,[82] be registered and allowed. It is interesting to note that this chapel was built with the aid of the squire of the parish, who was a strong churchman. On 6 July 1743, a lease for 99 years was granted to the Dissenters of land in Trefgarn Owen, whereon to erect a chapel, by Thomas Jones of Brawdy, J.P., and his son, John Jones, at an annual rent of 2s. 6d. Brawdy parish offers other examples of sympathy between Nonconformists and church-going landlords. The Reverend Stephen Hughes, who was ejected from his living of Meidrim, Carmarthenshire, in 1662, became an itinerant preacher, and was invited by John ap Rice of Rickeston, "to preach near Brawdy Church". In 1773, Brother Titherington, a Moravian, preached at Brawdy, "and was invited to visit Mr. and Mrs. Jones with whom he had conversation in a friendly manner. This is of good consequence on account of his [i.e. Mr. Jones'] influence in that part of the county". But Mr. Jones also had an eye to business, for his wife possessed an ancient house-organ which she wished to be rid of, and in 1786 it was offered to the Moravians for ten guineas.

The Moravians seem to have possessed sensitive ears for musical instruments, and politely declined the offer. The would-be vendor was John Jones, J.P., a large landowner, whose wife was Thomasine, daughter of Anthony Stokes of Rosemarket. Many other examples of this generosity abound.[83]

At the same time, the law was enforced, fairly enough, when Dissenters held meetings in unlicensed houses. Thus John Powell *alias* Howell of Llanfihangel Abergwesyn in Carmarthenshire, yeoman, was charged in 1740 for preaching in an unlicensed place called Llwyngoras ycha in Bayvil, between 9 p.m. and midnight, 12 March 1739-40 "as a Dissenting preacher or heathen, contrary to an Act of Parliament made in I William and Mary". He was committed by the Epiphany Quarter Sessions to the Great Sessions, where he was indicted for preaching at Llwyngoras "to the Terror and disturbance of several of His Majesty's Subjects". The following were present aiding and abetting him; David Harry, yeoman; John William, carpenter; James Owen, yeoman; Andrew Simon, carpenter, David James, carpenter; all of Nevern parish; George John, husbandman; William Bowen, pedler; both of Bayvil, and Evan George of Meline, labourer. John Powell was quite unrepentant and repeated his offence at Pontfaen on the 19 November following.

Towards the end of the eighteenth century the government was preoccupied with colonial problems and endless wars in Europe. The French bogey was a very real one, and enemy ships occasionally appeared off the west coast. The result was that several rumours were spread which were likely to impair the popular morale, and the authorities took steps to counteract these alarms. On 27 July 1779, Isaac Phillip of St. Martins, Haverfordwest, yeoman, said that, "an enemy privateer, meaning a Privateering Ship belonging to Certain foreign persons then and now at open War with our Sovereign Lord the King," had arrived within the Harbour mouth of Milford Haven. He was indicted at the Great Sessions for speaking "falsely, knowingly, wilfully and maliciously with Intention to excite great fear and terror among His Majesty's liege subjects, and to spread a false and malicious Report and alarm".

These alarms were not confined to Pembrokeshire, as is shown in an undated letter of this period (or perhaps shortly after 1793) written by Mrs. Jane Johnes of Hafod, Cardiganshire, to her brother, John Johnes of Dolau Cothi, She wrote "I have heard this moment that 14 sail of the French are off Aberystwyth and Aberaron. If you are able let me beg of you to come over and bring with you what arms you can, powder and shot. They will not sell any at Aberystwyth . . . I will defend the house as long as I can. Trust to God for the rest, and if I fail, hope to be happy hereafter . . . You need not bring any People with you. We have enough here if we had Arms". However, this very brave lady was informed later in the day that the alarm was over and the French gone. "Thank God for it," she said "I was not in a very pleasant situation, not a friend near me . . . " (Dolau Cothi MSS, in N.L.W.). The writer was the wife of that great and enlightened model landlord, Colonel Thomas Johnes, J.P.

If "Wolf" had been cried unnecessarily at times, the animal itself did actually arrive. On 22 February 1797, a French force of some 1,500 men, under General Tate, made an unopposed landing below Carreg Wastad and Aber Yelin in the parish of Llanwnda. That such a force could not be maintained or achieve any military object was obvious, and on 24 February, the enemy surrendered unconditionally to Lord Cawdor, commanding The Castlemartin Yeomanry, The Fishguard Fencibles and other miscellaneous militia units that had been hastily concentrated to meet the invader. No great damage had been done, few lives had been lost, and no general action had been fought, but the event produced a *cause celebre* which proved to be the last case of treason in Pembrokeshire.

Official circles believed that the French had been assisted by some country folk who had visited headquarters and volunteered information to the enemy. A hunt for "traitors" was immediately instituted, and it is interesting to note that the suspected persons were Nonconformists. John Thomas of Haverfordwest, merchant, was arrested on suspicion, and was held in gaol for a few weeks before he was liberated, no charge being made against him. Treglemais, home of a Baptist minister the Reverend John Reynolds, was thoroughly searched. When going through his papers, a bundle of Welsh manuscript sermons was found. Asked what they were, the reverend gentleman answered: "Sermons. Do read them. They will do you a lot of good!" After some questioning Mr. Reynolds was allowed to remain in peace. Thomas William of Caerlem in Llanwnda, and William Thomas, were also arrested, but released immediately they proved they were not Dissenters. Finally, two men were sent for trial. Both were well-known Nonconformists, Thomas John of Summerton in Little Newcastle, a farmer and Baptist minister, and Samuel Griffith, of Pointz Castle, a yeoman and Independent Congregationalist. They were charged with having aided and comforted the enemy and urging them not to surrender. Both were held in close confinement in Haverfordwest gaol, but certain privileges were granted to Griffith.

A baptism during the great revival

Samuel Griffith came from an old yeoman stock, and had served as High Constable of Dewsland Hundred, as a Collector of Taxes for Brawdy parish, was the lessee of the Newgale Turnpike Gate, and farmed the largest property in the district. He had been twice married and had a young family, one of his sons later serving with considerable distinction as an Army surgeon for over thirty years. Having heard of the landing, Griffith immediately sent ten of his workmen with the only gun that he possessed, to fight the invaders. He then set out early on 23 February, with his neighbours, Thomas Howell and John Propert of Lochfane, and rode to the southern boundaries of Pencaer, and returned home after an uneventful day. On the following day he rose very early, and, accompanied by his son, and John Roch of Trevanner, rode towards Pencaer. At Mathry Hill they were joined by Thomas Davies and his brother, John Davies, of Castle Villa. At Garn Gelli, Griffith and Thomas Davies ran into a French outpost, were captured and taken to Trehowell to General Tate, who treated them well. Thomas Davies was very much at home apparently, and sat on one side of the fireplace with a glass of liquor in his hand, and the enemy general on the other. Davies explained how they had been captured. He said that he was astonished at the general's good English, and coolly asked him how he spoke the language so well. Tate replied that it was because he was an American. When Griffith and Davies expressed a fear that the French might not allow them to return peaceably, Tate ordered an escort for them. Griffith had not spoken much at Trehowell for his eloquent friend from Castle Villa had held the floor most of the time. But on his way home he got a very fine opportunity to make up for his silence, for he met John Rees of Harglodd, who charged him with being a sympathiser of the French. This Griffith hotly denied, saying that he would fight for his King as long as he had life, and "high words passed between them".

Thomas John was at a Baptist meeting at Mynachlogddu on 22 February, and heard of the landing that evening. He decided to go to Fishguard on the following day to see what had really happened. Together with some friends, he went to the high ground in Llanwnda parish, and having seen the French from afar, he discreetly retired towards Scleddau, and stayed in that district for some time with the Fencibles. He returned home soon after seven, supped and went to bed, no doubt confident in his belief that one Fishguard Fencible was worth three of the Frenchmen who lurked among the cairns of Llanwnda. On the following day (24 February), he again sallied forth and witnessed the French surrender on Goodwick Sands. He then returned to his home, greatly relieved at the happy turn of events.

The trial took place at Haverfordwest on 7 September 1797, Counsel for the Crown were Messrs. Phillips, Dauncey, Pouchet, and Sergeant Williams, with Richard Foley[84] as solicitor. For the defence were, Counsel, Mills and Blackstone, with John Lort Phillips[85] as solicitor. Hugh Barlow of Lawrenny was foreman of the jury. The chief witnesses for the prosecution were French prisoners whose statements proved to be entirely in favour of the defence! There were indications that some of them had been offered money to testify against the accused. Others contradicted themselves most flagrantly, while one (with unimpaired morale) refused to take the oath, saying that he had come to Wales to fight and not to answer questions! The leading Counsel for the Crown then withdrew the case, but said that someone had influenced the witnesses. The Judge then addressed the court, and warned Thomas John to be more careful in future. John interrupted to say he could not promise as he did not know where he had transgressed. The Judge replied that he thought a word of advice was not inopportune, that the trial would not enhance John's character, that there were many disloyal subjects in the country, and that traitors should be removed. John and Griffith were immediately discharged, no evidence having been called against the latter.

There is no doubt that this case was the result of malice or perhaps of panic. Both Griffith and John had nothing to gain by a French victory. Both were substantial yeomen, God-fearing and devout, and could certainly not feel kindly towards an atheistic institution like the French Republic. The case should never have been tried, for it was plain from the beginning that the evidence was not enough to hang a dog – let alone a Dissenter.

The notes to this essay have been written in order to identify the people who figured in the law-suits, and to shew the relationship between the different families. The laws against the Roman Catholics and Dissenters are so well-known, that I have not considered it necessary to discuss them in detail. This is offered as a contribution to an interesting period that saw the passing of the old order, and the inauguration of a new. It is my pleasant duty to acknowledge my indebtedness to my friend, Major John Cookson, B.A., formerly of the 3rd The King's Own Hussars, for the benefit of his scholarly and discerning comments and his ever-ready assistance.

FOOTNOTES

[1] The only other example in the Papers of Great Sessions, is a petition in Welsh demanding a reduction of corn prices in 1801, when John Ladd, Mayor of Newport, Pembs., led a vociforous mob to the mansion of Llwyngwair, to ask the support of George Bowen, J.P., who was "not at home" to the visitors. Several minor examples also occur in the Plea Rolls.

[2] Alice was the widow of Thomas Hankey and daughter of Thomas Havard of Hereford. Thomas Bowen was High Sheriff in 1603.

[3] Their son, Thomas Tooley of Arnolds Hill was a Catholic and a Royalist. On 25 December 1648 he compounded for delinquency in adhering to, and assisting, forces raised against Parliament.

[4] The Woolfords or Wolfords were wealthy glovers and skinners in Haverfordwest, and related to the great landowning families of Warren and Marychurch.

[5] Eldest son of Ernestus Musgrave of Llanina, Cards. He became a mercer in Haverfordwest and a prominent Quaker. His daughter, Susanna, married Evan Bowen, son of Evan Bowen, senior, of Prendergast.

[6] Of Prendergast, corvisor.

[7] In 1664, Humphrey Williams, Quaker, was committed to goal until he paid a fine of £5 "for his Contempt in putting on his hatt in Court".

[8] Of Puncheston. The Symmins family were prominent Quakers.

[9] He died in 1686, and left issue by his wife, Alice Foley of Ridgeway.

[10] Of Eastington, a cadet of Philipps of Picton Castle. He died in 1651/2.

[11] Of St. Brides. He had a distinguished career as a "Shoni bob ochor" (the Welsh equivalent of the Vicar of Bray) and served both Parliament and King with equal merit. He was finally a Royalist. The Laugharne family motto, "Ostentare jugulum pro capite alterius," dates from the days of Henry VII. Vide D.N.B. The general's kinsman, John Laugharne of St. Brides, was a stout Roundhead, and was described as "good hearty old gentleman".

[12] Of Johnston and Scovaston. High Sheriff in 1643 and 1644. He was a strong Royalist and father of Hugh Butler, "a grand Malignant". He followed King Charles into exile after Worcester.

[13] Of Peithyll, Cards., brother of Rees Lloyd of Trefach, Pembs., whose son, John Lloyd of Trefach married Elizabeth, elder daughter of Alban Owen of Henllys. Walter Lloyd married Joyce Lloyd of Forest and had issue.

[14] Of Henllys, son of George Owen the Pembrokeshire historian. He married Joan Bradshaw of St. Dogmaels and was father of David Owen.

[15] Son of Alban Owen. He married Anne daughter of Robert Corbett of Ynysymaengwyn, Merioneth. For a pedigree of the Owen family see *Trans. Hon. Cymmr. Soc.,* 1943-44.

[16] Of Orielton, near Pembroke.

[17] One of the Royalist defenders of Pembroke Castle in 1648. Probably of Greenhill near Pembroke.

[18] Of Eweston in Brawdy, a cadet of the St. Brides family.

[19] Of Greenhill.

[20] Of Vaynor.

[21] Colonel James Philipps of Tregibby was M.P. for Cardiganshire in 1654 and 1659, and High Sheriff in 1649. He was M.P. for Pembrokeshire in 1655. Born in 1594, he was alive in 1670. His second wife "the Matchless Orinda" (Catherine Fowler 1631-64). His character is neatly summed up in the *The Cambrian Register* for 1795. The Tregibby family was a cadet of Philipps of Picton.

[22] Richard Vaughan of Golden Grove was the second Earl. He was President of the Council of the Marches. A prominent Royalist; he died on 3 December 1686.

[23] He was also a competent antiquarian. He died about 1655. See my article on "Griffith of Penybenglog" in *Trans. Hon. Cymmr. Soc.* for 1938.

[24] This family was Royalist and Roundhead in turn.

[25] Richard le Hunte of Artramont near Wexford, Ireland. He married Mary Lloyd, daughter of coheiress of David Lloyd of Cilciffeth, by Mary Wogan his wife. This marriage brought him one third of the vast Pembrokeshire estate of the Lloyds.

[26] Younger son of Perrot Ap Rice of Rickeston in Brawdy, and Scotsborough near Tenby. He married Abigail daughter of Thomas Newsham of Abersannan, Carms.

[27] Of Eastmoor. He was a younger son of Henry Lort by Judith White, his wife, and married Alicia, daughter of Sir John Philipps of Picton Castle. An unflattering description of him appears in *The Cambrian Register.*

[28] He was in Pembrokeshire with Cromwell in 1648, and assisted in the siege of Pembroke Castle.

[29] Document in Haverfordwest Corporation Archives.

[30] He died by accident at the Tappot Pit in Prendergast in July, 1665. His descendants became respectable landowners, and served as High Sheriffs and magistrates.

[31] Of an ancient Pembrokeshire family. His will was proved on 1 December 1691.

[32] Born at Amroth in 1623. He held Llangwm and other livings in the county, and preached before Cromwell at Pembroke in 1648. After his ejection in 1662, he retired to Dredgeman Hill where he died in 1691. He was fortunate to secure the support of the influential Sir Herbert Perrott of Haroldston, who referred to him in his will, dated 21 June 1682, as "my loving friend" and bequeathed him £5. His son, Constant Phillips, married Grace, daughter of Richard Ford by Mary Wogan of Stone Hall.

[33] This family was originally of Walwyns Castle, and was descended from Holland of Conway, north Wales.

[34] Son of John Phillipps of Molleston by Jane Elliott, his wife. A cadet of Philipps of Picton Castle.

[35] Son of John Elliott by Mary Came, his wife. The family owned considerable estates in Narberth and Earwere. He died in 1682.

[36] Son of Morris Jones by Lettice Owen of Wenallt, his wife.

[37] He came from co. Bucks., and married Rachel, daughter of Sir William Wogan, Knt. He died circa 1681.

[38] Sybil Protheroe was the executrix of Compton Wogan (brother of the Regicide) in 1668.

[39] Matriculated at Magdalen College, Oxford, in 1655. Archdeacon of St. Davids from 1667 to 22 June 1678, when he died aged 48.

[40] Of Boulton Hill, Steynton. A landowner of ancient family.

[41] A family of rich merchants and landowners. He died on 1 June 1672.

[42] Of Eweston, a landowner. He founded Trefgarn Owen Congregational Chapel, and built the first meeting house on his estate. He died on 30 March 1725, at the advanced age of 90.

[43] A member of an old South Pembrokeshire family. He died in 1715, and was ancestor of Colonel Samuel Ferrior, 1st Life Guards, who was killed at Waterloo at the head of his regiment which he was leading to the charge.

[44] This family appeared in Pembrokeshire during the Civil War, and received grants of land at Narberth.

[45] Second son of Henry Poyer of Grove near Narberth, and died before 1710. An ancient family, the Poyers engaged in the tanning industry on a large scale, and had factories at Canaston. Of this stock was Colonel John Poyer, sometime Mayor of Pembroke, and who defended its castle with General Laugharne and

Colonel Powell, against Cromwell. The three officers were condemned to death, but afterwards it was decided that only one should die, and that lots should be drawn. Poyer drew the blank, and was shot at Covent Garden in 1649. His descendants bear the motto, *Sors est contra meo,* in honour of their Royalist ancestor. The mother of "Beau Nash" was a Poyer of Grove.

[46] Inventory of his goods for probate was exhibited at Carmarthen in 1708. His home was at Great Hook in Brawdy.

[47] Son of Revd. Peregrine Phillips of Dredgeman Hill.

[48] Son of William at the Battle of Colby Moor on 1 August 1645.

[49] A cadet of the St. Brides family. Administration of his goods was granted at Carmarthen in 1699 to his second wife, Dorothy, daughter of William Bowen of Williamston. His first wife was Elizabeth, daughter of David Owen of Henllys.

[50] Of Bangeston. High Sheriff in 1665. He was one of the founders of the old Pembroke Grammar School. His will was proved on 17 July 1694.

[51] Son of Richard Roberts of St. Davids: matriculated at Jesus College, Oxford, in 1665, aged 19; Vicar of Llanddewi Felffre, 1673; Rector of Nolton, 1678; Rector of Llanddewi Aberarth, Cards., 1687; Rector of Llanfallteg, Carms., 1691; he corresponded with the noted antiquary Edward Lhuyd. An interesting letter from him to Bishop Gibson is quoted in Camden's *Britannia,* (edn. Gough, 1789, p. 522).

[52] King William was an unsuccessful military commander, and most of his campaigns ended in failure.

[53] Mr. Francis Green stated that he was probably the son of John Evans of Llangoedmore, who matriculated at New Inn Hall, Oxford, on 8 December 1682, aged 18. His will was proved at Carmarthen on 18 March 1731/2.

[54] Descended from very ancient Pembrokeshire families. Among his ancestors were the martial Gwrwared of Cemais, Vaughan of Pontfaen, George Owen Lord of Cemais, and Philipps of Picton Castle. He was the eldest son of John Mathias (died 1683) by Joan Lloyd of Cilciffeth, and married Mary, daughter of Thomas Phillips of Trellewelyn, near Fishguard. He died before April 1733, when administration of his goods was taken out. He was grandfather of the famous Moravian, David Mathias (died 1808, aged 83), and ancestor of Colonel H. H. Mathias who led the charge of the Gordon Highlanders on the Heights of Dargai in 1897. His sister, Ursula, married John Owen of St. Kennox.

[55] Son of John Owen the elder, by Ursula Mathias, his wife. He was descended from George Owen, Lord of Cemais.

[56] Of Redstone. Isaac Philpin and Elizabeth, his wife were alive in 1716 when their son William was married.

[57] Brother of John Owen the elder. His wife was Mary, daughter of Thomas Hawkwell of Llawhaden by Mary Barlow, his wife.

[58] Of Ridgeway. He married a daughter of John Jones of Vaynor. John Foley had been outlawed by a writ from the King's Bench in 1691 for contempt of court. The Foleys had been Royalists, and five of that name were slain at the Battle of Colby Moor on 1 August 1645.

[59] A member of an old landed family who had turned to trade. He died on 21 May 1699, and was buried in the grave of his father, Maurice Bateman, in Narberth Church. On his tombstone are carved the family arms of [*sable*] three escallops between a chevron [*argent*], with a dove as a crest.

[60] Younger son of George Barlow of Slebech by Joan Lloyd of Cilciffeth: captain, later colonel, in Lord Peterborough's Horse. His lordship was a Catholic and a close friend of James II.

[61] Son of George Barlow of Slebech by Joan Lloyd; created a Baronet in 1677 High Sheriff in 1681. He lived mainly at Minwear. His will was proved in London in 1695. Twice married, he left six children.

[62] A cadet of Wogan of Wiston; High Sheriff in 1672. His wife was Katherine, daughter of James Philipps of The Priory, Cardigan, by whom he had 15 children. He died in 1702.

[63] Descended from the Mordaunt baronets of Massingham, Norfolk. He married Anne, daughter and heiress of Hugh Butler of Scovaston, and had 21 children. His father-in-law gave immense trouble, due to his annoying practice of secretly selling properties he had settled on the marriage of Mr. and Mrs Mordaunt. This was Hugh Butler, the "grand Malignant" of the Civil War.

[64] Son of William Bowen of Williamston; succeeded to the Upton estate. He married, 1st, a daughter of John Barlow of Cresswell; 2nd, Martha, daughter of Owen Edwardes of Trefgarn. His will was proved in 1715.

[65] Howell of Trenewydd, Crunwere parish, was a landowning family. The Revd. John was anon-juror; Robert was his brother, and married Mary, daughter and heiress of George Phillips.

[66] A cadet of St. Brides; son of Vaughan Laugharne of Pontfaen by Anne Hawkwell, his wife. He married Mary, daughter of his kinsman, Hugh Laugharne of Eweston.

[67] An attorney. He married Mary, daughter and heiress of Edward James of Clydau, by Diana, daughter of the Revd. Griffith Roberts of Llanddewi Felffre by Cecil, daughter of Sir William Wogan, Knt.

[68] Sons of David Morgan of Blaenbylan, by Elizabeth Bell of Arnolds Hill. William Morgan's will was proved in 1703. Morris Morgan was of Ffynnone Bychan, and married Anne Howell of Trenewydd. They were the squires of Clydau parish, and their parish priest, Evan Evans, was also of their way of thinking.

[69] Sir John Barlow must have found it particularly difficult to adjust himself to the new regime, for his family had been prominent Royalists. His great-grandfather, John Barlow, had been Royalist Master of Ordnance, and captain of a troop of horse, and "a church papist". Captain John Barlow's younger sons, William and Charles, left England as a result of the King's defeat, and both were killed in the Venetian service fighting the Turks; while his two daughters became lady abbesses in France.

[70] Of Bush, near Pembroke, son of Sir John. Essex Meyrick was born about 1635, and was of Gray's Inn in 1656. He was Mayor of Pembroke in 1661, 1677, and 1688. His wife was Jane Corbett of Ynysymaengwyn, by whom he had 8 children.

[71] Son of John Scourfield by Mary Philipps of Picton; High Sheriff in 1663; he married Mary, daughter of Sir Hugh Owen of Orielton; he died in 1696.

[72] He paid 8 hearth taxes in 1670. His estate passed to his daughter Anne, wife of Lewis Wogan of Wiston, and their daughter, Anne Wogan, married Thomas Lloyd of Bronwydd, Cards., who came to live at Cilrhiwe.

[73] Son of James Bowen by Alice Rowe of Linney; High Sheriff in 1682; he married Dorothy, daughter of Essex Meyrick of Bush.

[74] Son of Rees Bowen by Sybil Wogan of Stone Hall. By his will proved in 1703, he left Upton to his kinsman, John Bowen of Benton.

[75] Vicar there in 1683. James Lloyd of Cilrhiwe, by his will dated 1703, appointed him guardian of testator's grand-children, Bridget and Catherine Wogan.

[76] The records of this Society cover the period 1726-1760. Amongst its members were the Laugharnes, Barlows, Warrens, Philipps, Meyrick and Stepney, all of Pembrokeshire; the Mansels, Gwynne of Taliarus and Gwempa; Hancorne and Cornwallis, of Carmarthenshire; Popkin and others of Glamorgan. The Society's rules included allegiance to the King, and membership of the Church of England.

[77] Son of "the good Sir John" of S.P.C.K. fame. He was a prominent and able member of Parliament, a scholar, and a genealogist. There is no doubt about his Jacobite leanings, and he once produced a very magnificent pedigree which shewed that he was descended from the original British royal family, and had a better claim to the throne than the Electors of Hanover! When in his native county he lived mainly at Kilgetty which became the centre of Pembrokeshire Toryism. He greatly increased the number of voters in that district, and "the Black Hundred" of Kilgetty was used by him to defeat his Whig opponent, Hugh Owen of Orielton. He died in 1764, aged 63. His son, Sir Richard, was created Baron Milford in 1776.

[78] Son of John Philipps of Pentypark by Anne Scurlock his wife, born 1710. He was High Sheriff in 1734 and 1787. His wife was Jane Pryse of Gogerddan, Cards., and his daughter Mary, married Lord Milford. He was a hearty squire of the old school, but much given to intrigue. He died in 1794.

[79] In Llanrhian Parish.

[80] A village in Llanrhian parish. This district was closely associated with early Dissent. Two of the local landowning families, Thomas of Longhouse and Rogers of Carnachenwen (both extinct) were eminent Methodists, although the latter family traced its material fortune to a rascally smuggler who operated at Goodwick. From Trefin came the ancestors of Henry Richard of Tregaron, *Apostol Heddwch,* and of Captain Griffith Dedwith, the great Methodist of Borth-y-gest in north Wales.

[81] Treglemais, an ancient manor in Llanhowell parish, for many generations the home of the Reynolds family, which produced a large number of nonconformist ministers.

[82] A Congregational chapel in Brawdy parish. The first chapel was built between Trefgarn Owen and Grinston, at a spot called Cnwc yr Afar, but in 1743 it was built on its present site. That great marauding Papist, Owain Glyndŵr, was Lord of the Manor of Trefgarn Owen, which passed to his kinsfolk, the Newports of High Ercall, Salop.

[83] Minute Books of Pembrokeshire Quarter Sessions.

[84] Of Ridgeway.

[85] Of Lawrenny.

HIGHWAYS – REPAIRS AND TOLLS

1791. An Act for amending, widening and keeping in repair, the roads leading from the Town of Haverfordwest, through the town of Fishguard, to the town of Newport, in the county of Pembroke; and also from the town of Fishguard to the city of St. Davids in the said county of Pembroke.

The several roads from Haverfordwest, by Tangiers, Silver Stream, and Triffleton Bridge, through the town of Fishguard to Newport, and also from Fishguard towards St. Davids to Jordanston Water, and thence to St. Davids "are very ruinous, and in some seasons of the year almost impassable to passengers, and cannot be effectually repaired, widened and rendered commodious for travelling by the present Methods provided by the Law. The following are appointed trustees to put this Act into execution . . . Lord Milford, Wm. Knox, John Phelps, Richard Bowen, Samuel Fenton, Edward Waters, James Rees", etc., etc. A list of fifty-one persons, including six Clerks.

QUALIFICATION OF TRUSTEES

To be in receipt of £50 p.a. from lands, his own dejure uxoris, or heir apparent of a person having £100 p.a. from such states, or possessing personalty of value of £1,000.

Trustees to meet at Guildhall in Haverfordwest on first Monday in May next to put this Act into operation. Treasurer, clerk and collectors of Tolls, Surveyors to be appointed.

NO INNKEEPERS ENTITLED TO BE AN OFFICER

Turnpikes to be erected across roads as Trustees think proper, and also a Toll Gate house if they think necessary, together with a garden to be enclosed next to such house.

TOLLS

For every horse or beast drawing any Coach, Berlin, Landau, Chariot, Chase, Caravan, Chair, Hearse or Litter . . . 6d.

For every Waggon, Wain, Cart, or any other such Carriage, drawn by not more than 3 horses 3d., and for any horse more than three . . . 1d. for every such horse.

For every Horse, Mare, Gelding, or Ass, mule - laden or unladen and not drawing . . . 1d.

For every drove of Oxen, Cows or other cattle, 10d. per score; and so in proportion for any lesser number.

For any drove of Calves, Sheep, Lambs, Hogs or swine, 5d. per score, and so in proportion for any lesser number.

REFUSAL TO PAY

Power for Collector to seize and distrain Carriage, Horse, or beast and if not paid after three days, to be sold.

No carriage, horse, animal etc., to be charged more than once per day between Haverfordwest and Fishguard and Jordanston Bridge and St. Davids.

Tolls may be lessened with consent of the Creditors.

EXEMPTION FROM THE TOLLS

Carriages carrying stones, gravel, and other materials for repairing said roads, or any other roads within the parish where road lies; or for beasts going to pasture or watering places, or for letters carried by Royal Mail. Horses and carriages taking people to Church on Sundays, or chapel or any other place of religious worship, or attending funerals. Or carrying clergy when on parochial duties; or horses of officers and soldiers on duty; or carriages and horses carrying voters for MP elections, on day before and after the election day as well. Or horses or carriages passing 500 yds away from the roads.

After 1st. Jan 1795 no person shall be entitled to the said exemptions for any carts or carriages having the buildings of the wheels thereof fastened or secured by nails projecting over the surface of the Iron or Binding, commonly called Rose Headed Nails.

No gate to be erected between Fishguard and Newport till 3 miles are repaired, or between Fishguard and St. Davids till 5 miles are repaired. No gate shall be erected between Crows Nest and Silver Stream, or below end of Kilarth Lane and Triffleton Bridge. Penalty on Tollkeeper for permitting private passage to evade tolls.

Tolls may be leased to any persons for any term not exceeding three years. Materials to be got in for repairing the roads, or river, or brook or in private grounds. Causeways to be made.

Remove annoyances . . . trees near roads, bushes etc.

Roads may be widened, turned and altered and lands purchased for the purpose; but houses and other buildings not to be injured, or yard, garden, orchard, plantation, trees, or avenue without the consent of the owner.

No toll to be taken between Jordanston Water and St. Davids, till £450 is paid to the Treasurer for repairing that road.

PERSONS LIABLE FOR STATUTE WORK ON ROADS, in the parishes and continue to do so. Statute work may be compounded for.

Justices to apportion the Statute work. County bridges to be repaired as before. Roads to be measured and mile stones erected, stones or posts to be set up with inscriptions on them denoting distance from any town or place; if they think proper erect posts with inscriptions at places where roads lead off turnpike roads. No timber and stone to be drawn on the road (mill stones excepted) otherwise than on wheel carriages.

Proceedings of Trustees to be entered in books. This Act shall commence to take place on 2nd May 1791, and remain in force for 21 years.

Fighting over the tolls

TURNPIKES AND ROADS

Excerpts from the Fishguard Turnpike Trust (formed on May 2nd 1791/2)

2nd. August. Agreed with Thomas George mason to erect a dwelling house for a gatekeeper at end of town of Fishguard, 20 ft. long, 13 ft. broad, 7 ft to the square, 1 chimney, 2 windows, doors hinges, lock etc., for £17, to be completed by 1st. Oct.

1792. Sept 20th. That road from Ford bridge to end of St. Dogwells parish boundary to be proceeded upon under directions of J. Tucker, who is desired to order the hedges to be taken down. Ordered Mr. Stokes to be appointed Clerk of the Turnpike Trust at salary of £20 per annum.

1792. Nov 1st. Roderick Meyler keeper of gate at salary of 5 shillings a week, with house and garden erected for him.

1793. 16th. Dec. That the gates of Scleddy and Fishguard be advertised. That the old road from Scleddy Isha be stopped. That a new gate be set up at Scleddy, of the breadth of 10 feet, and that the present gate there be moved and set up elsewhere, With two keys and a lock.

1795. Oct. 1st. Martha David wife of Thomas David be appointed keeper of Prendergast gate with annual salary of 5s. per week.

Tolls received for 36 weeks from Oct. 14th to 17th June 1802.
> Scleddy Gate £7 15s.
> Fishguard Gate £17 4s. 4d.
> Morfa £10 19s. 1d.

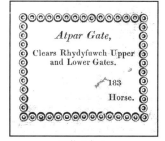

Subscriptions to Fishguard Turnpike Trust, Feb. 1791.
> Lord Milford, Lord Cawdor, Hugh Barlow £100 each.
> Wm. Knox £300;
> J. F. Barham, G. Vaughan and J. Phelps £200 each.
> R. Bowen, J. Tucker, T. Tucker, J. Harris, £100 each.
> W. Knox. £100.
> G. Vaughan £75.
> J. Rees Stokes £150. Mrs. Anne Edwards £30.
> Total £1,855.

Toll ticket

1750. Certificated, dated 26 April 1750 by Thomas Jones of Brawdy, JP, that he has agreed by the order of the Q.S. with Stephen Esmond of Camrose, mason, to repair Roch bridge for £5. 5s., and to keep it in repair for 7 years. A bond for performance signed by Stephen Esmond.

Road Map of the road from London to St. Davids. 1762. "He does not mention Solva, but marks a road leading to the north of that village to St.Davids ye worst way. The way is marked by hills, after the fashion of Speed, and our Traveller has improved on the old saying '17 hills and 16 miles to St. Davids from Haverfordwest'; for upon counting his hills finds he has 22 of them.

1770. Jury present, Wm. Mortimer, Farmer; Thomas Burry, Joseph Bowen and John Phillips, labourers; Evan Harry, shoemaker, Wm. Clement, weaver, all of St. Davids, John Rees and H. Rees of Whitchurch labourers on 12th Jan, assaulted and destroyed hedges and fences erected on land owned by Gilbert James Gent, and in the possession of J. Edward, Yeoman. They broke and prostrated them.

Verdict . . . Not Guilty.

1786. 20th Nov. Peter Williams gent., Thos Stephens yeoman, and J. Morgan, yeoman, all of Mathry did obstruct a road from Abercastle to St. Davids by building a hedge of earth and stone 5ft. high, 8ft. broad, and 30ft. in length.

In the Country

Bygone Farmers . . . Country Law . . . Hands on the land

[Fascinating fragments of history crop up in F.J.'s papers, here is one such nugget. – *Ed.*]

The writer of the following was the son of George Williams of Trearched. His mother's maiden name was Elizabeth Gough, daughter of Gough of Llanrhian. His father died when William was three years old.

"I, John Williams, finding it a great inconvenience that my ancestors did not write down remarkable observations and occurrences that happened to them here given the following relating to my own life. I was born October 20th, 1770. In my youth I was sickly. In my early age I was put to a country school and then to St. Davids. I made but poor use of my time. When I came of age I felt the loss of it. I was brought up by my mother, my only guardian. I went to Haverfordwest School when I was 15 years and succeeded in arithmetic so far as was sufficient for farming business. In my 17th year I left school and came home to assist my mother in business. The land she had in hand was Trearched. Our estate was Trearched, Trewalter Llwyd a house and garden at Trevine, the personal property, the stock and crops, £200. I soon applied myself to farming, and was trying to find out what was the most advantageous plan at that time. The work that was then first done was improving Trearched meadows by fallowing and sowing two crops of corn in them.

"After 1787 the east side of Parc-uch-Lawety (sic), hedge was fixed with stones and in another year Parcanlaw(sic) west hedge was likewise done. In 1791 Parc-y-ream (Parc y rhedyn), was hedged and made into a field. In 1792 Clintbach (Clun-bach) was enclosed. In 1792 the old hedges were gone out of repair and were made new, trees were planted. The greatest part of them died except a few that stand in the southwest garden. In 1793 I was married to Margaret, daughter of William Davies of Pencoed and Martha his wife daughter of Thomas of . . . . At which time my mother and I made an agreement. We had in cash £630, besides £124 that Mother had after her Aunt from Llanrhian. The agreement was that I had Trearched and £460. Total cash I had to begin was £794 . The latter end of the year the ox house was made. March 21st Dorothy was born. A hedge was made of the lower bank field. In 1795 Rediner field was made in the same year. Martha was born

November 30th, 1796. I took great delight in planting and planted the following pieces. Wainbeck, Gardd Cartios, Upper Wilting gardd, Helygucha. That same year the old Hall was taken down. The east pine end rebuilt, the staircase made and partitioned at the expense of Trevelgar and Mother borrowed money to pay for one half of it. The alterations I made in farming was to plough lay ground for corn. In 1789 my uncle, Mr. Llewellyn of Tregwynt (before the Harrises) bought Tresisillt and in the previous year Mary was born 1788 January 13th.

"The old custom was to fallow the ground for wheat. The rotation of crops was wheat, barley, oats, barley and lay ground. I found that by dressing the land well and manuring, the crops were not much better. What I thought first was to manure the land with lime. About the 26th year of my age I began to consider what effect it had. All my neighbours used it as manure, but could not say which way it improved the soil. It is certainly found to kill chick weed and some others. The query is whether anything can kill weeds and nourish grass, as they are so near in nature. Lime certainly does not show itself the first year as dung and compost does. The work was done in 1797. In the following year the garden hedge was made. In May I travelled to Bristol. The view I had of the country was but little, as I went there in 28 hours in a mail coach. Then Bath and back. I found great ingenuity of men, my business was to purchase Tresisillt as I had a favour of my uncle. Its cost was £1,150. The money I paid……. was £25 was left on account and £200 I gave my bond for. I had then after settling with him £359 at interest. In this summer Croft Mesrdorth was drained.

"Certain good points to follow principally. 1. To live in the fear of the Lord. 2. To speak fair words to all. 3. To make good use of one's time, for what is not employed will be seen the want of. 4. To ponder and take second thoughts in actions of importance or bargaining.

"In 1798 the kitchen was built. In 1799 the hedge joining . . . was made. In 1800 my Mother died at Olmarch. The value of her stock and crops was about £60. I had after her Trewalter and Olmarch, except £425 she owed me".

[Further notes. John Williams died on 21 March 1847 and Margaret, his wife, died 10 April 1850. He is buried at Croesgoch, his mother at Llanrhian and his wife at Llanreithan. Little did John Williams think that when mortality tugged at his sleeve urging him to leave a brief outline of his life that we should be allowed through our eyes such a fascinating glimpse of a bygone life. With a little imagination it is possible to see between the lines and I was left with some admiration and affection for what must have been a good man.] *Editor*

"I well recall from my early childhood visiting farmhouses. One was sure to see three pictures on the walls; namely that of Queen Victoria in pride of place, secondly William Gladstone – the Minister the Queen most disliked, and thirdly, a Baptist minister of the bewhiskered variety – thereby combining loyalty, political attachment and religious conviction." *F.J.*

The Extraordinary Evans Family

Due south from Mathry in a fold in the hills lies Mabws, formerly a residence of the princes of south Wales. Now a farmhouse, it was for many generations the home of the Evans family. The later generations at Mabws were remarkable for their varied achievements. One son became Editor of *The Sunday Times,* another became Master of the West India Docks and another was a minor poet who founded the journal *The Country Gentleman.* Another went to South Africa where he introduced Angora goat farming on a large scale. To keep his flocks under control he invented what was called "Evans Patent Fencing" known to us as barbed wire. His African farm consisted of nearly a quarter-of-a-million acres and when he died the obituary writer described it as "the largest farm in the world". His sister, Rebecca, born in 1833, became the first woman to lecture publicly in Britain.

※　　　　※　　　　※

David Lloyd George's family also hailed from the Mathry area. So in the 1914-18 War, Great Britain was lead by a Welshman and men died in millions on barbed wire invented by another Pembrokeshire man.

※　　　　※　　　　※

Excerpt from F.J.'s diary from a description of a journey made in August 1936

The weather was very fine and sunny and the old county looked its best. We stopped at Scollock Farm where we saw an interesting sight. The late Mr. Llewellyn of Scollock made a mint of money and before he died he decided to raise a lasting monument to himself and his good wife. He sent photographs and measurements to Italy to a sculptor who made on his instructions a fine monument in white marble to them. The statues of John Llewellyn and his wife are life size and most excellently executed. They are a perfectly natural and a fine looking pair. John then got the Bishop of St. Davids to consecrate a corner of the meadow next to the house. There the old yeoman and his wife lie buried, with their statues looking towards the homestead where they lived and toiled. The inscription on the monument gives the following information.

"Erected in loving memory of Martha Llewellyn; the dearly beloved wife of John Llewellyn, born at Bletherston, the 19th day of August 1840. Died at this farmhouse the 1st day of December 1906. Also of John Llewellyn, who was born at this house the 5th day of May 1846. Died March 21st 1918. Peace perfect peace. By the blessing of God on their joint industry and thrift they bought this farm and hand it down without encumbrances to their heirs. Endeavour to pull together as they did. Union is strength. As you would that men do to you, do also to them likewise. Love God and keep the Commandments, that you may prosper in this life, and have no fear of death."

※　　　　※　　　　※

Scarborough 1841. These three cottages are said to have been built from the timbers of an unfortunate ship the *Scarborough* that was wrecked on the nearby coast.

Wages of the Pembrokeshire Land Worker in about 1300

Weeding . . . wheat, 1d. per acre; oats ½d. per acre. Thatching and staking Corn . . . 2d. a day. Pitching corn to the stack . . . in the hayguard 2d. a day . . . Pitching in the common fields into the cart 1 and 1½d. per day. Carter 3d. per day. Washing and shearing sheep 1d. per score. Winnowing Corn of all kinds 2d. for every 7 sieves. Thrashing wheat 2d. per quarter. Thrashing oats 4d. per 5 quarters. This extract illustrates the gradual break-up of the Feudal system and a transition from servile labour to a system on money payments for labour.

❋   ❋   ❋

Prices in 1764. 2 sheep . . . 2s. Pair of gloves 3d. . . . breeches 10 shillings, ¼ tobacco 3d. . . . coat 10/- load of lime 3/6d. . . . . Wages . . . Martha James for one year 30/- plus grey apron. Shoes 2/6d. . . . gown 5/6d. N.B. Wicker coffins were still in use.

❋   ❋   ❋

Field names at Tankeston (Tancredston)

Hill Meadow, Upper Moor, Little Hill, Hayguard Meadow, Lower Croft, Small Meadow, Hollum Croft, Church Park, Hollum, Bollum, Upper Croft, Middle Croft, Park Pant, Park y filly, Park y big, Longland, Park Cerrig, Mountain Penfeidir, Waun Goch, Red Moor, Park Glas.

❋   ❋   ❋

Pointz Castle field names, Moeldir, Pen quarrel, Rhyd las, Pen porth, Park dan dre, Park quarrel, Park Castell (by the old fortification) Park y hoel, Weirglodd fach, Stonyland, Mynydd fach, Park y bont, Park John Harry, Park pen groes ucha and isha, Bwlch gwyn, Park Scarborough, Park Scarborough isaf, Fflanydd, Park Mawr, Park y lan, Park y mount.

❋   ❋   ❋

"Arles or Ernes" or earnest money was given to a servant on hiring, e.g. the Shuttleworth accounts for September 1590, "4d. earnest money was paid unto a cook to serve at the next Assizes". Many other examples – 4d., 12d., the King's shilling when enlisting in the army. Also called "God's Penny" or *ernes*.

❋   ❋   ❋

Pentyparc – The Batty Attic

When I called at Pentyparc in 1981 the house was in excellent state, but what amused me was to find that one of the attics housed a large colony of bats.

❋   ❋   ❋

Penally Court

In 1852, R. Waters, Esq., lived at Penally Court and was Mayor of Tenby. The next owner was John M. Griffith and his daughter, Mary May Griffith, who when aged 25 in 1896, was appointed by Queen Victoria as Superintendent of the Royal Dairy at Balmoral.

© S.R.

Pencaer

Early Home of Dewi Emrys

SEVERAL places enjoy the glory or suffer the notoriety that a single event has thrust upon them. Such is Pencaer, promontory of crags, glens and windswept farmlands in north west Pembrokeshire. It was here that the last invasion of Britain took place in February 1797, when, after a few days of alcoholic abandon fourteen hundred Frenchmen surrendered to the local levies and, so legend tells, to red-shawled Cambrian matrons whose natural curiosity on that occasion has been interpreted as burning patriotism by their admiring descendants.

But Pencaer has more to offer than the memory of one spectacular event. Aloof from the invading crowd of visitors, travellers and hucksters who frequent the more accessible towns and villages of the county, it has retained its traditional style of life to a marked degree, and its inhabitants still tread the paths that many generations of their forebears had known. Perhaps the spirit of the place is nowhere invoked so effectively as in one of Dewi Emrys's essays: "My childhood was spent on the heather-clad hills of Pencaer in north Pembrokeshire, where nature was as unsophisticated as the people. My earliest Eden was the laden glen that never echoed the shriek of a locomotive, and my first woodland mirrors were lucent pools that had only reflected the God-made glories of heaven and earth".

One does not pass through Pencaer to reach anywhere. For it leads to nowhere. Pencaer is a land's end, girdled by the waves of St. George's Channel, embattled on the landward side by a ridge rising like some grey dragon's back, from the pip-squeak hummock of Garn Fathach to the corrugated crown of Garn Fawr towering above Pwll Deri.

These high places – there are twenty-one bearing the description 'carn' – give a special character to Pencaer. Some of their names contain echoes of the Mabinogion and the Age of Saints, while their slopes hold the graves of gold-torqued chieftains of pre-Christian days. From the peaks we can see the whole of the parish which, with the northern part of St. Nicholas pressing into Llanwnda's flank like a ploughman's thumb, encloses the land we call Pencaer, something over four miles from east to west, and half that distance from north to south. Whitewashed farms and cottages, velvet-green folds below Carn Coed, the carns, ancient stone walls and straggling hedges of thorn and furze, the bellcote of the venerable parish church, the tree-lined drive of Penysgwarne, the hermit outposts Carncoed, Penrhyn, Globo Fawr, Plas-y-binc, Pantybeudy; and the friendly heather everywhere, all convey the feeling that we have reached a land unchanged and unchanging, a relic of early Dyfed, a traditional tapestry, happily now preserved within the confines of our National Park.

I found that the best way to absorb the atmosphere of this land, to receive the message it has to impart, was to follow the trail of the cairns, starting in the east at Garn Wen on the confines of Pen Cw. On this outcrop sprawl the broken remains of several megaliths, and at nearby Penrhiw a massive cromlech still stands in the spot where gnarled Celtic hands first raised it some two thousand years ago. The older folk still speak of the "Viking funeral" when the body of a squire of Penrhiw was borne down to a boat on Goodwick beach, rowed by tenants across the waters of Fishguard Bay to Pwllgwaelod, and finally laid to rest in the churchyard on the Cwm yr Eglwys strand.

From Carn Wen the land slopes by Cile, Craig Elir, and Carn Hendy, to the dented coastline where Penanglas thrusts boldly into the sea. Tradition declares that a secret tunnel connected Aberanglas to the house of Penrhiw, a haunt of smugglers, whose chief, "Old Rogers", amassed sufficient wealth to purchase respectability, afterwards sealed by marriage with a daughter of a county family. A sense of seclusion, sometimes a little disturbing, settles on those who walk these lonely cliffs, by Carn Fathach, and by Maen Jaspis where the purple-red vein of jasper reminds us that it is of such that the gates of Paradise are wrought.

We must pause a while at Parc Ffynnon Wnda on Penfeidir land, for here is the holy well of the local saint, a shrine that has known the hymns and supplications of generations of Christians – *Sanctus Gwnda ora pro nobis* – now neglected, shrouded over with weeds and brambles, and silent, save for the muted melody of its waters as they trickle through bracken and bush towards the dingle of Penycwm.

A short walk brings us to Carn Wnda on whose western brow stands the cromlech Carreg Samson, where, we are told, slumbers the giant who in mighty rage had hurled skywards a massive boulder which landed at Goetan nearly a mile away.

Below the Carn, the hamlet of Llanwnda clusters around the church, dedicated to Gwnda, saint and philosopher, whose wise sayings are preserved in the yellowing folios of a manuscript in the British Museum. Giraldus Cambrensis occurs in the list of its vicars. Several Celtic crosses in the walls, and the rude construction, attest the undoubted antiquity of the fabric. On one side of the churchyard, burial gardens, silent roofless cells, enclose the tombs of gentles of long ago, Harries of Penrhiw, Williams of Carne Coch, and the Mortimers of Penysgwarne and Tre Howel, descendants of mail-clad Norman barons, whose exclusiveness even in this final acre strives vainly to show that Death is no leveller.

Beyond winding Feidir Eglwys we arrive at Castell, a little dwelling built snugly in the armpit of a prehistoric fort called Castell Gladys after a heroine of these parts. On the coast, a few fields from the fortification, the sequestered cove of Abergladys also preserves her memory, while further inland she is commemorated by the name Yet Ladis, a narrow pass on the ridge, haunted at the witching hour by two ladies accompanied by a fearsome hound, spectral sentinels of the approach to her former home.

Llanwnda church

Southwards, beyond Garn Cowil and Garn Gelli and Fron (where lived the ancestors of the late Sir Clement Price Thomas), is Rhosycaerau, early home of Dewi Emrys. The *caerau* at the fringe of the open wind-whipped moor have long since disappeared and in their place stands a weather-tiled chapel, where Dewi's father had ministered, an early "mother church" belonging to the Independents. Not far away are the Cotts whose *baban diwrnod oed* inspired the muse of Ceiriog, and the farmlands of Carne Coch, Cnwc y Wrach, Ffynnon Dridian, Caer Segan and Trefelgarn.

On Carn Brisgarn are remains of a cromlech and a curious megalith known as Cader y Cawr, reputed throne of yet another boulder-throwing giant; then on to Garn Folch and the ruined site of Tref Cilhwch where primitive tribesmen had huddled within stone-built cots. We are now in the very heart of Pencaer; everywhere along the slopes the heather runs like purple waves, there are burgeoning furze bushes alive with golden bloom, low hedges rambling in no apparent pattern, and faint grass-grown pathways leading to abandoned holdings and ruined dwellings. Isolated farms court the peace of the coastal strip; Dritwg, Penrhyn, Mesur Hirion, Trefisheg, Caerlem, one with the chilly name of North Pole, another with the more sanguine one of Good Hope.

Just below the cottage of Tai Bach Gwalchmai is another relic of the ancient faith, St. Degan's holy well, source of a shy rill which winds its brief course to the sea below the headland of Cnwc Sant Degan where the name Capel Degan denotes the site of hallowed ground. Degan escaped to this hermitage when a great disaster led to the inundation of the fair lowland that once bordered Pencaer, and the hoof marks of the steed that bore him to safety can still be seen by those determined to interpret certain indentations on rocks hereabouts. His memory survived well into modern times, and his shirt, allegedly possessing miraculous properties, was carefully preserved on a local hearth as late as the eighteenth century. Of his chapel no trace remains and we cannot avoid the melancholy reflection that another house of God, namely Salem, a disused Nonconformist chapel between Carn Glotas and Ffynnon Degan, will soon share the fate of Degan's fane.

The fields beyond Capel Degan belong to Tresinwen, cradle of the ancestors of David Lloyd George, and in the present century once home of the scholarly Dr. B. G. Charles. Beyond the cove of Porth Sychan we can see the last farm on the headland, remote Llanwnwr, Brontën in its grey aloofness. Here too, a medieval chapel had served the district, but today only faint traces of the burial ground remain to proclaim its former existence. Beyond the furthermost tip of the headland, on the islet of Ynys Michael, stands the light-house of Strumble, a guide and warning to mariners – Pencaer's sole concession to modern architecture. In its vicinity, places called Carreg y Wrach, Pwll Ffwlied and Ogof y Drwg retain echoes of a more superstitious age.

From Carn Gilfach the ridge ripples on towards Garn Fechan, from where we breast the slopes of Carn Fawr rising to a height of over 670 feet. This is the roof of Pencaer, where we can enjoy an extensive, almost a bird's-eye view of the greater part of the land over which we have walked. Around its crest are stone and earthen ramparts of the powerful hill-fort built during the Iron Age, perhaps earlier, and still in a good state of preservation.

On the lower slopes, at Talygaer farm, is an equally well-preserved circular stone-built pigs' cot, the only one of its kind left in Dyfed.

No longer are the people of Pencaer obliged to build bastions against warlike marauders. On one side of Carn Fawr stands a youth hostel built in a style fully in sympathy with the traditional buildings of the district: on the other side, the unpretentious roadside chapel of Harmony and its manse, for many years home of "Arianglawdd", pastor, bard, antiquary, winner of eisteddfodic laurels. Further afield rise the roofs of old manorial messuages – Trefayog, Trellys, Tresisillt, now flourishing farms, while above Abermawr, the rook-haunted residence of Tregwynt remains the sole survivor of the spacious days of squirearchy. Near the fern-covered earth fort of Castell Poeth is the hamlet of Trefasser Gledde Goch. Local folk have always liked to believe that the name preserves the memory of the eminent Asser, cleric and friend of Alfred the Great, at whose court he spent most of his days. Whether indeed it was Asser's birthplace or whether the place-name inspired the acceptable belief, I cannot say, but it was most certainly the boyhood home of a distinguished churchman of our time, namely the Right Reverend Dr. J. J. A. Thomas, formerly Bishop of Swansea and Brecon.

Beyond the western flank of Carn Fawr, down the abrupt, difficult slope, a surprising cauldron of boisterous spume and spray, a "magic casement opening on the foam", meets our gaze; Pwll Deri, abode of legend and mystery, that drew from Dewi Emrys the joyous melody that still lives on the lips of his countrymen.

Pwll Deri is formed like an heraldic lunette, the northern horn ending in the promontory fort of Dinas Mawr, the southern horn slipping away past Carn Ogo to the blunt nose of Pen Bwchdy. Within their embrace, and protected by precipitous cliffs, are the inlets of Ogof March and Aber Twn, the stark rocks of Trwyn y Badau and wave lashed Carreg y Gerwinau, while a little further south are Godor Mabli and Pwll Crochan that mark the southern limit of Pencaer. Access to the pebbly beach is particularly hazardous, although somewhere down the cliff face winds a secret way known to adventurous rum-runners of long ago. But it is denied to us, and we must relish the scene as Dewi Emrys relished it:

Rown i'n ishte dwe uwchben Pwllderi,
Hen gatre'r eryr a'r arth a'r bwci.

And it is above Pwll Deri that we, too, linger. On the spot where Dewi brooded above wave and crag stands a long grey stone, raised in his memory by a group of admirers, engraved with the terse inscription, "Dewi Emrys 1881-1952", and a couplet from his famous poem. Simple words, a simple stone. These commemorate no simple man, but one who was a strange compound of complexity and naturalness, conformity and rebellion, homeliness and sophistication, whose mind wandered and sang like the meandering rivulets of the Pencaer of his youth, and sometimes rose in erratic notes like the wayward gusts that sweep over Pwll Deri and the open moorland above. It was this primeval scene that recalled to his mind the strange phantom that haunts these cliffs; the *bwci* that lurks in the minds of all, even of those who aver that they cannot believe what they cannot explain.

Perhaps, one dark night we ourselves may meet the *bwci* which has lived in folk-memory for nearly five hundred years.

In the time of Henry VIII, Gruffydd, Lord of Trellywelyn, owned all the land of Pencaer and a vast estate stretching away through mid-Pembrokeshire to the bridge of Llanglydwen in far-off Dyffryn Taf. A violent feud broke out between him and the nobles of Cemais. The latter planned to raid Trellywelyn, kill its owner, and carry away his cattle and wealth. One autumn evening mounted raiders assembled in Cwm Gwaun, but as it was too light for their purpose they lingered at an alehouse near Fishguard until the first owl-calls summoned them to resume their vengeful pilgrimage. One Howel bach, a hunchback servant of the Lord of Trellywelyn, happened to call, and soon divined the in-

tentions of the armed men. He slipped away, and at dusk reached the plas to warn his master. Hurriedly they collected the jewels and plate, which they buried in a secret place in the garden, barely in time, for the raiders were charging towards the house. Gruffydd and Howel escaped through the groves of Manorowen, over the moorlands and ridges, till they came to the refuge of Carn Ogo above Pwll Deri. Here the fugitive lord afterwards lived, food being brought to him from the neighbouring farms by his devoted retainer. When he died, Howel buried him in a cleft within the cave. Later, when he felt that his own years were numbered, Howel made his way to the cave and laid himself down at the side of the master he had served so long. It is told in Pencaer that peasants who ventured to this secluded spot at vesper time on the eve of the feast of St. Michael, have seen a tall cloaked figure standing watch on Carn Ogo and at his side the crouched form of faithful Howel bach.

PRIZE PEMBROKESHIRE PORKERS

PEOPLE born outside the Premier County, thereby missing the privilege of being "Pembrokeshire men born and bred", sometimes laughingly refer to us natives as "Pembrokeshire Pigs". It has often struck me that these people imagine that our pigs are just ordinary little porkers – something similar to those that live in other parts of the Principality. However, in his sketch I propose to introduce them to some real pigs, trusting that they will thereafter remain for ever silent, or, at least, that they will utter the phrase "Pembrokeshire Pigs" as an acknowledgement of their own unfortunate inferiority!

The first pig I beg to introduce to you was a regular Goering of his day, and this is the way that *The Cambrian* of 7 February 1807, informed a startled public of what was going on in the pleasant Hundred of Castlemartin: "A pig of the old Pembrokeshire breed, reared by Lord Cawdor, was slaughtered a few days since at Stackpole Court; its height was 3 feet 5 inches, girth 8 feet 1 inch, length from the nose to the root of the tail 6 feet 7 inches, and weighed when alive 50 score 17 lbs. The four quarters with the head weighed 43 score 17 lbs., and the rough fat 45 lbs. The meat was distributed amongst His Lordship's cottagers and labourers."

The next pig was a mere tiddler compared with Lord Cawdor's outsize pet, but would still make a good standard-bearer for the county. I introduce him to you from the pages of *The Shrewsbury Chronicle* of 17 February 1826: "Mr. James MacLauren, of Clyn Kemes (sic) in the parish of New Moat, Pembrokeshire, killed a Pig, weight 36 score and 5 lbs., a cross between a thorough Berkshire and old Welsh kind, three and half years old." Readers will do well to note how the Editor of the *Chronicle* uses a capital letter for Pig as a mark of respect to the Clyn Kemes product.

Ten years rolled by, ten years of silence and the Welsh nation, after the shocks of 1807 and 1826, returned to their normal life and laughter was again heard in the mountains and vales of Cambria. It would appear that they had forgotten Pembrokeshire entirely, or else had returned to their scoffing ways and, possibly, the phrase "Pembrokeshire Pigs" was again bandied about. But retribution was at hand.

On 9 January 1836, the blow fell, and the peace of a thousand households was shattered. White-faced Welshmen spoke with bated breath to their neighbours, and in the inns men drank their ale and said but little. For on that date *The Merthyr Guardian* published the following bulletin: "On 6 January 1836, a hog belonging to Mr. Edw. Pritchard of the Nelson Hotel, Milford, was slaughtered, which weighed the enormous weight of 45 stone 6 lbs. It measured from snout to the heel, after being hung up 7 feet 10 inches; depth on breast, 2 feet 2 inches. Thickness of flesh on back, 12 inches; breadth over the back, 18 inches."

The pride of Pembrokeshire

So much for the Pembrokeshire Pigs! These large sizes however, were not confined to pork alone, and we read in *The Glamorgan Gazette* for 6 September 1834: "On Saturday last a calf of only 3 months old was slaughtered in Milford Market by Mr. John Lloyd, contractor to H.M. Revenue Cruisers in this port, of the enormous weight of 80 lbs. per quarter: the calf was reared by Mr. William Greenich, of South Neeston."

In these days of rationing [1941] it is good to know that the Pembrokeshire soil can produce good fare and plenty of it. Exactly a century ago, a householder asking for a pound of potatoes at Newport, might receive only half a potato! To explain this somewhat unusual phenomenon I will quote *The Welshman* of 8 October 1841: "A potato weighing 2 lbs. 9 ozs., circumference one way 22 inches, and other way 19 and half inches, was something in shape similar to an infant child, with his arms and legs off, and of the female kind. It was grown in the garden of Mrs. Lloyd, of the Castle Inn, Newport, Pembrokeshire."

I give full permission to anyone who may wish to prove to the uninformed that Pembrokeshire is the Premier County, to use the above instances which I am sure will convert the most stubborn unbeliever!

※   ※   ※

Piggy Postscript

The song *Y Mochyn Du,* sung to the tune of *Lili Lon* was once very popular in Wales.   It was written by John Owen, a servant boy at Crosswell in north Pembrokeshire to celebrate the death in the parish of a black pig. Later in life the author became the Revd. John Owen of Burry Port and he is said to have been greatly ashamed of having produced so frivolous a composition in his youth.

※   ※   ※

On 1 September 1631 John Philipps of Molleston, Thomas Philipps of Martletwy, gentlemen, with four others, assigned hogs, wine and 'wild honey' within the forest of Narberth to John Barlow of Slebech, Esq.

※   ※   ※

Misc . . . A bat is a Rod 12ft. long containing half of a linear perch of the Bishop's measure. With this bat or rod the farmers measured land. Two bats in length, and two in breadth will make a perch.

※   ※   ※

A Crymych farmer received this note from the butcher: "Can't kill you today, killing myself. Will you kill tomorrow?"

A typical farming landscape

SOME FARMERS OF BYGONE PEMBROKESHIRE

BRITISH people have long been accustomed to colonising and making fertile vast tracts of land all over the globe. All the projects of reclamation and irrigation have been rendered possible by the plough, the axe, the pick and shovel. In short, the Empire owes as much to its husbandmen, plain homely and sturdy farmers, as to its naval and military leaders – whose names and exploits are worthily recorded in our history. Yet the colonisation of Britain, which is a history of our farming community, has not been brought home to the people of these islands, and the significance of the struggles and experiments, failures and successes of farmers and landowners is now only being slowly recognised by the modern inheritors of English soil. This essay is an attempt to present the record of some men and societies who have in bygone days contributed to agricultural improvements in the county of Pembroke. This has been done for England by Professor Scott Robertson and Mary Elliott Hobbs in *Great Farmers* and it is to be hoped that in time a similar work will be produced for the Principality. It is a work that entails exacting labour and its preparation will cover a good many years. The methods by which marsh lands and tracts of heath were made to produce food and to support families is certainly worthy of permanent record. This script deals only with the fringe of the subject and a very small corner of the country.

The early eighteenth century saw a general effort being made to improve agriculture. These efforts, largely uncoordinated, represented only a small section of the farming community. However, from about 1750 there was a genuine awakening and a determined effort made by landowners and farmers to improve the condition of the land and stock. Societies were formed, rewards were offered for crops and cattle, and the Royal Society encouraged husbandry by offering premiums for good works. The results were often noted by travellers, such as Warner (*Walks in Wales*, 1798, pp. 339-342), who describes the conditions in north Pembrokeshire in 1798. He writes: "Our object was Eglwyswrw, a small village in Pembrokeshire, about six miles from Kilgarran, where we had already bespoken accommodations for the night. The road to this place carried us through a rich country, which, unlike any thing we had hitherto seen in Wales (excepting in the vale of Clwyd), exhibited a general system of good husbandry. We observed with much satisfaction the admirable effects of this system in the appearance of the lands, and the heaviness of the crops, but were still more gratified by the comfort and decency amongst the little farmers and labouring poor.

"Perhaps, throughout the whole British Empire, there is no spot where the peasantry exhibit more happiness than in the northern parts of Pembrokeshire. Their families, on an average, consists five people, provided for in the following manner – the father generally employed through the whole year by the same farmer, who allows him during the eight summer months

Thatched cottage and toll gate

four pence per day, and for the remaining four months threepence per day. He eats, however, his meals, breakfast, dinner and supper, at the farmers', and is usually allowed beside a jug of skimmed milk. The mother employs all the time not dedicated to domestic labours in knitting, or more commonly in making pieces of flannel, to be disposed of at some of the neighbouring fairs, of which there are several annual ones in every Welsh town; out of the profits of this, the rent of the cottage is usually paid. No increase of wages to the labourer takes place in general at harvest, as he expects to be recompensed in another way. But this is optional on his part; and if he choose money, the farmer gives him eight pence per day during that season. If not, he is paid what the people in this country call an huggling, a practice of the following singular nature – at Christmas, the farmer pays off a little debt which his labourer may have contracted at the millers' and presents him with three large, coarse loaves, and two large wheat loaves (each about two gallons) together with a quarter of good mutton. Thus assisted, the Pembrokeshire peasant partakes, in some little degree, of those gifts of a bountiful Providence, which the higher classes of society in other countries monopolize entirely to themselves. He sees himself brought to something like a rational level with his fellow creatures, perceives that he has a state in society and feels that the practice of certain duties results from this situation, all which convictions operate upon him as powerful motives to decency and integrity, cheerfulness and content. The cottages of this part of Pembrokeshire generally let at fifteen or eighteen shillings per annum each having a small plot of ground attached to them which enables the tenant commonly to keep a pig and very often a cow."

The north of the county was divided among a large number of landowners owning estates of something like 1,000-2,000 acres on average. In most cases the proprietors were also occupiers and ran a home farm themselves. Such were the Bowens of Llwyngwair, Warren of Trewern, Lloyd of Cwmgloyne, Lloyd of Bronwydd, Harries of Trevaccoon, Gower of Castell Maelgwn, and many others. When a family became extinct or left its ancestral seat for any other reason the incomers were usually good, substantial yeomen who farmed well and successfully. Such was Bribwell (now Blaiddbwll) in north Pembrokeshire formerly home of the Reynolds, descendants of the famous family of

Griffith of Penybenglog, which went to a Parr of Haverfordwest by marriage to the heiress of that place. Edward Williams writes of the place about 1795/6: "Bribwell a large old mansion, large Spanish chesnuts, Elms, &c., a large field of Barley in helm the crop abundant, some were opened for carrying but the quantity of Straw was great and of the most luxuriant growth the ear was generally small and the grains far from being fine, ten grains in length was the largest ear I could find. Stubble already consumed by the clover and inter-mixed natural grass to such a degree that I very much doubted whether the corn had grown on that field where it stood in helm till I was told it had by one of the workmen, about 1 or 2 tons per acre might have been mown on this field. I never saw such luxuriancy of herbage of such rapid growth in my life. The soil of this district is luxuriantly productive of grass." (Llanover MS. No. 69. N.L.W.)

A characteristic of Pembrokeshire farming at this period was to keep small stacks or helms of corn in the fields and not to carry them to the haggard. Travellers always noted this and commented thereupon. Thus, in 1801, a tourist in Haverfordwest writes: "Mr. David Reese, our Landlord [the Castle Inn] being a very communicative Man, I seized the opportunity of enquiring the reason why the Farmers stacked their Corn in the fields, and he answered, that in general they were not very nice in cleaning their fallows, and consequently the weeds were so numerous, that it required much time to dry them, and therefore if stacked in a large rick they would heat and fire, but that it was very safe even for three Months in the field, if the small stacks were well made. I do not approve of this mode of Agriculture as at best it is double trouble and expense, for each of these little stacks have a course thatch. Provisions are very dear at Haverford West, Beef 8d. Mutton 7d. and Veal fluctuating from 4½d. to 8d. as they can get it, Butter is sold for 12d., per lb. and that very indifferent. He likewise informed me that the Farmers, altho they lived in so strange and penurious a manner, were many of them opulent Men and rode excellent Horses, there was much game and good hunting in the neighbourhood. . . ." (*Tour.,* N.L.W. MS. 1340c. Wed. 9 Sep., 1801)

About this time the conditions of farming in Pembrokeshire were fairly advanced, and this was mainly due to the lead given by progressive farmers like John Mirehouse, Lord Cawdor, Thomas and Charles Hassall, and James Ackland.

Also, agricultural societies and farmers' clubs had been established in the county under the patronage and guidance of enlightened landowners, who improved their properties by encouraging their tenants, and these were responsible for great improvements in Pembrokeshire. The earliest one was "The Society for Agriculture of Pembrokeshire", formed in 1784 by Mr. Knox, of Llanstinan; others were: "The Society for the Encouragement of Agriculture, etc. in Pembrokeshire" (1806); "The Farmers' Club of Narberth" (1804); "The Pembroke Agricultural Society", formed on August 9 1817; "The Dewsland Agricultural Society " (1843) – the first secretary being Levi Griffith of Rickeston in Brawdy; "The Pembrokeshire Agricultural Association", formed in 1843; and the "Agricultural Society for the Tenants of Bronwydd", under the benevolent patronage of the Lord Marcher of Kemes.

Ploughing matches were also popular features in the last century and they were held annually at the following places (amongst others): Narberth (1804), Pembroke (1817), Norchard (1833), Dungleddy (1834), Tenby (1841), Roose (1841), Dewsland (1842), and Lawrenny (1844). Most of these were held under the auspices of the various societies and helped to make the ploughman's life more interesting and useful. There were also various cattle shows from early times, but they do appear to have been as popular in Pembrokeshire as they were in Carmarthenshire and Glamorgan.

One of the most successful farmers in the county was John Mirehouse of Brownslade, in Castlemartin. The Mirehouse family was from the north of England, John's father being the Revd. Thomas Mirehouse, Canon of Peterborough, son of John Mirehouse of Miresdyke, Westmoreland. He was educated at Clare College, Cambridge, where he graduated B.A. in 1774, and proceeded M.A. in 1777, and was a Fellow of his College. He married Mary, sister of Sir John Edwards, Bart., of Greenfields, Montgomeryshire, by whom he had seven children, the eldest being John (known as "Taffy" Mirehouse), a famous lawyer and Common Sergeant of the City of London, 1833-1850.

John Mirehouse was a well-known and popular landowner, magistrate and High Sheriff (1806), he fulfilled all the duties of a conscientious country gentleman. His fame as a progressive farmer spread throughout the land and the improvements he effected on his property in Castlemartin are a memorial to his foresight and energy.

A pioneer who was not discouraged by temporary setbacks, he gave a lead and an example to the county. He spent his whole life seeking ways and methods to improve the land until his whole estate bore the unmistakable imprint of his practical knowledge. He was considered to be one of the most successful gentlemen-farmers in the kingdom.

Three things that characterised Brownslade when Mirehouse arrived were lack of shelter from the Atlantic gales (as there were no trees), certain low swamps, and fairly dry pieces of limestone soil that lacked water. The house and buildings were in need of repair and improvement, and altogether the prospect of living at Brownslade then might easily have repelled any one. But not John Mirehouse.

Firstly he decided that he must protect his land and crops from the violent blasts from the Atlantic. About 1780-85 he started strengthening the fences and planting young trees along them. However, he found that the winter storms rendered this useless and his work was undone. He persevered, and built walls with flat stones up on top of them, forming a rude embattlement. This simple method was found to break the force of the gusts very effectively. On seeing Mirehouse's success in this, Campbell of Stackpole, and other local land-owners adopted this method of building sheltering walls on their land. Earth mounds were also raised at Brownslade with thick wattled work on them to shelter the plantations and thorn fences until they were well established

Gale-force winds

and of sufficient strength to weather the Atlantic gales. In time he had provided shelter for his cattle, crops and home. He rebuilt Brownslade and laid out very fine gardens and lawns. His neighbours warned him that he was risking losing a good deal of money and that his labours were not likely to be successful owing to the open and windswept character of the land. However, the success with which his coppices grew in their shelters turned Brownslade into a pleasant house, and his gardens ranked with the best in the county.

Part of his lands required a good deal of water, and when the weather was fairly dry the soil suffered considerably. To overcome this, he built a large reservoir which he connected by means of covered pipes to small ponds in the fields. This reservoir provided water for about 150 acres of pasture. The ponds were small and carefully made of stone and mortar and the water in them was frequently changed, so that it was always fresh and clean for the stock. Mirehouse disapproved of the idea of large ponds with trees planted around them, since the cattle would stand in the ponds under the shade of the trees during the hot spells and thus foul the water. Shade he provided by planting trees in other parts of the fields.

Facing the sea were some sandy dunes and on them, small burnet, with an abundance of yarrow, grew in some profusion. Mirehouse grew luxuriant fences of osier willow on the banks facing the Atlantic, and behind them kept a flock of South Down sheep for folding on the blowing sands, in order to assist the vegetation and to make the arable sandy lands of a finer texture.

Where John Mirehouse made a name for himself was in drainage of the marshes that once characterised the district. About a mile from Brownslade, between two small hills near the shore, was a morass about two miles long by about a quarter of a mile wide. He decided to drain this uninviting area and, by applying the principles of deep drainage, he succeeded in reclaiming some 274 acres. It cost him a good deal of labour and in the beginning he was almost led to believe that the undertaking was too much. However, by great perseverance, he attained his object, and part of the marsh was converted into the most valuable land in Castlemartin. One hundred acres was arable, the remainder pasture, and before 1800 this land, formerly a hopeless swamp, was worth fifteen shillings an acre. The whole undertaking only cost him £500 in hard cash. This enterprise won for him the Gold Medal of the Society for the Encouragement of Arts, Science and Commerce, which was awarded to him in 1800. It must be remembered that this scientific drainage was carried out successfully by Mirehouse long before the famous James Smith of Deanston Farm, who commenced operations in 1823.

On this reclaimed soil Mirehouse grew very fine wheat, coleseed and turnips, while the pasture yielded fine crops of hay and supported numerous head of his Castlemartin breed of black cattle. About 1795 he sowed 1½ bushels of oats on one acre of this land and harvested 96 Winchester bushels from it. This extraordinary return proves the exceptional fertility of the soil. He grew root crops pretty widely in order to clean the ground, especially coleseed, which he grew on an extensive scale on the reclaimed gorse. He found that it was more suitable than turnips and less affected by the fly. In this soil it grew from three to five feet high and gave much shelter to the feeding sheep. When mangled by the sheep this coleseed was not injured by succeeding frosts as turnips usually were, and they sprouted afresh however bare they were nibbled. Mirehouse sowed about two pounds to the acre and found that the cost was something like turnips. He was one of the first farmers in the county to grow turnips on a large scale, and in 1776 Brownslade was one of the few farms which produced good turnip crops. The earliest grower of turnips that is known in the county was a

The Welsh Black

forebear of the writer, one John Roberts of Tregidreg, in Mathry, who grew crops of turnips (and also flax) in 1754, and possibly earlier. Mirehouse got his turnip land ready fairly early and began to sow on 16 June, without fail, despite the condition of the weather. It was some considerable time before turnips became a popular farm produce.

Mirehouse used three types of harrows – the drag harrow, which was a large framed one with a diagonal iron bar on the surface; the diamond harrow, which was made up of four square ones joined together and drawn diagonally by the corner; and two single harrows consisting of several small ones tagged together, which he found excellent for use on rough lands. He introduced improved ploughs to West Wales, and bought two from Montgomeryshire, completely geared for £2 apiece, and four others of lighter materials for £1 17s. 6d. each.

Mirehouse summed up corn growing in the county in the following words : "Pembrokeshire has a great superabundance of wheat and oats; wheat in the southern and oats in the northern and north western parts. Of course, those grains are exported to Liverpool, Bristol, Sussex and Dorsetshire in pretty large quantities. The consumption of the lower and many of the middle classes of the inhabitants, is entirely barley; and I have some reasons for thinking, that although there may be an exportation of this grain from some parts of the county it is more than counterbalanced by importation in others, either as barley or malt; and therefore, upon an average of 7 years, I do not think Pembrokeshire supplies itself with its own consumption of barley though it makes considerable exports of wheat and oats." (Report by Revd. Walter Davies, pp. 488-9.) He grew very fine crops himself. At that time smut was common in Castlemartin wheat, and Mirehouse worked hard to eradicate it. He found that English wheat escaped it in the first year, but was afterwards liable to it. The native Welsh wheat, claimed in other parts to be quite immune from it, was found to be quite as liable to it when sown on Castlemartin soil. Mirehouse deprecated the use of medicated brine and other panaceas and claimed that clear water had been more effectual than anything to cure the seed of smut.

In a district, low lying, and inclined to be very damp, he experimented with stackyard frames to keep his corn from contact with the earth and to allow a current of air passing under them. At Brownslade he built walls of stone and mortar some two feet high with horizontal flues and perpendicular orifices at proper distances the whole length of the flues. In making the stack, poles or other substances were placed in the orifices and drawn upwards as the stack advanced in height – and by this means the finished stack was thoroughly ventilated – which was most essential in a climate so naturally humid. He was angered by the method of haymaking in Pembrokeshire. The farmers, having cut the hay, let it lie for a day or two, according to Mirehouse "thrown about in a very slovenly and idle manner". It was then collected into small cocks and left like that for another day, when the cocks were opened and scattered again. The master of Brownslade held that this method resulted in the harvested hay being of an inferior quality owing to overlong exposure to sun, dews and rain.

He kept good cattle and his herds were praised by noted breeders of the day. It was the old black breed of the county that grazed the pastures of Brownslade. The black breeds of Roose and Castlemartin had been kept pure until the opening of this century. The latter have more quality and less bone and are shorter legged and not so big as the Roose beast. The Castlemartin lacked fineness of horn, but it is a favourite saying: "Don't buy me a bull without a good thick horn – his stock feed and come to the weight best." The Castlemartin cows are generally good, and like most Pembrokes, with white spots, and white under the belly – and horns yellow with a black tip. Varieties of old Castlemartin bred in Dewsland were the Llanreithan blacks (Harries) and the Mabws breed (Evans).

Mirehouse was popular with his tenants and the labouring poor. In 1798/9, when prices were very high, it was feared that there would be riots in Pembroke and the adjoining villages, and Lord Cawdor seriously considered calling out the militia. But Mirehouse and Adams of Holyland, staunchly supported the poor people, and succeeded in lowering the market prices of essential foods. In October 1803 beef in the Pembroke market was fourpence a pound and labourers' wages eightpence a day. At this time, the price of provisions were lower in south Pembrokeshire than any other part of Wales, owing entirely to the firmness of Mirehouse and other landowners in the district, who furnished their cottages with necessaries at the normal rates during the time of scarcity. He did not believe in raising the labourers' wages – his idea being that it was better to keep down the price of provisions. Malkin, writing of Mirehouse in this connection says "Yet there is nowhere a more contented set of cottagers than in Pembrokeshire, because they have many privileges conceded by their employers which place them on a level with the increased demands of the times without raising their pride or tempting their morals by an addition of pecuniary payment". Mirehouse believed in granting leases for one life only. He inserted restrictive clauses to prevent the tenants exhausting the soil, and held out the prospect of a renewal to the son of the lessee. This stimulated good farming in both farmer and son and served to keep the same families on the same farms for generations.

TO
LABOURERS.

WANTED several LABOURERS who can undertake the making of HEDGES on PORTFIELD, for inclosing Lands allotted to "The Trustees for the "Freemen of the Borough and County of the Town "of Haverfordwest."

☞ The Hedges are proposed to be let to Labourers by the Perch, and Particulars may be obtained on application to WM. PHILLIPS, Hill-Street, Clerk to the said Trustees, any time before TUESDAY, the 14th day of JANUARY instant.

Haverfordwest, January 7th, 1840.

Joseph Potter, Printer, Haverfordwest.

John Mirehouse of Brownslade, died on Saturday, 29 March 1823, and "had the consolation of being surrounded in his last moments not only by his family, but by six of his servants, three of whom had lived with him upwards of forty, and the remainder above twenty years". He had farmed over 2,000 acres of land in Castlemartin and his name had become a proverb of good farming in West Wales.

The neighbours of Brownslade were the Campbells of Stackpole, who were also notable farmers. The three most outstanding in the efforts to improve farming in the Castlernartin hundred were: John Campbell, created Baron Cawdor of Castlemartin in 1796; John Frederick Campbell, first Earl Cawdor (died 1860); and the second earl who died in 1898. Under the fostering influence and example of this family, the Castlemartin district became known as "the garden of the county". The Stackpole family were foremost in forming farmers' societies and gave valuable prizes to encourage the agricultural population.

One of the first tasks to which the family applied that industry usually associated with the name Campbell, was the draining of the Castlemartin gorse and the low lying bogs on the Stackpole property. This was effected with considerable success and the family then introduced the Dutch plough for use on the reclaimed soil. This plough had a broad wing and firm share, with a long taper point, circular traversing coulters, curved earth-board, single tail, and a sliding gauge to the beam to regulate the depth of the furrow, with a swivel at the point of the beam to regulate the width (Hassall). The soil of the reclaimed gorse was extraordinarily fertile, and from its tillering property thin sowing was a necessity. On one occasion 96 bushels of oats were gathered from twelve gallons of seed per acre on this reclaimed soil. At Stackpole, wheat was sown at three Winchester bushels per acre, barley 3½ bushels, but on the best lands there 2½ bushels were found sufficient.

Speaking of this country in his *Report*, Hassall says: "The property of this valuable tract is in very few hands. From Freshwater East Bay, along the southern coast by Freshwater West, round the south cape of Milford Haven, and up the Haven for several miles; comprehending a tract of country of about fourteen miles in length and of various breadths from seven to four, including the entire parishes of Stackpole, St. Petrox, Bosherston, St. Twinnels, Warren, Castlemartin and Angle, together with a considerable part of the parishes of Roscrowther, Pwllcrochan and Pembroke, containing about 16,000 acres, is the entire property of Mr. Campbell of Stackpole Court, and forms one of the finest and best connected estates that has ever fallen within my observation in any part of the Kingdom; being all valuable land, without the intervention of mountain waste or common."

The Castlemartin gorse was formerly a tract of several hundred acres covered with rush, sedge or coarse unprofitable grass. John Campbell obtained an Act of Parliament to drain and enclose this tract. He drained it by making deep ditches – most of which were planted with willows and other suitable trees. The greatest part of it was immediately tilled preparatory to its being converted into meadow. The improvement was effected by paring with a plough of the type used in the Cambridgeshire fens, and burning as a preparation for coleseed; after which a crop or two of corn has been taken to bring the soil fit to receive grass seeds. Hassall, in his *Report*, says: "No agricultural improvement that I have been a witness of in the course of extensive and long experience, has succeeded

Orielton

better than this undertaking; which promises in a very few years to become some of the most valuable land in the county. It is now the entire property of Mr. Campbell of Stackpole Court."

The owners of Stackpole were foremost breeders of the famous Castlemartin black cattle, and they helped to improve the breed. In 1794, Pembroke bulls sold from 8 to 12 guineas, and in 1802 yearling bulls were sold for 18 guineas. The Castlemartin oxen were used as draught beasts, and they were well-known for their good going. Nearly all the old time tourists who came to the county refer to the reckless speeds of these ox-drawn chariots. It was a popular saying that in a chariot race drawn by oxen, it was Pembrokeshire against All England for a thousand guineas! John Hook Campbell of Bangeston, Lord Lyon King at Arms (died 1795), uncle of the first Lord Cawdor, introduced the old Leicester cattle into the county, but they were not kept pure, and a cross of them was kept at Stackpole and Brownslade in 1802. The Campbells also introduced the Suffolk punch into the county late in the eighteenth century and, crossed with the native breed, produced very good results. There were some of these Suffolks still at Stackpole in 1802, but they seemed much inferior to the best Montgomery kind.

The family helped to establish a number of cattle shows and agricultural societies in the county. Lord Cawdor and Sir John Owen of Orielton, were patrons of the Pembroke Farmers' Club formed in 1817. In 1824, Lord Cawdor helped to establish three annual cattle fairs at Carew (1 May, 2 August and 9 November). He was an exhibitor at these early shows and won several prizes. At the show of cattle, sheep and pigs of the Pembrokeshire Agricultural Society at Haverfordwest on Tuesday, 4 August 1807, the following prizes went to his lordship : Best two-year-old heifer, best yearling ram, two year-old ram, and the best pen of two-year-old ewes. In 1808 he scored successes with his heifers, yearling rams and ewes. In 1812 he was again to the fore with yearling bulls and ewes.

Two of the best-known agriculturists in Wales were Thomas Hassall of Cilrhiwe (ob. 8 November 1813), and Charles Hassall of Eastwood, near Narberth (ob. May 1814). They established themselves in Pembrokeshire in the latter half of the eighteenth century and became well-known as progressive farmers, land agents, secretaries of agricultural societies, and authorities on enclosures. Of the two, perhaps Charles was the more accomplished. He had gained favour in the eyes of Lord Cawdor and the Honourable Charles Greville, one of the founders of Milford, and became subsequently an important man in the county. For some time he was steward to the Llanstinan Estate (Knox), but owing to some disagreement he was dismissed from that appointment. He appears to have been an extremely able person with considerable force of character. Sir Thomas Picton of Poyston (killed at Waterloo in 1815), fought a duel with him with pistols at thirty paces and narrowly missed being killed in the encounter.

He held a number of public appointments in connection with surveying and farming generally. In 1791 he was selected surveyor to the South Wales Association for the Improvement of Roads. He was employed by the Government in 1795 in making a survey of an immense tract of waste land called the Great Forest of Brecknock (at one time belonging to the Duke of Buckingham, but forfeited to the Crown), to ascertain what parts of it were capable of being improved by cultivation. He was an active Commissioner for Enclosures for the counties of Pembroke, Carmarthen and Glamorgan, and also acted in that connection for Merionethshire in 1809. An authority on drainage, he assisted Sir John Owen of Orielton, to drain the Ten Marshes. Naturally, enclosures aroused a good deal of controversy and in 1810 the following note was anonymously sent to Hassall:

To the encouragers of Inclosures – A Hint.

> *It is a Sin in Man or Woman*
> *To steal a Goose from off a Common,*
> *But who can plead that man's excuse,*
> *Who steals a Common from a Goose.*

The "Answer to the Hint by C. Hassall" is as follows:

> *He stands in need of no excuse*
> *Who feeds an Ox where fed a Goose –*
> *Expels a base encroaching Crew,*
> *And gives each honest Man his due,*
> *Who bids the Ocean keep its Bounds*
> *And not intrude on People's Grounds*
> *Witness the Marshes near this Town*
> *So lately cloathed in dreary brown;*
> *But now are always to be seen,*
> *In gay and everlasting Green.*

The honours of that exchange go to Hassall, I feel. "The marshes near this Town" were the Tenby marshes.

In 1794 there appeared a *Report – A General View of the Agriculture of the County of Pembroke with observations on the means of its Improvement, by Charles Hassall. Drawn up for the consideration of the Board of Agriculture and Internal Improvement.* This report is a comprehensive survey, clearly and simply written, and shows an intimate knowledge of the county. It is surprising that Hassall, who was a non-Pembrokeshire man, should have been so shrewd an observer of the character of the people of Little England. His report covers nearly all aspects of agriculture and also certain other industries of the county, such as coal. He had travelled widely and observed in England and Wales, and his suggestions for improvements are sound and practicable. Hassall was a master of his job. It is in this report that we find reference to the first agricultural society in Pembrokeshire. He writes (pp. 36-7): "A Society for the encouragement of Agriculture, Manufactures and Industry, was instituted in 1784, under the patronage of Mr. Knox; which flourished for the space of six or seven years, and then became extinct; inasmuch that the premiums obtained in consequence of the advertisement of the Society, the last year of its existence, have not as yet been settled." Charles Hassall was a methodical man and did his best to teach farmers to keep proper records. Farmers, whose only account books were their right and left pockets, now kept ledgers which shewed them exactly where they stood and how and where they made profits.

In 1793 he had prepared a similar report on agriculture in Carmarthenshire which is full of valuable material. Hassall was also a citizen soldier and was appointed Major of Pioneers in Pembrokeshire in 1803, and the captains of the Hundreds (divisions of the county) had to make all their returns to him. He played a leading part in bringing Lieut.-Colonel Thomas Knox to book after his conduct in connection with the French landing near Fishguard in 1797. Charles Hassall of Eastwood died on Tuesday morning, 16 May 1814 at the comparatively early age of 60, and a mural tablet was erected to his memory in Narberth church.

The other brother, Thomas Hassall, was an equally active and energetic personality where agricultural improvement was concerned. He lived at the old country house of Cilrhiwe, in a fairly hilly and barren district, but by his extensive and judicious pursuits he improved the locality out of all knowledge. About 1802 he obtained a premium from the Society for Encouragement of Arts for reclaiming about 1,000 acres on his several upland farms. This mountain land he first enclosed into fields of ten to fifteen acres each. He then pared and burned the sod, adding to the ashes 160 bushels of lime per acre, and cropped as follows: "On 'the better' soils: 1 wheat, 2 peas, 3 white oats with red clover 8 lbs., white clover 6 lbs., hayseeds 2 bushels, or ryegrass 1 bushel, and mowed the first year's grass, as sheep would have destroyed it, especially on the light soils." "The lighter soils" were a vast alluvial mass of schistose shell combined with nearly all the varieties of the tract, whether of stones or soils, and on these he spread loam four inches deep. "The peaty soils" were drained where necessary, pared, burned and limed; always sowing the seed under the first furrow as more ploughing would have injured the soil by making it too light. On the "lowland soils," as far as the dung manure extended, he gave 80 loads an acre, with the ashes, and fallowed, sowing wheat under second furrow; and laid these down with the barley and seeds. This extensive tract in its natural state was of very little value, and grew only furze, fern and heath, etc. (*Report,* Revd. Walter Davies, 1796).

Wastrell's improved field gate, 1818

He was an active and intelligent commissioner under the Enclosure Acts for the counties of Pembroke, Carmarthen and Cardigan, was secretary of the Pembrokeshire Agricultural Society, and all shows were organised by him. He was a systematic man and kept meteorological notes for his district, making a special study of rainfall. Perhaps not as colourful a personality as his brother, Charles, he was held in high regard by landowners and farmers, and his advice and assistance was eagerly sought. Thomas Hassall died at Cilrhiwe on 8 November 1813, greatly respected by all who had known him.

We will now turn to the agricultural societies which we mentioned earlier in this essay. The most enterprising of these was "The Pembrokeshire Society for the Encouragement of Agriculture and Internal Improvements", and its shows were generally held at Haverfordwest. Members of the Society usually met at the Castle Inn, White Hart Inn, Narberth, and Eglwyswrw, where they adjudged the premiums. The exhibitors were mostly gentry and yeomen, and between 1806 and 1812 the following appear constantly as prize-winners: Cawdor, W. H. Scourfield, Henry Davis of Mullock, Evans and Eaton of Crinow, John Bateman of Sodston, Lord Kensington, Richard Mathias of Lochmeyler, Ferrior of Pierson, William Charles and John Crymes, Thomas Hassall, Davies of Penycoed, Thomas of Whiteley, and Llewhellin of Ambleston (cattle and sheep); William Francis of Longridge, used to exhibit a remarkably fine boar of Berkshire breed, which he kept for the benefit of his neighbours. In 1807 George Roch of Butter Hill, John Bateman of Robeston Wathen and James Thomas of Kilpaison, won prizes for turnip crops, John Hammett of Castell Maelgwn, Esq., M.P., took the five guinea premium for clover seed.

Labourers in husbandry were also catered for and premiums given for servants who had served long and faithfully in the service of one master, for those who had reared children without parish relief, for the best Welsh ploughman and best English ploughman. Prizes also went to draftsmen living in Pembrokeshire who produced the best specimens of skill in making implements of husbandry, such as ploughs, harrows, hoes, etc. Thus; in 1806, William Paget, wheelwright, and William Vicars, blacksmith, of Rush Acre, near Narberth, produced two chaffcutters, two ploughs, a pair of moss and seed harrows, two "hell rakes", and a winnowing machine, all of most excellent contrivance and workmanship, for which they were awarded three guineas. In the same year, Peter Davies, carpenter, and David Cornock, smith, got a premium of one guinea for a Beverston plough of first class craftsmanship, while Francis Bevan, carpenter, and Benjamin Howell, smith, received a similar premium for a Rotherham plough.

A Wastrell plough

In 1807, Thomas Matcher, labourer to the Revd. Mr. Grant of Nolton, and Morris Williams, labourer to William Evans of Bletherston, shared a guinea for having done 31 years' service apiece with their respective masters and three guineas were awarded to George Rowe, servant of John Phillips-Laugharne, for rearing children without parochial aid.

The secretary of the Society in 1805-07 was Charles Hassall, who was succeeded by his brother, Thomas. The chair was taken by Col. W. H. Scourfield, John Bateman, William Francis, the Revd. David Bird Allen, John Phelps of Withybush, and others. Among the judges we find Morris Williams of Cwmgloyne, the Revd. Thomas Bateman, rector of Dinas, and the Hassalls. The Society also held fairs of cattle, sheep, horses and pigs, and in 1805 Charles Hassall advertised that the Society would hold such fairs at Pembroke (12 April 1806) and at Haverfordwest (14 April 1806).

The first reference to a ploughing match in West Wales is in 1807, when the Society granted prizes for ploughing to the farm servants of the following gentlemen – Col. W. H. Scourfield and Richard Mathias of Hayston. The early ploughing matches appear to have been well organised and produced considerable improvement in tillage. On 3 November 1808, the Pembrokeshire Agricultural Society and the Narberth Farmers' Club met to witness a ploughing match in a large field on the farm of Mr. James of Camphill, near Narberth. Eleven ploughs started for the Welsh prizes and six for the free prize for English (Little England) and Welsh ploughmen. The servants of the following were the winners – 1. John Herbert Foley of Ridgeway; 2. Nathaniel Phillips of Slebech; 3. William Evans of Bletherston; 4. George Roch of Butter Hill; 5. Mr. Thomas of Egremont; 6. William Evans of Bletherston; 7. John Harding of Clynderwen; 8. Mr. Davies of Raturno. The free prize went to James Fair, servant to John Harding. The weather was uncommonly fine that day, and a large company of gentlemen and farmers had gathered to witness the proceedings. The ploughing was of a high standard, "exceeding every expectation, and the prejudice in favour of the old system vanishing like vapour before the radiance of the sunbeam. After the ploughing was over the company proceeded to a sale of some new Leicester ewes belonging to Lord Cawdor, which, being finished, they sat down to an elegant dinner at the White Hart Inn, where the evening was most agreeably spent in conversation on agricultural subjects, and the utmost harmony and good humour pervaded the societies" (*The Cambrian,* 12 November 1808).

How long this Society continued to exist I am unable to say, but the few records relating to it suggest that it took a leading part in improving the livestock of the county as well as toning up agriculture generally. The attitude of the Society to cattle breeding is well summed up in the notice of January 1806, signed by Thomas Knox pro the secretary, "The Candidates for Premiums offered for Bulls, Heifers, Sheep or Pigs, are requested to take notice that the size of the animal will not influence the Society in the distribution of the Premiums, but the form and fashion will always be considered as entitled to a preference; this notification is thought necessary in order to encourage Breeders of Stock from every part of the county to exhibit their best animals at these shows".

The Pembroke Farmers' Club for the encouragement of Agriculture and Internal Improvement was a virile and progressive association, and was responsible for considerable improvements in the farming of south Pembrokeshire. Instituted on 9 August 1817, under the patronage of Sir John Owen of Orielton, Bart., and Lord Cawdor, it was fortunate enough to receive the interest and support of such enlightened landowners as the Adams of Holyland, Allen of Cresselly, Bowling of Bulliber, Butler of Chappell and Leach of Corston. Its policy was to improve cattle breeding, corn-growing, and especially to encourage the smaller farms and labourers. No person possessing freeholds over the value of £200 per annum were to receive any pecuniary premiums offered by the Club. This was particularly encouraging to those who entered the lists against such a redoubtable farmer as Lord Cawdor. Abraham Leach of Corston, was the prime mover in this matter. Meetings were regularly held to discuss agricultural topics and to seek ways and means of general improvements.

One of the foremost of the members was Mr. David Freeman of Crickmail (described in *The Welshman* of 1842 as "probably the best farmer in the County of Pembroke"), who won numerous prizes with his black cattle. Other redoubtable sons of the Castlemartin soil were the Jermins of Brothirhill, William Greenish of Cleggars, Llewellin of Merrion Court, Davies of Hayes (a family of famous horsemen) and many others.

One of its ploughing matches took place on 5 November 1825 at Mr. Henton's farm in Yerbeston, when eleven ploughs started at eleven in the forenoon. The first prize went to the ploughman of Joseph Lewis of Lacery, using an iron plough, the second to the ploughman of William Greenish of Cleggars, using a chain plough, and the third to the ploughman of David Freeman of Crickmail, using a Scotch plough. In 1835 the number of competitors had greatly increased, and at 10 a.m. on Saturday, 12 December, twenty crack teams started on the farm of Pierce Llewellin at Merrian Court. They turned over their half acre apiece by two in the afternoon. The prizes, varying from £1 to eight shillings, were won by the ploughmen of the following: Nicholas Bowling of Bulliber, Thomas Drinkwater of Castlemartin, George Bowling of Pembroke, Pierce Llewellin, Pierce Butler of Chapel, and Sir John Owen of Orielton, Bart., M.P. Afterwards, fourteen farmers entered into a sweepstake of one shilling each to draw the straightest single furrow, which was given to John Davies of Hayes.

At the ploughing matches of the Pembroke Farmers' Club, new and improved ploughs were tried out with good results. On the principle that the proof of the pudding is the eating thereof, it was proved to the local farmers that some of the new fangled devices were worthy of adoption. Experiments were also carefully made at these meetings. On 3 December 1842, a match was held in Pembroke when twenty iron Castlemartin ploughs, one wooden Rotherham, and a two-wheel plough by Ransom started to plough their "one acre". The judges, Messrs. Roberts of Loveston, Richard Llewellin of Nash, and Drinkwater of Castlemartin, awarded the prizes to the ploughmen

God speed the plough

The winning team

of the following farmers: Pierce Llewellin, Isaac Williamson of Orielton, Bowling of Bulliber, Benjamin George of Windmill; David Freeman of Crick-mail and Griffith of The Priory. The two wheel plough, which was drawn by a beautiful pair of greys owned by Nixon of Portclew, attracted much attention, particularly to the aparent lightness of draught. The spring gauge was sent for, and on being applied to the plough, the index pointed at 3 cwt. as the average power required; it was then fixed on a swing plough and the index showed that 4 cwt. was required to turn a furrow of the same size. This created some sensation, but it was discovered that the plough was of a deep pitch, and consequently required a considerable pressure on the handles. The instrument was afterwards applied to three other ploughs and the draught was nearly the same as with the wheel plough.

The Society held numerous meetings in course of the year to award premiums and discuss farming topics. At a meeting held in The Golden Lion, Pembroke, on 2 November 1833, an improved plough was produced and drawn for, the winner being Mr. Drinkwater. It was then decided to produce an improved pair of harrows, to be drawn for in the following May. The premiums for the greatest number of acres and the best turnips cultivated on the drill system went to Mr. Freeman. It was evident that great attention had been paid to this crop by keeping it clean and free from weeds, but the turnips were very small. About this time the Society introduced a most commendable rule that no servants were to be hired without satisfactory testimonials accompanying them from their last masters.

At a dinner held in February 1841, at The Dragon Inn, Pembroke (John Adams of Holyland, in the chair, and N. A. Roch, vice-chairman), David Freeman and Mr. Parcell led a discussion on the best method of preventing smut in wheat. A premium was awarded to Pierce Llewellin for the best hunting colt bred by members. It was decided that the subject for discussion at the next meeting was to be "The best method of feeding cattle, stall-feeding or otherwise".

At the meeting held at The Lion Inn, Pembroke in November 1841, a long and interesting discussion was held on the merits of different manures. The majority were in favour of nitrate of soda, but there were a number of James Pigg's supporters there with their cry of "muck's your man". The subject for the next discussion was "The best and most economical method of keeping horses". Mr. B. Wilson won the sweepstakes for the largest turnips and he produced twelve which weighed together 134 pounds. The prizes for sheep shearing went to the servants of John Adams of Holyland and Ben George of Windmill Hill for colts and hunters: William Ormond of Coedrath, Richard Jermyn of Brothirhill, and Pierce Llewellin. Mr. Lewis of Norchard had the premium for the best pen of two-year old South-Down ewes; Pierce Butler and Pierce Llewellin for the best Leicesters. Premiums were also awarded to servants in husbandry for work and character, and for rearing children.

In August 1842, Pierce Butler was president at a meeting when the topic was, "The System of Agriculture best adapted to the soils of Pembrokeshire". It was admirably argued by Messrs. Waters of Penally, Lewis of Norchard, Bowling of Bullibar, David Freeman and others. Later on in that year the society produced a new turnip drill, which was drawn by William Ormond.

The Pembroke Farmers' Club was a live movement in the south of the county and undoubtedly did a great deal to improve agriculture in those parts. It was the district where Mirehouse, the Lords Cawdor, Mr. Ackland and the baronets of Orielton held sway, and they were all leading farmers in their time.

The Narberth Farmers' Club was also a live and flourishing affair and did much to stimulate agricultural matters in that locality. This flourishing society was fostered by such landlords as Foley of Ridgeway, Harding of Clynderwen, Phillips of Slebech, Scourfield of Moat and others. As the district was on the Welsh-English border of the county, competitions were held between the Welsh and English ploughmen. What the ancient Flemings and Welsh did with the sword they now did with ploughshares.

Early in November 1804, a ploughing match was held on the farm of John Herbert Foley of Ridgeway, on a piece of old ley that had not been broken-up for upwards of fifty years, each ploughman having a pair of horses without a driver. As soon as the ground had been measured out (about three-eighths of an acre each) eleven ploughs started for the Welsh prizes and three for the free prize for Welsh and English. The weather was very fine and a large gathering witnessed the event. The prizes went to the ploughmen of the following gentlemen: William Evans (Shropshire plough), John Thomas, the secretary (Shropshire plough), John Harding, the president (Suffolk plough), and a pair of leather breeches (value six shillings) to another servant of William Evans with a Shropshire plough. The free prize of two guineas was divided between the servants of William Francis and Nathaniel Phillips. The former, an Englishman (i.e. a Little Englander), with three horses and a driver, with Lord Somerville's plough, did his work in a highly satisfactory manner, and the latter, a Welshman, with a pair of horses without a driver, showed equal skill. "After the match the company repaired to Narberth to dinner, when the glass circulated briskly, and 'Success to the Farmers' Club,' 'Speed the Plough,' 'The Memory of the late Duke of Bedford,' 'Sir John Sinclair' and 'Lord Somerville,' were severally drunk with applause, and the remainder of the evening was spent with the utmost hilarity." (*The Cambrian,* 24 November 1804.) After the ploughing match in November 1806, near Narberth town, with pairs of horses and no drivers, the club reported that "the ploughing in general was very good and the judges had great difficulty in determining the prizes. Great progress has been made in ploughing; and the generality of farmers who were averse to this mode of ploughing are now fully sensible of its incomparable superiority. After the business of the day was over the members of the club, with other gentlemen, dined at the White Hart Inn, where the evening was spent with much pleasantness and good humour".

These dinners, following the events in the field, did much to bring farmer and landlord together.

The Narberth Club encouraged sheep farming and did a good deal in introducing the Leicestershire breed into the county. These Leicester sheep were then crossed with the native Pembrokeshire breed and the result proved most satisfactory. Among the leading lights in the sheep world in 1800-10 we can count David Rees, landlord of The Castle at Haverfordwest, also a successful and enterprising farmer, Thomas of High Toch, and Eaton of Crinow. The Club offered prizes for shearers, and shearing matches were held annually under the auspices of the Society.

David Rees was a popular figure and held the respect of the "County," since his inn was built by the Barlows for political purposes. Apart from running the tavern Rees had a considerable farm and introduced several new methods and improvements. After each harvest home he used to hold elegant entertainments on his farm for the benefit of his servants and neighbours. At these "feasts" he awarded prizes to the industrious labourers whom he encouraged in their craft. Dancing followed the repasts, which continued very often until after 4 o'clock in the morning, thus adding a touch of "Merrie England" to this remote county.

The Acklands of Boulston and Amroth, have been mentioned earlier as enlightened landowners. They experimented on their estates and held ploughing matches, sometimes at considerable expense to themselves. At the beginning of the last century, James Ackland of Amroth Castle, had a flat piece of 38 acres upon his farm which was wet and boggy, and in winter was nearly covered with water. The soil was about ten inches of peat upon clay and it produced only the coarsest aquatic grasses.

Ackland set about reclaiming this plot of ground, and it was drained, pared, burned, and limed abundantly. It produced the following crops in turn: turnips, wheat, barley, oats, with clover and ryegrass. The hay harvests were most abundant – five acres were mowed as early as 10 May, and the second crop in the beginning of July, both together amounting to 98 cart loads which came to five tons of hay per acre. Neither was there any occasion to sow any grass seed further as a good natural grass grew in abundance. The value of this piece of ground was increased from £4 10s. per acre to at least 40 guineas as a result of Mr. Ackland's industry.

On 17 December 1833, a ploughing match was held at Norchard under the patronage of Robert Innes Ackland of Boulston, when the judges were Abraham Leach of Vaynor, Robert Dempster of Cornel, and Mr. Protheroe of Wiston. Sixteen ploughs entered the lists and the prizes went to the servants of Messrs. Evans of Clarbeston, Hitchlimp of Boulston Farm, Robbin of Parkfield, Currie of Rosehill (agent to Baron de Rutzen of Slebech) and Abraham Leach, Esq. Afterwards, Mr. Ackland regaled the company to a dinner at Norchard Farm house, and in an address to the gathering, he stated that as long as he lived he would support the farmers of Pembrokeshire to the utmost.

The Dungleddy ploughing matches started in 1833, and here the chief supporter was Sir Richard Bulkeley Philipps, Bart., M.P. of Picton Castle. The chief prize-winners were the servants of Messrs. Gwyther of Farthingshook, Hitchings of Boulston, Furlong of

Churchill, Robbin of Portfield, Currie of Rosehill, Isaacs of Shoalshook, Hughes of Toch and Smith of Knock. Sir Richard Philipps always sent his ploughmen to these matches, and they brought home several prizes.

The Tenby ploughing matches were held at Astridge (1841), Gumfreston, Knighton, etc., and received support from landowners and farmers like the Collens of Molleston, Waters of Penally Court, Ormond of Wedlock, Thomas Lewis of Norchard and George Hughes of Park House.

The Lort-Phillips family of Lawrenny, fostered ploughing matches in the home district, and the Allen of Cresselly, also lent their support. They appear to have had unusually large "fields," as, for instance, in February 1844, when thirty ploughs started for the prizes.

The Hundred of Roose – ancient home of the Flemings – had its ploughing matches, and good farmers have always been bred in this division of the county. The matches were held at Copeston, Herbrandston, Steynton, Barretts Hill, etc. The leading lights were Squire R. B. Child of Newton, Brown of Thornton, Will Davies of Capeston, Greenish of Neeston, Marychurch of Johnston, Devereux of Sodbury, Laningan of Hasguard, and James of Broadmoor.

The earliest reference I have seen to Roose ploughing matches is in 1841, but they were probably held prior to that date. They had very large fields, 38-40 ploughs generally entering the lists.

The hundred of Dewsland also had its Agricultural Society and its ploughing matches. The Society was formed in 1841, and Levi Griffith of Rickeston, in Brawdy, was its first secretary. The mainstays were the Griffith family of Pointz Castle and Rickeston, Harries of Trenichol, Gwyther of Brawdy, Rheynish of Eweston, Reynolds of Treglemais, Mortimer of Trewellwell, Steel of Hayscastle, and others. At a ploughing match held at Tregadogan, near Solva, in 1842, twenty-two ploughs started for the prizes, which were won by John Harries of Trewillim, Thomas Beynon of Lochvane, Richard Thomas of Newhouse, John Phillips of Trenewydd, and William Howell of Pointz Castle.

We find inventors sending specimens of their handicraft to Pembrokeshire for demonstration purposes and as an advertisement. Thus, in 1805, a threshing machine, on an entirely new principle was exhibited at Trevaine Farm near Tenby. It was made by Perkins & Son of Stockton-upon-Tees, and its merits were that it threshed more cleanly and with greater ease than any other machine and cleared 200 Winchester bushels a day. Improvements in design of implements was greatly encouraged by the societies, who gave premiums to the local craftsmen, smiths and carpenters, chiefly for producing implements of an improved nature.

I trust that this brief record will show to the people of today that great and commendable efforts were made to improve agriculture in the last century by men whose names are almost forgotten by us who reap the benefit of their labours but the form and fashion will always be considered as entitled to a preference; this notification is thought necessary in order to encourage breeders of stock from every part of the county to exhibit their best animals at these shows.

AGRARIAN DISORDERS AT PEMBROKE

date early but unknown

THE years following upon 1795 brought scarcity of foodstuffs in the country and this led to high prices which were beyond the means of the poorer classes. The result was riots, and troubles disturbed the life of the county, and the militia had to be called out to restore order. In Castlemartin were two distinct parties – the farmers who were supported by Lord Cawdor of Stackpole on the one hand, and the people who were supported by Adams of Holyland and Ackland of Earwere and Boulston. I have come across some letters relating to the affair, and extracts from them are herewith presented to Pembrokeshire readers for the first time.

Major Joseph Adams
The first letter was written from Holyland on Sunday 8 November 1795, by Major Joseph Adams, to John Campbell of Stackpole Court, afterwards, Lord Cawdor. Joseph Adams was born in 1742, and entered the regular army where he rose to the rank of Major. He married Elizabeth, daughter of the said John Campbell, by whom he had a son, Alexander Adams, who became a Lieutenant-General. Descendant of an ancient and illustrious county family, Joe Adams as he was generally known, was a popular figure in the life of Little England and took a leading part in the formation of the Pembroke and Castlemartin Yeomanry (now the 102nd Field Regt. RA in which I held a commission for some time). In this letter we hear the first reference to the coming storm. He writes, "there was yesterday at Haverfordwest an assembly of the Justices of the Peace for considering the Duke of Portland's letter to the Lord Lieutenant relative to Corn. I conversed with some of them, and it was the general opinion of those, there is not enough for the consumption of this county in it. The great Barley District, St. Davids, is worse this year than the last, as Mr. Harries of Criglase says who has the Tithes of that District, and though the appearance at Harvest was favourable yet on Threshing it proves to yield poorly . . . "

Before December of the same year things were coming to a head and Joe Adams attributes a good deal of the trouble to the farmers and factors who, despite the shortage, were intent on exporting the scarce commodity. In a letter dated 8 December 1795, Joseph Adams puts the matter clearly to John Campbell, and takes his stand by the people or, "the lower orders of People" as he calls them. He states: "I thank you for your kind letter which I read yesterday and perfectly agree with you in opinion relative to the Exploitation of Corn , the supplying the Markets, and also that no language should be held to irritate a Mob but unhappily great cause was give for alarm by Roch of Paskeston and Hervey of Angle buying up wheat to export. The Report from the Magistrates to the Duke of Portland's letter was that wheat is the shortest crop, and there is certainly not enough in this County for its consumption. If then the Middle Class are sufferers will they not Complain? and their Complaints go a great way to irritate the lower orders of People who have most intercourse with them. The farmers had withheld from Supplying the Market for a fortnight to enhance the Price then too great, and notwithstanding every Argument of Policy and Interest to them they would not be prevailed on Until the People grew tumultuous. Now they are justly Alarmed as also are The Corn Factors, the Farmers have promised a Constant Supply to the Markets and the Factors will not export. So good is come from Evil. You seem to think that Party or jealousies were the cause, but I do assure you I never saw all Ranks, Parties, or Classes of People so irritated (Farmers and Factors excepted) and all joining in the same Language. The Heat is now, thank God, allayed, and I trust no cause will be given to revive it, for then no one can pronounce what consequence will ensue. Your name had been glanced at, as acting in contradiction to the spirit of the resolutions you brought forward at the Quarter Sessions, by letting Bangeston to Harvey. I told Mr. Mirehouse (of Brownslade, one of the finest farmers and model landlord of his times) of it, and afterwards it was reported he was concerned with Harvey. I desired Mr. Hand to tell him of it that he might justify himself. Enclosed is his letter to me and my answer. Since Harvey has declared Mirehouse is not concerned, but you'll see by M's letter to me there was a Plan which M. says you are acquainted with. I mention this as I am zealous for your Honor and I think I should not act right by you in not acquainting you with it. The Fencible with Capt. Ackland, and the Yeomanry paraded on Saturday last, and will again next market day, so that I hope all will be quiet, but I repeat, it depends on the supplying the Markets, and no exploitation. . . ."

Major Dudley Ackland
The next notice we have is contained in the letter written to John Campbell by Major Dudley Ackland of Pembroke, afterwards of Boulston. Ackland was born in Philadelphia

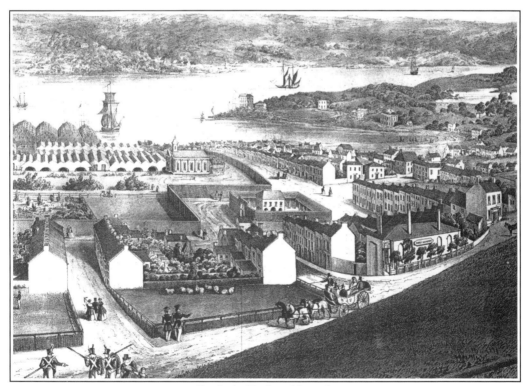

Pembroke Dock and barracks

in 1748, entered the regular army and rose to be a major in the 91st Regiment. In 1783 he married Jane, daughter of F. Innes of Coleraine, Ireland. He settled in Pembroke town for some years, and in 1797 he purchased Boulston and built the modern house. He died in 1809. Like Joseph Adams he sided with the people in opposition to John Campbell, and in his letter dated at Pembroke, 10 March 1796 on his return from Earwere, he states ". . . I should have wrote you an account of the Field Day had our meeting been such as I expected it would when I last wrote to you, but the day turned out so exceedingly cold and windy and only sixteen attending, we made a very short business of it; and appointed another meeting that day fortnight, which will be next Tuesday, when I hope we shall do better. I shall wait your Orders for our meeting weekly or once a fortnight whichever you please. My Brother's account of the conduct of the Troop and his own Company is highly flattering to both, and I have no doubt but they would have supported the Magistrates and their officers properly – however I sincerely hope neither the one or the other will ever be brought to the disagreeable necessity of Firing upon poor Creatures who have certainly great reason to complain: for I am convinced and so are all your Friends here that the Scarcity at Pembroke is Artificial and not Real, and that two thirds of the Corn remains unthreshed and that it is owing to the Avarice of the Farmers our Markets are so high.

"I have the mortification to find on my return to Pembroke, that mutton is at 5d. a pound, (the same as I paid in London and Bath all the Winter for the best), and here I have had some at nine months old. This is so glaring an Imposition, that we have come to a Resolution of not buying it till the price falls. Annexed you a Copy of the Resolutions which is signed by all the principal People here and we mean to send it to Haverfordwest for the same purpose. In this business the Farmers are alone to blame, for the price of the sheep is so high to the Butcher that he cannot get above a Shilling or eighteen pence for his trouble. In short every order of People here are dissatisfied with the attempts to impose upon them, and do not allow that Farmers here have a right to charge as much as in England where the price of labour is double and the Rent of Farms much higher: and what is remarkable there never was known any Winter to be more grass in the Country than the last. Mr. Painter has just told me that the price of sheep at Pembroke is £33 a score . . . ."

Butter is a great luxury

The copy of the Resolution states that the undersigned will not submit to the "Injurious Combination against the Public . . . the means of absolutely starving the lower order of Industrious Tradesmen and Labourers"; they will not suffer beef to be sold at more than 4½d. per lb., and butter at 9½d. per lb. They will boycott the farmers and the market till these prices are agreed to.

A Pembrokeshire market day

This letter apparently left John Campbell unmoved, and on 27th March, Dudley Ackland writes an ultimatum to Stackpole Court and tenders his resignation as an officer of the Castlemartin Yeomanry. He writes that the principal people of Pembroke are solid in support of the Resolution mentioned above, and "we are determined to go on, and not to recede(?) as long as there is a possibility of holding out – notwithstanding the threats of sending the Mutton to another market. You say Butter is a Luxury. I grant it is, but it is such a one as the poor of this Country have always indulged in, and it cannot be supposed they can live on Barley Bread alone . . . for the Farmers by making Fortunes on their ruin, will be enabled to pay more Rent and so establish it forever. I should tire you to mention the extortionate price of many things in the market. I shall only say that a sucking pig such as I suppose could be bought for two shillings some years ago now sells for eighteen and nineteen shillings, and they are mostly bought by the very lowest Order of People, who raise one or two in order to pay their Rents. I again repeat that there is no scarcity when Barley is brought to Market by Waggon Loads, and afterwards put up in Store because it will not fetch more than it sells for in London, and while your House at Bangeston is filled with wheat etc. by a Fellow (Hervey) who I believe does not belong to this Country and who never was before a Corn Factor. After all I have said you will see the necessity there is for my begging you will have the goodness of accepting of my Resignation as your Lieutenant, and recommend another in my room . . .".

❊   ❊   ❊

Pantseason, also Pantsaison

In 1799 one of the family, Col. John James fought a duel on the field called Fortune's Frolic, killed his opponent and had to flee to the continent. He returned to Pantsaison and died in 1819.

DEWSLAND NOCTURNE

Written 1961

IT WAS a cool September evening when I left the hospitable fireside of a farmhouse in the Brawdy district and made my way through a narrow thorn-lined lane that led past a ruined gatehouse to the highway beyond. The westering sun had dipped into the waves beyond St. David's Head, leaving mauve-red farewell streaks in a sky that had blazed with imperial splendour but an hour or so before. A few stars hung above, twinkling outriders of the moon yet to rise, twilight had faded into darkness, but as I strode along I could still discern before me the grey roadway, flanked by high banks and eastward-bowing wind-whipped thorn trees and gorse bushes, silent sentinels that had defied tempestuous rages from St. George's Channel. I had a fair way to go. My road was to take me through parts of six Pembrokeshire parishes – Brawdy, Llandeloy, Llanreithan, St. Lawrence, St. Edrins, Mathry – the very heart of the Hundred of Dewsland, ancient patrimony of the patron saint whose cathedral church some eight miles westward nestles in a hidden hollow on the banks of Alun Water, the stream that still bears the name of a Celtic god.

I am genuinely fond of walking, though there are few who would own to such diversion, for the art of walking is no longer with us. Our medieval forebears would toil cheerfully to the shrine of St. Thomas at Canterbury or to the holy well of the Blessed Virgin of Penrhys, while their descendants at the beginning of this century would trudge willingly for ten miles and more to attend a *Gymanfa* or to seek the pleasures of Portfield Fair. Today, a man who walks instead of travelling by car or bus or train, is regarded as a pretty poverty-stricken wretch, and one who will deliberately walk from pure choice an eccentric, a potential poacher or a harmless professor maybe. It is permissible for a man to walk a few hundred yards from his home to the village shop, chapel or tavern, without exciting comment, but he who sets out for a mile or more, and at night too, is a suspicious character and must have some explanation ready to account for his movements. The civilian infantryman is "out". Yet such am I, a walker from choice, an anachronism, my sole object that evening to reach the hearth of my cousin's hilltop farm standing amidst a sparse copse that rose like the last despairing hairs on an elder's skull.

As I have said, this was the very heart of Dewsland, a land of farms, cottages, hamlets, a featureless plateau intersected by deep romantic glens such as Rholwm, Trebwrnallt, Pontyrhafod, Trenichol, Gegin Ffwlbert, a few bald hills like Penlan Mabws and Mathry, a countryside through which byroads and lanes wander as crazily and casually as the myriad rills that ripple through its windswept acres.

In the murmuring gloom I could see white council houses rising spectre-like at Trefgarn Owen and, a little further on at Llandeloy, houses that sheltered folk without beautifying the land, artificial hamlets called into being by tidy planners who knew the map but not tradition. For the Welsh, the true Welsh that is, are not village-minded, and even where villages or hamlets have existed they are rarely compact communities, like those of England, wreathed around a village green, a church, or some such social centre, but random, untidy, accidental. The scattered cottages that stood, a generation ago, at the roadsides and in the meadows are now condemned cabins, roofless rubble amidst a miniature wilderness where gardens once had bloomed, gardens full of cabbages, potatoes, gooseberry and currant bushes, apple trees, sage, lilac, primroses, the "old man", and in whose sheltered nooks little square wooden beehives stood like miniature Swiss chalets. A few stunted trees, their fruit turned sour, degenerate fruit bushes, relentless throttling brambles are the sole memorials. They greeted me in the gloom, wan but friendly ghosts, for the pedestrian surely belonged to their world and maybe his end too would be as melancholy. I passed one such deserted hamlet, straggling Penfeidir, ruinous and mournful as if a squadron of Hunnish cavalry had swept through; yet less than a hundred years ago a dozen families had lived, struggled, quarrelled and loved and died within those walls, and from such cots had gone forth men like the Revd. Shon Clun, saintly "Rowlands Madagascar", and scholarly Dr. Thomas Nicholas. Condemned they were as "insanitary", a menace to public health; nevertheless large sturdy families had been reared in most of them, lively children who grew up tough as teak and, as parish registers and tombstones show, to ages well beyond the allotted span. I myself had known many of these greybeards, resourceful, secretive – they would have survived in a desert – hardy, gnarled old fellows, many of whom retained their vigour to within a few weeks of the final count. They had been poured out of these cottages into the service of the farms where they toiled from dawn to dusk, devouring their victuals like foxhounds, sleeping soundly on their truckle beds above stables, until they married and acquired a cot of their own. A pretty tough crew.

Although the breed is by no means extinct, I knew that I would greet none of them on my road. They no longer tread their homeward way, but vegetate cosily in synthetic villages surrounded by taps, wireless sets and electric fires; they no longer walk or hobble, for sons and grandsons are also their chauffeurs.

Here and there among the trees an uncurtained window would reveal a bluish-white light and I knew that, within, a semicircle of subdued mutes listened carefully to the works of far-off folk, to music, to words sometimes wise, sometimes amusing, sometimes trivial. When a door opened or a set was turned on fiercely, I could distinguish un-Welsh accents, classical compositions or jazz, for sounds carry far in the night air. Half a century ago, the musical box and the gramophone were the sole sources of "canned" entertainment, while the piano, organ, accordion, mouth organ and the "gewgaw" produced the melodies of homely performers. Evening entertainment was not confined to music, for the telling of tales, legends, traditions, the reciting of poetry and scripture found ready and appreciative audiences. The oral literature that I imbibed on the hearths of my grandparents at Grinston and Clawddcam has remained among my most cherished possessions and helped to guide my footsteps into the delights of historical research, which in turn has given a deeper meaning and an added significance to my appreciation of both past and present. Modern techniques and advances, however, must not be condemned; there is no doubt that horizons are widened and the hedge of parochialism removed, so that the joys and advantages of a wider culture have been made available to the most remote and outlandish dwelling. Sentimentality butters no buns. But reforms and improvements may well carry disadvantages in their train. There is reason to suspect that our generation no longer strives to achieve as old-time social conditions obliged its predecessors to do, for today the fruits are presented to us on a plate, and we hold out our hands instead of using them. The loss or weakening of creative urges and instincts, however modest and limited their scope and achievements, must inevitably contribute to the devitalizing of national character.

Nothing illustrates the social revolution that has taken place more than the sounds of evening, or the lack of them. As I walked along past Hook, Berry Bush, Rhosgranog, my mind went back to the evening walks I had taken on these same roads some fifty years ago when barely out of my frock, and I found no difficulty in recalling the sounds that had been so familiar a feature of those far-off days. For the countryside then was full of sounds. In the storehouse of my mind I could still hear the songs and eisteddfod pieces – *The Tempest, Worthy is the Lamb, Cartref* – being practised at the firesides of farms and cottages, the deep roar of a lusty bass, the piercing wail of a determined soprano, the tremulous treble of an uncertain child, when numerous family choirs composed of parents and sons and daughters wrestled with the intricacies of tonic sol-fa and old notation. For families

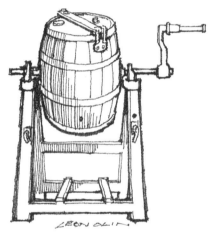

A butter churn

were large then, they fashioned their own joys and sorrows, and contributed melodies practised on hearths for the delectation of public audiences at church halls, chapel vestries and eisteddfod tents. Then they created, today they listen. Families have dwindled in size; today one child is modish, two children are permissible, but three or more are likely to invite condolences rather than congratulations.

People sang at their work as well as at their ease, more especially in the evening. Among my earliest attractions was the friendly nasal tune of the separator in the dairy attended by the housewife or her daughters who warbled as if their lives depended on their performance, and the resounding slaps that accompanied the final stages of butter-making that could be heard for great distances, as if some powerful parent were chastising a particularly well-developed infant. The separator rusts on some scrap heap; the farmer now sells his milk and buys his butter.

On Sunday nights, and on some week-nights, one would pass crowds of people, old and young, on their way from church and chapel, linked arm-in-arm singing hymns, old, accustomed, haunting – O *fryniau Caersalem, Bydd myrdd o ryfeddodau* and others – but those who still go to worship no longer walk and sing, but are swept along in motor cars. One old character, Billy Richard, who laboured throughout his life on the farm of Mr. Nicholas of Hayscastle, never missed the Sunday evening at Trefgarn Owen chapel, winter or summer, fine or stormy. After the service he trudged away on his own and at Grinston crossroads just below my grandfather's farm, he would strike up his favourite hymn

Dechrau canu, dechrau canmol,
Ym mhen mil o filoedd maith.

It never varied, and he sang his way on along the cavernous darkness of the sunken road that winds past Rholwm, Trebwrnallt, Castle Hill, until he reached the gates of Hayscastle.

Footsteps on the road – long a merry accompaniment of our civilisation – are no longer heard. They seem old-fashioned today, and when we do happen to hear them we pause, we listen, as to an unfamiliar intrusion. Footsteps! Footsteps that I knew so well – the gravel-crunching stride of the farmer, the sharp clattering of women's clogs like castanets on kitchen floors, the blithe patter of the feet of boys playing hoop by moonlight (a delightful pastime of my youth), perhaps the laboured tread of a benighted tramp (what became of *Trampyn Mawr, Toe the Line* and *Harcourt?),* and occasionally the vigorous oaths and horrid belching of a drink-laden rustic rolling homeward to his bed or perchance to sudden slumber in some sheltered ditch. On many a late evening, one might be forgiven for imagining that a company of infantry was on the march when thirty or forty people who had been harvesting or threshing at a farm took the road to their various abodes. These footsteps are the minstrels of yesteryear, for the countryman, if he walks at all, is now rarely heard; the wellington has evicted the hobnailed boot and the wooden clog.

In addition to sounds that told of human beings were those generated by machines, revolutionary enough when I was young, almost extinct today. Perhaps the one whose passing I mourn most was the mumbled drumming of the threshing machine, like some gigantic humming-bird, insistent, interminable, and the joyous hysterical shrieks of the engine's whistle which told the countryside that the last sheaf had been pitchforked aloft. The tinkle of bells on push-bikes and the squeaks of brakes told of some swain on his way to a sportive rendezvous or perhaps of a constable with a sharp eye for nocturnal "strays".

Veritable music to my childish ears was the clip-clop of hooves on the road as a trap and pony passed by, and the powerful, stamping, pounding tread of great shire horses that drew heavy carts with iron-banded wheels rolling like the tumbrils of an enthusiastic revolution, to the accompaniment of gay jingling harness and the hoarse encouraging cries of the drivers. They have been replaced by lorries and cars and rubber tyres. And there was the covered waggon driven by Essex of Trefgarn, our main link with the outer world, with civilisation as understood and practised at Haverfordwest. At night, the horses turned into the fields tended to congregate near the hedges that lined the road, and when passing, one often heard the stampede of hooves as the animals, in a little panic, made towards the open pasture. They are gone, and we can travel many miles without seeing one of those noble animals, once the pride of every farm and a measure of its prosperity. With the passing of the horse, the blacksmiths and carpenters at Penfeidir, Llandeloy and Penycwm damped their glowing

Down memory lane

fires, those islands of rural friendship, and closed for ever the workshops that had served the land for so long.

Another sound that attracted me enormously was the low gurgling of many waters over the pebbly fords of Mabws, Troedyrhiw, Pontyrhafod, Castle Villa, Trefanner, Gignog, Lochmeyler, Llandeloy and New Inn. They too are silent, their waters now flow through culverts beneath the dry macadam, their music muted, and the rough-hewn wooden handrails on which we carved our initials gone forever. No more will venturesome extroverts splash along their stony beds to prove that their boots are watertight, and no one now ensnares the "shilgots" that dart like brown lightning among the boulders below the footbridge. And the laboured hiccuping-beats of the mill-wheels turned by those waters are also silent – the mill of Brawdy a dreary ruin, Felin Stwper, a calm hermitage, and of the mill of Priskilly, where my father was born, all that remain are some reed-covered mounds and vagrant bushes.

As I walked on I suddenly realised that I had not seen or passed a single person on my road, only the ghosts of long, long ago who had risen to keep me company. Once a car had hurried by and I saw the lights of several others stabbing the blackness like silver swords, rising and falling in the distance, and heard the whine of an engine as it breasted a slope or an unpractised driver laid violent hands on a protesting gear. The economic and social, and to some degree the religious, history of a community can be conveyed through the media of sounds. These, or their absence, tell of the great changes that have taken place during our lifetime and we, being so occupied with our own little affairs, have often failed to realise the significance of what has taken place around us. But sounds never pass away, they lie coiled in our consciousness, slumbering yet never entirely asleep, and leap into our waking lives, sometimes unbidden, sometimes in response to some chance note that the tuning-fork of memory might strike. Some are cheerful, merry, encouraging, and tell of gaiety, laughter, wedding-bells; others are sombre, untoward, disturbing and tell of gravesides, farewells, tears, disasters.

As I neared the end of my journey, another note, now familiar to all Dewslanders, invaded my thoughts. A late lone 'plane, its recognition lights winking ceaselessly, droned powerfully overhead. Men of my generation have become sound-conscious for good reasons, for once there were sounds that presaged death and horror, relief and joy, and for me they are always associated with dark cloud blanketed nights, sinister dusks, grey dawns. Once experienced those sounds of darkness are not easily forgotten – the swish of footfalls through dew-soaked grass, the click of the safety catch, anxious whispers, the pause and intense peering through bushes. Do we hear voices? Are they guttural? On again, then down. A plane circles menacingly above and red revealing flares momentarily light up the trees, hedges, hummocks and our own nakedness. Ping, ping, seemingly from all directions. Ours? Theirs? Crump, crump, crump. A sobbing curse from a Durham miner as he claws the turf. Theirs all right. Something has gone wrong. Cries in the gloom – "Stretcher bearers, stretcher bearers!" "Seen the Captain?" "For Christ's sake any of you blokes seen Mr. Banks?" "Yes, Sarge, been carried back." Lucky devil. Steady now, push on. A hatless gunner officer staggers through the acrid smoke. He has been ordered to collect what infantry he finds, and all the odds and sods he can lay hands on, and hold the right flank where a counter-attack is coming in. "Hello Sergeant! S Company? How many men have you got?" "About twenty left, we bloody well carried the can sir." "Right Sergeant, better get them to line that hedge." "Very good sir. Come on you, get fell in, get weaving." Fumbling in the dark, the weary officer takes out a message-pad and starts to write a "sitrep" as he had been taught when on a course at Salisbury Plain where the sun shone cheerily over Long Barrow, where the larks sang and there was no one to shoot back.

Those doom laden sounds tortured a dark night just such as this, also in September, almost twenty years ago, near a place called Salerno. But this was Dewsland, heartland of my ancestors, home of my youth, where no terrors lurked. I heard the 'plane change its tune, cough once or twice as if clearing its throat, before making peaceful landfall on the long green rides of Brawdy airfield.

The Odd Contrasts of War - Excerpt from F.J.'s World War II Manuscripts

Burnt out tanks hull down in yellow daisies at Kasserine, mounds with wooden crosses in the corner of a cornfield near the banks of Medjerda. A green lizard over a foot in length that suddenly faced me as I crouched behind a crag on the Goubellat Plain, and the smell of wild thyme in the hills above Medjer-el-bab.

Grinning gunners slogging through acrid fumes to feed the thunder of the guns at Kaze Mezour. The cork forest at Sedjanane, the exotic flowers on the corniche roads near the Bay of Cavallo. The pine trees of Aisi Dralam. A wrecked anti-tank gun among the ruins of a Temple of Imperial Rome.

25 pdr. guns of F.J.'s regiment in action
(Imperial War Museum photograph. Ref. NA851)

Direct hit on German Mk. 4 tank.
(I.W.M. official photograph. Ref. NA757)

Unloading guns onto Salerno Beachhead
(I.W.M. official photograph. Ref. NA6632)

Aftermath of the Battle of Beja.
(I.W.M. official photograph. ref. NA 1042)

CHAPTER VI

A REVIEW OF PEMBROKESHIRE MILITARY MEN

THE CITIZEN SOLDIERS OF PEMBROKESHIRE – 1936

THE history of the old volunteers of Pembroke awaits the historian and when this is written it will be found to be a glorious and stirring chapter in the life of the county. Pembrokeshire has given some distinguished soldiers to the service of the Empire - Sir Gelly Meyrick, Rowland Laugharne, Admiral Thomas Tucker, Sir Thomas Picton, Sir Richard Foley, the Philipps, Bowens and Barlows, the fighting Foleys of Ridgeway, "Tiger" Davies and "Navarino" Davies of Capeston, and many others.

THE ROYAL PEMBROKE FUSILIERS

The Volunteers and Territorials of Pembrokeshire derive their military tradition and descent from the Royal Pembroke Fusiliers, a militia regiment first raised in 1588 – one of the most glorious years in the annals of British history. We will pass over the intervening centuries, until we come to the beginning of the last century.

THE R.P.V.I.

I have been fortunate to find certain information concerning the Royal Pembrokeshire Volunteer Infantry covering the period 1803-1806, which contains some interesting items, and gives considerable data regarding the members thereof and their rate of pay. The R.P.V.I. was contemporary with the Pembroke and Castlemartin Yeomanry, with which Major Joseph Adams was connected.

The officers of the Royal Pembrokeshire Volunteer Infantry on 24 June 1804, were the following:- Lord Kensington, Colonel Commandant; Lieut.-Col. Allen; Major H. W. Bowen; Captains the Lord Cawdor, Leach, Mathias, Philipps, Bowling, Allen, Probert, Harries and Skyrme; Adjutant Salmon; Paymaster Henry Rees; Surgeon Thomas, (Surgeons Mate, Voyle); Q.M., Potter. Geo. Hassell, Esq., at Great George Street, London was the General Agent for the Corps. Unfortunately the papers rarely give the Christian names or initials of the officers, and this renders it somewhat difficult to place them. However, it is possible to obtain the dates of their commissions from the War Office, and this would help considerably to reveal the identity of the officers to modern readers.

The pay roll of the R.P.V.I. in 1804 gives us the number of officers, N.C.O.s and men of the corps. The pay in the following list is *per diem*: One colonel, £1.2s. 6d.; two lieutenant colonels, 15s 8d.; eight captains, 9s 5d.; seventeen lieutenants, 5s 8d.; ten ensigns, 4s 8d.; one adjutant, 8s 0d.; one quartermaster, 5s 8d.; one surgeon, 9s 5d.; one surgeon's mate

3s 0d.; one paymaster, 15s.; one sergeant major, 2s 0¾d.; one Q.M.S., 2s 0¾d.; forty-five sergeants, 1s 6¾d.; forty-six corporals 1s 2¼d.; nineteen drummers, 1s 1¾d.; eight-hundred and eighteen privates, 1s. This shows that the force in 1804 comprised of 973 all ranks, while the numerical strength on 1 December 1806 (excluding officers), was 1,010 N.C.O.s and men. This was highly creditable to Pembrokeshire when we remember that there were other volunteer bodies contemporaneous with the R.P.V.I. Every parish and village had its volunteers, the little hamlet of Kilgetty contributing a full company of its own.

The Adjutant's pay in 1803 was six shillings a day, but this was increased by two shillings in the following year, while a sergeant major's pay rose from 1s 6d a day in 1803 to 2s 0¾d in 1804.

The troops assembled once a year (if not more), but unlike their present-day counterparts, did not always confine their soldiering to the sunny days of summer, e.g. we read that ten companies of the R.P.V.I. were on permanent pay and duty from 25 November 1804, to 1 December 1804.

The estimates for pay and other expenses incidental to a military force were signed by Lord Kensington in the following way: "I do hereby certify upon my Word and Honour as an Officer and a Gentleman, that I have carefully examined the foregoing, which is a just Estimate to the best of my knowledge and Belief."

It is interesting to note that there is no mention of a chaplain to the Force. I wonder whether it is safe to assume that the spiritual level of those days amongst troops was sufficiently high to dispense with the services of a priest!

There are undoubtedly many old commissions granted to officers still in our country houses, as well as other relics, such as uniforms and arms. I possess some ancient swords used by the former volunteers of Pembrokeshire. To be an officer in the Pembrokeshire Militia, a property qualification was necessary. The following is a typical application: "I, Thomas Jones of the Town and County of Haverfordwest, Esquire, do hereby Certify that I am Seized of in fee in my own right of an Estate in Land and Tenements of the

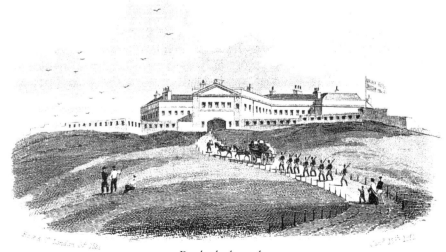

Pembroke barracks

yearly value of one hundred and fifty pounds. Situate in the parish of Llanvairnantgwynn in the said County of Pembroke, so as to Qualify me to be and act as a Lieutenant in the Militia for the said County of Pembroke. Witness my hand this Twenty Seventh day of December 1786 (signed) Thos. Jones."

The commission of George Harries of Tregwynt (parish of Granston) who was a captain in the Pembrokeshire Militia, is still extant. It is dated 30 September 1779. His son, another George Harries, was a captain in the Carmarthen Militia, his commission being dated 30 May 1803.

Much information regarding the different forces in Pembrokeshire may be gleaned from the records of the affair of 1797. A letter of 15 April 1797, written to Lt. General Rooke, was signed by officers, who named the forces to which they were posted. From this we know that at this period there was:

1. Pembrokeshire Yeomanry Cavalry.
2. Pembrokeshire Militia.
3. Pembrokeshire Prov. Cavalry.
4. The Local Volunteers.
5. The Lord Milford's.
6. The Fishguard Fencibles.

Our ancestors were patriots and trained in the defence of their native shores. The foregoing shows how strong the volunteer movement was in the county.

THE CASTLEMARTIN YEOMANRY

One of the last persons to wear the old full dress of the Castlemartin Yeomanry Cavalry was the late Sir Owen Scourfield. At a parade of the Pembrokeshire Yeomanry some years ago at Penally, Sir Owen appeared in the blue and silver uniform of the old regiment, and a very imposing figure he made. He commanded the Yeomanry at one time, and up to his death he took a keen interest in its activities. When they were in camp at Penally, the Rt. Hon. David Lloyd George, M.P., visited the three squadrons and presented long service medals to non-commissioned officers and men.

At a meeting of gentlemen of Pembrokeshire at London on 19 April 1794, with Lord Milford, Lord Lieutenant of the county in the chair, John Campbell of Stackpole Court submitted a plan for raising two troops of volunteer cavalry for the defence of our shores. These troops were to consist of gentlemen and Yeomanry and such persons approved of by the Lord Lieutenant. One troop was to be connected with the Hundreds of Castlemartin and Narberth and the other with the Northern Hundreds of the county, and each troop was to be 50 strong including all ranks. Officers were to receive commissions from the Lord Lieutenant. Horses and clothing were to be provided without expense to the Government and Lord Milford was to open a fund in London to further the project.

The moving spirit behind this was John Campbell, eldest son of Pryse Campbell of Stackpole Court. He was born about 1753, educated at Eton 1763-67, and entered Parliament. He was created Baron Cawdor of Castlemartin on 21 June 1796.

On 9 May 1794, Capt. Henry David and Lieutenant Alex Fotheringham appear in the War Office List as officers of the Pembroke Troops of Fencible Cavalry. In July and August of the same year the following appear as officers of the Pembroke Troops of Gentlemen and Yeomanry – Captains Richard Lord Milford and John Campbell, Lieutenants Dudley Acland and Cornet John Lloyd. In the War Office List of 15 July 1803, we find Captain Joshua Roch, Lieutenant John Grant and Cornet George Clayton Roch of the Gentlemen and Yeomanry Cavalry. Joshua Roch commanded the Dungleddy Troop in which John Grant served, the other Comet and Paymaster being William Philipps Allen, the Q.M. was Richard Barzey, with six N.C.O.s, one trumpeter and 54 men. Thus the original establishment of 50 all-ranks was exceeded. The title Castlemartin Yeomanry was not always followed since Lord Cawdor in 1797 signs himself as "Captain, Pembroke Yeomanry Cavalry".

The newly-raised force was soon called upon to give an account of itself in the field. On 22 February 1797, a force of about 1400 Frenchmen effected a landing near Fishguard. The Castlemartin Yeomanry, mustering 50, were ferried across from Pembroke and linking with the Fishguard Fencibles and other volunteer units marched to meet the enemy. But issues were not joined and the French surrendered to Cawdor on the 24th.

In 1853, Queen Victoria granted the battle honour "Fishguard" to the Castlemartin Yeomanry, and this was the first battle honour carried by a Volunteer unit of the British Army.

Later on the unit increased to at least five Troops. In 1804-05, they were officered as follows - Captain Lord Cawdor's Troop was commanded by Capt. "Joe" Adams with Capt. Matthew Campbell, Lieutenants John Bowling and Henry Leach, Cornets James Child and John Jones, Quartermasters Stephen Davies and George Davies; 8 N.C.O.s, 2 Trumpeters, and 69 O.R.'s. a troop commanded by Capt. Henry Stokes with Lieutenant Richard Rees and Cornet William Miller Williams; a troop commanded by Capt. Morris Williams, of Cwmgloyne, with Lieutenant and Paymaster Thomas Hassell, and Comet Thomas James: a troop commanded by Capt. John Price with Lieutenant Thomas Batine; a troop commanded by Capt. John Rees with Lieutenant George Davies, Cornet Thomas Edwards and Q.M. John Lewis. It appears that the whole was under command of Lt.-Col. Sir Hugh Owen, Bt., Orielton, at that time.

In June 1804, General Gascoyne reviewed the following at Portfield, Haverfordwest: Lord Cawdor's two troops of Yeomanry Cavalry, Sir Hugh Owen's three troops, Capt. Howell's troop, Col. Roch's troop, the Huntingdon Regiment of Militia, Lord Kensington's Volunteers commanded by Col. Ackland, Capt. Hardings's Infantry, Capt. Mathias's, with a small train of Artillery – in all some 3,000 troops. "The Cavalry performed the sword exercise and went though their manoeuvres to the General's satisfaction." Later, in November of the same year "the celerity, precision and steadiness of the same troops greatly impressed the general". The strength of the Pembrokeshire citizen army in 1806 was as follows: Castlemartin Yeomanry (Capt. John Adams) 94, the Dungleddy Troop (Lt.-Col. J. Roch) 66, the Fishguard Fencibles (Lt.-Col. Thomas Lloyd) 570, Loyal Llandissilio Volunteers (Capt. John Harding) 132, Milford Artillery (Capt. Hon. C. F.

Major de Rutzen with his troops

Greville) 90, Loyal Prendergast Infantry (Capt. John Mathias), 111, Haverfordwest Fusiliers (Capt. W. H. Scourfield) 67, Pembrokeshire Militia (Col. Lord Kensington) 1,053, and Pembroke Infantry (Capt. F. Mansell) 176.

In November, 1801, the N.C.O.s and troopers of the Dungleddy Troop of Volunteer Cavalry, presented, at Portfield, a valuable sword to their commander, Col. Roch, as a testimonial of their esteem.

In January, 1820, the Lord Lieutenant signed the following commissions in the Yeomanry: Robert Innes Ackland to be Captain, Richard Bulkeley Philipps Grant to be Lieutenant, William Bevans Williams to be Cornet, and Davies Griffiths to be Quartermaster. In July, 1834, C. P. Callen was appointed Cornet to the 2nd Troop of Castlemartin, and Yeomanry Cavalry vice Lewis Mathias, resigned.

In June, 1835, after their eight days duty at Portfield, they were inspected by General Sir George Cockburn, who addressed them thus: "In sincerity I speak it, that as an old Cavalry officer I have witnessed the performance of many troops of Yeomanry Cavalry in other places, but I never before saw men perform their various evolution's as yours have done this day . . . and should we meet on active service, I trust the Castlemartin Yeomanry will evince the same valour which once compelled a foreign enemy to surrender to their prowess". In July 1841, the Castlemartin, 160 strong, under Major Bowling were inspected on Portfield by Sir Charles Dance. They marched down High Street, three abreast led by the band playing *Le Petit Tambour* in lively style. About this time west Wales was disgraced by agrarian outrages and the Castlemartin was called out to quell the disturbances. Captains Mansell and Leach were stationed with Troops at St. Clears for a while in February, 1843.

A military review on Tenby Sands in the 1930's

In 1841 a song was written in praise of the Castlemartin and goes to the air of "Green grow the rushes, Oh." It is a pleasure for me to preserve this song from oblivion by publishing it in this volume.

THE CASTLEMARTIN YEOMANRY

Now many a day has passed away
Since first we marched to Fishguard's shore
With foreign foes war's game to play
What Yeomanry ne'er did before;
Yet on we sped by courage led
With noble Cawdor took the field,
Whose skill and spirit at our head
Invaders soon compelled to yield.

Our rallying word: A good broad-sword,
A nag to bear us fresh and free –
Our ranks enlarge
Then sound the "Charge!"
Bold Castlemartin Yeomanry,
And better men there need not be
Who proudly start from Pembroke's heart,
Her Castlemartin Yeomanry.

Still at our post it is our boast,
To be when any danger's near,
When enemies assail our coast,
As Frenchmen once approached us here;
And would they know, again we'll show
With arms as strong and hearts as good,
What patriot fires in Welshmen glow
Warmed by their ancient British blood.
Then give the word:-
A good broad-sword, etc.

Though war's rough trade now wants no aid
From us, as here its course is run;
Yet called, we'll meet it – not afraid
To do as we before have done;
Who would not fly the weak or shy,
Or who with him in friendship blend,
Whose heart and hand would fail to try'
His home and kindred to defend?
Be still our word:
A good broad-sword, etc.

In later years the Castlemartin became known as the Pembroke Imperial Yeomanry and took the field in the South African War where it suffered casualties and acquitted itself honourably. In the war of 1914-18 the Yeomanry again did its duty right well and saw service in the East. In 1921 the unit was converted to Artillery and formed the 102nd (Pembroke and Cardiganshire) Field Artillery.

The uniform of the old Castlemartin Yeomanry was blue with white facings.

THE PICTON SOLDIERS

Thanks to Brian Picton Swann's research we are able to incorporate many additional facts to the Picton history to give a more comprehensive picture. Mr. Swann's original contributions are in italic type. *Major Francis Jones would, I am sure, have applauded Mr. Swann's skill and dedication in updating and editing his unfinished essay.*

A fascinating aspect of families is genius or superior qualities in certain generations. A family may continue century after century without producing one person of eminent ability. In others a sudden flowering of genius lasts for a few generations. In some genius is transmitted down many generations so that a family have a natural aptitude towards certain professions or trades.

In the case of genius as embodied in Cecil, Shakespeare, Burns and Lloyd George, there is nothing in their ancestry to indicate the source of superlatively gifted ancestors. In the case of sons possessing the same gifts as the father we see the operation of heredity.

An example of the sudden emergence of talent is seen in the family Picton of Poyston in Pembrokeshire. Few know that General Sir Thomas Picton was one of four brothers holding army commissions at the same time, and that both his uncle and one of his brothers, also attained the rank of General. The Pictons of Poyston were minor squires.

Poyston, then a modest property, originally belonged to a family named Howell, whose heiress, Alson, married John Reynolds. There was a son, John Reynolds who was one of the coroners for Pembrokeshire in the early half of the seventeenth century. The coroner married, before 1630, to Elizabeth, daughter of John Voyle of Filbeach by his wife, Cecil Dawkin of Gower. After her husband's death, Elizabeth remarried a Picton of whom nothing is known. They had three children – John Picton, Joan, who married a William Morgan, and Gwenllian, who married a Thomas.

John Picton lived in the parish of Rudbaxton; Poyston seems to have been owned by his half-brother, James Reynolds, and although described as "gentleman" in his will dated 1 May 1666, and proved on 13 September of that year, that document contains no reference to landed property. John married before June 1650, Elinor Hayward, daughter of a neighbour, George Hayward of Flether Hill, a minor squire, and Anne Buckley his wife. Apparently there had been some disagreements between the families, for the father-in-law by his will dated 30 June 1650, bequeathed £100 to Elinor Picton provided she and her husband relinquished all claims against testator's son, George Hayward.

From the marriage of John Picton and Elinor (Hayward) there were two children, a son John, and a daughter Margaret, who married James Wogan of Goodhook in Uzmaston parish, a younger son of John Wogan of Wiston. John Picton, the son, a minor in 1666, appears to have acquired Poyston, possibly from his Reynolds relations although no evidence of the transaction has survived. He also owned at least seven farms in the neighbouring parish of Ambleston which he settled on his issue in 1710. In a steady and unspectacular way the family was prospering.

John Picton married twice. The identity of his first wife is unknown, and by her he had an only child, John Picton later of Pembroke, *who married Corbetta Meyrick of Bush,* who died in 1734. His second wife was Phoebe Mary Pritchard, daughter of the Revd. Dr. Thomas Pritchard, Prebendary of Mathry, Archdeacon of Llandaff, by his wife, Phoebe Field, second daughter of the Rt. Revd. Theophilus Field, Bishop of St. Davids. *It was possibly through this marriage that Poyston was acquired, as the will of Dr. Thomas Pritchard (PCC 1646/7) states "The love and bounty of my Revd. Father in lawe, Bishop Field, by virtue of which the greater part of the money which purchased Poyston did aryse to me".* By her he had two sons, Thomas born 1685, and William *(died 1764 leaving one son, John who also died unmarried).* John Picton's will dated 13 March 1716, was proved at Carmarthen on 16 October 1719. His will shows that he had increased the family estate. In addition to the lands in Ambleston and Rudbaxton, he owned properties in the parishes of Martletwy and Yerbeston which he devised to his younger son, the remainder to his elder son and heir. Phoebe Mary survived her husband but a short time and her will, dated 24 December 1719, was proved at Carmarthen on 8 August 1722.

The elder son of the second marriage, Thomas Picton, succeeded to Poyston. *He married firstly, Anne Meyrick in 1712, she died in 1713.* Like his father, he then took a bride from the parsonage. She was Frances Bowen, baptised at St. Mary's, Haverfordwest, on 10 September 1689, younger daughter of the Revd. James Bowen, rector of Rudbaxton by his wife, Frances, daughter of Arnold Thomas of Haverfordwest. *They married at Prendergast in 1716.* The Revd. James Bowen graduated from Jesus College, Oxford, was rector of Rudbaxton in 1671, rector of Leweston in 1681 and Canon of St. David's Cathedral in 1688. He died on 24 October 1700, aged 63.

Thomas Picton died on 4 July 1727, at forty-two, his will dated 26 June 1727, being proved on 25 September following. Frances survived her husband by nearly half a century and died on 15 November 1775, aged eighty-six. Both were buried at Rudbaxton. They had five children, namely, John, who died on 22 October 1727, aged seven years; Thomas who succeeded to Poyston, and whom we shall consider later; William, an army officer, of whom more later; James, who died young; and Elizabeth, who married in 1737 to John Warren, younger son of John Warren of Trewern.

This generation showed ability in an unexpected direction. As we have seen, of the four preceding ancestors, two had married with the minor squirearchy, and two into clerical families. Thus it was a departure from family tradition when the younger son, William, embarked on an army career. William Picton was born in 1724. His first commission is unknown, *but he was promoted on 16 January 1748 to Lieutenant in Colonel Henry Skelton's Regiment (later to become the 12th Foot). He was Quartermaster of the Regiment*

Sir Thomas Picton, G.C.B.

from 1752-1755 when he was transferred to the command of one of the fifty new companies of Royal Marines which were raised in that year. By July of the following year he had transferred back to the Army and became a Captain-Lieutenant in Skelton's Foot (the 12th Foot), being promoted Captain on 25 August 1756. He served with the regiment in Germany under Lord Granby in 1761, was promoted Major on 12 April of the following year. On his appointment as Lt. Colonel, he was received in audience by King George III, who congratulated him on his distinguished services in Germany. He was Lieutenant Colonel of the regiment from 21 August 1765 to 1773. He was stationed at Gibraltar in 1773 and 1783. On 6 September 1777, he received the rank of Brevet Colonel in the Army, and on 14 January following, became Colonel of the 75th Foot (Prince of Wales' Regiment), which he raised principally from Dyfed and which contained many Welsh officers. On 21 April 1779, he was removed to the Colonelcy of his old regiment, the 12th, and commanded it for the rest of his life. Further promotions came rapidly. On 20 November 1782 when commanding the Grenadier Company of the 12th, in Germany during the Seven Years War, he was thanked in Army Orders by Prince Ferdinand for his behaviour at the affair of Zierenburg. He was promoted Major General, on 19 October 1793, and on 1 January 1798, General in the Army. He died in London on 14 October 1811, in his eighty-seventh year and was buried in a vault in the church of St. George's, Hanover Square. He left his large fortune to his favourite nephew (Sir) Thomas Picton. He had served in the Army for sixty-six years, fifty-four years in the 12th Foot (1756-78, 1779-1811). His memorial in Rudbaxton church says that he had, "served in Flanders, in Germany, and at the siege of Gibraltar (1778) against the combined fleets of France and Spain, and at the destruction of the battering ships on the 13th day of September 1782". To have achieved this high rank without being rich or having Army connections meant he was an outstanding officer whose abilities and character impressed his superiors. He had opened a new door for the Pictons and, as we shall see, obtained commissions for four of his nephews which led to fame if not to fortune.

The General's elder brother, Thomas Picton succeeded to the Poyston estate. He was a country gentleman, being a Justice of the Peace and High Sheriff of Pembrokeshire in 1749. He married Cecil, daughter and heiress of the Revd. Edward Powell of Llandow, an ancient Glamorganshire family. Her mother was Cecil, born 1729, daughter of Edward Turberville of Sutton and also heiress of her mother Cecil Loughor of Tythegston and heiress of the Ewenny Priory (later Abbey), estate. This marriage allied the Pictons to the ancient aristocracy, for the Powells were descendants of the medieval chieftain, Einon ap Collwyn, while the Turbervilles, who had intermarried with the families of Carver, Stradlings, Talbot and Gainge, were of Norman extraction. The Powells came of an equally distinguished stock, descended from Einon ap Collwyn and intermarried with the Vaughans of Tyle Glas, Herberts, Barzet, Nelson and Cave.

A romantic air wreathed the union, for Picton and Cecil eloped and were married in Reynold's cave at Tresilian in Llantwit *Major in 1750.* This marriage, and the career of General William Picton were to have far reaching effects on the future of the Poyston family. Thomas Picton *died in 1790 and his widow in 1806. They* had *fourteen* children:

1. Richard Turberville Picton *baptised 1751* – see later.

2. Thomas Picton, baptised 13 May 1753, died an infant *buried 14 November 1757.*

3. William Picton baptised 20 July 1755, buried 5 January 1757.

4. William Picton, baptised on 8 May 1758 – see later

5. (Sir) Thomas Picton, born 24 August 1758 – see later.

6. (Revd.) Edward Picton, baptised 13 July 1760 – see later.

7. (Major General) John Picton, baptised 176**1** – see later.

8. Elizabeth, baptised 28 April 1754, died 3 February 1830 unmarried aged 76.

9. Frances, baptised 30 May 1756; married William Morris of Mount Pleasant, near Carmarthen, and died without issue on 10 April 1836, aged 80.

10. *Charlotte baptised 21 June 1759. Married John Beete and they emigrated to New York. They visited Thomas Picton in Trinidad when he was Governor there. They had two children, John Picton Beete who joined the Army in the 21st Foot in 1820, transferred to the 54th Foot, but left the Army in 1843 and settled in Prince Edward Island. He inherited Iscoed under the will of his cousin John Williams alias John Picton in 1883. He returned to Wales and died in 1887 aged 88. He had two sons and one daughter who inherited the Iscoed estate in 1909. Charlotte's daughter, Mary Caroline Beete (1849-1927) married James Brogden and had a daughter Lucy Caroline Brogden. Charlotte was widowed and remarried James Gardiner in 1814 in New York. She was still living in 1853.*

11. *Jane Picton, no record of her baptism exists in the Rudbaxton registers, but she was brought to church on 10 June 1765. She married Henry Stokes in 1818, and was a widow and childless when she died in September 1848.*

12. *Cecil baptised 22 May 1763; married 1795 Revd. George Jenkins. They had seven children.*

13. Catherine, baptised, 9 September 1763; married 1796, John Warlow, son of Arthur Warlow of Lochturffin, Pembrokeshire. *They had five children.* John Warlow conducted business as a wine and brandy merchant in Haverfordwest, and in 1799 bought Castle Hall, a residence near Milford Haven. His business failed in 1804; Castle Hall was sold, and he emigrated to the West Indies where he died in 1814. His widow died on 28 June 1838, aged sixty-eight.

14. *Anne Picton, baptised 27 December 1764. She married Francis Williams of Cotts, Prendergast in 1801. He had a distinguished career in the Royal Marines. They had one son and two daughters. The son John, born 1807 became an M.D. and succeeded to Iscoed under the will of his uncle, Revd. Edward Picton. On 14 April 1853 he presented a Bill of Complaint in the Court of Chancery, joining 29 Picton descendants asking for authority to raise, by sale or mortgage of the Iscoed estate a sum sufficient to pay the legacies outstanding under the will of Sir Thomas Picton. This document provides a detailed record of the Picton family at this date. His will was dated 1882, and he left his estate to his uncle John Picton Beete.*

The eldest son, Richard Turberville Picton, was commissioned as Ensign in the Army on 8 January 1768, transferred as Ensign to his uncle's regiment, the 12th Foot on 3 February 1769. Later he became a Lieutenant, and then Captain on 25 September 1778. He served as Brigade Major at the siege of Gibraltar where he distinguished himself, but his health being impaired he had to retire between 1790/91. On the death without issue of his kinsman, Richard Turberville of Ewenny on 25 January 1771, he succeeded to that estate and took the name, Richard Turberville Turberville *in 1797*. He settled at Ewenny, and was High Sheriff of Glamorgan and a J.P. for that county in 1804. He married a distant kinswoman, Elizabeth, daughter and co-heiress of the Revd. Gervase Powell of Llanharran, rector of Llanfeigan (Brec.), and vicar of Merthyr Tydfil. He died on 2 July 1817, leaving two sons and a daughter, who all, successively, owned Ewenny, but died without issue. The eldest son, Richard Turberville, was made a Captain in the Royal Glamorgan Militia on 5 September 1808 and died in 1848. The next son, Gervas Powell Turberville, born in 1790, went from Westminster School to the Royal Military Academy, and joined the 12th Foot as Ensign on 12 February 1807 and became Lieutenant on 13 August following. Gervas served with the 12th in the West Indies *(India)* in 1808, Captain on 14 March 1811, Major in 1825 and Lieutenant Colonel of the regiment from 8 October 1830 until he retired on 28 August 1835. He was made a Knight of the Guelphic Order of Honour in 1836 and served as High Sheriff of Glamorgan in 1851 and Gervas Turberville died childless on 16 June 1861, aged 71.

The career of Sir Thomas Picton is well known and only requires a brief summary here. Educated at Haverfordwest Grammar School, he became an Ensign in the12th Foot on 14 November 1771. *He was sent to the Military Academy of Louis Lochee in Chelsea.* Two years later, he joined his regiment at Gibraltar and in March 1777, was promoted Lieutenant. On 26 January 1778, he was promoted Captain into the 75th (or Prince of Wales Regiment of Foot), and returned to England. When the 75th was disbanded at Bristol in 1783, Picton quelled a threatened mutiny for which he received the Royal approbation. After this he returned to Poyston where he spent twelve years on half-pay. In 1794 he went to the West Indies where he was appointed to the 17th Foot (afterwards known to a majority as the 68th), and also as AOC to the Commander in Chief, Sir John Vaughan. For his distinguished services in the capture of St. Lucia he was promoted Lieut. Col. After further active service in the islands he was appointed Military Governor of Trinidad. He proved a vigorous and effective ruler, and on 22 October 1801 was promoted to Brigadier General. *He was forced in 1802 to take part in the experiment of tripartite government of Trinidad along with new fellow Commissioner William Fullarton and Admiral Sir Samuel Hood. This proved a total failure, and Fullarton collected evidence to prosecute Picton for alleged torture and misconduct whilst Governor.* The trial took place in the years 1806-10 and vindicated him. He was promoted Major General on 25 April 1808. In 1809 he took part in the capture of Flushing. In January 1810 he went to Portugal where he was given command of the 3rd Division, took part in the battle of Busaco (1810), and the defence of the lines of Torres Vedras. On 15 October 1811, he was appointed Colonel of the 77th (Middlesex Regiment) and took part in capture of Ciudad Rodrigo and Badajoz (both in 1812). He was wounded at Badajoz and invalided to England, suffering from fever. In Spring 1813 Picton returned to the Peninsula, having been made a KB by the Regent on 1 February. On 4 June 1813 he was promoted Lieut. General in the Army and took part in the battle of Vittoria in 1813. Having forced the passes of the Pyrenees he returned to England in July 1813 and took his seat as

M.P. *for Pembroke borough* and received the thanks of the House for his services. In December Picton returned to Spain to command Third Division, took part in the fighting in France and in the capture of Toulouse in April 1814. In the armistice following the abdication of Napoleon and on the break up of the Third Division, the officers subscribed £1,600 for a service of plate to him but he was disappointed at not being given a peerage. On 24 June 1814, he received for the seventh time the thanks of the House of Commons and returned to Wales. Upon the extension of the Order of the Bath at the beginning of 1815, Picton was promoted to be a Knight Grand Cross.

In June 1815 he joined the Army at Brussels and was appointed to command the Fifth Division. He took part and was wounded at Quatre Bras and died of his wounds. His body was brought home and he was buried in the family vault at St. George's, Hanover Square, on 3 July 1815, aged fifty-seven. He was unmarried and left no legal descendants. On 29 June 1815, the House of Commons ordered a monument to be raised to his memory at public expense in St. Paul's Cathedral. A memorial was raised at Carmarthen and unveiled August 1828.

Sir Thomas Picton died unmarried but while in Trinidad had four natural children by his mulatto mistress Rosette Smith. They were left legacies in his will written nine days before his death at Waterloo. The eldest, Thomas Picton Rose came to Neath in 1812 and was apprenticed to a doctor and became a MRCS in 1821. He eventually became an Assistant Surgeon in the Army and in 1824 was posted to the R.A.C.C. but died at sea on route to the Cape.

The third brother, Edward Picton was the only one to receive a university education. He matriculated from Brasenose College, Oxford on 4 June 1778 at the age of seventeen, proceeded to B.A. from New College in 1783 and took Holy Orders. He shared his brother's passion for the military life, and was commissioned as Chaplain in the 12th Foot on 19 May 1784, and served with the regiment until 1792 *when he resigned.* In 1798, he was presented by his eldest brother to the vicarage of Great St. Brides super Ely, with the curacy of Wick, Glamorganshire. In 1815 he succeeded to the Iscoed estates under the will of his brother Sir Thomas, where he settled for the rest of his life. He was a Deputy Lieutenant and Justice of the Peace of that county and for Pembrokeshire and Glamorgan. He married Charlotte Maria Edwardes of Rhydygors near Carmarthen, but had no issue. He died on 26 August 1835 in his seventy-fifth year and was buried at St. Ishmaels. The inscription on his monument describes him as, "Descended paternally from the Pictons of Poyston, and maternally from the De Tur Bervilles of Ewenny who settled in Wales shortly after the Conquest, and were established for centuries in the Principality. He by them was connected with the chief families of this country". His wife, survived him. *They had no issue, and the Iscoed estate passed to his nephew John Williams, son of his youngest sister, Anne Picton, who then took the name of Picton.*

The youngest son, John Picton, was commissioned Lieutenant on 26 January 1778 in the 75th Foot which his uncle had raised and of which he was Colonel. He did not remain long in the 75th which was disbanded in 1783 and he was placed on half pay. He was transferred to full pay on 28 April 1784 as Lieutenant to the family regiment, the 12th Foot. He became Captain on 27 October 1790 and served with distinction in Flanders in

1794 *and on the retreat through Germany to Bremen in April 1795. He was paymaster to the Regiment for much of the campaign.* The Duke of York mentioned him in his despatch written from Arnhem on 28 October 1794, "Captain Picton of the 12th Regiment was also wounded in a sally from Nimeguen on the morning of the 28th". On the 16 June following he was promoted Major. In 1797 he accompanied his regiment to India and served there and in the East Indies for several years. In December 1798, when stationed at Madras, he fought a duel with his commanding officer, Colonel Henry Harvey Aston, a brave but eccentric man. Both deloped and the affair had no effect on his subsequent career. He became a Brevet Lieutenant-Colonel in the Army on 1 January 1801, Lieutenant Colonel of his regiment on 30 November 1809 and Brevet Colonel on 25 July 1810. He was employed as Major General on the Staff, and in August 1814 was second in command in the Isle of France. Shortly afterwards he returned to his house, Cartlett Cottage at Haverfordwest, where he died, suddenly, on 5 January 1815 after retiring to bed in apparently perfect health. He was fifty-three years old and unmarried. *He also had two natural children.*

The remaining son, William Picton, was baptised in 1757. In the family account left by Col. Thomas Picton Milner it is related that one of the brothers "Being threatened by a flogging ran away from home and was never heard of again". When Sir Thomas Picton was serving in the Peninsula, a Spanish Officer appeared and inquired concerning the 23rd Foot, a Welsh Regiment. He reputedly bore a strong likeness to the General who made strenuous efforts to locate him. It may be that this was the missing brother.

Mention should be made of the children of John and Catherine Warlow:

1. Thomas Warlow, *born 1797 – died Meerut, India 1824.* He entered the H.E.I. Company's army as a cadet in Bengal in 1815 and became a second Lieutenant in 1817. He was mentioned in the despatches of Sir D. Marshall for his conduct at the capture of Mundiah by Bengal troops in 1818 and in the following year, took part in operations on the Indian frontier and was promoted to Lieutenant. He became a Captain on 28 September 1827.

He married Mary Prudence Ord, by whom he had three sons:

i. Thomas Picton Warlow (b. 1827) who entered the Royal Artillery, and was a Lieutenant Colonel commanding the Pembroke Dock Garrison in 1869; became Inspector of Small Arms, Birmingham and in 1867 he succeeded to the Ewenny Abbey estate *on the death of Elizabeth Turberville,* and assumed the name of Turberville. He was D.L. and J.P. of Glamorganshire and High Sheriff in 1876. *He died without issue in 1891.*

ii. William Warlow (born 1803), *his early career was spent in the Hussars but he* entered the medical profession and became a Member of the Royal College of Surgeons. He married Miss *Charlotte* Bellairs, by whom he had a daughter, Elizabeth

Sir Thomas Picton

Caroline who married Captain J. B. Edwards of Rhydygors, Carmarthen. *They had several children.*

2. Catherine Warlow, *baptised 1800 at Haverfordwest,* married in 1822, Grismond Philipps of Cwmgwili, an officer of the 23rd Foot, (LWF) who had served in the Peninsula War and at Waterloo. *They were the forebears of the Philipps of Cwmgwilli, Carmarthenshire.* The grandson of this marriage, Colonel Sir Grismond Picton Philipps, C.V.O., of Cwmgwili, was Lord Lieutenant of Carmarthenshire until his recent death.

3. Cecil Warlow, *born 1801. She married William Evans, solicitor of Haverfordwest and had issue. He died in 1849 and she in 1872.*

Ref. [1] W.W.H.R., X. pp. 43-54.

THE PEMBROKE YEOMANRY
Copy of orders in 1807

The following will interest many old members of the Pembroke Yeomanry. This regiment no longer exists, and passed out after the Great War. It is a copy of the orders dated 10 June 1807, when the Corps was known as the Castlemartin Yeomanry Cavalry.

"On Field Days the gentlemen of the Corps are all required to attend punctually at the time and the place stated appointed by the Commanding Officer. Each must appear in the field with the arms, clothing and accoutrements which he shall have received as mentioned in the following list: Helmet and feather, black stock, uniform jacket, blue overalls (except when leather breeches are ordered) gloves, boots and spurs, sword and belt, sword knot, military bridle, collar, holsters and straps, pistol, goat skin, cloak.

"When horses are sick or hurt, must nevertheless attend dressed in their uniforms and wearing their swords. No excuse will be accepted for gentlemen's absence unless they are disabled by any hurt or sickness, or are out of the County of Pembroke or on the other side of Milford Haven. Members of the Corps being unprovided with excuses shall be fined according to the rule here given, each time they shall so offend: Captain £1. 1s.; Lieutenant 9s.; Cornet, 8s.; Quarter Master, 3s.; Sergeant, 2s. 6d.; Corporal. 2s. 6d.; Private 2s. 6d.; Trumpeter, 2s. 6d.; Farrier, 2s. 6d." So it can be seen that the attendance of a private was considered just as important as the attendance of a sergeant. The orders were signed by Joseph Adams, Captain.

Capt. Adams lived at Holyland, Pembroke, and it was he who had charge of General Tate who commanded the French when they landed at Fishguard in February 1797. He was well-known to Baron Cawdor and other gentlemen of the county as "Joe Adams".

A Pembrokeshire recruiting officer?

CHAPTER VII

SOME ANCESTRAL HALLS
AND THEIR FAMILIES

SLEBECH HALL

SOME years before the last war, the Baron de Rutzen and I were rummaging in an attic at Slebech Park[1] when we came across a small framed silhouette of a man attired in what we considered to be the dress of the early nineteenth century. Nothing was known of his identity, but after cleaning it we were able to read on the back this faded inscription: "Sir Alan Cameron, Lieut. Gen. KCB., of the Erracht branch of the House of Lochiel, who with the aid and assistance of his father in law Nathaniel Phillips of Slebech Park Esquire raised the 79th or Cameronian Highlanders & afterwards commanded them in the Peninsula."

This determined me to investigate the history of Nathaniel Phillips and Sir Alan Cameron, and in course of my researches I came across several matters of national as well as local interest. Much of what is printed below is based on notes I made at that time from the muniments in Slebech, afterwards deposited in The National Library by the Baron de Rutzen.[2]

Phillips and Cameron

Nothing is known of the ancestry of Nathaniel Phillips, except that his father's Christian name was also Nathaniel, and there is no evidence to suggest that he was in any way connected with the numerous West Wales families bearing the surname Phillips. The coat of arms used by him: *quarterly, gules and argent, in the first quarter an eagle displayed or*, proved that he himself claimed no kinship with a Welsh family. Neither do we know his place of birth. Born on 10 June 1730, he grew up to become a planter in Jamaica where he engaged in the sugar trade and its by-products, owning Phillipsfield, Suffolk Park, Boxford Lodge, Pleasant Hill and other valuable properties worked mainly by coloured slaves. By industry and application he amassed a fortune and his worldly successes may be traced in the Slebech muniments.

On 18 June 1761, Nathaniel Phillips married at Jamaica, Anne, daughter of Richard and Anne Swarton. The union was of short duration for Anne died on 6 October 1766 and was buried in the chancel of the church at Kingston. The only surviving child of the marriage, Anne, born 2 November 1765, was for many years heir apparent to her father's vast fortune.

In the late 1770s Nathaniel spent some time in England and took a house in Gloucester Place, Portman Square, London. He returned frequently to Jamaica to attend to business. In 1785 he fought a duel and killed his man in a dispute concerning the conviction of one of his slaves, an affair described in detail in the documents that have survived. It was some time after this event that he settled permanently in Britain.

I now turn to the gentleman whose silhouette I saw in the attic, Alan Cameron. Readers will recall how the chieftain, Lochiel, led his clansmen in the short and disastrous rising, the "Forty-Five", and how the Camerons broke through Barrel's Regiment of Foot at Culloden. The second-in-command of the clan at that battle was Donald Cameron of Erracht. Donald's direct forebears had been long associated with war and violence and few of them had died in their beds. His father had been killed at Sheriffmuir in "The Fifteen", his grandfather had fought on the losing side at the Boyne in 1690, his great-grandfather had fallen during inter-clan strife in 1660 and his great-great-grandfather had been hanged for cattle-lifting in 1630. After Culloden, Donald Cameron took to the heather and the hills and after several years of privation as a homeless wanderer, accepted the government's terms and returned to his ancestral hearth.

Alan Cameron, the son of this Donald, was born in 1753 at Erracht in Inverness-shire. He is said to have been educated by private tutors before proceeding to St. Andrews. A liberal education does not seem to have modified in any way the restless spirit bestowed on him by his ancestry. Hardly had he returned home than he quarrelled with a kinsman, Cameron of Morsheirlich, a Jacobite lately returned from wanderings on the Continent. As a result of the quarrel Alan called him out. Morsheirlich, a much older man and an expert swordsman, tried to persuade the challenger to abandon the challenge. However, he insisted on the meeting and the affair was settled with swords on the banks of the river Lochy on an early autumn morning. The challenger, who received some slight wounds, succeeded in fatally wounding Morsheirlich so that he died shortly afterwards. As a result Alan had to flee to escape the vengeance of the dead man's family and for two years lived in Mull and Morven under the protection of his maternal kinsfolk, the Macleans.

In 1773, he emigrated to America, and two years later obtained a commission in a provincial regiment, The Royal Highland Emigrant Corps, commanded by his kinsman, Colonel Alan Maclean of Torloisk, then engaged in operations against the American colonists. In course of the campaign he undertook a mission to raise and organise a force recruited from Red Indian tribes, but was captured and imprisoned in a vaulted cell in Philadelphia as an abettor of Indian atrocities and was very badly treated. After two years he succeeded in escaping, but as he dropped from the prison wall he fractured both ankles. He was befriended by one Phineas Bond who nursed him and afterwards assisted him to regain the British lines. He then returned to his native Erracht and was placed on half-pay.

In 1779 occurred an event that was to have a profound influence on his subsequent career. He met Anne Phillips, the young daughter of Nathaniel Phillips, the Jamaica merchant, and fell in love with her. The father frowned upon the idea of a match, in view of his daughter's age and the fact that Cameron had little to offer and had, apparently, no prospects. But Cameron was not to be denied and he and Anne eloped to Gretna Green where they went through a form of marriage. Such is the family tradition. However, the registers of Marylebone church in London reveal a more prosaic story, and record that on 16 September 1779 Anne Phillips was married by banns to Alan Cameron of Erracht in

Scotland. This does not entirely dispose of the runaway match, for I am informed that several Gretna Green marriages were subsequently regularised by a church ceremony.

The *Historical Records of the Queen's Own Cameron Highlanders* published in 1909 contains an excellent reproduction of a miniature of Anne and a silhouette of her husband, the latter being identical with the one described at the beginning of this essay.

They had seven children: Phillips, born in 1782; Donald; Nathaniel born at London in 1787; Ewen: Marcella: Anne and Diana. During their early married life they lived partly at Erracht (where Alan had acquired a lease which unhappily involved him in a feud with his clan chieftain) and in Gloucester Place, Portman Square, where the Jamaica merchant had settled. Alan still pined for military adventure, but remained unemployed.

In 1793 Cameron's great chance came. On 17 August of that year he received letters of service for raising a corps of highlanders. The regiment was to be raised without the usual allowance of levy money; it was to be recruited within three months and when established, to be designated the 79th or Cameron Volunteers with Cameron as its commander.

The raising of a regiment involved a considerable outlay of money, far beyond the resources of Cameron's purse. However, Nathaniel Phillips rose nobly to the occasion and as a result of his practical help and the great popularity of his son-in-law in the Highlands, the 79th was quickly formed, and on 3 January 1794 embodied at Glasgow as an effective corps consisting of 1,000 men officered by old half-pay officers of the American War, with Alan Cameron as Lieutenant-Colonel Commandant. When we reflect that this was achieved without any government bounty, it is clear that the measure of Nathaniel Phillips' assistance must have been decisive.

The subsequent conduct of the unit, both under its old designation of 79th Foot (Cameron Volunteers) and its newer one of Queen's Own Cameron Highlanders, provides a distinguished chapter in the annals of British arms. In 1794 the regiment served in Ireland where it received its uniform, and a distinctive tartan of the pattern known as the "Erracht Cameron", specially designed by Mrs. Anne Cameron.

Alan Cameron led the regiment through the severe campaign of 1794/5 in Flanders where it acquitted itself well. In 1796 it served in the West Indies and took part in the recapture of Martinique. Casualties and disease reduced its strength drastically and in 1797 the battalion was broken up and 210 of the men drafted to The Black Watch. Alan Cameron and his officers returned to the Highlands and with further help from his father-in-law raised a second 79th Regiment, 780 strong, in 1798. In the following year the 79th was in Holland where it fought in Moore's brigade,

Slebech Hall

performing particularly well on the Helder where Cameron was wounded. In 1800 it was at Ferrol and Cadiz, and in 1801 landed at Aboukir and took part in the battle of Alexandria. In 1804 Cameron received permission to raise a second battalion of the 79th and within six months had recruited a regiment of 800 men. Both units were placed under his command and subsequently did splendid service in the Peninsular War. Cameron covered the retreat of Sir John Moore at whose special instance he had been promoted to Brigadier-General.

The 79th fought at Talavera, Busaco, Fuentes d'Onoro and throughout the campaign in Spain, and later at Waterloo where it formed part of Kempt's Brigade in the 5th Division commanded by Sir Thomas Picton.

Alan Cameron was promoted Major-General in July 1810, but soon afterwards ill-health obliged him to return to England. He saw no further active service. In January 1815 he was made K.C.B. on the extension of the Order of the Bath and in August 1819 was promoted Lieutenant-General. He died at Fulham on 9 March 1828.

Sir Alan's four sons all served in their father's regiment. Phillips Cameron rose to be Lieutenant-Colonel and commanded the unit at Fuentes d'Onoro in 1811 and died of wounds after the battle. Donald, the second son served as a Captain. Ewan, a Lieutenant, died after Talavera in 1809. The only son to survive was Nathaniel Cameron who became Lieutenant-Colonel of the second battalion of the 79th, which he commanded during the period 1813-15. He died on 20 April 1860, aged 83. Nathaniel was also the only member of the family who left descendants. He married at Marylebone in November 1812 a West Wales wife, namely Letitia Pryce Cuny, daughter of the Revd. John Powell Cuny, rector of St. Brides, Pembrokeshire. After retiring from the army he lived for some time at Dan-y-graig near Swansea. His daughter, Mary Anne Cameron, married in April 1835 John Wyndham Bruce (brother of the first Baron Aberdare), and their eldest son, Alan Cameron Bruce-Pryce (died 1908) of Blaen-y-cwm, Monknash, Glamorgan, left a large family (see *BLG*).

So much for the connection between Nathaniel Phillips and Sir Alan Cameron. I shall now proceed to explain how it was that the silhouette of the latter came to Slebech in Pembrokeshire.

Phillips and de Rutzen

Nathaniel Phillips had taken a house in London shortly before 1779. After he had retired from personal direction of his Jamaican concerns, he entertained the idea of acquiring an estate in Wales where he would settle down as a country gentleman. He came in contact with William Knox, a similar *nabob*, who some years previously, had bought the Llanstinan and Slebech estates in Pembrokeshire. In 1792 he entered into negotiation for the sale of the Slebech estate, and by 1795 had bought it and was resident there.

An estate was not the only acquisition he made in Pembrokeshire. About this time he decided on a second matrimonial venture. He was 66 years of age and had been a widower for 30 years. His choice fell on the attractive daughter of a Pembrokeshire parson, Mary Dorothea Phillips, then a minor about 19 years old. They were married, by licence, at St. Mary's, Islington, in February 1796. The great difference in their ages proved in no way prejudicial to what turned out to be a happy and successful union. The marriage allied him to the older landed families in West Wales and no doubt contributed to the ease with which Nathaniel Phillips fitted into local society. In the same year as his marriage he was picked High Sheriff and placed in the Commission of the Peace for the county. An amiable and kindly man, "Nat" Phillips, settled down as to the manner born and became a popular and useful member of the community. Richard Fenton describes a fete and a ball he attended at Slebech, his most vivid memory being of the sewin landed from the river Cleddau below the house and carried straight to the frying pan.

Mary Dorothea's father, the Revd. Edward Philipps, was a younger son of Thomas and Dorothy Philipps of Lampeter Velfrey, whose family was a cadet of the ancient and influential house of Philipps of Picton Castle, whose head at this time was Lord Milford, Lord Lieutenant of the county. Edward matriculated at Pembroke College, Oxford, on 14 December 1754 at the age of 17, and graduated Bachelor of Arts in 1758. He took Holy Orders and was rector of Begelly from 1767 to 1778 and of Lampeter Velfrey from 1778 until his death on 2 April 1793, aged 56. He married Catherine Harries (marriage bond dated 5 December 1774) and she died on 6 May 1803, aged 55. Both were buried at Lampeter Velfrey where a memorial to them was erected by their daughter, Mrs. Mary Dorothea Phillips of Slebech. The Revd. Edward Philipps was also a magistrate, and owner of a considerable property. He had seven children – Thomas Philipps of Neeston Hall, Pembrokeshire; John Philipps of London; Mary Dorothea wife of Nathaniel Phillips; Cecilia, wife of William Charles Allen of St. Brides who adopted the additional name of Philipps; Elizabeth, who had a passion for genealogical researches, married firstly, in 1808 Aldborough Richardson of Upper Wimpole Street, London, and secondly in 1832, Lieut.-Gen. Sir Henry King, fourth son of the second Earl of Kingston and had two little girls who died in infancy.

After having been heir apparent for many long years Mrs. Anne Cameron of Erracht found herself dethroned from that pleasant and enviable position. For Nathaniel and Mary Dorothea had four children – Mary Dorothea, born on 15 January 1797, whose christening on 20 August was attended by the Duke of Rutland, who noted in his journal "Mr Phillips is a West Indian, and has amassed an immense fortune"; Nathaniel, born in 1798 was educated at Eton and graduated at Christ Church, Oxford on 16 October1817 became High Sheriff of Pembrokeshire in 1820 and died unmarried on 20 July 1824 at the Hotel of the Arms, Amsterdam, from concussion and bruises occasioned by a severe fall; Louisa Catherine born in 1801, married on 11 February 1819, Thomas William, Viscount Anson, created Earl of Lichfield in 1831, and had issue; and Edward Augustus, born in 1802, died unmarried on 15 February 1830 and was buried at St. Marylebone, London.

Nathaniel Phillips, the father, died on 30 December 1813, at the age of 83. He was buried in the churchyard of the old parish church, hard by the mansion, but in 1860 his remains were removed to the vault in the new church of Slebech which stands on the side of the main road to Haverfordwest. His will, dated 9 November 1813, was proved in the Prerogative Court of Canterbury on 18 April in the following year. The main part of his fortune passed to the children of the second venture, his estate being charged with legacies totalling £37,000, of which £7,000 was for the Camerons. After the death of the sons, Nathaniel and Edward Augustus, reported above, the whole estate passed to Mary Dorothea and her sister, the Countess of Lichfield, as co-heiresses.

After the loss of her husband, Mrs. Phillips settled down to the cares of her young family. After Waterloo they spent much time in France and Italy, particularly in Rome where the widow rented a villa and entertained English visitors and the Roman society among whom she moved freely. In 1819, her younger daughter married Lord Anson and as her sons were still receiving their education, she was left with Mary Dorothea as her constant companion. They spent much time in Rome in 1821/22, and it was then that another nobleman appeared on the scene, one more romantic and colourful than the British peer who had already become Mrs. Philipps' son-in-law.

He was Charles Frederick, Baron de Rutzen. According to a letter written by him, his ancestor was one Augustus Edlen descended from a member of the German family of Von Frenz, who married the last of the Von Rutzens whose name, title and coat-of-arms he adopted,[3] and those lands he added to his own. On 26 December 1657 Augustus received an acknowledgement of nobility from Wladislaus IV, King of Poland, which was recorded in the manifesto of the Land Tribunal of the Principality of Samogicia. He is described in the family archives as hereditary lord of the estates of Polasche in the circle of Telshe in the Principality of Samogicia in Imperial Russia. From him the family has a proven descent.

Augustus died in 1677 and his will, dated on 18 January of that year was recorded in the records of the Principality of Samogicia on 11 May. He was succeeded by his son, Michael Frederick, who married one Ida Berthe. The will of Michael Frederick, dated 28 January 1738, was registered on 7 February in the same Land Tribunal. He was succeeded by his son, John Frederick, a minor, who in 1794 married Frederica Elizabeth, daughter of Charles Frederick von Suenger of Niederbartan in the Duchy of Courland. Courland lay on the southern side of the Gulf of Riga, and is today comprised in Latvia; Samogicia lay to the south of Courland, and is now comprised in Lithuania. Thus the Rutzens were "Baltic barons". They started to use the particle "de" instead of von towards the end of the eighteenth century.

Baron John Frederick, described in the family papers as "Patron President of the Ecclesiastical Lutheran Evangelical Council of Kroettingen", sold his hereditary estate of Polasche on 20 April 1793 and purchased other properties in Courland. He took a prominent part in local government and administration. On 19 September 1823 Leopold XII granted a Patent of the Military Order of St. John of Jerusalem to Baron John Frederick de Rutzen, "a nobleman of Curland", the original of which remains among the Slebech muniments. He died on 2 January 1832 and was buried at Maszutten, leaving the following children – Baron Charles Frederick von (de) Rutzen, born 3 March 1795 at Niederbartan in Courland, Baron Charles von (de) Rutzen, living in 1859, and married to Olga, niece of Prince Potemkin and Baron Henry William von Rutzen, to whom a confirmation of the arms and of the nobility of the Rutzens was granted by an ukase of the Senate, Department of Heraldry, on 16 October 1849 and who died at Maszutten, one of the family estates, on 2 November 1863, leaving a son, Baron William de Rutzen.

Baron Charles Frederick, the eldest son, is the man who married Miss Mary Dorothea Phillips. He wrote a draft autobiography, of which only a section of 24 folios seems to have survived.

According to this memoir, Charles Frederick spent most of his early life on the parental estates and before 1817 made an extensive tour of Europe. In 1819 he was living mainly at Libau in Courland and paid a brief visit to England. We learn, too, that his father had established private "express line" of two horses, a groom and post-boy, in each town, so that he could ride quickly to any part of the country. After 1815 there was much political intrigue concerning partitioned Poland and several secret societies formed, but the de Rutzens remained faithful to the settlement. A Lithuanian duke of considerable talents and estates and a close friend of Baron Charles Frederick, became a leading member of one of these societies, but as a result of a hot discussion on the matter their friendship came to an end and all attempts to effect a reconciliation proved fruitless. Despite this, Charles Frederick retained his admiration for the fine qualities of his erstwhile friend. Early one September morning in 1820 he heard from an authoritative source that the Duke had been denounced and that detachments of lancers were to surround his residence that evening at half past eleven of the clock when they were to impound all incriminating documents and arrest the owner. Memories of their days of friendship outweighed those of political hostility in the mind of Charles Frederick and he decided to warn the intended victim. As the matter was too urgent and too dangerous for him to send warning by letter, he decided to go himself. Disguised as a huntsman he mounted his horse and at a quarter past eight in the morning set out at a wild gallop along his father's pony "express line". After a most exciting ride and after many relays of sweating horses had carried him 165 English miles, this Lithuanian Paul Reviere arrived at the Duke's castle at exactly seven o'clock in the evening – that is, he had accomplished the long ride in under eleven hours. He was correctly, but coldly, received by the man he had come to warn. The Duke showed no emotion at the news but quietly thanked the baron and asked him to take some champagne. This he politely declined, took his leave, and rode away to a distant house where he spent the night. During the following morning he contacted an uncle living nearby, who gave him a carriage to carry him home to Maszutten. The Duke profited by the warning, burnt all incriminating papers and was able to prove his "innocence" when the troops arrived. In January 1821, Charles Frederick received a letter of thanks from him in which he also asked the baron to honour him by accepting "the enclosed". This proved to be a bill, dated 1 January 1821, for 200,000 silver roubles, nearly £36,000 in English money. The galloping baron answered that he was happy to learn that matters had turned out so well and returned the bill "as it must have been meant for Hirsch," an outstanding jockey of the day!

According to the memoir he went to Rome early in 1821. He does not state why he went there, but the late Mrs. Foley-Philipps of Ridgeway, whose knowledge of the family history was considerable, informed me that the baron had held a minor post in the Russian embassy. At any rate we know that he had a fair amount of leisure and moved in the fashionable circles of that city. It was a fortunate journey for the young baron, for there he found Mary Dorothea Phillips of Slebech, whose dower was to more than compensate him for his haughty rejection of the Duke's silver roubles.

Let the baron now tell us in his own words: "Shortly after my arrival at Rome, I dined with Chevalier d'Italinsky the Russian Minister – and Medem – Count Medem (Paul) – asked me after dinner, what I was going to do. I said I was going home to get up Boccacio for my Italian master for tomorrow. Oh, if that is all, said Medem, come with me to a Mrs. Phillips, a remarkable handsome English woman, without much English nonsense. She speaks very good French, knows everybody and has a charming daughter who, moreover, is considered the best Pianist in the whole of Rome. It is Mrs. Phillips's at-home tonight, and we are sure to meet the cream of the beau monde. It was late when we arrived – the rooms were nearly full. Presently there was a simultaneous move – a sort of gentle press towards another room. Miss Phillips was going to play. The instant she touched the Piano, there was a breathless silence, yet no ostentatious prelude, only the favourite Waltz of the day at once; but with such a band like power and precision and a truly soul stirring expression. The suppressed 'Brava's' were more than an ovation. Had this little Waltz been so plaid in Public, all the bouquets would have been at her feet. Miss Phillips was rising, when a very handsome young man, who was sitting by the Piano, shewed her a Cahier of Notes: she looked at them shrugged her shoulders and was going. Being, however, much entreated by this man & some others that were standing round, to play on, she again looked at the Notes, read some parts with marked and visible attention – then looked imploringly & apologetically around and after a short, sharp and appropriate prelude, began the piece, which was one of Rossini's overtures, just come out. At the first turning over, the man that sat by her bungled – at the second, he was evidently by some bars out, and this disconcerting Miss Phillips a good deal, I stepped forward, asked to be allowed to turn over, as the light was very much in that gentleman's face – which, in fact, was the case – and being attentive, of course, got through satisfactorily, so that Miss Phillips, when she had done, said to me, 'Oh mille remerciment, je vois que vous êtes musicient'. I said, unfortunately I was not, and a Lady, who, I afterwards learnt was Lady (Countess) Compton (Northampton) coming up & saying to Miss Phillips, 'Well done Mary', I retired – indeed there was nothing else for it, as every one wished to say his say.

"A few days after Mrs. Phillips's soiree, I was riding with the three Miss Bolds, chaperoned as usual by Lord Walpole and I think Prince Sapieha and Lord Stanley – the present Lord Derby. In the Piazza del Popolo there came towards us at a stepping dashing pace, a superbly appointed phaeton, in whose charioteer, when he familiarly nodded to our party, I recognised the handsome young man that sat by Miss Phillips at the Piano. The horses were such magnificent animals & such marvelous fine steppers, that I did not look at the driver till he was close by. I asked Miss Bold who it was. 'Oh Lord Miltown', and so saying she turned to Walpole and said 'has he proposed?' 'Poor Mil, I know, is very sick', was the answer, 'but I don't think he has yet plucked up courage enough; but, perhaps, she is only doing as her sister did. Anson was kept in fear & trembling ever so long'. At length I made it out that all this was about Miss Phillips.[4]

"Rome was immensely gay that winter. Grandees and belles, Balls & parties without end, & Mrs. & Miss Phillips everywhere. At one of Countess Apony's great Balls, at the Austrian Embassy, I was standing between Prince Leopold the present King of the Belgians and the Duke of Devonshire, as a Cotillion was being danced. When the Ladies had to look for partners, Miss Phillips came up to me les yeaux baisses, droped me a gracious courtsy, clapped her hands, and we left walsing. Whirling round she noticed the Prince and said (*Oh there is Prince Leopold just come. You must take me to him* – [this is crossed out, and the following French words substituted]) Voila le Prince arrive. Non, Madame, il-y-a desu quelque temps qu'il a parler an duc de Devonshire & moi. This seemed to shock her, and she asked me to take her up to the Prince to apologise for having interrupted the conversation and not having made her obeisance to him as she ought to have done, the Prince having been at her sister's place in Staffordshire when she was there – and I think she said she had also met him at Trentham, the Marquis of Stafford's. Had this not been my first dance with Miss Phillips – her charming & ladylike manner when conversing with the prince, would have made me recollect it. At our next meeting – I really forget now what assembly – Miss Phillips said to me in English 'How is it you never dance' 'Les Madam, chez nous le dance que quant on leurs saffle'. 'Does that mean you expect to be asked? No doubt so excellent a lodger has a right to make his own terms!' I tried to make the best of this unfortunate, and as she construed it conceited speech of mine, but her badinage and jeux d'esprit laid [?me] completely prostrate notwithstanding I kept my own ground, I mean I did not answer in English, and I was really glad when Prince Felix Schwarzenberg (he died as Prime Minister of Austria) led her off to a Quadrille. Potoky, Sapieha's cousin, was charmed with her wit and (?), and at my ignoring English, notwithstanding Miss Phillips declared she would never speak to me again in French, as the Miss Bolds had told her that I spoke English like and indeed better than most English.

"Miss Phillips insisted on speaking English as she said she had understood I might pass anywhere for an Englishman. By way of episode I would say here that, being well aware that no English could surpass though they might equal me in French, and knowing the great importance of a superior knowledge & command of languages & the disadvantage of the contrary, I very reluctantly gave in: besides I had ever made it a rule never to speak English to any one out of England; Miss Phillips, however, made that resolution go to the wall."

And there the Baron's fragment ends. It is a pity that the complete memoir has not survived, but the foregoing tells us clearly where and how the Baron met his future bride.

Anyway, not long after their first meeting the Baron proposed and was accepted, whether in English or French we do not know. They were married by Special Licence at Colwich, Staffordshire on 30 October 1822 by the Revd. Frederick Anson, rector of Sudbury in Derbyshire. The witnesses who signed the register were Lord Vernon and Lord Anson, the latter being the bride's brother-in-law. Among the wedding presents received by Mary Dorothea, was a diamond ring from her brother-in-law Lieutenant-General Sir Alan Cameron.

The marriage settlement, executed on 22 October 1822, was made between the following parties: 1. John Frederick, Baron de Rutzen in the Duchy of Courland and his eldest son,

Charles Frederick, Baron de Rutzen; 2. Mary Dorothea Phillips, spinster; 3. The Rt. Hon. Thomas William, Viscount Anson, Nathaniel Phillips of Slebech Hall (brother of the bride) and Roger Harries of Bernard Street, Russell Square, Middlesex, merchant. By this settlement the prospective bride agreed to convey £10,000 (charged on the Jamaica estate) to the trustees, for the uses of the marriage; the trustees were to advance that sum or part thereof on security of a mortgage of the de Rutzen estates of Laukozam, Maulgrauschen and Maschutten, in the territory, or under the Government, of Lithuania in Russia, which estates were then in mortgage or otherwise secured to Baron John Frederick. The Baron Charles Frederick was to charge his estates with £2,000 as dower for his bride.

The marriage was blessed with seven children. The Baroness continued to charm her family and friends with her musical talent, and a haunting little melody of her own composition called "Slebech Hall" has survived. They lived first at Brighton until 1829 when they moved to Bedford Square, London. By the death of her brother, Edward Augustus Phillips, in 1830, the Baroness and her sister, Lady Anson, became co-heiresses to the estates in Jamaica and Slebech.

In 1830 the de Rutzens came to live at Slebech to fit into a way of life that differed greatly from that of fashionable European capitals and watering places. The Baron now had to undertake the duties and responsibilities of an English country gentleman. The Slebech estate had become the property of Mary Dorothea and her husband, comprised over 3,700 acres lying in the parishes of Slebech, Minwear, Newton, Martletwy, Robeston Wathen, Narberth and Lampeter Velfrey. It produced a rental of £5,300 per annum. The estimated value of the extensive woodlands alone amounted to over £70,000.

The house, then known as Slebech Hall, largely if not wholly rebuilt by a former proprietor in the 1770s, was a substantial building in the form of a square with a circular tower at each corner and a wing containing domestic offices on its north side. The demesne land, nearly 1,300 acres in extent, was park-like in character, laid out with trees and plantations, while the river Cleddau, about 300 yards wide, flowed nearby. The river was navigable as far as Blackpool bridge (built by the de Rutzens about 1830), and all craft entering within the bounds of the estate had to pay toll to the owner and to load or discharge cargoes at Blackpool Quay. The fishery on the river also belonged to him. The tolls and fishery were let for £40 per annum. Owing to its seclusion the area abounded in wild fowl of all description and a very large heronry in the wood near the mansion, was the only one on the Milford Haven estuary at that time.

The Baron and his wife were Lords of the Manors of Slebech, Minwear, Newton, Narberth and Robeston Wathen, and of the Manors or Reeveships of Lampeter Velfrey and Llanddewi Felffre.

The manorial dues and renders were small, but the mineral rights always had a potential value, while the sporting rights were extremely valuable and immediately available. The Baron insisted on these perquisites and had to recourse to law to enforce some of them. In the town of Narberth he built a hotel, "The de Rutzen Arms", and also a market house and enjoyed tolls of the weekly market and of the fairs held in that town. The Baron shared a passion for the chase with his Pembrokeshire neighbours and was a noted

The unwelcome Pembrokeshire immigrant

performer with rod and gun. He preserved game on a big scale, and in 1835 added to them by importing black fowl from Russia. Some of his activities were influenced by his continental background, sometimes to the discomfiture of his tenants. To add to his pleasures he imported animals that had long been extinct in England. Among these were wild boar. In November 1834 he arranged for the Duke of Brunswick to send him two wild boar, aged 1½ or 2 years, in a cage via Hamburg. The boar were let loose in the Canaston woodlands and provided good sport for the Baron, but their presence was deeply resented by the farmers and tenants, and as a result of their hostility, the Baron, much to his disgust, had to discontinue importing them. He agreed to destroy them all provided he could do so in his own way – by more intensive hunting. It seemed to the farmers, however, that they took "an unconscionable time a-dying", and the Baron enjoyed several more years of exciting sport before the last boar was bowled over. At one time he even toyed with the idea of importing wolves!

As Lay Rector he was entitled to the Rectorial Tithe rent charges of Slebech, Minwear and Newton, and was patron of the livings of those parishes. All these, of course, he enjoyed in right of his wife. His somewhat autocratic actions involved him in trouble with ecclesiastical authority. The three churches were in a state of disrepair. That of Slebech, which had been used during the Middle Ages by the Knights of St. John, lay between the mansion and the river. From 1766 it had been a continual expense and after the death of Nathaniel Phillips in 1813, the fabric deteriorated sadly. Rather than repair it, the Baron decided to build a new parish church at a distance from the mansion, and on 3 October 1838 the Baroness laid the foundation stone. The church was finally finished and consecrated in 1848, towards the building of which the de Rutzens had contributed very substantially. On either side of the entrance porch, carved in stone, are the heads of the Baron and Baroness, that of the former being particularly lifelike.

In 1844 the Baron obtained an Order in Council which provided for the consolidation of the three parishes for ecclesiastical purposes. He then selected a site for a new church to be built for the parishioners of Minwear and Newton, but nothing more was done. After this, the three old churches became totally derelict, that of Minwear being deliberately dismantled by order of the Baron. These activities led to his appearance in the Court of Arches in 1861. Judgement was given against him. He was ordered to restore the old church of Minwear and to pay costs of the lawsuit.

He helped to further education in the parish, converted an old blacksmith's shop into a schoolroom, contributed £6 to the master for teaching the labourers' children, and gave him a house, and culm valued at £3, a generosity recorded in the report of the Commission on Welsh Education in 1847.

The family continued to make visits to London where they had many friends, some in exalted places. Among these were Queen Adelaide (wife of William IV), the Duke and

Duchess of Kent and their daughter, "the young Victoria", who ascended the Throne in 1837. Among her possessions was a piece of jewellery described as "Queen Victoria's hair set in a Diamond Brooch, graciously presented by Her Majesty to Baroness de Rutzen". She was also friendly with the Baroness Lehzen, Queen Victoria's companion and confidante and with the Duke and Duchess of Marlborough. They also maintained contact with their friends and relations on the Continent, among others the de Rutzens, Zachlehner of Memel, Baron de Grotthus, Marquis and Marchioness de Prouleroy and the Duke of Brunswick. The Baron and Baroness, taking their children with them, made at least one visit to Courland, some time before 1833.

In 1860 the Baroness fell ill. On 18 May she made her will and on 14 June she died and was buried privately in the vault in Slebech new church. In the will she requested that the remains of her father be removed from the old parish church and placed near her in the vault in the new church, and on 2 August this was done.

The Baron felt her loss keenly, for the marriage had been a most happy one, husband and wife being utterly devoted to each other and to their children. After her death he lived at intervals at different places in Europe, sometimes accompanied by his daughter, Emmeline. While at Dresden he was taken ill and died there on 15 August 1874. His remains were brought back to Slebech and placed in the vault alongside those of his wife.

Baron John Frederick de Rutzen and Mary Dorothea his wife had the following issue:

1. Baron Frederick Leopold Sapieha Manteuffel, born at Brighton on 10 June 1825 and baptised at the Royal Chapel. He succeeded his father at Slebech, was a Justice of the Peace and served as High Sheriff of Pembrokeshire in 1871. He was particularly interested in the volunteer movement and in 1847 became Cornet in The Pembroke Yeomanry, of which he became Major-Commandant in 1864 and Lieutenant-Colonel in 1871. He resigned the command in 1878 and in May of that year was appointed Honorary Colonel of the regiment. He died unmarried on 20 May 1890 aged 64 and was succeeded by his brother, Rudolph;

2. Baron Rudolph William Henry Ehrard, born 6 September 1828, baptised at Brighton on 8 October 1828. He was a B.A. of the University of Cambridge and became a barrister of the Inner Temple (1864). He was a Justice of the Peace for Pembrokeshire and served as High Sheriff in 1895. He died unmarried on 18 April 1915 and was succeeded by his nephew Alan;

3. Albert Richard Francis Maximilien – see later;

4. Eugene Ferdinand Ulrich Stanislaus, born 27 July 1834, baptised at Slebech on 7 September following. He married on 10 December 1892, Agnes daughter of Thomas Penman, and died without issue on 29 September 1916;

5. Minna Frederica Phillipa, born 23 September 1823, died 29 June 1825;

6. Frederica Maria Louisa, born 30 January 1827, baptised at Brighton 30 March following; married, 20 August 1850, Richard Ilbert Phillips of Lawrenny, Pembrokeshire. She died on 1 November 1904 leaving issue. (See Lort-Phillips of Lawrenny in *BLG.*);

7. Emmeline Charlotte Catherine, born 24 March 1832, baptised at Slebech on 13 May following; she died unmarried in August 1892.

Albert Richard Francis Maximilien de Rutzen was born on 27 January 1830 and baptised at St. James's, Westminster, on 3 April following. He was a B.A. of the University of Cambridge, and became a barrister of the Inner Temple (1857). He embarked on a legal career. From 1872 to 1876 he was stipendiary magistrate for Merthyr Tydfil, and for some years deputy-chairman of Quarter Sessions for Glamorgan, then became Metropolitan Police Magistrate for Marylebone 1876-91, Westminster (1891-97), Marlborough Street (1897-99), Bow Street (1899-1901) and was Chief Magistrate there from 1901. He was a Justice of the Peace and Deputy Lieutenant for Pembrokeshire, and Justice of the Peace for Glamorgan, Berkshire, London and the Home Counties. He was knighted in 1901. He formed the subject of one of "Spy's" famous cartoons.

On 11 September 1872 he married, at Llandeilo church, Horatia Augusta Stepney Gulston, eldest daughter of Alan James Gulston, J.P., D.L., of Derwydd, Carmarthenshire. Sir Albert died on 22 September 1913, his wife on 23 February 1924 and were buried in the family vault in Slebech church. They had five children:
1.   Alan Frederick James – see later;
2.   Emmeline Augusta Louisa, married on 10 November 1913, Sir Frank Hilliard Newnes, Baronet, of London. She was a Dame of Grace of St. John of Jerusalem, and died without issue on 8 October 1939;
3.   Gwendoline Mary, married on 10 August 1911, Lieutenant-Colonel Reginald Ernest Maffett, Duke of Wellington's Regiment, and had issue;
4.   Alberta Dorothea, died an infant, 22 December 1877;
5.   Violet Frances, married 24 April 1903, Sir Watkin Randle Kynaston Mainwaring, C.B.E., of Hafod y Coed, St. Asaph, second son of Salusbury Kynaston Mainwaring of Otley Park, Salop, and has issue.

Alan Frederick James de Rutzen, born 4 July 1876, succeeded to Slebech on the death of his uncle, Baron Rudolph, in 1915. At that time he was serving abroad in the Middle East as a lieutenant in The Pembroke Yeomanry. In July 1916, a detachment under command of Lieutenant Baron de Rutzen left The Pembroke Yeomanry at Wadi Natrum to join the Imperial Camel Corps. The detachment saw immediate action, and on 7 August, the Baron was killed at the battle of Kattia, near El Arish, in the Sinai desert.

He had married on 28 April 1908, Eleanor Etna Audley Thursby-Pelham, daughter of Captain Pelham Thursby-Pelham of Abermarlais Park, Carmarthenshire, by Emily Florence only daughter of Henry Foley, D.L. After her husband's death she married on 2 December 1918 to Captain George William Fisher Foley-Philipps. She died on 3 December 1945.

Baron A. F. J. de Rutzen left an only son, John Frederick Foley de Rutzen, born on 27 January 1909. He was educated at Eton College and in the University of Cambridge. On 23 May 1918 he received Royal Licence for himself and the heirs male of his body, on succession, to use the title Baron de Rutzen within His Majesty's Dominions.

A talented man, he had an original turn of mind and a gift of expression. Widely read, particularly in history, he also wrote poetry of no mean order. He believed in the traditional virtues associated with the life and conduct of a country gentleman, namely attachment to the lands he owned and to the tenants who rented them, and the discharge of those public duties that custom had long imposed on leading families in the community. Accordingly, he had a deep and practical interest in agriculture and estate management, was in the Commission of the Peace for the town and county of Haverfordwest, and for some time a member of the Pembrokeshire County Council. Stimulating, always sincere and frank, his mere presence made one feel more alive.

During the second world war he served in the Welsh Guards, and saw active service in North Africa and Italy. I met him in Hunts Gap before Beja when his battalion came to reinforce the brigade in which I was serving, at a very critical moment, and later, on the banks of the Medjerda. Our paths crossed again in Italy when my regiment supported the Welsh Guards in the fighting for Cerasola. I never saw him again. Major the Baron de Rutzen fell in action near Battaglia in the Gothic Line on 11 October 1944.

By his wife Sheila Victoria Katrin, daughter of Sir Henry Philipps, Baronet, of Picton Castle, whom he married on 28 July 1932, he had an only child, Victoria Anne Elizabeth Gwynne de Rutzen. She married on 3 May 1957 to Francis Dashwood, eldest son of Sir John Lindsay Dashwood, Baronet. The widowed Baroness de Rutzen married on 8 October 1947, Lieut.-Col. the Hon. Randal Plunket who afterwards succeeded as the nineteenth Lord Dunsany.

The pageant of the de Rutzens has ended. They moulder in the vault of the church which had been built mainly at their cost and the last of the Barons lies among Italian hills far from his Pembrokeshire home, but in the land where his ancestor first met the heiress of Slebech. Little did I dream, when I looked at the silhouette in the attic, to what paths my enquiries were to lead me; the sugar plantations of Jamaica, the Scottish Highlands, a prison in Philadelphia, Gretna Green, the Peninsula and Waterloo, the plains of Courland, Rome, and Slebech above the waters of Cleddau – they read more like incidents from a novel by Buchan, than materials for a factual chronicle devoted to the performances of real men and women. Yet it is one of the pleasures that comes the historian's way, to find the silver chain that binds what seems no more than a jumble of successive and isolated events into a coherent and significant whole.

Francis Jones

FOOTNOTES

[1] See Francis Jones "Some Slebech Notes" *The National Library of Wales Journal*, Vol. VII, No. 3 Summer 1952.

[2] See an able review of this collection by Dr. B. G. Charles, N.L.W. Vol. V, No. 3 Summer 1948,

[3] The German family of von Rutzen bore *or, a boar's head couped sable an annulet gules in its ear.* (R. Holme, *Academy of Blazon.* 1688 II, ix: 181 *Rietstap* Pl. CCXIV). The Barons de Rutzen of Slebech bore *or a double-headed eagle displayed sable, on an inescutcheon argent a boar's head and neck couped sable, an annulet or in the sinister ear:* supporters, *dexter, a gryphon, sinister, a lion crowned;* over the shield a baron's coronet.

[4] The love-sick charioteer was Joseph, fourth Earl of Milltown, who in 1828 married Barbara daughter of Lord Castle Coote. Viscount Anson (later Earl of Lichfield) had married Louisa Catherine Phillips in 1819.

POYSTON HALL

THE earliest references are "ville de Poytyngeston" in 1476 and "Poythenston" or "Poytington" in 1480. The name is probably a corruption of "Poytyns farm", certainly a Henry Poytyn was living in the Haverfordwest area in 1340. By 1592 the place was referred to as "Poiston" or "Poyston", later it became known as "the hall house of Poyston" (1671) or just "the Hall" (1679).

It is difficult to determine the form of the house that existed here before the eighteenth century, probably whatever it was became incorporated within the structure of the rear service rooms of the house. Still visible are several blocked-up windows and a doorway, with possible evidence of vaulting. The batter visible on the kitchen chimney stack suggests antiquity. The site is also suggestive of age, being low down, not far from water. A will in the early eighteenth century refers to an "oak room".

The three-storey front of the house with its Georgian symmetry is obviously eighteenth century. It faces south at a right angle to the axis of the old house. Thomas Picton, the owner of Poyston in the middle years of that century, sold two farms, Scollock (192 acres) and Triffleton (69 acres) for over £600 in the 1750s, so perhaps this financed his building. Certainly he had a large family so the size was useful. Superficially the house now looks much as it did in his time because although it was later totally upgraded and improved in the nineteenth century, the refurbishment respected the Georgian feel of the house. The Georgian interior was probably fairly plain with modest room sizes. The stairs to the top floor and some internal doors survive from this period. Externally there is still some slate hanging (a typical Pembrokeshire vernacular feature) dating from then together with zig zag brick cornicing under the eaves at the rear of the house. There are two small vaulted cellars under the front hall. Up until the Victorian changes there was a stone porch with some classical decoration, banded rustication in the stucco up to the first floor string course and a bust of General Picton mounted over the middle window over the porch.

In the mid 1800's the house, along with Withybush House, was acquired by William Owen, a highly successful architect, builder and joiner who had decided to completely retire from trade and become a gentleman. His son, Henry Owen, eventually settled at Poyston and it was during his time that the last phase of development took place. He added the dining room with the galleried library above making an impressive room two storeys high and embellished with heraldic crests, a gilded overmantel displaying the Owen crest and a collection moulded fireplace with Dutch tiles. He thoroughly overhauled the rest of the house

Poyston Hall

adding panelling, a stained glass window by Dix on the stairs, an ornate plaster fireplace and overmantel celebrating the battles of General Picton in the front hall. He added many "high tech" features of his age including a bathroom, an acetylene gas generating plant, the hydraulic ram system which pumped water up to the greenhouse, and an electric wind direction indicator linked to the dragon weather vane on the library roof. He also added an attractive lodge (now called The Rose Gate) and gates and piers at the end of the front drive. This drive was known as The Avenue and whilst it was improved by Henry Owen, its route is identical to that shown on the 1830's tithe assessment map. An interesting feature almost now disappeared was a stone and iron bridge that crossed the public road and linked Poyston, via a path to Withybush House, the other Owen property.

There is a story that the ghost of General Picton dressed in a cloak and carrying a sword appears on the front drive on the anniversary of his death at Waterloo. Also associated with the legend of General Picton is the blackened skull of a horse that still exists under the floor of the drawing room. This is supposedly his horse from the battle of Waterloo. Tradition has it also that the rest of the horse is buried under the big lawn.

The grounds amount to 15 acres. Laid out in the eighteenth century the whole is surrounded by a belt of trees. Below a partially walled kitchen garden, lawns slope down to a small lake that in Victorian times boasted a boat house. There are several ornamental trees still surviving, the best being a tulip tree growing close to the dining room.

Ref: D. Ellis, Poyston.

EXTRACTS FROM AN ARTICLE WRITTEN IN 1954

STONE HALL, the house of William Wogan. On the evening of 15 November 1603, while the servants sat around the fire, one Thomas Phillip Dafydd Gwyn of Eglwyswrw, called and asked for shelter. He was given supper and a corner of the stable loft where the servants slept. By the morning however, Gwyn had disappeared – and so had Bailiff Winter's jerkin, the ploughman's breeches and other clothing, together with a sum of 8s.6d. Gwyn was traced through the hostelries of Letterston, Little Newcastle and Pontfaen and was eventually caught at an inn at Eglwyswrw, with 5d. in his pocket. He was brought before William Warren of Trewern and sent to gaol at Haverfordwest.

LLANREITHAN. It was said that Llanreithan was once famed for its honey; that it was besieged during a local war; that a Jacobite who had lived there had run away to London, and that the ghost of a former occupier haunted a nearby stream. Research among the records of Llanreithan had revealed that among the effects of Arthur Laugharne in 1699 were about 40 beehives, an unusually large number for that period. The last squire, John Laugharne, who shared the Barony of Cemais with the Lloyds of Bronwydd, kept an armed gang to ward off his creditors, and was the last person in Pembrokeshire to keep a Fool, known as Joe Llanreithan. After John Laugharne's lands were sequestered in 1744, he left for London, and although there is no record of the reason for his departure his neighbours considered it likely that he took part in the Rebellion. After his death in 1755 he was buried at night in an unknown place.

RIDGEWAY AND THE FOLEYS

THE historic house of Ridgeway in Pembrokeshire stands on high ground rising northwards from the main A40 highway. It faces south, overlooking the woodlands of Canaston and Minwear, the demesnes of Picton Castle and Slebech Park. To the west is Wiston with its remains of a twelfth-century castle built by Wizo the Fleming, and some two-and-a-half miles eastwards is Narberth, whose ruined fortress was the former home of the powerful medieval family of Mortimer. The river, Eastern Cleddau, and its tributary the Syfynwy, both well-known for fishing, pass close to Ridgeway. The county town of Haverfordwest is about six miles away. In very early times a track ran along the Ridgeway and also a pilgrim's road leading to St. Davids where the shrine of the Patron saint attracted vast crowds.

Ridgeway lies in the parish of Llawhaden, a district rich in archaeological remains. It was heavily populated in Celtic times as shown by the remains of eight earth-castles in Drim Wood, Pilcornswell, Gelli and Vaynor, and the pre-Christian tumuli at Dingstopple and St. Kennox.

Later, the parish formed part of the Barony of Llawhaden belonging to the Bishops of St. Davids who had a seat in the House of Lords by virtue of this Barony. A short distance to the northwest of Ridgeway, on a precipitous bluff commanding an extensive view is Llawhaden Castle built entirely of hewn stone during the period 1250-1300 by a Bishop of St. Davids who was also secular lord of the Lordship of Llawhaden. It stands on the site of an older Norman fortification which had been captured and destroyed by the Welsh princes in 1192.

The Bishops held their courts here, and the parishioners were responsible for guarding prisoners, and assisting in hanging condemned men "at the sound of the horn". The castle was garrisoned and strengthened during Owain Glyndŵr's revolt (1399-1415), and continued to be inhabited until the time of Bishop Barlow (1536-47), who dismantled it. The remains are impressive, and the moat that protected it in medieval times still exists. The Bishops maintained a large park within the parish in which a valuable herd of red deer roamed as late as 1536.

The parish church dating from the fourteenth century is dedicated to St. Aidan. Immediately north of Ridgeway House are the remains of a *hospitium,* founded by Bishop Beck in 1287, to assist pilgrims on their way to the shrine of St. David. St. Kennox was once home of the famous Vicar Prichard, author of the *Welshmen's Candle*, in the reign of James I. Among the landowning families were those of Hawkwell, Meares and Skyrme, whose heraldic devices decorate the plate in the parish church. Llawhaden also had fairs from early times, a privilege granted by the Bishops.

Ridgeway, the principal house in the parish, retained its importance for over 700 years, during which it remained in possession of the descendants of the first owner. Although a substantial building, little remains of the original structure and it was largely rebuilt towards the middle of the eighteenth century, and this is the house that exists today.

Richard Fenton, the Pembrokeshire historian who visited it about 1800, says: "Ridgeway, the elegant residence of my estimable friend, J. R. Foley, Esq. amidst groves chiefly of his own planting and though in so elevated an exposure of a growth productive of great ornament as well as shelter. From this eminence the prospect is delightful. In front you look down on all the woods of Canaston, Slebech, and Mynwear, with the richly-cultivated farm of Canaston, intersected with hedgerows; and from the lawn to the north you catch a view of the ruins of Llawhaden Castle, seen in point the most striking of any."

The Foleys of Ridgeway took a leading part in local life. In 1383 Bishop Hoton of St. Davids granted lands to John Foley who is described as "Constable of our Castle of Llawhaden and Master of our Works". During the wars of Owain Glyndŵr (1399-1415) John Foley commanded the castle which had been strengthened, provisioned and garrisoned.

In the time of Henry VIII, Bishop Barlow tried to take possession of Ridgeway and the case was heard before the King in person. The Bishop's attempt failed and the King confirmed the estate to the Foleys for ever, subject to a nominal payment to the Church.

In 1615 Richard Foley, being armed with a caliver, was a member of the Train Band of the Hundred of Dungleddy. Enthusiastic royalists, five of the Foleys were killed at the battle of Colby Moor fighting under the banner of Charles I.

In 1661 William Foley paid a Benevolence of 20 shillings, and nine years later Richard Foley paid three Hearth taxes for the house of Ridgeway. In 1691 John Foley of Ridgeway was declared an outlaw for contempt of court. In the Parliamentary election of 1714, John and Richard Foley voted for their neighbour, Sir George Barlow of Slebech.

They owned extensive property in various parts of Pembrokeshire and in 1719 John Foley was elected an Alderman of Newport. In 1737 Richard Foley subscribed five guineas towards a new organ in St. Mary's church, Haverfordwest.

Thomas Foley, entered the Navy and rose to the rank of captain, and accompanied Anson on his voyage round the world in 1744. His nephew achieved far greater fame. This was Sir Thomas Foley, born at Ridgeway, in 1757. He entered the Navy, took part in numerous sea battles, and received sufficient "prize-money" to enable him to buy the Abermarlais estate in Carmarthenshire. He became one of "Nelson's Captains", and fought at Toulon (1795), Cape St. Vincent (1797), his ship *Goliath* led the British fleet in the battle of the Nile (1798), and was prominent in the battle at Copenhagen (1801). He was a personal friend of Nelson. He was promoted to the rank of Admiral and Knighted in 1815. He married a younger daughter of the Duke of Leinster. Sir Thomas died in 1833 and was buried in a coffin made from the timbers of one of the ships he had commanded.

In the summer of 1802 Lord Nelson accompanied by Sir William and Lady Hamilton, made a journey to Milford Haven. From Monmouth they travelled along the highway known today as the A40 route. He was entertained by his friend Sir Thomas Foley at his town residence called Foley House which still stands in Goat Street, Haverfordwest. On the return journey, Nelson and his party called at Picton Castle. From there they went to Ridgeway where the tree-lined drive was illuminated by lanthorns and candles. They were entertained by the Admiral's older brother, John Herbert Foley and his wife. The youngest member of the Foley family, a little girl aged six years, was somewhat overawed in the presence of the august visitor but after Nelson had taken her on his knee and dropped some grapes into her mouth she felt more at home again. There were three Foley sisters at this time – Angela Emily, who married the Revd. William Vernon of Hanbury Hall, Lucy, and Jessie, who married Mr. T. T. Vernon also of Hanbury Hall.

John Herbert Foley was a friend of the historian Fenton, and served as High Sheriff of Pembrokeshire in 1795. His younger brother, Richard Foley, a barrister-at-law, published a book entitled *The Practice of the Court of Great Sessions* in 1792. Another member of the family, William Henry Foley, was High Sheriff of Carmarthenshire in 1870.

The last descendant of the Foleys at Ridgeway was Sir Richard Foley-Philipps, Baronet, who died in 1965.

The house is said to be haunted by the ghosts of the Foley Cavaliers who had fallen at Colby Moor, and there are tales of phantom horsemen galloping along the old drive.

BRIMASTON – TREOWMAN

Written in 1984

In early times the name of this large property (now two farms called Brimaston Hall and Grange) was variously rendered Bremerston (1326) Bromaneston (1373), Bromandston (1568). To Welsh speakers it is Treowman. In 1739 a Circulating Charity School (25 pupils) was held in "Trefowman alias Brimeston". In 1292 and 1326 it was Episcopal manor of the Bishop of St. Davids, and in the latter year was leased to Peter Russell, and during the time of that family became a lay manor. John Russell, last of the male line, left an only child, the heiress Elizabeth Russell who brought Brimaston to her husband Richard Laugharne of St. Brides. During the eighteenth century it became the property of Ford of Stone Hall in the neighbouring parish of St. Lawrence.

The last member in the main line of that family, Miss Mary Ford of Brimaston died in 1798. The two substantial farms were farmed by tenants and leaseholders and finally freeholders – Watts 1624, 1770-1862 Harries of Brimaston Hall, Morse 1748-1834, and in late nineteenth and twentieth centuries by Jenkins and Lloyd of Brimaston Hall, and Morris of Brimaston Grange. A Methodist chapel stands in the hamlet.

REFERENCES

P.R.O. Anc. Deeds E210. No. 24, 709;
Pembs. RO;
Land Tax 1786;
Black Book of St. Davids, 1326;
N.L.W. Poyston Deeds;
Sir A. Wagner, Coll. of Arms;
Geo. Owen Ms;
Francis Jones, *Hist. Journal of the Church in Wales 1969.*

CASTLE VILLA – CASWILIA

TUCKED away in the northernmost corner of the parish of Brawdy, the farmhouse of Castle Villa stands on a gentle slope above the west bank of the stream that forms the boundary with the parish of St. Lawrence, and at the entrance to the yard are remains of a fortification of the Iron Age, known as Castell Wilia from which the place takes its name. In deeds and documents, down to the early nineteenth century, the name was usually given as Castell or Castle Vilia or Wilia which has developed in modern days to the hybrid Castle Villa in written form, although it is still rendered by local people as Caswilia, thus remaining faithful to the original orthography.

Below the house, and near the spot where the stream crosses the road, known variously as Dŵr Caswilia and Dŵr Trewilym, there was at one time a corn mill, but this has totally disappeared. Across the wooded dingle, some three or four bowshots away is Trewilym sometimes written as Williamston in old documents, a former manorhouse, home of a medieval family named Dru, and afterwards home of the last of the old Castle Villa stock. The stream which here forms the boundary of Brawdy parish, flows southwards past Trewilym, Trebwrnallt (Tancredston), Gignog and Pont-y-garn, until it reaches the sea at Newgale. Due to mistaken reading by an eighteenth century cartographer, it has been marked on subsequent maps as "Brandy" instead of Brawdy brook, and although this triumph of consonantal mutilation continues to disfigure modern maps, natives of the district still refer to it as *afon Niwgwl*. The Commissioners of Ancient Monuments in their report on Pembrokeshire, contributed further to etymological lunacy by describing it as Bran ddu Brook!

Although much destroyed and almost obliterated on its eastern and southern sides, the fortification of Caswilia had been an important refuge. Consisting of an inner enclosure, 150 feet by 100 feet in diameter, it was defended by two, and in places by three earthen banks and ditches. A description made about the year 1900, states that the defences "where best preserved, consist of a rampart 3 feet above the interior, with two other ramparts in front; the outer has no ditch; their crests are 10 feet and 3 feet below the first. The ditches are shallow, the outer one, the deepest, being only 3 feet below the ground outside. On the north-west side, between the inner and the second bank, an additional bank has been interpolated for some distance. It is now 2 feet only above the first ditch, and 3 feet between it and the second line. This bank, for a distance of 50 feet from the entrance, has been replaced by a terrace occupying a similar position to that of Merrion (parish of Warren), though smaller" *(Ancient Monuments Report, County of Pembroke, p. 25)*. In its complete form it must have been a large and formidable fortification. The upper and more perfect portion of it is now overgrown with bushes and trees. This hill-fort may well date from the Iron Age period, and that it was a site of settlement from early times is confirmed by other relics found nearby, namely two megalithic monuments now preserved within the porch of the church of Brawdy. The first of these, 110 inches high, once served as a gatepost at Caswilia and bears, in ogam characters, the inscription MAQ(I) QAGTE. Sir John Rhys suggested the possibility that the name was associated with that of Mac Cecht, a name well-known in Irish legend. As there are several traces of Irish settlement in Dewsland still preserved in place-names like Breudeth (Brawdy), Emlych, Lleithir and Castell Mwrtach, and in early traditions, the suggested connection is by no means far-fetched. The other, 84 inches high, once served as a footbridge over a stream on the farm, and fortunately, it was noticed by Edward Lluyd's correspondent in the period 1680-1700, when a sketch was made of the ogam inscription, which read VENDOGNI, and the Latin one which read VENDAGNI FILIV . . . NI. Both are described in the *Ancient Monuments Report,* p 29, and in Nash-Williams, *Early Christian Monuments of Wales,* nos. 296, 298. These names probably commemorate some of the early settlers at Caswilia, men of importance, perhaps local chieftains of the 5th and 6th centuries A.D.

Of the later medieval mansion no trace remains above ground, but it is believed that the farmhouse, a strongly stone-built structure occupies the site. A few relics suggesting its earlier status have been found. About 1905 two pieces of what seem to have been a trefoil-headed window were found in the ruins of a fowl-house and many fragments of carved and dressed stones have been discovered in the vicinity of the homestead; two iron cannon balls, weighing about four pounds each, were found in a fosse of the old earthwork, and a coin of 1573. The house ceased to be used as a residence in the first half of the seventeenth century, and was probably dismantled about that time, or possibly reduced in size and adapted to farming usage.

Like so many gentry residences of Pembrokeshire, Castle Villa has its ghost. It is said that during the twilight hours the clatter of hooves are heard on the yard above, and some claim to have seen a mounted figure galloping up the slope and uttering a wild cry as he clears the entrance gate, his cries and the hoofbeats growing fainter as he disappears. The phantom rider is said to have been a former squire forced to flee for his life during an attack made by his enemies. Another tale speaks of a cloaked figure prowling among the outbuildings, a revenant squire come to seek a great treasure buried in a secret place at or near the old house. Less welcome was the appearance at Dwr Caswilia of the Devil himself, "*y gwr drwg*", who, ironically, often queered his own pitch by frightening passing midnight revellers into sobriety, and hardened sinners to the paths of repentance. Another less lethal wraith was "*y Ladi Wen*" seen perched on the handrail of the foot-bridge over the stream, said to be awaiting the return of a wandering lover.

The Family of Morris

The earliest owners of Castle Villa of which I have knowledge were the Morrises who lived there in the latter part of the fourteenth century. The name is spelt in contemporary documents variously as Morris, Mores and Morrice, and the fact that a permanent surname had been adopted at that period suggests that either the family was of English origin, or was a Welsh one which had adopted the English fashion of nomenclature. As none of the Welsh gentry families adopted permanent surnames until well on in the Tudor period, it seems not unlikely that the Morrises were of English extraction.

The extent of the estate at this time is not known, but the family's seat was at Castle Villa, with properties in Brawdy parish and in neighbouring parishes of Llanreithan,

St. Lawrence and St. Edrins were acquired over a period of years through purchases or judicious marriages by eldest sons.

Henry Morris the earliest known ancestor, still living at Castle Villa in 1407, had two sons, David and John, both mentioned in early deeds. On 5 May 1398, Henry Wise of Westfield and his wife Joanna Russell (of Brimaston), made a settlement of 15 messuages and 5 carucates in Letterston and Tredduog (in St. Edrins). Shortly afterwards the grantor's son, William Wise, granted Tredduog to Sir William Thomas, knight, who then conveyed it to Richard Wogan and William Parry, and they in turn conveyed it to "David Morys of Castell Villia" whose seal to the deed displayed the family arms of three towers. At that time the owner of Cerbyd (Llanhowel) had an interest in the estate, and by a deed executed at "Castle Vilia" in 1406, Ievan ap Ievan ap David ap Philip Thomas "of Kerbyt," granted 3 bovates in Castro Vilia and Penryn to John son of Henry Morris "de Castrovilia", with remainder to John's wife Alice, heiress of Henry Martin. Penryn, now a small-holding, once formed part of the demesne lands.

On 5 August 1431, Johanna, former wife of Peter Jordan, conveyed a messuage at "Redegely in Brody" to David Morris, a transaction that was to figure in a lawsuit over a century-and-a-quarter later which showed that this Johanna was an ancestress of the Castle Villa family, but the exact connection is not given. David Morris must have lived to a fairly good age, for some twenty years later, on the Friday after the feast of the Exaltation of the Holy Cross in 1451, Thomas ap David ap Ievan ap Philip granted a messuage in Western Grenton (now one of the Trefgarn Owen farms in Brawdy) to "David Morice of Castelvilia", reserving power to exact from the property the sum of 33s 4d to be paid to "my friend and lawful attorney," David ap Philip de Browdy, whom he appointed to deliver seisin to the grantee.

David Morris's wife Isobell, was the daughter of Thomas Laugharne of St. Brides by the coheiress, Joan Crabhall. Isobell outlived her husband and became the wife of Henry Perrot, a landowner whose seat was at Caerforiog near Solva. David Morris was followed by his son, Thomas, who is stated in an early manuscript in the College of Arms, London, to have married Margaret Howell who probably came from Talbenny parish, as suggested by a deed executed in 1497 whereby she granted all her lands and tenements in Talbenny and Howelston to her son (filio suo), Henry Morris of Castelvilia. Thomas Morris had three children – 1. Henry Morris of whom I shall speak later. 2. John Morris, to whom Henry Perrot of Caervoriog and Isobell Laugharne, his wife in 1483 granted "the mansion of Castelvilia," in exchange for a tenement in Tredduog, a toft in Menevia (St. Davids) and lands in Whitchurch. 3. A daughter (who married Lewis ap William ap Llywelyn of Trerhos, St. Lawrence).

Henry Morris succeeded to the Castle Villa estate, and by an arrangement with his brother, to the residence. According to Dwnn's pedigrees (ibid. i. 61, 169), Henry Morris married Elizabeth, daughter of Sir James ab Owen of Pentre Ifan by Jane, daughter of Jenkin Perrot of Caerforiog near Solva. Sir James, an important public figure, was knighted before 1512, in which year he was appointed Deputy of the Barony of Cemais. The Pembrokeshire Plea Rolls for 1543-4, record that "Henry Mores de Castell Villya in the lordship of Pebidok, (Pebidiog) gentleman", was summoned by Lewis Perkin gentleman, for £20 due on a bond signed at "Castell Villia" on 8 September 1538. Pebidiog was the original name of the episcopal lordship later known as Dewsland.

Henry's only son, Richard Morris, never succeeded to the estate, for he died during his father's lifetime, before 1545 – "*obiit ante pater*" says David Edwardes. Richard's wife was Katherine, daughter of Sir John Wogan of Wiston by Ann Phillips of Stone Hall in St. Lawrence – "*Katrin gwraig Ric Morys o gastell vilia*" *(Peniarth MS 140,* folio 78). She afterwards married John Scourfield of New Moat who lived at Castle Villa which his wife held for her life. Richard Morris had two daughters, Elizabeth, died unmarried, and Anne, the ultimate sole heiress of Castle Villa, to whom we shall return later.

The family of Scourfield
According to the earliest recorded pedigree, signed by John Scourfield on 14 October 1591 (Dwnn, *op cit,* i. 110, 175), the family stemmed from Sir Fulke Scourfield of Kendal, Westmorland, whose descendant, William married Elizabeth, daughter and heiress of Robert Wyard, widow of John Herle. Now, the Herle family held lands in Pembrokeshire and Breconshire during the Middle Ages, and it is possible that William Scourfield's marriage to the widow Herle, was the reason for his coming to West Wales. William's son, John was twice married, both wives being members of well-established local families. The first, Jenet, was daughter of Harry Howell of Llys-y-fran (living about 1380), son of Phillip Howell and grandson of Howel Fychan of Woodstock in Ambleston. The second wife was Joan Joyce, whose family had been settled at Prendergast near Haverfordwest for several generations. John Scourfield's eldest son by the first wife was Jenkin, described as of New Moat, and as husband of Jenet Broughton; their son Piers, also described as of New Moat, married Joan, daughter of Richard Jones of Haverfordwest and from this point onwards the descent is warranted by contemporary documents.

No evidence has been found to support the statements of the pedigree in its higher reaches, but it seems reasonable to accept as authentic the marriages from Elizabeth Herle onwards. The earliest reference that I have seen is contained in a deed dated 1439 preserved in the Public Record Office *(Ancient Deeds,* E 210, 5537, 10848), which mentions a John Skorffyll, junior, of Nova Mota, son of John Skorffyll the elder of the same place by Isabel, his wife. The next deed refers to Pyrs Scourfield in 1516 *(ibid.* A, 12249), and another to Henry Scourfield of New Moat, gentleman, in 1537 *(ibid.* 4549-50). The Pembrokeshire Plea Rolls (No. 10), describe the last-named as Harry son and executor of Peter Scourfield of New Moat who had died prior to July 1552. It should be noted that the Christian names Peter and Piers were interchangeable at this period. The said Henry, or Harry, married Etheldreda Butler of Trecadwgan near Solva, and was father of William, who, as we shall see, married Ann Morris, heiress of Castle Villa.

The coat-of-arms borne by the Scourfields of New Moat and Castle Villa, was *gules three greyhounds courant argent, collared or,* with a greyhound as crest, holding in its jaws a scroll inscribed with the Welsh word *Ffyddlon* (Faithful). They are recorded in this wise by Dwnn and by George Owen of Henllys, who adds a *chevron argent* to the escutcheon.

Although the arms are a play upon the surname, the greyhounds "scouring the field", a modern version found in the mid-nineteenth century states that when King John on a visit to Pembrokeshire was entertained by a Scourfield at a hunting party, he greatly admired the prowess of a particularly fleet white greyhound which his host afterwards presented to him. The arms are said to commemorate the event.

Greyhounds

The Scourfields and Castle Villa

As we have seen, the marriage of John Scourfield of New Moat to Katherine (Wogan) widow of Richard Morris of Castle Villa, brought him into association with that property which his wife enjoyed for her life. Several references occur to him in the Papers of Great Sessions: in September 1545, John Scourfield sued Rice Hendy of Haverfordwest, for the sums of 33s 4d and £3 13s 4, respectively; and in the same year Owen Tucker of Sealyham sued John Scourfield for £20 due on a bond whereby John had covenanted to pay the said sum due on a moiety of the farms of "Lettysdown, Lann, and Seynt Eddryn in the Hundred of Dewysland". In September 1551 William Wolfe clerk, sued John Scourffylde, for £9 and 5 marks due on bonds, and Wolfe further sued John Scurffild and Lewis Sar of St. Lawrence, husbandman, for trespassing on his lands in St. Lawrence and committing damage to the extent of £10. In the sessions of July 1554, the executors of the will of the above-named William Wolfe sued Marcus ap Owen of Roblingston and his surety, John Scourfield, for £40 due on a bond; in the same court John Scurfyld sued Henry Wathen, Watye Wathen and David ap Bynon, all of Pointz Castell, husbandmen, for £5 4 0, and he sued James Vaughan of Cilgerran, gentleman, for £4 10 0; and in September of the same year Julian Barlow, widow of Roger Barlow of Slebech, esquire, sued John Scurfyld for £10 15 0: in the sessions of July 1557 John Scurfelde sued John Butler of Coedkenles, Thomas ap Rees of Rycardston, and Owen Prichard of Fagwr goch, for sums of £7, £5 11 8, and 40s, respectively. In all these cases John is described as of "Castelvilie", "Castell Villia", or "Castell Velya", gentleman.

Shortly before 1554 another and closer connection was forged between the family and Dewsland, when William Scourfield, younger brother of the said John, married Anne Morris, sole heiress of the Castle Villa estate. This marriage resulted in the bride's mother also becoming her sister-in-law! The union took place before June 1554, as a lawsuit held in that month described William and Anne as man and wife. The lawsuit is of particular interest for it confirms the heiress's pedigree for five generations. The matter concerned a claim made by William Scourfield and Anne his wife against Thomas ap Ieuan and Jennett his wife, to a yearly rent – charge of 7 shillings issuing out of a messuage at "Redegely in Brody".

The plaintiffs stated that Johanna formerly wife of Peter Jordan, "remotest ancestress of the said Anne," had executed a deed dated 5 August 1431, produced in court, whereby

Johanna conveyed the tenement and rent-charge at Rhydygele to David Morris, from whom it descended to his son and heir, Thomas Morris, then to Thomas's son and heir, Henry Morris "who lived in the time of King Henry VIII", and then to Henry's grand-daughter, Anne, who was daughter and heiress of Richard Morris, who was son and heir of the said Henry. The defendants denied that the rent-charge amounted to 7 shillings, claiming that they were liable to paying only a yearly token rent of one penny. The result of the suit is not recorded. In the same court, William Scourfield and Anne sued Thomas Voyle for possession of 5 acres of land in Merles (Marloes), which had descended to Anne from her grandfather, Henry Morris, "his family having owned them from time immemorial", and had come to Anne as daughter and heiress of Richard Morris, son and heir of Henry.

The Pembrokeshire gentry of Elizabethan days often invested spare capital in shipping. William Scourfield of Castle Villa was one of these, and about 1555-6, he bade a fond farewell to his young wife and boarded the good ship *Trinity* of Milford, bound for France. She proved to be the ship that never returned. The years rolled by with no news and Anne concluded she was bereaved. An heiress, bereaved or no, never lacks suitors, and she shortly acquired as her husband, one of Pembrokeshire's leading landowners, Morgan Philipps of Picton Castle, no less. They lived together happily, and the union was blessed with a child, a little girl.

Alas, an enormous boulder plopped into the placid waters of their contentment for a bronzed and bearded William Scourfield suddenly appeared at the portals of Castle Villa. He had been captured by the Moors off the coast of Barbary, and after seven long years in infidel hands, had escaped. He found no adoring wife to listen to his wondrous relation, but to his chagrin learnt that she was now the chatelaine of Picton Castle. He immediately demanded the return of his wife. Being extremely fond of the many-acred Anne, Morgan Philipps refused, and told him to clear off back to Barbary; whereupon Scourfield sought redress in the law courts, with the result that Anne was restored to him. There is no record of Philipps' reactions, but he lost no time in seeking another spouse, and this time made no mistake, for he married Elizabeth Fletcher, whose spinsterhood was above suspicion, being the undoubted unmarried daughter of the Registrar of the diocese of Bangor. Neither are Anne's feelings recorded, but we do know that she returned dutifully, and, haply, lovingly, to the hearth of Castle Villa. Such is the essence of an account written by Morgan's descendant, Bulkeley Philipps, who died in 1766.

Striking confirmation of Scourfield's maritime adventure has been found in our

The return of William Scourfield

national archives. The *Calendar of Patent Rolls 1560-3,* includes a licence issued on 6 February 1563 enabling William Scourfield to gather alms in the cities of London and Bristol for paying the ransom of the "said William Skurfeld, and John Rychard, Robert Maner, William Pollett, John Allen, and Dennys Keyny, poor mariners, late of Hereford West, South Wales, who (with six others deceased) had been for seven years captives of Merocus of the infidels of Barbaria, their ship, *The Trynytie* of Milford, bound for France, having been driven on to that coast by misfortune of weather". The experience of cruel sea and dusky infidels effectively deflated William's itch for travel, and thenceforth we find him anchored to the more peaceful pastures of Castle Villa.

After his return, the name of William Scourfield, usually described as of Castell Villia, gentleman, appears often in the courts of Great Sessions, claiming money due on bonds, as in 1569, when he sued his kinsman, James Scourfield for £20, and three years later when he sued Phillip Lloyd of Trefgarn for trespassing on his lands at Hayscastle. In 1572 William, his brother John, both of Castle Villa, and their brother Morris of New Moat, attended a court at Haverfordwest, to give evidence against the mayor, Lewis Harries, in a suit concerning the town's boundary with Prendergast. During an adjournment the three brothers were drinking with company in an alehouse when a quarrel broke out, during which a man named Watts threw a lump of cheese at another named Strong and then attacked him with a dagger. The others intervened and disarmed him, and in order to be rid of him returned his weapon. Watts then left the alehouse, followed by William Scourfield who tried to persuade him to return to make friends with Strong, whereupon the angry Watts again drew his dagger and wounded the would-be peacemaker in the arm *(Arch Camb* 1896, p. 209).

He owned property in Haverfordwest, and a deed in the Eaton Evans and Williams Collection, shows that on 13 October 1589, William Scourfield of Castellvillia, gentleman, granted a lease to Mathew Synnett, son and heir of John Synnett deceased, of some old walls and a burgage in Hill Street near the lands of the town chamber, upon which walls the late John Synnett had built a house.

William Scourfield died on 20 October 1592. By Anne he had the following children:

1. John Scourfield, son and heir.

2. William Scourfield.

3. Anne, married John Meyler of Trewallterwen, St. Edrins parish, son of Thomas Meyler. She is described in the prenuptial settlement dated 17 July 1573, as "one of the daughters of William Scourfield of Castelvilia"; the deed stated that her father had paid her portion to the bridegroom who covenanted to settle the capital messuage of Trewallter(wen), a meadow in Tredduog of a yearly rent of 8 shillings, a tenement called Howellston and a tenement called Williamston (Trewilym) in St. Lawrence, to the uses of the marriage (N.L.W. *Lucas Deeds).* John Meyler died about 1611 (in which year his will was proved), leaving four sons and four daughters.

4. Daughters, names unknown.

John Scourfield who succeeded to the estate, was called "the younger" to distinguish him from his uncle John "the elder" of New Moat. He married Jane, daughter of a local landowner, Llewellin Lloyd of Llanstinan, son of Morgan Lloyd. The parties to the prenuptial settlement made on 29 February 1583-4, were William Scurfyld of Castelvillia, gentleman, Anne his wife (parents of the bridegroom), John Scurfilde the elder of New Moat, gentleman, and Katherine his wife, of the one part, and Llewelyn Lloyd of Llanstinan (father of the bride) and John Philipps of Bentebargh (Pentypark), gentleman, of the other part; whereby the following properties were settled to the uses of the marriage:

"The manor of Saynt Eddryns, 6 messuages and tenements and a chief rent of 17s 1d, in St. Edrins parish; lands in Trerosse (Trerhos) and Williamston (Trewilym) in St. Lawrence parish: the capital messuage and lands of Caystellvilia and Roskeneven and a water grist mill belonging, of the annual value of £12; and lands in Howelston and Talbenny and a grist mill there. The Castle Villa estate was described as comprising the manor of Saynt Eddryns, 28 messuages, 2 mills, 1,000 acres of land, 100 acres of meadow, 1,000 acres of pasture, 40 acres of wood, 500 acres of furze and heath, lying in the parishes of Brawdy, St. Edrins, St. Lawrence, Llandeloy, Llanreithan, Mathry, and Talbenny, and also a chief rent of 17s 1d. Jane's portion of £100 was to be paid by instalments, to be completed by 1592" (N.L.W. *Lucas Deeds,* 3309, 3776).

The settlement shows that the Castle Villa estate comprised some 2,640 acres, which is typical of the extent of the numerous Welsh estates in earlier times. Incorporated with the property was Rhoscynefin, a farm that once stood near the former Llandeloy-Llanreithan vicarage, the field adjoining being still called Parc Rhoscynefin.

The marriage proved distressingly brief, for John Scourfield the younger, died in his father's lifetime, at Castle Villa on 20 May 1588, leaving an only child, Anne. Thus, for a second time a daughter of the family became heiress to her grandfather. The widowed Jane married again, within four years, to Thomas Mathias of Glastir, in Nevern parish, by whom she had two daughters. She predeceased her husband, who moved to Llangwarran, being the first of his family to settle there, and who married a second wife, Ursula, daughter of George Owen of Henllys, Lord of Cemais, from whom the present family of Llangwarran descends.

The young heiress, Anne Scourfield, was one of the few women whose coat-of-arms was included by George Owen of Henllys in his armorial of Pembrokeshire magnates. Seven coats were marshalled on her shield – 1. Scourfield, with the difference of a second son. 2. Butler of Trecadwgan. 3. Cantelupe. 4. Tancred. 5. Morris of Castle Villa, *argent three towers triple-towered azure.* 6. Lloyd of Llanstinan. 7. Thomas Madog (whose heiress had married Morgan Lloyd of Llanstinan). The components of this heraldic achievement commemorate some of Anne's more remote ancestors whose heiresses had married into the Morris and Scourfield families.

Castle Villa, described as consisting of a messuage and two carucates of land, was held by fealty, homage, scutage and payment of 10s, as of the manor of Tancredston, the lord of which was John ap Rice of Rickeston (Treicert) in Brawdy. Accordingly, the wardship of the infant heiress, Anne, passed to ap Rice, which meant that he could dispose of her in marriage (if still a minor) as he thought fit. Her nearest kinsfolk, the Scourfields, had their own ideas about this, and decided that she should marry her second cousin, Thomas, younger son of John Scourfield of New Moat by his wife Katherine, daughter and heiress of Richard ab Owen of Lochmeyler.

The little girl's guardians – her mother (who by now had married Thomas Mathias), John Scourfield of New Moat and John Meyler of Trewallterwen, placed her in the care of a local freeholder William Walter Glyn of Trebrithin in Manorowen parish, to be "maintained and nurtured according to her rank". To this arrangement, John ap Rice had no objection, but as lord of the manor continued to retain her legal wardship. Suddenly, on 6 May 1592, a posse of mounted men consisting of William Scourfield (the ward's grandfather), John Scourfield and John Jenkin, both of New Moat, and John Meyler (the ward's uncle), descended on Trebrithin, abducted the ward, carrying her away despite the pleas and objections of William Walter Glyn and his household. As the object of the abduction was clear, John ap Rice immediately intervened, and in the autumn of 1592, and again in the following year, sued the abductors in the courts of Great Sessions, also demanding the return and custody of the messuage of Castle Villa and 120 acres of land in Brawdy and Llanreithan parishes, which were held of plaintiff by military service, and to which the young girl was heiress. The result of the lawsuit is not given, but one fact emerges, namely that Anne certainly married Thomas, younger son of John Scourfield the abductor, which represented a victory for the Scourfield family.

The marriage achieved with such labour proved disastrous. Thomas plunged into a life of dissipation and, finally, broke the entail on the Castle Villa estate, and sold it. A contemporary observer, George William Griffith of Penybenglog, wrote: "This Thomas Scourfield in the right of Anne his wieffe was possessed of a great estate, who, although he lived but a shorte space after his marriage, yet he by his disordered lieffe in being given too much to companie keepinge wasted and spent all his said wive's estate and died very poore . . . and sold away all to his brother William Scourfield."

Glimpses of the rake's progress are found among the papers of Great Sessions and other documents. In 1608 Thomas and his wife mortgaged the outlying parts of the estate, namely 9 messuages in Easter and Wester Howelston, a little messuage at the quay there, a parcel of wood, and a mill, all in Talbenny parish, to Thomas Lloyd of Cilciffeth, esquire, for £160. On 10 March 1608/9, they granted a lease for 21 years at a yearly rent of £10, of the capital messuage of Castle Villia, Rhos Kynhevin (Cynefin), and Castell Villia Mill, to Thomas ap Rice of Rickeston, which the lessee assigned on 31 May 1611 to William Barlow of Cresswell. Shortly afterwards, Thomas and Anne left Castle Villa, and settled at neighbouring Trewilym.

In April 1609 Richard Bateman of Haverfordwest, mercer, sued Thomas Scourfield for £6 9 5d due on a bond; in September, Jenkin ap Ieuan sued him and his brother William both described as of Trewilliam, for £4; and in the same year Thomas Lloyd of Cilciffeth esquire, was further concerned in the mortgage with Thomas and Anne Scourfield relating to 10 messuages, one grain mill, and 264 acres in Easter and Wester Howellstone in Talbenny, while another mortgage of 2 messuages related to one corn mill, 2 gardens, 2 orchards, and 613 acres in Brawdy and Llanreithan parishes. In September 1609, Thomas appears, for a change, as a creditor, when he sued Hugh Thomas of Priskily in Mathry parish, yeoman, for £6 due on a bond.

A continuation of the downward ride is revealed by transactions of the following years. In March 1610 he mortgaged a messuage and 61 acres in Trerhos, alias Patricksford, and St. Lawrence to Thomas Lloyd of Cilciffeth and in September, Thomas and his wife mortgaged 3 messuages and 260 acres in St. Edrins and St. Lawrence to one Ievan Griffith, gentleman, and a messuage and 64 acres in Trerhos alias Patricks Ford, to John Wogan, gentleman. On 10 June 1611, Thomas and Anne Scourfield, described as of Williamston, made a mortgage of Castle Villia, Rhoskynhevin, the Castle Villia mill, and Williamston ("in the former tenure of Lewis John Powell Goch and now of the said Thomas Scourfield"), to Thomas ap Rice, esquire, in the sum of £100 to be repaid at Michaelmas 1618, "in the hawle of the capital messuage or manorhouse of Rickardston in the parish of Brow-die". In July of the same year he was again concerned with Thomas ap Rice in respect of "3 messuages, a grain mill, 3 gardens and 713 acres in Castell Velia, Brawdy, Llanreithan, Trewilym, and St. Lawrence; and with James Scourfield, gentleman, in respect of 2 messuages, 3 tofts, 2 gardens, and 101 acres (6 acres being woodland) in Trehayle, Clyn y Foorne and Treftheog, in St. Edrins parish". In 1612, 1613 and 1614 he was raising further mortgages on the above properties, and, in addition, on "the manor of Treddiog alias Tretheog, with Ieuan Griffith, Arnold Tancke, and John Wogan". Very occasionally he appears in the courts as a creditor in respect of small sums, such as in September 1615 when he sued John Hewes and Gwenllian his wife, administrators of the goods of John David, deceased, for money for a gelding he had sold to deceased.

The end came in 1615. On 20 July of that year, Thomas and Anne Scourfield of Williamston, with consent of Thomas ap Rice, esquire, mortgagee, sold Castell Villia, the water grist mill, and "the decaid messuage called Rhos Kynhevin", to his elder brother, William Scourfield of New Moat, for £320. The lease of these properties, originally granted on 10 March 1608/9, was then surrendered by William Barlow of Cresswell, to William Scourfield for £55.

The purchaser, Thomas's elder brother William Scourfield, was a wealthy man, and in addition to owning the New Moat estate as heir of his father, was also "right heire to Llochmeyler (his mother being sole heiress of that estate), and by purchase from his brother and his wife, now enjoyeth Castlevilia" – so wrote George William Griffith about 1620. William served as High Sheriff of Pembrokeshire in 1617, and married Jane, daughter of George Owen of Henllys, by whom he had issue. He died on 22 March 1622.

After the sale the unfortunate Thomas remained at Trewilym, probably as a tenant, and retained some few scraps of his once extensive estate. We do not know the date of his death, but according to the antiquary of Penybenglog he "died very poore". A torn document in the Lucas collection suggests that his death took place late in the reign of James I or early in that of Charles I. This document, written some few years after 1624, is a grant to John Scourfield of New Moat, son and heir of William, from Anne Scourfield described as "widow of Thomas Scourfield of Williamston", of a messuage in the township of "Perskylly alias Pryskylly Vach" (which had been demised to Thomas and Anne by

William Scourfield of New Moat on 20 November 1610), and a messuage in the village of Llandelwy (demised to them by the same William on 3 February 1611/12).

Thus despite all vicissitudes, the chances of marriage, and unpredictability of character, Castle Villa remained in the Scourfield family, and continued to form part of the New Moat estate for a further three-and-a-half centuries, until after the Second World War when Lieut.-Colonel D. G. Davies-Scourfield, M.C., sold the property to a Mr. Pettijohn, who later sold it to Messrs. Ackroyd, the present owners.

The tenants of Castle Villa

Castle Villa ceased to be used as a residence after the departure of Thomas Scourfield, and was let to a succession of respectable tenants, and the house adapted to the requirements of farming. The first tenants of whom I have note was John Bowen, a kinsman of the Bowens of Robleston, later of Camrose. In 1621 and 1622, John Bowen of Castle Villa, gentleman, was sued in the courts of Great Sessions by William Hake of Haverfordwest, corvisor, for £3 3s. 1d., and by Alderman William Thomas of the same town, for £30; and in 1625 John Bowen "of Castle Villia alias of Camrose" gentleman was sued by John Tanke for £10, and by Thomas ap Rice, esquire, for £2.

As we have seen, part of Castle Villa was held of the lay manor of Tancredston of which the ap Rice family were lords; the other part of the property was held of the Episcopal manor of Dewsland, of which the Bishops of St. Davids for the time being were temporal lords. An interesting lawsuit in 1627 states that part of Castle Villa, then consisting of the farm, a toft, a grain mill, and 320 acres of land, had been held by William Scourfield of the Lord Bishop by military tenure; William died at New Moat on 22 March 1622, leaving the lands to his son John, then a minor and a ward of the bishop; on 4 November 1622 the bishop assigned the lands to the ward's mother, Jane, who leased Castle Villa on 13 March 1626 to William Laugharne of Llangwarran for a term of two years. The tenants at this time were John and William Bowen, gentlemen, and Lewis John ap Howell and Anne, his wife. However, Lewis John and Anne claimed to hold their part of the property in fee simple, and to have leased it to the Bowens, who, they alleged, had pastured cattle on the lands to the damage of £40. Accordingly in September 1627, William Laugharne instituted an action against the Bowens to recover the damages. John Bowen's son, Mathew, moved to Pembroke where he was still living in 1685.

The next tenant of whom I have knowledge was John Owen described as "of Castle William, husbandman", who died in 1649 and was followed by his son, Robert Owen, yeoman, who also held a neighbouring messuage, "in the townred and fields of Williamston alias Trewilym". After him came John Protheroe described as of Castel Villia, husbandman, assessed at two hearths in 1670, and who died in 1697 leaving a widow and a son. Shortly afterwards two yeomen became tenants, Thomas Davies and John Bateman. In 1766 Thomas Davies's son Daniel, who had married John Bateman's daughter, had the unhappy experience of seeing his father-in-law expire before his eyes. The inquest held at Castle Villa on 13 December before the coroner, William Jones of Llether, revealed that John Bateman, who had gone to help with ploughing, was holding "the plow as customary and when he had plowed a couple of furrows he called to the plow driver to stop the team, which he did; his son-in-law Daniel Davies, being at hand and perceiving him totter and fall, ran to help him, but he became 'lifeless' and was carried back to Castle Villa".

The Davieses held the farm on long leases which qualified them to vote in parliamentary elections. Thus in 1765 and 1768 Daniel Davies voted for Philipps of Picton Castle, and in 1812 his son, Thomas Davies, voted for Campbell of Stackpole. The property was held on leases for lives which were renewed to the family from time to time. For example, on 5 January 1801 Henry Scourfield esquire, then residing at Robeston, granted a lease for three lives to Thomas Davies of Castle Willia, farmer, of the farms of Castlewilliam (sic) and Rhoscynefin, at a yearly rent of £67 10s. 0d., rendering yearly eight fat hens at Christmas, providing two teams to carry coal or culm for the landlord, and to keep a dog or bitch and a fighting cock. Phoebe Davies, the last of her family, married Joseph Harries, son of James Harries of Trenichol, who settled at his wife's home, and voted for Greville in the election of 1831. They were followed by their son, George Harries, who left an only child and heir, Phoebe Davies Harries who, in 1894, married Walter Morris of Chapel farm near Pembroke. Their children were the last of the family to hold Castle Villa where their forebears had farmed for nigh on two-hundred-and-fifty years.

When I called at Castle Villa in November 1974, the farmhouse was being renovated. Apart from the removal of a block in the rear of the building, its external appearance has been little disturbed, while two new dormer windows placed in the roof over the kitchen wing, have improved not only its internal amenity, but its visual attractiveness. It was a dry day with a cold invigorating breeze.

Towards the evening I stood on the highest rampart of the *castell* crowned by a rook-thronged copse, surveying the scene as sentinels of distant ages may well have done, perhaps with wildly beating hearts. Northward across an open windswept moorland I could see the farm of Clawddcam with little clusters of sheep huddled near the hedges below the yard, the chapel of Blaenllyn and its secluded graveyard where many of my kinsfolk rest, the tall mansion of Trehâl amid sheltering trees, and the roof of Treddiog, an old manor-house long shorn of its tenurial authority; the furzy hump bank called Rofft Trewilym effectively screened from view the isolated church of St. Edrins, but to the southward I could see the homestead of Trewilym on a wooded slope, and the land rolling away towards Tancredston and the Gignog, to the high ground of Rindaston beyond.

Here was a strangely peaceful landscape with a distinct air of antiquity, seemingly largely unchanged since the days of the medieval Morrises and Elizabethan Scourfields whose footsteps we have traced. As I gazed over the unspoilt prospect, the lines of R. L. Stevenson came to mind:

> *Grey recumbent tombs of the dead in desert places,*
> *Standing-stones on the vacant wine-red moor,*
> *Hills of sheep, and the homes of the silent vanish'd races,*
> *And winds austere and pure.*

CHAPTER VIII

OF GHOSTS AND GHOULS, OF HAUNTINGS AND HORRORS

HOUNDED DOWN AND HANDED DOWN

TO CASUAL readers the study of genealogy appears to be merely a dry collection of dates of births, baptisms, deaths and marriages, with some rather pretty crests and escutcheons described in language beyond the ken of the ordinary layman. But to the student who goes deeper there lies a field of romance which often proves that truth is stranger than fiction. Sometimes whilst researching I have found a skeleton in a cupboard or some long forgotten scandal, as well as romance and high adventure.

I am convinced that these old family records, so reticent and reserved, hold matter of great interest. I have tried to "get behind" these dates, with the result that I have collected quite a number of interesting tales. In the private records of my own family, the Joneses of Brawdy, I found that two of the menfolk "dieyed in ye darkness of night, of a great fear". Believing that behind those words lay a matter of interest, I made a search and stumbled across a remarkable tale. Here is the story.

The ancient Jones of Brawdy family is a haunted clan. According to one legend, a member of the family who was notorious for his misdeeds was walled up alive in the old church which is entered from the yard of Brawdy house. His horrid bearded visage is said to appear on the pillar to glare at children who misbehave themselves in Brawdy church.

Another family ghost is traceable to the early eighteenth century. The central character was one William Jones, a younger son of the house. This young sprig grew up to be a turbulent character and was associated with several dubious enterprises. He took a deep interest in smuggling and illicit contraband was hidden in a hollow wall in the house. Parts still survive to be seen today. Though short, he was of Herculean strength and this, allied with an uncontrollable temper, made him feared by many people in the district. His relatives regarded him as a very black sheep indeed. He was a superb and bold horseman and would ride recklessly along the roads and the country folk often had to scurry for safety from the hooves of his horse.

One night while galloping home the young man rode down and killed a small child near Newgale. According to the tale he was then cursed by an old hag who had the second sight. She said that he and his descendants would be haunted by the Devil in the guise of a black hound before death. Soon after this, the reckless man left Pembrokeshire.

About forty years after the tragic event, a coastal trader sailed into Solva harbour. A member of the crew, an old man of forceful personality, was paid off. He obtained employment with a Mr. Raymond and settled in a small cottage. Soon afterwards he courted

Solva harbour

and married a young woman of the district who bore him children.

He had travelled the world as a sailor, it seemed, and he hinted that he hailed from north Wales. However, many locals recognised the family likeness to the Joneses of Brawdy. One night, deep in drink in a Solva tavern, he openly told people who he was, adding that he would as soon ride them down as carouse with them. One night shortly afterwards, the local doctor was called to his bedside. He found the old reprobate shrieking: "Send the hound away, send the hound away." He died shortly afterwards and was buried at Tregroes churchyard. The horrid hound of death is described as being the size of a young calf, with great glaring eyes, a large lolling tongue, and wolf-like fangs. It pads around as if it had been running hard. This spectral canine continued to appear to his descendants before their death. It was certainly seen by my grandfather when he died in 1919.

On the original draft of this article Francis Jones had written: "It is an interesting tale, and perhaps may be printed when I am an old man". 1933.

I have done as he wished. *[Editor]*

Hugh Charles-Jones writes: My father's long working life was devoted to truth and proof. So I have no reason to doubt the authenticity of the paranormal experience which he experienced. Like most historians he was often plagued with a missing link to a family pedigree on which he was working. On this occasion he seemed to have come to a blank wall. Vital information – the essential key to a long genealogy - needed one fact for the whole picture to fall into place.

It was shortly after my birth when he taught in Tenby and we lived in Saundersfoot. My father decided to leave the problem on his desk and to go out for a long walk in the woods. He hoped that the sea views and the woods towards Monkstone Point would ease the frustration of his historical impasse. The fresh air and the early morning sunlight cheered him up and he got into a brisk stride. But at the back of his mind the puzzle still niggled away. Then in the corner of his eye another walker appeared and after a few strides was alongside my father. He said good morning to the man, who answered, and they walked on together in step. My father told the man why he was out walking; that his researches had come to a full stop. He noticed that the man seemed to be averting his face, but that was a casual impression. In those days I fancy that people were far more forthcoming to strangers than they are today. The man said to my father "Well, if you go to St. . . . churchyard, and go to the third row of graves you might find an inscription on a grave in the third row from the end wall". They strode along in silence for a few more paces and then his companion dropped back. He looked back and the path was empty. My father assumed the man had taken a different turning. He did wonder though, why he hadn't said goodbye.

A few days later he visited the churchyard which was mentioned. After scraping away at the moss and lichen on a tombstone he found the information for which he was searching.

OF FATHER, SON, GRANDMAMMA AND THE GHOSTS

MY father's life was briefly touched by a ghostly Pembrokeshire apparition as you have just read. Another strange experience concerned his mother. She was staying with my mother and her children whilst my father was fighting in the Second World War. She told us all, "I have the strangest feeling that Francis is back in this country". This was strange. We had just got an airmail letter with no hint of his return. The next day he came home. He had suddenly been pulled out of the Italian front line by an unexpected posting to the War Office in London.

So I am the fourth generation to have a supernatural experience. Mine came about like this. My cousin, Graham Barrett and his wife, Pam, owned a delightful Pembrokeshire country house. They worked hard and turned it into an hotel, restoring it to its old splendour and comfort. It was the sort of place that features in *Country Life* magazine. It stood on a wooded hill having been built in the early 1800s, probably on a much older site. Around it were formal gardens, stables with cobbled floors, an old coach house and there was also a huge walled kitchen garden. The front drive was flanked by rhododendrons. The families of James, Barlow, Rice, Colby, Phillips and Lord Kensington had all owned it at some time.

I called on my cousins to find them most upset. They had booked a badly needed holiday, but the relief manager had let them down. Being self-employed, my time was my own, so I volunteered to look after the place for them. As it was November the high holiday season was over; there were experienced dining room staff and as I don't drink alcohol I thought I could manage. The guest bedrooms would be empty. A big attraction for me was that I could ride out Graham's thoroughbred hunter. They could go skiing whilst I enjoyed the place – a good deal all round.

One night when the last dinner guest and the staff had left, my companion and I settled down. We relaxed before a log fire, listening in the small hours to Neil Diamond's music. It was a wild night, high winds swayed the trees and rain lashed the windows.

Then we heard a different type of rhythm. The clump, clump, clump of hobnailed boots above our heads. It marched along the upstairs passage into my cousin's bedroom above. Louder, it stamped about. Silence. Then a sudden creaking, as if a heavy body had thrown itself on a bed. I felt not fear, but intense curiosity. Seconds later the whole performance was repeated. Then it dawned on me that the upstairs was entirely carpeted and my cousin's room, which contained a safe, was locked. I grabbed a shotgun ran upstairs and tried the door. It was locked fast. By now my mind whirled with puzzlement, fear and anger. The loaded shotgun was a great comfort. I yelled, "Come out, I have a loaded gun". Only the howling wind answered. Thus ended my musical *tête-à-tête;* my companion left abruptly and I was now alone. The fact that my bedroom being next to my cousin's was thought provoking, so I took the shotgun to bed with me, locked the door and jammed a chair under the handle.

Next morning I rode out, returning to have coffee with the cleaning ladies. Shyly, one asked "I saw the shotgun in your room, has there been any trouble?" I told them what had happened.

Round eyed, they twittered with excitement, "It was the ghost, none of us would ever spend the night there". Tell me about it, I thought. Instead I boasted, "Oh, it's just a bloody poltergeist. Don't you worry, I'll soon sort *that* out". At that there came a shattering crash from the reception hall. The girls shrieked and I rushed out. There on the floor, surrounded by broken glass, lay a picture. Apparently it had jumped clean off the wall. During the next few nights the shotgun and I got very close indeed. When Graham and Pam returned I didn't tell them anything. There seemed no point in alarming them. Neither did I tell my parents. A short time later they sold the place.

Years later in 1996, my wife and I published my father's book *Historic Houses of Pembrokeshire and their Families.* I had a telephone call ordering a copy. The address struck a chord. It was my cousin's old house. My son, Guy, and I delivered the book to the brooding mansion. The present owner was a charming woman. I gently broached the subject "I, um, er, had a curious experience when I stayed here". She cut in straight away. "You mean the ghost!" She seemed proud of it and talked eagerly about it. Her husband had begun to alter the cellars. There were some weird noises in the night – and when they investigated, a freezing black cloud emerged. They left the cellar as it was after that. People often felt that they were being intently watched. On turning round they caught flashes of something disappearing. The phones, external and internal, never worked properly, yet a guest's mobile phone inexplicably rang all night even when put under a mattress. I believed every word she said. I read the other day that the house had been sold yet again.

Postscript

My father told of his strange experience. I have now told of mine. To my knowledge I am the fourth generation at least to have encountered the inexplicable. I hope I may have turned the tables on the ghastly Brawdy hound. Whilst being a Master of Foxhounds it was my turn to haunt hounds.

Tregaman

Major Jones records an event in 1602 which deserves mention: "Thomas Young; killed at Eglwyswrw Faire upon Ascension day 13th May 1602 by John Bowen and Hugh Bowen the sonnes of James Bowen his uncle, brother to his mother, who were both executed for the same act at Haverford west XVIIIth of July anno prd." (*Protheroe* IV.)

Trevaccoon – Trefacwn

DIANA OF THE CHASE

SHORTLY after the first world war I came to know a very dear old lady named Margaret Hughes, living in the village of Goodwick, on the north Pembrokeshire coast. She was the unmarried daughter of a bygone miller of Trellewelyn Mill in the neighbouring parish of Manorowen, and had spent her entire life in the district. Possessing a lively intelligence and retentive memory, she was the repository of unwritten traditional treasures which she delighted to share with those who showed an interest in the why's and wherefores of local history.

Here is one story that Margaret Hughes told me. I remember it particularly, because in an unexpected way I was personally associated with the final chapter. It is a tale of tree-embowered Trellewelyn, seat of the Phillips family, whose lineage traced to the courtly splendours of medieval royalty, and whose estates were said to have stretched from the sands of Goodwick as far inland as the bridge of Llanglydwen on the Carmarthenshire border. But later, the house crumbled and decayed in the dell below Manorowen, so that now there is little to indicate it has been anything other than a farmhouse of the better type.

Margaret described how it had been raided by a marauding band from the woodland lairs of Cwm Gwaun, and how the lord of Trellewelyn buried his plate and jewels in a secret spot, which his ghost still haunts, waiting until he meets a descendant to whom the hidden hoard will be revealed. This powerful family ended in an heiress, known as "Miss Martha of Trellewelyn", a high-spirited, pranksome lass, in whom Nature had happily wedded enchanting beauty with the adventurous and fearless qualities that marked the ancient race from which she sprang.

She was a noted Diana of the Chase. She kept a pack of hounds, kennelled where the house of Drim stands today, and many are the tales of wild Valkyrie-like rides which ended in the death of a fox on distant Dinas Head, and even, so I was told, on Preseli Top itself. Possessing the fleetest of greyhounds she coursed the hare over the slopes of Carne Coch, through the bracken of Cnwc Sandy and across the wind-swept moors of Tregroes. She excelled with the fowling piece, and was equally expert with rod and line.

Eventually Miss Martha married, left Trellewelyn, and was not seen again. Margaret Hughes never knew the name of her husband, nor the name of the place where she had gone to live, except vaguely that it was "something like Bush". What happened to her? Did she continue to fly over Pembrokeshire fences, harass fox and hare and fowl? I made several attempts to trace her subsequent history, but no book, manuscript, or memorial afforded the slightest clue. The lady had vanished. Nearly twenty years later I came to Haverfordwest where I spent a happy time scheduling the archives within the walls of the massive fortress that broods grimly over the town. While there, I made the acquaintance of an elderly antiquarian, and one afternoon he invited me to his house to see some items in his private collection. I arrived in due course, and together we pored over the relics in his study – a bundle of Latin charters, a folio of pedigrees, seventeenth century pistols, a sabre used at Waterloo, some beautiful heraldic seals cut in silver and in stone, and various trinkets. He picked up a small signet ring engraved with a lion rampant, and said: "This belonged to a lady who was concerned in a peculiar episode in our family past." He said that a collateral ancestor married an heiress, and settled near Haverfordwest. In due course they had a child, on whom they lavished their love and affection.

Now the husband was in the habit of making visits to London, but declined to reveal the reason for them. Naturally enough, this disturbed the wife. One day, her husband having departed for London, she followed in order to discover the cause of his suspicious behaviour. Having found the coffee house where he stayed, she was relieved to find that his business proved of an entirely innocent nature. After a few days together they took the westward road for home.

On their arrival a weeping maid informed them that their child had suddenly fallen ill, and died on the previous day. They never recovered from the blow. Each bitterly upbraided the other. The husband blamed the wife for leaving the child, the wife blamed the husband for his secretiveness.

Thereafter, they lived in separate parts of the house, and a second staircase was built to ensure that they should not come face to face. She became a solitary, and died in 1772. They lived, he said "at Withybush, just outside this town. Her name was Martha Phillips of Trellewelyn. Would you like to see her?" He led me through the hall, and opened the door of the dining room. I stood before a portrait, done in the Gainsborough manner, of a fine lady in a flowered silken dress, pale, blue eyes, distant, and somehow rather eerie. Here, at long last, was my Diana of the Chase. As I gazed with delight and wonder, the portrait seemed to cloud, and before my eyes arose another face – that of a homely, beshawled little Welshwoman, daughter of the bygone miller of Trellewelyn Mill.

THE OLD GENTLEMAN AT CAREW – 1931

VERY few people of my acquaintance have a good word for the Old Gentleman who presides over that awful place where eternal fires glow and where even the largest snowball has no chance of survival. Indeed he has served (and still does) as an admirable subject of many an eloquent sermon and his name is often invoked by people whose emotions are apt to become uncontrollable. However, readers will be interested to know that this personage had once a seat in the county of Pembroke and that his neighbours thought highly of their local "squire". Apparently celibacy did not appeal to him and he had a wife who helped him to guard a valuable treasure hidden in the gloomy vaults of the ancient castle of Carew.

In September 1767 a visitor to Carew Castle writes, "The vaults here are very fine, in them say the Common People here, did Sir John [Perrott] bury his money the last time he went to Court (suspecting that he should not return), and gave it in charge to the

Devil, who true to his trust has kept possession ever since, and by Thunder and Lightening obliged those who have begun to dig for it to desist; this Devil however is a most Gentlemanlike Devil, always speaking English and no Welsh, and appearing well dressed: he is married also, and his Wife lives with him in the Castle. These and a hundred more stories did our Guide tell us, firmly believing them every one, and moreover saying that he had often conversed with the

Carew Castle

Devil, who, he said, was always well dressed, and wore a Gold Laced Hat, was always perfectly civil and obliging, never having done harm to any creature, so that nobody was afraid of him". To see if this belief was general the visitor questioned a number of local people about it and found that they all firmly believed the tale.

It will be seen from this quotation that the Old Gentleman was a cut above the Welsh people and that he had not sunk so low as we are sometimes apt to imagine – *for he spoke no Welsh.* This is a serious outlook and is undoubtedly an "insult to Wales". It now remains for the Welsh Nationalists to take the matter up and to insist on a Welsh-speaking official in that region of raging fires.

CURSE ON TRECWN

THE strategic position of Pembrokeshire has been recognised by military experts for many centuries. In medieval times it was used as a base for the subjugation of Ireland, and as a Marchership to keep the turbulent Welsh of the mountain districts in check. In later years its importance was realised by the Admiralty and Milford Haven has played no insignificant part in the naval annals of Britain.

The works in Trecwn, a sequestered and remote district in the Pembrokeshire hills, recall a family history which is full of romance and strange coincidences.

Trecwn is a beautiful Tudor mansion which still retains the characteristics of that great period in house building. Fenton, in 1811, wrote: "Trecoon, in point of situation, yields to very few spots in the county, as possessing every ingredient of fine scenery, being situated on the edge of a steep hill, having a higher at its back, sheltering it from the north, above the narrow vale."

The history of the families of Trecwn makes interesting reading and although their lands have now passed to the nation, their history will remain ever green because of a certain prophecy which the centuries have borne out. In 1369 there flourished in West Wales a powerful chieftain called Llewelyn y Coed, or Llewelyn of the Wood, since his dwelling was in the midst of wooded land. This chieftain is the ancestor of such families as those of Bowen of Llwyngwair, Philipps of Picton and Owen of Trecwn.

In the beginning of the six-teenth century, Owen ap David, a descendant of Llewelyn y Coed, settled at Trecwn. It is said that he ruthlessly destroyed many local habitations in order to render his lands more suitable to the arts of the chase.

An ancient hag, with the reputation of a witch, thereupon cursed him, saying that, though the lands would remain in his descendants, the name of the family would constantly change owing to lack of male heirs. This has been strikingly exemplified by the subsequent history of the family.

The grandson of this Owen ap David was Owen Johns, who entertained Lewys Dwnn, the Welsh Deputy Herald at Trecwn in 1591. He was a coroner for the county of Pembroke and Seneschal of the High Court of the Barony of Kemes. The surname was now Johns, but his sons in the Welsh fashion called themselves Owen. The last of the Owens, however, was an heiress, Ursula, who married John Vaughan, of Farthings Hook, the father of John Vaughan of Trecwn, High Sheriff of Pembrokeshire in 1710.

The Vaughans of Trecwn were an influential family, being related to the well-known clans of Wogan, Corbett and Owen of Orielton, and it appeared as if the Vaughans would break the curse of the ancient beldame. However, the last of the Vaughans died without issue, leaving the Trecwn estate to his three sisters – Lettie, the wife of John Thomas of Cilciffeth, from whom descended the Gwynnes of Court and the Mortimers, Martha and Dorothea, who in 1754, married Joseph Foster Barham and had a son, also named Joseph Foster Barham.

On the death of Martha Vaughan in 1803, Joseph Foster Barham, her nephew, inherited the estate. Thus, although the lands remained in the family, another change had taken place in the name.

The Barhams were descended from Sir Randall FitzUrse who, in 1170, with three other knights, slew Thomas à Becket on the steps of the High Altar in Canterbury Cathedral. He fled the country and his estates came to a relative who assumed the name of Barham. Later, one of the family married a member of the ancient Northumberland border clan of Foster.

Joseph Foster Barham of Trecwn, was M.P. for Stockbridge and a man of some accomplishment. In 1792 he married Lady Caroline Tufton, daughter of Sackville, eighth Earl of Thanet. His three sons died without issue and the estate fell to his daughter, Caroline, who had married the Revd. Saunderson Robins, Rector of Shaftesbury. Thus the name of Barham of Trecwn appeared to be about to follow in the wake of those of the earlier owners of the place. However, Capt. Francis Williams Robins, of the 60th Rifles (son of the Revd. S. Robins), assumed the name and arms of Barham and became owner of the Trecwn Estate.

Lawn Meet at Trecwn

Yet ill-fate still dogged the

house. On the death of Capt. Barham in 1926 he was succeeded by Cyril Hugh Sackville Barham, who settled at Trecwn, the seat of his Welsh progenitors. In May of 1933, the county was shocked to hear of the death, in a motor accident near Oxford, of Mr. Barham, his wife, and his son and heir. This tragic chance closed the strange history of the ancient house of Trecwn, and, after nearly 450 years of vicissitudes, the descendants of Llewelyn y Coed finally severed their connection with a district which had known them for so long under different names. *"Sic transit gloria mundi!"*

[For further information on Trecwn see *The Historic Houses of Pembrokeshire and their Families.* Trecwn was demolished by the Admiralty. – *Ed.]*

❊   ❊   ❊

Parish skullduggery

The livings of Llandeilo, Llangolman and Maenclochog, were granted by David de Rupe, son and heir of Gilbert de Rupe, to the Abbey of St. Dogmaels. The grant had been made without Royal Licence, but on 30 October 1320, the Abbot received a royal pardon for this omission. Llandeilo later became a lay manor, but in 1898 no emoluments were derived from it, and the manorial courts discontinued. The parish was united to Maenclochog by Order in Council 11 July 1877. Some ruins of the old church are still to be seen near the farmstead. The earliest-known family there was that of Cardigan, who remained till early in the seventeenth century. Its successor was the Griffith family. Griffith ap Thomas, (died c. 1649-52), had some remarkably enterprising sons who left the old homestead.

In 1642 John Griffith of London became treasurer and solicitor to Thomas Howard, Earl of Arundel, who became Earl Marshal in 1646; William Griffith was Groom of His Majesty's Chamber in 1642 and Thomas Griffith became ancient of a Company in Ireland in that year. Another brother, Maurice Griffith, *agricola,* stayed at home and was executor of his father's estate in 1652.

The next family there was that of Melchior, one of whom had married a daughter of Cardigan of Llandeilo in Elizabethan times. The Melchiors, a Welsh family, came from Newport, the first of this unusual name being Melchior ap Ievan ap Howel ap Gwallter, who died on 3 April 1591 and was buried in Newport church on Easter Day. His sons adopted their father's Christian name as their permanent surname. The Melchiors continued to farm Llandeilo until well into this century. Although they were custodians of St. Teilo's skull, they nevertheless sold the holy relic in 1927, for £50 it is said. In 1950 the Cheetham family lived there.

❊   ❊   ❊

Miss Tasker

The famous Tasker's school that served Haverfordwest and district for generations and still flourishes under the name of Tasker-Milward, was originally endowed by Miss Mary Tasker of Fletherhill. A local tale related that Mary Tasker had long narrow strips of cloth placed on the road so that she should not soil her shoes when she walked from Fletherhill to Rudbaxton church. These strips were of blue cloth edged with scarlet – colours later used in the early school uniform of the school she had founded.

JACOBUS

A Short Story

AFTER an absence of almost twenty years I decided to return to Wales and looked forward to renewing old friendships and forming new ones, for at the age of fifty the native is not too old to return and is usually still sufficiently active and receptive to enable him to adapt himself to new or changed conditions. My choice fell on a West Wales county town, in former days the administrative capital of a wide area, and which continues to enjoy a position of eminence among the towns west of Cardiff.

My first problem was to find somewhere to live. I had almost despaired of obtaining a place in the town when a stroke of luck terminated my anxieties. An empty house lay tucked away within the ruined walls of the ancient castle and through the good offices of friends I obtained a temporary tenancy of it.

First built in the reign of the Red King, the castle stood on a knoll overlooking a river crossing that in those days possessed strategic significance. More than once it had fallen to Welsh attacks led by the warlike princes of Dinefwr, only to be recovered by the Anglo-Normans who could ill afford to allow their position to be weakened by the loss of so important a base. Three English kings had rested within the walls; on two occasions the standard of Glyndŵr had fluttered from its ramparts. Welsh archers had mustered there before departing for the field of Agincourt, Royal Justiciars had held courts there, and Chamberlains, who received taxes from unwilling hands, cast up their accounts within the safety of its towers.

After the Middle Ages, decay. An engraving made during the reign of George II showed that it had become a mere shell. In the year the French stormed the Bastille a prison rose on the site of this Welsh castle and during Victoria's reign the police were also established there. All these, in turn, departed, and on the foundations of the demolished prison, a block of offices rose just before the second world war. A high wall cut off the medieval part, still an imposing fragment, from the modern buildings.

Thrilling tales told of secret passages along which bygone burgesses escaped to the safety of vaults beneath the castle, also used by enterprising smugglers who carried thither kegs of brandy and rum from boats which came with the flow tide when nights were dark.

Immediately inside the impressive medieval gateway, flanked by two well-preserved towers, between high walls, stood the little house, and there my wife and I came to live. It faced south and beyond it stretched a garden ending at a ruined drum-tower.

Quiet, secluded, it suited us admirably, and we felt something of a thrill to be surrounded by over eight hundred years of history – and exciting history at that. We shared this sanctuary with pigeons which we tamed so that they ate out of our hands, a cloud of chattering sparrows of amazing voracity, bats that darted like black lightning in the twilight and a solemn owl who lived in a cavity behind the house maintaining a stand-offish attitude despite all our efforts to befriend him.

We came there early in the year and the flowers we planted in tubs and boxes made a colourful picture when summer came, giving pleasure to ourselves and sustenance to the bees who quickly found them. Here we dwelt in a walled bower, a cloister of peace and repose.

The house, as I have said, faced south. At the back were the bedrooms whose windows looked out on the great wall of the keep, at its foot a small courtyard, the sole access to which lay through a long passage running through the house. Nothing grew on the lower half of the wall; a heavy creeper, home of a myriad of thrushes, covered the upper half.

The distance across the courtyard, from the rear of the house to the wall of the keep, was about twelve feet. The morning sun warmed this hidden nook, but the most attractive sight came at night when the moonbeams thrust into the shaft so that the grey stones shone and the green leaves glistened as if they had been dipped in silver. My bed faced the window and it became one of my simple pleasures to gaze out on this fairyland of silvery peace before dropping off to sleep.

I had gone late to bed on the evening of a Sunday in May. Well past midnight, the moon shone on high so that I required no other light to guide me to bed. I soon fell asleep.

How long I had lain sleeping I do not know, before I found myself gazing through the window. The moonlight still bathed the walls; I could see everything clearly and recall noticing a crevice from which a solitary wall-flower curved upwards. I raised my eyes to the top of the window, and saw beyond the twigs and leaves of the thick creeper like some giant's beard, still and glistening. Complete silence, not a breath of wind.

Suddenly the leaves and branches shuddered convulsively, and a long thin object, resembling a snake seemed to glide down the wall. It hung still for a moment, a dark line against the whitened stones. It moved again, and looking up I discerned further rustling movements among the growth in the upper part of the wall. Slowly, a pair of white shoes came into sight, then legs encased in red stockings, then a cloak of the same colour surmounted by a wide floppy hat adorned with a long feather and I watched a man descending until he disappeared into the courtyard below.

A feeling of alarm assailed me. Was it a burglar? Before I could move, the rope wriggled once more and a second figure, similarly clad, came swarming down.

Curiously enough, the appearance of the second man dispelled my anxiety and I no longer thought of burglars. Instead, an overwhelming curiosity to learn more about my unconventional nocturnal callers consumed me. For both men were attired in clothes of the seventeenth century. I had not glimpsed their faces as their backs were towards me when they came down the rope. I decided to go to the window to see what was going on. The distance to the bottom of the courtyard was about fourteen feet or so and I peered cautiously round the curtains we never drew, so that those below would not spot me. There, in the bright moonlight I saw them; crouched low at the foot of the keep, their backs humped, the long feathers in their hats tossing as they moved.

As they were close against the masonry and their movements concealed by the cloaks, I could not observe very well what they were at. I noticed one on his knees who seemed to be trying to dislodge a stone at the base of the wall. Whatever their ploy, they worked silently, quickly, with the utmost concentration. I watched fascinated, I suppose for about five minutes, perhaps more. Whatever they were after they knew exactly where to look for it I recall musing, and I became more curious than ever to discover their errand.

After a while one of the crouching figures stood back and the other still kneeling, plunged an arm into a cavity and drew out something which he concealed within the folds of his cloak. Together they pushed back a great stone which fitted exactly into the cavity. Having done this they stood upright and turned towards the dangling rope.

To avoid being detected I stepped back further into the room, stood at the foot of the bed, and waited. Slowly a man came into sight, climbing laboriously, encumbered by something he carried. Very deliberately he continued upwards and I could see the toes of his buckled shoes taking advantage of every cranny and ledge that scarred the wall. With the help of these footholds and the rope he reached the top and passed over the ramparts.

The second man hove into view; he moved much more quickly, even hurriedly I thought, and I noticed he had wound the rope around his body in the manner of mountaineers. He climbed hand over fist at a fine rate and would soon be gone. And then, as I watched his legs disappearing, it suddenly happened. A jerk, and a body came hurtling down and hung limply against the wall; the rope was no longer around his shoulders, but around his neck. He hung there for some seconds, and then, the body swung round so that it faced right into my bedroom, at the level of the window. I gazed in intense horror, for the man, complete in all other ways, had no face – only a white blank, as white as the moonlight that lit the grotesque scene. The body swung slowly, horribly, and was still.

The shock proved so great that I staggered back overcome with a feeling of nausea. Somehow I managed, my eyes riveted on the ghastly sight, to climb on to the bed, when mercifully I passed out.

In the morning my wife woke me, with a concerned chiding for having slept outside the blankets, thus risking a cold. Feeling rather tired and a little chilled, I got up. After a few minutes the memory of the events of the night came flooding into my mind. I rushed to the window. Nothing unusual met my gaze. A thrush warbled on the rampart, the flowers drank in the morning sun and I could see no signs of disturbance at the foot of the wall. For a while I stood thoughtfully and decided to dismiss it all as a ridiculous though highly unpleasant dream, not worth mentioning to my wife whose practical personality rarely welcomed fantasies of such a nature.

Now, I must tell you that every morning I walk to a tobacconist's shop situated about twenty paces from the barbican. Shortly after nine o'clock I went to get my customary cigarettes, but found that the shopkeeper had not arrived. Rather than wait, I walked to another shop which I knew opened promptly at nine. The woman who served me said, "Excuse me sir, as you are fond of old things, can you tell me what this is?", handing me a coin. I recognised it at once as a Jacobus, a coin of the reign of James the First. "Where did you find this?" I enquired. She replied "Shortly after we opened this morning a stranger came in and ordered some tobacco. He gave me this and left immediately. At first I thought it might be an Irish coin, we get lots of them here and went after him, but failed to see him outside". I explained to her the value of her acquisition, adding that if she ever felt like selling it, I would be obliged if I were given the first offer. She said she would do that and put the coin away on a shelf behind her.

As I walked back to the house, the coincidence struck me like a cannon ball. Jacobus! Two men in seventeenth century clothes! What had they been after at the foot of the wall? I hurried home and told my wife the whole story. After I had finished she said "Well, let's go and see whether the wall has been disturbed".

"That's that," I said, "Just a silly dream to teach me to go to bed earlier in future." As I made to go, my wife who had turned to take a closer look, clutched my sleeve and pointed in silence. I bent down. There close to the wall, glinting among the fallen leaves, lay a solitary Jacobus coin!

THE HAUNTED BELL

ONE late summer's evening some years ago I started to tramp from Solva to Goodwick. The night was clear and the moon was a good friend to a belated traveller lighting up the whole countryside. I marched on, enjoying every mile of it since I was a young man and did not tire quickly. I stopped for a moment to fill my old pipe with some Rigers', always my favourite baccy, but to my great dismay found that I had used up all my matches, while the nearest shop was still some miles ahead. However, I decided to push on and call at the first house I came across to obtain a light for my pipe. A little further on I saw in some fields on my right, a cottage and without looking for gates, climbed over the hedge and made my way across the fields. All was quiet save for the occasional screams in the distance of some poor rabbit caught in one of those vile metal traps which are used by church and chapel-going farmers and trappers. In less than two minutes I was knocking at the cottage door. Within I heard the slow movements of a person getting up from a chair, and then slow, heavy footsteps coming towards the door. It was opened by a very old man.

I apologised for the rather late intrusion and explained my mission. Being a hospitable man – they are all hospitable in Dewsland – he asked me in and I was soon sitting on a form in the recesses of the *simne fawr*. The ancient was a lonely bachelor but very sociable and he greatly welcomed a chat, and although the hour was late, he asked me to stay a little while to rest and have a talk. I was by no means averse to this and we had an interesting conversation. He had known my great-grandfather, William Jones, and told me many things about old and extinct families and amusingly recounted how the new-rich of the district had made their money! He was a philosophical genealogist and had some strange and remarkable theories on the rise and fall of families. I jotted down afterwards many of his sage remarks, which will duly appear in the "Guardian" as he is gone from our midst many a day. He was a very decent man, this old labourer in his cottage and I liked him tremendously. His outlook and mine were much the same.

"I like to be as my fathers were
In the days ere I was born".

Those simple lines sum up our philosophy.

The culm fire gave good heat and light and I noticed that there was a small sheep bell hanging on the wall behind the fire. It excited my curiosity somewhat and he took it down for me to see. It was an old bell and cracked, while the tongue had been taken out.

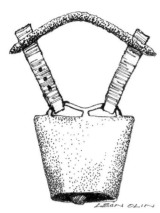

The haunted bell

Said he: "That bell has a strange and tragic history which I have not related to many people." This made me very curious to hear his tale and after he had filled his pipe and lit up, he told me the following story:

Very many years ago, a Mr. James lived at Lochmeyler in the parish of Llandeloy. The family had come there after the heiress of the Bowens had married a Scourfield. Where the James's stock hailed from I cannot say, but they were settled there for some generations and there are descendants still living in the district. One of the squires had a young son who was the pride of his parents and a very popular gentleman. At one of the fairs held at Tancredston he met Miss Griffith, the daughter of a very respectable yeoman who lived at Treindeg, in those days a small mansion. Mr. James would gallop his horse very often afterwards through Llandeloy past Tancredston and Hayscastle Tump to see his lady love at Treindeg. The lambing season came on and Miss Griffith kept one of the lambs as a pet and its frolics were the amusement of the house. However, the lamb was capricious and sometimes it would stray from the house and could only be found with difficulty, and so Mr. James said he would bring a little bell to hang around its neck. Miss Griffith was naturally charmed to find that her lover took such an interest in her pet and looked forward to having the bell, which would remind her of his love, and at the same time give her an indication of her pet's whereabouts.

Well it so happened that Cromwell's men had come to Roch Castle and many of the troops had been billeted on the farms. There were some very strong Royalist gentlemen in Dewsland and the Ironsides took great care that there should be no rising. It was dangerous to travel at night, since the patrols showed scant respect for nocturnal pilgrims. But Mr. James was not to be denied and he decided to walk over to Treindeg one evening, since a man on horseback is easily seen and heard, and he wished to avoid meeting any patrols. So he crossed the field as quietly as he could with the little bell in his hand. Among the distant trees he could see lights burning and he knew that Miss Griffith was waiting for him.

However just before he came out to the lane that leads to Treindeg, he fell when crossing a small ditch and the sheep-bell in his hand rang out a merry little tune. Immediately, he heard shouting from the road about twenty yards away and in the darkness he could hear men running towards him ordering him to stop. Mr. James, however, ran towards the friendly mansion, but with his running the little bell again tinkled. Some shots rang out and the young gentleman fell dead.

The noise had attracted the attention of the people of Treindeg and they came out with lanthorns to the spot where a group of soldiers were standing over the body of the dead man. Miss Griffith came with them and in the dim light of the lanthorns she stooped down and kissed her lover's forehead. The little bell lay beside him and this she picked up and took with her to the house. Within a few months they buried her. She had died of a broken heart.

My people were serving men at Treindeg then and have always lived in the district. One night the old *Plas* caught fire and was burned to the ground. One of my ancestors helped to save some things from the fire and that bell was one of them, and it has remained in my family ever since. You can still see the ruins of the old mansion, which was never re-built.

My father told me that the little bell was haunted by the dead man's spirit and used to tinkle a kind of dirge on certain nights. He heard it a number of times but I have only heard it once. I had been very busy hedging one winter's day and it was late when I came to this old cottage for my supper. After having partaken of food, I took out my pipe to enjoy

"After having partaken of food . . ."

a smoke. The hard work of the day and the heat of the fire soon made me very drowsy and I slept several hours, for when I awoke the candle had burned itself out and the fire was only just smouldering. The clock was striking the hour of midnight. Then before I could move, I heard a little movement in the *simne fawr*. I next heard the little tinkle of that bell. It tinkled for about a minute and then all was silent again. As I was living here alone and being religious and rather elderly, I took the tongue of the bell out and it has been at rest ever since.

I took the bell in my hand. It looked an ordinary thing, but what a tragic tale was connected with it. The ancient was so pleased to have such an appreciative audience and to meet with one who loved the old things, that he gave me the bell as a present.

I never saw him again and he has been gathered to his fathers, but I still have the bell in my possession and it lies before me now as I write this essay.   *Written in 1934*

※   ※   ※

The prisoner of Tresisillt

An old story on *Llafar Gwlad* states: Once upon a time a mermaid used to inhabit the shores of Pencaer. She used to come out of the water and perch herself on a rock on the end of the land of Tresisillt (Tresysayllt), sometimes prancing about, gambolling and combing her long abundant hair. Many people saw her and one succeeded in capturing her and she was taken as a prisoner to the farm of Treseissyllt, where she was placed in a barrel of water. For some time she did nothing but shriek. Suddenly she desisted and cast a spell over the place and the people fearing magic released her; she returned to the sea and was seen no more. The spell she cast over the place was that no child should be born alive at Tresisillt again.

THE GOLD OF THE SEA

The perilous sea

"Aye, there's much gold on the sea floor", said the old cottager to me as we stood together looking across the sea from the rock above Pwll Deri in Pencaer. I had made a pilgrimage on an ancient push-bike to the St. Nicholas churchyard in order to copy down inscriptions from certain tombstones. Afterward I left the bike in a hedge and trudged over the fields – a glorious trespasser

heady with the wine of my new discovery – towards the rugged coastline of Pencaer. It was here that I met a most cultured gentleman – a farm labourer of the old school, who had lived a happy life, courteous and hospitable, contented and religious. I felt that a chat with him would be a tonic and so indeed it was.

Casual conversation led to the talk about gold on the sea-floors and this resulted in the tale about the Armada ship. Possibly the story has no real connection with the 1588 adventure, but related to some shipwreck of later years. But that I do not know and neither does he. Still his tale was an arresting one.

After our hard-living, hard-swearing sea-dogs had made the King of Spain look a fool, the whole world of history knows that some remnants of his once mighty fleet tried to round our island and get home again. It is a fact that at least one of these galleons was wrecked on our Pembrokeshire coast and there are tales that one struck the iron-bound coast of Pencaer and was accordingly plundered by the inhabitants of that headland who lived up to the old tag *Pencaer, lle gwael i fagu da, ond lle da i fagu lladron*, which interpreted is: Pencaer, a poor place to raise cattle, but a good place for breeding thieves!

It was a stormy night when our galleon, with a broken rudder, was tossing aimlessly in the St. George's Channel. Raked by England's cannon, the great vessel was carried helplessly towards the rocks of Pwll Deri, the waves completing what Drake and Hawkins had started. The captain ordered all the gold ingots, doubloons and other treasures in the ship, to be placed in a casket which was put into an open boat. With some difficulty the boat was lowered to the rough seas and manned by some sturdy sailors. A junior gentleman of Spain was put in command of the precious cargo with instructions to make the shore safely if possible and bury the treasure in a convenient spot. The captain remained true to his command and perished with the rest of his men when the vessel struck the Pencaer coast. The little boat was tossed about by the merciless waves, but its crew manfully attempted to make Abermawr safely. In vain, however, and in the darkness they were driven into a small aber nearby and the crew perished with the exception of the young nobleman who had fastened the casket by a chain to his arm.

The inhabitants of that part of Owen's Pembrokeshire had however seen the lantern burning in the little boat and had gathered to see it meeting its inevitable end. They rescued the officer from the waves with a broken arm and a cracked skull. The young man, however, recovered after a long illness and tribulation, and was allowed to live unmolested among the Pencaer *Cymry*, where he eventually married and had issue. Local lore has it that a certain family is the descendant of this union and I have spoken to some of them , one of whom, in his cups, will tell you as he has told me, that his ancestors came from a castle in Spain. His name certainly has an alien ring.

But what of the casket, you will ask? Aye, what of the treasure of the galleon? And this is what they will tell you. A certain yeoman, a man of the ancient blood and authority, accompanied the Welsh spoilers that stormy night, and it was he, by priority of position, who took the unopened casket and safely brought it to his home at Llan . . . . His descendants – fairly well-to-do folk – are still at this farm and it is said, when none of the relations are near, that the wealth of the casket enabled their Elizabethan ancestor to buy lands and tenements in the district. The day following the storm, the natives reaped a good harvest from the wreck of the galleon and the iron casket of the previous evening was forgotten in the scramble for blankets, furniture and other contraband.

> *"For why? Because the good old rule sufficeth them;*
> *the simple plan, that they should take who have the power,*
> *And they should keep who can".*

THE GOLD AT CWRT

COURT or Cwrt is a small mansion near the village of Llanychaer. A long and beautiful drive leads to the house, winding uphill above the river Gwaun. The house is in a pleasant spot, surrounded by grand old trees, with a huge walled garden behind it. It is a typical small country house of Wales, a square building with a pillared entrance to the hall and a fine lawn before it.

It was the seat of the Gwynnes who lie buried in Llanychaer graveyard. A fine race, they made ideal squires and were much loved in the district. They had intermarried with the Thomases of Posty, also a clan of good standing in north Pembrokeshire. One of the ladies of Cwrt, Miss Lettice Gwynne, married John Morgan Mortimer, of Penysgwern, gent., and she was buried in 1871 in the burial garden of the Mortimers at Llanwnda. Their son, the Revd. Thomas Gwynne Mortimer, M.A., R.D., of Court, was vicar of Castelbythe, and a bachelor, he was the last of the old line. He died in 1903. Since then Court has been let as a farm and is inhabited today by a very respectable farming family.

Our tale takes us back to the days of the Gwynnes. There are different versions of the story told in the district, but an uncertain tale often presents itself in slightly different form, according to the taste and subject to the imagination of the raconteur. I give this version as it was told me by an old lady of four score years and six, whose memory takes us back nearly to the time that my story was born.

The Gwynnes were, in many ways, a remarkable family of original ways and manner. They also, according to local tradition, kept a great deal of gold in the house – sovereigns, nowadays a profitable trade. These sovereigns were so numerous that they could not be kept in an ordinary drawer or the proverbial stocking and so the Gwynnes had them placed in a very large sieve, which was put into an old oak coffer in the hall of Cwrt. For many years this was the bank of the squires, and although the knowledge of this was pretty well-known, such was the honesty of the servants and the respect of the district that the sovereigns were as safe in the old coffer as in any modern strong house. The squires hunted and entertained and enjoyed their rural sway, with never a thought of the burglar and the rogue.

But the peace of a de Coverley household may be broken and the trust of a family shaken, the knowledge of the gold of the Gwynnes had aroused a certain interest somewhere and the moss-trooping instinct of the mountaineer is strong. One day there was occasion to open the coffer – those vexatious taxes you know – and to the intense astonishment not unmixed with anger, the Gwynnes saw that there was but a handful of coins in the sieve. Some knave had carried away a large fortune from the coffer, and had left neither trace nor mark to give rise to a suspicion. The mysterious disappearance of the sovereigns was never satisfactorily solved. Whether a covetous servant or a penurious neighbour or a man with a sense of injustice we shall never know.

But with the disappearance of the gold from the coffer a local proverb arose. Perhaps somewhat malicious and cynical in its portent: *Dyna aur y Cwrt yn dangos.* When a householder or farmer bought any land or property the country folk would smile and wisely say: "There is the gold of Cwrt showing itself!"

Llangwarren demesne

THE COINS OF LLANGWARREN

MANY are the strange stories that surround our old country houses, and to me some of the most attractive of these are connected with hidden treasure. I have heard four of these stories in the course of my wanderings and researches – the treasure trove of Llangwarren, near Letterston; Llanreithan, near Croesgoch; Court, above Llanychaer and Trewern in Cemais.

Llangwarren is a pleasant mansion not far from the village of Letterston and has been for many centuries the seat of the Mathias family, which has occupied and still occupies a prominent position in Pembrokeshire annals. Nearby are the houses of Heathfield where the Harries family once lived, Jordanston Hall, where the ancient family of Vaughan made its home in olden times and Priskelly, where John Harries, the last member of that Welsh Jacobite association the Society of Sea Serjeants, died in the opening years of the last century. Llangwarren house has been altered during the past decades by various squires to make it suit the requirements of the times. And it is in connection with one of these renovations that my tale is told.

About 1818 several alterations were made at Llangwarren, and in the course of this work it was decided to block up a certain window. There was a seat under this window – a common feature in old houses – and the wall there was not very thick, and so it was planned to pull it down from the outside, to the level of the floor. A ladder was placed against the wall early one morning and the workmen started on their work. One of the men, whom we will call William, mounted the ladder and commenced removing some of the stones. For no reason apparent to his mates, he came down, telling them "We had better go in to breakfast now as we are a little late. You go on. I shall follow you as soon as I remove this gravel that has got inside my boot". The workmen, whose open air vocation gave their appetite a good edge for a morning meal, trooped off towards the servants' quarters leaving their foreman engaged with his boot. After their meal they returned, but saw no sign of William, and thinking nothing amiss they carried on with their job. Then they saw a broken earthware pitcher and nearly 30 gold sovereigns scattered about. The gold pieces were coins of the reign of James I, Charles I and of Louis XIV, some of them having been cut into two so as to represent half pieces. Then they realised the significance of William's absence and considered him either a lucky man or a canny rogue.

Nothing further was heard of William for a long time. He seemed to have vanished entirely and was never again seen in the places of his youth. One day, many years afterwards one of these workers of my tale, when at Haverfordwest, visited an inn of repectable appearance, and ordered a tankard of ale. Picture his surprise when he recognised in the person of the corpulent and prosperous landlord, no other than William, the old foreman who had directed the renovations at Llangwarren House many years before.

Y Bwch du

It is said that long ago this rocky place was inhabited by large herd of wild goats. Their chief was *Y Bwch Du*, the black he-goat, a strong black, agile animal. He led them till he died, it is said, of old age. The herd, however, retained possession of their rocky tract of land for about 80 years afterwards and then measures began to be taken against them. They had one weakness; they would sweep down at night into the crops and wreak much damage. Then they retired to their rocky fastness once more. When threatened by dogs and huntsmen they used to swim from Pen-y bwch du to Abermawr and Morfa, and then return to their old haunt when the crisis was over. However, they were struck down by rifle and trap. But even so there were said to be hundreds there in the 1880's. About four years ago they damaged the crops again and twelve were shot. Now it is said that only two or three still live as their ancestors had done on the Bwchdy.

ST. EDRINS

Written in 1936-37

IN THE middle of green fields, surrounded by "the grass of madmen", stands the little parish church of St. Edrins in the Dewsland Hundred of Pembrokeshire. It has been built on high ground, and its huge tower out of all proportion to the rest of the building, is a prominent landmark. Although visible to almost every traveller to St. Davids, it is rarely visited, but it is well worthy of a pilgrimage.

Local tradition states that the church originally stood in a field near the farm of Treddiog, and ancient manuscripts support this, since many references are found to St. Edrins, "the church of Trefduawg". Thus in 1190, Phillip de Barri (brother of the famous Geraldus Cambrensis), was witness to Robert Fitz Elidor's grant of "the church of Trefduawk" to St. Davids, for the repose of his soul, and that of his friend, Milo de Cogan, a famous knight of early Norman days. This grant was confirmed in 1278 by Bishop Richard Carew. In the Taxation of 1291, "Ecclesie de Treffdyauc" is assessed at £3. 6s 8d four tenths for the King, the amount payable being 6s. 8d.

As the years rolled on the little church appears to have fallen on bad times, but in 1846, it was rebuilt, "towards the erection of which" reads the mural tablet, "Her Majesty Queen Adelaide contributed the munificent sum of £100".

The church possesses objects of unusual interest. In the porch is the old font, which once formed part of a stile on the north side of the churchyard. It was supported by an octagonal shelf, now missing. In the north wall of the chancel there is a plain Latin cross in relief, bearing the Greek signs of Alpha and Omega; while by its side is a fragment of a cylindrical pillar with a cross carved thereon. The stone in the south wall has, in relief, a plain Latin cross.

The fourth cross is a simple and dignified reminder of a young man's sacrifice. It is a plain wooden cross with the dried clay of a foreign field still on it, bearing the inscription: "2nd Lieut. L.G.T. Thomas, Att. M.G.C". This was the cross which, on a French battlefield, marked the last resting place of Lionel George Theophilus Thomas, killed in action at Ypres on 20 September 1917, aged nineteen years. He was the only son of Mrs. Thomas, J.P. and the late Mr. T. E. Thomas, J.P. of Trehale in the

St. Edrins church

parish of St. Edrins, a descendant of the ancient family of John of Carwen and Trehale.

In the churchyard is an old Celtic cross incised within a circle on a grey upright stone. It is said to mark the grave of an early Welsh chieftain who had accepted the teachings of the Master.

But perhaps the most interesting of all is "the grass of madmen" *(porfa 'r cynddeiriog)*. Around the walls grows a curious thin reedy grass which, it is claimed, will cure anyone afflicted with hydrophobia. When a man or animal was suspected of having rabies this grass was given to the stricken one to eat. This has been done within living memory and is said to be a certain cure. In 1811 there was a stone trough in the chancel wall for offerings after the grass had been eaten, being the perquisite of the parish clerk.

The parishioners say that during the troublous days of the Civil War, a large sum of gold was buried in the churchyard but never recovered. Any attempt to locate it is said to draw a terrible storm of thunder and lightning over the district. Thus do the Unseen Powers guard the treasure of St. Edrins.

The graveyard soil, which is said to preserve bodies, is light and sandy. The true tale of the "Supervisor of Trehale" has a bearing on this. In bygone days there lived at Trehale a supervisor of the malt tax, who apparently had committed some breach of his trust. Fearing the vengeance of the law he rarely left the house and habitually had a loaded pistol and naked sword on the table before him to combat any attempt to apprehend him. However, his sins were overlooked and he was allowed to end his days in peace. He was buried at the west end of the church. Some sixty years later, in 1846, the great tower was added to the church and in digging the foundations the workmen came across the coffin of the supervisor. The body was in excellent state of preservation, on his coat being the large gold brooch he was wont to wear, and at his side a sword and pistol. The coffin was then buried in another part of the churchyard and has not been disturbed since.

We now leave the little church with its legends and traditions, with the cross of the young squire within and the cross of the Welsh chieftain without, leaving St. Edrins to the ancient peace of green fields and hedgerows, wondering "How many beads have here been told, How many matins here been sung!".

Francis Jones and Ethel Charles were the last couple to be married at St. Edrins.   It is now a private house. – *Editor.*

To Ethel

The sun above and scudding skies
Hold a glory of their own,
But all this pride is nothing to
The love that we have known.

Francis Jones
Pengorse, 1931

GHOSTS AND LEGENDS

MY wife Caroline and I have a hand-written book filled with legends, descriptions of castles, cottages, smugglers caves, ghost stories, battles and a wide sweep of historical data. It is dated 1926. In the Author's foreword, F.J. (then 16 years of age) wrote: "During the Xmas vacation of 1923 the pleasant task of gathering old traditions and legends (hitherto not recorded), of the districts of Fishguard, Goodwick and Pencaer was allotted to me, and it was a very pleasant work to carry out." Here are a few extracts from his researches.

※   ※   ※

Legends are of the greatest value and it is hoped they will continue to hold a place in the affections of their owners. In the old days these traditions and tales were told before the fireside to children to amuse or interest them. Today more books and papers are available and, together with radio and television, they are ousting the old beliefs. I remember in the old days the story telling and the singing that went on in Pembrokeshire. When you walked along the road at night you would often hear the sound of singing coming from a cottage or a farmhouse. Today these sounds are still, the family is silent, listening to the wireless or watching television, so the old stories will die-out before long, unless we collect them and write them down in order to preserve them.

※   ※   ※

The Gilfach is a farmhouse on the slope of Carn Folch. People say that Gilfach is a contraction of the proper name "Cilhwch" but this is not a very probable suggestion. Whilst a man was riding a horse in Gilfach yard he rode through the pond and the horse stumbled; to explain the cause of this, the pond was drained. In it was found an air-tight iron coffin which was pulled out. It was opened and found to contain human bones, but they crumbled away when handled and exposed to the air. Whose body it was no one could say as there was no evidence to say who it was that lay in the iron coffin.

※   ※   ※

Another Pembrokeshire family, the Philipps of Kilbarth, were also continually seeing harbingers of doom. It appears that all members of the family were "fey," seeing ghost funerals, ghost ships on the river Cleddau and even phantom tombstones.

※   ※   ※

There is still a tradition amongst the oldest people in the neighbourhood of Maenclochog, that when the Devil offered all the nations of the earth to our Lord if He would prostrate Himself, the Devil expressly reserved to himself Little Newcastle (Casnewy-bach), and Maenclochog. Afterwards he gave up Little Newcastle, but retained Maenclochog to this day.

The ghost of Trefaser crossroads. This crossroads was once haunted by an unseen being and a rumour current among the peasants states that one inhabits it to the present day. This ghost comes to the crossroads on certain nights, its nocturnal haunts were the rocks and bushes; when near Trefaser crossroads it gave vent to the most terrible and bloodcurdling shrieks which frightened all who heard them very much. This was at midnight on certain dates.

※   ※   ※

The Gate of the Ladies. This is a gate opening from the head of the old road to another road in the furthest corner of the land of Panteurig, between Carn Fach and Carn Fechan. Tradition: two ladies dressed in white (*ladi wen*) used to appear here at midnight on certain nights and stood there on their cold nocturnal vigil. They were waiting for a certain person to tell them the whereabouts of a great treasure on Pencaer, but he has not turned up. One of the ladies left and her place was taken by a black hound. It is said that they still wait for this person.

※   ※   ※

Horse Heads . . . In the year 1883, the stone steps leading into the chancel of Steynton church were taken up. Not more than a foot beneath the surface and immediately under the chancel arch, was found a human skeleton, three horses heads and an iron pike. More horses heads were found by workmen whilst laying a new floor in the dining room at Jordanston Manor. It appears that in every old house it was customary to bury the skeleton heads of horses so as to produce an echo or a better sound in the rooms. Poyston Hall also has a skeleton horse-head beneath its drawing room floor.

※   ※   ※

Having been found guilty at Trellys, the offender was sentenced to a term of imprisonment at Felindre. Felindre is between Llanwnda and Tremarchog and there are many stories concerning the prison of Felindre. This names explains itself: *Felin* is a mill, and *dre* is town. Hence the town of the mill. There was a mill in Felindre in those days and sentenced offenders had to tread the mill to grind the flour. But if the condemned was rich enough to pay the jailer, then he would be let off the tread mill. As time went on feudal privilege decayed and the court of Trellys stopped and the jail at Felindre was no longer used.

※   ※   ※

In south Pembrokeshire the charm for a wart was to rub the wart with a black snail, then affixing the snail on a prickle of the white hawthorn and leaving it until it drops off, when the wart was expected to drop off likewise.

Another charm was to rub the wart with a small stone, then wrap the stone up in paper and drop it at a cross- road. It was supposed that whoever picked up this stone had the wart transferred to him. Secrecy was required in both cases otherwise the charm lost its virtue. Children will never pick up a small parcel still, for fear of the transference of warts.

※   ※   ※

Lights that appear to old Welsh families before a death: If lights are small and pale blue in colour they predict the death of a child; if large and ruddy, then an adult; if large and pale olive then an old person long ill and decrepit.

An interesting Pembrokeshire coat of arms. This is the Toad of Trellyffant (literally: the town of the Toads), and the legend was known as early as the fifteenth century. The name probably perpetuates the presence of toads there at some remote period.

Mention must be made of the medieval chieftain who lived once near Dinas called Llyffan Gawr. The second element may thus be a personal name, that is the *tref* of Llyffain (*Tref* had an economic significance under the old Welsh land tenure). The earliest known reference to the legend is contained in a work by Giraldus Cambrensis in 1188. He records the memory in his usual vivid manner: "In our time a young man, native of this country, during a severe illness, suffered as violent a Persecution from toads, as if the reptiles of the whole province had come to him by agreement; and though destroyed by his nurses and friends, they increased again on all sides in infinite numbers like Hydra's heads. His attendants, both friends and strangers, being wearied out, he was drawn up in a kind of bag, into a high tree [which was] stripped of its leaves and shredded of its bark. Nor was he there secure from the venomous enemies, for they crept up the tree in great numbers, and consumed him even to the very bones."

Another reptile tale (tail). Moreiddig's mother (Arddun, daughter of Jestyn ap Gwrgant), was sleeping peacefully on a green sward on a fine summer's day, when a snake crept into her mouth and thus into her body, and that when her child was born, this horrid creature was entwined around its neck. It is also stated that the place of this birth was afterwards called the *dychrynllyd*, "the frightful place", later corrupted into Llechryd. Pembrokeshire folk say the events took place on the Cardiganshire side and Cardiganshire folk vice versa.

Hoaten. In 1786 Great, Middle and Little Hoaten were owned by Thomas Skyrme of Vaynor, and let to farmers. On the lawn of Great Hoaten rests a huge iron anchor, said to be a relic of the Spanish Armada.

Llwynbedw. The ghost of Llwynbedw is said to be that of a lady who had been drowned at Glanpwll-du just below the plas. In the evening, the sound of a rapidly driven coach could be heard from the house. It stopped at the entrance and a ringing of the house bells followed. Residents could hear the swishing of the ghost's skirts as she darted from room to room. One bedroom was never used, as those who had slept there claimed that, "something" disturbed their repose. As a result the occupiers found great difficulty in recruiting house servants from the district where tales of the, "Lady of Llwynbedw" were well-known. Mr. Peter Gwynne Hughes lived there for many years, his sleeping hours seemingly undisturbed.

Prendergast. The only relic of the early days to have survived is "The Lady of the Ghyll", a ghost in the form of a vaporous cloud, said to walk along a footpath in Prendergast; the small tract of land that harbours her is called "The Ghyll".

⁂   ⁂   ⁂

Sealyham was the home of the Tucker family. An eighteenth century Tucker – Admiral Thomas Tucker, R.N., achieved renown by killing the notorious pirate "Blackbeard" in the West Indies. He went on to capture Spanish ships with rich cargoes and died in 1766.

The ghost of a woman in white used to haunt the drive, the tradition being that a daughter of the house, Grace Tucker, had fallen in love with the coachman. Her angry father is said to have built a small cottage off the drive with barred windows in which he consigned his daughter "to cool her off". This little building, Major Jones reports, became a ruin, but had for a time been used by Captain John Owen Tucker-Edwardes as kennels for his hounds. He was the first man to breed Sealyham terriers. Mrs. C. O. Higgon once told Major Jones that she and a friend had actually seen the ghost gliding across the drive on a winter's evening in 1987.

⁂   ⁂   ⁂

Trevaccoon – Trefacwn. The late Mr. Francis Green, whose mother was a Harries, told Major Jones of a tradition that one of the Hardings had ploughed up a "rich treasure" in a field on Porth Eiddy land afterwards known as "Parc Harding". What the nature of this treasure was and what became of it is not mentioned.

⁂   ⁂   ⁂

The Gwrach-y-rhibyn, a hag like creature with scaly wings, is a dreadful old hag with long matted hair, a hooked nose, piercing eyes, a crooked back, long arms with claw like fingers. She is said only to haunt families in whom there is a genuine strain of old Welsh blood.

⁂   ⁂   ⁂

Walwyns Castle is an interesting edifice. Some say that the word is derived from Gawine or Garwaine, one of the Knights of Arthur's round table. About 80 years ago some people were digging a grave in Walwyns Castle churchyard; a body of gigantic size with a laurel of leaves over the skull was found. But no one knew who it was.

⁂   ⁂   ⁂

Enoch Lale was an old man who lived at Cwm Felin, a cottage (now in ruins). He had a dream a considerable time before 1797. He saw three ships filled with soldiers, with masts as high as the crags and their pennants swept the cliff tops. He told his dream to many people, but they gave little credit to it, believing that something was playing on the old man's imagination. But on 22 February 1797 they remembered Enoch Lale.

CHAPTER IX

MATTERS ECCLESIASTICAL, PRIESTS, PARSONS AND PARISHIONERS

MEDIEVAL RECORDS RELATING TO THE DIOCESE OF ST. DAVIDS

D URING periods of vacancy the temporalities of the See of St. Davids were taken into the hands of the King who appointed keepers to administer them until such time as they were delivered to the newly-appointed bishop. Accounts of their stewardship rendered by the keepers were enrolled among the national archives. The following, preserved in The Public Record Office, consist of such records, namely:-

I.   Account of Bogo de Cnoville, 1280.
II.   Inventory of the goods of Thomas, Bishop of St. Davids, 1293.
III.   Extent of the Lands of the Bishopric of St. Davids, 1327.
IV.   Extent of the Lands in England of David, Bishop of St. Davids, 1327.
V.   Account of John Gogh, 1350.

The information they contain varies considerably, but taken together these documents provide useful data, some unique, of the possessions and sources of revenue of the bishops during the years 1280-1350. In this prefatory note, attention will be drawn to the nature and contents of the documents.

The first is the account rendered by Bogo de Cnoville (or Knovill) who kept the temporalities from 1 April 1280 to 10 June 1280, the See being then vacant by the death of Bishop Richard de Carew which had taken place on the former date.[1] His successor, Thomas Beck (or Bek), elected bishop on 3 June 1280, received the royal assent on 17 June and was consecrated on 6 October following.[2] The keeper, a Shropshire knight who had rendered eminent services to the King, stood high in the royal favour. On 10 June 1280 he was appointed to hear and determine pleas and complaints touching the Bishop of St. Davids and the tenants of his bishopric,[3] and in January 1280/81 received the appointment of Justiciar of West Wales, the seat of his government being Carmarthen Castle.[4] Bogo's account as keeper of the temporalities is not detailed and he contented himself with recording totals of the receipts which came to £87 8s. 1½d. for the seventy-one days of his stewardship and the expenses, taking care to note his own, which stood at £16 15s. 0d. Among the entries was the rent of *Calemay* (Calan Mai), a customary rent payable every third year, which continued to be paid on some episcopal manors for centuries following, and *Leyr Wyt,* a fine paid to the lord for incontinence or adultery; the fair at St. Davids, held twice yearly, lasted to within living memory; the reference to the janitor in Llawhaden Castle reminds us that here was the chief prison of the bishop and shows that the castle was a going concern in 1280, prior to the advent of Thomas Beck during whose episcopacy it is usually alleged to have been built. But of the castle of Landogwit (Llandygwydd, Cards.), nothing remains and this is the sole reference that I have seen to it, and the description may be a scribal slip.[5]

Bogo de Cnoville did not account for all the temporalities, for, as he states, the manors of *Landou* (Llanddew, Brec.), *Graclan* and *Neweuton,* were in the keeping of Humphrey de Bohun, Earl of Hereford, and the manors of Glascon (Glascwm, Brec.) and St. German (Rad.) in that of Roger de Mortimer, both of whom accounted, separately, to the King.

The second document, an inventory of the goods of Thomas Beck, contains details which throw some light on the agricultural interests of the See. As noted earlier, Beck was elected bishop on 3 June 1280 and consecrated on 6 October following.[6] He sang mass for the first time in the diocese at Strata Florida on 1 or 2 February 1281 and was enthroned in his cathedral church on the Feast of St. David in that year. Previously he had held appointments in the Royal Household and as bishop, entertained the King and Queen when they visited St. Davids, *peregrinationis causa,* on 26 November 1284, the weight of the expenses on that occasion being such as to cause him to apply later to his chief guest for an easement. He created the offices of Chancellor, Sub-dean, and Succentor at St. Davids, established colleges at Llangadog, (afterwards moved to Abergwili) in 1284 and Llanddewibrefi in 1287, a hospital at Llawhaden and obtained from the King a grant of two weekly markets in his cathedral city. His interest in the protection of the Holy Places, (his brother Anthony Beck, Bishop of Durham, was Patriarch of Jerusalem), is indicated by the fact that he took the Cross in 1290 and journeyed to the Holy Land.

Bishop Beck died on 12 May 1293. The election of his successor, David Martin (brother of Nicholas Martin, lord of Cemais), received the royal assent on 28 July 1293.[7] During the short vacancy the See was in the keeping of the lord Ralph de Broughton who, assisted by two of the King's deputies, William de Bruer and John de Forneis, prepared an inventory of the goods of the late bishop.

The deceased prelate had farmed on an extensive scale, possessing 2,348 animals of all kinds. The emphasis was on cattle and sheep, typical of Welsh farming in medieval times. The stud *(equitium)* forms an interesting feature and judging from its place in the inventory, seems to have been located in south Pembrokeshire between Llawhaden and Lamphey, notable then as now for rich pastures and grain-producing areas. Of the 66 horses, 46 were mares and one stallion was kept. Little is known of the breeding of horses in medieval Wales, but there is evidence that some of the Welsh princes and marcher Lords kept valuable studs and some of the Welsh armies in pre-conquest days contained a cavalry arm.

The reference to goats on Ramsey Island (Ynys Dewi) is significant, inasmuch as it confirms the tradition, still persisting in the Hundred of Dewsland, that the former bishops once kept flocks of such animals there.

It will be noticed that the bishop owned a large number of cattle at Llanddewibrefi, 174 of all kinds, described as being "in custody" of Griffith ap Eynon, Cadwgan ap Yevan, and Lleucu daughter of Adif, whose herds are specified separately. These may have been servants of the bishop, but, on the other hand, the entry may be an example of an ancient custom in West Wales, called "dairy farm" or "dairy bargain", whereby the owner leased the cattle, the lessees paying one third (this sometimes varied) of the profits annually to the lessor by way of rent. Many references have been found to this custom, particularly in Dewsland, where it persisted to quite recent times, the present writer having spoken to people who started their farming careers through this method in the latter half of the last century. As the formula, "in custody of," does not occur elsewhere in the document under discussion, it seems to indicate a particular arrangement and I would suggest, tentatively, the possibility of some form of a "dairy bargain".

It has been possible to tabulate the livestock. My original analysis was detailed; for instance horned cattle were subdivided into bulls, cows, calves, heifers, oxen, bullocks, steers and draught animals, but owing to the limitations of space I have given below only the *totals* of each type. "Beasts of burden" and "draught animals (45 in all), are included under "Horned Cattle" in this table.

	Horned Cattle	Horses	Sheep	Pigs	Goats	Geese	Totals
Landou	16	–	160	–	–	–	176
Newton	6	–	–	–	–	–	6
Abran	54	1	230	5	–	–	290
Llanfihangel	7	–	–	–	–	–	7
Llanegwad	23	1	–	–	–	–	24
Berwick	14	–	–	–	–	–	14
Llawhaden	69	–	–	–	–	–	69
stud	–	66	–	–	–	–	66
Lamphey	52	12	–	77	–	14	155
Menevia	10	–	120	–	–	–	130
Ramsey Island	44	–	44	–	70	–	158
Pointz castle	33	–	247	–	–	–	280
Brimaston	11	–	136	–	–	–	147
Wolfscastle	13	–	210	–	–	–	223
Castlemorris	17	–	–	–	–	–	17
Trefin	31	–	254	–	–	–	285
Llanddewi (Gower)	16	1	–	–	–	–	17
Llandygwydd	28	–	24	–	–	–	52
Adpar	24	–	–	34	–	–	58
Llanddewibrefi	174	–	–	–	–	–	174
Totals	642	81	1,425	116	70	14	2,348

The prices were fairly constant throughout the diocese. The value of draught animals varied from 2s. 6d. to 6s. 8d. per head; oxen from 1s. 8d. to 6s.; bulls from 2s. to 3s.; cows from 3s. to 5s.; bullocks and heifers from 1s. 6d. to 2s. 6d.; stallions 6s.; mares from 4s. to 13s. 4d.; foals and colts from 4s. to 10s.; sheep from 4d. to 12d.; ewes from 8d. to 12d.; lambs from 2d. to 2½d.; pigs from 2d. to 1s. 6d. In some instances the total values do not agree with the price given per head, but despite these discrepancies it is possible to form a reasonable idea of the overall prices.

St. David's Cathedral

Owing to the method of making the grain entries, it has been very difficult to produce a wholly satisfactory analysis. In some places quantity is described by weight, in others by measure and by acreage. It is possible that a *cribrum* at St. Davids differed from its counterpart at Warren, a "stack" and a "stang" could vary in different places, while an acre might be a "Welsh" acre or a standard one.[8] In one case (the Prebend of Brawdy), eight stacks are recorded, but the type of grain is not indicated. Thus it is not always possible to compute precise figures. The term *cribrum* meaning a sieve *(cribro-are,* to riddle, sieve), or a dry measure, occurs commonly in medieval records and is to be compared with *gogeretta* which seems to be a Latinised form of Welsh *gograid,* measure of corn, sieveful, but the conversion of *cribrum* into the Standard measure obtaining in 1293 is hardly possible[9]. Perhaps the word *crib* was actually current for a *basket* for measuring corn, for a sieve could hardly have been so used. Accordingly, wherever the form *cribrum* appeared in the Latin text, I have rendered it as *crib* in my translation below.

Nevertheless, we can form a general idea of the main crops grown and their distribution. Oats easily come first, being grown in 22 out of the 24 places listed: then comes wheat, grown in 12 places, barley in 11 and rye in 10. Peas were grown in 8 places, beans in 5.

St. Mary's College, St. Davids

The analysis I have attempted is as follows:

Place	Oats	Wheat	Barley	Rye	Hard Corn	Beans	Peas
Landou	60½a	–	–	8q	28½	–	–
Newton	20a	–	–	–	6a	–	–
Abran	45a	–	–	–	22½	–	–
Llanfihangel	12a	–	–	–	6a	–	–
Llanegwad	34a	–	–	–	–	–	–
Berwick	24q	1½q	1a	2a	–	–	2a
(Ferwig)	26a	1a					
Llawhaden	129a	–	–	14a	–	–	–
Lamphey	85½a	40c	36a	–	–	21a	23a
		124a					
Ramsey Is.	17a	10a	3a	–	–	–	–
		1stg					
Pointz castle	84a	50a	12a	8a	–	–	8a
		8c	10c				
Brimaston	47a	–	–	2a	–	–	–
Wolfscastle	40a	–	–	1a	–	–	–
Castlemorris	40a	–	–	1½a	–	–	–
	1st						
Trefin	79a	15a	2a	5a	–	–	–
Llanddewi	24q	9½q	2a	–	–	–	–
	41a	2b					
	15a						
Llandygwydd	60q	–	–	12q	–	–	–
	60a			15a			
Adpar	60a	–	–	6a		1st	
Stackpole	9c	22c	30c	–	–	–	5c
Manorbier	8c	30c	45c	–	–	6c	–
Jameston	6c	27c	25c	–	–	6c	–
Carew	90c	70c	–	–	–	20c	
Brawdy preb.	(8 st, type of grain not specified)[10]						
Warren	8c	35c	20c	–	–	10c	–
Marloes	–	1st	–	–	–	–	–

a – *acre.* b – *bushel.* q – *quarter.* c – cribrum. st – *stack.* stg – stang.

St. Davids

In addition to the foregoing, 11 cribs of wheat malt, 13 of barley malt and 9 of oat malt were entered at Lamphey; 12 of oat malt at Ramsey, 2s.; and 3 quarters of barley malt at Llanddewi.

Oats varied in price, from 15s. 6d. to 4s. per acre, being constant at 4s. per crib; wheat varied from 2s. 6d. to 5s. per acre, constant at 3s. 6d. per crib; barley from 3s. to 5s. per acre, constant at 2s. 9d. per crib; rye from 3s. to 8s. per acre; beans at 4s. and 5s. per acre and peas at 2s. per acre.[11]

In addition there are a number of miscellaneous items such as implements of husbandry and other gear. A cart with iron-bound wheels at Landou was worth 6s. 8d., an iron harrow at Llanegwad was worth 2s. 6d., the "boat for sand" worth 40s. at the Berwick (Ferwig), was probably employed for the transport of sand by sea, to be used by farmers as a fertiliser perhaps or for the use of masons. At Trefin a boat with decayed gear, and 11 nets for herring fishing, indicates a local industry still followed by some people in that locality.

Several place-names deserve attention, and I have appended notes to them in the appropriate sections below. The Prebend of Brawdy in Dewsland, of which Warren in south Pembrokeshire formed a part in 1293, should be noted. Little is known of this prebend except that it had been appropriated to the Bishop's table prior to the episcopate of Thomas Beck[12] and this entry reveals that contributions to it came from lands in Brawdy, Bryngwyn, Grinston, Eweston, Tankardston (all in Brawdy Parish), Hayscastle and Rindaston (both in Hayscastle Parish) and Warren.

We now turn to the third record, an extent of the temporalities of the See vacant by the death of Bishop David Martin. He died on 9 March 1328 and the election of his successor, Henry de Gower, received the royal assent on 1 May 1328,[13] so that this record was compiled between those dates or shortly after the last-mentioned one. Although described as an extent of the lands of the bishopric, it is clear that in its present state it does not include all the lands and revenues by any means. Either the keeper (whose identity is unknown to me) who made the return was responsible only for those manors extended, or the record is incomplete. The following manors and their value are given: St. Davids, £13 18s. 6d.;[14] Trefin £6 4s. 8d.; Llandygwydd £1 6s. 8d.; Lamphey £11 9s. 4½d.; Llawhaden £9 0s. 11d.; Castlemorris £5 16s. 2d.; Wolfscastle £5 3s. 1d.; Landou £7 18s. 10d.; and New Moat, £6 3s. 0d.; making a total of £77 1s. 2½d.

The fourth document, of the same period, describes the lands in England held by the late Bishop Martin, their value being about £6 13s. 10d. It is the only description of the English properties I have seen for this period.

The fifth and last document is a very brief return of the value of the temporalities in 1350. On 4 September 1349 Bishop John de Thoresby was translated from St. Davids to the See of Worcester and on 11 September, Reginald de Brian was elected Bishop of St. Davids, the temporalities, as stated in this document, being delivered to him on 15 January 1349/50. They were held for the brief period 4-15 January 1349/50 by

John Gogh, clerk, and Walter de Bergh, their value for those eleven days amounting to £2 3s. 7d., a figure based on the value for one whole year, namely £104 17s. 0d.

John Gogh, a King's clerk, had been presented to the Prebend of Brawdy on 27 February 1347. He vacated the prebend before 23 November 1349, when the King ratified it to the bishop and on 20 March 1350 Gogh was appointed Archdeacon of St. Davids. He also held the prebends of Abergwili and Llanddewibrefi, and other livings in England.[15]

I wish to record my gratitude to the following gentlemen who helped me with the production of this essay, namely, Mr. R. E. Latham, M.A., of the Public Record Office, Dr. B. G. Charles, M.A., and Mr. Walter Morgan, M.A., both of The National Library of Wales.

FOOTNOTES

[1] *West Wales Hist. Recs.,* IV. 272. Carew had been bishop Since 1256.

[2] *ibid.*

[3] *Welsh Assize Roll,* ed. J. Conway Davies, p. 94.

[4] He held on various occasions the posts of Sheriff of Salop, constable of Montgomery, Steward of Carmarthen and Cardigan and frequently represented the Crown in law suits in Wales and the Marches.

[5] According to *The Black Book of St. Davids,* 1326, Cymmrodorion Record series 1902, p. 200, the buildings at the manor of Llandygwydd consisted of five houses, viz., the hall, chamber, kitchen, stable and grange.

[6] See *DNB* and *DWB.*

[7] *West Wales Hist. Recs.,* IV, 272.

[8] For a discussion of weights and measures see W. Rees, *South Wales and the Marches* 1284-1415, pp. 280-2.

[9] I thank Mr. R. E. Latham, M.A. of the Public Record Office for his kindness in allowing me to use his manuscript index of medieval terms and for many additional Welsh references to these terms, and Dr. B. G. Charles of the National Library for valuable guidance. The word *gwagar* is still used for a sieve in south-west Wales.

[10] Their total value came to £17.12.0, i.e. £2.4.0. per stack.

[11] Distribution of cattle and grain and prices should be compared with data in *The Black Book of St. Davids,* 1326; see also J. Conway Davies, "The Black Book of St. Davids" in *The National Library of Wales Journal,* vol. IV, Summer 1946, pp. 158-176.

[12] See *West Wales Hist. Recs.* V. 165-6.

[13] *West Wales Hist. Recs.,* IV. 272; *Black Book,* p. i. intro.

[14] One entry states that there is a meadow on Ramsey Island worth 5s. per acre, but does not give the acreage of the meadow. I have included the price for one acre, but the *Black Book* (pp. 14, 16) shows that the Bishop held much more land there. This total, therefore, must be taken as approximate.

[15] *West Wales Hist. Recs.,* v, pp. 161, 165-6.

SOME FACETS OF RELIGIOUS LIFE

1824. St. Elvis Church is entirely without seats or pews. Floor of earth and uneven. There is no chancel and no railings. There is a small table at the East end. There are no interments in the parish. The windows are in sad condition. Roof in very bad order and it was never pointed within, walls good, but need to be whitewashed. The church is altogether in bad order. No chalice, Flagon, Paten or linen. There is a desk which needs repair, no cushion, no pulpet no Bible. There are register books for christenings and marriage only. There is a stone bench round the wall of the church covered with matting. No bell, no churchyard. This parish claims a right to be exempt from attending the Bishops court. Ford the incumbent is in his 89th year, lived in a house close by the chapel yard. Communion 4 times a year. I am obliged to perform the service of the Chapel in my own house, because the chapel is so dilapidated and dangerous to enter. Ford Chapel receives £77 interest yearly from the Augumentation of the Kings Bounty. "Witness my trembling hand this 4th Oct. 1824." *Clerk.*

Fragment of a letter written in 1811. "In Pembrokeshire there is a religeous cult called Jumpers. They are most ignorant Enthusiasts. After their extempore sermons they jump and dance about the room in the most extravagant manner 'till they are quite exhausted'. In these paroxysms some indecent Familiarities between the Sexes are said to take place, the usual conclusion of many religious transports."

※   ※   ※

Extract from Tour in Wales 1805, p.82, calls the Jumpers "a set of fornicating sons of b......s".

※   ※   ※

"Llanfair Parish clerk is an old woman, but [she] cannot read, write or sing, who also acts as sexton".

※   ※   ※

The Vicar of Brawdy John Wilcox, 24 September 1807. "The sacrament is monthly administered and never in my time for 50 years any alms or oblations given, No alms given to the poor of the parish, as they are all poor. Congregation very irregular, sometimes over 300, sometimes nil. No. of communicants about 20."

※   ※   ※

St. Lawrence. The vicar keeps a Sunday school and 7 children attend. No Nonconformist chapels in the parish, but several near the parish of Anabaptists, Independants, Methodists, and Welsh Methodists. Many in the parish are joined with them, and others are carried away with the wind of doctrine to hear them.

※   ※   ※

Parish reports for the Bishop's Visitation sometimes reveal aspects of bygone days. *Viz.* Llanfair 1810. Incumbent Revd. Wm Edwards lives at Mount Pleasant Haverfordwest. Curate, J. Pugh of Trehowel. Services in general Welsh. We have had no male parish Clerk for fifty years, but an old woman whose name is Dorothy Jenkin, she does what she can of the office, for which there had never been a fixed salary, but it is the custom in the Parish for every Farmer to give her a little meal or money as they think proper.

※   ※   ※

"That scoundrel Bishop Barlow stripped the lead off the roof of St. Davids Palace and also of Llawhadan Castle in 1536, it is said out of the sale of [the] lead to portion his five daughters. He proposed likewise appropriating the lead of the cathederal roof. But Henry VIII was not one to suffer the monument of this proud father that Miss Anne, Miss Betty and Miss Maggie (and two sisters) might have good dowers."

※   ※   ※

8 September 1398. Guy the new Bishop "walking from the chapel commonly called Fethen church after masses heard and prayer poured forth, as is the custom with bare feet as far as his city of St. Davids where he was met by the clergy and escorted to the high altar of the Cathederal".

"Wake up in the back there"

The "Waker of Sleepers", carried a long wand in church. At one end there was a bunch of feathers or a fox's brush, at the other, a wooden knob. With the feathers he gently tickled the face of a lady dozing, but should a man be found asleep he received a colossal crack from the knobbly end. Both methods were effective, but sometimes caused unseemly mirth and chuckles amongst those of the congregation who were awake to witness the operation.

※   ※   ※

Trenewydd: In 1786 Robert Morgan lived at Trenewydd. His relation, Frances Elizabeth Morgan, was the first woman in Wales to become a doctor.   She was born in 1843 and died in Brighton in 1927.

※   ※   ※

Llanrhian: 1813. "How many inhabitants in your parish?" inquires the Bishop. This reply is given, "Having lost my horse by an unfortunate accident, and not receiving your queries in time, I have not been able to make the necessary inquiry".

※   ※   ※

Brawdy, East and West. "and no alteration hath taken place into the language within the memory. A Sunday school kept by myself at 7 am and 1 pm beginning before Divine Service. The weekly school is kept by a Master paid by the parents. 98 people. About 300 attend church, sometimes less, there are but few that do not attend the church sometimes. About 40-50 communicants at the Lords supper monthly".

※   ※   ※

Many years ago a retired schoolmaster was a lay reader in the church of Uzmaston, who had a habit, when reading the lessons, of explaining any unusual word. A very good idea, probably the results of his having been a teacher. One Sunday he read, "And he said to the harlot . . ." he stopped and said "Harlot, harlot, . . . or as we say about here "whore, whore".

※   ※   ※

In Pembrokeshire it was customary up to the close of the last century to walk bare foot to church on Good Friday, as had been done since pre-Reformation days.

※   ※   ※

Sermons could be extremely long. In the reign of Charles II one was preached for three-and-a-half hours. When the cleric concluded, he saw only one young apprentice remained in the church.

※   ※   ※

In the Puritan period hour-glasses were often placed near the pulpits – (Some churchgoers today must often regret that this has been discontinued. – *Ed.)*

※   ※   ※

With the decay of Catholicism, the people's education suffered, and widespread illiteracy resulted. Vicar Pritchard wrote: "Big books can well be read by an English tanner's daughter; In Wales, a squire's daughter cannot even read her 'pater'."

St. Davids 1810 . The parish of St. Davids is a large one. It is divided into four parts, for each of which there is an overseer of the poor appointed. Its average length I calculate to be about six miles, and its average breadth about three, exclusive of Ramsey Island. I reside in the Prebendal House, viz the Archbishop of Brecon's house at St. Davids. Services in Welsh except on last Sundays in month, when it is in English . . . it may be proper to add that two Wesleyan ministers have been lately haranguing here at private homes.

※   ※   ※

Great Sessions 3 September 1663. That there is a common conventicle or private meetings of the Quakers upon the last Thursday of every month, under pretence of Holy Worship at the house of David Richard his sonne.

※   ※   ※

Tregroes: Henry Morgan Esq., of Tregroes who was a strong supporter of the Hermon Baptist Chapel, Fishguard, always gave a sovereign in the collection which he modestly covered with a penny.

※   ※   ※

The Parson's Perks: In 1834 Trewern was let to the Revd. David George. One morning during his tenancy, after a bad storm, some damage was discovered to a chimney stack. When a mason was sent to investigate and make repairs he had to climb up the kitchen chimney but lost his way and ended up in a secret chamber above the porch which was filled with treasure – silver plate and valuables – probably hidden there at the time of the Reformation and forgotten. It is said that the parson and the workman made a pact and from time to time the parson would take a piece up to London, sell it and divide the proceeds with the mason.

※   ※   ※

This is a tale of a nonconformist Pembrokeshire grocer. Like many Nonconformists, he pretended to be very pious and godly and used to assemble his assistants and maids every evening for prayers and scriptural readings.

"Mary, hast thou closed the shop?"
"Yes Master."
"Hast thou sanded the sugar?"
"Yes Master."
"Hast thou watered the treacle?"
"Yes Master".
"Then thou canst come to prayers."

Chapter X

LITIGATION, VEXATIOUS MATTERS AND VARIOUS WRONGDOERS

THE TRAIL OF THE FUGITIVE

WHETHER fact or fiction, few tales are more absorbing than those relating to escapes and hurried journeys. A journey taken at leisure is a comfortable, unexciting affair, however illustrious the travellers, however important their purpose. The sight of a law-abiding traveller homeward-bound on a mountain road barely attracts attention any more than that of a fox padding noiselessly along a woodland drive. But place a brace of detectives on the heels of the former or a pack of hounds on the trail of the latter, and the whole picture, including our own attitude, is immediately transformed. The pace becomes breathless; ingenuity, cunning, persistence, courage, all bubble to the surface, and if the subsequent chase be long and arduous it assumes the nature of an odyssey, a saga, in which the onlooker often identifies himself with the quarry. Such hurried journeys have engaged the interest of mankind from earliest times – the flight into Egypt, the march of the Ten Thousand, Carey's ride to Edinburgh, the escapes of Bonnie Prince Charlie and Lord Nithsdale, the flight to Varennes, and nearer our own day the escape of the young Churchill from the Boers – such events never fail to fire the imagination and to enlist our sympathies. They tell of struggles against overwhelming odds, of men who played against the loaded dice, and who, whether submerged in disaster or crowned by final success, often displayed qualities of heroism which ennoble even a cause with which we might profoundly disagree.

Into this class falls the tale of James ap Griffith ap Howel of Castell Maelgwn whose tumultuous life, persecutions, and wanderings entitle him to a prominent place in the calendar of escapes and hurried journeys. James – I shall refer to him only by his first name throughout my narrative unless quoting from original source – came of an ancient Carmarthenshire family tracing its lineage to Elystan Glodrudd, eleventh century prince of the territory between Wye and Severn, one of the first Welsh states to be overrun by the encroaching English and the land-hungry Norman. Among Elystan's numerous descendants was Grono Goch of Llangathen who stood high in the royal favour, being Constable of Dryslwyn Castle in 1280-81, Forester of Glyn Cothi in 1301, and holder of lands in Caio by demise from the Earl of Cornwall locum tenens of the King in 1307. To Lewys Dwnn, Grono was a "royal captain" of Edward I, who slew Saliner the Frank, whose armorial bearings, a silver shield adorned with a red charger's head with gold snaffle, he added to his own. Henceforth the family occupied an influential position in Carmarthenshire and south Cardiganshire.

The great-grandson of the redoubtable Grono, namely Thomas ap David of Llangathen, had three sons – Rhys who settled at Abergwili, Thomas Fychan of Llether Cadfan, whose grandson became Esquire of the Body to Henry VIII, and David. This David married Marged, daughter of Iorwerth ap Rhys Chwith a prominent Cardiganshire landowner, and went to live at Gwernan in the parish

Castle Maelgwyn

of Troedyraur. From the marriage there were two sons, Griffith ap David of Cryngae in Emlyn who married Gwenllian, daughter of Griffith ap Nicholas of Dinefwr, and Howel ap David who lived at Gwernan and at Cefncoed in Llangathen. Famed for his open-handed hospitality, Howel ap David extended patronage to the bards, and Lewis Glyn Cothi who flourished in the period 1447-86, addressed two poems of praise to him and lamented his death in elegaic verse. By his wife Agnes, daughter of the Pembrokeshire knight Sir Thomas Perrot, Howel had three sons. The eldest of these, Griffith ap Howel, married as his second wife, Sage daughter of Thomas ap Griffith ap Nicholas, sister to Sir Rhys ap Thomas, K.G. Their only child, James ap Griffith ap Howel of Castell Maelgwn in the north Pembrokeshire parish of Manordeifi forms the subject of my tale.

The descent is as follows:

Grono Goch, Constable of Dryslwyn 1280-81, Forester of Glyn Cothi 1301

Griffith ap Grono Goch

David ap Griffith

Thomas ap David

David ap Thomas

Howel ap David

Griffith ap Howel married secondly, Sage, sister of Sir Rhys ap Thomas, K.G.

James ap Griffith ap Howel of Castell Maelgwn (The Fugitive) was the son of Sage and Griffith ap Howel.

In view of what occurred later, note must be taken of James's connection with the great House of Dinefwr (Dynevor), whose brightest ornament, Sir Rhys, was his uncle. James owned Castell Maelgwn (which was his chief residence), the lordship of Ysbyty in Cardiganshire, Llanddewibrefi in the lordship of the Bishop of St. Davids, and lands in Arwystli and Cyfeiliog in mid-Wales.

James married twice. By his first wife Maud, daughter of Morgan ab Evan Llewelin Gwilym Lloyd, he had an only child, Jenkin, who took the permanent surname of Powell, and lived at Penrallt in the lordship of Emlyn, either in north-east Pembrokeshire or north-west Carmarthenshire. By his second wife, Elizabeth (or Elen), daughter of Owen ap Philip Fychan, whom he married a little before 1518-19, he had two daughters, Sage and Elizabeth.

Such was the family background of the chief actor in the drama. He comes to the forefront of the stage at the time of the tragic fall of his kinsman, Rhys ap Griffith, grandson of the man who had done so much to ensure the success of the founder of the Tudor dynasty at Bosworth.

'Captaynes and Ryngleders'

Sir Rhys ap Thomas died in 1525. His son and heir, Sir Griffith, who had held an appointment in the household of Arthur, Prince of Wales, died in his father's lifetime. Accordingly, Sir Rhys was succeeded by his grandson, Rhys ap Griffith, a youth of some seventeen years, recently married to the Lady Katherine Howard, daughter of the second Duke of Norfolk. Owing to his youth, or more probably to the royal attitude, Rhys did not succeed to his grandfather's offices of Justice and Chamberlain of South Wales, which were granted to Walter Devereux, Lord Ferrers. This led to friction between Ferrers and Rhys which came to a head in 1529 when the latter, accompanied by armed retainers, forcibly resisted the new Justice's attempts to hold Sessions in the town of Carmarthen. As a result Rhys was arrested, together with about eighty of his supporters, among them the "captaynes and ryngleders" who had led and directed the riots. In November of that year Rhys appeared before the Court of Star Chamber, and both he and Ferrers were severely censured for their conduct and ordered to remain at amity and to make peace between their warring retinues.

But the matter did not end there. Ever mindful of his family's primacy in Wales, Rhys continued to consider ways and means of embarrassing Ferrers towards whom his hostility had by no means been diminished by his experiences in the Star Chamber, and he became involved in more dangerous activities, or at least activities that could be interpreted as such by a hostile observer. And so in October 1530 he was arrested on charges of high treason and thrown into the Tower. He was tried, found guilty on the flimsiest evidence, and beheaded on Tower Hill on 4 December 1531, while his enormous landed possessions worth £10,000 a year, together with personal property valued at £30,000 passed into the King's hands. It was a political trial, Rhys's real offence probably being his adherence to Catholicism and his declared opposition to Anne Boleyn whom the King had determined to marry.

James of Castell Maelgwn shared in the fall of his kinsman, with whom he had been "verie familiar together". Apparently he had not been personally involved in the disturbances at Carmarthen in 1529, but was mulcted in large sums for other misdemeanours, the nature of which are unknown. However, he had been actively associated with some of Rhys's later movements, and the extent of his complicity is suggested in the warrant sent by the King to Lord Ferrers on 7 October 1530 for the arrest of "James ap Griffyth ap Howell (who) hath not only dysobeyed sundry our lettres and commandyments, but also fortefyed himself in South Wales within the Castell of Emlyn as our rebell and dysobeysaunte Subjecte", together with "his partakers and adherents being within the said castell". He was arrested and lodged in the Tower. Among those who effected his capture was James Leche, sometime mayor of Carmarthen, who received a pension in September 1535, "in respect of his old service in the apprehension of James Griffith Aphowell, traitour and outlawe"[1] While James lay in durance, Rhys, already in custody within the same grim fortress, tried to enlist his help, for the indictment against Rhys states that he dispatched one Edward Lloyd to "Jacobo ap Gruffith ap Howell nuper domino de Castell Maelgom in Wallia, gentilman", to persuade him to enter into a conspiracy. James is alleged to have agreed to act as Rhys's agent by selling or mortgaging the lordship of Emlyn to John Hughes of London in order to raise money on his behalf.

In the event, no indictment was preferred against James, and it is clear that he turned King's evidence. The nature of his testimony is not known but it could not have contained anything likely to have lessened the penalty which the victim was called on to pay. Nevertheless, this remains a blot on James's memory and earned him the undying hatred of the House of Dinefwr. When Henry Rice, great-grandson of Rhys, later petitioned for the restoration of the royal favour, he made several severe strictures on James, "a man of mean estate, having his chiefest stay of living from the said Rice", and said that he had once been "apprehended by the said Rice for counterfeating the Great Seal, and by him sent up to the lords of the Council, and committed to the Tower", so that his heart became "full of revenge". No evidence has been found to support those grave charges, while several charges contained in the petition can be proved to be totally unfounded. It must be remembered that Henry Rice's object was to whitewash Rhys, and to show that he had been led to his doom by the treachery of associates.

James's accommodating action did not lead to his immediate release, and he finally presented a humble petition praying for a pardon for past transgressions. On 20 June 1532 the King granted a pardon to "James Griffith ap Howell of Castell Malgwn in the county of Pembroke, alias of the lordship of Spyttye in the lordship of St. John in the county of Cardigan, alias of the lordship of Emlyn in the county of Carmarthen, alias of Llanddewibrefi in the lordship of the Bishop of St. Davids, and alias of Arwystli and Cyveiliog in Powys, gentleman". For this he had to pay a fine of £526 13s. 4d., an enormous sum in those days, which suggests the degree of his misdemeanours and the extent of his wealth and standing.

Marked man

Shortly after being pardoned, James returned to Castell Maelgwn, where we find him sending various sums of money to London to pay towards the fine. Nevertheless, he was a marked man and the government kept close watch on him. His politics were less in question than his religion, for James was a firm and sincere Catholic, a supporter of Queen Catherine, and hostile to Anne Boleyn, but as opposition to Henry's plans, whether based on religion or any other consideration, was liable to be interpreted as treason, or at least disloyalty, life was apt to be difficult for a man whose convictions were stronger than his discretion. James was an outspoken man as he himself admitted on a later occasion, and after the King's divorce had been formally announced on 23 May 1533, his position became precarious, if not impossible. About Whitsuntide, Queen Catherine sent a letter to him hinting that he should flee to Ireland. The lord of Castell Maelgwn was not slow in acting on the hint and, assembling his family and some faithful retainers, slipped out quietly on one dark night, and set forth through the hills to seek refuge in the house of his friend Rhydderch ap David ap Jenkin, in south Carmarthenshire, until a vessel could be found to convey them out of the country.

From this time onwards James's movements came under the close scrutiny of the King and his ministers, who, directly and indirectly, found means to harass him at every place he tried to seek refuge. Numerous references in State Papers enable us to follow the winding wake of the hunted man and the continual shifts to which he was put in order to preserve his life and liberty. We follow him from Wales to England, Ireland, Scotland, Flanders, Austria, Germany, France, Italy, to the courts of Emperor, Kings, and Dukes, to the ante-rooms of Chancellors and Cardinals, to obscure lodging-houses and dubious waterside taverns, an outlaw moving in the shadow of attainder, relentlessly pursued by the most powerful prince of renaissance Europe.

In his native Wales, James continued to enjoy the confidence of his friends, and also of the supporters of the executed Rhys, which suggests that his conduct during the trial of that unfortunate man had not been so nefarious as Henry Rice was to allege some eighty years later. Among those who rallied to him were Thomas ap Rhydderch of Cryngae, David Meredith of Kidwelly, Walter ap John, David Vaughan of Llether Ychen and Trimsaran together with his brothers Roger, Morgan, and Thomas, who had been concerned in the tumults of 1529. It became necessary for him to embark as quickly as possible for every moment's delay meant that the government's agents were closing on him.

On a dark night, David Vaughan led the fugitive to the shore at Kidwelly where a coal-boat lay ready to sail. The party consisting of James, his wife, Sage his daughter, John ap Morgan a kinsman, Lewis a mariner, John ab Evan Tew, John Owen a gunner, David William, Henry Ellington, and "John a pen berere,"[2] went aboard, and the boat sailed on the ebb tide bound for Uphill, a village near Weston-super-Mare on the Somerset coast. There they disembarked, and James then engaged a ship of some 16 tons burthen, manned by a master and five men. Posing as a merchant, he filled her hold with a cargo of beans which he proposed to sell at a profit at the next port of call. On the night of 2 June 1533, the vessel left for the little creek of Youghal in southern Ireland, which they reached four days later. There they remained for a seven-night during which the cargo was landed and sold. From Youghal they sailed for Drogheda, and when the vessel drew near the harbour, James told the master and crew that they were not to berth but to change course and sail at once for Scotland. They refused, whereupon James drove them under hatches where he confined them until they agreed to carry out his orders. The voyage continued without further incident and on 22 June the party landed at St. Tronyan's in south-west Scotland.

Hearing that the King of Scots was on his way there, James decided to await his arrival, and took lodgings in the house of a widow. He despatched two of his servants to Wales to acquaint friends of his safe arrival in the northern kingdom. The royal party arrived on 25 June, and James managed to obtain an interview with one of the courtiers, Lord Fleming, in the cloisters of St. Tronyan's whose abbot was the latter's brother. As a result James was presented to the monarch by whom he was warmly received.

But English eyes were watching and within a week or two, Lord Dacre, the Earl of Northumberland, Sir T. Clifford, Sir G. Lawson and Sir Thomas Wharton had sent letters to London with news about the fugitive "the gentleman of Wales" as they called him. The government acted promptly and the Commissioners of the Border remonstrated with the

King for receiving rebels, especially at a time when the two nations were proposing to enter into a treaty of friendship.

The Scots King ignored the remonstrance and when he left for Edinburgh on 1 July the fugitive and his retinue formed part of his train. At the capital James lodged in the house of a servant of the King's Secretary where he stayed a month, and is also said by one of the English spies to have been "appointed to a castle South West of Edinburgh". James had long discussions with the Secretary, the Chancellor, and Treasurer, whom he tried to persuade to give him a force of 3,000 men to accompany him to Wales "that he with the Lyon of Scotland should subdue all England". However, the Scots stopped short of hostilities, he received no men, but obtained grants from the Treasury to sustain himself and his party. The friendliness of the King may be partly explained by a circumstance which Sir Thomas Wharton, a Commissioner of the Border, conveyed in a letter to Cromwell on 11 July. He wrote: "The Scots King, hearing the woman named his (i.e. James ap Griffith's) daughter to be fair and about the age of 15 years, repaired to the said castle and did speak with the said gentleman, and for the beauty of his daughter as my espeiall (spy) saith, the King repaired lately thither again." The old, old story, it would seem. She was Sage, the elder daughter, whom we shall meet again.

Treacherous Servant

Royal dalliance was not what James had bargained for. Having received a report that he was well thought of in the court of Queen Mary of Hungary, then Regent of the Netherlands, he decided to cross into Europe. He obtained a passport from the Council of Scotland to go to Flanders, a sum of 160 crowns from the Treasury, and in July 1533 licence to leave the realm. A ship was found, but on the eve of departure James quarrelled violently with some stray Welshman he met in the capital, with the result that both had to appear before the Council. After the "local difficulty" had been solved, James set forth. He reached Newbotell (Newbattle) early in August then on to Dalkeith, and by the end of the month was at Leith.

While at Leith, James addressed a personal letter to Queen Mary, which, together with some other "writings", he handed to his servant Harry Ellington, who was to convey them to the Netherlands. The emissary was ill-chosen, for immediately on arrival at Antwerp he sought out Stephen Vaughan, one of Cromwell's most active agents on the continent, handed the letter and writings to him and offered to capture and deliver his unsuspecting master to the English government. Vaughan sent an account of the encounter together with James's letter, to Cromwell, and also dispatched the treacherous scoundrel to London.

Cromwell's response to the situation reveals the subtlety of his methods. Queen Mary the Regent was sister to the Emperor Charles V, a warm partisan of his aunt, the divorced Queen Catherine of England. Anxious to discover the lengths to which the Emperor was prepared to go in her support, the Minister considered that this information might well be obtained through the unwitting services of James ap Griffith ap Howel. Accordingly, Cromwell immediately sent Ellington back to the Netherlands with orders to deliver

James's letter to the Queen, to continue to act as if he were the loyal servant of James, and he was to transmit a copy of the Queen's reply and any other relevant information to Cromwell.

The projected double-cross did not come off. Ellington returned as directed, and on 1 December came to Brussels where he delivered the letter to the Bishop of Palermo, the Queen's Chancellor. In reply the Queen thanked "James Greffythe" for his goodwill towards her imperial brother, and for his "offers", regretted she could not send a vessel for him without the Emperor's command, but said that James would be welcomed in her domains. Ellington, with the letter in his scrip, proceeded to Antwerp, and on 8 December, being a Sunday, went to attend mass in a church in that town. His piety proved his undoing. As he came out, a Scot lately arrived from his homeland and a close associate of James, touched him on the shoulder and invited Ellington to accompany him. James had entertained some suspicions of Ellington, and the Scot having made numerous enquiries about his activities, discovered he had been to London and had shown his master's letter to Cromwell. Accordingly he trailed Ellington on his return and pounced on him as we have seen above. The Scot then informed the authorities of what he had gleaned, had Ellington arrested and taken to "the Pynbanke wheron they wolde apullyd me" so the wretch complained later. As a result he broke down and made full confession of his treachery. He remained in custody for some time, but was later released and was back in England in April 1534.

While all this was going on James remained in Scotland, probably in Leith, waiting for Queen Mary to send a vessel to convey him over the North Sea. He also tried to keep in touch with his Welsh friends and dispatched his servant, David Williams, with a message for them. The unfortunate messenger was marked by English agents, arrested in the house of one Thomas Lewis, and taken to answer interrogatories prepared by Cromwell himself.

How James and his followers left Scotland is not known, but he was at Lubeck in the domains of the Duke of Holste early in May 1534, and on the 12th of that month a watchful English agent sent news of his arrival to Cromwell. As Holste was a supporter of the Protestant cause, James departed before 25 May, and an agent informed Cromwell that "the Welshman" had left the Duke "and privily went his way, some say to Ferdinand, others to the Emperor".

Chapuys, the Emperor's ambassador, met James, and in September 1534 sent a favourable account of him to his master describing him as "a man of courage and good sense, and of the principal lineage in Wales, who could put the King (Henry VIII) to terrible confusion by his partisans". Nevertheless, the Emperor was not disposed towards active measures against England, and by the end of the year James was back in Flanders. In December, the spy, Stephen Vaughan, wrote from Antwerp to tell Cromwell that "My lord of Bure entertains Jamys Griffith ap Powell and his wife and has given them a house in Bure. The knave sent his wife to the Queen of Hungary with an interpreter to show his griefs. The Queen gave her 100 guylden".

Little is known of his movements in 1535. It was reported to Cromwell that he had been "twice with the Regent in Flanders", and English secret agents at Calais made an attempt to implicate David Lloyd ap Owen of Machynlleth, described as "one of the richest men in Wales", a known sympathiser with James, but the business fell through. He continued to send messengers to England, some of them pretty determined fellows, for a note made by Cromwell in 1536 relates to "the execution of him that came from James Griffith ap Howell which killed the two men at Hounslow".

The King alarmed

Judging from the great care taken in tracing his movements and counteracting his efforts, it is clear that the government regarded James as an important figure. To embarrass him, ambassadors and agents were instructed to prejudice continental courts against him by denigrating his character and lineage, bringing the most serious charges against him, and emphasising that he was a rebel. In 1536 the government was so seriously alarmed, that the King himself took a hand in matters. In March, Henry wrote three letters in his own hand, one to a secret agent, one to the Consuls and Senate of Nuremburg, and one to the Emperor Charles V. He requested the Senate "to arrest two criminals, James Griffith ap Powell, an English subject of low birth, guilty of treason, robbery, manslaughter, and sacrilege, who is travelling with a rebel named Henry Philip through Germany on his way from Flanders to Italy". He asked the Emperor to take the two "rebels" and hand them over as prisoners to the Archdeacon of Lincoln, England's ambassador at the Imperial court.

Wherever he went James found that the English were using every influence to induce the courts to arrest and punish him, and "in that behalf do high justice and to the King's grace of England high pleasure". Consequently he was constantly on the move seeking new patrons and greater security. But he never seems to have lost his nerve, adversity and persecution hardened his resolve, and although he did not succeed in putting any formidable plan into operation against England, he certainly caused much anxiety to the Tudor monarch and his ministers.

His Welsh supporters were also harassed, and if their recent conduct was above reproach then ancient peccadilloes were revived so that bygones were not allowed to rest. For example, on 30 April 1536, Bishop Lee wrote from Brecon to Cromwell that "David Vaughan, officer of Kidwelly in Wales, is accused by your servant Jenkin Lloyd for assisting the rebellion of James ap Howell Griffith". Vaughan was the man who had helped James to escape from Kidwelly in 1533.

The Henry Phillips, or Philip ap Henry, or Philip ap Henry Fychan as he was variously called, mentioned as James's companion in 1536, was a colourful character. He had been a wild and lively youth, and had fled to the continent after robbing his own father. He then appears as a student at Louvain university where he was known for his intelligence, wit, and command of languages, but continued to be involved in all manner of scrapes. A loyal Catholic, he helped the English priest Gabriel Donne to betray Tyndale to the imperial officers at Antwerp in May 1535, and was personally known to Cardinal Pole who was appointed legate to England in 1537. His connection with James became closer as he married the latter's daughter Sage, the little lady who had attracted the King of Scots.

The marriage took place at Regnisburg, and a letter dated 24 March 1538 tells she "was great with child". Nevertheless he was hardly an ideal son-in-law and at one time, even offered to betray James to his enemies.

In April 1537 James started from Wittenberg on his way to Nuremburg, and we hear no more of his doings for the remainder of that year. We pick up the trail again in the following year, when Thomas Theobald, in a letter from Augsberg on 24 March 1538, informed King Henry, that the fugitive calling himself "Sir James Greffeth" dared not show himself openly in Augsberg, that he passed through Ulmes "but tarried not", and added that he (Theobald) had met Henry Phillips who had offered to betray his father-in-law. Anyway the ambiguous son-in-law made his peace with the King, and by September 1540 had returned to England, and the minutes of the Privy Council record "the coming over of Philip ap Henry alias Philip ap Harry alias . . . Vaughan". On 29 June of the following year "Philipp ap Harry" received a pardon.

Despite the difficulties, James remained steadfast, and on no occasion offered to appease Henry or his relentless agents. Even the Protestant reformer Melancthon, who met him, was moved to compassion and in a letter to Vitus Theodorus, dated 6 April 1537 says that James had asked to be commended to Theodorus, and that "he formerly held land of his own in which he could raise 12,000 soldiers, and was, moreover, Governor of Wales, but spoke rather freely against the Divorce. To him was particularly commended the daughter of the Queen because she had the title Princess of Wales; and therefore he grieved at the contumelies put upon her. He was afterwards put in prison from which, after a year and three months, he escaped by making a rope out of cloth. I beg you to receive and console him; his exile his long, his misfortunes long, and he seems a modest man. Here he has asked for nothing". James's palpable exaggerations are understandable, and are certainly more respectable than the vicious reports spread about him by the English King and his agents. The hunted man, finding the Low Countries and Germany too hot to hold him, travelled to Italy where he hoped to find patrons, and, in particular, to enter the service of Cardinal Pole. He arrived in the peninsula in August 1538, stayed for a time in Bologna, and then made his way to Rome.

Having failed to lay their hands on him or to persuade continental rulers to arrest him, the government decided to deliver one last blow at their elusive quarry. Early in 1539 Parliament passed an Act of Attainder against a number of the King's enemies. Among them we read the name of "James Griffith Appowel, late of London", and on 3 June, Thomas Rolffe was appointed "auditor of the lands of James Griffith". The attainted man's only son who had remained at Castell Maelgwn, found himself bereft of all sustenance, and in 1540 "Jenkyn ap Jamys ap Gryffith ap Howell having noo lands nor other lyvyng of certyntie whereby he shuld lyve upon" petitioned Cromwell "out of his most habundant charytie to accepte and admiytte your poore orator into your lordship's service". Cromwell was pleased to grant him some minor office, the nature of which is not known[3].

After this we hear little of James's wanderings, and it would seem that the government no longer regarded him as capable of raising serious opposition to Henry in the courts of

Europe. He was still in exile in 1549 when Cardinal Pole wrote from Rome recommending "especially Captain Griffeto" to the Bishop of Ceneda, Papal Nuncio in France.

Home is the Fugitive

Whatever we may think of his loyalty, his religion, or his dubious acquaintances, no one can withhold admiration for his courage and his persistence in face of great odds, and few will suppress a feeling of satisfaction to learn that James did indeed "come into his own again", and returned to his Welsh home embosomed in the fair groves above the banks of Teifi. According to Henry Rice, who hated him at a distance of over half a century "James ap Griffith (a man banished for divers reasons and excepted in all pardons) did confess beyond seas to divers of his acquaintance this damnable practice of his against Rice ap Griffith, and being sore troubled in conscience he returned home with intent to acknowledge his offence and to submit himself to my grandfather Griffith ap Rice ap Griffith. And he (my grandfather not enduring to hear of him) retired himself into Cardiganshire, where he died most miserably; there are some yet alive will affirm this from my grandfather's mouth".

What we do know from a less prejudiced source is that James did return, and not with his tail between his legs by any means. Three suits listed in Early Chancery Proceedings in 1554-55 contain some significant evidence as to his activities. In the first suit James Griffith ap Powell of Castell Maelgwn alleged that David Mortimer and his under-tenant Henry Powell, unjustly retained a messuage and 100 acres of land at "Kilvoyer" in Manordeifi parish, which he (James) claimed to have bought, about 1517, from Thomas ap Price ap Hoskyn for £30. In defence David Mortimer alleged that he had a right to the premises as they had been mortgaged to £10, by Thomas' father, Rhys ap Hoskyn, before the sale, to Richard Griffith ap Rees whose daughter, Nest verch Richard, he (Mortimer) had married, and complained of James' power, "being the Ruler of these countreys where the premyses lyeth".

In the second suit James complained that about 26 years previously he possessed goods and chattels amounting to a great value, but "upon grett consideracons hym thereunto movinge att the time departed owt of this Realme" leaving the goods, some of which came casually into the hands of Swellin ap Griffith. He had brought an action against him but he only returned a brass pan, and together with one Jenkyn ap Swellin, offered to compound to satisfy complainant. James said that Swellin had taken 2 kine (worth 4 marks), 20 pieces of pewter vessels (worth 2 shillings each) and 20 bushels of wheat of English measure (worth 20 shillings) which he withheld from him. The defence alleged that James had already given a release for these goods on payment of £4.

In the third suit "James Gryffyth ap Howell of London esquire", said that he had held the rectory or parsonage of Ystrad in Cardiganshire for a term of years, and had appointed one Jenkin David ap David to collect the tithes and oblations. However, "aboute xxxiii yeres past your said orator was dryven and compellyd to departe oute of this Realme of England unto foren partyes" where he remained until his return some twelve months ago. At the time of James's enforced departure, Jenkin had tithes and profits amounting to £19 in value which he unjustly retained.

It will be noted that the throne was occupied at the time of the suits by Queen Mary whose cause James had espoused over twenty years before. Mary came to the Throne in July 1553, and in the following year we find James back at Castell Maelgwn, again "ruler of the country" in the Manordeifi area, so it is clear that he returned shortly after the accession of the Catholic queen, that his attainder was reversed, and that he received back part, if not all, of his lands, and certainly his old home of Castell Maelgwn.

That is the last notice I have found about James ap Griffith ap Howell. Whether eventually, after the accession of Elizabeth, he withdrew to Cardiganshire to die "most miserably" as Henry Rice affirmed, or whether he passed the evening of his life at Castell Maelgwn we do not know. Perhaps we may be permitted to assume the latter, and that his ashes lie within the hallowed ground of Manordeifi church whose summoning bell he had so often heard from his woodland home.   *[Written in 1970]*

FOOTNOTES

[1] In 1533 James made certain payments "consarnynge the hurtynge of William Vaughan of Kilgarron", which doubtless refers to the time of his capture.

[2] Perhaps of Penybuarth, not far from Newcastle Emlyn.

[3] The Golden Grove MSS, states that Jenkyn was also known as John Powell, and was Marshal of the King's Hall. If this is so, he may be the John Powell described in the Court of Augmentations records for 1548-54 as "Marshall of the King's Hall" holding a Crown lease of Cenarth Mill, and who brought an action against Thomas Bruyne, and 18 other men of the lordship of Emlyn for refusing to grind their corn at Cenarth Mill, according to custom.

DUELS

Wolfsdale

In 1620 Morgan ap Owen (Bowen) of Wolfsdale was committed at Haverfordwest Sessions by Sir John Stepney, the Mayor and Thomas Cannon for making an assult and an affray on his own father and William Jones with his "sword drawn in a very outrageous manner".

❊   ❊   ❊

Sod's Lore

In 1657 Lewis Warlow was one of the jury on the inquest on the body of David Rees. "The jury say that David Rees and Philip Husband on 22nd of March were in fields at Robleston, throwing clods of earth at each other in a jesting manner. The said Philip Husband with one clod of earth did casually strike the said David Rees in the body, from which strike the said David Rees languished from the 25th day of March to the 29th March on which day he died."

❊   ❊   ❊

A clean getaway

Examination of Vaughan Phillips, gent. of London, for killing Thomas Roach, gent. of London. Taken on 6 April 1683. A duel in a certain piece of ground called the Marsh near Haverfordwest on 4 April 1683. Deceased borrowed a sword from Mr. Bowen of Niston, gent. After he killed him Phillips went over a hedge and seeing Mathew Pryume on a horse, took hold of the bridle, leapt on the horse and rode away.

All's well that ends well

From the *Cambrian* 1805: Two gentlemen of Pembroke met a few days since, in the neighbourhood of that place to decide an affair of honour. After a bloodless exchange of shots, the friendly interference of the seconds produced an amicable adjustment of the business.

❊   ❊   ❊

A poor end

On 1 April 1839 there died at Tenby William Richards Esq., Mayor of that town, having been wounded in a duel with a gentleman named Mannicks. The dispute arose from some misunderstanding, a reference to the late election of Guardian under the Poor Law.

❊   ❊   ❊

A stark tragedy

On a Saturday in September 1799, at about four in the afternoon, a duel was fought in a field near Haverfordwest, between two youths under 20 years of age. The one, an articled clerk to an attorney, and the other, a tanner's son of that place. Unfortunately the latter was mortally wounded and expired the next morning leaving his disconsolate family in a condition bordering on madness. The second and the surviving party had fled and have not been seen since. We hear that the Coroner's Court have returned a verdict of murder against the absconding party. *(Salopian Journal.)*

❊   ❊   ❊

SAYINGS IN COURT

Free speech

1684. Words spoken by Howell Phillips of Broudy parish, husbandman before me Jasper ap Rid Esq, on 10th March last. Howell Phillips said that "he cared not a turd for an Justice of the Peace of this county, and that they were villains for persekution".

❊   ❊   ❊

Honesty rewarded

1667. "We whose names are under written, do certify unto your lordship that David Esmond of Camrose, labourer is a very poor man having a wife and five small children to maintain by his labour and industry. To the utmost of our knowledge he behaves himself fair and honest with all men, neither hath he committed harm against any man to annoy him, to the utmost of our knowledge, nor defrauded any man in bargaining, buying or selling; nor any eaves dropping, nor do not sleep be day and walk by night the annoyance of his neighbours. The 18th day of June, in the 6th year of King Charles II. Signed George Owen, John Bowen etc."

❊   ❊   ❊

A dead end

1770. Jury presents that there is a highway from the village of Hendre, but on 10th July at Llangar in Whitchurch parish; a hedge or wall was built across the road by persons unknown. That John Edward, yeoman, has obstinately refused to move it.

Crime report

Extract of Jury Presentments 1681-1693. The parish of St. Davids in the Hundred of Dewsland.

"We whose hands are hereunto published, being petty constables within the parish, do hereby certify that one Rees Williams of St. Davids, did within the month of 1 August past, did abuse, beat and break the blood of William Lewis, one of the petty constables of the said parish; and as far as other misdemeaners in our Warrent mentioned, we none of us have neither seen or heard of any Saboth breakers, Tennis players, Dancing, Bowling or Jumping or Tippling on the Lord's day. Nor any other assaulters, drunkards, Swearers, nor any other misdemeaners done or committed since the last quarter Sessions to the utmost of our knowledges. Given under our hands the 5th day September 1681. The marks of Harry Warlow, William Francis and six others."

❄   ❄   ❄

"Lewis Mathias of Llanreithan, comes in for unenviable rememberance in the 1690s being described as: "A litigious and contentious person, and one that doth generally oppress his neighbours by troublesome and vexacious law suits for triffling matters and one that lends money to severall persons upon corrupt and usurious Contracts to ye ruin of some of their Majesties poor subjects."

❄   ❄   ❄

Road closed

1628. Jury present William David of Llanwnda for not "scowering his ditches, near the highe waie from Jordan to Haverfordwest, in Parish of Letterston, and also for making a dunghill in the said highway to the annoyance of travellors".

❄   ❄   ❄

Making amends

1629. Petition of William David of parish Llanwnda on behalf of himself and parishioners "That at the last Great Sessions the parish was fined five marks for not repairing the highway from Differing Godick to Haverfordwest. It is now mended and ask for a discharge of the said fine".

❄   ❄   ❄

Westfield

Home of the Davies and Bowen families. William Davies made his will in 1728. He cut his elder sons off with the proverbial shilling " . . . t o my eldest son, John who has married a woman of ill fame and character – 1/-" and "to my idle and extravagent son, William 1/-". He left the bulk of his estate to another son, Charles, and a lesser share to his next son, Thomas who went into the Church.

❄   ❄   ❄

The bums rush(ed)

1654. Maurice Richard of Letterston, yeomen, Bailiff Itinerant of the County of Pembroke, took 2 horses and 1 mare, worth 20/- each, belonging to Gilbert Griffith to safe custody till a debt be paid. However Gilbert Griffith, and Charity his wife, Phillip Gough of Brawdy, and Anne wife of David Brewett of St. Davids, did beat and abuse the bailiff and rescue the cattle. Gilbert Griffith owed William Garnons gent, 35/- and 28/8d.

Penralltheiny

In the first half of the eighteenth century Penrallt-rheiny passed to a Miss Garnons, who married William Phillips of Fagwyr Eynon, Monington. Upon the death of their eldest son, William, in 1803, he left the estate to his second son, John, to the exclusion of the next in line (again named William), who was allowed an annuity of only £25. The reason for this somewhat unusual procedure is that William, shortly after birth, had been put out to be nursed with a woman who had a baby son of her own, and it was believed that she had substituted her own child for that of Penralltheiny.

❄   ❄   ❄

Another curious Pembrokeshire tale

A young baronet lay dying in the south of the county in 1809. He intended to leave his estate to his rightful heir, a cousin who would inherit the title. His mother however, disapproved of the cousin, and determined that the estate should go to J … L … This it is said she achieved by drawing up a new will in her son's name, forging his signature in front of witnesses in her son's bedroom a few hours after his death.   To salvage the consciences of the witnesses she put a live spider in the mouth of the corpse so that they could all truthfully say 'there was life in the body when the will was witnessed'.

SMUGGLERS
AND
MATTERS MARITIME

Extracts from F.J.'s researches

1438. Papal Registers, VIII pages *675/6.*

To the Bishop of St. Davids

MANDATE at the recent petition of Richard Wogan, John William, John Wych, Eynon ap David and John Teshely, priests, and William Morrice, clerk of the diocese of St. Davids "containing, that for a long time many pirates were lying in wait round about that part of the City of St. Davids which stretches towards the sea shore and waiting for an opportunity to spoil the cathedral church, which also is near the said shore, and the inhabitants of the City, especially laymen, met together and resolved to make an armed attack upon the pirates. But seeing themselves not strong enough implored the aid of all the clerks of the said church; and that thereafter they made an assault upon the pirates, in which a number were wounded, two only being killed, some captured, and the rest put to flight; and adding that although the petitioners were present at the said assault, and helped the citizens therein; they themselves neither killed or wounded any of the pirates . . . if he found that they were not guilty otherwise than as stated, to dispense the said clerk to be promoted at all, even holy orders and monister therein, and the said priests to maintain in their orders, to dispense them on account of irregularity if any, and rehabilitate them".

The Havens and Creeks of Pembroke

1566, dated at Prendergast 8 January. Survey of all creeks, havens and landing places. One of the commissioners Arnold Butler is dead, another commissioner John Bradshame is absent and dwelling in Radnorshire, therefore we, Thos. Catharne and Jno Rastall, executors to the best of their powers.

❋   ❋   ❋

Survey: Without the haven of Milford, upon the North side; – Goultropp and Bridebay, by estimation 6 households, Nolton 6 households, Solvaich none, Portclays none, Porthmore none. Trevine 6 households, Fiscard 20 households. Purclays, Trevyne, Solvach before mentioned are under the government of the Bishop of St. Davids, yet nevertheless no ship, vessel or boat in any of these places without authority to load and unload, but only of the Queen's Officers.

❋   ❋   ❋

Names of all ships, boats and vessells with the names of owners and masters Llanstinan: Llewellyn Lloyd, owner and master of a boat of 8 tons called the *Mary Grace* and sails with four men and useth to trade to Ireland, afishing, North Wales and upp Severn.

❋   ❋   ❋

Home Office Papers 1770. May 12th

Edward Stanley to Richard Sutton, On 2nd inst. The *Palham* cutter in the service of the customs of Beaumaris, being at anchor in Porthlisci Bay, Co. Pembroke, was attacked by two large smuggling cutters and a wherry, and, the officers being obliged to quit it, was boarded by the crew of the wherry. It has since been found at St. Davids, on shore between two rocks, with several holes in the bottom, and almost rifled of everything. The Commissioners have offered a reward of £200 for the conviction of any of the offenders. Asks that H.M.'s pardon may also be promised to such as shall discover any of their accomplices.

❋   ❋   ❋

Mr. B. Rees, tide surveyor of Tenby with his boat's crew seized 47 ankers of brandy, on Saturday last at Manobier, Pembrokeshire. 13 April 1804. – *The Cambrian*

Wm. Evans of Ceire, Pembrokeshire was apprehended and taken into custody on Friday last, for assaulting and obstructing the Supervisor of Excise at Tenby, whilst in the execution of his duty. 22 February 1806. – *The Cambrian*.

❋   ❋   ❋

15 March 1806. On Monday last in a dreadful gale was wrecked on the rocks of Penberry near St. Davids, the sloop *Resolution* (her first voyage) from Aberystwyth to Milford, and it is supposed every soul perished. The bodies of men have been washed up on shore and were buried yesterday at St. Davids in coffins made out of the mast of the wreck. The highest praise is due to Col. Roch's corps of yeomanry cavalry who immediately marched from Haverfordwest to the spot to protect the property and to give every assistance.

❉   ❉   ❉

25 October 1806. Driven on shore near Pencaer rocks in the parish of Llanwnda, Pembs., Two pieces of Deal Balk. One piece 52 ft. long, the other 38 ft. long; both in circumfrence 3 ft. 10 inches or there-abouts. Whoever has lost the same may have the timber by applying to William George at Rhosywern in the said parish on paying all expenses for Salvage and advertising.

❉   ❉   ❉

Lost in a violent storm

31 January 1807. The *Providence of Swansea,* Jenkins, Master, was lost in a violent storm on Thursday 22nd inst. near Fishguard. The crew of the unfortunate vessel prevented by the fury of the tempest from landing in their boats were hauled on shore by means of ropes, in which generous work many highly respectable persons assisted, some of whom plunged up to their necks in the sea. On reaching the shore dry clothes and every requisite assistance were afforded to the distressed seamen by their benevolent preservers, whose conduct on the occasion is above all praise. Amongst those most active to lend their friendly aid were Mr. Harris of Tregwynt, Mr. Morgan of Abercastle, Mr. Thomas of Tresisillt and several others who have derived a lustre from their prompt and humane exertions that can never be effaced from the grateful recollection of those whom they happily succeeded in rescuing from a watery grave. Read this and blush ye Wreckers on Glamorgan's Eastern coast.

❉   ❉   ❉

19 December 1807. The *Fidelity* of Fishguard, David Williams, Master, laden with hemp and timber and the *Mermaid* of Newport, Thos. Lloyd, master, laden with culm, were stranded on the 8th inst. at Traethmawr, near St. Davids. Great praise is due to Messrs John and William Beynon of Pembrey, Mr. Wm. Williams of Hendre Einon and Mr. Henry Phillips of Llanferran, for their great and unwearied exertions in

To the Humane and Benevolent.

THE PETITION

OF

JOHN LEWIS,

MASTER MARINER, OF THE VILLAGE OF SAINT DOGMELLS, IN THE COUNTY OF PEMBROKE

HUMBLY SHEWETH,

THAT your Petitioner was Master and principal Owner of the Smack "ANN" of Cardigan.

That in going through "Jack Sound," near Milford Haven, on the 17th day of July last, about 4 o'clock in the Morning, the wind suddenly died away, when the Current catched the Vessel, which Current, as well as the heavy Sea, or Swell then being, drifted the said Vessel towards the Shore.

That, in spite of our united exertions in rowing and pulling, (the said Vessel being at the time in a place where Anchors were of no service at all) the said Vessel inevitably drifted on the Rocks, called the Sledges, where she became a total wreck in a few minutes.

That your Petitioner had much to do to save both his and his crew's lives, whereby he lost all his Clothes, Money, and other Documents of value.

That your Petitioner, through this melancholy misfortune, lost more than he will ever be able to recover, as the Vessel was much in debt, and not Insured; and the said Vessel being all his and his family's dependance for livelihood.

That your Petitioner having had credit for the above debt when contracted, which time is almost expired.

Your Petitioner is therefore obliged to seek the aid of the humane and benevolent Members of Society, in order to discharge the Debt he lately contracted by repairing the said Vessel.

Your Petitioner, therefore, most humbly beg the Humane and Benevolent to take his distressing case into their serious consideration, and grant him what assistance they might think proper.

And your Petitioner, as in duty bound, will ever pray.

St. Dogmells, Oct. 4th, 1849.

We know the Petitioner, and we believe the statement made in the above Petition to be correct.

HENRY J. VINCENT, Vicar of Saint Dogmells;
GEORGE BOWEN, Church Warden;
DAVID DAVIES, Agent to Lloyd's, Cardigan;
DANIEL DAVIES, Minister of the Gospel, Cardigan;
HENRY THOMAS, Collector of Customs, Cardigan;
JOHN P. WILLIAMS, Minister of the Gospel, Blaenywaun;
WILLIAM PHILLIPS, Mayor of Cardigan;
THOMAS EDWARDS, Merchant, Cardigan;
WILLIAM WILLIAMS, Preacher of the Gospel, Cardigan;
DAVID REES, Preacher, Cardigan.

Isaac Thomas, Printer, St. Mary-Street, Cardigan.

assisting to save both vessels and cargoes, not only from the danger of the seas, but from the claws of those unfeeling monsters called wreckers, too commonly met with on the sea coast.

※   ※   ※

1809. Ebenezer Griffith of Llanrhian was apprenticed to serve at sea by Indenture dated 17 Jan 1809, for three years, to Henry Richards of Trefin, mariner. Description of Ebenezer: Aged 16 years, 5' 2", dark hair, fair complexion, with a mark on his right leg. Signed by – Samuel Harris J.P. and both parties.

※   ※   ※

Scotchwell
John Lort Stokes, born 1812, achieved fame as an Admiral who served on H.M.S. *Beagle* with Charles Darwin and was badly injured by an aboriginal who speared him. Admiral Stokes not only helped Darwin chart various areas of Australia but was later to command his own ship and sailed to New Zealand. The name "Cptn Stokes" is carved on the trunk of an old tree in the grounds.

※   ※   ※

9 April 1815. On morning of 26th inst., arrived at Milford the boat customs cutter, Capt. Prosser, with the smuggling cutter *Mary* of Guernsey, Capt. Phillips; which she captured yesterday after a very long chase in Caldy roads; the *Mary* had on board about 600 ankers of brandy and gin, which have been secured in the Custom House ashore. The crew (11 persons) are secured and are to be delivered over to the Navy.

※   ※   ※

5 May 1815 . . . On 3rd May the *Fox,* a Custom's cutter (Capt. Cuff) arrived at Milford with her prize, a beautiful vessel (about 13 tons burthen) called the San Euphenica of Gweek, Wm. Hoskyn master, which she captured near Land's End for having aboard 150 ankers of brandy and geneva. Two persons found on board her have been sent on board H.M. ship *Myrtle* for naval service. The other members of the crew had been put ashore to sell the cargo a short time before she was taken by the *Fox. – The Cambrian.*

※   ※   ※

Edward George, William Griffith, John Griffith, Henry David all of St. Davids swear that they were not present at the riot and unlawful assembly at a place called Newgale bay where in a most barberous manner the goods of a vessel cast away at sea, were, by the country people ransacked and plundered to the utter ruin of the owner . . . Note adds, "not to be proceeded against."

※   ※   ※

St. Davids: Thomas Williams, master and owner of a boat called *The Peter*, of eight tons and saileth with four men, and commonly tradeth to Ireland, N. Wales and upp Severn afishing. Thomas John ap Philip, owner and master of a boat of eight tons, and sails with four men and tradeth as before.

Queen's Rememberance's Roll Memoranda

"On the Northe side of these islands is a bay called Bride Baye, but no good harborowe, and Ramsers an Ilande where shippes may ryde at nede in grete stremes and there goeth owte the forlande called Saynte Davies Heade, which is a poynte righte agenst Waterforde Haven in Ireland . . . All this coaste is a naughtie baye, full of rocks and sand called of many the Sack of Wales . . . Ffrom Saynte Davies head is one Kennying to Ffyskarde where is a good Road at Sotherlye and Westerle wynds,but no haven for a shippe, it lieth agenst Westforde in Ireland, the country bare but of cattell and is under the Lord of Kemmeys."

❊   ❊   ❊

Names of Persons deputed by the Commissioners for the keeping and surveying of all harbours, creeks and landing places in County Pembroke, and the places appointed unto their several charges as followeth. From Dale to Solvaich, George Colton, John Renbote, John Tailor. From Solvaich to Fiscard, William Jones of Brodie, William Jones of Castle Moris, Owen ap Res, Saunders Watkyns, Thomas Perkyn of Pancare, Ieuon ap William, Thomas Perkyn of St. Davids.

❊   ❊   ❊

Coastal trade

A coastal vessel called the *Priscilla,* started to trade in 1751 between Bristol and Haverfordwest. The boat carried a mixed cargo and the captain kept a book of the orders he had received, which throws light on both economic and domestic matters. The orders were by Pembrokeshire people.

    Hair hat for cousin Morse's child 2/6d. Gold scales for Henry John of Caerwen 4/-.

    Dr. Davies of H'west, 2 blackbird cages, 2 linnet wire cages, and a fountain to each wire cage 2/6d Received no money.

    Mr. Davies of the Ship and Castle, H'west. 8 lbs tea. No money.

    Mr. Roch of Butterhill, one qt. of oil turpentine. No money.

    Mr. Davies of Crabhole, one qt. of spirit of wine, 1 quart oil turpentine, and one bundle of barrell hoops.

    Cousin Williams of Felindre, a looking glass 8" x 12", 8/6d

Other items were:

    "100 of tobacco" £4 5s. 6d.

    A bridle 2/-.

    2 dozen brooms, 2/-.

    14 lbs of currents 5/9d.

    2 lbs lump sugar 1/5d.

    2 lbs of tea, 10/-.

    1 lb of coffee 1/8d.

    3 lbs of soap 10d.

    3 second-hand books 10/-.

    Aesop's Fables 10d.

LEWIS OF HENLLAN

IN October 1861, the Revd. David Griffiths, professor in Accrington College, died. He had been born at Posty, Bletherston parish. He kept school at Ffynnon for some time. His last desire was to be buried at Trefangor. His body was brought to Narberth Road (Clynderwen), and he was taken to the cemetery. When they reached it the squire of Henllan, owner of the farm refused them leave to bury, until they acknowledged his right to the land and paid for the grave. They refused, and the grave was closed. The funeral then proceeded to Narberth, and a grave was opened in Bethesda cemetery where he was interred.

A number of the leaders of the Baptists met at Narberth, including Revd. Henry Price, and the Squire was again approached. The squire refused to compromise. A note was then published that there would be a re-burial at Trefangor. This took place on 4 November 1861. They found the gate to the cemetery locked and covered with thorns. The arrangements were in the hands of William Rees, solicitor, of Haverfordwest. He appealed for permission to enter but was refused. He asked the crowd to help him and soon the gate and thorns were removed. Service was held while the grave was being re-opened. Dr. Davies of Haverfordwest, Henry Rice, Rhydwilym, D. M. Evans, Llanelli, D. Davies, Blaenconin, and a student of Accrington took part.

Thereupon the squire of Henllan brought a lawsuit at Haverfordwest, and although the evidence was strong for the Baptists, the verdict was given against them. "Gwŷr mawr y Sir a drafodai'r achos!" It cost the Baptists about £500.

About five years later, while going through some old papers, the squire of Henllan found the deed regarding Trefangor. He saw that the Baptists were the true owners and he made this known. He did more, he gave a piece of land to enlarge the old cemetery, and gave £10 towards building a wall around it.

The Revd. Henry Rice wrote a poem on the Burial Garden of Trefangor in which he says that Griffith Howells, his wife, Anne, and their son, John lay there.

[Editor's note: The squire deserves credit. He was big hearted enough to admit he was wrong. His generous restitution speaks louder than words.]

THE MATHRY TITHE SUIT

The spellings of place-names in this article are those used by Major Jones

ON the top of the highest hill in the Hundred of Dewsland, Pembrokeshire, stands
the little village of Mathry,[1] which clusters around the ancient church dedicated to
the holy martyrs.   The earliest forms of the name Martre, Martru, Marthery and Mathri
are believed to derive from this dedication. The vicarage has been from earliest times in
the patronage of the Bishop of St. Davids and the stipend of the vicar was provided by the
prebendary of the Golden Prebend, as the prebend of Mathry was called on account of its
excellence. Perhaps its two most distinguished prebendaries were Giraldus Cambrensis,
who was collated to the prebend in 1175 by his uncle, Bishop David fitzGerald, and Jeremy
Taylor, D.D., the steadfast Royalist who was chaplain to Archbishop Laud and King Charles
I. The parish itself consists of some 7,271 acres and is a typical rural area far away from
railroads and factories, and the hurry and bustle of towns. Indeed the face of the district
has altered very little during the past one thousand years, and were Giraldus to return
today on a visit to the Golden Prebend he would have little difficulty in recognising the
sights that had met his eye in the year 1175[2]. To the north and north-east he would see
the trees of Tregwynt, ancient home of Sir Fromand Brown, knight, and still the home of
his descendants, the present family of Harries. Further to the north he would observe the
Llanwnda hills where he was once a parish priest.[2] Beyond Fishguard he would see the
grey age-old hills of Precelly (Preseli), and perhaps when regarding them a frown would
gather on his comely brow. For it was from those hills that the rugged moss-trooper,
William ab Gwrwared and his retainers, descended on the Golden Prebend, plundered it,
seized the prepositus of Giraldus there and held him to ransom. But, as Giraldus wrote,
the Lord and the Blessed David within three or four days administered vengeance on the
raiders, more especially on "William Abwurwaret", who was the ring leader.[3]

In 1195 another raid came from the same quarter and its perpetrators were punished
by a more earthly power, for in that year the Pope excommunicated William, son of Martin,
Nicholas de Avenal and others, who had by force seized the prebend of Mathry.[4] Looking
eastwards our prebendary would still see the trees of Llangloffan where Henry Dedwydd
lived in 1326 and where his descendants still live in this year of grace. He would also
recognise Castle Morris and Priskilly, two important centres in medieval Dewsland. To
the south, a mile or so from Mathry, he would recognise the house of Mabws, the old
home of a branch of the royal stock of Rhys ab Tewdwr – relations of Giraldus – and
which until recently was the home of descendants of the mighty Wogans, the most
illustrious of whom was "Rebecca Mabws", a lady whose literary genius caused something
more than a local stir in the last century. To the north-west his eye would alight on Trefelyn
and the Episcopal grange of Longhouse, both of which are still the homes of the Perkins
family, whose ancestors in Giraldus' day lived at nearby Carnachenwen. Beyond these
places, above the coast which is lapped by the blue waters of St. George's Channel, the
watcher would see Trefin, while further westwards he would see the craggy crests of
Penbery and Carn Llidi which stand as sentinels near the ancient cathedral of the See to

which Giraldus had so long aspired. On the southern slope of Mathry Hill his eye would alight perhaps on Tregidreg, but this would not cause a frown or smile or sigh to escape him, for the tenants of Tregidreg in Giraldus' time were doubtless faithful sons of the Church who did not fail to render just oblations to their parish priest.

The village and parish of Mathry has changed but little, and this is true of the whole physical face of the Hundred of Dewsland. The strife between Norman lord and Welsh prince, the Wars of the Roses, the Civil War and the Industrial Revolution, all by-passed this Episcopal lordship, leaving its peaceful dwellers to their daily toil, their weekly mass and their fortnightly suit at court. The nearest approach to excitement in the village of Mathry was provided by its market and fair, both of which flourished there in the days of Edward III. The market has lapsed but the fair continues. Fenton mentions some interesting matters in connection with the little village. He states that the church was "formerly dignified by a steeple serving for a landmark to mariners, from its situation on this conspicuous eminence, an exposure that proved the means of its destruction, it being blown down by a storm".

About 20 October 1693, the district received visitors who were far more destructive than William ab Gwrwared or the great Atlantic storms, for about that date a great plague of locusts appeared in the fields around Mathry and proceeded to reduce the value of the Golden Prebend by their devastations among the crops. The affair was sufficiently important for Mr. Edward Lhuyd to communicate an account of it to the Royal Society. After this the district lapsed again to its customary peace and quiet until the middle of the eighteenth century, when the serenity of Mathry parish was rudely disturbed by the recalcitrance of one of its parishioners whose conduct caused, to the vicar at least, as much apprehension as the ancient raiders had caused to Giraldus. The main actor on the stage was a yeoman called William Roberts. The storm-centre was Tregidreg.

Tregidreg is a farm lying on the south-western slope about a mile from the village of Mathry. The earliest-known farmer there was Walter ap Traharne, who, with his co-tenants, in 1326, held a carucate of land at "Trefkedryg", paying yearly at the Pentecost, one penny, and doing services of court.[5] Apart from occasional references in the Plea Rolls, nothing is

Rough justice

known of its tenants or owners until we come to the latter half of the seventeenth century. In 1680 the farms of Tregidreg and Trewalter were owned by the Price family, one of whom, the Revd. Robert Price, was vicar of Fishguard. About 1749/50 Tregidreg was leased by Edward Price to William Roberts of Mathry parish, and in 1788 was conveyed by Price to Thomas Tucker of Haverfordwest, who by his will of 1822 devised the property to William Fortune of Leweston. In 1823, Fortune granted a lease of the farm to David Thomas of Letterston, a relative of the Rhyd-y-Harding family.

William Roberts, who took a lease of Tregidreg in 1749/50, was a member of an old farming family long settled in the parish and which had faithfully adhered to the established Church. He was happily married with four children and was a respectable member of the community. However, about 1754, he seems to have developed some conscientious scruple to the payment of the tithe. The vicar then was the Revd. James Griffith, who had been presented to the living in 1742 which he held (with Granston and St. Nicholas), until his death in 1758. As a result of his refusal to meet his tithe obligations, William Roberts found himself involved in a lawsuit and the depositions throw an interesting light on the parochial life of Mathry towards the middle of the eighteenth century. The documents are preserved among the Exchequer Depositions in H.M. Public Records Office (E. 134. Hilary. 30 Geo. II. No. 2).

By virtue of a writ out of H.M. Court of Exchequer at Westminster, a commission was directed to John Hensleigh[6], John Stokes,[7] David Hughes[8] and Gilbert James,[9] to take the depositions of witnesses, in the case of James Griffith, clerk, plaintiff, versus William Roberts, defendant. These depositions were taken on 17 January 1757 at the house of Mathew Reynolds known by the Sign of the Three Cranes, in the parish of St. Mary, Haverfordwest. Five witnesses were examined. The first was John Jenkins of St. Nicholas parish, yeoman, aged 29 years or thereabouts, collector of the tithes of Mathry parish for the plaintiff. The second was William Phillip of Mathry parish, yeoman, aged 40 years or thereabouts, who had been for six years and more, clerk and sexton of Mathry parish and church. The third was James Griffith of Granston parish, yeoman, aged 23 or thereabouts. The fourth was Martha Phillips of Haverfordwest, widow, aged 72 years or thereabouts. She was the daughter of the late Revd. Thomas Selby,[10] who was formerly curate and afterwards vicar of Mathry. She was born in Mathry parish. The last witness was David George of St. Nicholas parish, yeoman, aged 33 years or thereabouts.

The defendant was alleged to have refused to allow the plaintiff to carry off his tithes, unless the oxen employed in the business were "muffled or muzzled" to prevent their eating defendant's grass as they drew the vicar's cart over the fields of Tregidreg. The main point of the interrogatories was to inquire whether there was a custom in Mathry parish for the rector, vicar, impropriator or farmer of tithes, "to muffle or muzzle" the cattle on such occasions.

The evidence showed that William Roberts of Tregidreg was legally bound to pay tithe of all hay, pigs, cheese, geese, eggs, hemp, honey, garden stuff, Easter offerings and also to pay a customary oblation of bread. However, he had on several occasions refused to render them although requested to do so. In 1753, he had growing at Tregidreg a crop of turnips and a crop of hemp, the tithes of which were worth ninepence and two shillings respectively. In

The unwelcome oxen

the following year his sow brought a litter of pigs, the tithe whereof was due to the plaintiff. He had in his family four persons of age to communicate and to receive the Sacrament of the Lord's Supper, for each of whom, according to the custom of the parish, William Roberts ought to pay yearly at Easter to the Vicar an oblation of a loaf or cake of bread baked "on a plank."[12] All these dues William Roberts refused, in the last case stating that it was "not fit to give the Children's bread unto dogs or words to that or the like effect".

The vicar appears to have been a patient man and had hoped that defendant's attitude would presently change. His hopes were dashed, however, and in 1754 matters came to a crisis. The defendant had 4½ acres of hay in one of his fields, the tithe of which was of the quantity of a cart-load and of the value of four shillings. John Jenkins, having tithed or "separated the tythe or tenth from the other nine parts of the hay", came with the vicar's team to cart it away, accompanied by James Griffith. Thereupon William Roberts, with his son and daughter and another person appeared on the scene. He objected to plaintiff's admission to his land and stood in the gap (which was the entrance to the field) with a pitchfork in his hand which he held against plaintiff's cattle. He refused them admission unless the cattle in the vicar's cart were muzzled "to prevent their eating the defendant's grass". Roberts' son and daughter and another person were present in the nature of reinforcements to assist him in case the plaintiff's cart and collectors should have attempted by force to enter the field. It is given in the depositions that no such custom of muzzling the cattle under these circumstances was known in the parish of Mathry. The vicarial team however had to depart without entrance to that field or to three other fields beyond, to which the only access was through the gap resolutely held by defendant and his commando.

Unfortunately there are no further records of the case, and the probability is that the proceedings were dropped. Whether the conscience of William Roberts was quieted by the legal expenses and whether he became reconciled to his persistent parson and yielded his plank bread and his pigling, and used his pitchfork to fill his vicar's cart, we can only conjecture.

The few other references we have of him show him as discharging his civic duties in a normal manner. In 1765 he voted in the Parliamentary election of Pembrokeshire for Philipps of Picton, but as his son, John, voted for Owen of Orielton in the same election, it would appear that the family of Tregidreg was making sure that it supported a winner. In the 1768 election only the son recorded his vote, which he gave in favour of the Orielton interest.

William Roberts was buried at Mathry on 17 May 1782, having been twenty years a widower. The son, John Roberts, carried on the farm, and in 1787 he was the assessor of the land tax for the parish. He died, leaving by his wife, Anne, six children, one of whom was Esther, who had been baptised at Mathry on 14 June 1772. In 1796 Esther Roberts married Henry Watts of Brawdy parish, by whom she had two children – James Watts of Llanhowel, a man much given to Calvinistic Methodism, and Sophia Watts, who in 1819 married Thomas Jones of Ponthenffordd, a descendant of Jones of Brawdy and great-great-grandfather of the writer of this essay.

FOOTNOTES

[1] For an informative note on this place-name see Owen's *Pembrokeshire,* ii, 290 fo. in addition to that note it should be stated that the forms *Marther* and *Marthry* are consistently found in the Pembrokeshire Plea Roll: and the Paper of Quarter Sessions until about 1800, when the spelling *Mathry* becomes standardised.

[2] For an actual record of the church and prebend see *West Wales Historical Records, ii,* 296 v, 187.

[3] *Work,* i, 320.

[4] *De Invectionibus, cap. xx,* p. 6o.

[5] *Black Book of St. Davids,* p. 103.

[6] Of Panteague, attorney; son of Henry Hensleigh by Mary Lewis of Lan. His wife was Catherine, daughter of the Revd. Thomas Philipps, vicar of Laugharne; *ob.* 28 January 1769, aged 64.

[7] Of Haverfordwest, attorney; son of John Stokes of Roch. Will proved 1770.

[8] Of Harmeston.

[9] Of Llanunwas, near Solva, attorney; *ob.*1806, aged 90.

[10] The will of the Revd. Thomas Selby was proved at Carmarthen in 1719, and the Inventory of his goods, shows that he also farmed. His wife, Mary, was the daughter of James Jones of Llether by Lettice Warlow.

[11] George Owen of Henllys states that acres of turnips were grown in Pembrokeshire prior to 1600. During the Civil Wars, some time prior to 1646, a certain Royalist freeholder - one Owen ap Owen of Llanycefn – serving in the regiment of Col. Thomas Butler, with others, plundered the Llanycefn dwelling house and lands of the Roundhead Griffith Twyning and destroyed his lands "sowed with Turneps, Passterneps, Carrotts, Cabadges &c." *(Chanc. Proc. C.,* 464/83.)

[12] Plank bread, *bara plank – a* thin, flat cake baked on a circular iron plate called a plank. Such bread was baked on Dewsland farms within living memory. The present writer recalls devouring it with relish on his grandfather's farm some thirty-five years ago, where it was baked as a normal part of the household food. The item *plank* appears often in the inventories of Pembrokeshire testators in the sixteenth and seventeenth centuries, the same word being used in both north and south Pembrokeshire. In 1741 John Thomas of Haroldston West was committed to gaol for stealing "one large Plank Cake made of Wheat" from the house of William James of Brawdy parish. *(Pembs.Gaol Files,* P.R.O.)

"Above the Law"

CHAPTER XI

SOME VANISHED PEMBROKESHIRE SPLENDOURS

TURBULENT TIMES . . .

Thomas ap Rice of Rickeston and Scotsborough

OF THE old families of Dewsland few were more prominent in the life of the county than the successive owners of Rickeston. We know nothing of the first settler there, Rickart, except that he gave his name to the place, but it is likely that he was of Norman ancestry and perhaps arrived about the same time as Tancred came to neighbouring Tancredston early in the twelfth century. From Rickart's tun developed the form Rickeston, while its Welsh equivalent survives as Treicert.

During the 1200's, Rickeston became the property of a family surnamed Le Moigne, sometimes written Le Mayne and Le Maen. According to Lewys Dwnn's *Heraldic Visitations*, "Gwenllian le Maen sol eyr of Ffylip le Mwyn O Dre Rickart" married Robert Martin whose name certainly points to a Norman origin.

The Martins continued at Rickeston for nearly two centuries, during which they acquired further properties by intermarriage with substantial landed families like Marlos, Ramsey, Dyer of Fishguard, and Warlow of Bernard's Well in Henry's Moat.

Thomas ap Rice was the eldest son of John ap Rice and his wife Katherine Perrot. The date of his birth is not given but he was High Sheriff of the county in 1610 and a Justice of the Peace. In 1598 he married Margaret, daughter of William Mercer of Lancashire. She died in childbirth on 1 May 1610, in her thirtieth year, "after she had lived twelve years in wedlock with me and borne ten children, of whom seven survive" – so said her husband who caused these facts to be inscribed on his monument in St. Mary's Church, Tenby. He married secondly, Alice, daughter of Lewis Thomas ap John of Cwmgwili near Carmarthen, but they had no issue.

Thomas ap Rice added to his inherited property. When he suffered a Recovery of his estates in the Great Sessions in 1627, his property consisted of 40 messuages, 10 cottages, 3 grain mills, 20 gardens, 10 orchards and 6,120 acres of land in Scotsborough, Cornish Down, Tenby, Knightston, Amroth, Begelly, Brawdy, Rickeston, Hayscastle, Tancredston, Llandeloy and Whitchurch. This by no means represented the whole estate as he owned further properties in St. Davids and Castlebythe.

Among properties he leased was Ramsey Island, about 400 acres in extent, which the Bishop had granted to him in 1619 for the lives of his (lessee's) children, Lettice, John and William, at a yearly rent of £3. Winter storms often isolated the island and the currents in the sound made the crossing hazardous enough in fair weather. These were not the only difficulties, for a survey made of the island in 1660 reported, "There are two little houses thereon, and though it be strong, yet often rob'd by pyrates".

Mr. ap Rice suffered as a result of such a visitation in 1633. About the first week in Lent of that year, one Gilbert William, who had charge of Thomas ap Rice's ferry boat, noticed a ship entering the sound. A short time afterwards the captain, "a Brittaine from France" (i.e. a Breton) accompanied by two men landed on the island and took away a sheep, after which the vessel set out to sea. In May the same vessel came to ride near "St. Davids Head at Whitsond bay", and this time it appears that the crew were aided and abetted by several local people. Gilbert was standing on the shore when members of the crew called on him to come on board. He did so and recognised not only the captain, but a gaggle of men from St. Davids parish – Thomas Phillip Goch, yeoman, Hugh Badcock, David Thomas Blethin, Richard Hergest and Maximilian Pardo, "one of the quire of St. Davids". When he told them he recognised the captain as the sheep-stealer, the St. Davids men asked him to be silent in the matter. In the meantime there were more arrivals, Thomas John Richard, Hugh Davy, Ieuan Phillip and Thomas Williams of Treleddyn who brought with him a couple of hens, a cock, a capon, which he hoped to sell, and a jar of milk which he wished to trade for wine. The ship then sailed and dropped anchor close to Ramsey and the captain with 30 men landed and "ranged over the island". About midnight they came aboard carrying with them four cheeses from the dairy house and one sheep. A little after sunrise on the following morning, Gilbert William was frightened out of his wits when the island was invaded by twenty-seven of the ship's company armed with pistols, swords, half-pikes and muskets. This time they took away some sheep, a lamb and eight cheeses, all belonging to Mr. ap Rice.

A Bill of Complaint exhibited by Thomas ap Rice in the Court of Star Chamber in 1615 illustrates the unruly conditions that obtained in Pembrokeshire in the early seventeenth century. He complained that several attacks of a barbarous nature had been made on his servants who went around in fear of their lives. It transpired that in January 1612, Thomas Richard, yeoman, James Bowen and Lawrence Bowen, gentlemen, Elizabeth Bowen otherwise Thomas, Alice Bowen, spinster, all of Llandeloy parish, and John Bowen of Camrose, gentleman, had conspired "to take awaie the lives" of his servants James and Thomas Williams. They manufactured a "most dangerous, unusuall, and sharpe weopon and instrument much like unto a Paddle staffe with a head of yron and steele fastned upon the same, beinge a foote in length and havinge a helve and staffe of three yards in length", with which they often threatened to kill the said Thomas Williams, and laid in wait sundry times to kill him as he went about his master's business. But "by the providence of Allmightie God (he was) preserved from their furie and outrage". Having failed to encounter their prey, they marched towards Rickeston armed with "longe Welsh hookes, forrest bills, and glaves", while one Thomas Richard was, "weaponed with the said paddle staffe". At Rickeston they found Thomas Williams feeding his master's cattle, whereupon they immediately attacked him and the said Thomas Richard wounded him so seriously that he was lamed and maimed and nearly died.

The attackers then withdrew, and awaited further opportunity to renew their assaults on the servants and tenants of ap Rice. They assembled at Llandeloy in October 1612 and set upon Owen David, one of the Rickeston servants, whom they grievously wounded.

Their next major effort took place on the Feast of the Circumcision of Our Lord, 1 January 1613, when divine service was being conducted in Llandeloy church. Among the congregation sat William Bowen of Llandeloy, gentleman, described as, "a verie aged man and tenaunte" to Thomas ap Rice. Outside in the graveyard a very different congregation assembled, at the maintenance and instigation of one James Bowen, consisting of John Bowen, Thomas Richard, John Richard and other riotous persons, all armed with long forest bills, pikes, staves, swords, daggers, rapiers, hangers and other offensive weapons. Suddenly they burst into the church and seized the unfortunate William Bowen when kneeling at prayers, saying they had a warrant for his arrest from Thomas Lloyd the High Sheriff. Thereupon they "did pull, lugg, hale, and dragg" the poor old man, sorely bruised and wounded him on his head and body and shed his blood copiously. Not satisfied with that, "in a riotous, prophane, and wicked manner (they) overthrew the Communion Table in the said church to the ground", and furthermore "did impiously and barbarously batter and deface the ffontstone in the said church". They then proceeded to "drive and force a nagg or horse" into the church, upon which they sat their victim and took him to the dwelling house of James Bowen where he was kept a prisoner that night and the following day. He was then hustled off to the house of Thomas Bowen at Robleston, where he spent a further day, after which his captors escorted him to the county gaol at Haverfordwest where he was thrown into a cell, bail being refused.

A further outrage took place on 16 April, when David Jenkin, petty constable of Llandeloy, called at James Bowen's house to demand a rate of 4 pence, assessed by Thomas ap Rice and other justices of the peace, towards the relief of poor and maimed soldiers. Bowen refused to pay, whereupon the constable tried to distrain by seizing household stuff to the value of the rate. This raised a hornet's nest. James Bowen, his wife Elizabeth, Alice Bowen and other riotous persons, all armed, hurled themselves on the hapless constable. Alice Bowen locked him in a room, "and did with a naked knife which she held in her hands, run at and stab at the saide constable", and would have killed him had not some neighbours arrived and, "prevented the fume of the said Alice and her confederates".

This was not all. On 12 August, James and John Bowen, and Thomas Richard, "still pursuing their outrageous courses against Thomas ap Rice, esquire, his servants, and tenants", invaded a parcel of lands called Hendre Ucha in Llandeloy parish held by David Jenkin who was, "quietlie loadinge, steadinge, and carryinge away of divers stacks of furres and whinnes latelie cutt, felled, and stacked for his necessarie fuel and firebote". They fell on the tenant and wounded him sorely. At a later day, joined by Elizabeth Bowen alias Thomas, and Lawrence Bowen, all fully armed, they forcibly entered the lands of John Bowen called Lochmeyler where they found the unfortunate David Jenkin somewhat recovered from his previous encounter, busy with hay loaded on, "cartes and steades" ready to be carried to the barn at Hendre. They seized the hay and when David Jenkin and John Bowen "quietly asked him to desist" the invaders, "inraged with furie and mallice", attacked and wounded them.

The Papers of Great Sessions reveal that a great deal of trespass accompanied by violence, sometimes leading to death, often occurred partly due to intermixed lands and disputed boundaries. Thomas ap Rice himself appears to have taken a hand in these expeditions and in 1628 a true bill was returned against him for stealing two loads of peas, valued at five shillings, from the servant of Rowland Watts of Hayscastle, husbandman.

During the Civil War, Thomas ap Rice played the role of a "Shoni bob ochor". In 1642 he was for Parliament, but before the end of the following year declared his intention to exert his utmost to reduce Pembroke town and castle to His Majesty's obedience, and in September was numbered among those who subscribed £2,000 for the King.

Thomas ap Rice, "being of great years", made his will at about three o'clock in the afternoon of 27 March 1650. He died shortly afterwards and his widow proved the will at Carmarthen on 22 April following. A further probate was granted in PCC in 1656. A very fine monument to Thomas ap Rice and his first wife, Margaret (Mercer), was placed in St. Mary's church, Tenby, where both were buried. She is shown lying at full length and just above her, Thomas ap Rice kneels on a cushion before a prie-dieu. The remains of the original colours indicate that his hair, beard and moustache were dark, while his wife had fair hair and dark eyes. On a panel below the effigies, are figures of their children, four boys and three girls, all kneeling in prayer. The monument is rich in heraldry and contains the arms of ap Rice, Martin, Marlos, Bateman, Perrot, Verney, Le Valans, Roch and also those of Mercer.

Scotsborough originally stood on the verge of an inlet called The Ritec. The area has been reclaimed from the sea, but is today a swamp through which the river Ritec continues to run. After the departure of the ap Rice's, Scotsborough was never inhabited by gentry and gradually decayed so that it was largely ruinous by the early part of the nineteenth century. The west front was converted into cottages to house a number of working people, but in or about 1824 an epidemic of smallpox broke out in these tenements and the occupiers fled in panic, never to return. The building soon became a total ruin. Scotsborough had been a large strongly fortified house and the loopholes in some of the walls are probably of pre-fourteenth century origin.

The fate of Rickeston, cradle of the race, is equally gloomy. Like the family, the mansion has disappeared and not a stone remains to mark the site. A plan of the property made in 1775 for James Jones, by Thomas Lewis and surveyed by Charles Hassall, shows the house to have been a large L-shaped building set amidst lawns, surrounded by trees, with a few outbuildings near by.

A new farmhouse with extensive out-buildings was built by Samuel Griffith, who died in 1824 and I have been told that a good deal of the stones and other materials from the old mansion were used for that purpose.

Scotsborough in decline

STACKPOLE COURT AND THE LORTS

(I wish to express my gratitude to the Earl Cawdor, descendant and heir at law of the main lines of the Lorts, for his kindness in allowing me the use of his extensive family muniments, on which, unless otherwise stated, this essay is based.)

THE seventeen parishes comprised in the westernmost part of the old palatine county of Pembroke have been noted for the number of prominent landowing families that took root there. In the parish of Angle on the tip of the peninsula, we find the Hall, home of the Kynners and later of the Mirehouses, who continue to reside there, and ruined Bangeston, former home of the Dawes. The fair face of the parish of Castlemartin has been scarred by the requirements of national defensive arrangements, so that ruins and in some instance only the name, remain of former residences like Bulliber and Brownslade, Pricaston and Linney. In Rhoscrowther stood Eastington, fortified home of the Perrots and Meares families, and in Pwllcrochan, Greenhill, where Powells from north Pembrokeshire settled. In Hundleton stands Orielton, ancient home of the Wyrriots and later of the Owens, who dominated political life in Pembrokeshire for nearly three centuries, and Corston seat of the Leach family. The farmhouse of Buckspool in Bosherton, was the home of the Adamses before they moved to Paterchurch in St. Mary Pembroke, and later to Holyland on the fringe of the town of Pembroke. In St. Mary's parish stood Golden Hill, home of the Powells and Cunys and Llanion and Bush, both occupied by the well-known family of Meyrick. In Lamphey the palace of the Bishops of St. Davids gave way to the Court, seat of Mathiases who still reside there and Portclew seat of a family with nothing ecclesiastical about them apart from their surname, Bishop. Near Nash church stands a house owned by the family of Davies, and in Cosheston Paskeston home of the family of Roch. Perhaps the best-known of these residences was Stackpole,[1] medieval home of a family of that name, which became known as Stackpole Court in late Tudor times when it became the property of the Lorts, from whom it was transmitted through an heiress to a Campbell of Cawdor in Scotland, in whose descendants it remained as one of our most distinctive stately homes till its demolition in 1963.

Stackpole Court

The house of Stackpole stood in the small parish of St. Petrox, close to the border of the parish of Stackpole Elidor (Elidyr), sometimes called Cheriton. The deer park belonging to the mansion, part of its demesne and the hamlet, lay in the latter parish. South of St. Petrox is the parish of Bosherston, known throughout the Middle Ages by its earlier name of Stack-pole Bosher.[2]

The earliest known owner of

Stackpole bore the Welsh name Elidor or Elidyr. His household included an unusual servitor whose strange dealings are chronicled by Giraldus Cambrensis in 1188.   In the *Itinerary* he tells us that a phantom appeared in the house of Eliodurus de Stakepole in the form of a red-haired young man who called himself Simon. First seizing the keys from the person to whom they were entrusted, he impudently assumed the steward's office, which he managed so prudently and providently, that all things seemed to abound under his care and there was no deficiency in the house. Whatever the master or mistress secretly thought of having for their daily use or provision, he procured with wonderfully agility and without any previous directions, saying "You wished that to be done, and it shall be done for you". He was also well acquainted with their treasurers and secret hoards and sometimes upbraided them on that account; for as often as they seemed to act sparingly and avariciously, he used to say: "Why are you afraid to spend that heap of gold or silver, since your lives are of so short duration, and the money you so cautiously hoard up will never do you any service?" He gave the choicest meat and drink to the rustics and hired servants, saying that those persons should be abundantly supplied, by whose labours they were acquired. Whatever he determined should be done, whether pleasing or displeasing to his master or mistress, for, as we have said before, he knew all their secrets, he completed in his usual expeditious manner, without their consent. He never went to church or uttered one Catholic word. He did not sleep in the house but was ready at his office in the morning. He was at length observed by some of the family to hold his nightly converse near a mill and a pool of water, upon which discovery he was summoned the next morning before the master of the house and his lady and receiving his discharge, delivered up the keys which he had held for upwards of forty days. Being earnestly interrogated at his departure who he was, he answered that he was begotten upon the wife of a rustic in that parish, by a demon in the shape of her husband, naming the man, and his father-in-law, then dead, and his mother still alive, the truth of which the woman upon examination, openly avowed.

While the existence of the demon steward may be doubted, that of his master is well established. Elidor founded the church of Stackpole Elidor and his equally pious son, Robert, granted to the commandery of St. John at Slebech two messuages and two bovates of land in Stackpole and to the Cathedral of St. Davids the church of Tredduog (St. Edrins in Dewsland) for the repose of his own soul and that of Milo de Cogan. These grants were made between the years 1180 and 1190. A Philip de Stackpole is said to have taken part in the invasion of Ireland in the time of Henry II. Several references are found throughout the Middle Ages to men bearing this territorial designation, but this does not mean that they belonged to the same family, for the description "de Stackpool" was given to whoever held the land at that place. In 1290 a Papal dispensation was given to Richard de Stakepol for marrying Lucy de Rannvilla of the diocese of St. Davids to whom he was related in the fourth degree. Medieval documents show that men of this name held lands at Alleston, Marledge, Merrion, Lamphey and Llawhaden.[3]   The name survived in south Pembrokeshire for many centuries and in 1589 one George Stackpull witnessed a grant of the farm of Easter Trewent to George Lort who then held Stackpole on a lease.

The last of the family to hold the property was Richard de Stackpool living in 1349, who married Margaret, sister of Richard de Turberville of Coyty in Glamorgan, and by her had two daughters, co-heiresses, named Isabella and Joanna. Isabella married Rhys ap Gruffydd of Llangathen in Carmarthenshire and died without issue. Joanna, who had inherited Stackpole as her share, married Sir Richard de Vernon, of Harlaston in Staffordshire.

There is no indication of the extent of Stackpole or its status in medieval times. Dr. Henry Owen's description of it as a "barony" is not borne out by any evidence. It certainly acquired manorial status in the fifteenth century and is included in George Owen's lists of Pembrokeshire manors,[4] compiled about 1590/5, when the lord of the manor of Stackpole is given as "Stanley".

Through marriage with Joanna, the Vernons acquired the property and held it for over two centuries. As they owned extensive lands in England, it is doubtful whether they ever resided on their Welsh estate. Sir Richard Vernon appears as a member of a commission to enquire into the King's debtors in Pembroke in 1400, but no other references have been found to participation in Pembrokeshire concerns. He died shortly afterwards and Joanna is described as widow in 1403.

The last male of the main line, Sir George Vernon of Haddon "King of the Peak", died in 1567 leaving two daughters, Dorothy, who married Sir John Manners, second son of the second Earl of Rutland, and Margaret, who married Sir Thomas Stanley of Winwick, second son of Edward, third Earl of Derby. Stackpole formed part of Margaret's dowry.

Towards the middle of the fifteenth century some difficulty arose relating to the ownership of Stackpole, the precise nature of which is not clear, but a document dated 15 February 1465 provides us with a final result of the wrangling that had taken place. This was the award of Walter Burghull and John ap Howell of the county of Pembroke, gentlemen, in the discord and debates between William Vernon, knight, and Richard Bennayth and "all manor of lyffelodies (livelihoods) being in variance betwene them" in Wales as well as in England.

The arbitrators, who were chosen by Thomas Frebody, attorney to both disputants, awarded to Richard Bennayth the manor of "Westbromewiche" in the county of Stafford and all other manors and lands which descended by way of inheritance through Agnes, wife of John Adam grand-dame of the said Richard Bennayth, her heir. To William Vernon, knight, they awarded the manor of Stackepoll in the county of Pembroke together with all other manors, lands and tenements in Wales which Gruffydd Nycholas, Hugh Bennayth and Henry Don held jointly of the gift of Dame Jane Vernon. The award was signed and sealed at Pembroke.

Few references have been found to the tenure of the later Vernons. In 1547 Sir George Vernon of Haddon in Derbyshire, patron of the parish church of Bosherston, granted the patronage to John Hynks and Hugh Bretherton, gentlemen and in 1563 granted several leases, usually for lives, of his Pembrokeshire properties. For instance, on 25 August of that year, he gave a lease of a messuage, a piece of ground called the Underwodd and a mill called Ye North Mylne, all in the town and fields of Stackpole Elydor, to Hugh Meare and his sons William and John, all of Sampstone in St. Petrox parish, at a yearly rent of £2 14s. 4d.

Sir Thomas Stanley died in 1576 and before October 1578, the widow had married William Mather.[5] They lived at Tonge Castle, Shropshire and in 1579 granted a large number of leases for lives of their Pembrokeshire properties to various tenants. Thus, on 2 March 1579,[6] William Mather of Tonge Castle, esquire, and "Dame Margaret his wife, late the wife of Sir Thomas Stanley, knight, deceased", granted a lease of Este Sampstone in St. Petrox parish to Hugh Meare and his sons, William and Thomas, for lives of lessee at a yearly rent of 24 shillings. In all these transactions the lessors appointed George Lort and Roger Lort to be their lawful attorneys to deliver seisin to the lessees.

The most important of the leases was that granted on 3 October 1578, when William Mather and Dame Margaret, his wife, leased "their castell, Capytall messuage, mansyon howse, and manor place of Stackpole, called the Castell or manor of Stackpole or Stackepole Courte, with its appurtenances, a pasture ground and meadow called Daire Parke, two little meadows called the Yest and West Meadows, a corn mill called the manor Mylne and the stream and water course thereto belonging, with all appurtenances belonging to the said castell and capital messuage of Stackpole, and a ground, pasture, or wood, called Throstell Woode, a close or pasture and the hill close lying in Stackpole Elydor, a messuage called Lodes Meade in Stackpole Bosher otherwise Bosherstone, and all the lands now in occupation of George Lort the elder, to hold for the lives of George Lort the elder, Roger Lort and George Lort the younger, for 'a certain yearly rent'."

The Rise of the Lorts

In Tudor times families established themselves in three ways – through successful participation in trade and industry (including husbandry), practice of the law and holding offices of profit under the Crown. Normally, advancement was a gradual process, sometimes extending over two or more generations, like the Whites of Tenby, Dawes of Pembroke and Laugharnes of Haverfordwest, medieval burgesses and tradesmen who invested profits in real estate and eventually founded county families with seats at Henllan, Bangeston and St. Bride's.   Occasionally advancement came through the efforts of one unusually-gifted individual who shot upwards like an arrow from a taut bowstring, examples of which are provided by Barlow of Slebech, Stepney of Prendergast and Canon of Haverfordwest. But the overwhelming majority of the Tudor gentry of Pembrokeshire had a different origin. They were folk of long lineage with roots deep in the medieval past, whose ancestors had lived on rural free-holds, having their being in the very womb of the motherland such as the families of Adams of Paterchurch, Bowen of Llwyn-gwair, Lloyd of Cilciffeth, Warren of Trewern, Wyrriot and Owen of Orielton, Philipps of Picton,

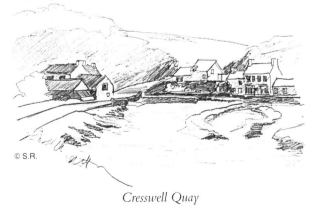

© S.R.

Cresswell Quay

Vaughan of Pontfaen, the swarming Wogans and dozens of others, little kings of rural parishes, who enjoyed the privileges bestowed by inherited acres and the security provided by kinship and connection.

Suddenly, in Elizabeth's reign, George Lort appeared, an English Melchisedech, without crusader, chieftain, princeling or heraldic trapping to buttress his ambition and to admit him to the brotherhood of the *petite noblesse de la campagne* of the Celtic west. Yet within twenty years of his arrival as steward of an absentee family he had acquired two valuable manors and a large number of farms in south Pembrokeshire, so that his possessions exceeded those of many of his longer established neighbours. Such incursion into the real estate market could not have been effected without a good deal of capital and perhaps luck. How and where did George Lort obtain the money? It is doubtful whether stewardship, or successful husbandry alone, could have been the source of the liquid assets, even if mortgages were involved, necessary to purchase in so short a space of time properties on such a scale as indicated by contemporary deeds and documents.

The earliest reference to the name, known to me, occurs in an entry stating that, "Sampson Lorte alias Lord," was a Bachelor of the Civil Law in the University of Oxford on 28 February 1519 and I have to thank Mr. Roland Thorne, M.A., of *The History of Parliament Trust*, for the production of this solitary, and significant, item. To have received a university education at that time argues that he came of a reasonably well-to-do family. He may have been Sampson Lort, a priest whose will, dated 22 December 1537, was proved by his brother, John Lort, in the following month. Testator expressed a wish to be buried in the chancel of Sheffield church and bequeathed the farm of Dronfeld and his "trotting gelding" to his servant and a "royall" to each of the children of his brothers and sisters. Thomas Lorde, vicar of Sheffield, perhaps a kinsman, witnessed the will.

But what is really significant is the Christian name and the alternative form of the surname. The unusual name Sampson occurs among the Lorts of Stackpole and the first two generations of that family consistently signed themselves as "Lort alias Lord". So it is not unlikely that the Bachelor of the Civil Law of 1519 belonged to the same stock.

According to general belief the Lorts came from Staffordshire, but enquiries at the record office of that county have revealed no trace whatsoever of such a family. Neither do the *Visitation* pedigrees of Staffordshire, Derbyshire, Shropshire, Cheshire, Lancashire, Leicestershire, Worcestershire, Gloucestershire and Herefordshire contain any references, and my friend Sir Anthony Wagner, Garter King of Arms, has no information relating to the family's origin.[7] That they were not an aristocratic or gentry family is clear; that they were extremely able men, architects of their own fortune is equally clear. Even the spelling of their name had not achieved finality at the beginning of the seventeenth century and George Lort and his sons are consistently described in contemporary legal documents as "Lort alias Lord". Indeed it was in such manner that members of the family subscribed themselves and not until the end of the reign of the first Stuart monarch did the name assume the final form of Lort.

On 17 November 1591, the deputy-herald, Lewys Dwnn, called at Stackpole and recorded George Lort's short pedigree. It started with one William Lord followed by his son Henry, who married Jonet, daughter of John Bagot of Blithfield, Staffordshire. Henry was followed by his son Thomas Lord, who married Elizabeth, daughter of William Brereton, a member of an ancient Cheshire family. But the pedigree rolls of those two illustrious houses reveal no trace of a Lort intermarriage. Thomas's son, described in the pedigree as "John Lort alias Lortt" of Knowlden in Staffordshire, married twice; firstly to Elizabeth, daughter of John Robinson, and secondly a daughter of one Robert Shenton.

By the first wife, John Lord of Knowlden had eight sons and one daughter, namely: Henry Lort, dead in 1591; Nicholas Lort of Stafford who married Anne Kowap and had four children; Humphrey Lort, who married Joan, and had three children; Roger Lort and John Lort, both dead in 1591, Robert Lort who married Alice Head and had five children; Anthony Lort dead in 1591; Elizabeth Lort who married William Acton; and George Lort ancestor of the Pembrokeshire line.

Owing to the arrangement of the pedigree it has not been possible to establish the seniority of George Lort, but I think he may have been a younger son. He was the first of the family to settle at Stackpole, describing himself as "High Steward, under William Mather, to Lady Margaret Stanley, in Stackpool", and signing his name as, "George Lorde al's Lorte". It would appear that he was appointed steward about the year 1578 when he obtained the lease of Stackpole Court as recited above. The deputy herald recorded the family arms as *argent a saltire vert and on a chief vert a saltire argent*, with *a gauntlet argent holding a saltire vert*, as crest, which, as we shall see, were later changed.

The earliest reference that I have found to him in Pembrokeshire, is in a deed dated 21 October 1575, whereby William Herbert and Mary Herbert, widow, leased six messuages, a mill and 182 acres in Stackpoole, to George Lort, gentleman, and his sons, Roger and George, for their lives. On 29 September 1577 the Lorts assigned the lease to Hugh Owen, Wiriot Owen and Sibilla Owen of Orielton. The lease was still operative in 1594, for on 8 September of that year, George Lort, the younger, assigned his life interest to his brother Roger who undertook to assume the assignor's responsibilities under the terms of the lease, and to acquit, discharge, and save harmless the assignor against any demands of William Mather, Dame Margaret his wife and the heirs and assigns of Sir Thomas Stanley, knight, deceased.

George Lort, sometimes described as "the elder", to distinguish him from one of his sons who bore the same name, prospered and acquired valuable leaseholds and freeholds from the absentee family of Herbert who owned extensive properties in south Pembrokeshire. William Herbert created Earl of Pembroke in 1551, owned lands in the county which passed to his second son, Sir Edward Herbert of Hendon, Middlesex and of Swansea. In 1587 Sir Edward bought Red Castle and the district of Powisland from Edward Grey. This castle was also described as Poole Castle and later as Powis Castle, the name it still bears. Sir Edward increased his interest in south Pembrokeshire by acquiring some of the properties of Sir John Perrot of Carew after the attainder of that worthy. He married Mary Stanley, daughter and heiress of Thomas Stanley of Standon, Herefordshire, sometime Master of the Mint and died on 23 March 1595 and was buried in Welshpool church. His son, William Herbert, who succeeded to the estates, was created a Knight of the Bath in 1603 and advanced to the dignity of Baron Powis of Powis in 1629. He married, before 1597, Eleanor, third daughter of Henry Percy, eighth Earl of Northumberland, by whom he had issue. Lord Powis died in 1656 and was buried at Hendon.

During the years 1595/8, William Herbert, described in contemporary documents as, "lord and owner of the manor of lordship of Castell Martyn", granted several leases of his properties in Pembrokeshire, such as "the Crooked Splott and Burford Haine to Thomas Beede, yeoman, a moiety of Lowlensland to John Poyer, husbandman and parcels of lands at Broomesford, South-towne, Stonebridge, 200 acres of burrows and 13 acres of corse to Francis Meyrick of Monkton, esquire, who afterwards assigned the lease to Rees Phillip Scarffe of Lamphey, gentleman".

George Lort also had his eye on Herbert properties, particularly those in the vicinity of Stackpole Court and on 13 November 1589, Sir William Herbert, then of Swansea, Lady Mary his wife, and Mary Herbert of Cardiff, widow, conveyed to him, absolutely, Ester Trewent (described in the Final Concord as a messuage and 260 acres) in the parish of Stackpole Elidor.

More important by far was Lort's purchase of the manor of Castlemartin. On 14 March 1598, William Herbert of Poole Castle alias Red Castle, esquire, son and heir of Sir Edward Herbert, deceased, granted to George Lort alias Lord, of Stackpole and his son and heir apparent, Roger, gentlemen, for the sum of £2,800, the manor or lordship of Castell-martyne alias Castlemartynn, with all its rights, courts leet, wreck of the sea, etc., etc., and premises attached to it, lying in the parishes of Castelmartyne, St. Twynnells, and Monkton, to hold in as ample manner as the grantor, his father Sir Edward and his grandfather William, Earl of Pembroke, had held and enjoyed them together with all deeds, writings, charters, court rolls, rent rolls, surveys, to be delivered to grantees (except certain lands once belonging to Nicholas Dawes, deceased, reputed to be copyholds of the said manor, now let at £8 per annum and in variance between grantor and Henry Dawes and Henry White). He covenanted to levy a fine, so that a perfect common recovery could be effected of the manor in the next court of Great Sessions, by the description of the manor of Castelmartin with its appurtenances, 140 messuages, 20 tofts, 2 dove-houses, 140 gardens, 7,450 acres, and an annual rent of £10. Herbert covenanted further that he, his wife Eleanor and his widowed mother Mary, would surrender all rights in the said properties, and also agreed to convey lands in Glamorganshire to the grantees. This grant was to include lands already in lease to tenants, namely the Mill Acre, New Medow and Tyr Bolke in the East Hundred of Castlemartin, Fryers Parke, Court Park, Middleton, Borrow, the Gryppe, the Escheat Lands, Plasseth, Kings Land, Long Shipping, Brownslade, East and West Gupton, all in Castlemartin parish and Goldborough in Monkton parish. George Owen of Henllys,[8] John Meyrick, Clerk of the Peace, Thomas Herbert and Richard Bowen, were witnesses to the document.

On the same day William Herbert the grantor, William Stanley of Hooton, Cheshire, esquire, eldest son of Sir William Stanley (who was eldest son of Sir Rowland Stanley of Hooton) and Thomas Jucks of Buttington, Montgomeryshire, entered into a bond in £1,000 to assure the manor of Castell Martyne to George Lort and his son Roger, and that grantor's wife, Lady Ellenor, would acknowledge a Fine of the property. On the following day, 15 March, George and Roger Lort alias Lord(e), gentlemen, George Owen of Henllys and Thomas Bowen of Stockton (co. Hereford), esquires, gave a bond in £3,000 to William Herbert for the payment of £1,600 to be made to him on 5 April following.

When the Final Concord was made in the Great Sessions for Pembrokeshire on 11 September 1598, the advowson of the vicarage of Castlemartin, four mills and a further 1,260 acres were added, bringing the total acreage to 8,800.

The alienation of the manor had been made without a licence having been obtained first from the Crown. The omission was brought to the attention of the authorities, who took a lenient view and on 6 June 1598, the Lorts receive a pardon for their part in the transaction of 14 March, the force of which was to remain unchanged and undiminished.

George Lort must have flourished exceedingly to have been able to acquire this valuable manor. What is more important, is that the purchase increased his social position considerably, the possession of a manor being a status symbol as well as a financial advantage.

Wealth he certainly had, for in October 1598, he set about acquiring further properties in south Pembrokeshire, again from an absentee family. The negotiations took some time, but on 7 December 1599, Sir Griffith Markham of Bestwood Park, Nottinghamshire and Dame Anne, his wife, Thomas Markham of Kirby Bellars, Leicestershire, esquire, and Mary, his wife, granted to George Lort(e) alias Lorde of Stackpole and Roger, his son and heir apparent, gentlemen, in consideration of £2,200 a moiety of the following properties: "the manor and lordship of Nangle alias Angle commonly called the Lordship of the Hall; the manor and lordship of Geffreston; 12 messuages, 2 cottages, and all coal mines in the said lordship of Geffreston in the parishes of Martheltwy and Begelly; a messuage and lands in the parishes of St. Mary's and St. Michael's, Pembroke; a parcel of Westdraughton and Fletcher's Park, the Fleete (in tenure of Francis Meyrick, esquire), 7 messuages, half a close and a mill place in Mouncton parish; 8 messuages and 6 oxlands called Yolton's Lands in Rhoscrowther parish and their sedge plots, burrows, and sheep 'leaznes'; an oxland called Colverhill in St. Petrox parish; a messuage and an oxland in Stackpoll Ellidor parish; 5 messuages in the parishes of Llanstadwell, Johnston and Talbenny, called Wilkinsmoor, Popehill and South-hill; a messuage in Rosemarket parish in tenure of William Walter, gent., a messuage inGreenhill and a third part of 4 messuages in Scurlockston in Pulcrochan parish; and 2 oxlands at Brotherhill in Cosseston parish". Among the witnesses were Henry Adams, John Meyrick, Clerk of the Peace, and John Leache.

Later, the grantors were joined by Francis Smithe of Ashby Solinell, Leicestershire, esquire, and Elizabeth, his wife, because the said Elizabeth's jointure was included in the properties under a conveyance from Sir Thomas Griffin, deceased, and his son, Rees Griffin. On 31 December 1598 all the grantors gave a bond in £4,000 to the Lorts and covenanted to levy a Fine and suffer a Recovery of the properties which were then to become the absolute freehold of the purchasers. On 1 February 1599 the Smithes conveyed their interest to the Lorts and on 25 March following the Final Concord was made, the property being described as a moiety of the manors of Jeffreston and Nangle alias Angle,

280 messuages, 30 cottages, 20 tofts, 3 mills, 4 dovehouses, 100 gardens, 80 orchards and 16,040 acres of land in the manors and parishes described in the deed of 7 December and the bond of 31 December 1598.

The only reference to any transactions outside Wales is contained in a deed of 22 April 1591, when Lort agreed to assign his interest in a lease of the capital messuage and farm in Finderne and Potlocke to Edward Turvey of Churleston, Leicestershire, esquire, and John Bradshawe of Packington in the same county, gentlemen.

George Lort, architect of his own fortune, did not live long to enjoy his manorial possessions. He died late in 1600 or early in 1601. He had been married twice. Firstly, before 1558, to Margery, daughter of John Eddow of Warwickshire by his wife, Elizabeth Goodman of Chester, by whom he had three sons; and, secondly, to Anne, daughter of Richard Knight, widow of Hugh Burrows of Dindon, Warwickshire, with her seven children, to which she added one son by George Lort.

The widow, Anne, made her will in 1607. She desired to be buried in St. Petrox church and bequeathed £5 each to Henry Lort and his wife; £10 each to John Lort, George Lort junior and Elizabeth Lort, children of "my son in law" (*recte* stepson); £20 to the children of her son, Sampson Lort of Bristol; and to her daughters Eies Borrowes wife of . . . Syddon of Leicester, Sarah Borrowes wife of John Deverox (Deverau) of Nangle, (Angle), and her cousin Robert Edoe, £20, £8, and £1 respectively; and she nominated her "son in law," Roger Lort, executor.

George Lort's children were as follows:

By Margery Eddow:

1. Roger Lort, son and heir. See later.
2. Thomas Lort, born about 1559 and matriculated at Gloucester Hall, Oxford, on 3 August 1578, aged19, graduated B.A. on 14 February 1581/2 and proceeded M.A. on 3 June 1584. He remained in the University probably as a teaching Fellow, and it was there he died unmarried and intestate in 1596. On 24 November of that year, administration of the goods of Thomas Lort alias Lord, was granted by Thomas Ravis, Professor of Sacred Theology in the University of Oxford, vicar, to deceased's father.
3. George Lort, the younger, lived at Linney, Castlemartin. On 20 October 1610, John Philipps of Picton Castle, esquire, assigned several messuages and lands in Lyney alias Linney (which were held by Rees Rotherche of Laugharne, esquire, the said John Philipps and Richard Phillipps of Carmarthenshire, under a lease for the life from Lady Dorothy, Countess of Northumberland[9] and for 21 years after her death), to be held for the same term. On 4 July 1622, Henry Dawes of Bangeston gave a lease in consideration of £40, to George Lort of Linney, gentleman, of a messuage called Knapped Hall in Castlemartin parish, for 21 years, at a yearly rent of 40 shillings, a couple of capons at Christmas, 12 pence in lieu of a day's leading of furze and the herriot of best beast. He married Anne, daughter of Nicholas Dawes of Bangeston, but had no issue.

By Anne Knight (nee Burrows):

4. Sampson Lort, who was apprenticed for seven years on 20 July 1597 to John Lort of the city of Bristol, draper. His brother, Roger gave a bond in £100 on 9 October 1599, to indemnify the draper should the apprentice take away any of his master's goods and wares. He married firstly, Anne, [10] daughter of Mathew Hareland or Haviland of Bristol[11] merchant, by whom he had Mathew Lort, living in 1609; and secondly, a Miss Nash. Eventually, Sampson returned to Pembrokeshire and lived in Tenby. He died in Ireland and administration of his goods was granted in PCC on 27 April 1631 to Robert Eddowe, described as "next of kin".[12]

Roger Lort of Stackpole Court

Apart from the fact that he joined with his father in buying the manors of Castlemartin, Jeffreston and Angle, little is known of Roger Lort before he succeeded to the property. His father died before November 1601, for on the 10th of that month, Roger Lort alias Lord, of Stackpool, gentleman, sold his moiety of five messuages called Wilkins Moor, Foxhill and South Hill in the parishes of Llanstadwell, Johnston and Talbenny, and a moiety of a messuage in Roosemarkett (occupied by William Walter, gentleman), to Hugh Butler of Johnston, esquire, and the deed recites that the properties had been conveyed by Sir Griffith and Dame Anne Markham and Thomas and Mary Markham, on 7 December 1598 to George Lort "since deceased", and that Roger had inherited his late father's interest in the properties. He made further alienation in 1605 and on 11 January of that year, conveyed to John White of Tenby, his moiety of two oxlands in Brotherhill in Cosheston parish, which the Markhams had also conveyed to George Lort and his son, Roger.   On 18 October, Roger and Abra, his wife, sold their "moiety of the manor or lordship of Nangle alias Angle and a moiety of the capital messuage, mansion house and manor-place of Nangle commonly called the Courte House or Hall of Nangle, and all franchises of the manor, together with a moiety of 8 messuages in Nangle parish", to William Kinner and John Deverox (au), mariners, of Angle, for £361 18s. 6d. On 14 May 1611 he granted a messuage called Kneghe (later Kneeth, now Neath), and 2 messuages in Farringenet in Rhoscrowther parish, to Henry White of Henllan, esquire.

The assigning of leases and mortgages was a favourite and profitable business and from them we are able to learn something of the devolution of properties. Thus, on 12 February 1596, William Herbert of Poole Castle, gave a lease to Francis Meyrick of Mouncton, esquire, of 12 acres of land at Bromesford, Southtown and Stonebridge, and a further 213 acres of "burrows and corse and hayne" in Castlemartin parish, for 21 years at a rent of £4 16s. 3d. On 24 February 1597, Meyrick assigned the lease to Rees Phillip Scarfe of Lamphey, and on 6 August 1600, Scarfe assigned it to Roger Lort alias Lord, of Stackpole, for a yearly rent of 100 bushels of barley and 200 bushels of oats. The payment of rent in kind, as distinct from duties, occurs often as a safeguard against inflation.

Another assignment to come the way of the Lorts was that which started its course on 5 January 1602, when the Crown gave a lease for 21 years at a rent of £3 12s. 0d. to Peter Morgan of London, of four tenements in Nangle (now Angle) (one being called Court House), a tenement in Pwllcrochan and another in Rhoscrowther, all of which formed part of the moiety of the manor of Nangle purchased from Sir Thomas Jones by Sir John Perrot, later attainted. Less than two months after he had received it, Morgan assigned the lease to John Canon of the Middle Temple and Richard Gwin of New Windsor, Berkshire. On 1 June 1604, Canon and Gwin assigned it to Roger Lort, who, later in that year, assigned it to William Kinner and John Deverox of Nangle for £40 18s. 6d. Doubtless each assignor made a profit on the transaction.

The earlier deed of sale of the castle and manor of Castlemartin and the advowson of the church of Castlemartin, was confirmed by Sir William Herbert and Elenor his wife, to Roger Lort alias Lord, esquire. The confirmation is undated, but must have been made after 23 July 1603 when Herbert was knighted. It also describes the property as the castle, manor, and advowson as well as 150 messuages, 20 tofts, 4 mills, 2 dovehouses, 150 gardens and 8,080 acres in Castlemartin, St. Twynells, Flimston, and Monkton, which differs, but not significantly with the figures contained in the grant of 1598. I have frequently discovered such discrepancies, especially in Final Concords and Fines and I assume that absolute accuracy was not necessary in such transactions.

When did the Lorts acquire the freehold of Stackpole? Several references occur to the "purchase deed" of the manor of Stackpole, but it has not been discovered among the muniments. Fortunately an entry in the Plea Rolls of the Great Sessions provides the information we need. It states that Edward Stanley, in consideration of £2,000 paid by Roger Lort and his son Henry, granted to them by deed dated 4 December 1611, "the manor of Stackpole Elider and Stackpole Bosher" to be held in perpetuity.

The Crown continued to maintain interest in the manor of Castlemartin and on 10 December 1608, the King issued Letters Patent by way of grant and confirmation in perpetuity, upon "the commission of defects, of the manor of Castelmarten in the West and East Hundreds of Castelmarten, formerly held by Jasper, Duke of Bedford, together with the patronage of the vicarage of Castelmartin, with all appurtenances, etc. to our beloved subject Roger Lorte alias Lord of Stackpole in St. Petrox parish", in consideration of a payment of £233 3s. 10d. The very fine wax impression of the Great Seal affixed to this instrument has been preserved intact. In effect this was a pardon for "defects", which may have been neglect to obtain licence for the alienation or some other formal requirement due to the King as the superior lord of the fee. Another example of carelessness, (perhaps he had hoped to get away with it), occurred when he made a grant on 20 August 1608, of "a messuage in the vill of Cloyne, another in Froynes Lake, a moiety of Froynes Mill (water corn), another in the vill of Castlemartin, another in Le Slade, and another in

Cocksey, all in the lordship of Castlemartin" (once held by Sir William Herbert of Red Castle, Montgomery, which came to him from his father, Sir Edward Herbert, who had received them from Sir John Perrot). Roger had neglected to obtain licence for the transaction and underestimated King James's devotion to the acquisition of money, with the result that he had to pay up and on 21 March 1612, the Monarch was graciously pleased to issue a Royal Pardon to his beloved but erring subject.

Throughout his life he was described as "Lort alias Lord", and signed his name in that manner. To avoid tedious repetition, I shall thenceforth refer to him as Lort, which was the form used by his son and descendants. Although a coat-of-arms had been recorded for the family in 1591, Roger continued to use a personal seal bearing the initials "R.L."

The Lorts already owned Pricaston, later to be held by younger sons of the family. On 13 November 1612 Roger granted a lease to his third son, George, of the capital messuage called Prickardston of 120 acres, 11 acres at Slade nearby, a 40 acre messuage called 'Lough Meyler' and a 40 acre messuage called Uphill both in the town of 'Prickardston', to be held for 500 years from the grantor's decease, paying to the lord of the manor of Castlemartin the sum of £4 10s. 0d. yearly, rendering a couple of capons at Christmas, doing suit of court, suit of mill at King's Mill, rendering the best beast as a heriot and keeping the premises in repair. The properties were to remain in possession of grantee and his heirs male and in default of such heirs, to revert to the lord of the manor and his heirs male.

Among the last leases he granted, one is of special interest since it involves features of a custom known in Pembrokeshire as a "dairy bargain", which continued as late as the nineteenth century. On 12 November 1612 Roger Lort, esquire, granted to John Filbedge of Castlemartin, husbandman, a lease, "for 21 years of Brownslade (82 acres), 100 lambs with their issues and profits and the pasture of 120 sheep in the burrows of the lordship of Castlemartin, paying yearly, for the first three years, 40 bushels of wheat and 40 bushels of barley, good, pure, clean, well-winnowed and marketable, to be measured by lessor's old bushel (containing eighteen and a half gallons), and to be delivered between the feast of All Saints and 1 March yearly at a place near and upon the river of Milford between the Nangle and the town of Pembroke, upon forty days' warning; and further, yielding yearly an additional 40 bushels of wheat and 40 bushels of barley, a couple of capons at Christmas, and doing suit of mill at Kings Mylne and Froynes Mylne, and rendering the best beast as a heriot or 20 shillings in lieu as the lessor should choose".

Some time before 1590, Roger Lort married Abra, daughter of Hugh Burrows of Findon, by Anne Knight. As Anne, the mother, afterwards became the second wife of George Lort, it means that Roger married his stepmother's daughter. In some of the genealogies she is called Abertha and Abraha, but in legal documents the name is spelt as Abra.

Apart from the fact that he was one of the county treasurers for Poor and Maimed Soldiers in 1605 and served as High Sheriff of Pembrokeshire in 1607, little is known of Roger's public life. He died on 17 May 1613. The will of Roger Lort alias Lorde of St. Pterox, was made on 13 May 1613. He bequeathed as follows: "To his uncle, Robert Eddowe, two messuages in Stackpole Bosher; to his wife Abra, the profits of Rowston, a small tenement there called St. John's Houlde Rowlton, and Kythill in Stackpool parish, for life; to his son George, Trebrwen, Corston, Kitell, messuages specified in a deed dated 30 November 1612, testator's interest in the moiety of a tenement in Rosecrowther parish and testator's manor or lordship of Castlemartin; to his son, John, Drydowne, in Castlemartin parish and six other messuages, he to pay annuities of £100 and £20 to testator's wife and son George, respectively; to his daughter, Anne, £500 when 16 years of age; to his brothers, Sampson Lort of Bristol and George Lort, £100 and £10 respectively; to his son, Henry, all the lands in the parishes of Stackpool Elider, Stackpool Bosher, St. Petrox and Castlemartin", and Roger appointed his son, Henry, executor and residuary legatee; he appointed his wife to be tutrix of his said children, Anne and George, Henry Griffith, clerk and Walter Philpin of Tenby to be their overseers.

The will was proved at Carmarthen on 7 June 1613. The Inquisition Post Mortem was taken on 11 January following.[13] By Abra, who survived him, he had seven children:

1. Henry Lort, said to be 23 years of age in 1614. See later:
2. John Lort who matriculated at Jesus College, Oxford, on 20 November 1607, aged 17. He was a student of the Middle Temple in 1610 and died without issue, probably when a young man:
3. George Lort, to whom his father granted Pricaston in 1612. On 20 November in the same year his father also granted him a lease of Lowlyns Slade and 48 acres belonging, and 60 acres in Myddelton and Escheat Lands (all in the tenure of John Poyer), for lessor's life at a rent of £4 3s. 0d. On 20 March 1613 his father granted Corston and Trebrowen and a moiety of Kytwill alias Kyten well, (now Kitewell), in Rhoscrowther parish, to Walter Philipin of Tenby and the Revd. Henry Griffith of St. Petrox, on trust to the use of grantor's third son, George and his heirs male; and on 30 November of the same year, Abra Lort alias Lorde, widow, tutrix and guardian of her son, George, a minor, gave a lease on her son's behalf, to Philip Leache of St. Twynnels, yeoman, of a messuage of 26 acres in the town and fields of Carew in St. Twynnels parish for 21 years, at a rent of 36s. 3d, rendering a couple of capons at Christmas and providing a horse and cart to carry corn, timber, salt, slates, beer, wine "or any other portable thing", for lessor, and the best beast for a heriot. George Lort remained a bachelor and after his death, the property reverted to his elder brother, Henry:
4. Susan and
5. Jane Lort, both dead in 1597 :
6. Elizabeth Lort, who married Griffith White, eldest son and heir of Henry White of Henllan by Jane Fletcher, his wife. By the prenuptial settlement, dated 15 April 1611, Henry and Jane White granted to Roger Lort of Stackpole and Henry Dawes of Bangeston, "the Henllan estate lying in the parishes of Rhoscrowther, Pwllcrochan, St. Michael's, Cosheston, Begelly, Mouncton, Loveston, Castlemartin, Tenby town and Spittal, to be settled to the uses of Griffith and Elizabeth and their heirs male, and in default to their heirs female". The marriage took place and they had thirteen children. Griffith White's will was proved in 1664; his wife died on 2 February 1668 and her will was proved on 3 May following.

7. Anne Lort, a minor in 1613, married Hugh Philipps of Jestynton, Rhoscrowther parish, second son of Sir John Philipps, Baronet, of Picton Castle. They lived afterwards at Minwear, finally at Martletwy. Hugh died in 1652 and his will was proved at Carmarthen on 20 April 1652. Anne died after 2 September in the same year, her will being proved on 6 March 1653. They had two sons and three daughters.

Henry Lort of Stackpole Court

Henry Lort succeeded in 1613. Like his forebears he concentrated his energies on administering the Stackpole estate and his only participation in public life was to serve the office of High Sheriff in 1619.

Some twenty years later he nearly became Sheriff again, this time much against his wishes. His son, Sampson, came to his aid by addressing a letter to the Lord Chancellor, outlining the reasons why his father should not be "pricked". The letter, containing some interesting sidelights on how sheriffs were selected at that time is worth quoting in full. It reads: "I humblie make boulde to entreate your Lordshipp's assistance by way of letter to a friend at Cort or some other shure course, if your Lordshipp cannot be heere in person, to keepe my father from being Shirriff either of Carmarthen or Pembrooke shire for this next yeare. It is an office of much trouble and expence and will doe him more harme this year than it could doe at anie other tyme in respect of those greate somes of monie which he is to pay the Kinge for fine of depopulcon, and in regard of his manie troubles not yet ended. I perceve our adversaries doth use what meanes they can to have him pricked for this yeere, and I verily beleeve they will prevayle unlesse by your Lordshipp's meanes it may be prevented. The usuall day for that business your Lordshipp may please to remember is Sunday next, and it is in your Lordshipp's goodness that we only relie conserninge this particular. I beseech your Lordshipp excuse my unmannerly bouldness heerein, and presentinge my humble service to your honor I take leave and rest your Lordshipp's most humble servant, Sampson Lort. London, this 31st of October 1639". To make certain that his Lordship sould have no worry about finding a substitute, Sampson obligingly enclosed a list of, "Names of sufficient gentlemen to be Shirriff of Pembrooke shire: Lewis Barelow of Criswell, George Carew of Carew, George Heaward (of Fletherhill), James Philipps of Benteba (Pentypark), Hugh Bowen of Upton, Nicholas Lewis of Hencastle, all Esquires. The like names for Carmarthenshire: John Lewis of Llangeler, Henry Jones of Llangadock, John Vaughan of Llanelthy, Phillipp Lloyd of Llangehangell Abercowin, Henry Middleton of Llanarthney, John Harris of Llandilovawer, George Vaughan of Penbre, David Lloyd of Llanegwad, all Esquires."

Sampson's letter did the trick and in 1639 Thomas Warren of Trewern was pricked for Pembrokeshire and Henry Jones of Abermarlais for Carmarthenshire. In such wise are matters quietly and genteelly arranged.

In 1611, before he had inherited, Henry bought from Richard Budd of London, for £130, two tenements in Rowlston (Rowston) worth £4 6s. 10d. per annum, Kightill alias Kittel (Kitton Hill) worth 26s. 8d. per annum, in Stackpole parish and a close of six acres in Temby alias Tenby called Fursey Park worth 9s. per annum, "formerly belonging to the hospitium or free chapel of St. John" all to be held of the manor of East Greenwich in free socage, for ever.

In 1618 he instituted a suit in the High Court of Chancery against two tenants of the manor of Castlemartin, William Hitching and Harry Rowe, who refused to work at the lord's hay harvest as they were bound to do by custom, and further alleged that they had managed to get the ancient records of the lordship into their hands, which they claim contained no references to the obligation. The defendants said that George and Henry Lort, lords of the manor, grandfather and father of complainant, had never demanded observance of such custom, to which Henry Lort replied that if the duty had not been asked for, it was due to the negligence of the bailiffs of the manor. Unfortunately the verdict is not given.

Henry Lort made numerous leases. On 11 December 1618 he granted a lease to Henry Leach of Castlemartin, yeoman, of a messuage and lands in Prickeston, and an acre of meadow called The Upper Acre in Brownes Foord, in Castlemartin parish, for 21 years, at a yearly rent of £8, with two couple of capons at "Christide", a heriot when due and doing suit of mill at Kings Mill and Frowens Mill. On 26 October 1621 he granted a lease of 21 years to Henry Lech of Lowlenslade in Castlemartin, husbandman (probably identical with the lessee of 1618) of Lowlenslade and all lands, some 50 acres, lying east of the Beare way which led from Prickeston to Castlemartin church and an acre on the west side of the same way butting against the cross and Prickeston hedge at the south end thereof, and also 2 acres of meadow at Brownes foord. The rent was to be rendered in suit and services, namely 25 bushels of good, sufficient, clean, dry, well-conditioned wheat (allowing 19 gallons to the bushel), and 25 bushels of barley, a couple of capons at Christmas, a best beast as a heriot when due, to keep the premises in repair, do suit of court at the manor of Castlemartin, suit of mill at Kings Milne and Frowen's Milne as lessor appointed, to send his cart and horses to carry corn, timber, slates, salt, beer, wine and any other portable thing to or from such places as lessor should appoint, and to deliver the said wheat and barley at lessor's house, or at any place of lading between the town of Pembroke and Nangle, at the election of lessor.

On 28 October 1620 he granted a lease of a cottage and a "hay" or close adjoining, and three acres of arable land in the townred and fields of Bosheston, to Ales Leach, widow and Thomas Leach, fisherman, for their lives, at four pence per annum. An example of payment of rent in kind is provided by a lease for 21 years which he gave to Thomas Butler of Myrrian, husbandman, on 18 June 1625, of a messuage and lands in the townred of Bosheston, for which lessee was to render yearly, 30 bushels of good, sufficient, sweet, dry and marketable wheat of 20 gallons to the bushel, a couple of capons at Christmastide, doing suit at the manor court of Stackpool, suit at the court mill, providing a cart and horse to carry timber and a heriot of the best beast.

"A couple of capons at Christmas"

On 1 March 1631, Henry Lort of Stackpole Court, esquire, granted three separate leases, by way of settlement, to his second and third sons, Sampson and John. To Sampson he gave a lease of "two capital messuages and lands called Rowstone alias Rowleston, and Kitteel alias Kightill, a messuage called Easter Trewent, two parcels of lands called Throstle Wood alias Thrustlewood, and Underwood, a water corn grist mill called Throstle Millne alias Thrustle Millne, a parcel of 5 acres being part of Myrledge alias Marladge, a parcel being part of Woodsend, all in the parish of Stackpole Elider, on the east side of the market way leading from the parish church of St. Elider to the town of Pembroke, and between Great and Little Salterne and the limestone and lime kilns there, with the use of such ways leading to the limekilns, and also for the carriage of 'coolme and coles' to the said quarries and limekilns". This lease was to be held for 99 years (beginning from the time of lessor's death) by lessee and then his heirs male, and in default, by John Lort, gentleman, and in default, by William Lort, youngest son of lessor. The rent was £3 6s. 8d. a year, the premises to be kept in repair. The seal attached to the deed shows *a cross* (Lort) *impaling a chevron between three stags' heads caboshed* (White of Henllan). The second lease was to John Lort, the third son, of "two messuages and lands called Fursdon alias Furston in Muncton parish, and a messuage called Woodsend, and part of Marledge, in Stackpole Elidor parish". This too, was for 99 years, to take effect from the day of lessor's death, to be enjoyed by John Lort and his heirs male and in default, to William Lort, lessor's youngest son, and his heirs male. For this a rent of £3 13s. 4d. was to be paid and the premises kept in repair.

The third lease, also to his son John, comprised "the capital messuage of Prickeston (121 acres), three messuages in Prickeston called Loughmeyler and Uphill (each of 40 acres) and Cornells End (6 acres), a messuage called Beedston (48 acres) at Broadcarse, and a close of 4 acres called Hunston Parke, all in Castlemartin parish, for 99 years commencing at the decease of lessor, paying a rent of £10, and for want of male heirs to lessee the rent to be paid to the said Sampson and his heirs male; suit of mill to be made at Kings Mill or Froynes Mill, suit of court at the manor of Castlemartin, and the premises kept in repair".

On 22 October 1634 he granted a lease "for 21 years of a messuage and lands called Lymston in Castlemartin, to Thomas Gwither, husbandman, at £7 rent and services, and the carriage of goods by a cart and horses". Some of these deeds were witnessed by Robert Eddow, seneschal of the manor of Castlemartin.

In 1620 he obtained from the Crown a further confirmation in perpetuity of the manor of Castlemartin lying in Castlemartin and St. Twynells, all manorial rights in the parishes of Stackpole Elidor and Bosherston alias Stackpole Bosher and St. Petrox and also the manor and lordship of Myrian (Merrion) in the parish of Warren with all its rights and privileges. Twelve years later, on 5 May 1632, he acquired some Crown lands, when Charles Harbord, Christopher Favall and Thomas Younge of London conveyed to him "a tenement in Nova Carew alias Newtowne in Carew parish, a tenement in West Williamston and a tenement called Williamston Elvor alias Elnor in Begelly parish (which grantors had obtained from the king on 29 January 1631), to be held of the manor of East Greenwich, co. Kent, in free socage and not in chief, for ever, rendering to the Crown twelve pence for the price of two capons and £6 4s. 0d. to the Exchequer at Westminster".

He had sufficient spare money to lay out in mortgages and on 4 November 1625 he loaned £1,500 to John Wogan of Wiston, esquire, who conveyed to him by way of security the lordship, manor, and capital messuage and demesne of Lawrenny and the advowson of Lawenny church. In due course the money was repaid and on 1 November 1628, Henry Lort and Judith, his wife, re-conveyed the property to Wogan.

About this time he seems to have been offered a knighthood, which he turned down, and had to pay £100 composition therefor at the Exchequer.[14]

He added further manorial franchises to his estate on 14 May 1631, when he bought a, "one-fourth part of the manor of Myrian (Merrion) in Warren parish" from Nicholas Turnor of Waymill, Devon, Anthony Larder of Clisthidon, Devon and William Fursden of St. Gerrance, Cornwall, for the sum of £266 13s. 4d.

On 13 September 1637 he acquired another manor, when John Voyle, gentleman, Lettice his wife, their son and heir apparent William Voyle, all of "Saint Ellvvews" (St. Elvis in Dewsland), Owen Edwards, Esquire, and Ethlu, his wife, John Edwards, gentleman,and Anne, his wife of Treffgarne, conveyed to Henry Lort, Esquire, and his second son, Sampson, for the sum of £1,220 the lordship or manor of Walton East with all appurtenances, in the parish of Walton East then occupied by the said John Voyle and twelve tenants, together with two water corn grist mills in the said parish, for ever. The record of Fine accompanying the transaction showed the manor and its appurtenances to consist of 20 messuages, 20 tofts, 2 water corn mills, 20 gardens and 290 acres.

In 1629 he started negotiations which in due course brought him an extensive property in north Carmarthenshire. On 24 September of that year Thomas Philipps of Abergwili and Sybil, his wife, Rowland Philipps and Jane, his wife, William Philipps of Coedgain and Ellenor, his wife, Mary and Anne Williams of Cilycwm, spinsters, David Edwards and Gregory Morris, agreed to convey to Henry Lort, esquire, the manor of Nantbai and the capital messuage and appurtenances of Ystrad-ffin, in Llanfair-ar-y-bryn parish, for sum of £4,420. But should the said Mary and Anne Williams decline to execute the conveyance Henry was to pay only two-thirds of the purchase money. In order to secure the promises further it was agreed that William Philipps should execute a lease of 99 years of the promises to Lort, that the tenants should all attorn to Lort and that Rowland and William Philipps should give him a bond in £9,000.

On 3 October in the same year Henry Lort granted a lease of the following properties to William Philipps of Coedgain: "Ystrad-ffin parcel, of the lordship or grange of Nantbai, where Gregory Morris lately dwelt; the water corn mill in Nantbai; 45 messuages and lands (named) a cottage and garden, two parcels of land, all in Llanfair-ar-y-bryn parish; and lands in the parishes of Cilycwm, Llandingad, Myddfai, Llanwrda, Conwilgaio (Conwyl Gaeo), and Llanfynydd, for 31 years, at £340 per annum, reserving to lessor the right to hold manorial courts with the perquisites thereof".

In 1633 a conveyance of properties in Llanfair-ar-y-bryn parish, described in the Final Concord as, "200 messuages, 300 cottages, 5 water corn mills, 260 gardens, 50 orchards and 15,480 acres" was made to Henry Lort by Lewis Gwyn and Mary, his wife and David Morris and Anne his wife.

At the same time he secured a hold on valuable property called Rushmoor in Llanfihangel Abercowin(Abercywyn) parish, Carmarthenshire. The owners, Philipps, were in need of money, and borrowed £2,000 from Henry Lort and on 3 October 1629 conveyed Rushmoor to him by way of security. The Philippses failed to pull out of the morass and in the next generation, as we will see, Rushmoor became the absolute property of the Lorts. In 1623 Henry had bought the Pembrokeshire lands of another Carmarthenshire landowner, Morris Bowen of Llechdwnny, who conveyed to him, "18 messuages, 6 tofts, 4 dovecotes, 20 gardens and 111 acres of land in Rhoscrowther, Mounction, Manorbier and Tenby"; while Morris Wogan of Milton assigned to him the remainder of the term, "of a lease of lands in Merrion (Warren parish)" which the said Morris Bowen had granted to Henry Wogan of Boulston in 1604.

From these transactions it is clear that Henry Lort was a rich man who could lay hands on large sums of ready money, a worthy representative of an equally capable father and grandfather.

He had some trouble with his powerful neighbour Hugh Owen of Orielton who overtly encouraged tenants of the manor of Castlemartin to dispute the terms of their tenure. These confederates, James Barrett, John Ferrior and Richard Poyer, asserted that they held Upper Chapel, Lower Chapel and other lands in Castlemartin, in fee, and not as copyhold of the manor. According to the custom of the manor, such lands were copyhold, held by the rod and had to be surrendered to the lord on death, or when they were sold, after which they were redelivered to the next tenant or purchaser, on payment of customary fees. When called upon to observe the custom, the three tenants refused, whereupon Henry Lort brought an action against them in the Court of the Council of Wales, and on 29 July 1637, the defendants were convicted "for their perjury and misdemeanours", committed to the ward of the porter of the Council, there to remain till they paid to the Receiver of Fines, £20 each by way of fine, £5 damages, and £6 12s. 0d. to Henry Lort as costs of the suit.

Manorial jurisdictions, unless carefully defined, duly enforced, and regularly recorded, could be eroded. Occasionally the lord of the manor might seek to extend his privileges and to acquire others likely to be beneficial to him. Henry Lort once made such an attempt. I have to thank Mr. Geoffrey Steele-Morgan of Haverfordwest for drawing my attention to the evidence relating to this contained in the State Papers volumes issued by the Public Record Office. In November 1629 a ship bound from Ireland was wrecked on the coast within the parish of Bosherston and all hands and cattle aboard perished. Henry Lort immediately seized the wreck, in his right as Lord of Castlemartin. Sir Thomas Cannon reported this to the government and urged that a commission be issued to enquire into the legality of Lort's action. It was conceded that he had right of wreck on the coastlands of the manor of Castlemartin, but the parish of Bosherston was extra-manorial so that Lort's jurisdiction did not extend to that part of the coastline. Henry Lort, who claimed to be ill, Judith, his wife and other members of his family, when called before the commissioners found reasons for not appearing, so that the commissioners had "to give over the execution of the commission". These delaying tactics are explained by Henry Lort's efforts to obtain a patent of wreck on the coast where he owned lands outside the manor of Castlemartin. One of his sons was reported to be in London, busily attempting to achieve this. Information concerning his activities reached the Earl of Pembroke, Vice-Admiral of south Wales and Lord Chamberlain, who wrote to their lordships on 23 April 1631 warning them of Lort's intentions which, the Earl hoped, they "will conceive may prove prejudicial". They took the hint, and informed the Attorney General of their desire to prevent Mr. Lort procuring the grant.

Henry seems to have possessed a knack of running into trouble. He grew large quantities of corn, which he sold in Pembrokeshire and other markets, both in Wales and England. In 1637 some local Justices of the Peace reported to the Earl of Bridgwater, President of Wales and the Marches, that Lort had transported corn into other parts of the kingdom despite an "extraordinary dearth" in Pembrokeshire. This was also reported to London and an order was issued to remove Henry's name from the Commission of the Peace.

Lort had expected that the matter would be examined at Ludlow, but the certifiers pressed that it should be determined in London. As a result Henry addressed a humble petition to the King, and stated that his "ancestors being English and lately planted in that county (Pembrokeshire) having bettered their estates there by increase of tillage that having last term had conferred upon him by the Lord Chamberlain the office of *custos rotulorum*", some of the complaining Justices of the Peace having suits of law with him, had "through envy" misinformed their lordships of the situation. He was ready to manifest that Pembrokeshire was a good corn country, that the inhabitants made their bread of barley, oats and rye, which sorts of grain he had not exported "this year"; that wheat, "which is little used by the common people," had been sold by his agents to those who wished to buy it; that, he had not transported any corn out of the kingdom, apart from one load in a small bark to Bristol and another to Beaumaris, which he sold under market price; that he still has "yet lying by him much more corn that the county will buy". He prayed to be admitted to clear himself, and in the meantime that the order for putting him out of the commission of the peace, be suspended.

On 7 July 1637, the Earl of Bridgewater reported to the Privy Council that having examined the complaint, he did not find any evidence to sustain it, apart from one shipment of corn made by Lort to Ireland in 1629; Roger Lort (Henry's son), confessed that his father had exported corn, out of his over-plus, in two barks to Bristol and Beaumaris, but proved that the markets of Pembroke and Tenby were well supplied by him and that he had more corn that the people required, "and it is demanded what should become of it he might not export it". No corn had been exported since the issue of the Lord Treasurer's warrant in respect of the affair.

In 1639 Henry Lort was again in hot water, this time for converting arable lands in Pembrokeshire into pasture, which had led to depopulation of the countryside. He admitted his guilt, and on 27 December he presented a petition to the King praying for the royal pardon. He stated that he had been questioned in the Court of Star Chamber regarding depopulations and conversion of arable lands into pasture. Having submitted himself to the Commissioners they compounded with him for £2,500, of which £1,500 had already been paid by him into the Exchequer, the remainder to be paid in June and December following; as Sheriff of Pembrokeshire, Justice of the Peace, Deputy Lieutenant and Deputy Custos Rotulorum, he had been employed for many years in the King's service, and had performed the duties "with all faithfullness"; being now "very old and infirm and desiring to die in peace", he prayed the King to pardon him for the depopulations and conversions, together with all offences with which he was charged and also all errors, misprisions and offences (if any had been) committed by him in the aforementioned offices and employments, according to the tenor of the general pardon issued at His Majesty's coronation. An endorsement states that the petition should be referred to the Attorney General's consideration who was to convey his opinion to the King.

In a similar petition addressed to the Lords Commissioners, Henry outlined his case, stating that he was, "a bed-ridden man desirous to quit himself of all business and die in peace", and hoped that he would receive as ample a pardon as that granted previously to Sir Thomas Cannon.

The result is not recorded, but it would be charitable to hope that he received the royal pardon, for he died some eleven months later.

Henry Lort married, Judith, daughter of Henry White of Henllan in Rhoscrowther parish (High Sheriff in 1592 and 1604), by Jane, daughter of Richard Fletcher of Bangor. As we have seen his sister, Elizabeth, had married Jane's brother, Griffith White. Starting life as merchants in Tenby the Whites made a fortune in the second half of the fifteenth century and then bought Henllan to which they added a large estate as the years went on.

Apparently Henry Lort was not happy with the state of the family armorials that Dwnn had recorded in 1591. Henry's seal to a deed of 1631 showed a cross, impaling his wife's coat of *a chevron between three stags' heads caboshed.* His adopted arms were officially granted to him by Sir John Borough, Garter King of Arms, on 7 July 1637; namely, *a shield per fesse azure and gules, a cross or,* and for a crest *an arm in armour embowed sable studded or, holding in gauntletted hand a cross or,* with the motto *Sequor meliora,* and at the same time the Lort family tree, compiled by George Owen, York Herald, was recorded in the College of Arms.[15]

The death of Henry Lort is recorded by his second son in an endorsement on a lease dated 1 March 1631, in these words: "Date November 24th 1640. Memorandum that on the eleventh day of November about eight of the clock in the morning in the sixteenth yeere of King Charles the first, King of England, etc, and in the yeere of our Lord God one thousand six hundred and fortie, my father Henry Lort Esqr the within named lessor died and departed his life. Teste Sampson Lort the within named lessee."

By her husband's death, Judith became entitled by way of dower to a third of the grange of Nantbai and of the properties specified in the deed of 3 October 1629 (quoted earlier), and of land in Stackpole. She was living in the town of Pembroke in 1647.

Henry and Judith Lort had seven children, namely:

1. (Sir) Roger Lort, eldest son and heir, born about 1608. See later.

2. Sampson Lort, matriculated at Wadham College, Oxford, on 3 November 1626, aged 17. He lived at Rowston, and at Eastmoor in Manorbier parish and took an active part in public life. He married and left issue:

3. John Lort, like his brothers took part in public life and established the line of Lort of Pricaston. He died in 1673:

4. Griffith Lort:

5. William Lort, who lived at Summerton in Monkton parish. On 14 April 1651, Thomas Powell of Pwllcrochan parish, gentleman, granted a messuage of 20 acres called the Hill in St. Michael's Pembroke, lands at the east gate of Pembroke town and five closes of 18 acres and other lands in St. Michael's, a ploughland called Collcate in the same parish and other properties in and about the town of Pembroke, to William Lort of Stackpool Elidor, gentleman. Administration of his goods was granted in PCC in 1658:

6. Abra Lort, married Thomas Bowen of Trefloyne, near Tenby. Bowen had studied at the Inner Temple in 1636 and afterwards came home to manage his property. He died before 1650. Abra survived him by over thirty years and made her will in 1679. They had issue:

7. Elizabeth Lort, married George Owen, son of John Owen of Trecwn, who matriculated at St. John's College, Oxford, on 13 November 1629, aged 16. He had no issue and Elizabeth afterwards married a Mr. Martin of Redland, Bristol.

Sir Roger Lort of Stackpole Court

Roger, eldest son and heir of Henry Lort, is, perhaps, the best known member of the family. He is among the few Pembrokeshire men to be accorded a place in the *Dictionary of National Biography.* In addition to making valuable additions to the family estate, he took an active part in public life and although a Royalist at heart, his dexterity during the trouble years of the Civil Wars and the Commonwealth, ensured the survival of his family and estates, brought him offices under Cromwell and a baronetcy from Charles II. The Vicar of Bray could have been no more adept.

Roger, born in 1608, matriculated at Wadham College, Oxford, on 3 November 1626 at the age of eighteen years. He graduated B.A. on 11 June 1627 and in that year became a student in the Middle Temple. He was a Latin scholar of considerable merit, a poet, and in 1646 published his *Epigrammatum Liber Primus,* and according to a writer in the *Dictionary of National Biography* "the epigrams are not destitute of point". He was a Justice of the Peace for Pembrokeshire, served as High Sheriff in 1652 and on 15 July 1662 was created a baronet.

His two wives came from wealthy and influential families. The first, whom he married at St. Giles-in-the-Fields, Middlesex, on 10 May 1632, was the eighteen-year-old Hester Annesley, second daughter of Francis, Baron of Mountnorris, Viscount Valentia, by Dorothy,

The Bosherton lilies

daughter of Sir John Philipps of Picton Castle, Baronet. Hester's brother, Francis Annesley, afterwards created Earl of Anglesey, became Lord Privy Seal to Charles II. Born in Fishamble Street, Dublin, on 3 April 1613, and baptised on 18 April at St. John's church, Hester brought to her husband a marriage portion of £2,000. Under the terms of the post-nuptial settlement made on 1 April 1633, Henry Lort (father of Roger), granted to Sir Richard Philipps of Picton Castle and Griffith White of Henllan, the following properties:- "the capital messuage of The Moor, messuages called Kitehill, Layton, Lowelinges Slade, a capital messuage called Browneslade, messuages called Church Hay, Gupton, two messuages called Coxhay, a parcel of meadow called Browne-ffoorde, messuages called Clyne, Bulliber, Drydowne, Linny Rowe, all in Castlemartin parish; the manors and lordships of Stackpoole Ellider, Stackpoole Bosher, and Castlemartin together with the East and West Hundreds, with rights, franchises, etc., and messuages and lands belonging to them, in the parishes of St. Petrox and St. Twynells; the advowsons, donations, rights, of patronage and presentation of the churches of Stackpoole Ellider, Stackpoole Bosher, and St. Petrox, and the vicarage of the parish church of Castlemartin, in Pembrokeshire; the manors and lordships of Nantbay and Istradfyne, with rights, franchises, etc., and lands belonging to them, and all his properties in the parishes of Llanfairarybryn, Cilycwm, Cynwyl Gaio, Llanwrda, Llandingad, Myddfai, and Llanfynydd, in Carmarthenshire". These were to be held in trust for the use of the bridegroom and bride, for their lives (with dower of £300 yearly for Hester should she be widowed), and afterwards to Roger's heirs male and in default of such heirs, to the use of Sampson, grantor's second son, and in default, to John Lort the third son, to William Lort the fifth son, and to Griffith Lort the fourth son, in that order, and if the said sons had no heir male, the properties were to pass to grantor and his right heirs for ever.

Hester died in 1647, having borne her husband a son and four daughters.

In 1651 Roger married again, namely Joan, eldest daughter of Humphrey Wyndham of Dunraven Castle, Glamorgan, by whom he had one son and one daughter. By the pre-nuptial settlement made on 7 June 1651, Roger agreed to settle his estate to the uses of the marriage, to provide £600 yearly for Joan for life, and charged the estate with £4,000 to be shared among any younger daughters when they reached the age of 18. Joan's portion was £2,000.

The marriage took place before 20 July, for on that day the post-nuptial settlement was executed, when Roger Lort and Joan, his wife, granted to John Elliott, esquire, and Thomas Elliott, gentleman, both of Earewere, the following properties, to be held on trust for the uses of the marriage:- " the Moor, Kytehill, Layton, Lowling slade, the capital messuage of Brownslade, Church Haye, Gupton, a meadow called Brownford Mead, two messuages called Coxhaye, Cloyne, Bulliber, Drydowne, two tenements in Lynny Rowe, Parston alias Peirceston, Prickaston (in tenure of John Lort), eleven other messuages (unnamed), a parcel of lands at Downs and Westfield, two mills called King's Mill and Froynes Mill, a tenement and meadow at Stenbridge, several other parcels of lands with houses and gardens in the occupation of thirteen tenants, and copyhold and corse gale rents in the lordship of Castlemartin, all of which lay in the parishes of Castlemartin, St. Twynells, and Mouncton, within the lordship of Castlemartin. Accordingly, a fine was suffered on 1 September of the settled estates described as the castle and manor of Castlemartin , 150 messuages, 20 tofts, 4 mills, and 8,800 acres of land, a yearly rent of £10, common of pasture, and the advowson of the vicarage of Castlemartin, in Castlemartin, St. Twynnels, Flimston, and Mouncton. On 22 September 1651 Roger Lort and Joan his wife, executed a deed declaring that the premises were held to their uses for life, and afterwards to the heirs of their body.

On 20 July 1651 he made a settlement of his extensive estate in Carmarthenshire in order to establish it "in the name and blood of the said Roger Lort soe long as it shall please Almightie God to continue the same". The property was described as follows: In Llanfairarybryn parish, the lordship, manor, or grange called Nant Bay formerly part of the possessions of the dissolved monastery of Istrad Fleere, with courts leet, etc., the capital messuage called Istrad Fine, parcel of the lordship, wherein Thomas Williams, esquire, and Rice Williams, formerly dwelt, and wherein Thomas Phillips "now dwells", with demesne, lands, etc., belonging to Nant Bay and Istrad Fine, the tithes of those two places, a water corn mill in Nant Bay, and 47 messuages, three parcels of land, a cottage and garden; Cilycwm parish, forty messuages, and a water corn mill; Llandingat, Myddfai and Llanwrda parishes, four messuages, a garden, and a house and garden; Cynwyl Gaeo parish, fifteen messuages, a parcel of land, and a water corn mill; Llanfynydd parish, nine messuages, and a water corn mill; and other messuages held by seven tenants by leases granted to them by Thomas Williams alias Prees ab William late of Ystradfine, esquire, deceased".

These properties were to be held by John and Thomas Elliott of Earwere "as trustees, to the use of Roger and Joan for their lives, and afterwards to their heirs male, with dower to the said Joan and portions for her daughters".

Lort's conduct during the Civil War has attracted a good deal of adverse criticism. Like many others in that troublesome period, he changed sides, but whether as a matter of conviction or expediency is difficult to decide without firm evidence. As we shall see, there is a hint of deviousness in the manner in which he steered his course. What is abundantly clear is that he joined the winning side at the right time and reaped a personal harvest from both Crown and Parliament. Success in temporal affairs has much to do with timing and Roger Lort seems to have possessed a knack in this respect.

We first hear of Lort's civil war career in July 1642, when Parliament, without the King's assent, nominated Commissioners to put the Militia Ordinance (for raising troops) into execution. Among those nominated for Pembrokeshire was Roger Lort. However, when the King raised his standard in August, Lort took the Royalist side and in 1643 received from Lord Carbery, commander and head of the Royal Association in west Wales, a commission to raise and command a regiment. In the latter part of that year numerous declarations by loyalty were signed by the gentlemen of the county, three of them by Roger Lort and his brother, Sampson.

Roger's activities soon brought him to the notice of the House of Commons, who, on 19 April 1643, resolved to impeach Carbery and to send for Roger Lort as a "delinquent and for being active against the Parliament", and instructed the Deputy Lieutenants and magistrates to apprehend him.

Lort remained at large, and on 30 August challenged Tenby on behalf of the Royalist Association and through various threats and promises, induced the town authorities to submit. The town was then garrisoned for the King. Carbery had already garrisoned several strong-points, including Stackpole Court itself.

A Parliamentary force based at Pembroke, the only town of consequence not in Royalist hands, commanded by Rowland Laugharne advanced on Stackpole on 30 January 1644. Laugharne's force, consisting of some 350 foot and horse, supported by artillery borrowed from Parliamentary vessel, attacked the house. The fight lasted for eight hours, during which they engaged the defenders with small arms fire and directed "our ordnance at the house, but the walls thereof were so strong that they performed little execution; at last on our men gaining some part of the outer works near the walls, the enemy seeing the place no longer wardable, and themselves hard beset, yielded upon quarter, which was granted and nobly performed" – so wrote Captain Richard Swanley the naval commander, who had placed the guns at Laugharne's disposal. Leaving a small garrison in the house, Laugharne led the remainder of his force back to Pembroke, some three-and-a-half miles away.

The Lorts were now worried men.[16] Their house was in enemy hands and the military capacities of Laugharne were known to be formidable. On the day that Stackpole fell, Parliament had issued a Declaration promising to receive the nobility, gentry and others, into favour provided they abandoned opposition, took the Covenant and paid suitable fines. In March 1644 Roger Lort journeyed to London to make his peace with the new masters.

Roger's submission was accepted, and after consenting to serve on Parliamentary committees for the three counties of south-west Wales, he was freed from delinquency and sequestration, his fine of £1,000 remitted and restored to his real estate and goods. In June 1644 supported by his brothers, Sampson and John, he served on the county committee for Pembrokeshire, then engaged in raising troops for Parliament. After this the three brothers continued to give active support to Parliament. On 12 July 1648 an order to demolish the castle of Haverfordwest was signed by the three Lorts, and in March 1649, Roger and Sampson undertook to victual Parliamentary vessels that came to Milford and Tenby. Roger Lort disliked and distrusted John Poyer of Pembroke, and in order to forward schemes against him, went to London. This was in 1645, and Laugharne complained in a letter written on 13 September, that "Mr. Roger Lort, in our greatest exegiencie, deserted us, and in contempt of my commaunde for his staie, shipped himself off to London there . . . betoweth himselfe in disgorgeinge private ranckor and malice against those whose meritt will endure the este". As a result Roger was dubbed a "subtle ambidexter". Poyer, equally a "subtle ambidexter", as events were to show, imprisoned the three Lorts in Pembroke Castle for nearly a month in 1647, subjecting them to many indignities before being released.

An "information" laid against him by his ill-wishers and recorded in the State Papers on 12 February 1649 summarises his career during the time of the Civil War, as follows: That in 1641/2 Roger Lort with the King's Commissioners of array, joined the Marquis of Hertford, and became treasurer for the King; that he was made a Justice of the Peace, issued warrants to raise men and was principal actor in the Association of Pembroke, Carmarthen and Cardigan, and petitioned the Earl of Carbery to head it; that he subscribed to raise 400 "musqueteers" and had a commission to raise a regiment; he offered to raise money if the Earl secured Pembroke and Tenby, and subscribed warrants for forcing large sums from the inhabitants; in August 1643 he summoned Tenby to surrender, promising to ensure the major and burgesses to the value of his own estate, £30,000, and of his brother-in-law, Thomas Bowen's estate, £20,000, threatening to blockade them if they refused, by which juggling the town surrendered, whereupon he robbed the well-affected; in October 1643, he and others raised £2,000 which they took to Lord Carbery at Oxford, for fortifying Milford harbour. Roger summoned the men of Pembrokeshire to attend and aid him and delivered all arms in the county to Carbery; caused seven or eight garrisons to be fortified, including his own house which was stormed and taken by Major General Laugharne then commander for Parliament, causing the first bloodshed in that county; in 1644 he came to London, pretended to be for Parliament, and got himself appointed a committeeman for the counties of Pembroke, Carmarthen and Cardigan; and "has since been a subtle ambodexter", taking revenge on those who served Parliament, with the help of Rees ap Rees, formerly pilloried for false oaths and hangman to Gerard's forces, executing those who would not fight against Parliament and [he is] now appointed to the Sequestration Committee of the said three counties.

Included in the same "information" were Sampson Lort (Roger's brother), Colonel James Lewes (of Cilciffeth, *iure uxoris*), and John Elliott, whose alleged iniquities were eloquently outlined. Of Sampson, it was said that he had countenced malignants to seize the estate of Sir John Horsey at the suit of one James Ingrame, late underwriter of the Fleet, and he had been a malignant at Oxford and employed malignants in public offices; in April 1648, hearing of general insurrection, he directed his men to obey Colonel John Poyer, who with his approval and for many weeks, brought 36 bushels of corn weekly into Pembroke, notwithstanding their former engagements against Parliament.

Obviously the Lorts were not amongst the most popular of people but it is clear that the rodomontade recited above was the work of a splenetic Parliamentarian anxious to pay-off old scores. The authorities in London were more judicial and on 15 March 1649, they ordered the discharge of Roger, Sampson and their fellows, having noted that in 1643 they had surrendered and obtained the benefit of Parliament's declaration and since had borne arms and held office for Parliament and had actively opposed Laugharne, Poyer and Powell in the late insurrection.

Numerous reference to Roger's activities as a Justice of the Peace and Committeeman are found up to 1656. Afterwards his enthusiasm for the Commonwealth was less evident and it would appear that was returning to his former (and natural) loyalty.

That he benefited by defection to Parliament is shown by the way he avoided sequestration and by his purchases of sequestered lands of the less fortunate. An unflattering account of him occurs in a manuscript written about 1661 (printed in *The Cambrian Register,* 1795, p. 165), which reads "Roger Lort, of any principle or religion to acquire wealth; he fortified and defended his house against the parliament's seamen; but in preservation of no cause but his own. Hugh Peters was his welcome guest as long as Hugh was welcomed by Oliver Cromwell. Hugh had no sooner lost the one than the other. *Utilitas justi prope mater et aequi est".*

Roger Lort added considerably to his estate by acquiring freeholds and leaseholds. In 1630 Thomas ap Rees of Rickeston in Brawdy parish "granted the farms of Drydowne and Pencoed Mellyne (Meline) in St. Petrox and Castlemartin, to him. On 4 May 1632 Charles Harbord of London assigned to Roger Lort then of the Middle Temple, esquire, a Crown lease for 99 years dated 3 February 1630, of New Carew alias Newtowne and other tenements being parcel of the lordship of Castlemartin, the assignee to pay a rent of £6 4s. 0d. and 12 pence yearly in lieu of two capons". On 18 April 1642, Dennis Thomas of Carmarthen, mercer and Jane, his wife, granted the 67 acre farm called Lacerry in St. Twynnels parish to him for £200. In 1649 Thomas Williams of Gumfreston gentleman, sold the manor or lordship of Warren, the site of a windmill and other lands in Warren parish, to Roger and Hester Lort and their son, John, and on 1 August signed a bond for peaceful enjoyment of the properties.

On the last day of February 1652 he bought a messuage of 40 acres in Cathload (now Cartlett), Uzmaston parish, from Rowland Laugharne of St. Bride's, esquire, Anne, his wife and John, their son, for £193 12s. 0d. In 1655 he leased it to "Mr. Stephen Love, preacher of the Ghospell" for three lives at a rent of £12 2s. 0d., together with an assignment of a lease made to the Laugharnes by Dame Katherine Philipps of Picton Castle, widow, of lands now held with Lort's tenement of Cathload. Stephen Love died not long afterwards, and on 2 October 1658, his widow, Deborah, released all her claims in the messuage to Lort. In 1651 he bought from the Revd. Adam Hawkins of St. Ishmaels, clerk, a burgage and a malt mill in High Street, Tenby, for £40, to be held of the Crown manor of East Greenwich in free and common socage, charged with a chief rent of 13s. 4d. to the receiver of the manor. In 1653 Roger bought messuages called Loveston and Moor, the moiety of a corn mill and several cottages in Loveston parish, from George Adams, gentleman.

As example of profit gained through support of the Parliamentary cause is shown by the transaction relating to the sequestered barony or lordship of Llawhaden, part of the temporalities of the Bishopric of St. Davids. On 12 October 1647, Roger Lort, Herbert Perrott of Haroldston and John Elliott of Narberth, esquires, agreed to buy the lordship from the trustees authorised by ordinance of Parliament to convey same. They agreed to buy and hold the property in joint tenancy, with no benefit of survivorship and to transmit it to their several heirs on the same terms. They further agreed to borrow from Richard Lloyd of London, girdler, the sum of £246 towards the purchase price. The transaction took a long time to complete, but finally on 28 June 1650, Sir John Wollaston, knight, with five aldermen and fourteen citizens of the City of London, entrusted by several ordinances of the Lords and Commons of Parliament with the sale of the lands and possessions of late Archbishops and Bishops, for the use of the Commonwealth, granted to Roger Lort, John Elliott and Herbert Perrott, for the sum of

£1,068 13s. 11½d., the Barony of Llanhaden, appurtenances, courts, rights, privileges, rents and chief rents. It was an outright grant, to be held by the purchasers "for ever".

The permanency implied in the grant was rudely shattered by the Restoration ten years later, when the barony was handed back to the bishopric of St. Davids.

Roger acquired an interest in the lordship of Mouncton (Monkton), and it is likely that it formed part of the sequestered lands of a previous owner for in 1659 it was owned by Roger Lort and his friends John Elliott and Herbert Perrott who had been his partners in the purchase of the sequestered Barony of Llawhaden mentioned above. On 7 October 1659, these three gentlemen granted a lease to Roger White of Minwere, gentleman, "of the lordship of Mouncton, its rights and privileges, and the following appurtenances namely a meadow near the mansion house of the lordship, closes called Highe Crofte, adjoining Mouncton church, Poyers Parke, Dilas Close, Broadstolle Parke, Margaret's Meadow, The Storehouse close, The Long Haies, Easter Long Haies, and a 30 acre piece of 'mountain land' to be held for 99 years, at a rent of £20, and paying 40 shillings for a heriot".

Further properties in Carmarthenshire fell to his lap. As we have seen, his father already held a mortgage on the capital messuage called Rushmoor in Llanfihangel Abercywyn, belonging to the Philipps family. On 29 November 1651, Roger Lort loaned £600 to Richard Philipps and his sons John, Thomas, Henry, Owen and Edward, who conveyed Rushmoor to Lort by way of security until the money was repaid on or before 1 December of the following year and a proviso decreed that in event of non-payment, the property was to be conveyed absolutely to the mortgagee on payment of a further £600. They failed to make the payment and the mortgage was allowed to limp on until 29 January 1656, when the Philippses, in consideration of the further sum of £600, conveyed the property to Roger Lort. Quit-claims were later made by the sons of Richard Philipps and on 14 February 1661, Anne, Richard's widow, quit-claimed her interest in one-third of the property to which she was entitled by way of dower. Rushmoor, or Richmoor as it is also sometimes spelled in the deeds, was the home of the family of Philipps, minor squires, cadets of the house of Cilsant, who found themselves slipping down the social slope.

Another minor squire who parted with his lands in this way was David Powell of Ystrad Walter in Llanfair-ar-y-bryn. This too, came via the well-worn path of mortgage. It started in 1642 when David Powell, in need of ready money, mortgaged his property to Morgan Owen, Bishop of Llandaff. Ten years later, the property was still unredeemed. Powell, obtained a mortgage of a further £93 8s.4d., from the widow Anne Owens of Glasallt and on 2 January 1653 she assigned the combined mortgage, secured on Ystrad Walter and lands in Llanfair-ar-y-bryn and Llandingad, to Roger Lort. Matters did not improve for David Powell, and on 2 February 1653, in consideration of a sum of £680, he granted to Roger Lort, "the capital messuage, mansion house, and lands called Ystrad Walter, two other messuages and 13 parcels of land in Llanfairarybryn and Llandingad, for ever", and on 20 September 1654, Powell signed a final release and quit-claim of the properties. A similar fate befell David Morgan David of the parish of Talley, gentleman, who mortgaged two messuages and lands on 4 December 1646 to Nicholas Williams of Edwinsford for

£120, to be paid off at Michaelmas 1653. The mortgagee failed to produce the money and turned to Roger Lort for help. Roger agreed on 27 August 1656, to pay the money to Williams, and David Morgan David on his part agreed to convey the premises to Lort for ever and this was done on 15 October following.

The pattern is repeated in the case of Rees Pritchard of Abercrychan in Llanfair-ar-y-bryn parish, gentleman. On 12 January 1648 Rees and Lettice, his wife, mortgaged nine properties in Llanfair-ar-y-bryn to John Young, a Bristol mercer, and shortly afterwards they mortgaged Abercrychan in £120 to Major James Shelby and Frances, his wife. In a deed dated 10 May 1654, we are informed that Rees Pritchard "is necessited, to supply his present occasions", to sell outright to Roger Lort for £270 the properties mortgaged to Young and at the same time to assign to Lort the mortgage of Abercrychan, the equity of redemption of which was to remain in force. Not long afterwards, Rees Pritchard died and the remainder of the estate passed to his young son, Daniel Pritchard of Croft Hall in Llanfair-ar-y-bryn. Daniel had also been pushed-for-money and mortgaged nineteen properties in Llanfair-ar-y-bryn to one John Calverley of Eryholme, Yorkshire. He could not redeem the lands, and on 14 May 1659, sold them outright (described in the Final Concord as containing 300 acres) to Roger Lort for £825. The Abercrychan estate was to suffer further truncation on 4 July 1662 when Richard Pritchard (Rees's elder son), granted a messuage and parcel of land (already mortgaged to Lort), to Roger Lort (now a baronet), for £58.

He bought numerous other properties in north Carmarthenshire from minor land-owners, yeomen, and farmers, particularly during the period 1654-60; for instance in Llansawel parish from John Price of Abergorlech and Thomas Francis of Llansawel, gentlemen; in Cilycwm from David Jenkin, yeoman, and John Rees Morgan, Evan Rees Thomas, Richard Price of Ystrad-ffin, gentlemen; in Llanfynydd and Llandeilo-fawr from John Harries and Harry Harries of Coedygarth, gentlemen; in Llanfair-ar-y-bryn (in addition to those already detailed above) from Joan Gwyn, spinster; in Talley from David Morgan David; in Llandingad, Llanwrda and Cilycwm from Thomas Prydderch and Nicholas Rives; and in Llandyfaelog from Daniel Richard, gentleman, and Abigail, his wife. Several of these properties had been mortgaged to various people. He also bought three properties in Llanfair-ar-y-bryn from William Gwyn of Taliaris, esquire, for £109 4s. 0d.

The manor of Nantbai and the capital messuage of Ystrad Wallter were among the most important of the Carmarthenshire properties, particularly the former because of the minerals in its soil and during the following century his descendants reaped a rich harvest from the lead-mines they worked there.

He granted numerous leases, some for a term of years (usually 21), and some for lives. Here are instances. On 1 June 1652 he leased to Stephen Young of the village of Stackpole, "preacher of God's Word and Minister of the Gospel", and Hesther, his wife, "the messuage called Coed Melin in St. Petrox, for the lives of lessees, for £30 down and to pay £3 p.a. for the first three years of the lease. On 10 September 1655, he granted a lease for lives to Thomas William Thomas, yeoman, Margaret, his wife and their son, William Thomas

Williams, of the messuage of Llwyn Dynawed in Cilycwm, for £3 down, and a yearly rent of £3, a couple of capons, a bushel of oats, and to stall a beast yearly with sufficient and convenient fodder, to render a heriot of the best beast, do suit of mill at Cilycwm and carry stones and timber towards the mill's repair". On 18 April 1657 he gave a lease for lives to Abra and Jennett Leach, both widows, and John Leach, husbandman, of Castlemartin parish, "of the messuage of Lowlenslade and lands near the Beare way", for £10 down, rendering yearly 20 bushels of wheat and 20 bushels of barley (24 gallons to each bushel), by way of rent. On 20 April 1657 he granted a lease for 30 years to John Harries, esquire, and Henrie Harries his son and heir apparent, both of Llanfynydd parish, of five messuages, fifteen parcels of land, and a fishing weir on or near Gwern Vyda Vawr (Fedw Fawr), all in Llanfynydd parish, paying a yearly rent of £40, and rendering yearly a couple of capons or four shillings in lieu, two salmon and six "suins", a heriot of a best beast or twenty shillings on the death of a tenant, and to keep the premises in repair. He leased Ystrad Wallter on 27 January 1659 to Richard Price of Cilycwm, gentleman, and his sons, Edward and Rowland, for their lives, at £10 per annum, rendering two capons and a teal of wheat on 1 January, keeping a beast from 1 November to 1 May and paying £4 in lieu of a heriot.

Like his father, he had trouble with tenants who attempted to evade manorial rights. All freeholders in the lordship of Castlemartin held by copyhold, and when a holder died his heir paid a heriot, the lands had to be surrendered to the lord, which were then regranted by the rod, on payment of a due. Trouble arose when an owner held a number of properties, while the lord insisted that one should be paid for each holding. When Griffith White of Henllan, a very considerable landowner died, his son, Henry, declined to pay more than one heriot. Accordingly the matter was referred to the Justices of the Court of Great Sessions who found in Lort's favour and Henry White was ordered to pay a heriot for each tenement. The Justices found further, that as there were a great many parcels of land they should be reduced to eight copyholds and that in future White should be liable to pay eight heriots. At the same time, Roger Lort promised that at the death of Elizabeth and Mary, mother and wife respectively of Henry White, he would accept the sum of 40 shillings in respect of heriots due for such copyholds as they might possess at the time of death.

Prudence and industry of a careful parent and grandparent had ensured that Roger Lort started his career a wealthy man. Through his own shrewdness he ended his life as one of the richest and most important landowners in West Wales. His change of coat during the Civil War, subsequent acquisition of large properties and reversion to his first loyalty towards the end of the Commonwealth, have laid him open to the charge of deviousness, although such conduct was by no means uncommon among his fellow squires during that uncertain period. These manoeuvres did not endear him to some of his contemporaries as shown by the strictures I have quoted from the *The Cambrian Register*. Nevertheless he survived where others succumbed and his success was further capped by a baronetcy bestowed on him by King Charles II on 15 July 1662, an honour not wholly unassociated with his capacity to pay, for on the same day the Treasury acknowledged receipt of "the barony fee" of £1,095 paid by him.

Sir Roger Lort did not live long to enjoy the baronetcy and died on 10 March 1663. He desired to be buried in St. Petrox church "under my usual seat there". By his will, dated 13 January 1663, and proved in P.C.C. on 4 May 1664, he bequeathed as follows:- to the poor of Stackpool £10, together with a further £10 remaining his hands "from the will of my father"; to his eldest daughter Frances, £1,500 out of the profits of Nangle (Angle), "which I bought of Colonell Ashburnham, the Countess of Marlborough, and Mr. Miles Button"; to his second daughter, Hesther, £1,200 out of the profits of the lordship of Miriam (Merrion), and messuages in St. Florence parish and Redbart (Redberth) in Carew parish; to his third daughter, Anne, £1,000; to Joan, his youngest daughter, all his part of the lordship of Burton in Roose Hundred "which I lately bought of Mr. John Barlow of Slebech and Mr. Parrott ap Rice", also Sandyhaven (in occupation of Richard Stepney, esquire), Mullock and Sivers Hill, the corn mill called Mullocks Mill, and Trefach in Cemais "which I lately bought of Rice Lloyd, Gentleman"; these were to be enjoyed by his daughter, Joan, and his wife, Joan for her widowhood and by Joan, the daughter for a further 13 years after her mother's decease. To his second son Roger Lort, he left his realty in Carmarthenshire for ever. He recited that his dear brother-in-law, John Windham, barrister at law of Lincoln's Inn, had bought from Ashburnham and Button, on testator's behalf, for £3,900, the lordship of Nangle, the properties of Sandyhaven, the two Mullocks and Mullocks Mill, Ludsopp (Lydstep), New Inn, Redbart, houses and all walls and lands in Tenby, and he desired that his wife should enjoy them during widowhood.

When he died he owned 1,000 cows, steers and heifers, 10,000 sheep, 50 horses, corn worth £3,000, and goods valued at over £7,000, which, together with the real estate, shows him to have become one of the richest men in South Wales at that time. These figures were given in a Chancery lawsuit later in 1663 when the widow brought an action against Sampson and John Lort and their friends who were trying to retain much of the personalty which she claimed as her due, alleging that they had broken the agreement they had made with her on 24 March 1663, "in the chamber called the Doctor's Studdie in the house of Stackpoole Court".

After the funeral an unseemly wrangle developed concerning the expenses connected therewith, with the result that the heir Sir John Lort, brought an action against his stepmother, John Scurlocke and Roger White, and filed a bill of complaint on 27 September 1664 in the Chancery of the Great Sessions for Pembrokeshire. According to Sir John, his father had expressed a wish to be buried decently, without expense, but Dame Joan, "by whom Sir Roger Lort had several children upon whom he settled a great estate which of right belonged to plaintiff," said she would bear an equal share of the expenses and despatched the defendant White and her servant, John Freeman, to John Scurlock of Carmarthen, mercer, to buy mourning and other goods, to the value of £130. Plaintiff had no part in this and the funeral arrangements were made by Dame Joan, "to pleasure her own particular friends and relations".

The Dame replied that Sir Roger had died leaving a personal estate worth about £5,000 out of which the funeral expenses should be met, and denied promising to contribute towards defraying them. She said that plaintiff had declared he did not care what the cost would be so long as his "father was handsomely interred", and that "a banquet of sweetmeats would be more commodious than a dinner on ye funeral day". At his direction she wrote to Mr. Oakley of Carmarthen for sweetmeats and other necessaries and Freeman and White went to collect them. Plaintiff sent £12 towards payment. They returned with the sweetmeats and necessaries and also a quantity of cloth to be placed on the hearse.

White and Freeman told a similar tale, and John Scurlock agreed he had supplied the goods and that his mother-in-law, Mrs. Oakley, had been sent by Dame Joan to assist in the transaction. Scurlock's bill came to £125 9s. 11d.

It is clear that Sir John viewed with displeasure the handsome provision made in the will for his step-mother, step-brother and step-sister, and doubtless this had been partly the cause for his disinclination to meet the funeral expenses.

Dame Joan did not remain a widow for long and before 1666 had married Sir Edward Mansel, fourth Baronet, of Muddlescomb, Carmarthenshire, and brought her two children, Roger and Anne Lort, to live at her new home. The Mansels certainly benefited from the marriage, for on 2 October 1669 Joan and her husband gave a lease to Robert Mansel of Kidwelly, gentleman, of Bulliber, Drydown, and Cockhay, and an acre in Brownslade, in Castlemartin, for the lives of Francis and Mary Mansel, children of Anthony Mansel of Iscoed and Elizabeth Mansel, one of the daughters of John Mansel, late of Kidwelly, deceased, at a rent of £9 13s. 4d., 15 bushels of barley and seven bushels of wheat, of Pembroke town measure, yearly. Sir Edward Mansell died 1681. Dame Joan died on 8 October 1692 and was buried in St. Petrox church with her first husband, where her marble memorial is decorated with a lozenge bearing her family arms (Wyndham) in the centre, those of Lort on the dexter side and those of Mansel on the sinister. Fenton saw the monument, and chronicled a local legend concerning her – "There is a belief among the common people of these parts that this lady is often seen whirling round this vicinity in her carriage, with a headless coachman, headless horse, and herself headless; nay, she has been said to have rode in a fiery chariot from Tenby, and alighting on the farm-house of Samson, in the vale just below this church, to have crushed it".

The children of Sir Roger Lort, Baronet, were:

By his first wife, Hester (Annesley):
1. Sir John Lort, second Baronet, born 1638. See later.
2. Frances, married in May 1665, Rowland, son and heir of William Gwynne of Taliaris, Carmarthenshire and had issue. The pre-nuptial settlement dated 12 May 1665, stipulated that the wedding should take place within the four days following. Frances' portion was £2,000 and the bridegroom's father, "for settling the Inheritance of his reall estate upon his owne name, blood, and posterity for soe long time as itt shall please Almighty God", agreed to settle the property to the uses of the marriage and the issue and to secure a competent jointure for the bride. Displeased about the provisions of sister's marriage settlement, Sir John Lort brought an action against his brother-in-law and succeeded in "extending" his property in Llandeilo fawr and in 1672 Rowland Gwynne brought a counter-action against Sir John.

3. Hester who married Nicholas Adams of Paterchurch on 25 April 1665, the day after the pre-nuptial settlement had been signed, they had five sons and two daughters. She died at Bosherston on 10 November 1679 and was buried at St. Mary's Pembroke; Nicholas died on 10 May in the following year.

4. Anne, married a Mr. Whiting of London. The marriage took place after 1673, when Sir John Lort bequeathed £1,000 to "my sister Anne Lort". She was alive in 1698.

5. Dorothy, probably died young.

By his second wife, Joan (Wyndham):

6. Roger Lort, matriculated at Jesus College, Oxford, on 4 November 1670, aged fifteen. On 11 August 1660, his father conveyed forty-five properties in the Carmarthenshire parishes of Llanfair-ar-y-bryn, Llansawel, Talley, Cilycwm, Llandingad and Llanwrda, to Humprey Wyndham of Dunraven and John Wyndham of Lincoln's Inn, esquire, on trust, to the use of grantor for life, afterwards to his son, Roger Lort the younger and his heirs male, and in default of such heirs to successive sons begotten or to be begotten on Joan (Wyndham) his now wife, and in default, to the heirs male of grantor for ever. In the event, the younger Roger died unmarried, his mother had no more sons and the lands reverted to the main line. Roger died at Muddlescomb on 26 March 1675, and on 2 April was buried at St. Bride's, Glamorgan, the parish church of the Wyndhams of Dunraven. By will dated 24 March 1675, he left all his property to his mother and an inventory shows deceased's personalty to be worth £599.

7. Joan, married at Kidwelly on 11 September 1666, Rice Williams of Gray's Inn, later of Edwinsford. She died without issue and was buried in St Bride's Church, Glamorgan, on 22 November 1672. The widower married, secondly, Mary, daughter and co-heiress of John Vaughan of Llanelly. Rice was later knighted and died in 1694.

Sir John Lort, second Baronet

John Lort was born about 1638. No record of his admission to a university has been found, but at least he received some education associated with men of his quality, for on 27 June 1660 he was admitted to Lincoln's Inn. He must have had friends in high places and was knighted on 17 January 1662, some six months *before* his father received a baronetcy. In the following year the Earl of Carbery, President of the Council of Wales and the Marches, appointed him a Deputy-Lieutenant for Pembrokeshire. His period of knighthood proved almost as short as his father's baronetcy and on the latter's death on 10 March 1663 he succeeded to the hereditary dignity.

Sir John married Lady Susanna Holles, a bride with

Stackpole Court

a fortune of £4,000, daughter of the second Earl of Clare by Elizabeth, daughter of Horatio, Baron Vere of Tilbury. He had been given a licence from the Faculty Office on 31 January 1662 as, "Sir John Lort of Lincoln's Inn, bachelor, aged 23", to marry Lady Mary Stanhope of St. Paul's Covent Garden, spinster, aged 22, and at her own disposal. That marriage never took place and in the licence granted to him on 12 July 1663 to marry Lady Susanna Holles, he is described as bachelor, aged 26 *(sic)*.

The bride belonged to a distinguished family. Her grandfather, John Holles, had served against the Armada in 1588, held the appointment of Comptroller of the Household to the Prince of Wales in 1610-12, was created Baron Haughton in 1616 and Earl of Clare in 1624.

The parties in the pre-nuptial settlement made on 9 September 1663, were: 1. Sir John Lort, Knight and Baronet; 2. Arthur Earl of Anglesey, Sir John Vaughan (second son of the Earl of Carbery), Sir Erasmus Philipps of Picton Castle, Baronet; 3. Robert Raworth of Gray's Inn and Henry Hall of the Middle Temple, esquires; 4. John, Earl of Clare and his eldest son, Gilbert, Lord Haughton, Sir Edward Rosseter of Somerby, Lincolnshire, Knight, and John Wolfstenholme of London, esquire. By this document Sir John Lort settled the following properties (annual value included within brackets) to the uses of the marriage:

"The manor or lordship of Merrion (let at £62 17s. 2d.); a messuage in Easter Trewent and several messuages in Stackpool Bosher (£112 19s. 0d.); Trevelly and Carew farms both in Stackpool Bosher (£50 and £60); Merrion farm in Warren parish and Merledge farm in Stackpool Elidor (£40 and £50); several messuages in Ludsop, New Inn, Redbert and Tenby (£98 2s. 4d.); the lordship of Nangle (£206 5s. 4d.); the manor or lordship of Stackpoole, the capital messuage called Stackpoole Court and demesne lands (worth £1,000 yearly); and messuages belonging to that manor in Stackpool Elidor, Stackpool Bosher, St. Petrox and St. Twynnels (£188 8s. 0d.); messuages in Mouncton parish (£11 3s. 0d.); messuages in St. Twynells (£46 17s. 8d.); messuages, a water corn mill and a warren of 2,000 acres, all in Stackpool Elidor (£25, £35 and £80 respectively); Rawston in the same parish (£60); Prickeston in Castlemartin (£100); Furston and Woodsend in Mouncton and St. Petrox (£50); several messuages in Warren parish (£81) and in St. Petrox (£520 13s. 4d.); the advowsons, donations, presentations and right of patronage of the rectories of Stackpool Elidor, Stackpool Bosher and St Petrox and of the vicarage of Castlemartin".

These were entailed in strict settlement on Sir John and Susanna and the male heirs of their body and in default, to heirs female. On 10 October 1664, he executed a deed to secure his wife's jointure charged on specific properties of his Pembrokeshire estate.

Little is known about Sir John. A cryptic reference in a letter from George Frederick Beltz, Lancaster Herald, dated 17 March 1803, mentions Sir John Lort, "Styled in a memorandum now before me 'Prince of the Purple at Lincoln's Inn'," but the key to this mysterious description has yet to be found. He seems to have taken little or no part in public life.

He was not over enthusiastic about the generous settlement made by his father in respect of Dame Joan, the step-mother. Disagreements arose and at length these were referred to Arthur Earl of Anglesey, on behalf of Sir John and Sir William Syndham, Justice of the King's Bench, on behalf of Dame Joan. Articles were signed on 23 June 1664 and the following arbitration agreed to: that Sir John should pay £100 to Joan for the four dairies called Brownslade, Moor, Gupton and Church Hay, her interest in Carew dairy and as to a further £100 claimed by Joan to be due for corn in the ground at the four dairies at the time of Sir Roger's decease. This was to be referred to the voluntary oath of Sampson Lort of Moor who was to say whether there had been any previous agreement relating to the corn; that rents due from copyholders comprised in Joan's jointure should be examined to see whether Sir John had received them, what arrears were due, while Joan was to abate taxes on such payments; that Joan should have possession at Michaelmas next of the manor of Castlemartin and all lands comprised in her jointure, including the four dairies and her interest in the Carew dairy and that she could keep courts leet and other manorial jurisdiction and Sir John was to pay £180 to her for enjoying the dairies for the year ending next Michaelmas and she was to abate taxes thereon; that Sir John should enjoy all lands in the manor purchased in his name or jointly purchased with his late father and he was to permit Joan's steward to see and use the court-rolls in his custody and Joan was to have possession of all her jointure and the original purchase deeds of the manor.

No documents have been found to show that he added to the real estate. If the evidence of mortgages can be accepted, he was in need of ready cash on several occasions. Thus, on 30 December 1670, he borrowed £300 from his cousin John Lort of Pricaston, to whom he conveyed Wood and Underwood (being one hundred English acres), and a messuage and water corn mill in Stackpole Elidor, by way of security. Two years later Sir John turned to the same cousin for help, and on 13 August 1672 borrowed £1,360 at six per cent p.a. interest and conveyed to him, by way of security, the manor of Castlemartin, the advowson of the vicarage of Castlemartin and 49 other properties (including Pricaston, of which the mortgagee was tenant) in Castlemartin, St. Twynells, Flimston, and Monkton, and it was stated that Sir John's step-mother had dower interest in the properties by virtue of a settlement made by Sir Roger Lort in 1651 and Sir John convenanted that he or his heirs and assigns would repay the £1,360 and interest after the deaths of Dame Joan Mansel and Dame Susan Lort.[17]

The very few leases made by Sir John followed the normal pattern of that period. For example, on 29 September 1669 he granted a lease, in consideration of £30, of a messuage in the High Street of Tenby to William Driver, mariner, for 99 years at half-a-crown a year, lessee to keep the premises in repair; on 9 September 1664 he granted to John Thomas of St. Petrox, yeoman, a lease for 21 years of a house to be built by lessor near an old pair of walls in Stackpole town, formerly called the Oxe House, a close of ground of three acres, a garden in the Court and adjoining "the hay gard wall" of John Phillips, with liberty to enclose another garden not exceeding a stang out of the waste ground or green in the town of Stackpole, and to keep or pasture a cow upon some part of lessor's demesne, and ten sheep among lessor's flock, at a yearly rent of 40 shillings, doing suit of court, suit at Thrussel Mill, to work in the harvest for lessor who was to pay him, "the usual rate", to plant yearly ten young oak or ash upon some part of the leased lands and to keep the premises in repair.

Sir John Lort died between 29 January 1673, when he made his will, and 10 February 1673 when the inventory of his goods was compiled. He was aged about thirty-four years and was buried, at his express desire, near his mother's grave, in the church of Stackpole Elidor. He left the estate to his only son, Gilbert and his heirs, and in default to his only daughter Elizabeth and her issue, and in default to his cousin George Lort (son and heir of testator's uncle John Lort of Pricaston), with remainders to testator's brother Roger Lort, testator's cousin Thomas Lort of Moor, and, finally, in default of heirs, to testator's right heirs for ever; he desired that his son should be instructed by the Revd. William Lloyd, rector of St. Petrox and the Revd. Thomas Hitching, vicar of Stackpole Elidor. The will was proved in P.C.C. on 1 November 1673 by the widow, with power reserved to Sir Gilbert Lort.

Dame Susanna Lort, the widow, remained at Stackpole(pool) Court, for many years, bringing up her two children, Gilbert and Elizabeth, who were aged about three and eight years respectively when their father died. She granted several leases of land held in dower and occasionally granted some on behalf of her infant son. When Sir Gilbert came of age, she left Stackpole and took up residence at Turnham Green, Middlesex, where she lived from 1692 onwards. On 5 July 1692, she granted a release to her son, Sir Gilbert, "of the manor or lordship of Merrian, Merrian (Merrion) farm, Ester Trewent, several messuages (including Carew farm) in Stackpole Bosher; Trevally (Trefelly); messuages in Luddsop, New Inn, Redbert, and Tenby; the manor of lordship of Nangle, messuages in Nangle"; and all other properties she held in Pembrokeshire, so that he could "pass and suffer a common Recovery" in the Great Sessions of the said properties, provided that he paid his mother the sum of £20,000 before 26 September following. Dame Susanna died in 1710 and her will was proved in May of that year.

Sir Gilbert Lort, third and last Baronet

Born in Clare House, London, between one and two a.m. on Easter Day 1671 and baptised at St. Clement Danes on the Thursday following, Sir Gilbert had a long minority. By a deed dated 5 July 1692, he granted, "the capital messuage of Ystradffin and a parcel adjoining called Kae Mawr" (which had been leased by Roger Lort to Richard Price for life, and which lessor had surrendered to Sir Gilbert) and "Brysken helyg (Llanfynydd), to the said Richard Price of Ystradffin, gentleman, and Jonet widow of David Evan David of Llanfynydd, yeoman".

On 9 July following, Sir Gilbert granted a lease for a year to Stephen Morris of Clement's Inn and William Morgan of Chancery Lane, gentlemen, as a step towards barring the entail on the Pembrokeshire estate which included, in addition to the lands released by his mother on 5 July, the manor of Stackpole, Stackpole Court and demesne, several farms in Mouncton and St. Twynells, "a farm in Stackpole Elidor; Trefach, Y Tir Brith and parcels called Tyr y Brynar, and Tyr Jenkin Lloyd, being part of Trevach demesne, Penyrallt, a water corn mill called Velin Vach or Velin Wennid, all in Nevern parish", which had been purchased by Sir Roger Lort from Rice Lloyd, gentleman, and others; "Sandyhaven, the two Mullocks, Sivers Hill and a water corn mill called Mullocks Mill, in the parishes of St. Ishmaels and Burton; three-eighths of two messuages in the manor or lordship of Burton some time purchased by Mathew Prynne and Perrot ap Rice, gentlemen, and afterwards conveyed to Sir Roger Lort; parts and proportions of the manor or lordship of Burton in the hundred of Roose, and the advowson of Burton which Sir Roger had purchased from John Barlow of Slebech and George Barlow of Kilkiffith; a water corn mill, a warren of 2,000 acres, and Rawston, in Stackpole Elidor; Pricaston (in tenure of John Lort, esquire); Furston and Woodsend in Mouncton and St. Petrox; several farms in Warren and St. Petrox; the advowson of the rectories of Stackpole Elidor, Stackpole Bosher and St Petrox; Cathload (Cartlett in Uzmaston parish); Loveston, Moor, moiety of the advowson of Loveston and several messuages there; in Loveston parish, two closes called Easter and Wester Hill in Priors Hill, a parcel called Priory Marsh with the site of the Priory and Dove House, in the parish of St. Thomas, Haverfordwest, which Sir Roger Lort had purchased from Sir Francis Annesley, Baronet, and Arthur Annesley, esquire".

The hand of Sir Roger, the main architect of the importance of his family, was still evident at the end of the century as seen in the foregoing release. His name occurs again in a deed dated 1 June 1696, whereby Sir Gilbert granted to Daniel Richards of Carmarthen, gentleman, a lease (in obedience to a decree in Chancery in a suit between the lessor and lessee), of messuages in Llandyfaelog (formerly mortgaged by Daniel Richards and his father, to Sir Roger Lort) for the lives of lessee and his son, Daniel, at 10 shillings per annum, the premises to be surrendered in good repair to lessor or his heirs at the determination of the lease.

Two leases granted by Sir Gilbert contain some interesting provisions. On 28 April 1694 he gave a lease for nineteen years to "Samuel Smith of Manorbier parish, gentleman, of Rowleston and Kitehill in Stackpole Elidor and the liberty of building a limekiln at the Key at a place where Sir Gilbert's steward should appoint, with free liberty to dig limestone for use on the said tenements, at a yearly rent of £36, rendering a couple of fat capons every New Year's Day, a heriot of the best beast, sending carts for loading culm or for leading hay or corn, together with a man and bags sufficient for carrying corn, upon notice, and to keep the premises in repair, at Stackpole Quay, where the limekiln was to be built". On 30 April 1696 he granted a lease for 21 years to "Thomas William Rhydderch of Llanfairarybryn, yeoman, of Tir Gwern y Pwll in the grange of Nant Bai at a yearly rent of £7, rendering a teal of best oats of Llandovery Old Measure, two fat capons at Christmas, keeping a beast from 1 November to 1 May, the carriage of a teal of lime to the house or lands of Ystradffin, to pay a heriot of the best beast, doing suit at the courts leet and baron of the grange, suit of mill within the grange, carrying stones and timber for mill repair, paying a moiety of rates and assessments imposed by Act of Parliament, and the whole of other rates, keeping the premises in repair and not committing waste".

Sir Gilbert Lort never married. He died in his 28th year on 19 September 1698 and was buried on 27 September in Westminster Abbey, where a monument to his memory was erected by his sister, Lady Campbell. His will, dated 9 August 1698, was proved in P.C.C. on the 3 December following. He bequeathed all the Pembrokeshire and Carmarthenshire estates to the heirs male of his body, and in default to his stewards Richard Price and Richard Russell, gentlemen, upon trust, to the use "of my dear and honoured kinsman" John Duke of Newcastle, and "my friends," Thomas Owen of Gray's Inn and Edward Harley of the Middle Temple, esquires, for 99 years, to be held to the use of "my dear sister, Elizabeth Campbell, widow of Sir Alexander Campbell of Calder in the Kingdom of Scotland, Knight, and after her death, to the use of her son Gilbert Campbell and his heirs in tail, and in default to the daughters of his said sister in tail, and in default to testator's own right heirs for ever". To his "dear and loving mother," he bequeathed £600 for life, in augmentation of her jointure. He empowered the trustees to raise £3,000 for his niece, Susanna Campbell when 21 or on marriage. To "my aunt Anne Whiteing, my father's sister", he gave £10 yearly for life; to his servant John Shaw, his coachman Loveing Edwards, Edward Greene, his mother's gardener at Turnham Green, £10 each; to Mrs. Katherine Williams, £10, and a similar sum per annum for life; to Elizabeth. wife of Francis Bernard, £10; to the poor of Stackpole, £10, and the poor of Chiswick, Middlesex, £50; to his trustees the Duke of Newcastle and Thomas Owen, £100 each and to Edward Harley £80. He left his personalty (except arrears of rent), to his mother whom he appointed sole executrix.

The Heiress of Stackpole Court

Elizabeth, only sister and heiress of Sir Gilbert, succeeded to the family estates. Born in 1665, she married on 13 November 1689 a Scot, Sir Alexander Campbell of Cawdor Castle, M.P. for Nairnshire, son of Sir Hugh Campbell. Sir Alexander died on 27 August 1697 in his father's lifetime. Elizabeth died on 28 September 1714, aged 49, and was buried in Westminster Abbey. They had four surviving children:

1. Gilbert Campbell who died unmarried on 4 March 1710.
2. John Campbell, born in 1695 to whom the Lort inheritance came in 1714. He married and had issue:
3. Anne born about 1692, came of age in 1713, married Edmund Morris of Loddington, Leicestershire, esquire, and had issue:
4. Susanna, married in 1717, as his second wife, Sir James Campbell of Auchinbreck, fifth Baronet, and had three sons.

And so, after some one-hundred-and-twenty-years the family of Lort became extinct in the main male line. Its founder arrived in Pembrokeshire, a complete stranger "out of nowhere", and within twenty years had become a prosperous

The end of the line . . .

landowner, a manorial lord, whose sons and daughters by intermarriage with the older native gentry, consolidated the success so rapidly achieved by the father. The family flashed like a meteor through Pembrokeshire skies and its brilliance was as vivid in the reign of Dutch William as it had been in that of Good Queen Bess. No decadence or failure attended its setting and the last of the male line at Stackpole left intact an extensive and valuable inheritance, which descendants of his sister were to augment in the following centuries.

For a further hundred years the name of this talented stock was carried on by a cadet branch and although its history is not as spectacular as that of the parent line, it produced men whose careers were sufficiently important for inclusion in the *Dictionary of National Biography*. With the death of John Lort of Pricaston in 1800, the name ceased to adorn the chronicles of Pembrokeshire, but numerous descendants through female connections continue to occupy responsible positions in the county and elsewhere within the realm.

FOOTNOTES

[1] According to Dr. B. G. Charles, *Non-Celtic Place-Names in Wales,* p. 26, the name is probably derived from a Scandinavian form, meaning "the pool near the stack". The name is spelt in various ways until about 1700 when it took the final form, Stackpole, and for uniformity's sake, I shall use that spelling throughout this essay except when quoting from original documents.

[2] Elidor and Bosher are names of earlier owners. See Charles, *op.cit.,* pp. 4, 26.

[3] For a brief account of the "Lords of Stackpole" see *Old Pembroke Families* by Henry Owen, pp. 25-34.

[4] *Owen's Pembrokeshire,* Part II, pp. 400, 522.

[5] I have been unable to discover anything of Mather's origins, and the name does not occur in Visitation pedigrees.

[6] The "new style" of dating has been adopted throughout this essay.

[7] The Archivist of the City of Bristol, who very kindly assisted me, confirms the existence of Lorts in Bristol in later times, but this information throws no light on their origin and early development.

[8] Through his mother, Elizabeth Herbert, George Owen was second cousin to William Herbert the grantor.

[9] Dorothy, daughter of Walter Devereux, Earl of Essex, married Sir Thomas Perrott in July 1583. Sir Thomas died in February 1594, and later that year she married Henry (Percy) ninth Earl of Northumberland. She died on 3 August 1619.

[10] Dwnn calls her Anne daughter of . . . Chaberlyn.

[11] A note by Sir Thomas Phillipps of Middle Hill, states that on 10 February 1601, Roger Lort conveyed the manor of Christon, Somerset, to Matthew Haviland and his heirs.

[12] Related to Margery Eddow, George Lort's first wife. On 12 September 1610 Roger Lort appointed Robert to be his attorney to take seisin of lands in Castlemartin, and in 1616-26 he was seneschal of the manor of Castlemartin. Sampson had other kinsfolk in Bristol. Two of his uncles, Nicholas and Robert Lort, each had a son named John, one of whom was a mercer in Bristol.

[13] N.L.W. MS. 1362B

[14] B.M. Add Charter, 25745

[15] Contained in a MS of George Owen, York Herald, now in possession of Sir Anthony Wagner, K.C.V.O., Garter King of Arms, who kindly gave me a view of it.

[16] An echo of these troubles still linger in local memory. A cavern on the coast near Stackpole Quay, called "Lort's Cave", is said to have been Roger Lort's refuge on some occasion when pressed by his enemies.

[17] Sir John died before paying off the mortgage. An endorsement on the deed states that on 15 December 1692 "Sir Gilbert Lort, Baronet (Sir John's son and heir) agreed with George Lort (John Lort's son and heir) re the debt and interest".

CHAPTER XII

SOME PEMBROKESHIRE SPORTS AND SPORTSMEN

FRANCIS JONES wrote a feature article "Sports and Sportsmen of Bygone Pembrokeshire". These include of course, blood sports. I take the line that those who fear and would muffle the past are destined to fear for the future. So here are a few extracts recording "devil may care folk" from lustier days and it starts with hunting with hounds.

The first record of sport in the county is found in the "Mabinogian". It describes how Pwyll, Prince of Dyfed, set out from his palace at Narberth to hunt in Glyn Cuch, a sequestered valley in north Pembrokeshire . . . In a letter written on 17 December 1663, Hugh Laugharne of Leweston (now Eweston), in Brawdy sends a greyhound called "Wingfield" to one of his friends. "Wingfield is a 'Black dogge' with a white tipp on his tayle and a strip of white around his necke. I assure you he is of a very good kinde for either hare of foxe . . . "

❋   ❋   ❋

December 6. Cryer for crying [for] some lost hounds . . . one shilling.
April 1817. From Hunt records "Hester Williams at the recommendation of Governor Scourfield, for the loss of a cow sustained by her in consequence of her gate having been left open by the gentlemen of the hunt . . . £1".

❋   ❋   ❋

George Lort-Philipps was a Nimrod of the old school . . . as game a man as ever crossed the pigskin [saddle] and is still remembered for his great feats. Owing to a childhood accident he only had one leg and rode with a cork one. A very hard man to hounds, the Squire of Lawrenny died in 1866, his death having been directly caused by a fall in the hunting field in the previous spring.

❋   ❋   ❋

Polecat hunting gave Captain John Owen Edwardes of Sealyham much sport. He used to catch them in large numbers and all dog polecats he turned off at midnight and hunted them the following morning. One which he turned off at Letterston common ran as far as Pentypark and was marked under the garden wall, fully 8 miles and as straight as the crow flies. Another he turned off on a Saturday night forgetting all about the fact that Sunday was the following day. The pack ran him to Beulah and marked under a chapel wall. The congregation was either at its prayers or singing when twelve couple hounds appeared, notes that could be heard miles away.

Mr. Edwardes was a popular figure with all ranks as every true sportsman is. He once commanded a company of the Pembrokeshire Militia which were called out to suppress a lawless set known as the Rebecca Rioters about 1840. While helping to suppress them he found that it seriously interfered with his sport, thereupon he asked the leader of the rioters for a truce so that he could get in a day's hunting. To this, the rebel who must have been something of a sportsman himself, agreed. It was the Edwardes family that produced that excellent terrier, the Sealyham, named after its birth place.

❊   ❊   ❊

The hunt known to us as the Pembrokeshire hunt had quite an early origin. It is said that it was in existence in the late eighteenth century, and the tombstone of Joseph Williams in Freystrop graveyard records the death of one of its members. It reads:

> *"In memory of Joseph Williams,*
> *A brave and honest huntsman,*
> *Who died suddenly at Pill earth*
> *After a terrible fox chase.*
> *Oct. 26th.1786.*
> *Aged 32 years"*

❊   ❊   ❊

The Revd. Robert Ferrior was undoubtedly the greatest fox hunter that the cloth produced in Pembrokeshire. He held the living of Walton West from 1808 to 1849 and was a kindly and popular figure. He was known to all as Bob Ferrior and many tales are told of his original and eccentric ways. On one occasion when marrying a couple at Walton church, he paused in the middle of the ceremony, and looking steadily at the bride said "Art thou the daughter of Mrs. Pawlett of Natt's Hook?" "Aye Sir" said the startled bride. "Well," says Bob Ferrior "If thou'st make as good a wife as thy mother, thou'll make a good 'un".

He suddenly turned to his clerk and said "Where did we leave off Joe?" "I don't know sir" said Joe. Whereupon the Rector said: "Tut, tut. Never mind, let's begin again."

❊   ❊   ❊

Many of the squires held annual horse races and sports for their tenants and nearby farmers, one such detailed was a race by 15 stout fellows buried chin deep in sacks. The sports were succeeded by a sumptious dinner, when a turtle said to weigh about four hundredweight and the largest ever seen in Wales, graced the festive board.

Chasing the fox

The Newgale Races were formerly great events. I do not know when they started but they were held in the 1790's, and attracted people from all over the county. Good form was shown on 11 July 1804, when races were run for a silver cup, a saddle and an elegant bridle and whip. They were followed by rural sportsmen running in sacks, grinning through a gridiron for tobacco, and women running in gowns and ribbands. There was an annual Fair and Races at Waterstone in September. In 1825 the races started at midday, with six horses competing for a handicap prize of 20 lambs. The race was won by Counsellor, a four-year-old owned by Mr. Curre, agent of the Slebech estate. Three races were run in a field owned by Mr. Lewis Child of Newton House.

※   ※   ※

July 25 1808. Today in 1808. Newgale Races
"A large concourse of the nobility and gentry of the county were gathered on Newgale sands – Seven horses started for the Cup, which was won by Captain Spire's brown horse 'Jassy'."

   "The sports being concluded the gentlemen retired to partake of a sumptuous dinner at Sinnett's Hotel and the ladies hastened to the Marine Villa on the Hill to whom a general invitation had been given by its amiable inhabitant, Miss Stokes. Soon after dinner, the gentlemen joined the ladies at the Villa, when dancing commenced on the lawn to the music of a Pan Daean band stationed in the conservatory. Three military bands played martial music. Ices and the choicest fruits were later served to the company."

(From the *London Evening Star*)

※   ※   ※

A Bad Sport
18 May 1811. Considerable merriment has been excited in Pembrokeshire by the following recent occurrence. A smart young lass of sixty-five having been addressed by a gallant and gay Lothario of fourscore years in an unguarded moment unfortunately yielded to his pressing importunities, and became pregnant, nor is this her only misfortune, for the faithless man now refuses to marry her. Although the lady, in order to rivet his attentions, submitted to having the only two teeth remaining in her mouth drawn, they being too prominent and tending to disfigure her. She has, our informant adds, made the necessary deposition of her situation before a Magistrate in the neighbourhood.

※   ※   ※

Some freak races produced much mirth. In April 1835 an immense crowd from St. Davids, Solva, Trefin and Fishguard gathered to see a match made by George Williams of Ffynonne and John Morgan of Barry Island, two gentlemen of property in Dewsland. Williams (weight 11 stone), backed himself to run against Morgans (weight 22 stone, height 6 ft. 2 in.), carrying David Reynolds of Treglemes (weight 13 stone) on his back. Williams to go 100 yards and Morgan 50 yards. The wager was a quantity of cognac. For 30 yards the betting was 3 to 1 against small weight, but Morgan then fell and Williams dashed forward and won the match. Sometimes a man would be matched against horse flesh. In May 1801, a match was run between Lieut. Moore R.N. riding his celebrated mule Muley

Bey (got by Lord Milford's Spanish ass out of a blood mare) carrying l6 stone and Capt. John Stokes of the Huntington Militia on foot, over the turnpike road from Milford to Haverfordwest. The day was very wet and after a severe contest was won by the gallant Captain. The betting was 5 to 3 in favour of Lieut. Moore at the start; at the end of the first mile even betting and at the end of the third 6 to 4 in favour of Capt. Stokes. He was the son of Hugh Stokes Esq., of Hubberstone and he died in 1826 at the early age of 26 years. The defeated mule was sold in July 1805 to Dr. Britten of Birch Grove for the high price of 160 guineas.

※　　　　　※　　　　　※

Letter from F.J. published in The Times *in 1963*

Sir, When I was a small boy there lived in the Hundred of Dewsland in Pembrokeshire, an old man called *John y Wadden Wen* that is to say, John of The White Mole. He was a mole catcher by trade and a large percentage of the local male population sported waistcoats which testified to John's success in the chosen fields of his endeavour. On one occasion he trapped a perfectly white mole, never seen in these parts, before or since; and the song and dance he made about it gave rise to the sobriquet. I never learned his surname, but his sobriquet preserves the memory of a natural history curiosity of which we have no other record in Dewsland.

※　　　　　※　　　　　※

Mr. William Williams of Ivy Tower was a man of decided views. Writing in *The Cambrian,* 6 November 1817, the following: "Many self-made 'Esquires' of no Manors, or manners, without birth, station, service, or sufficient landed estate, have taken out certificates to kill game; ignorantly dreaming such a step a full power; for instance a Haberdasher of his own paper coinage, adorned wrongly with the arms of Philipps of Kilsant; and his honest clerk, who has since absconded much in debt – and I, William Williams of Ivy Tower, having some years past bought the manorial Rents and Rights of the said Lordship of St. Florence, as well as owning the principal estate therein, am so bereft of game there, that no inducement is left for me to appoint a Gamekeeper, however eligible. I therefore hereby publicly warn all Persons, not to ensnare, shoot, kill, Or hunt, – or pursue Game in my Manor afore-said, as they shall be prosecuted for and according to the circumstances of each trespass respectively."

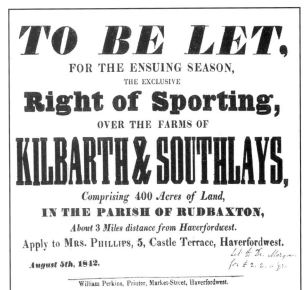

TO BE LET,
FOR THE ENSUING SEASON,
THE EXCLUSIVE
Right of Sporting,
OVER THE FARMS OF
KILBARTH & SOUTHLAYS,
Comprising 400 Acres of Land,
IN THE PARISH OF RUDBAXTON,
About 3 Miles distance from Haverfordwest.
Apply to MRS. PHILLIPS, 5, Castle Terrace, Haverfordwest.
August 5th, 1842.

William Perkins, Printer, Market-Street, Haverfordwest.

Sporting rights

F.J. writes: Wrestling, bare knuckle fighting, quoits and jumping were also favourable pastimes. During my youth I well remember some good jumping on the green at Llandeloy, but this is now a thing of the past. The internal combustion engine, wireless and modern banalities like the cinema are ousting the good old tough sports of our fathers. In his younger days my maternal grandfather, E. Francis of Clawddcam, was a first rate wrestler and I don't think he was ever downed. A short broadly built farmer, he threw my father's kinsman, Essex Harris, a giant over six feet tall and powerfully built, tossing him aside with great ease and broke his leg for him. Alas, those virile days are gone.

☀   ☀   ☀

Excerpts from Old Pembrokeshire Sports and Sportsmen

Sports in Pembs. At a meeting of the Common Council, Haverfordwest on 15 July 1734, "the resolution was passed forthwith with their Freedom as Burgesses of the Town.

Sir Edward Mansell Bt, Richard Gwyn, Richard Le Hunt, John Summers, Morgan Lloyd, Thos. Laugharne, Geo. Noble, John Powel, James Phillips, Esquires, and others gentlemen of the County of Pembroke who had entered into a Society for making annually in this town and have for eight years past contributed for a purse of 30 guineas to be run for on our Common of Portfield, which has brought vast numbers of people to the town, and great sums of money to the benefit and advantage of the people generally".

☀   ☀   ☀

The old gentry of Pembrokeshire were well-known for their heavy drinking after dinner. The following was told about one of the Lort-Phillips family. A number of the gentry were dining at a well known country house and by the small hours many bottles of good wine had been drunk. Certain gentlemen were peacefully reclining "lost to the world". Among those "out" was a squire of huge stature and who possessed a nose of good proportions. When they decided to part, all efforts were made to arouse the sleeping squire. He would wake up for a moment and then relapse almost immediately. Then Mr. Lort-Phillips said: "I know of a way to wake him up, but be prepared to run. Give me the tongs." He then put the tongs in the fire until they were fairly hot. Drawing the tongs from the fire he clamped the hot extremities around the prominent proboscis of the sleeping giant. The recipe was, I am told, most effective.

☀   ☀   ☀

Cegin Ffwlbert – The Polecat's Kitchen. This is a sequestered spot below Brawdy farm at the junction of the dingles from Rhyd-y-gele and Bont-fach. Possibly so called as it was the assembly place of sportive polecats.

COCKFIGHTING

COCKFIGHTING was one of the amusements of Carew people. The Cock Pit was in Well Hay, the chief promoter of the competitions at this time (1820's), was William Francis of the Parsonage. Cock fights were held in Spring, each side produced four or six cocks and the method was "fight the winner".

❋ ❋ ❋

William Francis was the inventor of the patent pill that still bears his name, and whose healing virtues still have a commercial value in the district. His tomb is due east of the church and the legend reads:

"In memory of William Francis Esq.,
of Carew Parsonage,
who departed this life
Aug. 7th 1827.
Aged 71 years.
There low he lies in lasting rest,
perhaps upon his mouldering breast,
Some spiteful (game) fowl builds her nest
To hatch and breed,
Alas nae maer he'll them molest."

From Spurrell's *History of Carew.*

❋ ❋ ❋

F.J. wrote *The History of Cock Fighting in Wales.* So far as is known it is the definitive work on the subject. Here are some extracts from the unpublished MSS., being written when the author was in the army.

"Sports of the field have always held an honourable place in the life of the people of Wales, but perhaps none ever commanded the affection of all classes so much as cock fighting – claimed to be the oldest sport in the world. It was organised better in these islands then in any other country in the world and the Welsh people showed that as breeders of fighting fowl they had little to learn from other nations. It was a man of Welsh extraction, Henry VII who founded the Royal cockpit, though the Monarchs were patrons of the sport long before the Tudor period. Welsh princes often made gifts of fighting cocks to English Kings, fitting presents from one warlike nation to another.

❋ ❋ ❋

The fighting cock is born to fight and he will show battle on the yard or field without the slightest encouragement from a human being.

John Evans commented in his *Tour through Wales*, "It is termed the Welsh Main and it doubtless arose from that determined and irresponsible spirit with which the Welsh enter into every kind of contest".

❊   ❊   ❊

The cockpit was usually a circular pit some twelve inches deep and varying greatly in diameter. The bottom was covered with turf called the "sod" or sometimes with matting. They were usually in the open, in fields, woods or lawns of private houses. There are also several pits in old Welsh churchyards which were convenient since many mains were fought on Sundays. Sometimes special buildings were erected called the Cock House.

❊   ❊   ❊

The big mains were usually fought for money e.g. for five guineas a battle and 100 gns. However, there were other prizes such as, silver bowls, tankards, cups and spoons. Also livestock such as horses, cattle, sheep and pigs; food such as meat, potatoes and furniture, beds, chairs and other household goods. Many mains were organised for charitable purposes, the money being given to poor families.

Entrance money was paid by spectators and all who entered birds had to be subscribers. The betting system was intricate and required a practised head to understand it. All bets had to be settled before leaving the pit.

❊   ❊   ❊

. . . the spurs varied in length, but were generally from 1¼ in. to 3 in. in this country. They were made of all sorts of metals; silver, steel, iron, copper and bronze. The making of silver spurs is a lost art and actually it was an alloy of silver that was used.

❊   ❊   ❊

The parish of Waldwyns Castle was a famous cocking centre and here the birds of South Roose contended for the honours. On Whit Monday 1836, arrests were made at Waldwyns Castle cock match, when the Master of the match the owner of the premises and the two "setters to" were hauled before William Cozens, J.P. of Sandyhaven. The complainants were the vicar and the overseer of the parish. The sportsmen were let off on promising never to fight cocks again.

❊   ❊   ❊

Pembrokeshire has always been famous for its breed of black cattle, but no less famous was its strain of black fighting cocks. They were known as the "Pembroke Hennies", because in plumage and build there was a marked resemblance between the male and the female of the species. They were black in colour and their fighting weight varied from 3 lbs. 6 oz. to 4 lbs. 10 ozs. and they were devastating performers in the pit. It was a savage and rapid fighter and contrary to popular belief could maintain combat over an extended period. The cockers of Pembrokeshire beat every county in Wales with their black devils as they were called and soon found it impossible to get opponents. Indeed, some English cockers refused to fight the Welsh unless they withdrew the black hennies from the pit. Whereupon the gentlemen of Pembrokeshire issued a challenge to the gentlemen of all England to fight over a period of five years for a considerable amount of money. There were no takers as far as is known.

Fighting-cocks were given names by their owners, e.g. Nelson, Brave Rodney, I'll show you How, Tommy's gone for the Groceries, Bessy Wants Him, Back Again, and Lasses be Honest. Some birds were named after famous racehorses of the day.

❋   ❋   ❋

There is an old ivy clad building immediately opposite Lambston Hall, now in a very ruinous condition called the cockpit. The Bowens of Camrose, a neighbouring seat, were great sportsmen and notable cockers. At Camrose there is still a very fine china bowl with a silver border that carries the Bowen crest of a lion rampant. This was a trophy won by the Bowen fighting cocks.

❋   ❋   ❋

Mr. James Tracey who had a shop at what is now 38 Main Street, Pembroke, used to prepare birds for battle. A sign over his shop read, "James Tracey, watchmaker and Taxidermist. Spurs made and fixed for Game Cock Fighting".

❋   ❋   ❋

Cocking was also well patronised in South Pembrokeshire. Major Loftus Adams of Holyland, the head of one of the oldest county families posseses a silver spoon with a game cock engraved on the flat handle which was won by a victorious Adams bird. Not far from Holyland is Bush, the seat of the ancient family of Meyrick. They were intrepid horsemen, foxhunters and racing men and also distinguished cockers. In the woods east of the house the remains of a large cockpit is still to be seen.

❋   ❋   ❋

Some cockfights were standing fixtures between parishes, towns, counties and families. In some instances, the dates were also fixed by custom, such as Easter Monday, Shrove Tuesday and race days. The feast days of the patron saints of the parishes were popular dates for the events.

❋   ❋   ❋

F.J. writes: My grandfather, John Jones of Grinstone, in Brawdy parish once kept some of the Pembrokeshire breed of fighting "hennies" which have now unfortunately nearly died out. He had a noted black "hennie" which, fighting with natural spurs, had never been beaten. This cock lived to a grand old age and seemed to get more savage as time went on. My Uncle William brought home a very fine young Indian game cock which was believed would soon rout the old warrior. The Indian however, proved to be a runner and on every occasion fled from the Grinstone cock. The sequel is interesting since it serves to show that the "runner" really possessed plenty of bottom. As the young 'un grew in strength and his spurs developed it showed signs of combativeness and one day got out and challenged the old black "hennie". The fight was long and furious and finally the old cock was struck in the brain and died, while the Indian gamecock stood over his prostrate form exulting and the air rang with his victorious crowing. But the old warrior died absolutely game.

Cocking was a great sport in schools as early as the time of Henry II and persisted until about 1800. The mains were usually staged in the schoolroom and the Main-master acted as controller of the sport. Every boy paid a fee called cock-pence and the money that Dicky Bulkeley had from his father for this purpose varied from 2d. to 4d. The winner of the school main was given the name "Victor" and had many privileges such as: the Victor could not be flogged for any misdemeanour during Lent; and he could save, if he pleased, any other boy from punishment merely by clapping his hat on the culprit's posterior to save him from the lash.

An interesting aspect of Welsh cocking was the superstition that attended it in certain districts where it was the custom to "charm" cocks before setting them. It is said that the most successful cockers fought the birds that resembled the "colour" of the day when the fights took place. If the day was cloudy, a blue cock was fought. If the sky was dark and lowering then a black, and on sunny days a black, red or golden duckwing was pitted. The charm was usually a verse from the Bible, written on a small piece of paper wrapped round the bird's leg, underneath the steel spurs. The verse was: "Taking the shield of faith, wherewith ye shall be able to quench all the fiery darts of the wicked.. . ." Another feature was the placing of freshly woven twigs of rowan beneath the sod of the pit, which was said to counteract the charms of conjurors. These pliant twigs were sometimes twisted into small rings. But the most potent of all charms used was a crumb taken from the Communion table of the parish church. The owner of the bird had to go into the church at midnight, search the table for the crumb. The crumb was then placed in the socket of the steel spur which was fixed on the cock's leg.

❊   ❊   ❊

Welsh cockers rose to the top of their profession. Howell Morgan was Cocker Royal to King George I and to the King of Denmark. He wrote a treatise called *The Cocker*. Good sport was always shown in the Principality, and John Harris wrote: "I have seen many mains in Wales, and very few plain cocks, a bad one never."

And here we bid adieu to the game cocks and cockers of old time Wales.

CHAPTER XIII

HERBERT VAUGHAN

THE MAN I KNEW

WHEN the *The South Wales Squires* appeared in 1926, I enjoyed the contents so much that I wrote an appreciation to a Pembrokeshire newspaper. Afterwards I received a pleasant letter from the author who modestly wrote that he felt I had over-praised the work, gently chiding me for the use of flowery adjectives. This marked the beginning of a friendship which I enjoyed until H. M. Vaughan's death shortly after the Second World War.

Herbert Millingchamp Vaughan, born in 1870, was the eldest son of John Vaughan, squire of Plas Llangoedmor near Cardigan. He went to school at Clifton and graduated at Keble College, Oxford, where he gained an M.A. When young he was elected Fellow of the Society of Antiquaries of London and devoted his life to historical research, local and national. For a few years in the 1890's he held a Territorial army commission in the Royal Monmouthshire Engineers Militia. In the first decade of this century he was appointed Justice of the Peace and thereafter was a familiar figure on the Bench in south-west Wales. In 1916 he served the office of High Sheriff of Cardiganshire. He was a member of the Cambrian Archaeological Association and of the Honourable Society of Cymmrodorion, to whose journals he contributed useful, instructive essays. His interests were wide-ranging. He lived for several years in Florence, where he studied and advised on the architecture of that city and of other parts of Italy. He was especially interested in the Stuart monarchs and in the Jacobite movement that characterised the sunset years of that Royal House in Great Britain.

Between 1906 and 1933 fourteen of Herbert Vaughan's books were published, the range of which indicate the catholicity of his interests. Towards the close of his life he wrote a fascinating autobiographical work, so far unpublished, and deposited in the National Library of Wales at Aberystwyth.

After the First Word War, H. M. Vaughan sold the Plas Llangoedmor estate and settled for the remainder of his life at 32 Victoria Street, Tenby. I was a schoolmaster in that town from 1930, which enabled me to spend much of my leisure in his amiable company which stimulated my studies on Welsh heraldry and genealogy. One of the main features of his home was the library containing historical and literary books, many concerning Wales. He gave me a free run of this splendid room, and it was there that I was introduced to Lewys Dwnn's volumes on Welsh heraldry and genealogy, constant companions of my later researches.

H. M. Vaughan was a tall, lean, impressive figure, usually clad in a long, enveloping overcoat and a generous scarf around the neck and shoulders. He was an extremely fast walker, but unfortunately his outdoor activities were curtailed by an internal disability, described in his autobiography. A delightful conversationalist, full of reminiscences of which his listeners seldom wearied, he wrote in the same style as he spoke – courteous, eloquent, often humorous, as exemplified in the pages of *The South Wales Squires*. A keen churchgoer, he was well-known as a lay reader throughout the Diocese of St. Davids. He served many years on committees of the National Library of Wales and National Museum at Cardiff, and he was an effective lecturer on a variety of subjects.

H. M. Vaughan certainly contributed much to his times and he assisted and inspired antiquarian and literary friends. He had been a landmark of my early days, and whatever I may be judged to have achieved in subsequent years will owe much to his invigorating and humane personality, particularly his readiness to help and guide.

During the last war he corresponded with me. His letters came to barracks in England, to battlefields in North Africa and Italy, and what a pleasure it was to receive these missives which strengthened the resolve and allayed the anxieties of the reader. The last time I saw him was shortly after the war in 1948, when, accompanied by Col. L. H. Higgon, Lord Lieutenant of Pembrokeshire, we called at his Tenby home. Although quite ill, clearly a tired man, he still conversed blithely and produced some of the sunshine of earlier days. A few weeks after our visit, Herbert Vaughan passed away peacefully.

I have spoken of events of long, long, ago. It is pleasant to return to the World of Yesterday, to meet again Herbert Vaughan and to relive those agreeable hours in his enduring company. "*Memoria est thesaurus omnium verum e custos.*"   *October 1987*

EXTRACTS FROM A TOUR THROUGH MONMOUTHSHIRE AND WALES IN JUNE AND JULY 1774

by H. P. Wyndham, second Ed.

At Haverfordwest, p. 65

Poultry and fish "were astonishingly cheap, and the very common cheese of the country sold from two-pence to three-pence a pound. This last article, indeed, was of so wretched a nature, that few Englishmen would venture to put a second morsel into their mouths. It is made from the combined milk of goats, sheep, mares and cows, and if any cheese should remain from the last year's stock, which is often the case, it is then chopped into minute pieces, and remixed with the new. It may easily be conceived that the cheese, by this means contracts such a hardness, as to be almost proof against the edge of a knife, and such a rankness, that train oil is sweet in the comparison".

At Haverfordwest, p. 67

"The women, even in the midst of summer, generally wear a heavy cloth gown, with a hood hanging from it behind; and instead of a cap, a large handkerchief wrapt over their heads is tied under their chins. They have sometimes, tho' rarely, a small beaver hat with a very low crown. On first seeing this fantastic head-dress I really imagined that there had been an epidemical swelling or toothache in the province!" The author thinks the custom may have come from the Flemings. The dress is peculiar to Pembrokeshire, for in other Welsh counties the women as well as men wear large beaver hats with deep crowns: some of the gentlewomen also wear these Welsh hats.

Fisgard, pp.79-80

"We found the accommodations so villainous at Fisgard, and Newport, that we prudently continued this day's stage, (tho' it was 39 miles) to Cardigan."

"As no wine was to be procured in the latter of these places, (Newport), we asked for some brandy to mix with our water; but the answer, here and in many other places on this coast, was, that they could get none, since the 'ruin of their trade with the Isle of Man' – meaning the smuggling frauds, which the later purchase of that island by the Government from the Athol family, has pretty effectually checked."

"Nefern church has no pavement in it, and the frequent burials, in the manner of St. Davids, have raised the ground within, seven or eight feet higher than it is without: In process of time instead of a church it will be only a sepulchre."

Page 81

Haverfordwest claims the merit of "having practised inoculation of the small pox, for time immemorial, before it was even known to the other countries of Britain: for where the London physicians, on the recommendation of a Turkish practise by Lady Mary Montague, were cautiously venturing the experiment on some condemned criminals, the more hardy native of Pembrokeshire dared to inoculate himself, without the assistance of either physician or preparation. Several letters in No. 375 of the Philosophical Transactions prove the truth of this fact, and these are dated so early as the year 1722".

※   ※   ※

Extract from a letter to F.J. 2 July 1935

"Dear Mr. Jones, I received your letter of June this evening. You will have my full sympathy in your effort to form a Historical Society for Pembrokeshire. Carmarthen has had a very vigorous one for years and Cardigan also has one, and we will not yield to either county in the richness of our antiquities. I am afraid that I cannot offer you much more than sympathy as I am 84-years-old and cannot hope that my strength of body and mind will last much longer." . . . David Salmon, Secretary, Historical Society of West Wales, Narberth.

CHAPTER XIV

JOTTINGS FROM
THE FRANCIS JONES ARCHIVES

HISTORICAL MISCELLENY

H.C.-J. writes:

MY FATHER was unable to imbue me with his passion for Welsh history. A rare failure for him, maybe a case of talent skipping a generation. That said, I humbly offer one contribution to his work. During our Windsor visits for the Knights of the Garter ceremony, we sometimes had a picnic at Runnymede. I quote from the great document signed there, The Magna Carta.

Clause 56. If we have deprived or dispossessed any Welshman of lands, liberties, or anything else in England or in Wales, without the lawful judgement of their equals, these are at once to be returned to them. A dispute on this point shall be determined in the Marches by the judgement of equals. English law shall apply to holdings of land in England, Welsh law to those in Wales, and the law of the Marches to those in the Marches. The Welsh shall treat us and ours in the same way.

Clause 57. In cases where a Welshman was deprived or dispossessed of anything, without the lawful judgement of his equals, by our father King Henry or our brother King Richard, and it remains in our hands or is held by others under our warranty, we shall have respite for the period commonly allowed to Crusaders, unless a lawsuit had begun, or an enquiry had been made at our order, before we took the Cross as a Crusader. But on our return from the Crusade, or if we abandon it, we will at once do full justice according to the laws of Wales, and the said regions.

Clause 58. We will at once return the sons of Llewelyn, all hostages, and the charters delivered to us as a security for the peace.

It seems the Welsh nation, its laws, culture, including genealogy was well established as an equal. Interestingly the only Clause mentioning Scotland (No. 59) says the Scots as liable to judgement "In our (English) court".

※   ※   ※

In 1168, the English King employed an interpreter to help him deal with the Welsh. This man, Iorwerth Goch, was paid £91 a year for his services. A handsome salary in those days showing the importance of his work.

※   ※   ※

Culpepper in his Herbal, says, "this furious biting herb (the common buttercup), has as many names as would fill a Welshman's pedigree".

William the Conqueror visited St. Davids in 1081. The next royal visitor was King John who stayed in Fishguard in 1210.

※   ※   ※

Major Sir Hugh Jasper Thomas, Knighted 1922, D.L., J.P. Born 22 April 1877. Son of Jasper Thomas, J.P. who married in 1904 Charlotte Eveline, daughter of Boyly Mathews, issue two sons, two daughters. Partner of James Thomas and Son, Land Agents. Mayor of Haverfordwest, 1909-10, Alderman of Pembrokeshire County Council, Trustee for Haverfordwest charities, Governor of County Hospital, Member of Territorial Force Association, etc. In April 1920, he bought the whole town of Milford Haven, valued at £1,250,000. He died in December 1924.

※   ※   ※

Garn Fawr is the highest spot on Pencaer and was very probably used as a watch tower by the old Britons. They could see all the sea, and so command any ships and give notice of their approach. On a very clear day eighteen parish churches can be seen from here; yet the church of Llanwnda parish in which Garn Fawr is cannot be seen at all.

※   ※   ※

The Normans, who occupied most of Pembrokeshire, respected the church, and Dewsland was allowed to enjoy the blessings of an unbroken and halcyon peace. Not a single stone castle was raised within its bounds, no Norman war cries disturbed its tranquillity, and the only military activities it knew was when the bishop led his tenantry to join the Royal Standard, carrying the relics of St. David before the marching host.

※   ※   ※

We now come to Haverfordwest, the caput of a great medieval lordship, and since the Act of Union in 1536, the county town of Pembrokeshire. It stands on the banks of the Cleddau which is tidal at this point. Although Haverfordwest is many miles from the sea, it was one of the most important ports in West Wales. The mayor still holds the title of Admiral of the Port, now the sole remaining memorial of its erstwhile maritime activity.

※   ※   ※

In 1468 Sir John Dunn, his wife Elizabeth and their daughter had their portrait painted by the celebrated Flemish artist Hans Memling. Known as the Chatsworth Triptych it was handed over to the nation by the Duke of Devonshire, and is now in the National Gallery. It is the earliest-known portrait of a Welshman.

※   ※   ※

The Lure of the Samphire, 1775
An inquest found that Thomas David, yeoman, on 20 September went out to the cliffs about a mile from St. Davids in order to gather Samphire. He fell over the cliff into the sea and was drowned.

The lure of the Samphire

"Grant in tail by Richard Picton Esq., to Thomas Perrot of Stephen Perrot esquire and Alice his wife, daughter of the grantor, of all his messuage, lands, and rents in Bickton in Rhos, at the quarterly rent of two greyhounds (leporarios), Monday after the conversion of St. Paul." This was embossed with Henry V's seal of arms. (Three pikes of a seal). *F.J. adds a beautiful drawing of the seal taken from ancient deeds in the Public Record Office.*

One cannot write about West Wales without mentioning King Henry VII, the first of the Tudor dynasty. Born in Pembroke Castle in 1457, he spent much of his youth as an exile in France. On 7 August 1485 he landed with an army at Dale in Milford Haven, and marched quickly to Haverfordwest, thence over the Preseli hills to Cardigan, which he reached on the 9th. He reached Llanbadarn on the 10th, and thence pushed on to Machynlleth through mid Wales, and finally to victory at Bosworth.

※ ※ ※

Windows even of wealthy people were either open to the weather or glazed with horn or oiled paper. Glass when obtainable was an expensive luxury even for the rich. Thus houses were cold in winter, this may account for the small windows still seen in ancient cottages and also for the practise of dividing the door in half. The upper part of the door let in light, the lower half closed excluded animals.

※ ※ ※

1736. Dr. Richard Pocock wrote: "Tenby is famous for the largest oysters in the world they are almost 7" over."

※ ※ ※

At Tenby when the High Sheriff's son married the rector of Tenby's daughter in 1877, garlands of flowers were hung across the High Street bearing pleasant mottoes while flags and banners fluttered from housetops in all directions. Children strewed flowers before the bride as they left the church.

THEY HAD A NAME FOR IT

Early Welsh life was tribal, and a pronounced emphasis was placed on the family. A freemen had to prove his ancestry to the ninth generation in order to hold land and participate in the councils of the state. Thus a Welshman's name was his title deed to property and his identity card in the courts. The law demanded that he should produce nine names, his own plus eight ancestors. Altogether he bore some nine names connected together by the little word *ap* or *ab*. This was essential in bygone days and useful in later days to the genealogist, but it proved an absolute nightmare to English lawyers and administrators. Apart from the spelling of the names and their number, the lack of a permanent label was apt to cause confusion. With the coming of the Tudors, Welshmen began to discontinue the traditional method and adopt permanent names. Added to this Rowland Lee, the great President of the Council of the Marches (died 1542) was no lover of things Welsh and he suppressed the Welsh mode of nomenclature whenever he could. The Act of Union of 1542 in abolishing gavelkind and making primogeniture the normal procedure rendered the long string of names unnecessary, and the natives (particularly the richer sort) adopted the English method. By the end of Elizabeth's reign (1603) most Welshmen used permanent surnames for legal purposes. However, the genealogical surnames did not entirely disappear. For instance, the old way persisted in remote parts of Cardiganshire down to 1800 and in North Wales to an even later date. Newly adopted names were taken from the bible, for example Samuel ap Griffiths ap Ieuan ap Cadifor who did not have a drop of Jewish blood in his veins would have descendants surnamed Samuel. A good example of this is the Pembrokeshire family who told me that their ancestor was Melchior, one of the wise men from the East.

A Welshman was not considered a gentleman of good blood, unless he could give the names of nine ancestors – father and son – in a direct line. The phrase *bonheddwr o'r nawfed ach* (a gentleman of the ninth generation) is still in current use in the Principality. This form of surname, while admittedly unwieldy, has proved a boon to Welsh genealogists. But on the other hand where a generation has been omitted by a scribe, the same has proved a dangerous pitfall. When speaking of a man, only two names were used, the son and father, e.g. in my own case, Francis ab James: while in some old deeds the whole list of names were given; the lawyers, in other instances merely gave the *two names,* omitting the *ab* or *ap.* Your true Welshman is clannish, as are all mountaineers, and conservative, and takes a deep pride in his ancestry and the humble farm labourer of the Welsh hills, can unhesitatingly take you back a century in his family tree – a thing which many modern plutocrats and even intelligent Englishmen are unable to do. The Welshman lives in the past; the Englishman in the future; that explains the difference in their character.

Until a comparatively recent date no surnaminal adjunct was used in Wales, beyond *ap* or son, as in David ap Howell, now very naturally corrupted into Powell. A more ancient form of *ap* is *hap.* This *hap* constantly occurs in charters of the time of Henry VI. It was unusual even a century ago to hear of such combination as Evan-ap-Griffith-ap-David-ap-Jenkin, and so on to the seventh or eighth generation, so that an individual carried his pedigree in his name. To burlesque this ridiculous species of nomenclature some seventeenth century wag described cheese as being "Adam's own cousin-german by its birth, Ap-Curds-ap-Milk-ap-Cow-ap-Grass-ap-Earth!"

※   ※   ※

The following anecdote was related to me by a native of Wales: An Englishman riding one dark night among the mountains, heard a cry of distress proceeding apparently from a man who had fallen into a ravine near the highway and on listening more attentively heard the words, "Help, master help" in a voice truly Cambrian. "Help! What, who are you?" inquired the traveller.

"Jenkin-ap-Griffith-ap-Robin-ap-William-ap-Rees-ap-Evan", was the response. "Lazy fellows that ye be" rejoined the Englishman, setting spurs to his horse, "to lie rolling in that hole, half a dozen of ye! Why in the name of common-sense don't ye help one another out?"

Even the gentry of Wales bore no hereditary surnames until the time of Henry VIII. That monarch who paid attention to heraldic matters strongly recommended the heads of Welsh families to conform to the usage long before adopted by the English as more consistent with their rank and dignity. Some families accordingly made their existing *sire*names statutory, while a few adopted the surnames of English families with whom they were allied as the ancestors of Oliver Cromwell, who thus exchanged Williams for Cromwell, which thenceforward they uniformly used.

※ ※ ※

In medieval times there was no legal obligation to sign deeds and documents. It was necessary to attach or seal the deed in the presence of witnesses whose names were entered by the scribe. Signiatum to deeds before 1500 were extremely rare. Recently I came across an ancient deed in London which bears the signature of a Pembrokian in addition to his seal. This I believe is the earliest-known signature of a Pembrokeshire man. The instrument is dated "Monday next after the feast of St. Laurence, 23rd Edward III, whereby John Harold, Lord of the town, and patron of the church of Haroldston appointed William Wasmeyre my bailiff" . . . 1422.

FAMILY MISCELLANY

In reply to an appeal to buy a book entitled *A Beginners Guide to Growing Old*, F.J., then in his late seventies, replied: "I do not want your book as I am a slow learner."

※ ※ ※

Up to scratch

"Fleas! Fleas! In the days of my Pembrokeshire childhood, almost every household was inflicted by the pernicious insects. They seemed to fasten particularly on people's necks, with the result that the small red circle showed where they had feasted was visible for a whole day before it disappeared. To counteract these attentions, people used to put a sprig of *hen ŵr* (Old Man's Beard) around the neck, or under the pillow, since it was anathema to fleas. Fleas are particular it seems, for there were some people whom they would never touch. I was one of those fortunate beings and although I shared beds with several fleas in my time (especially in North Africa during the war) I was never bitten. Whether this immunity was due to respect accorded me by these creatures or my own body smell, or even to some lethal quality in my blood, I do not know. My good fortune enabled me to listen with equanimity to the tales of sufferers and indeed, to derive a mild satisfaction from the consciousness of my superiority. In the land of fleas, he who secures immunity is King." *F.J.*

※ ※ ※

F.J. notes an occasion when a nurse reported to a doctor that a very sick patient was "Hanging on like grim death".

※ ※ ※

Shortly after my work had appeared on BBC's Pick of the Week for the fifth time in 18 months (a record which still stands), my father said: "Well, I suppose you are pretty expert at lucid elocution." I did not deny this at all. "Right Hugh, say Peggy Babcock very quickly." I nearly strangled my tonsils in a failed attempt . . . Dear reader, YOU try it. *H.C.-J.*

HINTS TO HISTORIANS . . . ?

and jottings from F.J's Notebooks

THE importance of personal contacts cannot be underestimated. The budding antiquary has to gain the friendship and support of informed people, usually much older than oneself, who can direct one to productive sources and often introduce one to their custodians – "well allied and friended" in Tudor parlance. Then, there is the recognition of the central subject and its cognate matters, a particularly important aspect – for one can often wander away from the main theme into by-roads that offer more seduction than instruction, although a few may enhance and decorate the central theme. It is wiser to stick to the M-road than swerve into a beguiling "slip-road". I can speak from experience; many years ago I was engaged on writing a study of Religion in Medieval Wales, but after writing a score or so pages, several reference to pilgrimages to holy wells gripped my fancy, with the result that I tore up what I had written and proceeded to write a book on The Holy Wells of Wales – a victory for the "slip-road".

※   ※   ※

History does not wholly reside in yellowing parchments and manuscripts; it lies all around us, in architecture, castle, country houses, cottages, church, bridges, early fortifications, field patterns, and so on. Thus it becomes necessary to develop powers of observation, and to cultivate awareness. Some are naturally endowed with this gift, others can acquire it. When I walk into Carmarthen I always endeavour to spot something new for it is easy to overlook objects when walking, perhaps wrapped in one's thoughts. I gaze at rooftops, eves, type and shape of chimneys, of windows, of surrounding rails, gates, courtyards, door-knockers and so on, for it is surprising what remains to be discovered even among familiar scenes. Always be ready to discover something new. The antiquary must loiter with intent. Occasionally we uncover the wholly unexpected. As Columbus might have reported back to Queen Isabella of Spain – "Well . . . er . . . er . . . we did not exactly find India, but there was this other promising piece of land!" He never realised he'd discovered a whole new continent, but the point is he did not go home empty-handed. Indeed we can make our entire life a voyage of discovery. Life is often a disorderly cruise, and sometimes we put into strange harbours. Cultivate curiosity – it was lack of curiosity that killed the cat. We must persevere and persist; the secret of success is to soldier on.

Another aspect of the antiquary's itinerary is to publish the results of his discoveries – in books, essays, lectures, broadcasts, even by after-dinner talks provided the port has not gone round too often. Antiquaries owe an obligation to the public which they can discharge by the printed word.

When composing, it is vital that the language should be absolutely clear, without ambiguity, or any possibility of an interpretation contrary to the writer's intention. Be on guard against slip-shod sentences or lack of clarity. On one occasion I attended a party where a joyous lady was recounting an amusing experience, and ended by saying: "I hadn't laughed so much since grandpa died." Only last week I had a letter from my grand-daughter who lives in Switzerland. The address written in the child's own hand gave my name, house, and town, followed by the words "South of Wales" – where is "South of Wales"? I had visions of desperately bobbing up and down in a coracle in mid-Bristol Channel mercilessly driven towards the devouring sands of Cefn Shidan. It is all too easy to stumble into ambiguity, as a recent notice posted up in a Government office shows – "Executives without a secretary may take advantage of the typists in the typing pool." On the other hand it is possible to express self-revealing truth with engaging tautology, such as the notice painted on a board over the entrance gate to the farmyard of Coch-y-barlys which I saw a few weeks ago – "Please close the gate. If the gate is not closed it will remain open."

❊   ❊   ❊

In 1939 I was mobilised with the Yeomanry; in due course I was overseas. Despite the carnage and vicissitudes of war, the magic carpet continued to bear me along. In North Africa I was able to see at first hand the remains of Classical antiquity, Roman amphitheatres, temples, baths and Arab remains of equal interest; during the few months I was stationed in Palestine I visited many hallowed sites with which I had been made familiar from my early Biblical reading. I entered the Holy Sepulchre in Golgotha, now canopied by a splendid church, where I received a Certificate of Pilgrimage from the hands of the Custodian, together with a piece of the rock taken from that hill of anguish, and a leaf from a tree in Gethsemane. Then, in the Italian campaign my few off-duty hours enabled me to savour the ruined splendours of Imperial Rome, the Appian Way and its wayside burial vaults and shrines, fabled Scylla and Charybodis and the mournful remains of Herculanium and Pompeii.

❊   ❊   ❊

I was befriended by the Lord Lieutenant, Sir Evan Davies Jones who lived at Fishguard, to whose residence he often invited me to browse in his library and to be regaled to a dish of tea. On one such occasion he gave me a truly wondrous present, the scarce 14 volumes of

West Wales Historical Records. I still recall the thrill of strapping them to the carrier of my bicycle and riding merrily homewards through the streets of Fishguard and along the flat road of the seaside Parrog. From the Parrog the road rose sharply towards Goodwick, so I pedalled hard to take the rise.

The next thing I experienced was the amazing sight of my front wheel suddenly appearing on high before my unbelieving eyes, like a steeple-chaser taking off at Beecher's Brook . . . such is the weight of historical learning when strapped to the back of a bike.

Letter of Elizabeth, Wife of William, First Earl of Northampton

Written c. 1618 when she was expecting him to become an Earl

"My Sweet Life,

"Now I have declared to you my mind for the settling of your State, I supposed, that that were best for me to bethink or consider with myself what allowance were metest for me. For considering what care I ever had of your estate, and how respectfully I dealt with those, which both by the Laws of Nature, and civil polity, Wit, Religion, Government, and Honesty, you my Dear, are bound to; I pray and beseech you to grant me, your most kind and loving Wife, the sum of £1600 per annum quarterly to be paid.

"Also I would (besides that allowance for my apparrel) have £600 added yearly (quarterly to be paid) for the performance of charitable Works, and those things I would not, neither will be countable for.

"Also I will have three Horses for my own Saddle, that none shall dare to lend or borrow; none lend but I; none borrow but you.

"Also I would have two Gentlewomen lest one should be sick or have some other Lett. Also believe, that it is an undecent thing for a Gentlewoman to stand mumping alone, when God hath blessed their Lord and Lady with a great estate.

"Also when I ride a hunting or a hawking, or travel from one House to another; I will have them attending. So for either of those said Women I must and will have for either of them a Horse.

"Also I will have six or eight Gentlemen: And I will have my two Coaches, one lined with Velvet to myself, with four very fair Horses; and a Coach for my Women, lined with swett Cloth; one laced with Gold; the other with Scarlet, and laced with watched Lace and Silver, with four good Horses.

"Also I will have two Coachmen, one for my own Coach, the other for my Women.

"Also at any time, when I travel, I will be allowed not only carroches and spare Horses for me and my Women; but I will have such carriages, as shall be fitting for all, orderly; not pestering my things with my Women's nor theirs with Chambermaids, nor theirs with Washmaids.

"Also, for Laundresses, when I travel, I will have them sent away before with the Carriages, to see all safe. And the Chambermaids I will have go before with the greens that the Chambers may be ready, sweet and clean.

"Also, for that it is undecent to croud up myself with my Gentleman Usher in my Coach, I will have him to have a Convenient Horse, to attend me either in City or Country. And I must have two footmen. And my desire is, that you defray all the Charges for me.

"And for myself (besides my yearly allowance), I would have twenty Gowns of apparrel; six of them excellent good ones, eight of them for the Country, and six other of them very excellent good ones.

"Also I would have to put in my purse £2000 and £200; and so you to pay my Debts.

"Also I would have £6000 to buy me Jewels, and £400 to buy me a pearle chain.

"Now seeing I have been and am so reasonable unto you, I pray you do find my Children apparrel, and their schooling, and all my Servants, Men and Women, their Wages.

"Also I will have all my Houses furnished, and all my Lodging Chambers to be suited with all such furniture, as is fit; as Beds, stools, chairs suitable; cushions, carpets, silver warming-pans, cupboards of plate, fair hangings, and such like. So for my Drawing Chamber in all Houses I will have them delicately furnished, both with hangings, couch, canopy, glass, carpet, chair, cushions, and all things thereunto belonging.

"Also my desire is, that you would pay your Debts, build up Ashby House, and purchase Lands; and lend no Money (as you love God) to the Lord Chamberlain, which would have all, perhaps your Life from you. Remember his son, my Lord Walden, what Entertainment he gave me, when you were at Tilt-yard. If you were dead, he said, he would be a Husband, a Father, a Brother, and said he would marry me. I protest I grieve to see the poor man have so little Wit and Honesty to use his Friend so vilely. Also he fed me with Untruths concerning the Charter House: but that is the least, he wish'd me much harm; you know him. God keep you and me from him, and any such as he is.

"So now that I have declared to you what I would have, and what that is that I would not have, I pray, when you be an Earl to allow me £1000 more than now desired, and double Attendance.

"Your loving Wife,

"Eliza Compton."

❊   ❊   ❊

More Notebook Jottings . . .

1920. Pitt was asked by his banker, a certain Mr. Smith for the privilege of driving through Horse Guards. "No", said Pitt, "but I can make you an Irish Peer", and the next day Mr. Smith became Lord Carrington.

❊   ❊   ❊

1920. Memo. "Start a Heraldic Magazine. Editor Francis Jones, Esquire."

❊   ❊   ❊

1924. Dear Sir,

I saw your advertisement and offer in John O'London Weekly, and I send you a short story for publication if deemed to be of standard merit. I also enclose a stamped envelope in lieu of its possible rejection.

Hoping I shall have the honour of communicating with you in the near future,

I remain, Sir,

Yours Truly

Francis St. Iwan.

CHAPTER XV

THE PATAGONIAN PAPERS

H. C.-J. writes

MY FIRST impression of my grandfather was that he was a lunatic. I was a toddler in the 1930's when I first saw him pick up a strange squat tea pot with a long spout. He stretched his arm out high, tilted his head back, and then expertly poured a long jet of tea into his mouth. He told me he had got into this habit when he rode with his gauchos in Patagonia. I once tried this brew. It was green and sour, and I spat it out. *Ych a fi!* Dada also showed me his silver spurs and his whip and told me how he loved throwing the *bola* to capture cattle and horses. He kept his old poncho cape on his bed and I asked him about it. He told me how he had so often slept under it beneath the stars, his saddle as a pillow and his loaded rifle for company. He gave me his treasured pistol belt which is displayed near my desk.

Dada was a short man, and as a result of the crippling injuries he had suffered in a riding accident in Patagonia (which had forced him to return to Wales), he walked with a limp. So he was never without a walking stick with an ivory carving of, I think, a dog's head. He appeared grave, as if he was pondering important matters. Yet when he smiled his clear bright blue eyes lit up his face. His white mustachio was always neatly clipped and he was invariably neatly dressed. My brother Dedwydd and I watched him shaving one morning. A ritual which always fascinates small boys. He was delicately slicing through shaving soap and his shirt was open. My brother spotted terrible scars on his chest. "How did you get those Dada?" he asked. With that dreamy expression that always came to him when he talked about Patagonia he told this story:

Riding the Pampas

He was the horse master on his uncle's ranch. He would break horses in, and when he had enough saddle trained horses he would lead them over the Andes and sell them to warring factions for their cavalry. He often did this trek on his own. (In fact lone travel seems a family trait. My father did it. I did it. I thought it was a cursed nuisance this swanning off alone when my children did it too. Only a few years ago I enquired about my daughter Lucy, who had gone walk-about in India. I was told she was now in Kabul). Back to my grandfather. One night he was asleep in his lonely camp when he was awakened by vicious snarling and neighing's as a puma attacked one of his horses. He rushed to his little makeshift corral, and was in turn attacked by the "mountain lion" as he described it. He was bowled over, and writhed and struggled with the animal. He managed to unsheathe his knife and stabbed it to death. He lost a lot of blood in the struggle and stumbled about disoriented in the high altitude and eventually passed out. He was nearly dead when some Indians found him and nursed him back to life. The kindly Indians cut off one of the puma's paws and later gave it to the lucky survivor. Come to think of it, without those long-dead kind natives neither father nor I would have never been born. Whether that is a good thing in my case, I leave for readers to decide. Anyway the paw came to my father, who kept it on his desk. It is now on mine.

In the Francis Jones Archives we discovered my grandfather's writings. One, a narrative in Welsh of his life as a Patagonia settler. Our very good friend Gwylon Phillips kindly translated it. We think it an interesting personal offering which illustrates part of an exotic period of Welsh history.

AN ACCOUNT OF LIFE IN PATAGONIA CIRCA 1880

by James Jones, (FJ's father)

Most of the inhabitants of Wales have become aware by one means or another of the existence of the Welsh Colony (*Y Wladfa*) in Patagonia.

When we consider that it is only a little over seventy years ago that the Welsh began settling in that country and that its population is only about ten thousand, it is hard to think of another settlement in any country that has attracted as much interest and contrasting opinions amongst our nation than Patagonia.

Much has been written and asked about *Y Wladfa* in recent years by both supporters and critics. Some elevate the country to the clouds whilst others like to tread its very name into the dust. When I hear these contrasting views, I find it difficult to know what to say of the country. It is dangerous both to say too much or too little. Some people emphasise

James Jones, fourth from left, back row

the glories whilst others stress the darker side of everything. It is my intention to steer a middle course to these two extremes. I will attempt to tell the truth without bias. I don't want to encourage anyone to venture there against his will and I don't want to prevent anyone from journeying there if that is his wish.

I thought that a short history of the country depicting the way of life of the Welsh people there would be of interest to you, inhabitants of this land of song. They have made it a sort of New Wales.

With a view to its location, Patagonia is situated in the southern extreme of the great continent of America. It is almost a thousand miles in length and three hundred miles in width. The country was discovered in the fifteenth century by the great explorer, Magellan, who took the country in the name of the King of Spain, though at that time Spain had no interest in this place. In previous centuries, Spain colonised most of South America, but a little over a century ago, the colonists rose against the mother country and demanded independence. Having disposed of the burdens imposed by Spain, the inhabitants created nine or ten smaller republics and the southernmost of these is known as the Argentine Republic.

Patagonia forms the most southern part of the Argentine. It must be borne in mind that there is no relationship between the name and Pat, the Irishman and that Welsh settlers do not wish to be known as "Pats" either. Patagonia means "the land of the people of Big Feet", after Magellan came across a tribe of native Indians with inordinately large feet.

The land of Patagonia is very arid. The eastern part is made up of highland that the natives call the Plain or Camp. The plain is a vast tract of plateau land covered throughout with thorn bushes. Grass, such as it is, grows hither and thither in clumps and appears dry, rough and tufty; but the land is not desert. In truth, large tracts of the great plain of Patagonia contain the best land in the world. The drawback is the lack of rainfall. Given sufficient water, hundreds of square miles which appear dry and barren would flower like a rose. The country looks wonderful in the rainy seasons and parts of Patagonia are not dry at all. In the hinterland amongst the high Andes where the rivers rise, there is a plentiful supply of rain with greenery in abundance. Indeed, the western slopes of the Andes provide as much rainfall as we experience here in Wales.

The valley of the river Camwy (Chubut), where the Welsh pioneers settled, is amongst the driest land in Patagonia. There the farmer has to irrigate his wheat fields as the settlement is dependent on the waters of the Camwy which run through the valley.

The Welsh settlement in Patagonia was established in 1865 when the first party of emigrants put ashore on the rugged coast on 28th July. They were the Welsh pioneers; these worthy individuals who are still regarded a credit to the Welsh nation. Their great courage has been unyielding and the 28th July is still celebrated as a holiday in Gŵyl y Glaniad (The Landing Holiday). The original intention of the settlement was to enable those Welsh people who left their native shores, to live together as one rather than be scattered amongst foreigners in this part of the world. The intention was no doubt noble, and should engage the minds of Welsh patriots. The hero of the first emigrants was Principal Michael D. Jones from Bala, Meirionydd.

Dyffyn Camwy is fifty miles long and four to five miles wide and fairly flat. If it was not so, it would be difficult to irrigate. The valley extends in an easterly direction surrounded by bare hills. Upon those hills are the Great Plains of Patagonia. The source of the Camwy is in the Andes mountains from which the river flows four hundred miles to the southern Atlantic. The Camwy is a large river and is navigable up to the town called Rawson, the chief settlement, and it is this very river which at times has flooded the land and destroyed many homes and public buildings.

Some years ago, I, along with many others, had to flee for my life and not for the first time. I saw hundreds of comfortable homes washed away by a great flood which overwhelmed the town. Few properties survived the catastrophe. Plas Hedd, the charming home of Eluned Morgan, some two miles from Rawson, was left an untidy pile by the flood and its treasures give a free passage towards the Atlantic seven miles down river. Heart-rending scenes were witnessed there, but throughout, the unquenchable spirit of the Welsh was seen in abundance. Neighbour helping neighbour in one big family. It was there that I saw true fellowship at its zenith raised to its ultimate from the roots, and pure Welsh emanating from the lips of the thousands who camped as best they could on the hillside with the few belongings which escaped the torrents.

I learned an important lesson that day; not to complain too much, play one's part and place one's trust in the Lord. And in the days to come, the Lord was good to us and ensured years of plenty for the settlers for their courage and forbearing. And, who knows, that in the near future, the Welsh people of Patagonia will evangelise the whole of South America? I pray that it should be so.

As to the geography of the valley; in the upper reaches there are majestic cliffs stretching for sixty miles on either side of the river and beyond the cliffs narrow valleys run to the source high in the Andes.

The best soil on earth is to be found in parts of the Camwy valley although there is also plenty of poor land. But generally the valley is conducive to growing wheat and hay, as long as the soil is well tilled and irrigated. There are many poor farms, particularly in the lower reaches near the Atlantic. The root of all the failures that befell the settlers for the first twenty years was the aridity of the land. But major developments in recent years have ensured that the settlers' sufferings will not continue into the future. The settlers dug canals to irrigate every part of the valley and their eyes were opened to the advantages of regular watering in such an arid landscape. In bygone days they scattered seed more in hope than expectation. If it rained, the seed sprouted but without further rain the seedling withered. They were dark, heartbreaking days of much suffering. The settler accepted government handouts, but for long periods they existed by hunting small animals and gathering wild berries.

Some three years following the founding of the colony, one of the settlers succeeded in raising a rich crop of wheat by irrigation. The others were much heartened and quickly persuaded that with regular watering the valley could be fruitful The enormous task of digging canals and ditches to enable the water to reach every square yard of the parched land began. From that time, the settlers have slowly prospered and many today live in comfortable circumstances.

Dyffryn Camwy is wheat country. Few fruit and vegetables were grown in the early years, but more attention is now given to root crops. Ditches are dug from the canals to the fields and as soon as the first wheat field is flooded ditches are opened to enable the water to reach others. Some land requires a lot of water. There are areas which are irrigated just two or three times a season whilst others need twice that amount. Undulating land is more difficult to water without drowning the seed in the hollows, and consequently great care is taken when releasing the water.

Ploughing

In Patagonia there are different types of plough mainly made in the United States, some with seats and others similar to those we use in Wales. In my opinion the ploughs with seats are superior for the ploughman can avoid walking behind the plough in such heat. They will quickly become fashionable in Wales, too. The horses in Patagonia are much smaller than those here in Wales. They are similar to circus ponies and of every colour but many are more stubborn than mules and nasty with it and will resist other than when it suits them. In a pair, one will often pull well while the other frequently tries to retreat with all its might. Consequently the ploughmen require the patience of Job and frequently ploughing becomes a battle between the ploughman and his team. The lack of patience is certainly prevalent in Patagonia. If only the ploughman exercised a little patience with his horses they would respond in kind.

There was once a farmer in Patagonia who showed such a lack of temperament that he tied a large bag made from animal skins to the tail of his horse. The animal, believing that the bogeyman had got it, bolted towards the desert and was never seen again.

But there are excellent, as well as dire, qualities to Patagonian horses. If for example at nightfall following a day out on the plain, the farmer loses his way in the darkness, all he has to do is loosen the reins and sit quietly and the good steed will certainly return its owner to his own doorstep no matter how deep the night or rough the terrain.

Sowing and reaping

Seed is generally sown in September and ripens in February. Summer and winter are at different times in Patagonia than they are here in Wales. Christmas in the Argentine is in high summer and whoever likes to celebrate Christmas at that time, go to Patagonia. When the crop ripens no one is seen harvesting with a sickle or a scythe, as machinery is used to cut, bind and thresh. I saw a machine in Patagonia, cutting, clearing and threshing wheat simultaneously and all that the farmer had to do was to sew the sacks and the grain was ready for market.

Crops vary from a half to a ton and a half an acre depending on the quality of the soil, how the land was treated and the weather conditions. Some years ago an English businessman journeyed to Patagonia with his heart set on farming. He took some land on rent, prepared the soil and sowed his seed. As he was more at home with his pen than with his tools, watering became a problem, and much of his seed was drowned. At harvest time much of the crop was sparse and thin and the gentleman felt in low spirits due to his failure. One day in his wheat field with stick in hand he counted each stalk in a certain area. So disappointed was he with the result that he flung his stick in the heat of temper shouting, "To hell with you!"

As the wheat is ground it is fed into *ffetanau* (large sacks) each holding two hundred pounds, loaded into wagons drawn by horses and oxen and sold in the town's storehouses. In time the grain is shipped to the capital Buenos Aires, a voyage of eight hundred miles. The capital is a large city of two million people and one of the most important trading centres in South America.

The inhabitants of Buenos Aires enjoy riotous living even on the Lord's Day. Most of the people are Catholics but few attend Mass and the congregations are mostly composed of the fair sex. Drunks are rarely seen on the streets, and in this context, Buenos Aires can be held as a glowing example to other towns in the Argentine.

One of the strangest sights I saw in Buenos Aires was the method of churning butter. Two large earthenware jars, full of cream are placed in skin bags and placed each side of a mule which is driven through the streets until the cream is well and truly churned. The butter is then sold from house to house.

The houses of Patagonia

Most of the Welsh homes in Patagonia are brick-built. Some are built of stone and others of clay. In the early days of settlement most of the homes were built of brick dried in the sun without a kiln in sight. Today there are many palaces and substantial homes built of kiln-dried bricks. Clay which is mixed with sand, is found on most farms.

Formerly the roofing material consisted of simple rafters set at two foot intervals and covered with wattle or reeds carefully placed to hold the thatch which was finally covered with a mixture of clay and sand mixed with chaff and spread thickly on the thatch. Today zinc is much used as roofing material but slate is unheard of.

The old clay roofs were adequate enough save in times of summer thunder storms when families were often given a thorough drenching in their bedrooms but most of our countrymen have applied themselves to waterproofing their homes to withstand all weathers.

House furniture

Generally the houses were untidy compared with those in Wales. Furniture was sparse and functional with very few luxurious pieces. Today, things have changed. In the early days boxes served as tables, and chairs are few and far between even today when benches persist. The homes of the unmarried men are the untidiest of all. The table is a box, the chair is a box and so is his bed. Often the kettle doubles as a tea-pot and coffee-pot and an old tin will suffice as a sugar bowl. The frying pan is often utilised as a plate. These habits are due to apathy and indifference, not poverty, but again conditions have improved in recent years.

Trees

Trees are scarce in Patagonia. There is an abundance of willow on the banks of the Camwy, but many are as crooked as the river itself. Many poplars have been planted recently and they flourish and there is no shortage of thorn and bush to fuel the fire. A variety of red thorn provides fierce heat and most of the settlers have wood fires. Others use cow manure and I have visited places where dried manure was the only source of heat and it burned well with similar qualities to our peat.

Land and Conditions

Although the Welsh settlers laboured hard and long digging irrigation canals and ditches and suffered greatly due to having to rely on constant watering, there are certain advantages as well as a few drawbacks for the farmer. Imagine emigrating to the United States or Canada and taking a farm. The holding could be deep in the forest and it would take more than a generation to clear the land completely for grassland and crop growing. It is not so in Patagonia. Thorn indeed thrives on some farms but clearing thorn is simple compared with clearing forests of mature trees. In addition one would be a settler amongst people of every nation and race and language with feelings of *hiraeth* for the old country.

In Patagonia, although eight thousand miles from the land of his fathers, a settler feels that he is in Wales. Welsh is spoken on the hearth; Welsh is the language of his neighbour; public and private worship is in Welsh and he is greeted in Welsh on the highways and byways. Even the animals look after themselves. Farmers share labour to provide winter fodder for the animals, but cattle and horses in Patagonia forage for themselves, summer and winter.

One certain disadvantage is the lack of social gatherings. The population is sparse and is spread so thinly throughout the valley that life can become tedious and filled with melancholy especially for those who previously enjoyed entertainment. No man enjoys living like a hermit every day of his life. Man is a social animal. Families do not suffer in this respect as individuals do or unmarried men. In some aspects the family is a social gathering in itself, but the bachelor or spinster, the widow and the widower has no one to socialise with – with the exception perhaps of the cat and dog or his horse.

Family life is not only cheaper but is so much more enjoyable. Bachelors here in Wales can live cheaply enough within the social circle without a care in the world, whilst the head of the family labours to sustain his loved ones. In Patagonia the family is a bonus, not a burden; the father does not have to battle to provide for his family, his family provides for him. In other words, it is easier for a man to look after his family than to look after himself.

But pity the poor bachelor, wife-less and leading a solitary existence. He must wander far to buy his provisions and to have his clothes washed. The alternative is to fend for himself. Cooking for oneself day in day out is a miserable chore. The bachelor life in Patagonia is a miserable one and the settlers call it *Cadw Batch*. My advice is to marry before emigrating. Young maidens are few and far between in Patagonia with four or five boys to each one. A shy innocent boy is given little chance and I must have been one of these when I was there.

Patagonia is a land for families and there is little comfort for a young man. The circumstances are very different there compared with those in Wales. I remember being invited to tea by a bachelor who felt hard done by on his own and was thoroughly disenchanted by having to cook for himself. I entered the home and the kettle was boiling on the hob. In his eagerness and frustration, he burned his hand when reaching for the kettle and it fell into the fire. He reached for it again and in temper, with a hefty swing of his leg, he kicked the kettle through the door shouting, "Go you old scoundrel!" If he had a wife, his hand would be fine and I would not have had to wait half an hour for a cup of tea.

Although life is lonely for the settlers and especially so for the single man, it cannot be said that any of the settlers is eager to return to Wales to labour in the pit or quarry. He owns his farm and regards himself as lord of the manor. The farmer is his own master. He labours in his own fields with the freedom to do as he will. He can leap on to his horse, gun in hand and dogs at his side, and ride deep into the bush in pursuit of game and he regards himself as much a gentleman as any squire here in Wales.

The collier underground in the south or the quarryman in Merioneth has not an inch of land and owns no animals except perhaps for a "fancy dog" or cat. A man in Patagonia is an important freeholder, owning a spread of perhaps three hundred acres with herds of cattle and many horses. It is not surprising therefore that he regards himself as, "someone," with little thought of returning to the old country to labour in the pit or quarry.

Although the Welsh are in the majority in Patagonia, the customs of the people differ considerably from those in Wales. For example, take the custom of courting. In his excellent lecture, "Courting, Marriage and Life", Dr. Jones refers to the different ways of courting seen in Wales such as courting at the fireside or courting arm in arm or in bed. In Patagonia, courting is carried out on horseback. It is on horseback that couples journey to meet each other and to whisper words of love and carry on as young people will.

The horse is central to life in Patagonia. Everyone loves riding – especially the young. It is unusual to go about on foot. In this respect the settler imitates, as they have in other ways, their Argentine neighbours who are reluctant to walk even twenty yards.

The settlers go to chapel on horseback where one may see forty, fifty or even sixty horses tied up as if the gathering inside was made up of horse-soldiers. Dogs attend worship and often disrupt the service in the most disgusting ways. It would be abhorrent in Wales to find a dog in the house of God, but regrettably familiar enough in Patagonia.

I remember one settler complaining to the Congregational Minister regarding the habit of allowing dogs to follow their master to church. He was told by the reverend gentleman to leave well alone, it was the dog who sustained the ministry!

It grieves me to report that there are many who give little thought to the soul and who prefer temporal interests. Having said that and in considering the many disadvantages present the religious feeling in Patagonia remains fairly satisfactory. One cannot expect, in such a sparsely populated country, to see congregations similar in size to those in Wales.

Hospitality

The hospitality extended by the settler in Patagonia is legendary and offered to all-comers. It is one of the great traditions of the people. Imagine being on a journey on the plains and just happening to come across a homestead. Your welcome from the lady of the house would be warm and wholesome. The kettle would be on the hob and moving on without partaking of a cup of tea would not be entertained for a moment. If one happened to be out at night miles from home, overnight hospitality would be extended without the thought of payment.

The wild animals of Patagonia

Among the wild animals of Patagonia are the guanaco or the Patagonian camel, the ostrich, the puma, (the Patagonian lion), the wild cat, the fox, skunk, armadillo and the hare. The most notable, without doubt, is the guanaco which is difficult to describe properly. It is a

yellowish-red creature somewhere between a sheep and a camel. It measures five to six feet in length and stands about four foot high. The Indians, particularly, spend a great deal of time hunting the guanaco but often without success as it is such an elusive and fast creature. A gentleman named Gallegos gave the following description of the guanaco. "You are strange animal, you neigh like a stallion, you have the wool of the sheep, the neck of a camel, the feet of a deer and as fleet of foot as a devil."

"*You are a strange animal . . .*"

The puma is another notable animal of Patagonia, a kind of lion. Grey or yellowish-grey in colour and five to six feet in length. It cannot be said that the puma has the fierceness of the African lion, but it is particularly harmful to sheep.

The Indians

Having given a short but imperfect description of the Welsh in Patagonia, it would perhaps not be amiss to relate something of the Indian and his customs today. Very few Indians visit the settlers in Dyffryn Camwy. Some years ago, the Argentine government sent troops of soldiers to round up the Indians. The government maintained that the nomadic Indian population of the plains hindered development in the hinterland. The raids resulted in the Indians laying down their weapons and accepting the government's proposals. From that day until this, the Indian is under close supervision of soldiers in reservations. In the south they camp at a location called Santa Cruz, while in the north they live in the neighbourhood of Valchea. They are free to hunt as before and are given licences to trade with the white man. Nowadays very few Indians come to the Welsh settlements; other settlements are more convenient. Years ago, their tents would be pitched here and there in the valley, and some would visit farmsteads and ask for bread or other supplies and to trade.

The Indian is very fond of the well baked bread of the Welsh housewife and the Welsh name *bara* has become part of their native language. The Indians in Patagonia trade animal hides and ostrich feathers in return for bread, flour and other supplies. When trading, they normally stay in the settlement for a month before returning again to the Plains.

The best kind of friendship exists between the Welsh and the Indians. The fact that the small communities have kept the peace with the aboriginals whilst never-ending feuds were fought with other nationalities in every part of America, will be to the great credit to our Nation as long as water runs.

The Indians live in tents made of animal skins. They are physically bigger than the Welsh, generally six- to six-and-a-half feet tall and solidly built. The skin colour varies, some have dark complexions whilst others are as fair as Europeans, but most Indians are a kind of yellowish-red.

I once saw two daughters of the chief Galletsh. They were as fair of face as any Welsh girls here. Perhaps they are the descendants of Madog ap Owain Gwynedd. The Indians have thickly matted dark hair, worn long by both male and female. They all paint their faces as protection for the skin against the wind and the heat of the sun The male Indians wear a *Cheripa* – a kind of undergarment or trousers made from linen, a piece of cloth or any material at hand. The girls wear a kind of petticoat but the upper garment is common to both sexes. It is a magnificent garment stretching from head to foot. It is made from animal skins sewn together with great skill by the females and one side is painted a shade of red. The hair is worn next to the skin. It is little wonder that the Indians look so grand and dignified, and the old sailors called Patagonia the "land of giants".

For food, the Indians depend entirely on hunting and the animal skins provide clothes, bedding and tents. They possess stallions and mares in great numbers which they slaughter and eat at feasts to celebrate child-birth or marriage.

A young brave having fallen for a maiden will send horses as a gift to his prospective in-laws, and they, in return, if the match is approved, will reciprocate. The marriage ceremony is patriarchal in nature and reminds us of the ceremony when Isaac married Rebecca.

Religion of the Indians

The Indians don't worship idols as do their African and Asian brothers. They believe in the existence of two gods or spirits, one benign and the other belligerent. The one is responsible for creating all things good while the other, which they call *Gualicha,* needs habitual sacrifice to appease him. It is he who is responsible for strife among the brethren, diseases and all other tribulations. For example, when a brave has a headache his head is placed between the doctor's knees who shrieks in his ear to enable the evil spirit to depart.

It can be said that the Indian prays hardly at all. Some maintain that they worship the Sun as in Peru, but this assertion is unproven, although they do greet a new moon. The Indians also offer sacrifices to *Gualicha.* Following a wedding feast, the heads, backbones and tails as well as the liver and hearts of horses are taken to a hill-top and left as a sacrifice.

When an Indian dies, all his possessions are burned and the corpse tied in material and buried in a sitting position. Stones are then piled on the grave to form a cairn, especially in the instance of the burial of a man of influence or a chief. Similar rituals were accorded to Welsh princes – who has not heard of Carnedd Llewelyn! However, the fact that such little effort has been made to bring the Good News of the Gospel to these unfortunates grieves me.

The South American Missionary Society does good work among the Indians of Tierra del Fuego, but nothing for the Indians of Patagonia. Catholic Missionaries have a presence among the Indians there, and isn't that a disgrace to us Protestant Welshmen? Is it not shameful that we let the work of looking after the spiritual needs of the Indians fall into the hands of Catholics!

To close this essay, I would like to draw your attention to the following. There will be some who intend going to Patagonia with a view of settling in Dyffryn Camwy. The truth is that all the farms in the valley have been taken years ago. But let no-one lose heart. There is good land and fertile valleys in the foothills of the Andes and gold and other minerals have been discovered there. When the railroad is built, the land would be ideal to receive thousands of prospective Welsh farmers. Many Welsh people have settled at a location called Cwm Hyfryd. It is a good and pleasant land which I visited and in which I stayed for a time. I enjoyed looking at the wild natural beauty and who would not desire to live in a fertile valley like that, with the high Andes rising to the clouds above our heads and the peaks covered in everlasting snow. Wouldn't it be wonderful to hear the ancient language of the Briton forever on the lips of the inhabitants!

James Jones

H.C.-J. writes . . .
It must be rare for a man to publish writings by his grandfather, father, himself and his son. The following poem was written by my son, Guy, aged thirteen for Christmas 1997 – thus this book contains literary work from the pens of four successive generations of a Pembrokeshire family.

Home is a place where I can do what I want,
When I want, and how I want,
Where I am free to play when I want,
Where I can go whatever happens.
It's a place of privacy,
A place that I can call my own,
And most of all, a place I can call home.

Guy Charles-Jones (aged 13 years)

Patagonia – home on the range

Relocated – The Jones of Brawdy ranch in Patagonia

Chapter XVI

MY UNFORGETTABLE PEMBROKESHIRE COMPANION

By Hugh Charles-Jones

AS a child I reached up for my father's hand and he took me out on journeys. When he was old and frail he reached out to me; the cycle was closing. It was my turn to take him out, but I still listened to him with child-like respect. I was a professional interviewer, yet I never recorded my father's words. He seemed infinite, of endless knowledge; stories flowed from him as if from an inexhaustible lake. Now he is gone and so much went with his passing. He leaves much to history and his own life is an addition to posterity.

For many years I interviewed, filmed, recorded and wrote about interesting people - Royalty, prime ministers, film stars, artists, writers, sportsmen and famous raconteurs in many different countries. My father stands in that company in his own right. "You don't know what you've got 'till it's gone" goes the song. I now know what that means. Time was when Mamma and Daddy seemed permanent in my life. Now I am trying to turn my ghosts into friends. It is so painful though. On my mother's death, my father not only lost a loving wife but also his driver. So I often drove him to Windsor Castle and The House of Lords for his ceremonial duties. As dear to his heart, were the expeditions we made into his beloved Pembrokeshire. I little knew then that these trips were future cherished memories. They were not mere journeys as he expounded on the countryside they became unique. A kind of "drive-by shooting" into history.

"Slow down, slow down boy," he'd say, oblivious of juggernauts inches behind. "Now you see that house in the trees there. Well, in 1674, quite recently really, a strange family called the Bowens lived there. One day the heir was riding past a gibbet . . . ." So the stories, legends and histories poured out with a youthful enthusiasm. There seemed not a bridge, a river, a chapel, or farmhouse, a castle or cottage that he didn't know something about. He even pointed out sites where there was nothing to see. Yet he could recreate the ghost of a bygone mansion and describe long dead families, their scandals, feuds and adventures right down to present day descendants. He was a skilled writer, an accomplished lecturer with a phenomenal memory. These gifts combined as his eyes dwelt on the countryside. I heard effortless tours de force and I never recorded a word of it. To be wise after the event is a sickening thing. The tales he told were not just a dry monologue of fact. They were laced with humour and laughter. He particularly enjoyed visiting the places of his youth, Clawddcam, Brawdy, Goodwick, Trefin and Grimston. The old Welsh oral tradition was the foundation of Daddy's phenomenal memory, his parents both had it too. "I remember learning to walk with my arm around our collie dog here," he told me when we were looking at his birthplace in Trefin. So I no longer fume behind cars full of grey heads as they crawl through country lanes as he and I did. Maybe they are also on sentimental journeys to the havens of their youth when life seemed endless.

Once we passed an insignificant cottage on the Haverfordwest road. "A boy went to the 1914-18 war from there," he said. "The parents got the dreaded telegram saying he had been killed. The mother refused to believe it. For the rest of her life when the weather was fine she'd sit outside looking down the road waiting, waiting for her son to come back. How sad that was." Whenever I pass it now, I think of three people; the dead soldier, his mother and my father. All dead. It was sad then, and is still to me today.

F.J. always seemed to have plenty of time. It was some years before I discovered how he did this. In his army days he told me he could get up, bath, shave and be dressed for the day in three-and-a-half minutes. He was usually at his desk writing at six in the morning.

Bathtime for officers of the Welch Regiment by Fred May. 1937

One of the advantages of being a writer is that in a few paces from the bedroom to desk and he's at work. By nine o'clock when most arrived at offices, scratching their heads and calling for coffee, my father would have three hours of uninterrupted work under his belt. That done for over 60 years the accumulation of output comes in the "super-human" class. His powers of concentration were honed to an awesome degree. He was the best manager of time I ever met. Every day had a purpose, a plan. Yet he was always able to cope with the unexpected in an almost leisurely manner and saw humour in most subjects. He was not a blinkered scholar but was always alert for the slightest nuance of human behaviour. He and my mother had that priceless knack of making the most mundane things little events of humour and interest. Once I dropped into a Little Chef for coffee. He looked at the menu and started to invent strange dishes from it. Then he decided to change the name Little Chef to "Icklesheff". Of a waitress he whispered to me, "she looks like a Medici princess gone to seed!" Of a fellow diner: "Look at that fat man digging his grave with his knife and fork AND he's holding his knife like a fountain pen!" Sometimes he would be silent with a far away look. Then with a sigh of contentment out came his inevitable note book and pencil and down went a code word for an article, essay or even a funny joke. His pocket diary was another essential tool. He had private nicknames for people. A man unfavoured by nature he called the Gremgoil, a cross between a gremlin and a gargoyle. There was the Anxious Man, Neanderthal Man, the Prince of Plagiarists, the Jester, the Bed Hopper and the Genius, as well as many others in Welsh. The Man with the Elgin Marbles in his mouth was another.

As we walked towns or villages together, people would cross the road to talk to him. He always seemed to have a system about his conversations. How was so and so; what was the outcome of this and that meeting; was the restoration of an old house finished, as well as any topical gossip. I had the notion that this seemingly trivial information had been filed away for possible future reference. I remarked to him once, "I suppose knowledge is power." "Most certainly," he replied, looking at me in surprise as if I had just pointed out something childishly obvious. He always dressed well on our trips, highly polished brown shoes, flannel slacks, a tweed jacket (watch chain in lapel) and a brown trilby hat over his long wavy silvery hair. If it was cold, the outfit was covered by a long thick tweed overcoat fashionable in the Twenties which nearly reached the ground. Driving him once, he said, "go up there, there's a house I want to see."

"Daddy, it's a one-way street."

"Do as you're told. Take no notice, just get there."

My father had that Welsh family tradition that friends and family had obligations and rights. The right to call at any time, even without warning, to walk in, sit down and be entertained. The obligation was also to be "on call" as it were for any visitors to our homes. So often he and I would sit on farmhouse settles, on ornate drawing room chairs and in prim Pembrokeshire parlours in remote parishes. He was treated as a benign baron inspecting his estates. He might not have owned land but he had a huge estate consisting of acres of his manuscripts. I sat during many long complicated conversations in English and Welsh. They were about family genealogies, local legends, heraldry, poetry, parsons, kings and kilns, deeds, plans, old books and diaries. Always he was thorough, painstaking and, above all, enthusiastic, with an unquenchable quest for truth, accuracy and proof. He gave of himself endlessly and effortlessly. The older he got, the more he knew. He took much from life, but he put so much more back into it which is why I resent the gap he has left behind.

Being on so many committees he often had rail journeys to London and Cardiff. He told me of a set drill he had invented. If he was spoken to by a person he suspected of being a potential bore, he'd fish out his note book, then he'd say, "You simply must excuse me, I'm writing an article on French medieval ecclesiastic music."

My parents once took me to Llanstephan. They loved the castle, the beach and the coastal path. "Today," Daddy announced, "I will show you a Holy Well." We trotted obediently behind him on a long hike. Much later he said

Francis Jones visiting ancestral haunts – Llwyngwair

"It's just around that corner." We approached the sacred place. Aghast, we stared down. Someone had there attended to a bodily function. There was an odour but not of sanctity. "That," said Daddy, "is NOT a holy relic." He added, "The dirty infidel." We all laughed all the way home.

F.J.'s travels came to an abrupt stop when he was in his mid fifties. He was rushed into hospital after a massive blood haemorrhage. Mamma stayed with him night and day whilst he underwent three complete blood transfusions. When I visited him he complained about a previous visitor. "That man was far too gloomy to be allowed in hospitals, he just sat there looking at me with a long face," he said. He was still in intensive care then. As I was leaving he called me back. "Are you taking care of those riding boots I gave you?", he said. He and I knew that he wasn't really talking about the boots. It was his way of saying good-bye, just in case. He came home pale and weak, but the old vivacity still shone brightly. "We shall travel over the Preselis to the haunts of my Pembrokeshire youth," he imperiously announced a short time later. My mother drove us. We were passing a mist-shrouded mountain. "Stop the car," Daddy said. He got out, "I'm going to climb to the top," he said. We protested. Mamma said, "You're too weak, you'll collapse, Francis. Don't do it, please." I said, "Well, I'm coming with you, Pa." He cut us short. "When I thought I was dying, I swore that if I recovered I would go up there." he said. "What is more I shall do it on my own." He was no stranger to mists, having been through the gun smoke in Africa and Italy.

We watched the slight figure toil up the slopes and disappear into the mist. Mamma was beside herself, so I walked up to meet him, or to carry him down. Then he reappeared. He was exhausted, but looked thoroughly pleased. "You could at least have brought down some writing on pillars of stone," I said. I wonder what he thought about up there in his lonely personal pilgrimage – was it thanks for deliverance, maybe a prayer? I often wonder about it.

My father constantly haunted estate agents where he collected details and illustrations of old houses he was researching. He also often wrote potted histories of old houses for sale particulars. Shortly after Mamma's death, I met him in Haverfordwest. We walked slowly up the High Street. I happened to notice his socks as he struggled up the steps to an estate agent's office. They showed my mother's neat darns. It hit me with such anguish. I was grieved for my parents and that lonely cold bed that awaited my father at night. The bed they had shared for 54 years.

I took my father to give an address to a learned society of which he was President. It was a dreary winter's day and the rain was pouring down. So we whiled away some time in a gloomy hotel. For once I came up with a reasonably original way of passing the time. I wrote the first part of a short story. Passing it over to Daddy I asked him to finish it.

F.J. at historic Welsh house, 1971

It went: Two men were sitting in an hotel. They were bored to tears. The younger said, "I'll just pop out and buy something to read." On the pavement he shrank back to avoid being splashed by passing traffic. He bounced off a fat lady into the road where he was knocked unconscious by a van owned by Wee Willie Winkie, teddy bear makers. When he came to in hospital, he was asked his name. Still dazed he said "Wee Willie Winkie." I asked my father to finish the story describing how the two men were re-united. Try though he did, he couldn't come up with a logical ending. I finished the story. "The older man got worried and searched for his companion. He visited the police station and enquired. The desk sergeant, who was a Carmarthen man, asked, 'And who are you Sir.'

'I am Wales Herald Extraordinary,' was the answer.

The sergeant said, 'Duw, duw, you're the second loony I've had today.' So the two men were re-united in the local lunatic asylum". It was one of the rare times that my father congratulated me. I found it among his papers. I later learned he used to show it to his friends. He never told me that. It also reminds me that although he could be exasperating, infuriating, caustic, sarcastic on occasion, but boring – never.

No longer shall I have those thrilling little pangs of expectation which I felt whenever I approached my parents' home. The love, warmth, laughter and lively interest are memories now, their courage too. Certainly this book would never have appeared without their example. Amongst my father's archives I found a poem he wrote in his youth.

Here is a verse from it –

James

Francis ap James

Hugh ap Francis ap James

> *I will strike my harp's golden strings,*
> *I will chant of ancient things*
> *From books of magic rhyme,*
> *And be one of the faery band*
> *To journey to the Western Land*
> *Beyond the shores of Time.*

Prophetic? I hope so.

Hugh Charles-Jones

Guy ap Hugh ap Francis ap James

BIBLIOGRAPHICAL ABBREVIATIONS

Anc Mon Pembs	Ancient Monuments Commissioners Pembrokeshire
Arch Cam	Archaeologia Cambrensis
B.B. St. Davids	Black Book of St. Davids 1326
B.G. Charles NCPN	Non-Celtic Place Names, Dr. B.G. Charles, 1938, Ldn. Medieval Studies
Burkes's L. G. 1850	Burke's Landed Gentry, 1850 edn
C of A	College of Arms, London
Carms RO	Carmarthenshire Record Office
Carms Studies 1974	Carmarthenshire Studies, presented to Major Francis Jones, ed. T. Barnes and N. Yates, Carmarthen, 1974
Chancery Proc	Chancery Proceedings Ser. II 420/40
DNB	Dictionary of National Biography, 63 vols., Ldn. 1885-1900, reprinted Oxford 1921-22
DWB	Dictionary of Welsh Biography down to 1940, London 1959
Dwnn	Heraldic Visitations see Meyrick, Samuel Rush
Fenton Tour Pembs	An Historical Tour through Pembrokeshire, Richard Fenton. 1811
Fo	Folio
G. G. MSS	Golden Grove Manuscripts
ibid	See last reference
J.B.A.A.	Journal of British Architectural Association
L.T.	Land Tax lists
Laws Little England	Laws, Little England beyond Wales, edn. 1888
Lewis TDW	Lewis Samuel, A Topographical Dictionary of Wales. Vols. 1 & 2, London 1833, 4th Edn
MS	Manuscripts
NLW	National Library of Wales
PRO	Public Record Office
Papers of G.S.	Great Sessions
Pembs RO	Pembrokeshire Record Office
Pembs Arch Svy	Pembrokeshire Archaeological Survey
Pembs Hist	The Pembrokeshire Historian
Protheroe	Protheroe Beynon Collection
R.Comm on Land in Wales	Royal Commission on Land in Wales
RCAM	Royal Commission for Ancient and Historical Monuments in Wales, An Inventory of the Ancient Monuments in Wales and Monmouthshire, London 1917
Rees, *Beauties of S. Wales*	Rees Thomas, The Beauties of England and Wales, South Wales, Vol. XVIII, London 1815
S.C. (JF) 1988	John Francis Sale Catalogues
Steegman Portraits	A Survey of Portraits in Welsh Houses, Vol. II, J. Steegman, Cardiff 1962
Taylor's Cussion	George Owen, the Taylor's Cussion, London
Thos. Lloyd, *Lost Houses*	T. Lloyd, The Lost Houses of Wales, SAVE London 1986
Timmins Nooks Pembs	Nooks & Corners of Pembrokeshire 1895. Timmins
Trans Cymmrodor	Transactions of the Honourable Society of Cymmrodorion
V.L.	Voter's Lists
W.W.H.R.	West Wales Historical Records

NOTES